DOCUMENTS OF UNITED STATES
INDIAN POLICY

Documents of United States Indian Policy

Second Edition, Expanded

Edited by
Francis Paul Prucha

University of Nebraska Press • Lincoln/London

The paper in this book meets the minimum requirements
of American National Standard for Information Sciences—
Permanence of Paper for Printed Library Materials,
ANSI Z39.48–1984.

Library of Congress Cataloging in Publication Data

Documents of United States Indian policy.

Bibliography: p.
Includes index.
1. Indians of North American—Legal status, laws,
etc. 2. Indians of North America—Government relations.
I. Prucha, Francis Paul.
KF8205.D63   1990   346.7301'3   89-16408
ISBN 0-8032-3688-3   347.30613
ISBN 0-8032-8726-7 (pbk. : alk. paper)

Second paperback printing: 1991

Contents

Preface xi
Preface to the Second Edition xiii
1. George Washington to James Duane. September 7, 1783 1
2. Proclamation of the Continental Congress. September 22, 1783 3
3. Report of Committee on Indian Affairs. October 15, 1783 3
4. Treaty with the Six Nations. October 22, 1784 5
5. Treaty of Fort McIntosh. January 21, 1785 5
6. Treaty of Hopewell with the Cherokees. November 28, 1785 6
7. Ordinance for the Regulation of Indian Affairs. August 7, 1786 8
8. Northwest Ordinance. July 13, 1787 9
9. Committee Report on the Southern Department. August 3, 1787 10
10. Report of Henry Knox on White Outrages. July 18, 1788 11
11. Report of Henry Knox on the Northwestern Indians. June 15, 1789 12
12. Establishment of the War Department. August 7, 1789 14
13. Trade and Intercourse Act. July 22, 1790 14
14. President Washington's Third Annual Message. October 25, 1791 15
15. President Washington on Government Trading Houses. December 3, 1793 16
16. Establishment of Government Trading Houses. April 18, 1796 16
17. Trade and Intercourse Act. March 30, 1802 17
18. President Jefferson on Indian Trading Houses. January 18, 1803 21
19. President Jefferson to William Henry Harrison. February 27, 1803 22
20. Superintendent of Indian Trade. April 21, 1806 23
21. President Jefferson on the Liquor Trade. December 31, 1808 24
22. Treaty of Portage des Sioux. July 19, 1815 25
23. Governor Cass on British Traders. July 20, 1815 25
24. Secretary of War Crawford on Trade and Intercourse. March 13, 1816 26
25. Exclusion of British Traders. April 29, 1816 28
26. Secretary of War Calhoun on British Traders. March 25, 1818 29
27. Authorization of Indian Agents. 1818 30
   1. Manner of Appointing Agents. April 16, 1818 30
   2. Compensation for Indian Agents. April 20, 1818 30
28. Secretary of War Calhoun on Indian Trade. December 5, 1818 31
29. Civilization Fund Act. March 3, 1819 33
30. Abolition of the Government Trading Houses. May 6, 1822 33
31. Act for Regulating the Indian Trade. May 6, 1822 34
32. Johnson and Graham's Lessee v. William McIntosh. 1823 35
33. Creation of a Bureau of Indian Affairs in the War Department.
   March 11, 1824 37
34. Authorization of Treaties; Trade Regulations. May 25, 1824 38
35. Message of President Monroe on Indian Removal. January 27, 1825 39
36. Treaty with the Ponca Indians. June 9, 1825 40
37. Treaty of Prairie du Chien. August 19, 1825 42

38. Thomas L. McKenney on Trading Sites. February 14, 1826   43
39. Secretary of War Eaton on Cherokee Removal. April 18, 1829   44
40. President Jackson on Indian Removal. December 8, 1829   47
41. Senator Frelinghuysen on Indian Removal. April 9, 1830   49
42. Indian Removal Act. May 28, 1830   52
43. Treaty with the Choctaw Indians. September 27, 1830   53
44. Cherokee Nation v. Georgia. 1831   58
45. Worcester v. Georgia. 1832   60
46. Authorization of a Commissioner of Indian Affairs. July 9, 1832   62
47. Indian Commissioner Herring on the Indian Race. November 22, 1832   63
48. Trade and Intercourse Act. June 30, 1834   64
49. Organization of the Department of Indian Affairs. June 30, 1834   68
50. President Jackson on Indian Removal. December 7, 1835   71
51. Indian Commissioner Crawford on Indian Policy. November 25, 1838   73
52. Regulations regarding Liquor and Annuities. March 3, 1847   75
53. Indian Commissioner Medill on Indian Colonies. November 30, 1848   77
54. Transfer of Indian Affairs to the Department of the Interior. March 3, 1849   80
55. Organization of Indian Affairs in Oregon. June 5, 1850   80
56. Indian Commissioner Lea on Reservation Policy. November 27, 1850   81
57. Modifications in the Indian Department. February 27, 1851   83
58. Treaty of Fort Laramie. September 17, 1851   84
59. Indian Commissioner Lea on the Civilization of the Indians.
     November 27, 1851   85
60. Superintendent of Indian Affairs in California. March 3, 1852   86
61. Treaty with the Oto and Missouri Indians. March 15, 1854   87
62. Indian Commissioner Manypenny on Indian Affairs. November 22, 1856   89
63. Indian Commissioner Mix on Reservation Policy. November 6, 1858   92
64. Indian Commissioner Dole on Reservation Policy. November 26, 1862   95
65. Report of the President of the Southern Treaty Commission. October 30, 1865   96
66. Treaty with the Creeks. June 14, 1866   98
67. Report of the Doolittle Committee. January 26, 1867   102
68. Creation of an Indian Peace Commission. July 20, 1867   105
69. Report of the Indian Peace Commission. January 7, 1868   106
70. Treaty of Fort Laramie. April 29, 1868   110
71. House Debate on Treaty-Making Power. June 18, 1868   115
72. Resolutions of the Indian Peace Commission. October 9, 1868   116
73. Secretary of War Schofield on Transfer of the Indian Bureau.
     November 20, 1868   117
74. Indian Commissioner Taylor on Transfer of the Indian Bureau.
     November 23, 1868   118
75. Indian Commissioner Taylor on Indian Civilization. November 23, 1868   123
76. Authorization of the Board of Indian Commissioners. April 10, 1869   126
77. Instructions to the Board of Indian Commissioners. 1869   127
78. Secretary of the Interior Cox on Reservations and on the Peace Policy.
     November 15, 1869   129
79. Report of the Board of Indian Commissioners. November 23, 1869   131
80. Indian Commissioner Parker on the Treaty System. December 23, 1869   134
81. President Grant's Peace Policy. December 5, 1870   135
82. Cherokee Tobacco Case. December 1870   136

83. Abolition of Treaty Making. March 3, 1871   136
84. Indian Commissioner Walker on Indian Policy. November 1, 1872   137
85. Assignment of Indian Agencies to Religious Societies. November 1, 1872   141
86. Establishment of a Reservation by Executive Order. May 29, 1873   143
87. Indian Commissioner Smith on Indian Citizenship. November 1, 1874   144
88. General Sherman on Transfer of the Indian Bureau. January 19, 1876   146
89. Indian Commissioner Smith on Principles of Indian Policy. October 30, 1876   147
90. Indian Commissioner Hayt on Indian Police. November 1, 1877   151
91. Standing Bear v. Crook. May 12, 1879   151
92. Secretary of the Interior Schurz on Reservation Policy. November 1, 1880   153
93. Indian Commissioner Price on Civilizing the Indians. October 24, 1881   155
94. Indian Commissioner Price on Cooperation with Religious Societies. October 10, 1882   157
95. Report on the Mission Indians of California. October 10, 1883   158
96. General Sherman on the End of the Indian Problem. October 27, 1883   159
97. Courts of Indian Offenses. November 1, 1883   160
98. Ex Parte Crow Dog. December 17, 1883   162
99. Program of the Lake Mohonk Conference. September 1884   163
100. Elk v. Wilkins. November 3, 1884   166
101. Major Crimes Act. March 3, 1885   167
102. United States v. Kagama. May 10, 1886   168
103. Indian Commissioner Atkins on the Five Civilized Tribes. September 28, 1886   169
104. General Allotment Act (Dawes Act). February 8, 1887   171
105. Use of English in Indian Schools. September 21, 1887   174
106. Marriage between White Men and Indian Women. August 9, 1888   176
107. Indian Commissioner Morgan on Indian Policy. October 1, 1889   177
108. Supplemental Report on Indian Education. December 1, 1889   178
109. Inculcation of Patriotism in Indian Schools. December 10, 1889   180
110. The Board of Indian Commissioners on Civil Service Reform. January 10, 1891   182
111. Relief of the Mission Indians. January 12, 1891   182
112. Amendment to the Dawes Act. February 28, 1891   184
113. Civil Service Classification in the Indian Service. April 13, 1891   185
114. Army Officers as Indian Agents. July 13, 1892   186
115. Rules for Indian Courts. August 27, 1892   186
116. Indian School Superintendents as Indian Agents. March 3, 1893   189
117. Commission to the Five Civilized Tribes (Dawes Commission). March 3, 1893   189
118. Report of the Dawes Commission. November 20, 1894   190
119. Extension of Civil Service Rules. September 15, 1896   195
120. Curtis Act. June 28, 1898   197
121. Stephens v. Cherokee Nation. May 15, 1899   198
122. Citizenship for Indians in the Indian Territory. March 3, 1901   199
123. Indian Commissioner Jones on Indian Self-Support. October 15, 1901   199
124. Lone Wolf v. Hitchcock. January 5, 1903   202
125. Indian Commissioner Leupp on Indian Policy. September 30, 1905   203
126. Burke Act. May 8, 1906   207
127. Indian Commissioner Leupp on the Burke Act. September 30, 1906   208
128. Lacey Act. March 2, 1907   209
129. Indian Commissioner Leupp on Reservation Schools. September 30, 1907   210

130. Indian Commissioner Valentine on Indian Health. November 1, 1910 — 212
131. Indian Commissioner Sells, A Declaration of Policy. October 15, 1917 — 213
132. Citizenship for World War I Veterans. November 6, 1919 — 215
133. Bursum Bill. 1922 — 215
134. Indian Citizenship Act. June 2, 1924 — 218
135. Pueblo Lands Board. June 7, 1924 — 218
136. Meriam Report. 1928 — 219
137. Johnson-O'Malley Act. April 16, 1934 — 221
138. Wheeler-Howard Act (Indian Reorganization Act). June 18, 1934 — 222
139. Indian Commissioner Collier on the Wheeler-Howard Act. 1934 — 225
140. Indian Arts and Crafts Board. August 27, 1935 — 228
141. Oklahoma Indian Welfare Act. June 25, 1936 — 230
142. Indian Claims Commission Act. August 13, 1946 — 231
143. House Concurrent Resolution 108. August 1, 1953 — 233
144. Public Law 280. August 15, 1953 — 233
145. Termination of the Menominee Indians. June 17, 1954 — 234
146. Transfer of Indian Health Services. August 5, 1954 — 236
147. Relocation of Indians in Urban Areas. 1954 — 237
148. Senator Watkins on Termination Policy. May 1957 — 238
149. Secretary of the Interior Seaton on Termination Policy. September 19, 1958 — 240
150. Native American Church v. Navajo Tribal Council. November 17, 1959 — 241
151. A Program for Indian Citizens. January 1961 — 242
152. Declaration of Indian Purpose. June 1961 — 244
153. Task Force on Indian Affairs. 1961 — 246
154. Colliflower v. Garland. February 4, 1965 — 247
155. President Johnson, Special Message to Congress. March 6, 1968 — 248
156. Civil Rights Act of 1968. April 11, 1968 — 249
157. Report on Indian Education. November 3, 1969 — 253
158. President Nixon, Special Message on Indian Affairs. July 8, 1970 — 256
159. Return of Blue Lake Lands to Taos Pueblo. 1970 — 258
    1. Return of the Lands. December 15, 1970 — 258
    2. Remarks of President Nixon. December 15, 1970 — 259
160. Alaska Native Claims Settlement Act. December 18, 1971 — 260
161. Indian Education Act. June 23, 1972 — 263
162. Extension of Indian Preference in Employment. June 26, 1972 — 264
163. Menominee Restoration Act. December 22, 1973 — 264
164. Comprehensive Employment and Training Act. December 28, 1973 — 266
165. United States v. State of Washington. March 22, 1974 — 267
166. Indian Financing Act. April 12, 1974 — 269
167. Morton v. Mancari. June 17, 1974 — 270
168. Student Rights and Due Process Procedures. October 11, 1974 — 271
169. Establishment of the American Indian Policy Review Commission.
    January 2, 1975 — 272
170. Indian Self-Determination and Education Assistance Act. January 4, 1975 — 274
171. Passamaquoddy Tribe v. Morton. January 20, 1975 — 277
172. Indian Crimes Act of 1976. May 29, 1976 — 278
173. Indian Health Care Improvement Act. September 30, 1976 — 278
174. Final Report of the American Indian Policy Review Commission.
    May 17, 1977 — 281

175. Establishment of Assistant Secretary—Indian Affairs. September 26, 1977   284
176. Oliphant v. Suquamish Indian Tribe. March 6, 1978   284
177. United States v. Wheeler. March 22, 1978   285
178. Santa Clara Pueblo v. Martinez. May 15, 1978   287
179. American Indian Religious Freedom. August 11, 1978   288
180. Federal Acknowledgment of Indian Tribes. October 2, 1978   289
181. Tribally Controlled Community College Assistance Act. October 17, 1978   290
182. Education Amendments Act of 1978: Title XI—Indian Education.
      November 1, 1978   291
183. Indian Child Welfare Act. November 8, 1978   293
184. Archaeological Resources Protection Act. October 31, 1979   294
185. United States v. Sioux Nation of Indians. June 30, 1980   295
186. Maine Indian Claims Settlement Act. October 10, 1980   296
187. Statement on Indian Health Programs. March 2, 1981   298
188. Indian Land Consolidation Act. January 12, 1983   300
189. Indian Policy: Statement of Ronald Reagan. January 24, 1983   301
190. Federal Acknowledgement of Narragansett Indian Tribe of Rhode Island.
      February 2, 1983   302
191. Bureau of Indian Affairs Statement of Policy. 1984   304
192. Report of the Task Force on Indian Economic Development. July 1986   305
193. Amendments to the Alaska Native Claims Settlement Act. February 3, 1988   308
194. Report on BIA Education. March 1988   309
195. Lyng v. Northwest Indian Cemetery Protective Association. April 19, 1988   312
196. Tribally Controlled Schools Act of 1988. April 28, 1988   314
197. Indian Gaming Regulatory Act. October 17, 1988   316

      Appendix
A1.   Winters v. United States. January 6, 1908   319
A2.   Authorization of Appropriations and Expenditures for Indian Affairs
      (Snyder Act). November 2, 1921   320

      Selected Bibliography   323

      Index   327

Preface

These documents illustrate the history of the relations between the United States government and the American Indians from the founding of the nation to the present time. My intention has been to provide a collection of official and quasi-official records that will serve a purpose similar to that served by Henry Steele Commager's *Documents of American History* for United States history as a whole. Like Commager, I have interpreted the term *document* in a very narrow sense. This collection, therefore, is not a well-rounded history of Indian-white relations, told by means of assembled primary sources. It is not a selection of documentary material gathered to show Indian contributions to American society, to indicate wrongs and injustices done to the Indians, or to make some other particular point. Nor is it intended as a source for research by students in primary materials, as a more extensive collection might be.

This volume contains the essential documents which marked significant formulations of policy in the conduct of Indian affairs by the United States government, which (by legislative enactment, administrative decree, or judicial decision) were the vehicles for changes in the course of events, or which indicated fundamental reaction to such policies or actions. Students and teachers have here a convenient reference work, supplying in easily available form the text of the documents they need to know when dealing with the public history of Indian affairs. The collection is, therefore, partial and, even within the norms established, selective. Because of limitations of space many important documents had to be omitted and others had to be severely cut. For some classifications, such as treaties, only representative samples could be included. The documents have been reprinted exactly as they appear in the sources cited, with all the variations of spelling, punctuation, and capitalization. Occasional shifts have been made in placement of headings, however, and obvious typographical errors have been corrected.

Students are urged to extend their study beyond this small volume, to read the full documents from which extracts are taken, to investigate more thoroughly the legislative and administrative history which form the context of the documents, and to study the effect of the policies upon the Indian groups. A selected bibliography, which points out reference works and important books and articles, is included at the end of the volume.

FRANCIS PAUL PRUCHA, S.J.

Marquette University
Milwaukee, Wisconsin

Preface to the Second Edition

The selection of documents to include in this updated edition was difficult because of the increasing number of laws, court decisions, and administrative reports dealing with Indian affairs. The 1970s and 1980s were extremely active times, and the movement toward self-determination of Indian tribes has been rapid. All that could be done here is to offer a sampling of the extensive sources, with the hope that all really key documents have been included, with enough others to give a broad view to correspond with and carry through the various elements of policy and policy-making represented in the original edition.

Another problem was extracting pertinent and representative sections from the full documents, for as the documents have grown in number, so too have they grown in size. The Dawes General Allotment Act of 1887, perhaps the most important Indian law of the nineteenth century, covers less than four pages in the *Statutes at Large*, and the Indian

Reorganization Act of 1934, which reversed the policy of the Dawes Act, covers less than five pages. Compare those key documents with the Indian Self-Determination and Education Assistance Act of 1975 and the Indian Health Care Improvement Act of 1976, each of which runs for more than fourteen pages in the *Statutes*. Fortunately, many laws now have preliminary statements of findings and of policy, which indicate the reasons for the legislation. These statements have generally been included, even though it has been necessary to cut drastically the substantive elements of the laws. Students are urged again to examine the full documents from which the extracts are taken, and are reminded that the book is intended as a teaching tool, not as a source for research.

The selected bibliography has been brought up to date, and the new index includes references to the documents added for the second edition.

F.P.P.

1. George Washington to James Duane
September 7, 1783

At the end of the Revolutionary War the new nation faced Indian problems of considerable magnitude, for the Indian nations at war with the United States had no part in the Peace of Paris. In a letter to James Duane, George Washington outlined principles that were to form the basis for the Indian policy of the Continental Congress.

Sir: I have carefully perused the Papers which you put into my hands relative to Indian Affairs. . . .

To suffer a wide extended Country to be over run with Land Jobbers, Speculators, and Monopolisers or even with scatter'd settlers, is, in my opinion, inconsistent with that wisdom and policy which our true interest dictates, or that an enlightened People ought to adopt and, besides, is pregnant of disputes both with the Savages, and among ourselves, the evils of which are easier, to be conceived than described; and for what? but to aggrandize a few avaricious Men to the prejudice of many, and the embarrassment of Government. for the People engaged in these pursuits without contributing in the smallest degree to the support of Government, or considering themselves as amenable to its Laws, will involve it by their unrestrained conduct, in inextricable perplexities, and more than probable in a great deal of Bloodshed.

My ideas therefore of the line of Conduct proper to be observed not only towards the Indians, but for the government of the Citizens of America, in their Settlement of the Western Country (which is intimately connected therewith) are simply these.

First and as a preliminary, that all Prisoners of whatever age or Sex, among the Indians shall be delivered up.

That the Indians should be informed, that after a Contest of eight years for the Sovereignty of this Country G: Britain has ceded all the Lands of the United States within the limits discribed by the arte. of the Provisional Treaty.

That as they (the Indians) maugre all the advice and admonition which could be given them at the commencement; and during the prosecution of the War could not be restrained from acts of Hostility, but were determined to join their Arms to those of G Britain and to share their fortune; so, consequently, with a less generous People than Americans they would be made to share the same fate; and be compelld to retire along with them beyond the Lakes. But as we prefer Peace to a state of Warfare, as we consider them as a deluded People; as we perswade ourselves that they are convinced, from experience, of their error in taking up the Hatchet against us, and that their true Interest and safety must now depend upon *our* friendship. As the Country, is large enough to contain us all; and as we are disposed to be kind to them and to partake of their Trade, we will from these considerations and from motives of Compn., draw a veil over what is past and establish a boundary line between them and us beyond which we will *endeavor* to restrain our People from Hunting or Settling, and within which they shall not come, but for the purposes of Trading, Treating, or other business unexceptionable in its nature.

In establishing this line, in the first instance, care should be taken neither to yield nor to grasp at too much. But to endeavor to impress the Indians with an idea of the generosity of our disposition to accommodate them, and with the necessity we are under, of providing for our Warriors, our Young People who are growing up, and strangers who are coming from other Countries to live among us. and if they should make a point of it, or appear dissatisfied at the line we may find it necessary to establish, compensation should be made them for their claims within it. . . .

The limits being sufficiently extensive (in the New Ctry.) to comply with all the engagements of Government and to admit such emigrations as may be supposed to happen within a given time not only from the several States of the Union but from Foreign Countries, and moreover of such magnitude as to form a distinct and proper Government; a Proclamation in my opinion, should issue,

1

making it Felony (if there is power for the purpose and if not imposing some very heavy restraint) for any person to Survey or Settle beyond the Line; and the Officers Commanding the Frontier Garrison should have pointed and peremptory orders to see that the Proclamation is carried into effect. . . .

Unless some such measures as I have here taken the liberty of suggesting are speedily adopted one of two capital evils, in my opinion, will inevitably result, and is near at hand; either that the settling, or rather over-spreading the Western Country will take place, by a parcel of Banditti, who will bid defiance to all Authority while they are skimming and disposing of the Cream of the Country at the expence of many suffering Officers and Soldiers who have fought and bled to obtain it, and are now waiting the decision of Congress to point them to the promised reward of their past dangers and toils, or a renewal of Hostilities with the Indians, brought about more than probably, by this very means.

How far agents for Indian Affrs. are indispensably necessary I shall not take upon me to decide; but if any should be appointed, their powers in my opinion should be circumscribed, accurately defined, and themselves rigidly punished for every infraction of them. . . . No purchase under any pretence whatever should be made by any other authority than that of the Sovereign power, or the Legislature of the State in which such Lands may happen to be. Nor should the Agents be permitted directly or indirectly to trade; but to have a fixed, and ample Salary allowed them as a full compensation for their trouble.

Whether in practice the measure may answer as well as it appears in theory to me, I will not undertake to say; but I think, if the Indian Trade was carried on, on Government Acct., and with no greater advance than what would be necessary to defray the expence and risk, and bring in a small profit, that it would supply the Indians upon much better terms than they usually are; engross their Trade, and fix them strongly in our Interest; and would be a much better mode of treating them than that of giving presents; where a few only are benefitted by them. I confess there is a difficulty in getting a Man, or set of Men, in whose Abilities and integrity there can be a perfect reliance; without which, the scheme is liable to such abuse as to defeat the salutary ends which are proposed from it. At any rate, no person should be suffered to Trade with the Indians without first obtaining a license, and giving security to conform to such rules and regulations as shall be prescribed; as was the case before the War. . . .

At first view, it may seem a little extraneous, when I am called upon to give an opinion upon the terms of a Peace proper to be made with the Indians, that I should go into the formation of New States; but the Settlemt. of the Western Country and making a Peace with the Indians are so analogous that there can be no definition of the one without involving considerations of the other. for I repeat it, again, and I am clear in my opinion, that policy and oeconomy point very strongly to the expediency of being upon good terms with the Indians, and the propriety of purchasing their Lands in preference to attempting to drive them by force of arms out of their Country; which as we have already experienced is like driving the Wild Beasts of the Forest which will return as soon as the pursuit is at an end and fall perhaps on those that are left there; when the gradual extension of our Settlements will as certainly cause the Savage as the Wolf to retire; both being beasts of prey tho' they differ in shape. In a word there is nothing to be obtained by an Indian War but the Soil they live on and this can be had by purchase at less expence, and without that bloodshed, and those distresses which helpless Women and Children are made partakers of in all kinds of disputes with them. . . .

[*Writings of George Washington*, ed. John C. Fitzpatrick, 27:133-40.]

2

2. Proclamation of the Continental Congress
September 22, 1783

The most serious obstacle to peaceful relations between the United States and the Indians was the steady encroachment of white settlers on the Indian lands. The Continental Congress, following Washington's suggestion, issued a proclamation prohibiting unauthorized settlement or purchase of Indian lands.

By the United States in Congress assembled.

A Proclamation.

Whereas by the ninth of the Articles of Confederation, it is among other things declared, that "the United States in Congress assembled have the sole and exclusive right and power of regulating the trade, and managing all affairs with the Indians, not members of any of the states, provided that the legislative right of any State, within its own limits, be not infringed or violated." And whereas it is essential to the welfare and interest of the United States as well as necessary for the maintenance of harmony and friendship with the Indians, not members of any of the states, that all cause or quarrel or complaint between them and the United States, or any of them, should be removed and prevented: Therefore the United States in Congress assembled have thought proper to issue their proclamation, and they do hereby prohibit and forbid all persons from making settlements on lands inhabited or claimed by Indians, without the limits or jurisdiction of any particular State, and from purchasing or receiving any gift or cession of such lands or claims without the express authority and directions of the United States in Congress assembled.

And it is moreover declared, that every such purchase or settlement, gift or cession, not having the authority aforesaid, is null and void, and that no right or title will accrue in consequence of any such purchase, gift, cession or settlement. . . .

[*Journals of the Continental Congress*, 25: 602.]

3. Report of Committee on Indian Affairs
October 15, 1783

A select committee headed by James Duane, to whom papers relating to Indian affairs had been committed, made a report to the Continental Congress on October 15, 1783, which outlined procedure for dealing with the Indians in the North and West. The influence of Washington's letter to Duane can be seen throughout the document. The following extracts from the long report are the introduction, which is a sort of prologue of policy, and the section relative to trade regulations. Other sections deal with the particular steps recommended to the commissioners for setting up a boundary line and negotiating with the tribes. An almost identical report was submitted in relation to the southern Indians.

[The committee report:] That they have attentively considered the several papers referred to them, and have conferred thereon with the Commander in Chief. . . . That it is represented, and the committee believe with truth, that although the hostile tribes of Indians in the northern and middle departments, are seriously disposed to a pacification, yet they are not in a temper to relinquish their territorial claims, without further struggles. That if an Indian war should be rekindled, repeated victories might produce the retreat of the Indians, but could not prevent them from regaining possession of some part of the distant and extensive territories, which appertain to the United States; that while such temporary expulsions could only be effected at a great charge, they could not be improved to the smallest advantage, but by maintaining numerous garrisons and an expensive peace establishment; that even if all the northern and western tribes of Indians inhabiting the territories of the United States could be totally expelled, the policy of reducing them to such an extremity is deemed to be questionable; for in such an event it is obvious that they would find a welcome reception from the British government in Canada, which by so great an accession of strength would become formidable in case of any future rupture, and in peace, by keeping alive the resentment of the Indians for the loss of their country, would secure to its own subjects the entire benefit of the fur trade. That although motives of policy as well as clemency ought to incline Congress to listen to the prayers of the hostile Indians for peace, yet in the opinion of the committee it is just and necessary that lines of property should be ascertained and established between the United States and them, which will be convenient to the respective tribes, and commensurate to the public wants, because the faith of the United States stands pledged to grant portions of the uncultivated lands as a bounty to their army, and in reward of their courage and fidelity, and the public finances do not admit of any considerable expenditure to extinguish the Indian claims upon such lands; because it is become necessary, by the increase of domestic population and emigrations from abroad, to make speedy provision for extending the settlement of the territories of the United States; and because the public creditors have been led to believe and have a right to expect that those territories will be speedily improved into a fund towards the security and payment of the national debt. Nor in the opinion of the committee can the Indians themselves have any reasonable objections against the establishment recommended. They were, as some of them acknowledge, aggressors in the war, without even a pretence of provocation; they violated the convention of neutrality made with Congress at Albany, in 1775, and in return for proffered protection, and liberal supplies, and to the utter ruin and impoverishment of thousands of families, they wantonly desolated our villages and settlements, and destroyed our citizens. To stop the progress of their outrages, the war, at a vast expence to the United States, was carried into their own country, which they abandoned. Waiving then the right of con-

quest and the various precedents which might be quoted in similar instances, a bare recollection of the facts is sufficient to manifest the obligation they are under to make atonement for the enormities which they have perpetrated, and a reasonable compensation for the expences which the United States have incurred by their wanton barbarity; and they possess no other means to do this act of justice than by a compliance with the proposed boundaries. The committee are of opinion, that in the negotiation which they recommend, care ought to be taken neither to yield nor require too much; to accommodate the Indians as far as the public good will admit, and if they should appear dissatisfied at the lines which it may be found necessary to establish, rather to give them some compensation for their claims than to hazard a war, which will be much more expensive; but it is supposed that when they shall be informed of the estimates of the damages which our citizens have sustained by their irruptions, and of the expences which the United States have incurred to check their career, it will have a tendency to suppress any extravagant demands. . . .

And whereas the trade with the Indians ought to be regulated, and security be given by the traders, for the punctual observance of such regulations, so that violence, fraud and injustice towards the Indians, may be guarded against, and prevented, and the honor of the federal government and the public tranquility thereby promoted.

Resolved, That a committee be appointed with instructions to prepare and report an ordinance for regulating the Indian trade, with a clause therein strictly prohibiting all civil and military officers, and particularly all commissioners and agents for Indian affairs, from trading with the Indians, or purchasing, or being directly or indirectly concerned in purchasing lands from Indians, except only by the express license and authority of the United States in Congress assembled.

[*Journals of the Continental Congress,* 25:681-83, 693.]

4. Treaty with the Six Nations

October 22, 1784

Typical of the treaties of peace signed by the United States with the Indian nations after the Revolutionary War was the treaty with the Six Nations in 1784, negotiated at Fort Stanwix.

Articles concluded at Fort Stanwix, on the twenty-second day of October, one thousand seven hundred and eighty-four, between Oliver Wolcott, Richard Butler, and Arthur Lee, Commissioners Plenipotentiary from the United States, in Congress assembled, on the one Part, and the Sachems and Warriors of the Six Nations, on the other.

The United States of America give peace to the Senecas, Mohawks, Onondagas and Cayugas, and receive them into their protection upon the following conditions:

ARTICLE I. Six hostages shall be immediately delivered to the commissioners by the said nations, to remain in possession of the United States, till all the prisoners, white and black, which were taken by the said Senecas, Mohawks, Onondagas and Cayugas, or by any of them, in the late war, from among the people of the United States, shall be delivered up.

ARTICLE II. The Oneida and Tuscarora nations shall be secured in the possession of the lands on which they are settled.

ARTICLE III. A line shall be drawn, beginning at the mouth of a creek about four miles east of Niagara, called Oyonwayea, or Johnston's Landing-Place, upon the lake named by the Indians Oswego, and by us Ontario; from thence southerly in a direction always four miles east of the carrying-path, between Lake Erie and Ontario, to the mouth of Tehoseroron or Buffaloe Creek on Lake Erie; thence south to the north boundary of the state of Pennsylvania; thence west to the end of the said north boundary; thence south along the west boundary of the said state, to the river Ohio; the said line from the mouth of the Oyonwayea to the Ohio, shall be the western boundary of the lands of the Six Nations, so that the Six Nations shall and do yield to the United States, all claims to the country west of the said boundary, and then they shall be secured in the peaceful possession of the lands they inhabit east and north of the same, reserving only six miles square round the fort of Oswego, to the United States, for the support of the same.

ARTICLE IV. The Commissioners of the United States, in consideration of the present circumstances of the Six Nations, and in execution of the humane and liberal views of the United States upon the signing of the above articles, will order goods to be delivered to the said Six Nations for their use and comfort. . . .

[Charles J. Kappler, ed., *Indian Affairs: Laws and Treaties*, 2:5-6.]

5. Treaty of Fort McIntosh

January 21, 1785

A treaty of peace following the Revolutionary War was made with the northwestern tribes at Fort McIntosh early in 1785, in which the Indians acknowledged the protection of the United States and agreed to boundary lines. The treaty, however, had little effect; it had to be confirmed and augmented by the Treaty of Fort Harmar, January 9, 1789, in which provisions were made to pay the Indians for the lands ceded.

Articles of a treaty concluded at Fort M'Intosh, the twenty-first day of January, one thousand seven hundred and eighty-five, between the Commissioners Plenipotentiary of the United States of America, of the one Part, and the Sachems and Warriors of the Wiandot, Delaware, Chippawa and Ottawa Nations of the other.

The Commissioners Plenipotentiary of the United States in Congress assembled, give peace to the Wiandot, Delaware, Chippewa, and Ottawa nations of Indians, on the following conditions:

ARTICLE I. Three chiefs, one from among the Wiandot, and two from among

5

the Delaware nations, shall be delivered up to the Commissioners of the United States, to be by them retained till all the prisoners, white and black, taken by the said nations, or any of them, shall be restored.

ARTICLE II. The said Indian nations do acknowledge themselves and all their tribes to be under the protection of the United States and of no other sovereign whatsoever.

ARTICLE III. The boundary line between the United States and the Wiandot and Delaware nations, shall begin at the mouth of the river Cayahoga, and run thence up the said river to the portage between that and the Tuscarawas branch of Meskingum; then down the said branch to the forks at the crossing place above Fort Lawrence; then westerly to the portage of the Big Miami, which runs into the Ohio, at the mouth of which branch the fort stood which was taken by the French in one thousand seven hundred and fifty-two; then along the said portage to the Great Miami or Ome river, and down the south-east side of the same to its mouth; thence along the south shore of lake Erie, to the mouth of Cayahoga where it began.

ARTICLE IV. The United States allot all the lands contained within the said lines to the Wiandot and Delaware nations, to live and to hunt on, and to such of the Ottawa nation as now live thereon; saving and reserving for the establishment of trading posts, six miles square at the mouth of Miami or Ome river, and the same at the portage on that branch of the Big Miami which runs into the Ohio, and the same on the lake of Sanduske where the fort formerly stood, and also two miles square on each side of the lower rapids of Sanduske river, which posts and the lands annexed to them, shall be to the use and under the government of the United States.

ARTICLE V. If any citizen of the United States, or other person not being an Indian, shall attempt to settle on any of the lands allotted to the Wiandot and Delaware nations in this treaty, except on the lands reserved to the United States in the preceding article, such person shall forfeit the protection of the United States, and the Indians may punish him as they please.

ARTICLE VI. The Indians who sign this treaty, as well in behalf of all their tribes as of themselves, do acknowledge the lands east, south and west of the lines described in the third article, so far as the said Indians formerly claimed the same, to belong to the United States; and none of their tribes shall presume to settle upon the same, or any part of it.

ARTICLE VII. The post of Detroit, with a district beginning at the mouth of the river Rosine, on the west end of lake Erie, and running west six miles up the southern bank of the said river, thence northerly and always six miles west of the strait, till it strikes the lake St. Clair, shall be also reserved to the sole use of the United States.

ARTICLE VIII. In the same manner the post of Michillimachenac with its dependencies, and twelve miles square about the same, shall be reserved to the use of the United States.

ARTICLE IX. If any Indian or Indians shall commit a robbery or murder on any citizen of the United States, the tribe to which such offenders may belong, shall be bound to deliver them up at the nearest post, to be punished according to the ordinances of the United States.

ARTICLE X. The Commissioners of the United States, in pursuance of the humane and liberal views of Congress, upon this treaty's being signed, will direct goods to be distributed among the different tribes for their use and comfort. . . .

[Charles J. Kappler, ed., *Indian Affairs: Laws and Treaties*, 2:6-8.]

6. Treaty of Hopewell with the Cherokees

November 28, 1785

The United States signed treaties with the southern tribes at Hopewell, South Carolina, in 1785 and 1786. These treaties fixed boundaries for the Indian country, withdrew protection from white settlers on Indian lands, made arrangement for the punishment of criminals, and provided trade regulations. Typical of these agreements was the treaty with the Cherokees.

Articles concluded at Hopewell, on the Keowee, between Benjamin Hawkins, Andrew Pickens, Joseph Martin, and Lachlan M'Intosh, Commissioners Plenipotentiary of the United States of America, of the one Part, and the Head-Men and Warriors of all the Cherokees of the other.

The Commissioners Plenipotentiary of the United States, in Congress assembled, give peace to all the Cherokees, and receive them into the favor and protection of the United States of America, on the following conditions:

ARTICLE I. The Head-Men and Warriors of all the Cherokees shall restore all the prisoners, citizens of the United States, or subjects of their allies, to their entire liberty: They shall also restore all the Negroes, and all other property taken during the late war from the citizens, to such person, and at such time and place, as the Commissioners shall appoint.

ARTICLE II. The Commissioners of the United States in Congress assembled, shall restore all the prisoners taken from the Indians, during the late war, to the Head-Men and Warriors of the Cherokees, as early as is practicable.

ARTICLE III. The said Indians for themselves and their respective tribes and towns do acknowledge all the Cherokees to be under the protection of the United States of America, and of no other sovereign whosoever.

ARTICLE IV. [Describes the boundary line between the Indians and the citizens of the United States.]

ARTICLE V. If any citizen of the United States, or other person not being an Indian, shall attempt to settle on any of the lands westward or southward of the said boundary which are hereby allotted to the Indians for their hunting grounds, or having already settled and will not remove from the same within six months after the ratification of this treaty, such person shall forfeit the protection of the United States, and the Indians may punish him or not as they please: Provided nevertheless, That this article shall not extend to the people settled between the fork of French Broad and Holstein rivers, whose particular situation shall be transmitted to the United States in Congress assembled for their decision thereon, which the Indians agree to abide by.

ARTICLE VI. If any Indian or Indians, or person residing among them, or who shall take refuge in their nation, shall commit a robbery, or murder, or other capital crime, on any citizen of the United States, or person under their protection, the nation, or the tribe to which such offender or offenders may belong, shall be bound to deliver him or them up to be punished according to the ordinances of the United States; Provided, that the punishment shall not be greater than if the robbery or murder, or other capital crime had been committed by a citizen on a citizen.

ARTICLE VII. If any citizen of the United States, or person under their protection, shall commit a robbery or murder, or other capital crime, on any Indian, such offender or offenders shall be punished in the same manner as if the murder or robbery, or other capital crime, had been committed on a citizen of the United States; and the punishment shall be in presence of some of the Cherokees, if any shall attend at the time and place, and that they may have an opportunity so to do, due notice of the time of such intended punishment shall be sent to some one of the tribes.

ARTICLE VIII. It is understood that the punishment of the innocent under the idea of retaliation, is unjust, and shall not be practiced on either side, except where there is a manifest violation of this treaty; and then it shall be preceded first by a demand of justice, and if refused, then by a declaration of hostilities.

ARTICLE IX. For the benefit and comfort of the Indians, and for the prevention of injuries or oppressions on the part of the citizens or Indians, the United States in Congress assembled shall have the sole and exclusive right of regulating the trade with the Indians, and managing all their affairs in such manner as they think proper.

ARTICLE X. Until the pleasure of Congress be known, respecting the ninth article, all traders, citizens of the United States, shall have liberty to go to any of the tribes or towns of the Cherokees to trade with them, and they shall be protected in their persons and property, and kindly treated.

ARTICLE XI. The said Indians shall give

notice to the citizens of the United States, of any designs which they may know or suspect to be formed in any neighboring tribe, or by any person whosoever, against the peace, trade or interest of the United States.

ARTICLE XII. That the Indians may have full confidence in the justice of the United States, respecting their interests, they shall have the right to send a deputy of their choice, whenever they think fit, to Congress.

ARTICLE XIII. The hatchet shall be forever buried, and the peace given by the United States, and friendship re-established between the said states on the one part, and all the Cherokees on the other, shall be universal; and the contracting parties shall use their utmost endeavors to maintain the peace given as aforesaid, and friendship re-established.

In witness of all and every thing herein determined, between the United States of America and all the Cherokees, we, their underwritten Commissioners, by virtue of our full powers, have signed this definitive treaty, and have caused our seals to be hereunto affixed. . . .

[Charles J. Kappler, ed., *Indian Affairs: Laws and Treaties*, 2:8-11.]

7. Ordinance for the Regulation of Indian Affairs

August 7, 1786

An ordinance to govern the Indian trade was approved by the Continental Congress on August 7, 1786. The features it proposed—essentially a licensing system administered by superintendents and agents—were adapted from earlier British practice. This ordinance was never fully effective, but its provisions in modified form became the accepted elements of later laws passed by Congress to regulate trade with the Indian tribes.

Whereas the safety and tranquillity of the frontiers of the United States, do in some measure, depend on the maintaining a good correspondence between their citizens and the several nations of Indians in Amity with them: And whereas the United States in Congress assembled, under the 9th of the Articles of Confederation and perpetual Union, have the sole and exclusive right and power of regulating the trade, and managing all affairs with the Indians not members of any of the states; provided that the legislative right of any state within its own limits be not infringed or violated.

Be it ordained, by the United States in Congress assembled, That from and after the passing of this Ordinance, the Indian department be divided into two districts, viz. The *Southern*, which shall comprehend within its limits, all the Nations in the territory of the United States, who reside southward of the river Ohio; and the *Northern*, which shall comprehend all the other Indian Nations within the said territory, and westward of Hudson river: Provided that all councils, treaties, communications and official transactions, between the Superintendant hereafter mentioned for the northern district, and the Indian Nations, be held, transacted and done, at the Outpost occupied by the troops of the United States, in the said district. That a Superintendant be appointed for each of the said districts, who shall continue in office for two Years, unless sooner removed by Congress, and shall reside within or as near the district for which he shall be so appointed, as may be convenient for the management of its concerns. The said superintendants shall attend to the execution of such regulations, as Congress shall, from time to time, establish respecting Indian Affairs. The superintendant for the northern district, shall have authority to appoint two deputies, to reside in such places as shall best facilitate the regulations of the Indian trade, and to remove them for misbehaviour. There shall be communications of all matters relative to the business of the Indian department, kept up between the said superintendants, who shall regularly correspond with the Secretary at War, through whom all communications respecting the Indian department, shall be made to Congress; and the superintendants are hereby directed to obey all instructions, which they shall, from time to time, receive from the said Secretary at War. And whenever they shall have reason to suspect any tribe or tribes of Indians, of hostile intentions, they shall communicate the same to the executive of the State or States, whose territories are subject to the effect of such hostilities. All stores, provisions or other property, which Congress may think necessary for presents to the Indians, shall be in the custody and under the care of the said superintendants, who shall render an annual account of the expenditures of the same, to the board of treasury.

And be it further ordained, That none but citizens of the United States, shall be suffered to reside among the Indian nations, or be allowed to trade with any nation of Indians, within the territory of the United States. That no person, citizen or other, under the penalty of five hundred dollars, shall reside among or trade with any Indian or Indian nation, within the territory of the United States, without a license for that purpose first obtained from the Superintendant of the district, or one of the deputies, who are hereby directed to give such license to every person, who shall produce from the supreme executive of any state, a certificate under the seal of the state, that he is of good character and suitably qualified, and provided for that employment, for which license he shall pay the sum of fifty dollars, to the said superintendant for the use of the United States. That no license to trade with the Indians shall be in force for a longer term than one year; nor shall permits or passports be granted to any other persons than citizens of the United States to travel through the Indians nations, without their having previously made their business known to the superintendent of the district, and received his special approbation. That previous to any person or persons obtaining a license to trade as aforesaid, he or they shall give bond in three thousand dollars to the superintendant of the district,

for the use of the United States, for his or their strict adherence to, and observance of such rules and regulations as Congress may, from time to time, establish for the government of the Indian trade. All sums to be received by the said Superintendents, either for licenses or fines, shall be annually accounted for by them with the board of treasury.

And be it further ordained, That the said superintendants, and the deputies, shall not be engaged, either directly or indirectly, in trade with the Indians, on pain of forfeiting their Offices. . . . And the said Superintendants and deputy superintendents, shall each of them give bond with surety to the board of treasury, in trust for the United States; the superintendants each in the sum of six thousand dollars, and the deputy superintendents each in the sum of three thousand dollars, for the faithful discharge of the duties of their office.

And be it further ordained, That all fines and forfeitures which may be incurred by contravening this ordinance, shall be sued for and recovered before any court of record within the United States, the one moiety thereof to the use of him or them who may prosecute therefor, and the other moiety to the use of the United States. And the said Superintendants shall have power, and hereby are authorized, by force to restrain therefrom, all persons who shall attempt an intercourse with the said Indians without a license therefor, obtained as aforesaid.

And be it further ordained, That in all cases where transactions with any nation or tribe of Indians shall become necessary to the purposes of this ordinance, which cannot be done without interfering with the legislative rights of a State, the Superintendant in whose district the same shall happen, shall act in conjunction with the authority of such State.

[*Journals of the Continental Congress,* 31:490-93.]

8. Northwest Ordinance

July 13, 1787

The legislation which established the Northwest Territory, thus inaugurating the policy of organizing and governing the national domain west of the Appalachians, included a firm statement of good faith and justice in dealing with the Indians.

. . . Article the Third. Religion, Morality *and knowledge being necessary to good govern-* *ment and the happiness of mankind,* Schools and the means of education shall forever be encouraged. The utmost good faith shall always be observed towards the Indians, their lands and property shall never be taken from them without their consent; and in their property, rights and liberty, they never shall be invaded or disturbed, unless in just and lawful wars authorised by Congress; but laws founded in justice and humanity shall from time to time be made, for preventing wrongs being done to them, and for preserving peace and friendship with them. . . .

[*Journals of the Continental Congress,* 32:340-41.]

9. Committee Report on the Southern Department

August 3, 1787

The conduct of Indian affairs under the Articles of Confederation suffered because of conflicts between federal and state authority. The proviso in the Indian clause of the Articles gave the states grounds for independent action which seriously weakened the authority of the general government in dealing with the Indians. A special committee which investigated Indian troubles in the southern department in 1787 considered the action of the states to be the crucial problem in Indian affairs.

. . . . [The committee observe] that the encroachments complained of appear to demand the serious attention of Congress, as well because they may be unjustifiable as on account of their tendency to produce all the evils of a general Indian war on the frontiers. The committee are convinced that a strict enquiry into the causes and circumstances of the hostilities often committed in and near the frontier settlements ought to be made; that it is become necessary for government to be explicit and decisive, and to see that impartial justice is done between the parties; that Justice and policy as well as the true interests of our citizens, evince the propriety of promoting peace and free trade between them and the Indians. Various circumstances shew that the Indians, in general, within the United States want only to enjoy their lands without interruption, and to have their necessities regularly supplied by our traders, and could these objects be effected, no other measures would, probably be necessary for securing peace and a profitable trade with those Indians. . . .

An avaricious disposition in some of our people to acquire large tracts of land and often by unfair means, appears to be the principal source of difficulties with the Indians. There can be no doubt that settlements are made by our people on the lands secured to the Cherokees, by the late treaty between them and the United States; and also on lands near the Oconee claimed by the Creeks, various pretences seem to be set up by the white people for making those settlements, which the Indians tenacious of their rights, appear to be determined to oppose. From these contrary claims, difficulties arise which are not easily removed. The respective titles cannot readily be investigated: but there is another circumstance far more embarrassing, and that is the clause in the confederation relative to managing all affairs with the Indians, &c. is differently construed by Congress and the two States within whose limits the said tribes and disputed lands are. The construction contended for by those States, if right, appears to the committee, to leave the federal powers, in this case, a mere nullity; and to make it totally uncertain on what principle Congress is to interfere between them and the said tribes; The States not only contend for this construction, but have actually pursued measures in conformity to it. North Carolina has undertaken to assign land to the Cherokees, and Georgia has proceeded to treat with the Creeks concerning peace, lands, and the objects, usually the principal ones in almost every treaty with the Indians. This construction appears to the committee not only to be productive of confusion, disputes and embarrassments in managing affairs with the Independent tribes within the limits of the States, but by no means the true one. The clause referred to is, "Congress shall have the sole and exclusive right and power of regulating the trade and managing all affairs with the Indians, not members of any of the States; provided that the Legislative right of any State within its own limits be not infringed or violated". In forming this clause, the parties to the federal compact,

10

must have had some definite objects in view; the objects that come into view principally, in forming treaties or managing Affairs with the Indians, had been long understood and pretty well ascertained in this country. The committee conceive that it has been long the opinion of the country, supported by Justice and humanity, that the Indians have just claims to all lands occupied by and not fairly purchased from them; and that in managing affairs with them, the principal objects have been those of making war and peace, purchasing certain tracts of their lands, fixing the boundaries between them and our people, and preventing the latter settling on lands left in possession of the former. The powers necessary to these objects appear to the committee to be indivisible, and that the parties to the confederation must have intended to give them entire to the Union, or to have given them entire to the State; these powers before the revolution were possessed by the King, and exercised by him nor did they interfere with the legislative right of the colony within its limits; this distinction which was then and may be now taken, may perhaps serve to explain the proviso, part of the recited clause. The laws of the State can have no effect upon a tribe of Indians or their lands within the limits of the state so long as that tribe is independent, and not a member of the state, yet the laws of the state may be executed upon debtors, criminals, and other proper objects of those laws in all parts of it, and therefore the union may make stipulations with any such tribe, secure it in the enjoyment of all or part of its lands, without infringing upon the legislative right in question. It cannot be supposed, the state has the powers mentioned without making the recited clause useless, and without absurdity in theory as well as in practice; for the Indian tribes are justly considered the common friends or enemies of the United States, and no particular state can have an exclusive interest in the management of Affairs with any of the tribes, except in some uncommon cases. . . .

[*Journals of the Continental Congress*, 33:456-59.]

10.   Report of Henry Knox on White Outrages
July 18, 1788

Peace with the Indians could not be maintained so long as aggressive action by the frontier whites gave the Indians grounds for retaliatory incursions. The outrages perpetrated by the frontiersmen among the southern Indians caused an early crisis in Indian relations. The report of Secretary of War Henry Knox to the Continental Congress in July 1788 shows the nature of the problem and the suggestions made for overcoming it. The proclamation Knox called for was issued by Congress on September 1, 1788.

[The secretary of war reports] That it appears . . . that the white inhabitants on the frontiers of North Carolina in the vicinity of Chota on the Tenessee river, have frequently committed the most unprovoked and direct outrages against the Cherokee indians.

That this unworthy conduct is an open violation of the treaty of peace made by the United States with the said indians at Hopewell on the Keowee the 30th of November 1785.

That the said enormities have arisen at length to such an height as to amount to an actual although informal war of the said white inhabitants against the said Cherokees.

That the unjustifiable conduct of the said inhabitants has most probably been dictated by the avaricious desire of obtaining the fertile lands possessed by the said indians of which and particularly of their ancient town of Chota they are exceedingly tenacious. . . .

That . . . by an upright and honorable construction of the treaty of Hopewell the United States have pledged themselves for the protection of the said indians within the boundaries described by the said treaty and that the principles of good Faith sound policy and every respect which a nation, owes to its own reputation and dignity require if the union possess sufficient power that it be exerted to enforce a due observance of the said treaty.

That in order to vindicate the sovereignty

of the Union from reproach, your secretary is of opinion, that, the sentiments, and decision, of Congress should be fully expressed to the said white inhabitants, who have so flagitiously stained the American name.

That the agent of indian affairs should disperse among the said people a proclamation to be issued by Congress on the subject. That the said proclamation should recite such parts of said treaty as are obligatory on the Union and a declaration of the firm determination of Congress to enforce the same. That all persons who have settled on any of the said lands unless the same shall have been fairly purchased of the said indians shall be warned at their peril to depart previously to a day to be affixed.

That in order to carry efficiently into effect the determinations of Congress the commanding officer of the troops on the Ohio should be directed to make himself acquainted of the best routes by which a body of three hundred men could be transported most easily and expeditiously to Chota on the Tenessee river, and report the same to the secretary at war.

That in case the Proclamation of Congress should be attended with no effect that the said commanding officer should be directed to move as early in the spring of the next year as the season should admit with a body of three hundred troops to Chota and there to act according to the special instructions he shall receive from the Secretary at War. . . .

Your Secretary begs leave to observe that he is utterly at a loss to devise any other mode of correcting effectually the evils specified than the one herein proposed. That he conceives it of the highest importance to the peace of the frontiers that all the indian tribes should rely with security on the treaties they have made or shall make with the United States. That unless this shall be the case the powerful tribes of the Creeks Choctaws and Chickesaws will be able to keep the frontiers of the southern states constantly embroiled with hostilities, and that all the other tribes will have good grounds not only according to their own opinions but according to the impartial judgements of the civilized part of the human race for waging perpetual war against the citizens of the United States. . . .

[*Journals of the Continental Congress,* 34:342-44.]

11.   Report of Henry Knox on the Northwestern Indians

June 15, 1789

The disturbances between whites and Indians along the Wabash River created a crisis in Indian affairs. Secretary of War Henry Knox urged a just and humane policy which would recognize Indian rights to the soil, reject the principle of conquest, and compensate the Indians for lands ceded by them.

. . . . In examining the question how the disturbances on the frontiers are to be quieted, two modes present themselves, by which the object might perhaps be effected; the first of which is by raising an army, and extirpating the refractory tribes entirely, or 2dly by forming treaties of peace with them, in which their rights and limits should be explicitly defined, and the treaties observed on the part of the United States with the most rigid justice, by punishing the whites, who should violate the same.

In considering the first mode, an inquiry would arise, whether, under the existing circumstances of affairs, the United States have a clear right, consistently with the principles of justice and the laws of nature, to proceed to the destruction or expulsion of the savages, on the Wabash, supposing the force for that object easily attainable.

It is presumable, that a nation solicitous of establishing its character on the broad basis of justice, would not only hesitate at, but reject every proposition to benefit itself, by the injury of any neighboring community, however contemptible and weak it might be, either with respect to its manners or power. . . .

The Indians being the prior occupants, possess the right of the soil. It cannot be taken from them unless by their free consent, or by the right of conquest in case of a just war. To dispossess them on any other principle, would be a gross violation of the fundamental laws of nature, and of that distributive justice which is the glory of a nation.

But if it should be decided, on an abstract view of the question, to be just, to remove by force the Wabash Indians from the territory they occupy, the finances of the United States would not at present admit of the operation.

By the best and latest information, it appears that, on the Wabash and its communications, there are from 1500 to 2000 warriors. An expedition against them, with the view of extirpating them, or destroying their towns, could not be undertaken with a probability of success, with less than an army of 2,500 men. The regular troops of the United States on the frontiers, are less than six hundred; of that number, not more than four hundred could be collected from the posts for the purpose of the expedition. To raise, pay, feed, arm, and equip 1900 additional men, with their necessary officers for six months, and to provide every thing in the hospital and quartermaster's line, would require the sum of 200,000 dollars; a sum far exceeding the ability of the United States to advance, consistently with a due regard to other indispensable objects.

Were the representations of the people of the frontiers (who have imbibed the strongest prejudices against the Indians, perhaps in consequence of the murders of their dearest friends and connexions) only to be regarded, the circumstances before stated, would not appear conclusive—an expedition, however inadequate, must be undertaken.

But when the impartial mind of the great public sits in judgment, it is necessary that the cause of the ignorant Indians should be heard as well as those who are more fortunately circumstanced. It well becomes the public to inquire before it punishes; to be influenced by reason, and the nature of things, and not by its resentments.

It would be found, on examination, that both policy and justice unite in dictating the attempt of treating with the Wabash Indians: for it would be unjust, in the present confused state of injuries, to make war on those tribes without having previously invited them to a treaty, in order amicably to adjust all differences. If they should after-wards persist in their depredations, the United States may with propriety inflict such punishment as they shall think proper. . . .

The time has arrived, when it is highly expedient that a liberal system of justice should be adopted for the various Indian tribes within the limits of the United States.

By having recourse to the several Indian treaties, made by the authority of Congress, since the conclusion of the war with Great Britain, excepting those made January 1789, at fort Harmar, it would appear, that Congress were of opinion, that the Treaty of Peace, of 1783, absolutely invested them with the fee of all the Indian lands within the limits of the United States; that they had the right to assign, or retain such portions as they should judge proper.

But it is manifest, from the representations of the confederated Indians at the Huron village, in December, 1786, that they entertained a different opinion, and that they were the only rightful proprietors of the soil; and it appears by the resolve of the 2d of July, 1788, that Congress so far conformed to the idea, as to appropriate a sum of money solely to the purpose of extinguishing the Indian claims to lands they had ceded to the United States, and for obtaining regular conveyances of the same. This object was accordingly accomplished at the treaty of fort Harmar, in January, 1789.

The principle of the Indian right to the lands they possess being thus conceded, the dignity and interest of the nation will be advanced by making it the basis of the future administration of justice towards the Indian tribes. . . .

As the settlements of the whites shall approach near to the Indian boundaries established by treaties, the game will be diminished, and the lands being valuable to the Indians only as hunting grounds, they will be willing to sell further tracts for small considerations. By the expiration, therefore, of the above period, it is most probable that the Indians will, by the invariable operation of the causes which have hitherto existed in their intercourse with the whites, be reduced to a very small number. . . .

[*American State Papers: Indian Affairs,* 1:13-14.]

12. Establishment of the War Department

August 7, 1789

When the First Congress under the Constitution established the War Department, it placed Indian affairs under its jurisdiction, where they remained until the establishment of the Interior Department in 1849.

An Act to establish an Executive Department, to be denominated the Department of War.

SECTION 1. *Be it enacted* . . . , That there shall be an executive department to be denominated the Department of War, and that there shall be a principal officer therein, to be called the Secretary for the Department of War, who shall perform and execute such duties as shall from time to time be enjoined on, or entrusted to him by the President of the United States, agreeably to the Constitution, relative to military commissions, or to the land or naval forces, ships, or warlike stores of the United States, or to such other matters respecting military or naval affairs, as the President of the United States shall assign to the said department, or relative to the granting of lands to persons entitled thereto, for military services rendered to the United States, or relative to Indian affairs; and furthermore, that the said principal officer shall conduct the business of the said department in such manner, as the President of the United States shall from time to time order or instruct. . . .

[U.S. Statutes at Large, 1:49-50.]

13. Trade and Intercourse Act

July 22, 1790

Unrest on the frontiers threatened the peace of the young nation, and President Washington and Secretary of War Knox called on Congress to provide legislation to prevent further outrages. Congress replied in July 1790 with the first of a series of laws "to regulate trade and intercourse with the Indian tribes." These laws, which were originally designed to implement the treaties and enforce them against obstreperous whites, gradually came to embody the basic features of federal Indian policy.

An Act to regulate trade and intercourse with the Indian tribes.

SECTION 1. *Be it enacted* . . . , That no person shall be permitted to carry on any trade or intercourse with the Indian tribes, without a license for that purpose under the hand and seal of the superintendent of the department, or of such other person as the President of the United States shall appoint for that purpose; which superintendent, or other person so appointed, shall, on application, issue such license to any proper person, who shall enter into bond with one or more sureties, approved of by the superintendent, or person issuing such license, or by the President of the United States, in the penal sum of one thousand dollars, payable to the President of the United States for the time being, for the use of the United States, conditioned for the true and faithful observance of such rules, regulations and restrictions, as now are, or hereafter shall be made for the government of trade and intercourse with the Indian tribes. The said superintendents, and persons by them licensed as aforesaid, shall be governed in all things touching the said trade and intercourse, by such rules and regulations as the President shall prescribe. And no other person shall be permitted to carry on any trade or intercourse with the Indians without such license as aforesaid. No license shall be granted for a longer term than two years. *Provided nevertheless,* That the President may make such order respecting the tribes surrounded in their settlements by the citizens of the United States, as to secure an intercourse without license, if he may deem it proper.

SEC. 2. *And be it further enacted,* That the superintendent, or person issuing such license, shall have full power and authority to recall all such licenses as he may have issued, if the person so licensed shall transgress any of the regulations or restrictions provided for the government of trade and intercourse

14

with the Indian tribes, and shall put in suit such bonds as he may have taken, immediately on the breach of any condition in said bond: *Provided always*, That if it shall appear on trial, that the person from whom such license shall have been recalled, has not offended against any of the provisions of this act, or the regulations prescribed for the trade and intercourse with the Indian tribes, he shall be entitled to receive a new license.

SEC. 3. *And be it further enacted*, That every person who shall attempt to trade with the Indian tribes, or be found in the Indian country with such merchandise in his possession as are usually vended to the Indians, without a license first had and obtained, as in this act prescribed, and being thereof convicted in any court proper to try the same, shall forfeit all the merchandise so offered for sale to the Indian tribes, or so found in the Indian country, which forfeiture shall be one half to the benefit of the person prosecuting, and the other half to the benefit of the United States.

SEC. 4. *And be it enacted and declared*, That no sale of lands made by any Indians, or any nation or tribe of Indians within the United States, shall be valid to any person or persons, or to any state, whether having the right of pre-emption to such lands or not, unless the same shall be made and duly executed at some public treaty, held under the authority of the United States.

SEC. 5. *And be it further enacted*, That if any citizen or inhabitant of the United States, or of either of the territorial districts of the United States, shall go into any town, settlement or territory belonging to any nation or tribe of Indians, and shall there commit any crime upon, or trespass against, the person or property of any peaceable and friendly Indian or Indians, which, if committed within the jurisdiction of any state, or within the jurisdiction of either of the said districts, against a citizen or white inhabitant thereof, would be punishable by the laws of such state or district, such offender or offenders shall be subject to the same punishment, and shall be proceeded against in the same manner as if the offence had been committed within the jurisdiction of the state or district to which he or they may belong, against a citizen or white inhabitant thereof.

SEC. 6. *And be it further enacted*, That for any of the crimes or offences aforesaid, the like proceedings shall be had for apprehending, imprisoning or bailing the offender, as the case may be, and for recognizing the witnesses for their appearance to testify in the case, and where the offender shall be committed, or the witnesses shall be in a district other than that in which the offence is to be tried, for the removal of the offender and the witnesses or either of them, as the case may be, to the district in which the trial is to be had, as by the act to establish the judicial courts of the United States, are directed for any crimes or offences against the United States.

SEC. 7. *And be it further enacted*, That this act shall be in force for the term of two years, and from thence to the end of the next session of Congress, and no longer.

[*U.S. Statutes at Large*, 1:137-38.]

14. President Washington's Third Annual Message

October 25, 1791

President Washington carried his concern for a just Indian policy to Congress in his annual messages. In 1791 he outlined the essential elements of a policy to "advance the happiness of the Indians and to attach them firmly to the United States."

. . . . It is sincerely to be desired that all need of coercion in future may cease and that an intimate intercourse may succeed, calculated to advance the happiness of the Indians and to attach them firmly to the United States.

In order to this it seems necessary—

That they should experience the benefits of an impartial dispensation of justice.

That the mode of alienating their lands, the main source of discontent and war, should be so defined and regulated as to obviate imposition and as far as may be practicable controversy concerning the reality and extent of the alienations which are made.

That commerce with them should be promoted under regulations tending to secure an equitable deportment toward them, and that such rational experiments should be made for imparting to them the blessings of civilization as may from time to time suit their condition.

That the Executive of the United States should be enabled to employ the means to which the Indians have been long accustomed for uniting their immediate interests with the preservation of peace.

And that efficacious provision should be made for inflicting adequate penalties upon all those who, by violating their rights, shall infringe the treaties and endanger the peace of the Union.

A system corresponding with the mild principles of religion and philanthropy toward an unenlightened race of men, whose happiness materially depends on the conduct of the United States, would be as honorable to the national character as conformable to the dictates of sound policy. . . .

[James D. Richardson, comp., *Messages and Papers of the Presidents*, 1:96-97.]

15. President Washington on Government Trading Houses

December 3, 1793

Washington repeatedly stressed the importance of properly regulated trade with the Indians. In his Fifth Annual Message to Congress he suggested that the United States government itself should enter the trade, a recommendation later incorporated in the factory system.

. . . . After they [Congress] shall have provided for the present emergency, it will merit their most serious labors to render tranquillity with the savages permanent by creating ties of interest. Next to a rigorous execution of justice on the violators of peace, the establishment of commerce with the Indian nations in behalf of the United States is most likely to conciliate their attachment. But it ought to be conducted without fraud, without extortion, with constant and plentiful supplies, with a ready market for the commodities of the Indians and a stated price for what they give in payment and receive in exchange. Individuals will not pursue such a traffic unless they be allured by the hope of profit; but it will be enough for the United States to be reimbursed only. Should this recommendation accord with the opinion of Congress, they will recollect that it can not be accomplished by any means yet in the hands of the Executive. . . .

[James D. Richardson, comp., *Messages and Papers of the President*, 1:133.]

16. Establishment of Government Trading Houses

April 18, 1796

Washington's proposal for government trading houses was accepted as a trial measure in 1795, and in 1796 Congress established a system of Indian trading houses, which would provide "liberal trade with the several Indian nations." This so-called factory system was extended periodically until it was abolished in 1822.

An Act for establishing Trading Houses with the Indian Tribes.

SECTION 1. *Be it enacted* . . . , That it shall be lawful for the President of the United States, to establish trading houses at such posts and places on the western and southern frontiers, or in the Indian country, as he shall judge most convenient for the purpose of carrying on a liberal trade with the several Indian nations, within the limits of the United States.

SEC. 2. *And be it further enacted*, That the President be authorized to appoint an agent for each trading house established, whose duty it shall be, to receive, and dispose of, in trade, with the Indian nations afore-mentioned, such goods as he shall be directed by the President of the United States to receive and dispose of, as aforesaid, according to the rules and orders which the President shall prescribe; and every such agent shall take an oath or affirmation, faithfully to execute the trust committed to him; and that he will not, directly or indirectly, be concerned or interested in any trade, commerce or barter, with

16

any Indian or Indians whatever, but on the public account. . . .

SEC. 3. *And be it further enacted,* That the agents, their clerks, or other persons employed by them, shall not be, directly or indirectly, concerned or interested in carrying on the business of trade or commerce, on their own, or any other than the public account, or take, or apply to his or their own use, any emolument or gain for negotiating or transacting any business or trade, during their agency or employment, other than is provided by this act. . . .

SEC. 4. *And be it further enacted,* That the prices of the goods supplied to, and to be paid for by the Indians, shall be regulated in such manner, that the capital stock furnished by the United States may not be diminished.

SEC. 5. *Be it further enacted,* That during the continuance of this act, the President of the United States be, and he is hereby authorized to draw annually from the treasury of the United States, a sum not exceeding eight thousand dollars, to be applied, under his direction, for the purpose of paying the agents and clerks; which agents shall be allowed to draw out of the public supplies, two rations each, and each clerk one ration per day.

SEC. 6. *And be it further enacted,* That one hundred and fifty thousand dollars, exclusive of the allowances to agents and clerks, be and they are hereby appropriated for the purpose of carrying on trade and intercourse with the Indian nations, in the manner aforementioned, to be paid out of any monies unappropriated in the treasury of the United States.

SEC. 7. *And be it further enacted,* That if any agent or agents, their clerks, or other persons employed by them, shall purchase, or receive of any Indian, in the way of trade or barter, a gun or other article commonly used in hunting; any instrument of husbandry, or cooking utensil, of the kind usually obtained by Indians in their intercourse with white people; any article of clothing (excepting skins or furs) he or they shall, respectively, forfeit the sum of one hundred dollars for each offence. . . .

[*U.S. Statutes at Large,* 1:452-53.]

17.   Trade and Intercourse Act

March 30, 1802

The temporary trade and intercourse acts passed in 1790, 1796, and 1799 were replaced in 1802 by a more permanent measure, which was largely a restatement of the earlier laws. With occasional additions it remained in force as the basic law governing Indian relations until it was replaced by a new codification of Indian policy in 1834.

An Act to regulate trade and intercourse with the Indians tribes, and to preserve peace on the frontiers.

Be it enacted . . . , That the following boundary line, established by treaty between the United States and various Indian tribes, shall be clearly ascertained, and distinctly marked in all such places as the President of the United States shall deem necessary, and in such manner as he shall direct, to wit: [The boundary is described in detail.] . . . *Provided always,* that if the boundary line between the said Indian tribes and the United States shall, at any time hereafter, be varied, by any treaty which shall be made between the said Indian tribes and the United States, then all the provisions contained in this act shall be construed to apply to the said line so to be varied, in the same manner as said provisions apply, by force of this act, to the boundary line herein before recited.

SEC. 2. *And be it further enacted,* That if any citizen of, or other person resident in, the United States, or either of the territorial districts of the United States, shall cross over, or go within the said boundary line, to hunt, or in any wise destroy the game; or shall drive, or otherwise convey any stock of horses or cattle to range on any lands allotted or secured by treaty with the United States, to any Indian tribes, he shall forfeit a sum not exceeding one hundred dollars, or be imprisoned not exceeding six months.

SEC. 3. *And be it further enacted,* That if any such citizen or other person, shall go

17

into any country which is allotted, or secured by treaty as aforesaid, to any of the Indian tribes south of the river Ohio, without a passport first had and obtained from the governor of some one of the United States, or the officer of the troops of the United States, commanding at the nearest post on the frontiers, or such other person as the President of the United States may, from time to time, authorize to grant the same, shall forfeit a sum not exceeding fifty dollars, or be imprisoned not exceeding three months.

SEC. 4. *And be it further enacted*, That if any such citizen, or other person, shall go into any town, settlement or territory, belonging, or secured by treaty with the United States, to any nation or tribe of Indians, and shall there commit robbery, larceny, trespass or other crime, against the person or property of any friendly Indian or Indians, which would be punishable, if committed within the jurisdiction of any state, against a citizen of the United States: or, unauthorized by law, and with a hostile intention, shall be found on any Indian land, such offender shall forfeit a sum not exceeding one hundred dollars, and be imprisoned not exceeding twelve months; and shall also, when property is taken or destroyed, forfeit and pay to such Indian or Indians, to whom the property taken and destroyed belongs, a sum equal to twice the just value of the property so taken or destroyed: and if such offender shall be unable to pay a sum at least equal to the said just value, whatever such payment shall fall short of the said just value, shall be paid out of the treasury of the United States: *Provided nevertheless*, that no such Indian shall be entitled to any payment out of the treasury of the United States, for any such property taken or destroyed, if he, or any of the nation to which he belongs, shall have sought private revenge, or attempted to obtain satisfaction by any force or violence.

SEC. 5. *And be it further enacted*, That if any such citizen, or other person, shall make a settlement on any lands belonging, or secured, or granted by treaty with the United States, to any Indian tribe, or shall survey, or attempt to survey, such lands, or designate any of the boundaries, by marking trees, or otherwise, such offender shall for-

feit a sum not exceeding one thousand dollars, and suffer imprisonment, not exceeding twelve months. And it shall, moreover, be lawful for the President of the United States to take such measures, and to employ such military force, as he may judge necessary, to remove from lands, belonging or secured by treaty, as aforesaid, to any Indian tribe, any such citizen, or other person, who has made, or shall hereafter make, or attempt to make a settlement thereon.

SEC. 6. *And be it further enacted*, That if any such citizen, or other person, shall go into any town, settlement or territory belonging to any nation or tribe of Indians, and shall there commit murder, by killing any Indian or Indians, belonging to any nation or tribe of Indians, in amity with the United States, such offender, on being thereof convicted, shall suffer death.

SEC. 7. *And be it further enacted*, That no such citizen, or other person, shall be permitted to reside at any of the towns, or hunting camps, of any of the Indian tribes as a trader, without a license under the hand and seal of the superintendent of the department, or of such other person as the President of the United States shall authorize to grant licenses for that purpose: which superintendent, or person authorized, shall, on application, issue such license, for a term not exceeding two years, to such trader, who shall enter into bond with one or more sureties, approved of by the superintendent, or person issuing such license, or by the President of the United States, in the penal sum of one thousand dollars, conditioned for the true and faithful observance of such regulations and restrictions, as are, or shall be made for the government of trade and intercourse with the Indian tribes: and the superintendent, or person issuing such license, shall have full power and authority to recall the same, if the person so licensed shall transgress any of the regulations, or restrictions, provided for the government of trade and intercourse with the Indian tribes; and shall put in suit such bonds as he may have taken, on the breach of any condition therein contained.

SEC. 8. *And be it further enacted*, That any such citizen or other person, who shall attempt to reside in any town or hunting camp, of any of the Indian tribes, as a trader, without such license, shall forfeit all the merchandise offered for sale to the Indians, or found in his possession, and shall, moreover, be liable to a fine not exceeding one hundred dollars, and to imprisonment not exceeding thirty days.

SEC. 9. *And be it further enacted*, That if any such citizen, or other person, shall purchase, or receive of any Indian, in the way of trade or barter, a gun, or other article commonly used in hunting, any instrument of husbandry, or cooking utensil, of the kind usually obtained by the Indians, in their intercourse with white people, or any article of clothing, excepting skins or furs, he shall forfeit a sum not exceeding fifty dollars, and be imprisoned not exceeding thirty days.

SEC. 10. *And be it further enacted*, That no such citizen or other person shall be permitted to purchase any horse of an Indian, or of any white man in the Indian territory, without special license for that purpose; which license, the superintendent, or such other person as the President shall appoint, is hereby authorized to grant, on the same terms, conditions and restrictions, as other licenses are to be granted under this act: and any such person, who shall purchase a horse or horses, under such license, before he exposes such horse or horses for sale, and within fifteen days after they have been brought out of the Indian country, shall make a particular return to the superintendent, or other person, from whom he obtained his license, of every horse purchased by him, as aforesaid; describing such horses, by their colour, height, and other natural or artificial marks, under the penalty contained in their respective bonds. And every such person, purchasing a horse or horses, as aforesaid, in the Indian country, without a special license, shall for every horse thus purchased and brought into any settlement of citizens of the United States, forfeit a sum not exceeding one hundred dollars, and be imprisoned not exceeding thirty days. And every person, who shall purchase a horse, knowing him to be brought out of the Indian territory, by any person or persons, not licensed, as above, to purchase the same, shall forfeit the value of such horse.

SEC. 11. *And be it further enacted*, That no agent, superintendent, or other person authorized to grant a license to trade, or purchase horses, shall have any interest or concern in any trade with the Indians, or in the purchase or sale of any horse to or from any Indian, excepting for and on account of the United States; and any person offending herein, shall forfeit a sum not exceeding one thousand dollars, and be imprisoned not exceeding twelve months.

SEC. 12. *And be it further enacted*, That no purchase, grant, lease, or other conveyance of lands, or of any title or claim thereto, from any Indian, or nation, or tribe of Indians, within the bounds of the United States, shall be of any validity, in law or equity, unless the same be made by treaty or convention, entered into pursuant to the constitution: and it shall be a misdemeanor in any person, not employed under the authority of the United States, to negotiate such treaty or convention, directly or indirectly, to treat with any such Indian nation, or tribe of Indians, for the title or purchase of any lands by them held or claimed, punishable by fine not exceeding one thousand dollars, and imprisonment not exceeding twelve months: *Provided nevertheless*, that it shall be lawful for the agent or agents of any state, who may be present at any treaty held with Indians under the authority of the United States, in the presence, and with the approbation of the commissioner or commissioners of the United States, appointed to hold the same, to propose to, and adjust with the Indians, the compensation to be made, for their claims to lands within such state, which shall be extinguished by the treaty.

SEC. 13. *And be it further enacted*, That in order to promote civilization among the friendly Indian tribes, and to secure the continuance of their friendship, it shall be lawful for the President of the United States, to cause them to be furnished with useful domestic animals, and implements of husbandry, and with goods or money, as he shall judge proper, and to appoint such persons, from time to time, as temporary agents, to reside among the Indians, as he shall think fit: *Provided*, that the whole amount of such presents, and allowance to such agents, shall not exceed fifteen thousand dollars per annum.

SEC. 14. *And be it further enacted*, That if any Indian or Indians, belonging to any tribe in amity with the United States, shall come over or cross the said boundary line, into any state or territory inhabited by citizens of the United States, and there take, steal or destroy any horse, horses, or other property, belonging to any citizen or inhabitant of the United States, or of either of the territorial districts of the United States, or shall commit any murder, violence or outrage, upon any such citizen or inhabitant, it shall be the duty of such citizen or inhabitant, his representative, attorney, or agent, to make application to the superintendent, or such other person as the President of the United States shall authorize for that purpose; who, upon being furnished with the necessary documents and proofs, shall, under the direction or instruction of the President of the United States, make application to the nation or tribe, to which such Indian or Indians shall belong, for satisfaction; and if such nation or tribe shall neglect or refuse to make satisfaction, in a reasonable time, not exceeding twelve months, then it shall be the duty of such superintendent or other person authorized as aforesaid, to make return of his doings to the President of the United States, and forward to him all the documents and proofs in the case, that such further steps may be taken, as shall be proper to obtain satisfaction for the injury: and in the mean time, in respect to the property so taken, stolen or destroyed, the United States guarantee to the party injured, an eventual indemnification: *Provided always*, that if such injured party, his representative, attorney or agent, shall, in any way, violate any of the provisions of this act, by seeking, or attempting to obtain private satisfaction or revenge, by crossing over the line, on any of the Indian lands, he shall forfeit all claim upon the United States, for such indemnification: *And provided also*, that nothing herein contained shall prevent the legal apprehension or arresting, within the limits of any state or district, of any Indian having so offended: *And provided further*, that it shall be lawful for the President of the United States, to deduct such sum or sums, as shall be paid for the property taken, stolen or destroyed by any such Indian, out of the annual stipend, which the United States are bound to pay to the tribe, to which such Indian shall belong.

Sec. 15. [Detailed specification of courts having jurisdiction under the act.]

Sec. 16. *And be it further enacted*, That it shall be lawful for the military force of the United States to apprehend every person who shall, or may be found in the Indian country over and beyond the said boundary line between the United States and the said Indian tribes, in violation of any of the provisions or regulations of this act, and him or them immediately to convey, in the nearest, convenient and safe route, to the civil authority of the United States, in some one of the three next adjoining states or districts, to be proceeded against in due course of law: *Provided*, that no person, apprehended by military force as aforesaid, shall be detained longer than five days after the arrest, and before removal. And all officers and soldiers who may have any such person or persons in custody, shall treat them with all the humanity which the circumstances will possibly permit; and every officer and soldier who shall be guilty of maltreating any such person, while in custody, shall suffer such punishment as a court martial shall direct. . . .

Sec. 17. *And be it further enacted*, That if any person, who shall be charged with a violation of any of the provisions or regulations of this act, shall be found within any of the United States, or either of the territorial districts of the United States, such offender may be there apprehended and brought to trial in the same manner, as if such crime or offence had been committed within such state or district; and it shall be the duty of the military force of the United States, when called upon by the civil magistrate, or any proper officer, or other person duly authorized for that purpose and having a lawful warrant, to aid and assist such magistrate, officer, or other person authorized, as aforesaid, in arresting such offender, and him committing to safe custody, for trial according to law.

Sec. 18. *And be it further enacted*, That the amount of fines, and duration of imprisonment, directed by this act as a punishment for the violation of any of the provisions thereof, shall be ascertained and fixed, not exceeding the limits prescribed, in the discretion of the court, before whom the trial shall be had; and that all fines and forfeitures, which shall accrue under this act, shall be one half to the use of the informant, and

20

the other half to the use of the United States; except where the prosecution shall be first instituted on behalf of the United States; in which case the whole shall be to their use.

SEC. 19. *And be it further enacted*, That nothing in this act shall be construed to prevent any trade or intercourse with Indians living on lands surrounded by settlements of the citizens of the United States, and being within the ordinary jurisdiction of any of the individual states; or the unmolested use of a road from Washington district to Mero district, or to prevent the citizens of Tennessee from keeping in repair the said road, under the direction or orders of the governor of said state, and of the navigation of the Tennessee river, as reserved and secured by treaty; nor shall this act be construed to prevent any person or persons travelling from Knoxville to Price's settlement, or to the settlement on Obed's river, (so called,) provided they shall travel in the trace or path which is usually travelled, and provided the Indians make no objection; but if the Indians object, the President of the United States is hereby authorized to issue a proclamation, prohibiting all travelling on said traces, or either of them, as the case may be, after which, the penalties of this act shall be incurred by every person travelling or being found on said traces, or either of them, to which the prohibition may apply, within the Indian boundary, without a passport.

SEC. 20. *And be it further enacted*, That the President of the United States be, and he is hereby authorized to cause to be clearly ascertained and distinctly marked, in all such places as he shall deem necessary, and in such manner as he shall direct, any other boundary lines between the United States and any Indian tribe, which now are, or hereafter may be established by treaty.

SEC. 21. *And be it further enacted*, That the President of the United States be authorized to take such measures, from time to time, as to him may appear expedient to prevent or restrain the vending or distributing of spirituous liquors among all or any of the said Indian tribes, any thing herein contained to the contrary thereof notwithstanding.

SEC. 22. *And be it further enacted*, That this act shall be in force from the passage thereof. . . .

[*U.S. Statutes at Large*, 2:139-46.]

18.   President Jefferson on Indian Trading Houses
January 18, 1803

Jefferson sent a special message to Congress at the beginning of 1803, in which he urged a continuation of the government trading houses established in the Indian country. His policy of moving the Indians from a hunting economy to an agricultural state was strongly stated in the message.

Gentlemen of the Senate and of the House of Representatives:

As the continuance of the act for establishing trading houses with the Indian tribes will be under the consideration of the Legislature at its present session, I think it my duty to communicate the views which have guided me in the execution of that act, in order that you may decide on the policy of continuing it in the present or any other form, or discontinue it altogether if that shall, on the whole, seem most for the public good.

The Indian tribes residing within the limits of the United States have for a considerable time been growing more and more uneasy at the constant diminution of the territory they occupy, although effected by their own voluntary sales, and the policy has long been gaining strength with them of refusing absolutely all further sale on any conditions, insomuch that at this time it hazards their friendship and excites dangerous jealousies and perturbations in their minds to make any overture for the purchase of the smallest portions of their land. A very few tribes only are not yet obstinately in these dispositions. In order peaceably to counteract this policy of theirs and to provide an extension of territory which the rapid increase of our numbers will call for, two measures are deemed expedient. First. To encourage them to abandon hunting, to apply to the raising stock, to agriculture, and

21

domestic manufacture, and thereby prove to themselves that less land and labor will maintain them in this better than in their former mode of living. The extensive forests necessary in the hunting life will then become useless, and they will see advantage in exchanging them for the means of improving their farms and of increasing their domestic comforts. Secondly. To multiply trading houses among them, and place within their reach those things which will contribute more to their domestic comfort than the possession of extensive but uncultivated wilds. Experience and reflection will develop to them the wisdom of exchanging what they can spare and we want for what we can spare and they want. In leading them thus to agriculture, to manufactures, and civiliza-tion; in bringing together their and our sentiments, and in preparing them ultimately to participate in the benefits of our Government, I trust and believe we are acting for their greatest good. At these trading houses we have pursued the principles of the act of Congress which directs that the commerce shall be carried on liberally, and requires only that the capital stock shall not be diminished. We consequently undersell private traders, foreign and domestic, drive them from the competition, and thus, with the good will of the Indians, rid ourselves of a description of men who are constantly endeavoring to excite in the Indian mind suspicions, fears, and irritations toward us. . . .

[James D. Richardson, comp., *Messages and Papers of the Presidents*, 1:340-41.]

19.   President Jefferson to William Henry Harrison

February 27, 1803

In a private letter to William Henry Harrison, governor of Indiana Territory, Thomas Jefferson spoke candidly of his views on Indian policy. He showed a humanitarian concern for Indian welfare and expressed a hope that the Indians would be incorporated into white society, but he also suggested harsh reprisals for Indians who took up the hatchet.

. . . . from the Secretary of War you receive from time to time information and instructions as to our Indian affairs. These communications being for the public records, are restrained always to particular objects and occasions; but this letter being unofficial and private, I may with safety give you a more extensive view of our policy respecting the Indians, that you may the better comprehend the parts dealt out to you in detail through the official channel, and observing the system of which they make a part, conduct yourself in unison with it in cases where you are obliged to act without instruction. Our system is to live in perpetual peace with the Indians, to cultivate an affectionate attachment from them, by everything just and liberal which we can do for them within the bounds of reason, and by giving them effectual protection against wrongs from our own people. The decrease of game rendering their subsistence by hunting insufficient, we wish to draw them to agriculture, to spinning and weaving. The latter branches they take up with great readiness, because they fall to the women, who gain by quitting the labors of the field for those which are exercised within doors. When they withdraw themselves to the culture of a small piece of land, they will perceive how useless to them are their extensive forests, and will be willing to pare them off from time to time in exchange for necessaries for their farms and families. To promote this disposition to exchange lands, which they have to spare and we want, for necessaries, which we have to spare and they want, we shall push our trading houses, and be glad to see the good and influential individuals among them run in debt, because we observe that when these debts get beyond what the individuals can pay, they become willing to lop them off by a cession of lands. At our trading houses, too, we mean to sell so low as merely to repay us cost and charges, so as neither to lessen nor enlarge our capital. This is what private traders cannot do, for they must gain; they will consequently retire from the competition, and we shall thus get clear of this pest without giving offence or umbrage to the Indians. In this way our settlements will gradually circumscribe and approach the Indians, and they will in time either incorporate with us as citizens of the United States, or remove beyond the Mississippi. The former is certainly the termination of their history most happy for themselves; but, in the whole course of this, it is essential to cultivate their love. As to their fear, we presume that our strength and their weakness is now so visible that they must see we have only to shut our hand to crush them, and that all our liberalities to them proceed from motives of pure humanity only. Should any tribe be foolhardy enough to take up the hatchet at any time, the seizing the whole country of that tribe, and driving them across the Mississippi, as the only condition of peace, would be an example to others, and a furtherance of our final consolidation. . . .

[*Writings of Thomas Jefferson*, ed. Andrew A. Lipscomb, 10:369-71.]

20. Superintendent of Indian Trade
April 21, 1806

This law of 1806 continued the system of government trading houses begun in 1796. It also authorized a superintendent of Indian trade to direct the business. The office of superintendent was held by two men, John Mason (1806-16) and Thomas L. McKenney (1816-22), until it was abolished in 1822.

An Act for establishing trading houses with the Indian tribes.

Be it enacted . . . , That it shall be lawful for the President of the United States, to establish trading houses at such posts and places on the frontiers, or in the Indian country, on either or both sides of the Mississippi river, as he shall judge most convenient for the purpose of carrying on a liberal trade with the several Indian nations, within the United States, or their territories.

SEC. 2. *And be it further enacted*, That the President of the United States shall be authorized to appoint a superintendent of Indian trade, whose duty it shall be to purchase and take charge of all goods intended for trade with the Indian nations aforesaid, and to transmit the same to such places as he shall be directed by the President. . . .

SEC. 3. *And be it further enacted*, That the superintendent of Indian trade shall receive an annual salary of two thousand dollars, payable quarter yearly, at the treasury of the United States.

SEC. 4. *And be it further enacted*, That the President of the United States shall be authorized to appoint an agent for each trading house established under the provisions of this act. . . .

SEC. 5. *And be it further enacted*, That it shall be the duty of each of the said agents, to receive from the superintendent of Indian trade, and dispose of, in trade with the Indian nations aforesaid, such goods as may be transmitted to him by the said superintendent; to be received and disposed of as aforesaid, according to the rules and orders which the President of the United States shall prescribe; and every such agent shall take an oath or affirmation, faithfully to execute the trust committed to him; and that he will not, directly or indirectly, be concerned or interested in any trade, commerce or barter, but on the public account, and he shall render an account quarter yearly to the superintendent of Indian trade, of all money, goods, and other property whatsoever, which shall be transmitted to him, or which shall come into his hands, or for which, in good faith he ought to account; and he shall transmit duplicates of his accounts to the Secretary of the Treasury of the United States.

SEC. 6. *And be it further enacted*, That the superintendent of Indian trade, the agents, their clerks, or other persons employed by them, shall not be, directly or indirectly, concerned in exporting to a foreign country, any peltries or furs belonging to the United States, or interested in carrying on the business of trade or commerce, on their own, or any other than the public account, or take or apply to his or their own use, any emolument or gain for negotiating or transacting any business or trade, during his or their appointment, agency or employment, other than provided by this act, or excepting for or on account of the United States. . . .

SEC. 7. *And be it further enacted*, That the prices of goods supplied to, and to be paid for, by the Indians, shall be regulated in such manner, that the capital stock, furnished by the United States, shall not be diminished. . . .

SEC. 10. *And be it further enacted*, That the sum of two hundred and sixty thousand dollars, including the sums heretofore appropriated, and applied to the like purpose, and exclusive of the salary of the superintendent of Indian trade, and of the allowances to agents and clerks, be, and the same is hereby appropriated, for the purpose of carrying on trade and intercourse with the Indian nations, in the manner aforesaid, to be paid out of any monies in the treasury of the United States, not otherwise appropriated.

SEC. 11. *And be it further enacted*, That if any agent or agents, their clerks, or other person employed by them, shall purchase or receive from any Indian, in the way of trade or barter, any gun, or other article commonly used in hunting; any instrument of husbandry or cooking utensil, of the kind usually obtained by Indians in their intercourse with white people, or any article of clothing, excepting skins or furs, he or they shall respectively forfeit the sum of one hundred dollars for each offence, to be recovered by action of debt, in the name and to the use of the United States, in any court having jurisdiction in like cases. . . .

SEC. 12. *And be it further enacted*, That it shall be the duty of the said superintendent of Indian trade, under the direction of the President of the United States, to cause the said furs and peltry to be sold at public auction, public notice whereof shall be given three weeks previous to such sale, in different parts of the United States, making an equal distribution of the same, in proportion to the demand of the market, and as may be deemed most advantageous to the United States, and upon such terms and conditions as shall be prescribed by the Secretary of War: *Provided*, that there shall not be less than six annual public sales, of the said furs and peltry, and that the superintendent of Indian trade shall not hold more than two such sales in any state, during any one year. . . .

[*U.S. Statutes at Large*, 2:402-4.]

21. President Jefferson on the Liquor Trade

December 31, 1808

Federal restrictions on liquor trade with the Indian tribes extended only to territory under federal jurisdiction, not to the states. On December 31, 1808, President Thomas Jefferson wrote to the governors of the states and territories, urging them to restrain their citizens from selling liquor to the Indians.

SIR,—The General Government of the United States has considered it their duty and interest to extend their care and patronage over the Indian tribes within their limits, and to endeavor to render them friends, and in time perhaps useful members of the nation. Perceiving the injurious effects produced by their inordinate use of spirituous liquors, they passed laws authorizing measures against the vending or distributing such liquors among them. Their introduction by traders was accordingly prohibited, and for some time was attended with the best effects. I am informed, however, that latterly the Indians have got into the practice of purchasing such liquors themselves in the neighboring settlements of whites, and of carrying them into their towns, and that in this way our regulations so salutary to them, are now defeated. I must, therefore, request your Excellency to submit this matter to the consideration of your Legislature. I persuade myself that in addition to the moral inducements which will readily occur, they will find it not indifferent to their own interests to give us their aid in removing, for their neighbors, this great obstacle to their acquiring industrious habits, and attaching themselves to the regular and useful pursuits of life; for this purpose it is much desired that they should pass effectual laws to restrain their citizens from vending and distributing spirituous liquors to the Indians. I pray your Excellency to accept the assurances of my great esteem and respect.

[*Writings of Thomas Jefferson*, ed. Andrew A. Lipscomb, 12:223-24.]

24

22. Treaty of Portage des Sioux

July 19, 1815

At the conclusion of the War of 1812, in which many tribes of the Northwest had actively supported the British, treaties of peace were signed with the several tribes at Portage des Sioux, on the west bank of the Mississippi above the mouth of the Missouri, and at Spring Wells, near Detroit. This treaty with one group of Sioux is typical.

A treaty of peace and friendship, made and concluded at Portage des Sioux, between William Clark, Ninian Edwards, and Auguste Chouteau, Commissioners Plenipotentiary of the United States of America, on the part and behalf of the said States, of the one part; and the Chiefs and Warriors of the Siouxs of the river St. Peter's, the part and behalf of their said Tribe, on the other part.

The parties being desirous of re-establishing peace and friendship between the United States and the said tribe, and of being placed in all things, and in every respect, on the same footing upon which they stood before the late war between the United States and Great Britain, have agreed to the following articles:

Article 1. Every injury or act of hostility committed by one or either of the contracting parties against the other, shall be mutually forgiven and forgot.

Art. 2. There shall be perpetual peace and friendship between all the citizens of the United States of America and all the individuals composing the tribe of the Siouxs of the river St. Peter's; and all the friendly relations that existed between them before the war, shall be, and the same are hereby, renewed.

Art. 3. The undersigned chiefs and warriors, for themselves and their said tribe, do hereby acknowledge themselves and their tribe to be under the protection of the United States, and of no other power, nation, or sovereign, whatsoever. . . .

[Charles J. Kappler, ed., *Indian Affairs: Laws and Treaties*, 2:114.]

23. Governor Cass on British Traders

July 20, 1815

A source of irritation on the northwest frontier after the War of 1812 was the activity of the British traders, who still influenced the Indians within the territory of the United States. Lewis Cass, governor of Michigan Territory, writing to Acting Secretary of War A. J. Dallas from Detroit in July, 1815, described the danger and urged establishment of military posts to cut off the British traders.

. . . . The privilege which British traders have heretofore enjoyed of carrying on a lucrative commerce with the Indians is a subject, which will doubtless engage the attention of the Government. To this source may be traced most of the difficulties we have experienced in our intercourse with them. I have every reason to believe that the Indian Department opposite to us are about to adopt the same systematick course of measures, which they have so long and so successfully pursued but with renewed activity and increased exertion. A deputation of One influential Chief from each of the different tribes left Malden shortly since for the lower Province and another follows in a few days. What their precise object is we have not yet been able to ascertain, but such enquiries are making as will soon disclose it to us. There is little doubt however of its relating to a general, systematick and vigorous organization of their Indian Department. In the mean time a large quantity of goods have arrived at Malden to be distributed as presents and the agents and Subordinate Officers are more numerous than at any former period. These unerring indications give us timely warning that the same measures are to be adopted, the same lying system continued (pardon the epathet, could all the facts be presented to you, you would say that no milder term could be used) and the same plan of filling our Indian Country with their Agents and Interpreters and traders, which have at all former periods kept the North Western frontiers in a state of feverish alarm. I am aware that the Government is compelled to view the whole ground and that it may be necessary to grant to the British the privileges heretofore held among the Indians, in Order to secure to our own Country commercial rights more important to the nation at large. It is with a view to such a possible event that I submit these propositions to you. Their adoption will be found to counteract in a very considerable degree causes which have heretofore Operated without any check.

Should it be found necessary in a treaty of commerce to make such a stipulation, the evil would be diminished by allowing to British subjects this privilege under the same restrictions it is granted to American Citizens. This will secure to us the right of recalling them, when we find their machinations injurious or when their obvious purpose of trading is to cover a project for scattering disaffection among the Indians. There are three great channels of communication, by which traders may introduce their Goods into the Mississippi and Missouri Country from the British dominions. One is by the way of Chicago and down the Illinois; Another by the way of Green Bay up the Fox River and down the Ouisconsin. This has been the great thoroughfare along which goods have been taken. Immense quantities have been smuggled to the Mississippi and it is calculated that not more than One third part of those sold in the Indian Country, ever pay duties.

The establishment of a post at Green Bay and at Prairie du Chien will close this line of Communication. Another at Chickago will effect the same object upon the Illinois. There will then remain a route to be taken, which has heretofore been little used. It is up a small river which enters Lake Superior near the Grand Portage and along a number of small Lakes with portages to the heads of the Mississippi. I am informed by intelligent men that this is the only route, after closing those by Chicago and Green Bay, which is practicable.

If British Traders are eventually to be excluded a post near the Grand Portage will be necessary to effect this object. Should other considerations render their admission proper the post would still be necessary to ensure a collection of the duties and to enforce the regulations proper to be adopted. A display of the power of the United States in that remote quarter would be productive of Salutary effects upon the minds of the Indians. . . .

I am inclined to believe, if these posts are all established and proper regulations adopted at the various agencies, that British traders may be admitted without very serious inconvenience. Certain I am that their admission will not be attended with the same evils, which have heretofore been experienced. . . .

[Clarence E. Carter, ed., *Territorial Papers of the United States*, 10:574-75.]

24. Secretary of War Crawford on Trade and Intercourse

March 13, 1816

In reply to a Senate resolution, Secretary of War William H. Crawford submitted a forceful statement in support of maintaining the system of government trading houses, which after the War of 1812 came increasingly under attack from private trading interests. His concern for bringing the Indians into "the pale of civilization," especially through the institution of private property, was typical of his age and foreshadowed later emphasis on this essential means of civilization.

. . . . [Report of losses in the government trading houses.] It is probable that a more intimate acquaintance with the nature of the commerce, a more skilful selection of the goods, and of the agents employed in vending them, and a considerable increase of the capital invested in it, will, in a short time, produce a small and gradually increasing profit, after defraying all the expenses incident to the establishment, which are now payable out of the public treasury. Under the most skilful management, the profits cannot be an inducement for continuing the system now in operation. That inducement, if it exists at all, must be found in the influence which it gives the Government over the Indian tribes within our limits, by administering to their wants, increasing their comforts, and promoting their happiness. The most obvious effect of that influence is the preservation of peace with them, and among themselves. The exclusion of all intercourse between them and the whites, except those who have the permission of the Government, and over whose conduct a direct control is exercised, has insensibly contributed to this desirable object.

The amelioration in their condition desired by the Government has continued to advance, but in so slight a degree as to be perceptible only after a lapse of years. If the civilization of the Indian tribes is considered an object of primary importance, and superior to that of rapidly extinguishing their titles and settling their lands by the whites, the expediency of continuing the system now in operation, under such modifications as have been suggested by the experience already acquired, appears to be manifest. The success of such an experiment requires the exercise of all the influence which belongs to the annual distribution of annuities and presents, aided by that which must flow from a judicious supply of all their wants, in exchange for those articles which the chase and the increasing surplus of their stock of domestic animals, will enable them to procure. This influence, skilfully directed for a series of years, cannot fail to introduce among them distinct ideas of separate property. These ideas must necessarily precede any considerable advancement in the arts of civilization, and presuppose the institution of laws to secure the owner in the enjoyment of his individual property; because no man will exert himself to procure the comforts of life unless his right to enjoy them is exclusive.

The idea of separate property in things personal universally precedes the same idea in relation to lands. This results no less from the intrinsic difference between the two kinds of property, than from the different effects produced by human industry and ingenuity exerted upon them. The facility of removing personal property from place to place, according to the will or convenience of the owner, gives to this species of property (in the estimation of the huntsman) a value superior to property in lands, which his wants as well as his habits compel him annually to desert for a considerable portion of the year. To succeed perfectly in the attempt to civilize the aborigines of this country, the Government ought to direct their attention to the improvement of their habitations, and the multiplication of distinct settlements. As an inducement to this end, the different agents should be instructed to give them assurances that, in any treaty for the purchase of lands from their respective tribes, one mile square, including every separate settlement, should be reserved to the settler, which should become a fee simple estate after the expiration of a certain number of years of actual residence upon and cultivation of it. Perhaps an additional reservation of a quarter or half-section of land to each member of such family would add to the inducements not only to make such separate settlements, but to the raising a family. If measures of this kind were adopted by the Government, and steadily pursued for a series of years, while at the same time a spirit of liberality was exhibited in the commerce which we carry on with them, success the most complete might be confidently expected. But commerce with our Indian neighbors, prosecuted upon a contracted scale, and upon the principles of commercial profit, would tend not only to diminish the influence of the Government with them, but could not fail entirely to alienate their affections from it. A period has arrived when the trade must be greatly extended, or entirely abandoned to individual enterprise. To reserve the trade in the hands of the Government, whilst the wants of the Indians are but partially supplied, would be to make them feel its influence only in their privations and wretchedness. . . .

These views are substantially founded upon the conviction that it is the true policy and earnest desire of the Government to draw its savage neighbors within the pale of civilization. If I am mistaken in this point—if the primary object of the Government is to extinguish the Indian title, and settle their lands as rapidly as possible, then commerce with them ought to be entirely abandoned to individual enterprise, and without regulation. The result would be continual warfare, attended by the extermination or expulsion of the aboriginal inhabitants of the country to more distant and less hospitable regions. The correctness of this policy cannot for a moment be admitted.

27

The utter extinction of the Indian race must be abhorrent to the feelings of an enlightened and benevolent nation. The idea is directly opposed to every act of the Government, from the declaration of independence to the present day. If the system already devised has not produced all the effects which were expected from it, new experiments ought to be made. When every effort to introduce among them ideas of separate property, as well in things real as personal, shall fail, let intermarriages between them and the whites be encouraged by the Government. This cannot fail to preserve the race, with the modifications necessary to the enjoyment of civil liberty and social happiness. It is believed that the principles of humanity in this instance are in harmonious concert with the true interest of the nation. It will redound more to the national honor to incorporate, by a humane and benevolent policy, the natives of our forests in the great American family of freemen, than to receive with open arms the fugitives of the old world, whether their flight has been the effect of their crimes or their virtues. . . .

[*American State Papers: Indian Affairs*, 2:26-28.]

25. Exclusion of British Traders
April 29, 1816

Fear of the influence of British traders on Indians in the United States and desire to keep the profits of the Indian trade in American hands led to exclusion of noncitizens from the trade.

An act supplementary to the act passed the thirtieth of March, one thousand eight hundred and two, to regulate trade and intercourse with the Indian tribes, and to preserve peace on the frontiers.

Be it enacted . . . , That licenses to trade with the Indians within the territorial limits of the United States shall not be granted to any but citizens of the United States, unless by the express direction of the President of the United States, and upon such terms and conditions as the public interest may, in his opinion, require.

Sec. 2. *And be it further enacted*, That all goods, wares and merchandise, carried by a foreigner into the lands to which the Indian title has not been extinguished, for the purpose of being used in the Indian trade; and all articles of peltry, of provisions, or of any other kind purchased by foreigners from Indians or tribes of Indians, contrary to the provisions of this act, shall be and the same are hereby forfeited, one half thereof to the use of the informer, and the remainder to the United States: *Provided*, That the goods, wares and merchandise are seized prior to their sale to an Indian, or Indian tribe, and the articles purchased are seized before they are removed beyond the limits of the United States.

Sec. 3. *And be it further enacted*, That if a foreigner go into any country which is allotted or secured by treaty to either of the Indian tribes within the territorial limits of the United States, or to which the Indian title has not been extinguished, without a passport first had and obtained from the governor of one of the states or territories of the United States, adjoining the country into which he may go, or the officer of the troops of the United States, commanding at the nearest post on the frontiers, or such other person as the President of the United States may from time to time authorize to grant the same, he shall, on conviction thereof, pay a fine of not less than fifty or more than one thousand dollars; or be imprisoned not less than one month, or more than twelve months, at the discretion of the court.

Sec. 4. *And be it further enacted*, That trials for offences against this act shall be had in the courts of the United States of the territory in which the person accused may be arrested, or in the circuit court of the United States, of the district into which he may be first carried, after his arrest.

Sec. 5. *And be it further enacted*, That each and every person charged with a violation of the second section of this act shall, if arrested, be indicted and tried in one of the courts aforesaid, and that the conviction of the accused shall authorize the court to cause the goods intended to be sold to, and articles purchased from the Indians, belonging to him, or taken in his possession, to be sold, one half to the use of the informer, and the other to the use of the United States. But if goods intended to be sold or articles purchased from the Indians contrary to the provisions of this act, should be seized, and the owner or person in possession of them should make his escape, or from any other cause cannot be brought to trial, it shall and may be lawful for the United States' attorney of the territory in which they may be seized, or the district attorney of the United States, of the district into which they may have been first carried after they are seized, to proceed against the said goods intended to be sold to, or articles purchased from the Indians, in the manner directed to be observed in the case of goods, wares or merchandise brought into the United States in violation of the revenue laws.

SEC. 6. *And be it further enacted,* That the President of the United States be, and he hereby is authorized to use the military force of the United States whenever it may be necessary to carry into effect this act, as far as it relates to seizure of goods to be sold to, or articles already purchased from the Indians, or to the arrest of persons charged with violating its provisions.

[*U.S. Statutes at Large,* 3:332-33.]

26. Secretary of War Calhoun on British Traders
March 25, 1818

The 1816 prohibition against noncitizens participating in the Indian trade was relaxed by the president in 1818 to permit the use of foreign boatmen and interpreters. The new instructions were sent by the secretary of war, John C. Calhoun, to Lewis Cass, governor of Michigan Territory, on March 25, 1818.

SIR, Your Excellency was instructed by the President thro' a letter from this department of the 26th of Novemr 1817, to enforce the act of the 29th April, 1816, and not to grant licenses to trade with the Indians, to any except American Citizens. Farther information and reflection induce him to believe that much inconvenience will be experienced, unless permission be given to the American trader to employ in his trade with the Indians, foreign boatmen & interpreters; and he therefore directs your excellency to grant permits for them. But as great abuses may be experienced by entering as boatmen and interpreters, foreigners hostile to our country, who may be intended to have the principal control over the trading expedition; the President farther directs that, before granting permits, a descriptive list be furnished of all foreigners employed as boatmen and interpreters; and that a bond with security be taken, that the persons described in the list are in fact boatmen or interpreters, as the case may be, and are not intended to be employed in any other capacity. The list ought to be so minute as to identify the persons, and a duplicate ought to be furnished to the party concerned. The bond will be taken in the penal sum of $500, for each person on the descriptive list. For each foreign interpreter, an American citizen must be employed in order to be trained in the duties of an interpreter. You will also require bonds with security in half the amount of the value of the goods destined for the Indian trade, that they are the property of American Citizens. Your Excelly will give the necessary instructions to carry the above regulations into effect, to Major Puthuff and the other agents under your superintendance.

Foreigners who are odious to our citizens, on account of their activity or cruelty in the late war, are not to be admitted in any capacity.

[Clarence E. Carter, ed., *Territorial Papers of the United States,* 10:738-39.]

29

27. Authorization of Indian Agents
1818

Indian agents, who became the key officials in relations between the United States and the Indian tribes, were not formally authorized in the early decades of the nation's history but relied for their appointment on vague references in treaties or the trade and intercourse laws. In 1818, however, two measures regularized their status. One provided a method of appointment for agents, along with the superintendent of Indian trade and the agents at the trading houses. The other determined specific compensation for designated agents and for the trading house factors.

1. Manner of Appointing Agents
April 16, 1818

An Act directing the manner of appointing Indian Agents. . . .

Be it enacted . . . , That the superintendent of Indian trade, the agents and assistant agents of Indian trading houses, and the several agents of Indian affairs, shall be nominated by the President of the United States, and appointed by and with the advice and consent of the Senate.

SEC. 2. *And be it further enacted*, That from and after the eighteenth instant, no person shall act in either of the characters aforesaid, who shall not have been thus first nominated and appointed. And every agent as aforesaid, before he shall enter upon the duties of his office, shall give bond to the United States, with two or more sufficient securities, in the penal sum of ten thousand dollars, conditioned faithfully to perform all the duties which are or may be enjoined on them as agents as aforesaid. . . .

[*U.S. Statutes at Large*, 3:428.]

2. Compensation for Indian Agents
April 20, 1818

An Act fixing the compensation of Indian agents and factors.

Be it enacted . . . , That, from and after the passage of this act, Indian agents and factors shall receive the following salaries per annum, in lieu of their present compensation, to wit;

The agent to the Creek nation, one thousand eight hundred dollars.

The agent to the Choctaws, one thousand eight hundred dollars.

The agent to the Cherokees on Tennessee river, one thousand three hundred dollars.

The agent to the Cherokees on the Arkansas river, one thousand five hundred dollars.

The agent to the Chickasaws, one thousand three hundred dollars.

The agent in the Illinois territory, one thousand three hundred dollars.

The agent at Prairie du Chien, one thousand two hundred dollars.

The agent at Natchitoches, one thousand two hundred dollars.

The agent at Chicago, one thousand three hundred dollars.

The agent at Green Bay, one thousand five hundred dollars.

The agent at Mackinac, one thousand four hundred dollars.

The agent at Vincennes, one thousand two hundred dollars.

The agent at Fort Wayne and Piqua, one thousand two hundred dollars.

The agent to the Lakes, one thousand three hundred dollars.

The agent in the Missouri territory, one thousand two hundred dollars.

And all sub-agents, five hundred dollars per annum.

SEC. 2. *And be it further enacted*, That all factors shall receive one thousand three hundred dollars, and assistant factors seven hundred dollars, per annum.

SEC. 3. *And be it further enacted*, That the sums hereby allowed to Indian agents and factors shall be in full compensation for their services; and that all rations, or other allowances, made to them, shall be deducted from the sums hereby allowed.

[*U.S. Statutes at Large*, 3:461.]

28. Secretary of War Calhoun on Indian Trade
December 5, 1818

Regulation of the Indian trade was a continuing problem for the United States. In response to a request from the House of Representatives, Secretary of War John C. Calhoun submitted a long statement on a system for trading with the Indians. The following are key extracts. Included is a digression in which Calhoun expressed his views on the necessity of civilizing the Indians.

. . . . After giving the subject that full consideration which its importance merits, it appears to me that the provisions of the ordinance of 1786, with a few additions and modifications, particularly in the administrative part, so as to adjust it to our present form of government, are, for this division of our Indian trade, the best that can be devised. The provisions of the acts now in force in relation to licenses are not as well guarded or as efficient as those of the ordinance referred to. The introduction of the factories seems to have relaxed the attention of Government to the system of trade under license. I would then propose to assume the provisions of the ordinance referred to, as the basis of a system to open the trade with the contiguous tribes of Indians to individual enterprise. Instead, however, of appointing two superintendents, I would propose a superintendent of Indian affairs, to be attached to the War Department, with a salary of $3,000 per annum; the superintendent to be under the control of the Secretary of War, and to be charged, subject to such regulations as the President may prescribe, with the correspondence, superintendence, and general management of Indian affairs; and to be authorized, with the approbation of the Secretary of War, to grant licenses to trade with the Indians. Licenses to be granted to citizens of good moral character, and to continue in force till revoked. A sum not less than $100, nor more than $500, to be determined under regulations to be prescribed by the President, to be paid for the privilege of using it at the time of granting the license, and annually during its continuance; and bonds, with sufficient security, to be taken to conform to law and regulations. Licenses to be revoked by the President whenever he may judge proper. To trade without license, to subject to a fine not exceeding $1,000, and imprisonment not to exceed six months, with a forfeiture of the goods. Licenses to be

granted to trade at specified places, to be selected by the applicants, and not to be changed without the consent of the superintendent. All peddling and sales of spirituous liquors to be strictly prohibited. Each trading-house, or establishment, to require a separate license; and books to be kept at the establishment, in which the prices of the goods sold and the articles purchased should be regularly and fairly entered; and to be subject at all times to the inspection of the Indian agent, or such persons as the superintendent may appoint. . . .

But it will probably be objected that it is our interest, and, as we propose to monopolize their trade, our duty, too, to furnish the Indians with goods on as moderate terms as possible; and that the sum to be paid for a license, by acting as a duty on the goods sold under it, will tend to enhance their price. In answer to which it may be justly observed, that it is not a matter of so much importance that they should obtain their supplies for a few cents more or less, as that the trade should, as far as practicable, be put effectually under the control of the Government, in order that they may be protected against the fraud and the violence to which their ignorance and weakness would, without such protection, expose them. It is this very ignorance and weakness which render it necessary for the Government to interfere; and, if such interference is proper at all, it ought to be rendered effectual. Such will be the tendency of this provision. Its first and obvious effects will be to diminish more certainly, and with less injurious effect than any other provision which can be devised, the number of traders, and to increase the amount of capital which each would employ. The profit of a small capital of a few hundred dollars would scarcely pay for the license; while that on a large one would not be much diminished by it. Both of these effects—the diminution of the number of traders, and the increase of the capital—would add greatly to the control of the Government over the trade. It would be almost impossible to inspect the conduct, and consequently control the actions, of the multitude of traders with small capitals, diffused over the Indian country, and settled at remote and obscure places. The greatest vigilance on the part of the superintendent and his agents would be unequal to the task. By diminishing the number, and bringing each more permanently before the view of the Government, a due inspection and superintendence becomes practicable. . . .

The reasons for fixing the trading establishments are no less strong. By rendering them stationary, and compelling the proprietor to keep books, containing regular entries of all their sales and purchases, important checks will be presented to prevent fraud and exorbitant charges. It will also strongly tend to prevent collision between the traders, and, consequently, the creation of parties among the Indians for or against particular traders—a state of things unfriendly to their interest, and dangerous to the peace of the frontier. Besides, the trading establishments, being fixed, as they will be, in the most advantageous positions, will, in time, become the nucleus of Indian settlements, which, by giving greater density and steadiness to their population, will tend to introduce a division of real property, and thus hasten their ultimate civilization.

. . . . The time seems to have arrived when our policy towards them should undergo an important change. They neither are, in fact, nor ought to be, considered as independent nations. Our views of their interest, and not their own, ought to govern them. By a proper combination of force and persuasion, of punishments and rewards, they ought to be brought within the pales of law and civilization. Left to themselves, they will never reach that desirable condition. Before the slow operation of reason and experience can convince them of its superior advantages, they must be overwhelmed by the mighty torrent of our population. Such small bodies, with savage customs and character, cannot, and ought not, to be permitted to exist in an independent condition in the midst of civilized society. Our laws and manners ought to supersede their present savage manners and customs. Beginning with those most advanced in civilization, and surrounded by our people, they ought to be made to contract their settlements within reasonable bounds, with a distinct understanding that the United States intend to make no further acquisition of land from them, and that the settlements reserved are intended for their permanent home. The land ought to be divided among families; and the idea of individual property in the soil carefully inculcated. Their annuities would constitute an ample school fund; and education, comprehending as well the common arts of life, as reading, writing, and arithmetic, ought not to be left discretionary with the parents. Those who might not choose to submit, ought to be permitted and aided in forming new settlements at a distance from ours. When sufficiently advanced in civilization, they would be permitted to participate in such civil and political rights as the respective States within whose limits they are situated might safely extend to them. It is only by causing our opinion of their interest to prevail, that they can be civilized and saved from extinction. Under the present policy, they are continually decreasing and degenerating, notwithstanding the Government has, under all of its administrations, been actuated by the most sincere desire to promote their happiness and civilization. The fault has been, not in the want of zeal, but in the mode by which it has been attempted to effect these desirable objects. The Indians are not so situated as to leave it to time and experience to effect their civilization. By selecting prudently the occasion for the change, by establishing a few essential regulations, and by appointing persons to administer them fairly and honestly, our efforts could scarcely fail of success. Nor ought it to be feared that the power would be abused on our part; for, in addition to the dictates of benevolence, we have a strong interest in their civilization. The enmity even of the frontier settlers towards them is caused principally by the imperfection of the present system; and under the one which I have suggested, it will greatly abate, if not entirely subside. The natural humanity and generosity of the American character would no longer be weakened by the disorders and savage cruelty to which our frontiers are now exposed. A deep conviction of the importance of the subject, and a strong desire to arrest the current of events, which, if permitted to flow in their present channel, must end in the annihilation of those who were once the proprietors of this prosperous country, must be my apology for this digression. . . .

[*American State Papers: Indian Affairs,* 2:182-84.]

29. Civilization Fund Act

March 3, 1819

The United States government became increasingly concerned with the education of the Indian tribes in contact with white settlements and encouraged the activities of benevolent societies in providing schools for the Indians. Congress in 1819 authorized an annual "civilization fund" to stimulate and promote this work.

An Act making provision for the civilization of the Indian tribes adjoining the frontier settlements.

Be it enacted . . . , That for the purpose of providing against the further decline and final extinction of the Indian tribes, adjoining the frontier settlements of the United States, and for introducing among them the habits and arts of civilization, the President of the United States shall be, and he is hereby authorized, in every case where he shall judge improvement in the habits and condition of such Indians practicable, and that the means of instruction can be introduced with their own consent, to employ capable persons of good moral character, to instruct them in the mode of agriculture suited to their situation; and for teaching their children in reading, writing, and arithmetic, and performing such other duties as may be enjoined, according to such instructions and rules as the President may give and prescribe for the regulation of their conduct, in the discharge of their duties.

SEC. 2. *And be it further enacted,* That the annual sum of ten thousand dollars be, and the same is hereby appropriated, for the purpose of carrying into effect the provisions of this act; and an account of the expenditure of the money, and proceedings in execution of the foregoing provisions, shall be laid annually before Congress.

[*U.S. Statutes at Large,* 3:516-17.]

30. Abolition of the Government Trading Houses

May 6, 1822

The government trading houses or factories suffered economically during the War of 1812 and after the war were attacked by private trading interests. Although strongly supported by such officials as Thomas L. McKenney, superintendent of Indian trade, and Secretary of War John C. Calhoun, the factory system fell under the assault.

An Act to abolish the United States' trading establishment with the Indian tribes.

Be it enacted . . . , That the President of the United States shall be, and hereby is, authorized and required to cause the business of the United States' trading-houses among the Indian tribes to be closed, and the accounts of the superintendent of Indian trade, and of the factors and sub-factors, to be settled; and for that purpose, the President is hereby authorized to select, from among the Indian agents, or others, a competent number of fit and suitable persons, to be and appear at the office of Indian trade in Georgetown, in the District of Columbia, and at each of the trading-houses established among Indian tribes, on or before the third day of June next, or as soon thereafter as can conveniently be done, to demand and receive of and from the superintendent of Indian trade, and of the respective factors and sub-factors, all the goods, wares, merchandise, furs, peltries, evidences of debt, and property and effects of every kind which may be in their power or possession, by virtue of their respective offices, and justly due and belonging to the United States; and

33

the said agents, selected for the purpose aforesaid, shall be furnished with copies of the latest quarterly returns of the said superintendent, factors, and sub-factors, as rendered by them to the Treasury Department, and copies of any other papers in the said department which will show what is, or ought to be due and coming to the United States, from the said office of Indian trade in Georgetown, and from each of the trading-houses established among Indians. . . .

SEC. 2. *And be it further enacted*, That the goods, wares, and merchandise, which shall be delivered over to the agents of the United States, under the provisions of this act, shall be placed at the disposition of the President of the United States, subject, under his orders, towards satisfying or extinguishing the treaty obligations on the part of the United States, to keep up trading-houses with the Indians; also, towards the payment of annuities due, or to become due, to Indian tribes; also, in making the customary presents to tribes or individuals in amity with the United States; and the surplus, if any, may be sold to the best advantage, under the orders of the President, and the proceeds paid over to the treasury of the United States.

SEC. 3. *And be it further enacted*, That the furs, peltries, effects and property, received under the first section of this act, shall be sold in the manner the President may direct; the debts due and owing shall be collected under his orders; and all the money received from these sources, and all that shall be received from the superintendent of Indian trade, and from the factors and sub-factors, shall be paid over, as fast as received, into the treasury of the United States: *Provided*, That such sums may be retained and applied, under the orders of the President of the United States, as may be necessary to defray the expenses of carrying this act into effect.

SEC. 4. *And be it further enacted*, That, as soon as may be after the commencement of the next session of Congress, the President of the United States shall communicate to Congress the manner in which he shall have caused this act to be executed, showing the amount of moneys, furs, peltries, and other effects, and the amount and description of goods, wares, and merchandise, and the actual cash value thereof, received from the superintendent of Indian trade, and each of the factors and sub-factors, under the provisions of this act.

[*U.S. Statutes at Large*, 3:679-80.]

31.   Act for Regulating the Indian Trade

May 6, 1822

With the abolition of the government trading houses, the United States fell back on a system of Indian trade carried on only by private individuals and companies. A new law revised the licensing regulations, strengthened the provisions for restricting the liquor trade, set regulations for the distribution of annuities, and created a special superintendent of Indian affairs to reside at Saint Louis.

An Act to amend an act, entitled *"An act to regulate trade and intercourse with the Indian tribes, and to preserve peace on the frontiers,"* approved thirtieth March, one thousand eight hundred and two.

Be it enacted . . . , That the seventh section of the act, entitled "An act to regulate trade and intercourse with the Indian tribes and to preserve peace on the frontiers," shall be, and the same is hereby, repealed; and from and after the passing of this act, it shall be lawful for the superintendents of Indian affairs in the territories and Indian agents, under the direction of the President of the United States, to grant licenses to trade with Indian tribes; which licenses shall be granted to citizens of the United States, and to none others, taking from them bonds with securities in the penal sum not exceeding five thousand dollars, proportioned to the capital employed, and conditioned for the due observance of the laws regulating trade and intercourse with the Indian tribes; and said licenses may be granted for a term not exceeding seven years for the trade with the remote tribes of Indians beyond the Mississippi, and two years for the trade with all the

34

other tribes. And the superintendents and agents shall return to the Secretary of War, within each year, an abstract of all licenses granted, showing by and to whom, when, and where, granted, with the amount of the bonds and capital employed, to be laid before Congress, at the next session thereof.

SEC. 2. *And be it further enacted,* That it shall and may be lawful for the President of the United States, in execution of the power vested in him by the twenty-first section of the act of the thirtieth of March, one thousand eight hundred and two, aforesaid, to which this is an amendment, to direct Indian agents, governors of territories acting as superintendents of Indian affairs, and military officers, to cause the stores and packages of goods of all traders to be searched, upon suspicion or information that ardent spirits are carried into the Indian countries by said traders in violation of the said twenty-first section of the act to which this is an amendment; and if any ardent spirits shall be so found, all the goods of the said traders shall be forfeited, one half to the use of the informer, the other half to the use of the government, his license cancelled, and bond put in suit.

SEC. 3. *And be it further enacted,* That all purchases for and on account of Indians, for annuities, presents, and otherwise, shall be made by the Indian agents and governors of territories acting as superintendents, within their respective districts; and all persons whatsoever, charged or trusted with the disbursement or application of money, goods, or effects, of any kind, for the benefit of Indians, shall settle their accounts annually, at the War Department, on the first day of September; and copies of the same shall be laid before Congress at the commencement of the ensuing session, by the proper accounting officers, together with a list of the names of all persons to whom money, goods, or effects, had been delivered within the said year, for the benefit of the Indians, specifying the amount and object for which it was intended, and showing who are delinquent, if any, in forwarding their accounts according to the provisions of this act.

SEC. 4. *And be it further enacted,* That, in all trials about the right of property, in which Indians shall be party on one side and white persons on the other, the burthen of proof shall rest upon the white person, in every case in which the Indian shall make out a presumption of title in himself from the fact of previous possession and ownership.

SEC. 5. *And be it further enacted,* That it shall and may be lawful for the President of the United States, from time to time, to require additional security, and in larger amounts, from all persons charged or trusted, under the laws of the United States, with the disbursement or application of money, goods, or effects, of any kind, for the benefit of the Indians.

SEC. 6. *And be it further enacted,* That the President of the United States, by and with the advice and consent of the Senate, may appoint a superintendent of Indian Affairs, to reside at St. Louis, whose powers shall extend to all Indians frequenting that place, whose salary shall be fifteen hundred dollars per annum; and one agent for tribes within the limits of East and West Florida, with a salary of fifteen hundred dollars.

[*U.S. Statutes at Large,* 3:682-83.]

32.   Johnson and Graham's Lessee v. William McIntosh

1823

The plaintiffs in this case claimed title to land in Illinois on the basis of purchase from the Indians; the defendant, on the basis of a grant from the United States. The Supreme Court decided in favor of the defendant and in so doing discussed the nature of the Indian land title under the United States.

. . . The United States, then, have unequivocally acceded to that great and broad rule by which its civilized inhabitants now hold this country. They hold, and assert in themselves, the title by which it was acquired. They maintain, as all others have maintained, that discovery gave an exclusive right to extinguish the Indian title of occupancy, either by purchase or by conquest; and gave also a right to such a degree of sovereignty, as the circumstances of the people would allow them to exercise.

35

The power now possessed by the government of the United States to grant lands, resided, while we were colonies, in the crown, or its grantees. The validity of the titles given by either has never been questioned in our Courts. It has been exercised uniformly over territory in possession of the Indians. The existence of this power must negative the existence of any right which may conflict with, and control it. An absolute title to lands cannot exist, at the same time, in different persons, or in different governments. An absolute, must be an exclusive title, or at least a title which excludes all others not compatible with it. All our institutions recognise the absolute title of the crown, subject only to the Indian right of occupancy, and recognise the absolute title of the crown to extinguish that right. This is incompatible with an absolute and complete title in the Indians.

We will not enter into the controversy, whether agriculturists, merchants, and manufacturers, have a right, on abstract principles, to expel hunters from the territory they possess, or to contract their limits. Conquest gives a title which the Courts of the conqueror cannot deny, whatever the private and speculative opinions of individuals may be, respecting the original justice of the claim which has been successfully asserted. The British government, which was then our government, and whose rights have passed to the United States, asserted a title to all the lands occupied by Indians, within the chartered limits of the British colonies. It asserted also a limited sovereignty over them, and the exclusive right of extinguishing the title which occupancy gave to them. These claims have been maintained and established as far west as the river Mississippi, by the sword. The title to a vast portion of the lands we now hold, originates in them. It is not for the Courts of this country to question the validity of this title, or to sustain one which is incompatible with it.

Although we do not mean to engage in the defence of those principles which Europeans have applied to Indian title, they may, we think, find some excuse, if not justification, in the character and habits of the people whose rights have been wrested from them.

The title by conquest is acquired and maintained by force. The conqueror prescribes its limits. Humanity, however, acting on public opinion, has established, as a general rule, that the conquered shall not be wantonly oppressed, and that their condition shall remain as eligible as is compatible with the objects of the conquest. Most usually, they are incorporated with the victorious nation, and become subjects or citizens of the government with which they are connected. The new and old members of the society mingle with each other; the distinction between them is gradually lost, and they make one people. Where this incorporation is practicable, humanity demands, and a wise policy requires, that the rights of the conquered to property should remain unimpaired; that the new subjects should be governed as equitably as the old, and that confidence in their security should gradually banish the painful sense of being separated from their ancient connexions, and united by force to strangers.

When the conquest is complete, and the conquered inhabitants can be blended with the conquerors, or safely governed as a distinct people, public opinion, which not even the conqueror can disregard, imposes these restraints upon him; and he cannot neglect them without injury to his fame, and hazard to his power.

But the tribes of Indians inhabiting this country were fierce savages, whose occupation was war, and whose subsistence was drawn chiefly from the forest. To leave them in possession of their country, was to leave the country a wilderness; to govern them as a distinct people, was impossible, because they were as brave and as high spirited as they were fierce, and were ready to repel by arms every attempt on their independence.

What was the inevitable consequence of this state of things? The Europeans were under the necessity either of abandoning the country, and relinquishing their pompous claims to it, or of enforcing those claims by the sword, and by the adoption of principles adapted to the condition of a people with whom it was impossible to mix, and who could not be governed as a distinct society, or of remaining in their neighbourhood, and exposing themselves and their families to the perpetual hazard of being massacred.

Frequent and bloody wars, in which the

whites were not always the aggressors, unavoidably ensued. European policy, numbers, and skill, prevailed. As the white population advanced, that of the Indians necessarily receded. The country in the immediate neighbourhood of agriculturists became unfit for them. The game fled into thicker and more unbroken forests, and the Indians followed. The soil, to which the crown originally claimed title, being no longer occupied by its ancient inhabitants, was parcelled out according to the will of the sovereign power, and taken possession of by persons who claimed immediately from the crown, or mediately, through its grantees or deputies.

That law which regulates, and ought to regulate in general, the relations between the conqueror and conquered, was incapable of application to a people under such circumstances. The resort to some new and different rule, better adapted to the actual state of things, was unavoidable. Every rule which can be suggested will be found to be attended with great difficulty.

However extravagant the pretension of converting the discovery of an inhabited country into conquest may appear; if the principle has been asserted in the first instance, and afterwards sustained; if a country has been acquired and held under it; if the property of the great mass of the community orginates in it, it becomes the law of the land, and cannot be questioned.

So, too, with respect to the concomitant principle, that the Indian inhabitants are to be considered merely as occupants, to be protected, indeed, while in peace, in the possession of their lands, but to be deemed incapable of transferring the absolute title to others. However this restriction may be opposed to natural right, and to the usages of civilized nations, yet, if it be indispensable to that system under which the country has been settled, and be adapted to the actual condition of the two people, it may, perhaps, be supported by reason, and certainly cannot be rejected by Courts of justice. . . .

It has never been contended, that the Indian title amounted to nothing. Their right of possession has never been questioned. The claim of government extends to the complete ultimate title, charged with this right of possession, and to the exclusive power of acquiring that right. . . .

After bestowing on this subject a degree of attention which was more required by the magnitude of the interest in litigation, and the able and elaborate arguments of the bar, than by its intrinsic difficulty, the Court is decidedly of opinion, that the plaintiffs do not exhibit a title which can be sustained in the Courts of the United States; and that there is no error in the judgment which was rendered against them in the District Court of Illinois.

[8 *Wheaton*, 543, 587-92, 603-5.]

33.   Creation of a Bureau of Indian Affairs
in the War Department
March 11, 1824

Secretary of War John C. Calhoun, without special congressional authorization, set up a "Bureau of Indian Affairs" within his department and assigned the duties of the office to Thomas L. McKenney. McKenney held the office until dismissed by President Jackson in 1830. Congress confirmed the position, then designated "Commissioner of Indian Affairs," in 1832.

Department of War
March 11th, 1824

SIR: To you are assigned the duties [of] the Bureau of Indian Affairs in this Department, for the faithful performance of which you will be responsible. Mr. Hamilton and Mr. Miller are assigned to you, the former as chief, and the latter as assistant clerk.

You will take charge of the appropriations for annuities, and of the current expenses, and all warrants on the same will be issued on your requisitions on the Secretary of War, taking special care that no requisition be issued, but in cases where the money previously remitted has been satisfactorily accounted for, and on estimates in detail, approved by you, for the sum required. You will receive and examine the accounts and

37

vouchers for the expenditure thereof, and will pass them over to the proper Auditor's Office for settlement, after examination and approval by you; submitting such items for the sanction of this Department as may require its approval. The administration of the fund for the civilization of the Indians is also committed to your charge, under the regulations established by the Department. You are also charged with the examination of the claims arising out of the laws regulating the intercourse with Indian Tribes, and will, after examining and briefing the same, report them to this Department, endorsing a recommendation for their allowance or disallowance.

The ordinary correspondence with the superintendents, the agents, and sub-agents, will pass through your Bureau.

I have the honor to be,
Your obedient servant,
J.C. Calhoun

Thos. L. M'Kenney, Esq.

[*House Document* no. 146, 19th Cong., 1st sess., serial 138, p. 6.]

34. Authorization of Treaties; Trade Regulations

May 25, 1824

Fur traders on the Missouri River experienced hostility from Indians and demanded government action to protect their interests. Congress authorized the president to make treaties of trade and friendship with the tribes beyond the Mississippi and to provide a military escort for the commissioners. The act also included important provisions regarding the Indian trade, especially the designation of specific sites at which the trade had to be conducted.

An Act to enable the President to hold treaties with certain Indian tribes, and for other purposes.

Be it enacted . . . , That the sum of ten thousand dollars be, and the same hereby is, appropriated, to defray the expenses of making treaties of trade and friendship with the Indian tribes beyond the Mississippi: and that the said sum shall be paid out of any money in the treasury not otherwise appropriated.

SEC. 2. *And be it further enacted,* That, for the purpose of negotiating said treaties, on the part of the United States, the President shall be, and he hereby is, authorized to appoint suitable persons for commissioners, and to fix their compensation, so as not to exceed what has been heretofore allowed for like services.

SEC. 3. *And be it further enacted,* That the President shall be, and hereby is, authorized to appoint two sub-agents to be employed among the Indian tribes, on the waters of the Upper Missouri, whose annual salary shall be eight hundred dollars each, to be paid out of any money in the treasury not otherwise appropriated.

SEC. 4. *And be it further enacted,* That it shall be the duty of Indian agents to designate, from time to time, certain convenient and suitable places for carrying on trade with the different Indian tribes, and to require all traders to trade at the places thus designated, and at no other place or places.

SEC. 5. *And be it further enacted,* That the superintendent of Indian affairs at St. Louis, and his successors in office, shall possess all the powers, and be subject to all the duties of governors of territories, when exercising the office of superintendents of Indian affairs, and shall exercise a general supervision of the official conduct and accounts of Indian agents within his superintendency.

SEC. 6. *And be it further enacted,* That the sum of ten thousand dollars be, and the same is hereby, appropriated, to be paid out of any money in the treasury not otherwise appropriated, to enable the President of the United States to furnish a competent military escort to the commissioners authorized to be appointed by this act, if, in his opinion, the same shall be necessary.

[*U.S. Statutes at Large,* 4:35-36.]

38

35. Message of President Monroe on Indian Removal
January 27, 1825

In the 1820s white pressures against the Indians in the eastern states increased and in the southern states especially created a severe crisis in Indian affairs. Georgia, citing the compact with the federal government of April 24, 1802, in which the United States had agreed to extinguish the Indian land titles in the state as soon as it could be done peaceably and on reasonable terms in exchange for the state's western land claims, insistently demanded the removal of the Indians from within her borders. Although not accepting Georgia's position, President James Monroe proposed a voluntary removal policy as the best solution and urged the policy upon Congress in a special message.

To the Senate and House of Representatives of the United States:

Being deeply impressed with the opinion that the removal of the Indian tribes from the lands which they now occupy within the limits of the several States and Territories to the country lying westward and northward thereof, within our acknowledged boundaries, is of very high importance to our Union, and may be accomplished on conditions and in a manner to promote the interest and happiness of those tribes, the attention of the Government has been long drawn with great solicitude to the object. For the removal of the tribes within the limits of the State of Georgia the motive has been peculiarly strong, arising from the compact with that State whereby the United States are bound to extinguish the Indian title to the lands within it whenever it may be done peaceably and on reasonable conditions. In the fulfillment of this compact, I have thought that the United States should act with a generous spirit; that they should omit nothing which should comport with a liberal construction of the instrument and likewise be in accordance with the just rights of those tribes. From the view which I have taken of the subject I am satisfied that in the discharge of these important duties in regard to both the parties alluded to the United States will have to encounter no conflicting interests with either. On the contrary, that the removal of the tribes from the territory which they now inhabit to that which was designated in the message at the commencement of the session, which would accomplish the object for Georgia, under a well-digested plan for their government and civilization, which should be agreeable to themselves, would not only shield them from impending ruin, but promote their welfare and happiness. Experience has clearly demonstrated that in their present state it is impossible to incorporate them in such masses, in any form whatever, into our system. It has also demonstrated with equal certainty that without a timely anticipation of and provision against the dangers to which they are exposed, under causes which it will be difficult, if not impossible, to control, their degradation and extermination will be inevitable.

The great object to be accomplished is the removal of these tribes to the territory designated on conditions which shall be satisfactory to themselves and honorable to the United States. This can be done only by conveying to each tribe a good title to an adequate portion of land to which it may consent to remove, and by providing for it there a system of internal government which shall protect their property from invasion, and, by the regular progress of improvement and civilization, prevent that degeneracy which has generally marked the transition from the one to the other state.

I transmit herewith a report from the Secretary of War, which presents the best estimate which can be formed, from the documents in that Department, of the number of Indians within our States and Territories and of the amount of lands held by the several tribes within each; of the state of the country lying northward and westward thereof, within our acknowledged boundaries; of the parts to which the Indian title has already been extinguished, and of the conditions on which other parts, in an amount which may be adequate to the object contemplated, may be obtained. By this report it appears that the Indian title has already been extinguished to extensive tracts in that quarter, and that other portions may be acquired to the extent desired on very moderate conditions. Satisfied I also am that the removal proposed is not only practicable, but that the advantages attending it to the Indians may be made so apparent to them that all the tribes, even those most opposed, may be induced to accede to it at no very distant day.

The digest of such a government, with the consent of the Indians, which should be endowed with sufficient power to meet all the objects contemplated—to connect the several tribes together in a bond of amity and preserve order in each; to prevent intrusions on their property; to teach them by regular instruction the arts of civilized life and make them a civilized people—is an object of very high importance. It is the powerful consideration which we have to offer to these tribes as an inducement to relinquish the lands on which they now reside and to remove to those which are designated. It is not doubted that this arrangement will present considerations of sufficient force to surmount all their prejudices in favor of the soil of their nativity, however strong they may be. Their elders have sufficient intelligence to discern the certain progress of events in the present train, and sufficient virtue, by yielding to momentary sacrifices, to protect their families and posterity from inevitable destruction. They will also perceive that they may thus attain an elevation to which as communities they could not otherwise aspire.

To the United States the proposed arrangement offers many important advantages in addition to those which have been already enumerated. By the establishment of such a government over these tribes with their consent we become in reality their benefactors. The relation of conflicting interests which has heretofore existed between them and our frontier settlements will cease.

There will be no more wars between them and the United States. Adopting such a government, their movement will be in harmony with us, and its good effect be felt throughout the whole extent of our territory to the Pacific. It may fairly be presumed that, through the agency of such a government, the condition of all the tribes inhabiting that vast region may be essentially improved; that permanent peace may be preserved with them, and our commerce be much extended.

With a view to this important object I recommend it to Congress to adopt, by solemn declaration, certain fundamental principles in accord with those above suggested, as the basis of such arrangements as may be entered into with the several tribes, to the strict observance of which the faith of the nation shall be pledged. I recommend it also to Congress to provide by law for the appointment of a suitable number of commissioners who shall, under the direction of the President, be authorized to visit and explain to the several tribes the objects of the Government, and to make with them, according to their instructions, such arrangements as shall be best calculated to carry those objects into effect.

A negotiation is now depending with the Creek Nation for the cession of lands held by it within the limits of Georgia, and with a reasonable prospect of success. It is presumed, however, that the result will not be known during the present session of Congress. To give effect to this negotiation and to the negotiations which it is proposed to hold with all the other tribes within the limits of the several States and Territories on the principles and for the purposes stated, it is recommended that an adequate appropriation be now made by Congress.

[James D. Richardson, comp., *Messages and Papers of the Presidents*, 2:280-83.]

36.   Treaty with the Ponca Indians

June 9, 1825

In response to fur traders' pleas a military expedition was sent up the Missouri River in 1825 under General Henry Atkinson to overawe the Indians and to conclude treaties of peace with them. (See Act of May 25, 1824.) One of the treaties signed was with the Ponca Indians.

For the purposes of perpetuating the friendship which has heretofore existed, as also to remove all future cause of discussion or dissention, as it respects trade and friendship between the United States and their citizens, and the Poncar tribe of Indians, the President of the United States of America, by Brigadier General Henry Atkinson, of the United States' Army, and Major Benjamin O'Fallon, Indian Agent, with full powers and authority, specially appointed and commissioned for that purpose of the one part, and the undersigned Chiefs, Headmen, and Warriors, of the Poncar tribe of Indians, on behalf of said tribe, of the other part, have made and entered into the following articles and conditions, which, when ratified by the President of the United States, by and with the advice and consent of the Senate, shall be binding on both parties—to wit:

ARTICLE 1. It is admitted by the Poncar tribe of Indians, that they reside within the territorial limits of the United States, acknowledge their supremacy, and claim their protection. The said tribe also admit the right of the United States to regulate all trade and intercourse with them.

ARTICLE 2. The United States agree to receive the Poncar tribe of Indians into their friendship, and under their protection, and to extend to them, from time to time, such benefits and acts of kindness as may be convenient, and seem just and proper to the President of the United States.

ARTICLE 3. All trade and intercourse with the Poncar tribe shall be transacted at such place or places as may be designated and pointed out by the President of the United States, through his agents; and none but American citizens, duly authorized by the United States, shall be admitted to trade or hold intercourse with said tribe of Indians.

ARTICLE 4. That the Poncar tribe may be accommodated with such articles of merchandise, &c. as their necessities may demand, the United States agree to admit and license traders to hold intercourse with said tribe, under mild and equitable regulations: in consideration of which, the Poncar tribe bind themselves to extend protection to the persons and the property of the traders, and the persons legally employed under them,

whilst they remain within the limits of the Poncar district of country. And the said Poncar tribe further agree, that if any foreigner, or other person not legally authorized by the United States, shall come into their district of country, for the purposes of trade or other views, they will apprehend such person or persons, and deliver him or them to some United States' superintendent, or agent of Indian Affairs, or to the Commandant of the nearest military post, to be dealt with according to law. And they further agree to give safe conduct to all persons who may be legally authorized by the United States to pass through their country; and to protect, in their persons and property, all agents or other persons sent by the United States to reside temporarily among them.

ARTICLE 5. That the friendship which is now established between the United States and the Poncar tribe should not be interrupted by the misconduct of individuals, it is hereby agreed, that for injuries done by individuals, no private revenge or retaliation shall take place, but instead thereof, complaints shall be made, by the party injured, to the superintendent or agent of Indian affairs, or other person appointed by the President; and it shall be the duty of the said Chiefs, upon complaint being made as aforesaid, to deliver up the person or persons against whom the complaint is made, to the end that he or they may be punished agreeably to the laws of the United States. And, in like manner, if any robbery, violence, or murder, shall be committed on any Indian or Indians belonging to said tribe, the person or persons so offending shall be tried, and if found guilty shall be punished in like manner as if the injury had been done to a white man. And it is agreed, that the Chiefs of said Poncar tribe shall, to the utmost of their power, exert themselves to recover horses or other property, which may be stolen or taken from any citizen or citizens of the United States, by any individual or individuals of said tribe; and the property so recovered shall be forthwith delivered to the agents or other person authorized to receive it, that it may be restored to the proper owner. And the United States hereby guaranty to any Indian or Indians of said tribe, a full indemnification for any horses or other property which may be stolen from them by

41

any of their citizens: *Provided*, That the property so stolen cannot be recovered, and that sufficient proof is produced that it was actually stolen by a citizen of the United States. And the said Poncar tribe engage, on the requisition or demand of the President of the United States, or of the agents, to deliver up any white man resident among them.

ARTICLE 6. And the Chiefs and War- riors, as aforesaid, promise and engage, that their tribe will never, by sale, exchange, or as presents, supply any nation or tribe of Indians, not in amity with the United States, with guns, ammunition, or other implements of War. . . .

[Charles J. Kappler, ed., *Indian Affairs: Laws and Treaties*, 2:225-26.]

37.   Treaty of Prairie du Chien
August 19, 1825

Intertribal conflicts threatened the peace of the frontiers, and the United States sought to prevent such hostilities by having the Indian tribes agree to definite boundary lines and specific areas which each claimed. Tribes from the upper Mississippi were assembled at Prairie du Chien in the summer of 1825 to conclude such a pact.

Treaty with the Sioux and Chippewa, Sacs and Fox, Menominie, Ioway, Sioux, Winnebago, and a portion of the Ottawa, Chippewa, and Potawattomie Tribes.

The United States of America have seen with much regret, that wars have for many years been carried on between the Sioux and the Chippewas, and more recently between the confederated tribes of Sacs and Foxes, and the Sioux; and also between the Ioways and Sioux; which, if not terminated, may extend to the other tribes, and involve the Indians upon the Missouri, the Mississippi, and the Lakes, in general hostilities. In order, therefore, to promote peace among these tribes, and to establish boundaries among them and the other tribes who live in their vicinity, and thereby to remove all causes of future difficulty, the United States have invited the Chippewa, Sac, and Fox, Menominie, Ioway, Sioux, Winnebago, and a portion of the Ottowa, Chippewa and Potawatomie Tribes of Indians living upon the Illinois, to assemble together, and in a spirit of mutual conciliation to accomplish these objects; and to aid therein, have appointed William Clark and Lewis Cass, Commissioners on their part, who have met the Chiefs, Warriors, and Representatives of the said tribes, and portion of tribes, at Prairie des Chiens, in the Territory of Michigan, and after full deliberation, the said tribes, and portions of tribes, have agreed with the United States, and with one another, upon the following articles:

ARTICLE 1. There shall be a firm and perpetual peace between the Sioux and Chippewas; between the Sioux and the confederated tribes of Sacs and Foxes; and between the Ioways and the Sioux.

ARTICLES 2-9. [Designation of boundary lines between tribes and description of areas claimed by specific groups of Indians.]

ARTICLE 10. All the tribes aforesaid acknowledge the general controlling power of the United States, and disclaim all dependence upon, and connection with, any other power. And the United States agree to, and recognize, the preceding boundaries, subject to the limitations and restrictions before provided. It being, however, well understood that the reservations at Fever River, at the Ouisconsin, and St. Peters, and the ancient settlements at Prairie des Chiens and Green Bay, and the land property thereto belonging, and the reservations made upon the Mississippi, for the use of the half breeds, in the treaty concluded with the Sacs and Foxes, August 24, 1824, are not claimed by either of the said tribes.

ARTICLE 11. The United States agree, whenever the President may think it necessary and proper, to convene such of the tribes, either separately or together, as are interested in the lines left unsettled herein, and to recommend to them an amicable and final adjustment of their respective claims, so that the work, now happily begun, may be consummated. It is agreed, however, that a Council shall be held with the Yancton band of the Sioux, during the year 1826, to explain to them the stipulations of this treaty, and to procure their assent thereto, should they be disposed to give it, and also with the Ottoes, to settle and adjust their title to any of the country claimed by the Sacs, Foxes, and Ioways.

ARTICLE 12. The Chippewa tribe being dispersed over a great extent of country, and the Chiefs of that tribe having requested, that such portion of them as may be thought proper, by the Government of the United States, may be assembled in 1826, upon some part of Lake Superior, that the objects and advantages of this treaty may be fully explained to them, so that the stipulations thereof may be observed by the warriors. The Commissioners of the United States assent thereto, and it is therefore agreed that a council shall accordingly be held for these purposes.

ARTICLE 13. It is understood by all the tribes, parties hereto, that no tribe shall hunt within the acknowledged limits of any other without their assent, but it being the sole object of this arrangement to perpetuate a peace among them, and amicable relations being now restored, the Chiefs of all the tribes have expressed a determination, cheerfully to allow a reciprocal right of hunting on the lands of one another, permission being first asked and obtained, as before provided for.

ARTICLE 14. Should any causes of difficulty hereafter unhappily arise between any of the tribes, parties hereunto, it is agreed that the other tribes shall interpose their good offices to remove such difficulties; and also that the government of the United States may take such measures as they may deem proper, to effect the same object.

ARTICLE 15. This treaty shall be obligatory on the tribes, parties hereto, from and after the date hereof, and on the United States, from and after its ratification by the government thereof. . . .

[Charles J. Kappler, ed., *Indian Affairs: Laws and Treaties*, 2:250-54.]

38. Thomas L. McKenney on Trading Sites
February 14, 1826

The law of May 25, 1824, providing that Indian agents should designate "certain convenient and suitable places" for carrying on trade with the Indians, was opposed by traders, who found it too restrictive, and several attempts were made in Congress to repeal the act. In a report submitted to Secretary of War James Barbour, February 14, 1826, Thomas L. McKenney, head of the Indian Office, defended the act. His report was violently attacked by Robert Stuart of the American Fur Company, but the provision was retained in the laws governing trade with the Indians.

. . . . The fourth section of the aforesaid act is in the words following, to wit: "*And be it further enacted*, That it shall be the duty of Indian agents to designate, from time to time, certain convenient and suitable places for carrying on trade with the different Indian tribes, and to require all traders to trade at the places thus designated, and at no other place or places." . . .

The chief object of the Congress in adopting this provision was, doubtless, the protection of the Indians. In this point of view, the provision is as just as it is humane. Just, because the Indians have claims upon the Government for protection; and humane, because, without its interference, all experience testifies that they must be injured.

But the question is, does the provision in the section under consideration answer those great ends? An answer, to be conclusive, could be given only by a comparison of the state of excitements in the Indian country, and along our borders, prior to the operations of this act, and since it has been in force. But the act is of too recent origin to have disclosed any very striking effects in correcting the evils which it was intended to remedy. It is believed, however, that a comparative quiet has been produced by it already; that fewer murders have been committed among the Indians themselves, and by them upon the whites, since the trade has been restricted, than before. In my opinion, its operations have been salutary; and, if every thing which it was hoped to gain by it

43

has not been realized, it is owing more to the short period in which the act has been in operation than to any defect in its provisions. . . .

The source of all the difficulty is to be found in the necessity which the traders esteem themselves to be under to carry spirituous liquors into the Indian country; and it is from this source that so much wretched-ness and so many evils proceed. There are many persons engaged in this trade whose feelings, no doubt, revolt at the calamities which a traffic of this sort occasions; but the forbidden and destructive article is considered so essential to a lucrative commerce, as not only to still those feelings, but to lead the traders to brave the most imminent hazards, and evade, by various methods, the threatened penalties of the law. . . .

It is believed that sound policy, no less than justice and humanity, requires that it should be made a capital offence for any person to furnish spirituous liquors to Indians, *under any circumstances.* But, in the absence of such a provision, it does appear to me that the next best measure, viewed in connexion with existing prohibitory laws, is, to oblige those who may carry on trade with them to do so from certain designated places. These, however, ought to be made "suitable and convenient;" and so the law provides.

The existing obligation to locate and carry on trade at places which are known, and no others, and which are *previously designated,* does appear to me to bring the evils, which it is esteemed on all hands to be so important to remedy, more immediately within the eye of the officers of the Government and the grasp of the law, than any that has been heretofore devised. It is apparent, from the very statement of the case, that the chances of detection are greatly multiplied by the existing provision; and just in proportion as this point is gained will the evil diminish. The agents have a power over the vending of spirituous liquors in the one case, which they could never attain in the other. There needs no argument to prove this, as nobody, it is presumed, will dispute it. But the penalty is heavier in the one case than in the other; and this will operate as an additional check. Wherever the trader may be located, there is the whole amount of his property, in one confined and tangible place; whereas, when he roams the country at will, it is separated into smaller parcels, and borne about upon pack-horses. In the latter case, even if he is detected, (experience has proven, however, that, once in the forests, there is very little risk,) the levy might fall upon no more than the amount of what a single pack-horse would carry; and that, if forfeited, would be matter of small concern, and scarcely worth guarding. . . .

[*American State Papers: Indian Affairs,* 2:659-60.]

39. Secretary of War Eaton on Cherokee Removal

April 18, 1829

The federal policy of removing the eastern Indians to areas west of the Mississippi, strongly supported by President Andrew Jackson, brought sharp opposition from the Cherokee Indians, who argued for their right to remain where they were. One of the best statements of Jackson's position is the letter written by Secretary of War John H. Eaton on April 18, 1829, to John Ross, Richard Taylor, Edward Gunter, and William S. Coody, who comprised the Cherokee delegation.

Friends and Brothers,

Your letter of the 17th of February, addressed to the late Secretary of War, has been brought to the notice of this Department, since the communication made to you on the 11th Instant; and having conversed freely and fully with the President of the United States, I am directed by him to submit the following as the views which are entertained, in reference to the subjects which you have submitted for consideration.

You state that "the Legislature of Georgia in defiance of the laws of the United States, and the most solemn Treaties existing," have extended a jurisdiction over your Nation to take effect in June 1830. That "your nation had no voice in the formation of the confederacy of the Union, and has ever been unshackled with the laws of individual states because independent of them"; and that consequently this act of Georgia is to be viewed, "in no other light, than a wanton usurpation of power, guaranteed to no State, neither by the common law of the land, nor by the laws of nature."

To all this, there is a plain and obvious answer, deducible from the known history of the Country. During the War of the Revolution, your nation was the friend and ally of Great Britain; a power which then claimed entire sovereignty, within the limits of what constituted the thirteen United States. By the declaration of Independence and subsequently the Treaty of 1783, all the rights of sovereignty pertaining to Great Britain, became vested respectively in the original States, of this union, including North Carolina and Georgia, within whose territorial limits, as defined and known, your nation was then situated. If, as is the case, you have been permitted to abide on your lands from that period to the present, enjoying the right of soil, and privilege to hunt, it is not thence to be inferr'd, that this was any thing more than a permission growing out of compacts with your nation; nor is it a circumstance whence, now to deny to those States, the exercise of their original Sovereignty.

In the year 1785, three years after the Independence of the States, which compose this union, had been acknowledged by Great Britain, a treaty, at Hopewell, was concluded with your nation by the United States. The emphatic language it contains cannot be mistaken, commencing as follows—

"The Commissioners plenipotentiaries of the United States in Congress assembled, give peace to all the Cherokees, and receive them into favor and protection of the United States of America." It proceeds then to allot, and to define your limits and your hunting grounds. You were secured, in the privilege of pursuing the game; and from encroachments by the whites. No right however, save a mere possessory one, is by the provisions of the treaty of Hopewell conceded to your nation. The soil, and the use of it, were suffered to remain with you, while the Sovereignty abided, precisely where it did before, in those states within whose limits you were situated.

Subsequent to this, your people were at enmity with the United States, and waged war upon our frontier settlements; a desirable peace was not entered into with you, until 1791. At that period a good understanding obtained, hostilities ceased, and by the Treaty made and concluded, your nation was placed under the protection of our Government, and a guarantee given, favorable to the occupancy and possession of your Country. But the United States, always mindful of the authority of the States, even when treating for what was so much desired, peace with their red brothers, forbore to offer a guarantee adverse to the sovereignty of Georgia. They could not do so; they had not the power.

At a more recent period, to wit, in 1802, the State of Georgia, defining her own proper limits, ceded to the United States, all her western territory upon a condition which was accepted, "that the United States shall, at their own expense, extinguish for the use of Georgia as early as the same can be peaceably obtained on reasonable terms, the Indian title, to all the lands within the State of Georgia." She did not ask the military arm of the Government to be employed, but in her mildness and forbearance, only, that the soil might be yielded to her, as soon as it could peaceably be obtained, and on reasonable terms. In relation to Sovereignty nothing is said, or hinted at in the compact; nor was it necessary or even proper, as both the parties to the agreement well knew that it was a right which already existed in the state in virtue of the declaration of our independence, and of the Treaty of 1783, afterwards concluded.

These things have been made known to you frankly, and after the most friendly manner; and particularly at the making of the treaty with your nation in 1817, when a portion of your people stipulated to remove to the West of the Mississippi; and yet it is alleged in your communication to this Department, that you have "been unshackled with the laws of individual States, because independent of them."

The course you have pursued of establishing an independent, substantive, government, within the territorial limits of the State of Georgia, adverse to her will, and contrary to her consent, has been the immediate cause, which has induced her, to depart from the forbearance, she has so long practiced; and in virtue of her authority, as a Sovereign, Independent State, to extend over your country, her Legislative enactments, which she and every other state embraced in the confederacy, from 1783 to the present time, when their independence was acknowledged and admitted, possessed the power to do, apart from any authority or opposing interference by the general government.

But suppose, and it is suggested, merely for the purpose of awakening your better judgment, that Georgia cannot, and ought not, to claim the exercise of such power. What alternative is then presented? In reply allow me to call your attention for a moment to the grave character of the course, which under a mistaken view of your own rights, you desire this Government to adopt. It is no less than an invitation, that she shall step forward to arrest the constitutional act of an independent State, exercised within her own limits. Should this be done, and Georgia persist in the maintenance of her rights, and her authority, the consequences might be, that the act would prove injurious to us, and in all probability ruinous to you. The sword might be looked to as the arbiter in such an interference. But this can never be done. The President cannot, and will not, beguile you with such an expectation. The arms of this country can never be employed, to stay any state of this Union from the exercise of those legitimate powers which attach, and belong to their sovereign character. An interference to the extent of affording you protection, and the occupancy of your soil is what is demanded of the justice of this Country and will not be withheld, yet in doing this, the right of permitting to you the enjoyment of a separate government, within the limits of a State, and denying the exercise of Sovereignty to that State, within her own limits, cannot be admitted. It is not within the range of powers granted by the states to the general government, and therefore not within its competency to be exercised.

In this view of the circumstances connected with your application, it becomes proper to remark that no remedy can be perceived, except that which frequently, heretofore has been submitted for your consideration, a removal beyond the Mississippi, where, alone, can be asured to you protection and peace. It must be obvious to you, and the President has instructed me again to bring it to your candid and serious consideration, that to continue where you are, within the territorial limits of an independent state, can promise you nothing but interruption and disquietude. Beyond the Mississippi your prospects will be different. There you will find no conflicting interests. The United States power and sovereignty, uncontrolled by the high authority of state jurisdiction, and resting on its own energies, will be able to say to you, in the language of your own nation, the soil shall be yours while the trees grow, or the streams run. But situated where you now are, he cannot hold to you such language, or consent to beguile you, by inspiring in your bosoms hopes and expectations, which cannot be realized. Justice and friendly feelings cherished towards our red brothers of the forest, demand that in all our intercourse, frankness should be maintained.

The President desires me to say, that the feelings entertained by him towards your people, are of the most friendly kind; and that in the intercourse heretofore, in past times, so frequently had with the Chiefs of your nation, he failed not to warn them of the consequences which would result to them from residing within the limits of Sovereign States. He holds to them, now, no other language, than that which he has heretofore employed; and in doing so, feels convinced that he is pointing out that course which humanity and a just regard for the interest of the Indian will be found to sanction. In the view entertained by him of this important matter, there is but a single alternative, to yield to the operation of those laws, which Georgia claims, and has a right to extend throughout her own limits, or to remove, and by associating with your brothers beyond the Mississippi to become again united as one Nation, carrying along with you that protection, which, there situated, it will be in the power of the government to extend. The Indians being thus brought together at a distance from their brothers, will be relieved from very many of those interruptions, which, situated as they are at present, are without a remedy. The Government of the United States will then be able to exercise over them a paternal, and superintending care to happier advantage, to stay encroachments, and preserve them in peace and amity with each other; while with the aid of schools a hope may be indulged, that ere long industry and refinement, will take the place of those wandering habits now so peculiar to the Indian character, the tendency of which is to impede them in their march to civilization.

Respecting the intrusions on your lands, submitted also for consideration, it is sufficient to remark, that of these the Department had already been advised, and instructions have been forwarded to the agent of the Cherokees directing him to cause their removal; and it is earnestly hoped, that on this matter, all cause for future complaint will cease, and the order prove effectual.

[Office of Indian Affairs, Letter Book no. 5, pp. 408-12, Record Group 75, National Archives.]

40. President Jackson on Indian Removal
December 8, 1829

The executive branch of the federal government was firmly committed to the removal of the eastern tribes to the region west of the Mississippi by President Andrew Jackson. In his First Annual Message to Congress in December 1829 he set forth his views.

. . . . The condition and ulterior destiny of the Indian tribes within the limits of some of our States have become objects of much interest and importance. It has long been the policy of Government to introduce among them the arts of civilization, in the hope of gradually reclaiming them from a wandering life. This policy has, however, been coupled with another wholly incompatible with its success. Professing a desire to civilize and settle them, we have at the same time lost no opportunity to purchase their lands and thrust them farther into the wilderness. By this means they have not only been kept in a wandering state, but been led to look upon us as unjust and indifferent to their fate. Thus, though lavish in its expenditures upon the subject, Government has constantly defeated its own policy, and the Indians in general, receding farther and farther to the west, have retained their savage habits. A portion, however, of the Southern tribes, having mingled much with the whites and made some progress in the arts of civilized life, have lately attempted to erect an independent government within the limits of Georgia and Alabama. These States, claiming to be the only sovereigns within their territories, extended their laws over the Indians, which induced the latter to call upon the United States for protection.

Under these circumstances the question presented was whether the General Government had a right to sustain those people in their pretensions. The Constitution declares that "no new State shall be formed or erected within the jurisdiction of any other State" without the consent of its legislature. If the General Government is not permitted to tolerate the erection of a confederate State within the territory of one of the members of this Union against her consent, much less could it allow a foreign and independent government to establish itself there. Georgia became a member of the Confederacy which eventuated in our Federal Union as a sovereign State, always asserting her claim to certain limits, which, having been originally defined in her colonial charter and subsequently recognized in the treaty of peace, she has ever since continued to enjoy, except as they have been circumscribed by her own voluntary transfer of a portion of her territory to the United States in the articles of cession of 1802. Alabama was admitted into the Union on the same footing with the original States, with boundaries which were prescribed by Congress. There is no constitutional, conventional, or legal provision which allows them less power over the Indians within their borders than is possessed by Maine or New York. Would the people of Maine permit the Penobscot tribe to erect an independent government within their State? And unless they did would it not be the duty of the General Government to support them in resisting such a measure? Would the people of New York permit each remnant of the

47

Six Nations within her borders to declare itself an independent people under the protection of the United States? Could the Indians establish a separate republic on each of their reservations in Ohio? And if they were so disposed would it be the duty of this Government to protect them in the attempt? If the principle involved in the obvious answer to these questions be abandoned, it will follow that the objects of this Government are reversed, and that it has become a part of its duty to aid in destroying the States which it was established to protect.

Actuated by this view of the subject, I informed the Indians inhabiting parts of Georgia and Alabama that their attempt to establish an independent government would not be countenanced by the Executive of the United States, and advised them to emigrate beyond the Mississippi or submit to the laws of those States.

Our conduct toward these people is deeply interesting to our national character. Their present condition, contrasted with what they once were, makes a most powerful appeal to our sympathies. Our ancestors found them the uncontrolled possessors of these vast regions. By persuasion and force they have been made to retire from river to river and from mountain to mountain, until some of the tribes have become extinct and others have left but remnants to preserve for a while their once terrible names. Surrounded by the whites with their arts of civilization, which by destroying the resources of the savage doom him to weakness and decay, the fate of the Mohegan, the Narragansett, and the Delaware is fast overtaking the Choctaw, the Cherokee, and the Creek. That this fate surely awaits them if they remain within the limits of the States does not admit of a doubt. Humanity and national honor demand that every effort should be made to avert so great a calamity. It is too late to inquire whether it was just in the United States to include them and their territory within the bounds of new States, whose limits they could control. That step can not be retraced. A State can not be dismembered by Congress or restricted in the exercise of her constitutional power. But the people of those States and of every State, actuated by feelings of justice and a regard for our national honor, submit to you the interesting question whether something can not be done, consistently with the rights of the States, to preserve this much-injured race.

As a means of effecting this end I suggest for your consideration the propriety of setting apart an ample district west of the Mississippi, and without the limit of any State or Territory now formed, to be guaranteed to the Indian tribes as long as they shall occupy it, each tribe having a distinct control over the portion designated for its use. There they may be secured in the enjoyment of governments of their own choice, subject to no other control from the United States than such as may be necessary to preserve peace on the frontier and between the several tribes. There the benevolent may endeavor to teach them the arts of civilization, and, by promoting union and harmony among them, to raise up an interesting commonwealth, destined to perpetuate the race and to attest the humanity and justice of this Government.

This emigration should be voluntary, for it would be as cruel as unjust to compel the aborigines to abandon the graves of their fathers and seek a home in a distant land. But they should be distinctly informed that if they remain within the limits of the States they must be subject to their laws. In return for their obedience as individuals they will without doubt be protected in the enjoyment of those possessions which they have improved by their industry. But it seems to me visionary to suppose that in this state of things claims can be allowed on tracts of country on which they have neither dwelt nor made improvements, merely because they have seen them from the mountain or passed them in the chase. Submitting to the laws of the States, and receiving, like other citizens, protection in their persons and property, they will ere long become merged in the mass of our population. . . .

[James D. Richardson, comp., *Messages and Papers of the Presidents*, 2:456-59.]

41. Senator Frelinghuysen on Indian Removal

April 9, 1830

One of the strongest supporters of the Indian opposition to removal was Senator Theodore Frelinghuysen of New Jersey. He presented his arguments in a long speech in the Senate on April 9, 1830, during the debate on the removal bill.

. . . . God, in his providence, planted these tribes on this Western continent, so far as we know, before Great Britain herself had a political existence. I believe, sir, it is not now seriously denied that the Indians are men, endowed with kindred faculties and powers with ourselves; that they have a place in human sympathy, and are justly entitled to a share in the common bounties of a benignant Providence. And, with this conceded, I ask in what code of the law of nations, or by what process of abstract deduction, their rights have been extinguished?

Where is the decree or ordinance that has stripped these early and first lords of the soil? Sir, no record of such measure can be found. And I might triumphantly rest the hopes of these feeble fragments of once great nations upon this impregnable foundation. However mere human policy, or the law of power, or the tyrant's pleas of expediency, may have found it convenient at any or in all times to recede from the unchangeable principles of eternal justice, no argument can shake the political maxim, that, where the Indian always has been, he enjoys an absolute right still to be, in the free exercise of his own modes of thought, government and conduct.

In the light of natural law, can a reason for a distinction exist in the mode of enjoying that which is my own? If I use it for hunting, may another take it because he needs it for agriculture? I am aware that some writers have, by a system of artificial reasoning, endeavored to justify, or rather excuse the encroachments made upon Indian territory; and they denominate these abstractions the law of nations, and, in this ready way, the question is despatched. Sir, as we trace the sources of this law, we find its authority to depend either upon the conventions or common consent of nations. And when, permit me to inquire, were the Indian tribes ever consulted on the establishment of such a law? Whoever represented them or

their interests in any congress of nations, to confer upon the public rules of intercourse, and the proper foundations of dominion and property? The plain matter of fact is, that all these partial doctrines have resulted from the selfish plans and pursuits of more enlightened nations; and it is not matter for any great wonder, that they should so largely partake of a mercenary and exclusive spirit toward the claims of the Indians.

It is, however, admitted, sir, that, when the increase of population and the wants of mankind demand the cultivation of the earth, a duty is thereby devolved upon the proprietors of large and uncultivated regions, of devoting them to such useful purposes. But such appropriations are to be obtained by fair contract, and for reasonable compensation. It is, in such a case, the duty of the proprietor to sell: we may properly address his reason to induce him; but we cannot rightfully compel the cession of his lands, or take them by violence, if his consent be withheld. It is with great satisfaction that I am enabled, upon the best authority, to affirm, that this duty has been largely and generously met and fulfilled on the part of the aboriginal proprietors of this continent. Several years ago, official reports to Congress stated the amount of Indian grants to the United States to exceed 214 millions of acres. Yes, sir, we have acquired, and now own more land as the fruits of their bounty than we shall dispose of at the present rate to actual settlers in two hundred years. For, very recently, it has been ascertained, on this floor, that our public sales average not more than about one million of acres annually. It greatly aggravates the wrong that is now meditated against these tribes, to survey the rich and ample districts of their territories, that either force or persuasion have incorporated into our public domains. As the tide of our population has rolled on, we have added purchase to purchase. The confiding Indian listened to our professions

49

of friendship: we called him brother, and he believed us. Millions after millions he has yielded to our importunity, until we have acquired more than can be cultivated in centuries—and yet we crave more. We have crowded the tribes upon a few miserable acres on our southern frontier: it is all that is left to them of their once boundless forests: and still, like the horse-leech, our insatiate cupidity cries, give! give!

Before I proceed to deduce collateral confirmations of this original title, from all our political intercourse and conventions with the Indian tribes, I beg leave to pause a moment, and view the case as it lies beyond the treaties made with them; and aside also from all conflicting claims between the confederation, and the colonies, and the Congress of the States. Our ancestors found these people, far removed from the commotions of Europe, exercising all the rights, and enjoying the privileges, of free and independent sovereigns of this new world. They were not a wild and lawless horde of banditti, but lived under the restraints of government, patriarchal in its character, and energetic in its influence. They had chiefs, head men, and councils. The white men, the authors of all their wrongs, approached them as friends—they extended the olive branch; and, being then a feeble colony and at the mercy of the native tenants of the soil, by presents and professions, propitiated their good will. The Indian yielded a slow, but substantial confidence; granted to the colonists an abiding place; and suffered them to grow up to man's estate beside him. He never raised the claim of elder title: as the white man's wants increased, he opened the hand of his bounty wider and wider. By and by, conditions are changed. His people melt away; his lands are constantly coveted; millions after millions are ceded. The Indian bears it all meekly; he complains, indeed, as well he may; but suffers on: and now he finds that this neighbor, whom his kindness had nourished, has spread an adverse title over the last remains of his patrimony, barely adequate to his wants, and turns upon him, and says, "away! we cannot endure you so near us! These forests and rivers, these groves of your fathers, these firesides and hunting grounds, are ours by the right of power, and the force of numbers." Sir, let

every treaty be blotted from our records, and in the judgment of natural and unchangeable truth and justice, I ask, who is the injured, and who is the aggressor? Let conscience answer, and I fear not the result. Sir, let those who please, denounce the public feeling on this subject as the morbid excitement of a false humanity; but I return with the inquiry, whether I have not presented the case truly, with no feature of it overcharged or distorted? And, in view of it, who can help feeling, sir? Do the obligations of justice change with the color of the skin? Is it one of the prerogatives of the white man, that he may disregard the dictates of moral principles, when an Indian shall be concerned? No, sir. In that severe and impartial scrutiny, which futurity will cast over this subject, the righteous award will be, that those very causes which are now pleaded for the relaxed enforcement of the rules of equity, urged upon us not only a rigid execution of the highest justice, to the very letter, but claimed at our hands a generous and magnanimous policy.

Standing here, then, on this unshaken basis, how is it possible that even a shadow of claim to soil, or jurisdiction, can be derived, by forming a collateral issue between the State of Georgia and the General Government? Her complaint is made against the United States, for encroachments on her sovereignty. Sir, the Cherokees are no parties to this issue; they have no part in this controversy. They hold by better title than either Georgia or the Union. They have nothing to do with State sovereignty, or United States, sovereignty. They are above and beyond both. True, sir, they have made treaties with both, but not to acquire title or jurisdiction; these they had before—ages before the evil hour to them, when their white brothers fled to them for an asylum. They treated to secure protection and guarantee for subsisting powers and privileges; and so far as those conventions raise obligations, they are willing to meet, and always have met, and faithfully performed them; and now expect from a great people, the like fidelity to plighted covenants. . . .

It is a subject full of grateful satisfaction, that, in our public intercourse with the Indians, ever since the first colonies of white men

50

found an abode on these Western shores, we have distinctly recognized their title; treated with them as owners, and in all our acquisitions of territory, applied ourselves to these ancient proprietors, by purchase and cession alone, to obtain the right of soil. Sir, I challenge the record of any other or different pretension. When, or where, did any assembly or convention meet which proclaimed, or even suggested to these tribes, that the right of discovery contained a superior efficacy over all prior titles?

And our recognition was not confined to the soil merely. We regarded them as nations—far behind us indeed in civilization, but still we respected their forms of government—we conformed our conduct to their notions of civil policy. We were aware of the potency of any edict that sprang from the deliberations of the council fire; and when we desired lands, or peace, or alliances, to this source of power and energy, to this great lever of Indian government we addressed our proposals—to this alone did we look; and from this alone did we expect aid or relief. . . .

Every administration of this Government, from President Washington's, have, with like solemnities and stipulations, held treaties with the Cherokees; treaties, too, by almost all of which we obtained further acquisitions of their territory. Yes, sir, whenever we approached them in the language of friendship and kindness, we touched the chord that won their confidence; and now, when they have nothing left with which to satisfy our cravings, we propose to annul every treaty—to gainsay our word—and, by violence and perfidy, drive the Indian from his home. In a subsequent treaty between the United States and the Cherokee nation, concluded on the 8th July, 1817, express reference is made to past negotiations between the parties, on the subject of removal to the west of the Mississippi; the same question that now agitates the country, and engages our deliberations. And this convention is deserving of particular notice, inasmuch as we shall learn from it, not only what sentiments were then entertained by our Government towards the Cherokees, but, also, in what light the different dispositions of the Indians to emigrate to the West, and to remain on their . . . [ancient] patri-

mony, were considered. This treaty recites that application had been made to the United States, at a previous period, by a deputation of the Cherokees, (on the 9th January, 1809) by which they apprized the Governmment of the wish of a part of their nation to remove west of the Mississippi, and of the residue to abide in their old habitations. That the President of the United States, after maturely considering the subject, answered the petitions as follows: "The United States, my children, are the friends of both parties, and, as far as can be reasonably asked, they are willing to satisfy the wishes of both. Those who remain may be assured of our patronage, our aid, and our good neighborhood." "To those who remove, every aid shall be administered, and when established at their new settlements, we shall consider them as our children, and always hold them firmly by the hand." The convention then establishes new boundaries and pledges our faith to respect and defend the Indian territories. Some matters, by universal consent, are taken as granted, without any explicit recognition. Under the influence of this rule of common fairness, how can we ever dispute the sovereign right of the Cherokees to remain east of the Mississippi, when it was in relation to that very location that we promised our patronage, aid, and good neighborhood? Sir, is this high-handed encroachment of Georgia to be the commentary upon the national pledge here given, and the obvious import of these terms? How were these people to remain, if not as they then existed, and as we then acknowledged them to be, a distinct and separate community, governed by their own peculiar laws and customs? We can never deny these principles, while fair dealing retains any hold of our conduct. Further, sir, it appears from this treaty, that the Indians who preferred to remain east of the river, expressed "to the President an anxious desire to engage in the pursuits of agriculture and civilized life in the country they then occupied," and we engaged to encourage those laudable purposes. Indeed, such pursuits had been recommended to the tribes, and patronized by the United States, for many years before this convention. Mr. Jefferson, in his message to Congress, as early as 1805, and when on the subject of our Indian relations, with his usual enlarged

51

views of public policy, observes: "The aboriginal inhabitants of these countries, I have regarded with the commiseration their history inspires. Endowed with the faculties and the rights of men, breathing an ardent love of liberty and independence, and occupying a country which left them no desire but to be undisturbed, the stream of overflowing population from other regions directed itself on these shores. Without power to divert, or habits to contend against it, they have been overwhelmed by the current, or driven before it. Now, reduced within limits too narrow for the hunter state, humanity enjoins us to teach them agriculture and the domestic arts; to encourage them to that industry, which alone can enable them to maintain their place in existence; and to prepare them in time for that society, which, to bodily comforts, adds the improvement of the mind and morals. We have, therefore, liberally furnished them with the implements of husbandry and household use; we have placed among them instructors in the arts of first necessity; and they are covered with the aegis of the law against aggressors from among ourselves." These, sir, are senti-

ments worthy of an illustrious statesman. None can fail to perceive the spirit of justice and humanity which Mr. Jefferson cherished towards our Indian allies. He was, through his whole life, the firm unshrinking advocate of their rights, a patron of all their plans for moral improvement and elevation. . . .

I trust, sir, that this brief exposition of our policy, in relation to Indian affairs, establishes, beyond all controversy, the obligation of the United States to protect these tribes in the exercise and enjoyment of their civil and political rights. Sir, the question has ceased to be—What are our duties? An inquiry much more embarrassing is forced upon us: How shall we most plausibly, and with the least possible violence, break our faith? Sir, we repel the inquiry—we reject such an issue—and point the guardians of public honor to the broad, plain . . . [path] of faithful performance, and to which they are equally urged by duty and by interest. . . .

[*Register of Debates in Congress,* 6:311-16.]

42. Indian Removal Act
May 28, 1830

After bitter debate in Congress and in the public press, Congress passed an act authorizing the president to exchange lands in the West for those held by Indian tribes in any state or territory and appropriated $500,000 for the purpose. This act enabled President Jackson to proceed with the removal policy and to negotiate removal treaties with the southern tribes.

An Act to provide for an exchange of lands with the Indians residing in any of the states or territories, and for their removal west of the river Mississippi.

Be it enacted . . . , That it shall and may be lawful for the President of the United States to cause so much of any territory belonging to the United States, west of the river Mississippi, not included in any state or organized territory, and to which the Indian title has been extinguished, as he may judge necessary, to be divided into a suitable number of districts, for the reception of such tribes or nations of Indians as may choose to exchange the lands where they now reside, and remove there; and to cause each of said districts to be so described by natural or artificial marks, as to be easily distinguished from every other.

SEC. 2. *And be it further enacted,* That it shall and may be lawful for the President to exchange any or all of such districts, so to be laid off and described, with any tribe or nation of Indians now residing within the limits of any of the states or territories, and with which the United States have existing treaties, for the whole or any part or portion of the territory claimed and occupied by such tribe or nation, within the bounds of any one or more of the states or territories, where the land claimed and occupied by the Indians, is owned by the United States, or the United States are bound to the state

52

within which it lies to extinguish the Indian claim thereto.

SEC. 3. *And be it further enacted*, That in the making of any such exchange or exchanges, it shall and may be lawful for the President solemnly to assure the tribe or nation with which the exchange is made, that the United States will forever secure and guaranty to them, and their heirs or successors, the country so exchanged with them; and if they prefer it, that the United States will cause a patent or grant to be made and executed to them for the same: *Provided always*, That such lands shall revert to the United States, if the Indians become extinct, or abandon the same.

SEC. 4. *And be it further enacted*, That if, upon any of the lands now occupied by the Indians, and to be exchanged for, there should be such improvements as add value to the land claimed by any individual or individuals of such tribes or nations, it shall and may be lawful for the President to cause such value to be ascertained by appraisement or otherwise, and to cause such ascertained value to be paid to the person or persons rightfully claiming such improvements. And upon the payment of such valuation, the improvements so valued and paid for, shall pass to the United States, and possession shall not afterwards be permitted to any of the same tribe.

SEC. 5. *And be it further enacted*, That upon the making of any such exchange as is contemplated by this act, it shall and may be lawful for the President to cause such aid and assistance to be furnished to the emigrants as may be necessary and proper to enable them to remove to, and settle in, the country for which they may have exchanged; and also, to give them such aid and assistance as may be necessary for their support and subsistence for the first year after their removal.

SEC. 6. *And be it further enacted*, That it shall and may be lawful for the President to cause such tribe or nation to be protected, at their new residence, against all interruption or disturbance from any other tribe or nation of Indians, or from any other person or persons whatever.

SEC. 7. *And be it further enacted*, That it shall and may be lawful for the President to have the same superintendence and care over any tribe or nation in the country to which they may remove, as contemplated by this act, that he is now authorized to have over them at their present places of residence: *Provided*, That nothing in this act contained shall be construed as authorizing or directing the violation of any existing treaty between the United States and any of the Indian tribes.

SEC. 8. *And be it further enacted*, That for the purpose of giving effect to the provisions of this act, the sum of five hundred thousand dollars is hereby appropriated, to be paid out of any money in the treasury, not otherwise appropriated.

[*U.S. Statutes at Large*, 4:411-12.]

43. Treaty with the Choctaw Indians
September 27, 1830

The first of the removal treaties signed with the southern Indians after passage of the Removal Act of 1830 was that with the Choctaws at Dancing Rabbit Creek. It provided for an exchange of lands, guaranteed protection for the Indians, and specified annuities and other payments or services.

A treaty of perpetual friendship, cession and limits, entered into by John H. Eaton and John Coffee, for and in behalf of the Government of the United States, and the Mingoes, Chiefs, Captains and Warriors of the Choctaw Nation, begun and held at Dancing Rabbit Creek, on the fifteenth of September, in the year eighteen hundred and thirty.

ARTICLE I. Perpetual peace and friendship is pledged and agreed upon by and between the United States and the Mingoes, Chiefs, and Warriors of the Choctaw Nation of Red People; and that this may be considered the Treaty existing between the parties all other Treaties heretofore existing and inconsistent with the provisions of this are hereby declared null and void.

ARTICLE II. The United States under a grant specially to be made by the President

53

of the U.S. shall cause to be conveyed to the Choctaw Nation a tract of country west of the Mississippi River, in fee simple to them and their descendants, to inure to them while they shall exist as a nation and live on it, beginning near Fort Smith where the Arkansas boundary crosses the Arkansas River, running thence to the source of the Canadian fork; if in the limits of the United States, or to those limits; thence due south to Red River, and down Red River to the west boundary of the Territory of Arkansas; thence north along that line to the beginning. The boundary of the same to be agreeably to the Treaty made and concluded at Washington City in the year 1825. The grant to be executed so soon as the present Treaty shall be ratified.

ARTICLE III. In consideration of the provisions contained in the several articles of this Treaty, the Choctaw nation of Indians consent and hereby cede to the United States, the entire country they own and possess, east of the Mississippi River; and they agree to move beyond the Mississippi River, early as practicable, and will so arrange their removal, that as many as possible of their people not exceeding one half of the whole number, shall depart during the falls of 1831 and 1832; the residue to follow during the succeeding fall of 1833; a better opportunity in this manner will be afforded the Government, to extend to them the facilities and comforts which it is desirable should be extended in conveying them to their new homes.

ARTICLE IV. The Government and people of the United States are hereby obliged to secure to the said Choctaw Nation of Red People the jurisdiction and government of all the persons and property that may be within their limits west, so that no Territory or State shall ever have a right to pass laws for the government of the Choctaw Nation of Red People and their descendants; and that no part of the land granted them shall ever be embraced in any Territory or State; but the U.S. shall forever secure said Choctaw Nation from, and against, all laws except such as from time to time may be enacted in their own National Councils, not inconsistent with the Constitution, Treaties, and Laws of the United States; and except such as may, and which have been enacted by Congress,

to the extent that Congress under the Constitution are required to exercise a legislation over Indian Affairs. But the Choctaws, should this treaty be ratified, express a wish that Congress may grant to the Choctaws the right of punishing by their own laws, any white man who shall come into their nation, and infringe any of their national regulations.

ARTICLE V. The United States are obliged to protect the Choctaws from domestic strife and from foreign enemies on the same principles that the citizens of the United States are protected, so that whatever would be a legal demand upon the U.S. for defence or for wrongs committed by an enemy, on a citizen of the U.S. shall be equally binding in favor of the Choctaws, and in all cases where the Choctaws shall be called upon by a legally authorized officer of the U.S. to fight an enemy, such Choctaw shall receive the pay and other emoluments, which citizens of the U.S. receive in such cases, provided, no war shall be undertaken or prosecuted by said Choctaw Nation but by declaration made in full Council, and to be approved by the U.S. unless it be in self defence against an open rebellion or against an enemy marching into their country, in which cases they shall defend, until the U.S. are advised thereof.

ARTICLE VI. Should a Choctaw or any party of Choctaws commit acts of violence upon the person or property of a citizen of the U.S. or join any war party against any neighbouring tribe of Indians, without the authority in the preceding article; and except to oppose an actual or threatened invasion or rebellion, such person so offending shall be delivered up to an officer of the U.S. if in the power of the Choctaw Nation, that such offender may be punished as may be provided in such cases, by the laws of the U.S.; but if such offender is not within the control of the Choctaw Nation, then said Choctaw Nation shall not be held responsible for the injury done by said offender.

ARTICLE VII. All acts of violence committed upon persons and property of the people of the Choctaw Nation either by citizens of the U.S. or neighbouring Tribes of Red People, shall be referred to some authorized Agent by him to be referred to the President of the U.S. who shall examine into such cases and see that every possible degree of justice is done to said Indian party of the Choctaw Nation.

ARTICLE VIII. Offenders against the laws of the U.S. or any individual State shall be apprehended and delivered to any duly authorized person where such offender may be found in the Choctaw country, having fled from any part of U.S. but in all such cases application must be made to the Agent or Chiefs and the expense of his apprehension and delivery provided for and paid by the U. States.

ARTICLE IX. Any citizen of the U.S. who may be ordered from the Nation by the Agent and constituted authorities of the Nation and refusing to obey or return into the Nation without the consent of the aforesaid persons, shall be subject to such pains and penalties as may be provided by the laws of the U.S. in such cases. Citizens of the U.S. travelling peaceably under the authority of the laws of the U.S. shall be under the care and protection of the nation.

ARTICLE X. No person shall expose goods or other article for sale as a trader, without a written permit from the constituted authorities of the Nation, or authority of the laws of the Congress of the U.S. under penalty of forfeiting the Articles, and the constituted authorities of the Nation shall grant no license except to such persons as reside in the Nation and are answerable to the laws of the Nation. The U.S. shall be particularly obliged to assist to prevent ardent spirits from being introduced into the Nation.

ARTICLE XI. Navigable streams shall be free to the Choctaws who shall pay no higher toll or duty than citizens of the U.S. It is agreed further that the U.S. shall establish one or more Post Offices in said Nation, and may establish such military post roads, and posts, as they may consider necessary.

ARTICLE XII. All intruders shall be removed from the Choctaw Nation and kept without it. Private property to be always respected and on no occasion taken for public purposes without just compensation being made therefor to the rightful owner. If an Indian unlawfully take or steal any property from a white man a citizen of the U.S. the offender shall be punished. And if a white man unlawfully take or steal

any thing from an Indian, the property shall be restored and the offender punished. It is further agreed that when a Choctaw shall be given up to be tried for any offence against the laws of the U.S. if unable to employ counsel to defend him, the U.S. will do it, that his trial may be fair and impartial.

ARTICLE XIII. It is consented that a qualified Agent shall be appointed for the Choctaws every four years, unless sooner removed by the President; and he shall be removed on petition of the constituted authorities of the Nation, the President being satisfied there is sufficient cause shown. The Agent shall fix his residence convenient to the great body of the people; and in the selection of an Agent immediately after the ratification of this Treaty, the wishes of the Choctaw Nation on the subject shall be entitled to great respect.

ARTICLE XIV. Each Choctaw head of a family being desirous to remain and become a citizen of the States, shall be permitted to do so, by signifying his intention to the Agent within six months from the ratification of this Treaty, and he or she shall thereupon be entitled to a reservation of one section of six hundred and forty acres of land, to be bounded by sectional lines of survey; in like manner shall be entitled to one half that quantity for each unmarried child which is living with him over ten years of age; and a quarter section to such child as may be under 10 years of age, to adjoin the location of the parent. If they reside upon said lands intending to become citizens of the States for five years after the ratification of this Treaty, in that case a grant in fee simple shall issue; said reservation shall include the present improvement of the head of the family, or a portion of it. Persons who claim under this article shall not lose the privilege of a Choctaw citizen, but if they ever remove are not to be entitled to any portion of the Choctaw annuity.

ARTICLE XV. To each of the Chiefs in the Choctaw Nation (to wit) Greenwood Laflore, Nutackachie, and Mushulatubbe there is granted a reservation of four sections of land, two of which shall include and adjoin their present improvement, and the other two located where they please but on unoccupied unimproved lands, such sections shall be bounded by sectional lines, and with the consent of the President they may sell the same. Also to the three principal Chiefs and to their successors in office there shall be paid two hundred and fifty dollars annually while they shall continue in their respective offices, except to Mushulatubbe, who as he has an annuity of one hundred and fifty dollars for life under a former treaty, shall receive only the additional sum of one hundred dollars, while he shall continue in office as Chief; and if in addition to this the Nation shall think proper to elect an additional principal Chief of the whole to superintend and govern upon republican principles he shall receive annually for his services five hundred dollars, which allowance to the Chiefs and their successors in office, shall continue for twenty years. At any time when in military service, and while in service by authority of the U.S. the district Chiefs under and by selection of the President shall be entitled to the pay of Majors; the other Chief under the same circumstances shall have the pay of a Lieutenant Colonel. The Speakers of the three districts, shall receive twenty-five dollars a year for four years each; and the three secretaries one to each of the Chiefs, fifty dollars each for four years. Each Captain of the Nation, the number not to exceed ninety-nine, thirty-three from each district, shall be furnished upon removing to the West, with each a good suit of clothes and a broad sword as an outfit, and for four years commencing with the first of their removal, shall each receive fifty dollars a year, for the trouble of keeping their people at order in settling; and whenever they shall be in military service by authority of the U.S. shall receive the pay of a captain.

ARTICLE XVI. In wagons; and with steam boats as may be found necessary—the U.S. agree to remove the Indians to their new homes at their expense and under the care of discreet and careful persons, who will be kind and brotherly to them. They agree to furnish them with ample corn and beef, or pork for themselves and families for twelve months after reaching their new homes.

It is agreed further that the U.S. will take all their cattle, at the valuation of some discreet person to be appointed by the President, and the same shall be paid for in money

after their arrival at their new homes; or other cattle such as may be desired shall be furnished them, notice being given through their Agent of their wishes upon this subject before their removal that time to supply the demand may be afforded.

ARTICLE XVII. The several annuities and sums secured under former Treaties to the Choctaw nation and people shall continue as though this Treaty had never been made.

And it is further agreed that the U.S. in addition will pay the sum of twenty thousand dollars for twenty years, commencing after their removal to the west, of which, in the first year after their removal, ten thousand dollars shall be divided and arranged to such as may not receive reservations under this Treaty.

ARTICLE XVIII. The U.S. shall cause the lands hereby ceded to be surveyed; and surveyors may enter the Choctaw Country for that purpose, conducting themselves properly and disturbing or interrupting none of the Choctaw people. But no person is to be permitted to settle within the nation, or the lands to be sold before the Choctaws shall remove. And for the payment of the several amounts secured in this Treaty, the lands hereby ceded are to remain a fund pledged to that purpose, until the debt shall be provided for and arranged. And further it is agreed, that in the construction of this Treaty wherever well founded doubt shall arise, it shall be construed most favorably towards the Choctaws.

ARTICLE XIX. The following reservations of land are hereby admitted. To Colonel David Fulsom four sections of which two shall include his present improvement, and two may be located elsewhere, on unoccupied, unimproved land.

To I. Garland, Colonel Robert Cole, Tuppanahomer, John Pytchlynn, Charles Juzan, Johokebetubbe, Eaychahobia, Ofehoma, two sections, each to include their improvements, and to be bounded by sectional lines, and the same may be disposed of and sold with the consent of the President. And that others not provided for, may be provided for, there shall be reserved as follows:

First. One section to each head of a family not exceeding Forty in number, who during the present year, may have had in actual cultivation, with a dwelling house thereon fifty acres or more. Secondly, three quarter sections after the manner aforesaid to each head of a family not exceeding four hundred and sixty, as shall have cultivated thirty acres and less than fifty, to be bounded by quarter section lines of survey, and to be contiguous and adjoining.

Third; One half section as aforesaid to those who shall have cultivated from twenty to thirty acres the number not to exceed four hundred. Fourth; a quarter section as aforesaid to such as shall have cultivated from twelve to twenty acres, the number not to exceed three hundred and fifty, and one half that quantity to such as shall have cultivated from two to twelve acres, the number also not to exceed three hundred and fifty persons. Each of said class of cases shall be subject to the limitations contained in the first class, and shall be so located as to include that part of the improvement which contains the dwelling house. If a greater number shall be found to be entitled to reservations under the several classes of this article, than is stipulated for under the limitation prescribed, then and in that case the Chiefs separately or together shall determine the persons who shall be excluded in the respective districts.

Fifth; Any Captain the number not exceeding ninety persons, who under the provisions of this article shall receive less than a section, he shall be entitled, to an additional quantity of half a section adjoining to his other reservation. The several reservations secured under this article, may be sold with the consent of the President of the U.S. but should any prefer it, or omit to take a reservation for the quantity he may be entitled to, the U.S. will on his removing pay fifty cents an acre, after reaching their new homes, provided that before the first of January next they shall adduce to the Agent, or some other authorized person to be appointed, proof of his claim and the quantity of it. Sixth; likewise children of the Choctaw Nation residing in the Nation, who have neither father nor mother a list of which, with satisfactory proof of Parentage and orphanage being filed with Agent in six months to be forwarded to the War Department, shall be entitled to a quarter section of Land, to be located under the direction of the President, and with his consent the same may be sold and the proceeds applied to some beneficial purpose for the benefit of said orphans.

ARTICLE XX. The U.S. agree and stipulate as follows, that for the benefit and advantage of the Choctaw people, and to improve their condition, there shall be educated under the direction of the President and at the expense of the U.S. forty Choctaw youths for twenty years. This number shall be kept at school, and as they finish their education others, to supply their places shall be received for the period stated. The U.S. agree also to erect a Council House for the Nation at some convenient central point, after their people shall be settled; and a House for each Chief, also a Church for each of the three Districts, to be used also as school houses, until the Nation may conclude to build others; and for these purposes ten thousand dollars shall be appropriated; also fifty thousand dollars (viz.) twenty-five hundred dollars annually shall be given for the support of three teachers of schools for twenty years. Likewise there shall be furnished to the Nation, three Blacksmiths one for each district for sixteen years, and a qualified Mill Wright for five years; Also there shall be furnished the following articles, twenty-one hundred blankets, to each warrior who emigrates a rifle, moulds, wipers and ammunition. One thousand axes, ploughs, hoes, wheels and cards each; and four hundred looms. There shall also be furnished, one ton of iron and two hundred weight of steel annually to each District for sixteen years.

ARTICLE XXI. A few Choctaw Warriors yet survive who marched and fought in the army with General Wayne, the whole number stated not to exceed twenty.

These it is agreed shall hereafter, while they live, receive twenty-five dollars a year; a list of them to be early as practicable, and within six months, made out, and presented to the Agent, to be forwarded to the War Department.

ARTICLE XXII. The Chiefs of the Choctaws have suggested that their people are in a state of rapid advancement in education and refinement, and have expressed a solicitude that they might have the privilege of a Delegate on the floor of the House of Representatives extended to them. The Commissioners do not feel that they can under a treaty stipulation accede to the request, but at their desire, present it in the Treaty, that Congress may consider of, and decide the application. . . .

[Charles J. Kappler, ed., *Indian Affairs: Laws and Treaties*, 2:310-15.]

44. Cherokee Nation v. Georgia
1831

When Georgia extended her laws over the Cherokee lands, the Indians brought suit against the state. The Supreme Court refused to accept jurisdiction because it declared that the Cherokee Nation was not a "foreign nation" in the sense intended by the Constitution. John Marshall, who delivered the opinion, described the Indian tribes as "domestic dependent nations."

. . . . Mr. Chief Justice MARSHALL delivered the opinion of the Court.

This bill is brought by the Cherokee nation, praying an injunction to restrain the state of Georgia from the execution of certain laws of that state, which, as is alleged, go directly to annihilate the Cherokees as a political society, and to seize, for the use of Georgia, the lands of the nation which have been assured to them by the United States in solemn treaties repeatedly made and still in force.

If Courts were permitted to indulge their sympathies, a case better calculated to excite them can scarcely be imagined. A people once numerous, powerful, and truly independent, found by our ancestors in the quiet and uncontrolled possession of an ample domain, gradually sinking beneath our superior policy, our arts and our arms, have yielded their lands by successive treaties, each of which contains a solemn guarantee of the residue, until they retain no more of their formerly extensive territory than is deemed necessary to their comfortable subsistence. To preserve this remnant, the present application is made.

Before we can look into the merits of the case, a preliminary inquiry presents itself. Has this Court jurisdiction of the cause?

The third article of the constitution describes the extent of the judicial power. The second section closes an enumeration of the cases to which it is extended, with "controversies" "between a state or the citizens thereof, and foreign states, citizens, or subjects." A subsequent clause of the same section gives the Supreme Court original jurisdiction in all cases in which a state shall be a party. The party defendant may then unquestionably be sued in this Court. May the plaintiff sue in it? Is the Cherokee nation a foreign state in the sense in which that term is used in the constitution?

The counsel for the plaintiffs have maintained the affirmative of this proposition with great earnestness and ability. So much of the argument as was intended to prove the character of the Cherokees as a state, as a distinct political society, separated from others, capable of managing its own affairs and governing itself, has, in the opinion of a majority of the judges, been completely successful. They have been uniformly treated as a state from the settlement of our country. The numerous treaties made with them by the United States recognise them as a people capable of maintaining the relations of peace and war, of being responsible in their political character for any violation of their engagements, or for any aggression committed on the citizens of the United States by any individual of their community. Laws have been enacted in the spirit of these treaties. The acts of our government plainly recognise the Cherokee nation as a state, and the Courts are bound by those acts.

A question of much more difficulty remains. Do the Cherokees constitute a foreign state in the sense of the constitution?

The counsel have shown conclusively that they are not a state of the union, and have insisted that individually they are aliens, not owing allegiance to the United States. An aggregate of aliens composing a state must, they say, be a foreign state. Each individual being foreign, the whole must be foreign.

This argument is imposing, but we must

58

examine it more closely before we yield to it. The condition of the Indians in relation to the United States is perhaps unlike that of any other two people in existence. In the general, nations not owing a common allegiance are foreign to each other. The term foreign nation is, with strict propriety, applicable by either to the other. But the relation of the Indians to the United States is marked by peculiar and cardinal distinctions which exist no where else.

The Indian territory is admitted to compose a part of the United States. In all our maps, geographical treatises, histories, and laws, it is so considered. In all our intercourse with foreign nations, in our commercial regulations, in any attempt at intercourse between Indians and foreign nations, they are considered as within the jurisdictional limits of the United States, subject to many of those restraints which are imposed upon our own citizens. They acknowledge themselves in their treaties to be under the protection of the United States; they admit that the United States shall have the sole and exclusive right of regulating the trade with them, and managing all their affairs as they think proper; and the Cherokees in particular were allowed by the treaty of Hopewell, which preceded the constitution, "to send a deputy of their choice, whenever they think fit, to Congress." Treaties were made with some tribes by the state of New York, under a then unsettled construction of the confederation, by which they ceded all their lands to that state, taking back a limited grant to themselves, in which they admit their dependence.

Though the Indians are acknowledged to have an unquestionable, and, heretofore, unquestioned right to the lands they occupy, until that right shall be extinguished by a voluntary cession to our government; yet it may well be doubted whether those tribes which reside within the acknowledged boundaries of the United States can, with strict accuracy, be denominated foreign nations. They may, more correctly, perhaps, be denominated domestic dependent nations. They occupy a territory to which we assert a title independent of their will, which must take effect in point of possession when their right of possession ceases. Meanwhile they are in a state of pupilage. Their relation to the United States resembles that of a ward to his guardian.

They look to our government for protection; rely upon its kindness and its power; appeal to it for relief to their wants; and address the president as their great father. They and their country are considered by foreign nations, as well as by ourselves, as being so completely under the sovereignty and dominion of the United States, that any attempt to acquire their lands, or to form a political connexion with them, would be considered by all as an invasion of our territory, and an act of hostility.

These considerations go far to support the opinion, that the framers of our constitution had not the Indian tribes in view, when they opened the Courts of the union to controversies between a state or the citizens thereof, and foreign states.

In considering this subject, the habits and usages of the Indians, in their intercourse with their white neighbours, ought not to be entirely disregarded. At the time the constitution was framed, the idea of appealing to an American Court of justice for an assertion of right or a redress of wrong, had perhaps never entered the mind of an Indian or of his tribe. Their appeal was to the tomahawk, or to the government. This was well understood by the statesmen who framed the constitution of the United States, and might furnish some reason for omitting to enumerate them among the parties who might sue in the Courts of the union. Be this as it may, the peculiar relations between the United States and the Indians occupying our territory are such, that we should feel much difficulty in considering them as designated by the term foreign state, were there no other part of the constitution which might shed light on the meaning of these words. But we think that in construing them, considerable aid is furnished by that clause in the eighth section of the third article, which empowers Congress to "regulate commerce with foreign nations, and among the several states, and with the Indian tribes."

In this clause they are as clearly contradistinguished by a name appropriate to themselves, from foreign nations, as from the several states composing the union. They are designated by a distinct appellation; and as this appellation can be applied to neither of the others, neither can the appellation distinguishing either of the others be in fair construction applied to them. The objects, to which the power of regulating commerce might be directed, are divided into three distinct classes—foreign nations, the several states, and Indian tribes. When forming this article, the convention considered them as entirely distinct. We cannot assume that the distinction was lost in framing a subsequent article, unless there be something in its language to authorize the assumption. . . .

The Court has bestowed its best attention on this question, and, after mature deliberation, the majority is of opinion that an Indian tribe or nation within the United States is not a foreign state in the sense of the constitution, and cannot maintain an action in the Courts of the United States. . . .

If it be true that the Cherokee nation have rights, this is not the tribunal in which those rights are to be asserted. If it be true that wrongs have been inflicted, and that still greater are to be apprehended, this is not the tribunal which can redress the past or prevent the future.

The motion for an injunction is denied. . . .

[5 *Peters*, 15-20.]

45. Worcester v. Georgia

1832

Samuel A. Worcester, a missionary among the Cherokees, was imprisoned because he refused to obey a Georgia law forbidding whites to reside in the Cherokee country without taking an oath of allegiance to the state and obtaining a permit. The Supreme Court decided in favor of Worcester, maintaining that the Cherokees were a nation free from the jurisdiction of the state.

. . . . Mr. Chief Justice MARSHALL delivered the opinion of the Court.

This cause, in every point of view in which it can be placed, is of the deepest interest.

The defendant is a state, a member of the Union, which has exercised the powers of government over a people who deny its jurisdiction, and are under the protection of the United States.

The plaintiff is a citizen of the state of Vermont, condemned to hard labour for four years in the penitentiary of Georgia; under colour of an act which he alleges to be repugnant to the Constitution, laws, and treaties of the United States.

The legislative power of a state, the controlling power of the Constitution and laws of the United States, the rights, if they have any, the political existence of a once numerous and powerful people, the personal liberty of a citizen, are all involved in the subject now to be considered. . . .

The Indian nations had always been considered as distinct, independent political communities, retaining their original natural rights, as the undisputed possessors of the soil, from time immemorial, with the single exception of that imposed by irresistible power, which excluded them from intercourse with any other European potentate than the first discoverer of the coast of the particular region claimed; and this was a restriction which those European potentates imposed on themselves, as well as on the Indians. The very term "nation," so generally applied to them, means "a people distinct from others." The Constitution, by declaring treaties already made, as well as those to be made, to be the supreme law of the land, has adopted and sanctioned the previous treaties with the Indian nations, and consequently admits their rank among those powers who are capable of making treaties. The words "treaty" and "nation" are words of our own language, selected in our diplomatic and legislative proceedings, by ourselves, having each a definite and well understood meaning. We have applied them to Indians, as we have applied them to the other nations of the earth. They are applied to all in the same sense.

Georgia, herself, has furnished conclusive evidence that her former opinions on this subject concurred with those entertained by her sister states, and by the government of the United States. Various acts of her legislature have been cited in the argument, including the contract of cession made in the year 1802, all tending to prove her acquiescence in the universal conviction that the Indian nations possessed a full right to the lands they occupied, until that right should be extinguished by the United States, with their consent: that their territory was separated from that of any state within whose chartered limits they might reside, by a boundary line, established by treaties: that, within their boundary, they possessed rights with which no state could interfere; and that the whole power of regulating the intercourse with them was vested in the United States. A review of these acts, on the part of Georgia, would occupy too much time, and is the less necessary, because they have been accurately detailed in the argument at the bar. Her new series of laws, manifesting her abandonment of these opinions, appears to have commenced in December, 1828.

In opposition to this original right, possessed by the undisputed occupants of every country; to this recognition of that right, which is evidenced by our history, in every change through which we have passed; is placed the charters granted by the monarch of a distant and distinct region, parcelling out a territory in possession of others whom he could not remove and did not attempt to remove, and the cession made of his claims by the treaty of peace.

The actual state of things at the time, and all history since, explain these charters; and the King of Great Britain, at the treaty of peace, could cede only what belonged to his crown. These newly asserted titles can derive no aid from the articles so often repeated in Indian treaties; extending to them, first, the protection of Great Britain, and afterwards that of the United States. These articles are associated with others, recognising their title to self-government. The very fact of repeated treaties with them recognises it; and the settled doctrine of the law of nations is, that a weaker power does not surrender its independence—its right to self-government, by associating with a stronger, and taking its protection. A weak state, in order to provide for its safety, may place itself under the protection of one more powerful, without stripping itself of the right of government, and ceasing to be a state. Ex-amples of this kind are not wanting in Europe. "Tributary and feudatory states," says Vattel, "do not thereby cease to be sovereign and independent states, so long as self-government and sovereign and independent authority are left in the administration of the state." At the present day, more than one state may be considered as holding its right of self-government under the guarantee and protection of one or more allies.

The Cherokee nation, then, is a distinct community, occupying its own territory, with boundaries accurately described, in which the laws of Georgia can have no force, and which the citizens of Georgia have no right to enter, but with the assent of the Cherokees themselves, or in conformity with treaties, and with the acts of Congress. The whole intercourse between the United States and this nation, is, by our Constitution and laws, vested in the government of the United States.

The act of the state of Georgia, under which the plaintiff in error was prosecuted, is consequently void, and the judgment a nullity. Can this Court revise and reverse it?

If the objection to the system of legislation, lately adopted by the legislature of Georgia, in relation to the Cherokee nation, was confined to its extra-territorial operation, the objection, though complete, so far as respected mere right, would give this Court no power over the subject. But it goes much further. If the review which has been taken be correct, and we think it is, the acts of Georgia are repugnant to the Constitution, laws, and treaties of the United States.

They interfere forcibly with the relations established between the United States and the Cherokee nation, the regulation of which, according to the settled principles of our Constitution, are committed exclusively to the government of the Union.

They are in direct hostility with treaties, repeated in a succession of years, which mark out the boundary that separates the Cherokee country from Georgia; guaranty to them all the land within their boundary; solemnly pledge the faith of the United States to restrain their citizens from trespassing on it; and recognise the pre-existing power of the nation to govern itself.

61

They are in equal hostility with the acts of Congress for regulating this intercourse, and giving effect to the treaties.

The forcible seizure and abduction of the plaintiff in error, who was residing in the nation with its permission, and by authority of the President of the United States, is also a violation of the acts which authorize the chief magistrate to exercise this authority.

Will these powerful considerations avail the plaintiff in error? We think they will. He was seized, and forcibly carried away, while under guardianship of treaties guarantying the country in which he resided, and taking it under the protection of the United States. He was seized while performing, under the sanction of the chief magistrate of the Union, those duties which the humane policy adopted by Congress had recommended. He was apprehended, tried, and condemned, under colour of a law which has been shown to be repugnant to the Constitution, laws, and treaties of the United States. Had a judgment, liable to the same objec-

tions, been rendered for property, none would question the jurisdiction of this Court. It cannot be less clear when the judgment affects personal liberty, and inflicts disgraceful punishment, if punishment could disgrace when inflicted on innocence. The plaintiff in error is not less interested in the operation of this unconstitutional law than if it affected his property. He is not less entitled to the protection of the Constitution, laws, and treaties of his country. . . .

It is the opinion of this Court that the judgment of the Superior Court for the county of Gwinnett, in the state of Georgia, condemning Samuel A. Worcester to hard labour in the penitentiary of the state of Georgia, for four years, was pronounced by that Court under colour of a law which is void, as being repugnant to the Constitution, treaties, and laws of the United States, and ought, therefore, to be reversed and annulled. . . .

[6 Peters, 534-36, 558-63.]

46.   Authorization of a Commissioner of Indian Affairs

July 9, 1832

In 1832 Congress at last provided for an official specifically charged with the direction and management of Indian affairs. The commissioner succeeded the head of the Indian Office that had been established by the secretary of war in 1824. The same act absolutely prohibited the introduction of ardent spirits into the Indian country.

An Act to provide for the appointment of a commissioner of Indian Affairs, and for other purposes.

Be it enacted . . . , That the President shall appoint, by and with the advice and consent of the Senate, a commissioner of Indian affairs, who shall, under the direction of the Secretary of War, and agreeably to such regulations as the President may, from time to time, prescribe, have the direction and management of all Indian affairs, and of all matters arising out of Indian relations, and shall receive a salary of three thousand dollars per annum.

SEC. 2. *And be it further enacted,* That the Secretary of War shall arrange or appoint to the said office the number of clerks necessary therefor, so as not to increase the number now employed; and such sum as is necessary to pay the salary of said commis-

sioner for the year one thousand eight hundred and thirty-two, shall be, and the same hereby is, appropriated out of any money in the treasury.

SEC. 3. *And be it further enacted,* That all accounts and vouchers for claims and disbursements connected with Indian affairs, shall be transmitted to the said commissioner for admininstrative examination, and by him passed to the proper accounting officer of the Treasury Department for settlement; and all letters and packages to and from the said commissioner, touching the business of his office, shall be free of postage.

SEC. 4. *And be it further enacted,* That no ardent spirits shall be hereafter introduced, under any pretence, into the Indian country.

SEC. 5. *And be it further enacted,* That the Secretary of War shall, under the direction of the President, cause to be discontinued

the services of such agents, sub-agents, interpreters, and mechanics, as may, from
time to time, become unnecessary, in consequence of the emigration of the Indians, or
other causes.
[*U.S. Statutes at Large*, 4:564.]

47. Indian Commissioner Herring on the Indian Race

Extract from the *Annual Report of the Commissioner of Indian Affairs.*

November 22, 1832

The first man to hold the office of commissioner of Indian affairs authorized by Congress in 1832 was Elbert Herring. In his first report to the secretary of war he urged that the Indians be brought within the social system of the whites, especially in regard to private ownership of property.

. . . Some of the Indian tribes have proceeded to hostile acts, in the course of the
year past, against each other, and conflicts
have ensued, in which blood has been spilt in
defiance of the obligation imposed by the
guarantee of the United States, for the preservation of peace and tranquillity among
them. The instigators of such unwarrantable
proceedings, as well as the chief actors in
every instance of ascertained outrage, are
justly considered responsible to the Government for the transgression, and are invariably required to be given up to its authority
to answer for the offences.

It is difficult to restrain such aggressions,
growing out of ancient feuds, prompted by
an unchecked spirit of rapine, and a thirst for
warlike distinction, and, particularly, when
probable impunity furnishes an additional
incentive. To prevent outrage is, however,
far better than to punish the offenders; nor
should the expense attendant on the remedy
to be found in the employment of a sufficient
body of mounted rangers preclude its exercise. A display of military force, and the
certainty of speedy punishment, can alone
prevent a ready resort to rapine and bloodshed on the part of those who recognize no
restraint on plunder, no bounds to the grati-
fication of revenge.

On the whole, it may be matter of serious
doubt whether, even with the fostering care
and assured protection of the United States,
the preservation and perpetuity of the Indian race are at all attainable, under the form of
government and rude civil regulations subsisting among them. These were perhaps
well enough suited to their condition, when
hunting was their only employment, and
war gave birth to their strongest excitements. The unrestrained authority of their
chiefs, and the irresponsible exercise of
power, are of the simplest elements of des-
potic rule; while the absence of the *meum* and
tuum in the general community of possessions, which is the grand conservative principle of the social state, is a perpetual operating cause of the *vis inertiae* of savage life. The
stimulus of physical exertion and intellectual
exercise, contained in this powerful principle, of which the Indian is almost entirely
void, may not unjustly be considered the
parent of all improvements, not merely in
the arts, but in the profitable direction of
labor among civilized nations. Among them
it is the source of plenty; with the Indians,
the absence of it is the cause of want, and
consequently of decrease of numbers. Nor
can proper notions of the social system be
successfully inculcated, nor its benefits be
rightly appreciated, so as to overcome the
habits and prejudices incident to savage
birth, and consequent associations of ma-
turer years, except by the institution of separate and secure rights in the relations of
property and person. It is therefore suggested, whether the formation of a code of laws
on this basis, to be submitted for their adoption, together with certain modifications the
existing political system among them,
may not be of very salutary effect, especially
as co-operating with the influences derivable
from the education of their youth, and the
introduction of the doctrines of the christian
religion; all centering in one grand object—the substitution of the social for the
savage state. . . .

[*House Executive Document* no. 2, 22d
Cong., 2d sess., serial 233, p. 163.]

June 30, 1834

The final codification of the trade and intercourse acts was passed by Congress in 1834. It offered no sharp break with the past but embodied, sometimes in modified form, the principles that had developed through the preceding decades. The House Committee on Indian Affairs, which drew up the bill, relied heavily on a report submitted in 1829 by Lewis Cass and William Clark.

An Act to regulate trade and intercourse with the Indian tribes, and to preserve peace on the frontiers.

Be it enacted . . . , That all that part of the United States west of the Mississippi, and not within the states of Missouri and Louisiana, or the territory of Arkansas, and also, that part of the United States east of the Mississippi river, and not within any state to which the Indian title has not been extinguished, for the purposes of this act, be taken and deemed to be the Indian country.

SEC. 2. *And be it further enacted,* That no persons shall be permitted to trade with any of the Indians (in the Indian country) without a license therefor from a superintendent of Indian affairs, or Indian agent, or subagent, which license shall be issued for a term not exceeding two years for the tribes east of the Mississippi, and not exceeding three years for the tribes west of that river. And the person applying for such license shall give bond in a penal sum not exceeding five thousand dollars, with one or more sureties, to be approved by the person issuing the same, conditioned that such person will faithfully observe all the laws and regulations made for the government of trade and intercourse with the Indian tribes, and in no respect violate the same. And the superintendent of the district shall have power to revoke and cancel the same, whenever the person licensed shall, in his opinion, have transgressed any of the laws or regulations provided for the government of trade and intercourse with the Indian tribes, or that it would be improper to permit him to remain in the Indian country. And no trade with the said tribes shall be carried on within their boundary, except at certain suitable and convenient places, to be designated from time to time by the superintendents, agents, and sub-agents, and to be inserted in the license. And it shall be the duty of the persons granting or revoking such licenses, forthwith to report the same to the commissioner of Indian affairs, for his approval or disapproval.

SEC. 3. *And be it further enacted,* That any superintendent or agent may refuse an application for a license to trade, if he is satisfied that the applicant is a person of bad character, or that it would be improper to permit him to reside in the Indian country, or if a license, previously granted to such applicant, has been revoked, or a forfeiture of his bond decreed. But an appeal may be had from the agent or the superintendent, to the commissioner of Indian affairs; and the President of the United States shall be authorized, whenever in his opinion the public interest may require the same, to prohibit the introduction of goods, or of any particular article, into the country belonging to any Indian tribe, and to direct all licenses to trade with such tribe to be revoked, and all applications therefor to be rejected; and no trader to any other tribe shall, so long as such prohibition may continue, trade with any Indians of or for the tribe against which such prohibition is issued.

SEC. 4. *And be it further enacted,* That any person other than an Indian who shall attempt to reside in the Indian country as a trader, or to introduce goods, or to trade therein without such license, shall forfeit all merchandise offered for sale to the Indians, or found in his possession, and shall moreover forfeit and pay the sum of five hundred dollars.

SEC. 5. *And be it further enacted,* That no license to trade with the Indians shall be granted to any persons except citizens of the United States: *Provided,* That the President shall be authorized to allow the employment of foreign boatmen and interpreters, under such regulations as he may prescribe.

SEC. 6. *And be it further enacted,* That if a

64

foreigner shall go into the Indian country without a passport from the War Department, the superintendent, agent, or sub-agent of Indian affairs, or from the officer of the United States commanding the nearest military post on the frontiers, or shall remain intentionally therein after the expiration of such passport, he shall forfeit and pay the sum of one thousand dollars; and such passport shall express the object of such person, the time he is allowed to remain, and the route he is to travel.

SEC. 7. *And be it further enacted*, That if any person other than an Indian shall, within the Indian country, purchase or receive of any Indian, in the way of barter, trade, or pledge, a gun, trap, or other article commonly used in hunting, any instrument of husbandry or cooking utensils of the kind commonly obtained by the Indians in their intercourse with the white people, or any other article of clothing, except skins or furs, he shall forfeit and pay the sum of fifty dollars.

SEC. 8. *And be it further enacted*, That if any person, other than an Indian, shall, within the limits of any tribe with whom the United States shall have existing treaties, hunt, or trap, or take and destroy, any peltries or game, except for subsistence in the Indian country, such person shall forfeit the sum of five hundred dollars, and forfeit all the traps, guns, and ammunition in his possession, used or procured to be used for that purpose, and peltries so taken.

SEC. 9. *And be it further enacted*, That if any person shall drive, or otherwise convey any stock of horses, mules, or cattle, to range and feed on any land belonging to any Indian or Indian tribe, without the consent of such tribe, such person shall forfeit the sum of one dollar for each animal of such stock.

SEC. 10. *And be it further enacted*, That the superintendent of Indian affairs, and Indian agents and sub-agents, shall have authority to remove from the Indian country all persons found therein contrary to law; and the President of the United States is authorized to direct the military force to be employed in such removal.

SEC. 11. *And be it further enacted*, That if any person shall make a settlement on any lands belonging, secured, or granted by treaty with the United States to any Indian

tribe, or shall survey or shall attempt to survey such lands, or designate any of the boundaries by marking trees, or otherwise, such offender shall forfeit and pay the sum of one thousand dollars. And it shall, moreover, be lawful for the President of the United States to take such measures, and to employ such military force, as he may judge necessary to remove from the lands as aforesaid any such person as aforesaid.

SEC. 12. *And be it further enacted*, That no purchase, grant, lease, or other conveyance of lands, or of any title or claim thereto, from any Indian nation or tribe of Indians, shall be of any validity in law or equity, unless the same be made by treaty or convention entered into pursuant to the constitution. And if any person, not employed under the authority of the United States, shall attempt to negotiate such treaty or convention, directly or indirectly, to treat with any such nation or tribe of Indians, for the title or purchase of any lands by them held or claimed, such person shall forfeit and pay one thousand dollars: *Provided, nevertheless,* That it shall be lawful for the agent or agents of any state who may be present at any treaty held with Indians under the authority of the United States, in the presence and with the approbation of the commissioner or commissioners of the United States appointed to hold the same, to propose to, and adjust with the Indians, the compensation to be made for their claim to lands within such state, which shall be extinguished by treaty.

SEC. 13. *And be it further enacted*, That if any citizen or other person residing within the United States or the territory thereof, shall send any talk, speech, message, or letter to any Indian nation, tribe, chief, or individual, with an intent to produce a contravention or infraction of any treaty or other law of the United States, or to disturb the peace and tranquillity of the United States, he shall forfeit and pay the sum of two thousand dollars.

SEC. 14. *And be it further enacted*, That if any citizen, or other person, shall carry or deliver any such talk, message, speech, or letter, to or from any Indian nation, tribe, chief, or individual, from or to any person or persons whatsoever, residing within the United States, or from or to any subject, citizen, or agent of any foreign power or state, knowing the contents thereof, he shall forfeit and pay the sum of one thousand dollars.

SEC. 15. *And be it further enacted,* That if any citizen or other person, residing or living among the Indians, or elsewhere within the territory of the United States, shall carry on a correspondence, by letter or otherwise, with any foreign nation or power, with an intent to induce such foreign nation or power to excite any Indian nation, tribe, chief, or individual, to war against the United States, or to the violation of any existing treaty; or in case any citizen or other person shall alienate, or attempt to alienate, the confidence of any Indian or Indians from the government of the United States, he shall forfeit the sum of one thousand dollars.

SEC. 16. *And be it further enacted,* That where, in the commission, by a white person, of any crime, offence, or misdemeanor, within the Indian country, the property of any friendly Indian is taken, injured or destroyed, and a conviction is had for such crime, offence, or misdemeanor, the person so convicted shall be sentenced to pay to such friendly Indian to whom the property may belong, or whose person may be injured, a sum equal to twice the just value of the property so taken, injured, or destroyed. And if such offender shall be unable to pay a sum at least equal to the just value or amount, whatever such payment shall fall short of the same shall be paid out of the treasury of the United States: *Provided,* That no such Indian shall be entitled to any payment, out of the treasury of the United States, for any such property, if he, or any of the nation to which he belongs, shall have sought private revenge, or attempted to obtain satisfaction by any force or violence: *And provided, also,* That if such offender cannot be apprehended and brought to trial, the amount of such property shall be paid out of the treasury, as aforesaid.

SEC. 17. *And be it further enacted,* That if any Indian or Indians, belonging to any tribe in amity with the United States, shall, within the Indian country, take or destroy the property of any person lawfully within such country, or shall pass from the Indian country into any state or territory inhabited by citizens of the United States, and there

take, steal, or destroy, any horse, horses, or other property, belonging to any citizen or inhabitant of the United States, such citizen or inhabitant, his representative, attorney, or agent, may make application to the proper superintendent, agent, or sub-agent, who, upon being furnished with the necessary documents and proofs, shall, under the direction of the President, make application to the nation or tribe to which said Indian or Indians shall belong, for satisfaction; and if such nation or tribe shall neglect or refuse to make satisfaction, in a reasonable time, not exceeding twelve months, it shall be the duty of such superintendent, agent, or sub-agent, to make return of his doings to the commissioner of Indian affairs, that such further steps may be taken as shall be proper, in the opinion of the President, to obtain satisfaction for the injury; and, in the mean time, in respect to the property so taken, stolen or destroyed, the United States guaranty to the party so injured, an eventual indemnification: *Provided,* That, if such injured party, his representative, attorney, or agent, shall, in any way, violate any of the provisions of this act, by seeking or attempting to obtain private satisfaction or revenge, he shall forfeit all claim upon the United States for such indemnification: *And provided, also,* That, unless such claim shall be presented within three years after the commission of the injury, the same shall be barred. And if the nation or tribe to which such Indian may belong, receive an annuity from the United States, such claim shall, at the next payment of the annuity, be deducted therefrom, and paid to the party injured; and, if no annuity is payable to such nation or tribe, then the amount of the claim shall be paid from the treasury of the United States: *Provided,* That nothing herein contained shall prevent the legal apprehension and punishment of any Indians having so offended.

SEC. 18. [Depositions of witnesses.]

SEC. 19. *And be it further enacted,* That it shall be the duty of the superintendents, agents, and sub-agents, to endeavour to procure the arrest and trial of all Indians accused of committing any crime, offence, or misdemeanor, and all other persons who may have committed crimes or offences within any state or territory, and have fled into the

Indian country, either by demanding the same of the chiefs of the proper tribe, or by such other means as the President may authorize; and the President may direct the military force of the United States to be employed in the apprehension of such Indians, and also, in preventing or terminating hostilities between any of the Indian tribes.

SEC. 20. *And be it further enacted*, That if any person shall sell, exchange, or give, barter, or dispose of, any spirituous liquor or wine to an Indian, (in the Indian country,) such person shall forfeit and pay the sum of five hundred dollars; and if any person shall introduce, or attempt to introduce, any spirituous liquor or wine into the Indian country, except such supplies as shall be necessary for the officers of the United States and troops of the service, under the direction of the War Department, such person shall forfeit and pay a sum not exceeding three hundred dollars; and if any superintendent of Indian affairs, Indian agent, or sub-agent, or commanding officer of a military post, has reason to suspect, or is informed, that any white person or Indian is about to introduce, or has introduced, any spirituous liquor or wine into the Indian country, in violation of the provisions of this section, it shall be lawful for such superintendent, Indian agent, or sub-agent, or military officer, agreeably to such regulations as may be established by the President of the United States, to cause the boats, stores, packages, and places of deposit of such person to be searched, and if any such spirituous liquor or wine is found, the goods, boats, packages, and peltries of such persons shall be seized and delivered to the proper officer, and shall be proceeded against by libel in the proper court, and forfeited, one-half to the use of the informer, and the other half to the use of the United States; and if such person is a trader, his license shall be revoked and his bond put in suit. And it shall moreover be lawful for any person, in the service of the United States, or for any Indian, to take and destroy any ardent spirits or wine found in the Indian country, excepting military supplies as mentioned in this section.

SEC. 21. *And be it further enacted*, That if any person whatever shall, within the limits of the Indian country, set up or continue any distillery for manufacturing ardent spirits, he shall forfeit and pay a penalty of one thousand dollars; and it shall be the duty of the superintendent of Indian affairs, Indian agent, or sub-agent, within the limits of whose agency the same shall be set up or continued, forthwith to destroy and break up the same; and it shall be lawful to employ the military force of the United States in executing that duty.

SEC. 22. *And be it further enacted*, That in all trials about the right of property in which an Indian may be a party on one side, and a white person on the other, the burden of proof shall rest upon the white person, whenever the Indian shall make out a presumption of title in himself from the fact of previous possession or ownership.

SEC. 23. *And be it further enacted*, That it shall be lawful for the military force of the United States to be employed in such manner and under such regulations as the President may direct, in the apprehension of every person who shall or may be found in the Indian country, in violation of any of the provisions of this act, and him immediately to convey from said Indian country, in the nearest convenient and safe route, to the civil authority of the territory or judicial district in which said person shall be found, to be proceeded against in due course of law; and also, in the examination and seizure of stores, packages, and boats, authorized by the twentieth section of this act, and in preventing the introduction of persons and property into the Indian country contrary to law; which persons and property shall be proceeded against according to law: *Provided*, That no person apprehended by military force as aforesaid, shall be detained longer than five days after the arrest and before removal. And all officers and soldiers who may have any such person or persons in custody shall treat them with all the humanity which the circumstances will possibly permit; and every officer or soldier who shall be guilty of maltreating any such person while in custody, shall suffer such punishment as a court-martial shall direct.

SEC. 24. *And be it further enacted*, That for the sole purpose of carrying this act into effect, all that part of the Indian country west of the Mississippi river, that is bounded north by the north line of lands assigned to the Osage tribe of Indians, produced east to the state of Missouri; west, by the Mexican possessions; south, by Red river; and east, by the west line of the territory of Arkansas and the state of Missouri, shall be, and hereby is, annexed to the territory of Arkansas; and that for the purpose aforesaid, the residue of the Indian country west of the said Mississippi river shall be, and hereby is, annexed to the judicial district of Missouri; and for the purpose aforesaid, the several portions of Indian country east of the said Mississippi river, shall be, and are hereby, severally annexed to the territory in which they are situate.

SEC. 25. *And be it further enacted*, That so much of the laws of the United States as provides for the punishment of crimes committed within any place within the sole and exclusive jurisdiction of the United States, shall be in force in the Indian country: *Provided*, The same shall not extend to crimes committed by one Indian against the person or property of another Indian.

SEC. 26. *And be it further enacted*, That if any person who shall be charged with a violation of any of the provisions or regulations of this act, shall be found within any of the United States, or either of the territories, such offenders may be there apprehended, and transported to the territory or judicial district having jurisdiction of the same.

SEC. 27. *And be it further enacted*, That all penalties which shall accrue under this act, shall be sued for and recovered in an action of debt, in the name of the United States, before any court having jurisdiction of the same, (in any state or territory in which the defendant shall be arrested or found,) the one half to the use of the informer, and the other half to the use of the United States, except when the prosecution shall be first instituted on behalf of the United States, in which case the whole shall be to their use.

SEC. 28. *And be it further enacted*, That when goods or other property shall be seized for any violation of this act, it shall be lawful for the person prosecuting on behalf of the United States to proceed against such goods, or other property, in the manner directed to be observed in the case of goods, wares, or merchandise brought into the United States in violation of the revenue laws.

SEC. 29. [Repeal of previous acts.]

SEC. 30. *And be it further enacted*, That until a western territory shall be established, the two agents for the Western territory, as provided in the act for the organization of the Indian department, this day approved by the President, shall execute the duties of agents for such tribes as may be directed by the President of the United States. And it shall be competent for the President to assign to one of the said agents, in addition to his proper duties, the duties of superintendent for such district of country or for such tribes as the President may think fit. And the powers of the superintendent at St. Louis, over such district or tribes as may be assigned to such acting superintendent, shall cease: *Provided*, That no additional compensation shall be allowed for such services.

[*U.S. Statutes at Large*, 4:729-35.]

49.   Organization of the Department of Indian Affairs

June 30, 1834

In 1834 Congress regularized the organization and operations of the superintendents and agents responsible for Indian affairs, thus eliminating much of the confusion and vagueness that had plagued the Indian service.

An Act to provide for the organization of the department of Indian affairs.

Be it enacted . . . , That the duties of the governors of the territories of Florida and Arkansas, as superintendents of Indian affairs, shall hereafter cease, and the duties of the governor of the territory of Michigan, as superintendent of Indian affairs, shall cease from and after the establishment of a new territory, embracing the country west of Lake Michigan, should such a territory be established. And while the governor of the said territory of Michigan continues to act as superintendent of Indian affairs, he shall receive therefor, the annual sum of one thousand dollars, in full of all allowances, emoluments, or compensation for services in said capacity.

SEC. 2. *And be it further enacted*, That there shall be a superintendency of Indian affairs for all the Indian country not within the bounds of any state or territory west of the Mississippi river, the superintendent of which shall reside at St. Louis, and shall annually receive a salary of fifteen hundred dollars.

SEC. 3. *And be it further enacted*, That superintendents of Indian affairs shall, within their several superintendencies, exercise a general supervision and control over the official conduct and accounts of all officers and persons employed by the government in the Indian department, under such regulations as shall be established by the President of the United States; and may suspend such officers and persons from their office or employments, for reasons forthwith to be communicated to the Secretary of War.

SEC. 4. *And be it further enacted*, That the following Indian agents shall be appointed by the President of the United States, by and with the advice and consent of the Senate, who shall hold their offices for [the] term of four years, and who shall give bond, with two or more securities, in the penal sum of two thousand dollars, for the faithful execution of the same, and shall receive the annual compensation of fifteen hundred dollars.

Two agents for the Western territory.

An agent for the Chickasaws.

An agent for the eastern Cherokees.

An agent for the Florida Indians.

An agent for the Indians in the state of Indiana.

An agent at Chicago.

An agent at Rock island.

An agent at Prairie du Chien.

An agent for Michilimackinac and the Sault Sainte Marie.

An agent for the Saint Peter's.

An agent for the Upper Missouri.

And the following agencies shall be discontinued at the periods herein mentioned, that is to say:

The Florida agency, from and after the thirty-first day of December next.

The Cherokee agency, from and after the thirty-first day of December next.

The Indiana agency, from and after the thirty-first day of December, eighteen hundred and thirty-six.

The Chicago agency, from and after the thirty-first day of December next.

The Rock Island agency, from and after the thirty-first day of December, eighteen hundred and thirty-six.

And all other agencies, not provided for in this act, from and after the passing thereof: *Provided*, That the limitation of the said agencies shall not be construed to prevent the President of the United States from discontinuing the same at an earlier period. And the President shall be, and he is hereby authorized, whenever he may judge it expedient, to discontinue any Indian agency, or to transfer the same, from the place or tribe designated by law, to such other place or tribe as the public service may require. And every Indian agent shall reside and keep his agency within or near the territory of the tribe for which he may be agent, and at such place as the President may designate, and shall not depart from the limits of his agency without permission. And it shall be competent for the President to require any military officer of the United States to execute the duties of Indian agent.

SEC. 5. *And be it further enacted*, That a competent number of sub-agents shall be appointed by the President, with an annual salary of seven hundred and fifty dollars each, to be employed, and to reside wherever the President may direct, and who shall give bonds, with one or more sureties, in the penal sum of one thousand dollars, for the faithful execution of the same. But no sub-agent shall be appointed who shall reside within the limits of any agency where there is an agent appointed.

SEC. 6. *And be it further enacted*, That nothing herein contained shall be construed to require the re-appointment of persons now in office, until the expiration of their present term of service; but the commissions of all Indian agents and sub-agents, now in office, shall expire on the fourth day of March next, unless sooner terminated.

SEC. 7. *And be it further enacted*, That the limits of each agency and sub-agency shall be established by the Secretary of War, either by tribes or by geographical boundaries. And it shall be the general duty of Indian agents and sub-agents to manage and superintend the intercourse with the Indians within their respective agencies, agreeably to law; to obey all legal instructions given to them by the Secretary of War, the commissioner of Indian affairs, or the superintendent of Indian affairs, and to carry into effect such regulations as may be prescribed by the President.

SEC. 8. *And be it further enacted*, That the President of the United States may, from time to time, require additional security, and in larger amounts, from all persons charged or trusted, under the laws of the United States, with the disbursement or application of money, goods, or effects of any kind, on account of the Indian department.

SEC. 9. *And be it further enacted*, That an interpreter shall be allowed to each agency, who shall receive an annual salary of three hundred dollars: *Provided*, That where there are different tribes in the same agency, speaking different languages, one interpreter may be allowed, at the discretion of the Secretary of War, for each of the said tribes. Interpreters shall be nominated, by the proper agents, to the War Department for approval, and may be suspended, by the agent, from pay and duty, and the circumstances reported to the War Department for final action; and blacksmiths shall, in like manner, be employed wherever required by treaty stipulations, and such blacksmiths shall receive an annual compensation of four hundred and eighty dollars: and if they furnish their shop and tools, an additional sum of one hundred and twenty dollars; and their assistants shall be allowed an annual compensation of two hundred and forty dollars. And wherever farmers, mechanics, or teachers are requried by treaty stipulations to be provided, they shall be employed under the direction of the War Department, and shall receive an annual compensation of not less than four hundred and eighty dollars, nor more than six hundred dollars. And in all cases of the appointments of interpreters or other persons employed for the benefit of the Indians, a preference shall be given to persons of Indian descent, if such can be found, who are properly qualified for the execution of the duties. And where any of the tribes are, in the opinion of the Secretary of War, competent to direct the employment of their blacksmiths, mechanics, teachers, farmers, or other persons engaged for them, the direction of such persons may be given to the proper authority of the tribe.

SEC. 10. [Compensation, travel allowances, etc.]

SEC. 11. *And be it further enacted*, That the payment of all annuities or other sums stipulated by treaty to be made to any Indian tribe, shall be made to the chiefs of such tribe, or to such person as said tribe shall appoint; or if any tribe shall appropriate their annuities to the purpose of education, or to any other specific use, then to such person or persons as such tribe shall designate.

SEC. 12. *And be it further enacted*, That it shall be lawful for the President of the United States, at the request of any Indian tribe to which any annuity shall be payable in money, to cause the same to be paid in goods, purchased as provided in the next section of this act.

SEC. 13. *And be it further enacted*, That all merchandise required by any Indian treaty for the Indians, payable after making of such treaty, shall be purchased under the direction of the Secretary of War, upon proposals to be received, to be based on notices previously to be given; and all merchandise required at the making of any Indian treaty shall be purchased under the order of the commissioners, by such person as they shall appoint, or by such person as shall be designated by the President for that purpose. And all other purchases on account of the Indians, and all payments to them of money or goods, shall be made by such person as the President shall designate for that purpose. And the superintendent, agent, or sub-agent, together with such military officer as the President may direct, shall be present, and certify to the delivery of all goods and money required to be paid or delivered to the Indians. And the duties required by any section of this act, of military officers, shall be performed without any other compensation than their actual travelling expenses. . . .

SEC. 14. *And be it further enacted*, That no person employed in the Indian department shall have any interest or concern in any trade with the Indians, except for, and on account of, the United States; and any person offending herein, shall forfeit the sum of five thousand dollars, and upon satisfactory information of such offence being laid before the President of the United States, it shall become his duty to remove such person from the office or situation he may hold.

SEC. 15. *And be it further enacted*, That the President shall be, and he is hereby, authorized to cause any of the friendly Indians west of the Mississippi river, and north of the boundary of the Western territory, and the region upon Lake Superior and the head of the Mississippi, to be furnished with useful domestic animals and implements of husbandry, and with goods, as he shall think proper: *Provided*, That the whole amount of such presents shall not exceed the sum of five thousand dollars.

SEC. 16. *And be it further enacted*, That the President be, and he is hereby, autho-

rized to cause such rations as he shall judge proper, and as can be spared from the army provisions without injury to the service, to be issued, under such regulations as he shall think fit to establish, to Indians who may visit the military posts or agencies of the United States on the frontiers, or in their respective nations, and a special account of these issues shall be kept and rendered.

SEC. 17. *And be it further enacted*, That the President of the United States shall be, and he is hereby, authorized to prescribe such rules and regulations as he may think fit, for carrying into effect the various provisions of this act, and of any other act relating to Indian affairs, and for the settlement of the accounts of the Indian department. . . .

[*U.S. Statutes at Large*, 4:735-38.]

50. President Jackson on Indian Removal

December 7, 1835

President Andrew Jackson held firm in favor of Indian removal. In his annual message to Congress in December 1835 he renewed his arguments for the removal policy.

. . . . The plan of removing the aboriginal people who yet remain within the settled portions of the United States to the country west of the Mississippi River approaches its consummation. It was adopted on the most mature consideration of the condition of this race, and ought to be persisted in till the object is accomplished, and prosecuted with as much vigor as a just regard to their circumstances will permit, and as fast as their consent can be obtained. All preceding experiments for the improvement of the Indians have failed. It seems now to be an established fact that they can not live in contact with a civilized community and prosper. Ages of fruitless endeavors have at length brought us to a knowledge of this principle of intercommunication with them. The past we can not recall, but the future we can provide for. Independently of the treaty stipulations into which we have entered with the various tribes for the usufructuary rights they have ceded to us, no one can doubt the moral duty of the Government of the United States to protect and if possible to preserve and perpetuate the scattered remnants of this race which are left within our borders.

In the discharge of this duty an extensive region in the West has been assigned for their permanent residence. It has been divided into districts and allotted among them. Many have already removed and others are preparing to go, and with the exception of two small bands living in Ohio and Indiana, not exceeding 1,500 persons, and of the Cherokees, all the tribes on the east side of the Mississippi, and extending from Lake Michigan to Florida, have entered into engagements which will lead to their transplantation.

The plan for their removal and reestablishment is founded upon the knowledge we have gained of their character and habits, and has been dictated by a spirit of enlarged liberality. A territory exceeding in extent that relinquished has been granted to each tribe. Of its climate, fertility, and capacity to support an Indian population the representations are highly favorable. To these districts the Indians are removed at the expense of the United States, and with certain supplies of clothing, arms, ammunition, and other indispensable articles; they are also furnished gratuitously with provisions for the period of a year after their arrival at their new homes. In that time, from the nature of the country and of the products raised by them, they can subsist themselves by agricultural labor, if they choose to resort to that mode of life; if they do not they are upon the skirts of the great prairies, where countless herds of buffalo roam, and a short time suffices to adapt their own habits to the changes which a change of the animals destined for their food may require. Ample arrangements have also been made for the support of schools; in some instances council houses and churches are to be erected, dwellings constructed for the chiefs, and mills for common use. Funds have been set apart for the maintenance of the poor; the most necessary mechanical arts have been introduced, and blacksmiths, gunsmiths, wheelwrights, millwrights, etc., are supported among them. Steel and iron, and sometimes salt, are purchased for them, and plows and other farming utensils, domestic animals, looms, spinning wheels, cards, etc., are presented to them. And besides these beneficial arrangements, annuities are in all cases paid, amounting in some instances to more than $30 for each individual of the tribe, and in all cases sufficiently great, if justly divided and prudently expended, to enable them, in addition to their own exertions, to live comfortably. And as a stimulus for exertion, it is now provided by law that "in all cases of the appointment of interpreters or other persons employed for the benefit of the Indians a preference shall be given to persons of Indian descent, if such can be found who are properly qualified for the discharge of the duties."

Such are the arrangements for the physical comfort and for the moral improvement of the Indians. The necessary measures for their political advancement and for their separation from our citizens have not been neglected. The pledge of the United States has been given by Congress that the country destined for the residence of this people shall be forever "secured and guaranteed to them." A country west of Missouri and Ar-

kansas has been assigned to them, into which the white settlements are not to be pushed. No political communities can be formed in that extensive region, except those which are established by the Indians themselves or by the United States for them and with their concurrence. A barrier has thus been raised for their protection against the encroachment of our citizens, and guarding the Indians as far as possible from those evils which have brought them to their present condition. Summary authority has been given by law to destroy all ardent spirits found in their country, without waiting the doubtful result and slow process of a legal seizure. I consider the absolute and unconditional interdiction of this article among these people as the first and great step in their melioration. Halfway measures will answer no purpose. These can not successfully contend against the cupidity of the seller and the overpowering appetite of the buyer. And the destructive effects of the traffic are marked in every page of the history of our Indian intercourse.

Some general legislation seems necessary for the regulation of the relations which will exist in this new state of things between the Government and people of the United States and these transplanted Indian tribes, and for the establishment among the latter, and with their own consent, of some principles of intercommunication which their juxtaposition will call for; that moral may be substituted for physical force, the authority of a few and simple laws for the tomahawk, and that an end may be put to those bloody wars whose prosecution seems to have made part of their social system.

After the further details of this arrangement are completed, with a very general supervison over them, they ought to be left to the progress of events. These, I indulge the hope, will secure their prosperity and improvement, and a large portion of the moral debt we owe them will then be paid. . . .

[James D. Richardson, comp., *Messages and Papers of the Presidents*, 3:171-73.]

51. Indian Commissioner Crawford on Indian Policy
Extract from the *Annual Report of the Commissioner of Indian Affairs*
November 25, 1838

Commissioner of Indian Affairs T. Hartley Crawford had strong views on Indian policy, which he expressed in his annual reports. In 1838 he wrote, among other things, about manual labor schools, allotment of Indian lands to individual Indians, and confederation of the Indians in the West.

. . . . The principal lever by which the Indians are to be lifted out of the mire of folly and vice in which they are sunk is education. The learning of the already civilized and cultivated man is not what they want now. It could not be advantageously ingrafted on so rude a stock. In the present state of their social existence, all they could be taught, or would learn, is to read and write, with a very limited knowledge of figures. There are exceptions, but in the general the remark is true, and perhaps more is not desirable or would be useful. As they advance, a more liberal culture of their minds may be effected, if happily they should yield to the influences that, if not roughly thrust back, will certainly follow in the wake of properly directed efforts to improve their understandings. To attempt too much at once is to insure failure. You must lay the foundations broadly and deeply, but gradually, if you would succeed. To teach a savage man to read, while he continues a savage in all else, is to throw seed on a rock. In this particular there has been a general error. If you would win an Indian from the waywardness and idleness and vice of his life, you must improve his morals, as well as his mind, and that not merely by precept, but by teaching him how to farm, how to work in the mechanic arts, and how to labor profitably; so that, by enabling him to find his comfort in changed pursuits, he will fall into those habits which are in keeping with the useful application of such education as may be given him. Thus too, only, it is conceived, are men to be christianized; the beginning is some education, social and moral lives, the end may be the brightest hope: but this allusion ought not, perhaps, to have been made; upon it I certainly will not enlarge; it is in better hands. Manual-labor schools are what the Indian condition calls for. The Missionary Society of the Methodist Episcopal Church has laid before the department a plan, based upon the idea suggested, for establishing a large central school for the education of the Western Indians. Into their scheme enter a farm, and shops for teaching the different mechanic arts. Experience, they say, has shown them, after much opportunity for judging correctly, that separate schools for the respective tribes, though productive of much good, are not so useful as one common school for the benefit of all would be. They assert truly that a knowledge of the English language is necessary, and they think that it can be best acquired in an establishment of the latter description. I would not hazard a different opinion; and yet it may not be improper to state that the funds which have been set apart for education purposes belong to the several tribes, without whose consent the Government could not devote them to a general school; and this the society admits. There is no disposition to discourage the efforts of those who choose to labor in this work of benevolence. On the contrary, there is, as there should be, an eagerness to meet any advance which promises greater facilities for improving the mind and morals of the Indian. Upon success in this department hangs every hope. All that can be done to encourage and cheer on those who have devised this scheme of goodness and charity, I think, should be done. But, whatever reform may be deemed advisable in the direction and economy of the separate schools, it appears to me that if the proposed central school shall be established, they should be kept up too. They may, perhaps, be more numerous than is necessary or advantageous; they may be too expensively conducted, or more scholars ought to be taught for the money expended, or they may be badly located; but each, or all, of these objections may be obviated, and the schools improved. For such minor institutions, would not the central school be able to furnish teachers? Could not the Government, in consideration of any pecuniary aid it might render, exact, as a condition, that a certain number of young Indians of capacity should yearly leave the central school qualified to be instructers, who shall make compensation for their own education by teaching as long as might be thought a suitable return? After such a plan had been in operation three or four years there would be an annual supply. . . .

There is one measure that, in my judgment, is of great importance; it has heretofore attracted the attention of Congress, and I hope will meet with favor. As any plan for the government of the western tribes of Indians contemplates an interior police of their own, in each community, and that their own laws shall prevail, as between themselves, for which some of their treaties provide, this, as it seems to me, indispensable step to their advancement in civilization cannot be taken without their own consent. Unless some system is marked out by which there shall be a separate allotment of land to each individual whom the scheme shall entitle to it, you will look in vain for any general casting off of savagism. Common property and civilization cannot co-exist. The few instances to be found in the United States and other countries of small abstracted communities, who draw their subsistence and whatever comforts they have from a common store, do not militate against this position. Under a show of equality, the mass work for two or three rulers or directors, who enjoy what they will, and distribute what they please. The members never rise beyond a certain point, (to which they had reached, generally, before they joined the society,) and never will while they remain where they are. But if they should, these associations are so small and confined as to place their possessions in the class of individual estates. At the foundation of the whole social system lies individuality of property. It is, perhaps, nine times in ten the stimulus that manhood first feels. It has produced the energy, industry, and enterprise that distinguish the civilized world, and contributes more largely to the good morals of men than those are willing to acknowledge who have not looked somewhat closely at their fellow-beings. With it come all the delights that the word home expresses; the comforts that fol-

low fixed settlements are in its train, and to them belongs not only an anxiety to do right that those gratifications may not be forfeited, but industry that they may be increased. Social intercourse and a just appreciation of its pleasures result, when you have civilized, and, for the most part, moral men. This process, it strikes me, the Indians must go through, before their habits can be materially changed, and they may, after what many of them have seen and know, do it very rapidly. If, on the other hand, the large tracts of land set apart for them shall continue to be joint property, the ordinary motive to industry (and the most powerful one) will be wanting. A bare subsistence is as much as they can promise themselves. A few acres of badly cultivated corn about their cabins will be seen, instead of extensive fields, rich pastures, and valuable stock. The latter belong to him who is conscious that what he ploughs is his own, and will descend to those he loves; never to the man who does not know by what tenure he holds his miserable dwelling. Laziness and unthrift will be so general as not to be disgraceful; and if the produce of their labors should be thrown into common stock, the indolent and dishonest will subsist at the expense of the meritorious. Besides, there is a strong motive in reference to ourselves for encouraging individual ownership. The history of the world proves that distinct and separate possessions make those who hold them averse to change. The risk of losing the advantages they have, men do not readily encounter. By adopting and acting on the view suggested, a large body will be created whose interest would dispose them to keep things steady. They would be the ballast of the ship.

Plans have at various times been proposed for a confederation of the Indian tribes west of the Mississippi, embracing those who shall hereafter remove. I incline much to doubt the expedience of such a measure. It could only be executed with the consent of the tribes that might become members of it. The Choctaws have twice signified their disinclination to it. The treaty with the Cherokees of December, 1835, discourages it. The idea of such a bond between dependant communities is new. The league could only be for regulation among themselves, and not for mutual protection, which is the usual object of such combinations. They have no common property to secure, or common interest to advance. Any plan I have seen is based upon the power of the President to reject their articles of association, which exhibits strikingly their true position. They may be likened to colonies, among whom a confederation does not exist. They are governed, and their legislation, by each community for itself, is supervised and controlled, by the parent country. When they contemplate a different attitude, they confederate. A general council of the Indians might pass resolutions of a pacific character, or to arrest actual hostilities, and to regulate their intercourse with each other, but this could be done better by Congress, leaving to each tribe the management of its own internal concerns, not interfering with treaties or laws. There are inherent difficulties in the dissimilar conditions of the tribes. Some of them are semi civilized, others as wild as the game they hunt. Some are rich, others poor. Some number but a few hundred souls, others more thousands. We cannot frame for them, much less could they do it, articles of confederation which would bring into council a just representation of the different tribes. If you allot so many representatives to a tribe, looking to its population, the smaller would be swallowed up in the larger. If you limit to a certain number, or within or between two numbers, you are unjust to the larger tribes, which a combination of the smaller, with fewer motives to rectitude, might control. A small proportion of all might come into the confederation, and these separated from each other by bands who would not join in the arrangement, and would not on any principle be bound by the resolves of the general council. We owe duties to ourselves. Cogent reasons for not giving to these neighboring communities more concentration than they have must be seen. While they are treated with all kindness, tenderness even, and liberality, prudential considerations would seem to require that they should be kept distinct from each other. Let them manage their internal police after their own views. One or more superintendents, and as many agencies as may be deemed proper, with such regulation of their intercourse with each other, and such guards for their protection, as Congress shall think fit to prescribe, would, it appears to me, meet the emergence. Through the officers thus stationed among them, they could make their complaints known, and ask redress for grievances, which would be afforded when it was proper. It is not understood that the deliberations of the council could result in any act that would be valid, until approved by the chief magistrate, which does not lessen the force of what has been said.

It would perhaps be judicious not to pay a compliment at some hazard, especially where it would not be appreciated, but to assert directly for general purposes the authority which actually exists, and which must, upon any suggestion that may be adopted, be really felt and acknowledged. At some future period, if circumstances should be so changed as to call for a territorial government, or for any other alteration in the system, the United States can, in the guardian position they occupy, make such modification as sound judgment and an anxious desire to benefit the Indians shall dictate.

[*Senate Document* no. 1, 25th Cong., 3d sess., serial 338, pp. 450-51, 454-56.]

52. Regulations regarding Liquor and Annuities

March 3, 1847

Two significant changes in Indian policy were made by an act of Congress in 1847. One strengthened the procedures for eliminating the liquor trade among the Indians. The other provided for distribution of annuities to heads of families rather than to tribal chiefs, in the hope of lessening or eliminating the influence of traders on the tribal leaders.

An Act to amend an Act entitled "An Act to provide for the better Organization of the Department of Indian Affairs," and an Act entitled "An Act to regulate Trade and Intercourse with the

75

Indian Tribes, and to preserve Peace on the Frontiers," approved June thirtieth, eighteen hundred and thirty-four, and for other Purposes.

Be it enacted . . . , That the limits of each superintendency, agency, and sub-agency shall be established by the Secretary of War, either by tribes or geographical boundaries; and the superintendents, agents, and sub-agents shall be furnished with offices for the transaction of the public business, and the agents and sub-agents with houses for their residences, at the expense of the United States; and, with the assent of the Indians, be permitted to cultivate such portions of land as the President or Secretary of War may deem proper.

SEC. 2. And be it further enacted, That the twentieth section of the "Act to regulate Trade and Intercourse with the Indian Tribes, and to preserve Peace on the Frontiers," approved June thirtieth, eighteen hundred and thirty-four, be, and the same is hereby, so amended, that, in addition to the fines thereby imposed, any person who shall sell, exchange or barter, give, or dispose of, any *spirituous* liquor or wine to an Indian, in the Indian country, or who shall introduce, or attempt to introduce, any *spirituous* liquor or wine into the Indian country, except such supplies as may be necessary for the officers of the United States and the troops of the service, under the direction of the War Department, such person, on conviction thereof before the proper District Court of the United States, shall in the former case be subject to imprisonment for a period not exceeding two years, and in the latter case not exceeding one year, as shall be prescribed by the court, according to the extent and criminality of the offence. And in all prosecutions arising under this section, and under the twentieth section of the act to regulate trade and intercourse with the Indian tribes, and to preserve peace on the frontiers, approved June thirtieth, eighteen hundred and thirty-four, to which this is an amendment, Indians shall be competent witnesses.

SEC. 3. And be it further enacted, That the eleventh section of the "Act to provide for the better Organization of the Department of Indian Affairs," approved June thirtieth, eighteen hundred and thirty-four, be, and

the same is hereby, so amended as to provide that all annuities or other moneys, and all goods, stipulated by treaty to be paid or furnished to any Indian tribe, shall, at the discretion of the President or Secretary of War, instead of being paid over to the chiefs, or to such persons as they shall designate, be divided and paid over to the heads of families and other individuals entitled to participate therein, or, with the consent of the tribe, be applied to such purposes as will best promote the happiness and prosperity of the members thereof, under such regulations as shall be prescribed by the Secretary of War, not inconsistent with existing treaty stipulations. And no such annuities, or moneys, or goods, shall be paid or distributed to the Indians while they are under the influence of any description of intoxicating liquor, nor while there are good and sufficient reasons for the officers or agents, whose duty it may be to make such payments or distribution, for believing that there is any species of intoxicating liquor within convenient reach of the Indians, nor until the chiefs and head men of the tribe shall have pledged themselves to use all their influence and to make all proper exertions to prevent the introduction and sale of such liquor in their country; and all executory contracts made and entered into by any Indian for the payment of money or goods shall be deemed and held to be null and void, and of no binding effect whatsoever. . . .

SEC. 5. And be it further enacted, That in aid of the means now possessed by the Department of Indian Affairs through its existing organization, there be, and hereby is, appropriated the sum of five thousand dollars, to enable the said department, under the direction of the Secretary of War, to collect and digest such statistics and materials as may illustrate the history, the present condition, and future prospects of the Indian tribes of the United States. . . .

SEC. 7. And be it further enacted, That for compensation of a special agent and two interpreters for one year, to enable the War Department to keep up such a communication with the said Indians as may be necessary towards the preservation of a good understanding with them, and securing peace on the frontier, the sum of three thousand six hundred and fifty dollars be, and the same is hereby, appropriated out of any money in the treasury not otherwise appropriated, and that the sum of ten thousand dollars be, and the same is hereby, appropriated to carry into effect the treaty with the Camanche and other tribes of Indians. . . .

[*U.S. Statutes at Large,* 9:203-4.]

53. Indian Commissioner Medill on Indian Colonies
Extract from the *Annual Report of the Commissioner of Indian Affairs*
November 30, 1848

As white population surged westward and emigrants from the older states cut through Indian lands on their way to the Pacific coast, plans to consolidate the Indians materialized. An early and forceful proposal to form two concentrated colonies of Indians in the West was put forth by Commissioner William Medill in 1848.

. . . . While, to all, the fate of the red man has, thus far, been alike unsatisfactory and painful, it has, with many, been a source of much misrepresentation and unjust national reproach. Apathy, barbarism, and heathenism must give way to energy, civilization, and christianity; and so the Indian of this continent has been displaced by the European; but this has been attended with much less of oppression and injustice than has generally been represented and believed. If, in the rapid spread of our population and sway, with all their advantages and blessings to ourselves and to others, injury has been inflicted upon the barbarous and heathen people we have displaced, are we as a nation alone to be held up to reproach for such a result? Where, in the contest of civilization with barbarism, since the commencement of time, has it been less the case than with us; and where have there been more general and persevering efforts, according to our means and opportunities, than those made by us, to extend to the conquered all the superior resources and advantages enjoyed by the conquerors? Of the magnitude and extent of those efforts but little comparatively is generally known.

Stolid and unyielding in his nature, and inveterately wedded to the savage habits, customs, and prejudices in which he has been reared and trained, it is seldom the case that the full blood Indian of our hemisphere can, in immediate juxtaposition with a white population, be brought farther within the pale of civilization than to adopt its vices; under the corrupting influences of which, too indolent to labor, and too weak to resist, he soon sinks into misery and despair. The inequality of his position in all that secures dignity and respect is too glaring, and the contest he has to make with the superior race with which he is brought into contact, in all the avenues to success and prosperity in life, is too unequal to hope for a better result. The collision is to him a positive evil. He is unprepared and in all respects unfitted for it; and he necessarily soon sinks under it and perishes. It must be recollected, too, that our white population has rapidly increased and extended, and, with a widening contact, constantly pressed upon the Indian occupants of territory necessary for the accomodation of our own people; thus engendering prejudices and creating difficulties which have occasionally led to strife and bloodshed—inevitable between different races under such circumstances—in which the weaker party must suffer. Hence, it is to natural and unavoidable causes, easily understood and appreciated, rather than to wilful neglect, or to deliberate oppression and wrong, that we must in a great measure attribute the rapid decline and disappearance of our Indian population. Cannot this sad and depressing tendency of things be checked, and the past be at least measurably repaired by better results in the future? It is believed they can; and, indeed, it has to some extent been done already, by the wise and beneficent system of policy put in operation some years since, and which, if steadily carried out, will soon give to our whole Indian system a very different and much more favorable aspect.

The policy already begun and relied on to accomplish objects so momentous and so desirable to every Christian and philanthropist is, as rapidly as it can safely and judiciously be done, to colonize our Indian tribes beyond the reach, for some years, of our white population; confining each within a small district of country, so that, as the game decreases and becomes scarce, the adults will gradually be compelled to resort to agriculture and other kinds of labor to obtain a subsistence, in which aid may be afforded and facilities furnished them out of the means obtained by the sale of their former possessions. To establish, at the same time, a judicious and well devised system of manual labor schools for the education of the youth of both sexes in letters—the males in practical agriculture and the various necessary and useful mechanic arts, and the females in the different branches of housewifery, including spinning and weaving; and these schools, like those already in successful operation, to be in charge of the excellent and active missionary societies of the different Christian denominations of the country, and to be conducted and the children taught by efficient, exemplary, and devoted men and women, selected with the approbation of the Department by those societies; so that a physical, intellectual, moral, and religious education will all be imparted together.

The strongest propensities of an Indian's nature are his desire for war and his love of the chase. These lead him to display tact, judgment, and energy, and to endure great hardships, privation, and suffering; but in all other respects he is indolent and inert, physically and mentally, unless on occasions for display in council, when he not unfrequently exhibits great astuteness and a rude eloquence, evincing no ordinary degree of intellect. But anything like labor is distasteful and utterly repugnant to his feelings and natural prejudices. He considers it a degradation. His subsistence and dress are obtained principally by means of the chase; and if this resource is insufficient, and it be necessary to cultivate the earth or to manufacture materials for dress, it has to be done by the women, who are their "hewers of wood and drawers of water." Nothing can induce him to resort to labor, unless compelled to do so by a stern necessity; and it is only then that there is any ground to work upon for civilizing and Christianizing him. But little, if any, good impression can be made upon him in these respects, so long as he is able freely to roam at large and gratify

his two predominant inclinations. Nor can these be subdued in any other way than by the mode of colonization, to which reference has been made. When compelled to face the stern necessities of life and to resort to labor for a maintenance, he in a very short time becomes a changed being; and is then willing, and frequently eager, to receive information and instruction in all that may aid him in improving his condition. It is at this stage that he begins to perceive and appreciate the advantages possessed by the white man, and to desire also to enjoy them; and, if too far advanced in life for mental instruction himself, he asks that it may be provided for his children. Such is the experience in the cases of several of the tribes not long since colonized, who a few years ago were mere nomads and hunters; and, when settled in their new countries, were opposed to labor and to anything like schools or missionaries; but who are now desirous of both the latter for the benefit of their children and themselves, and are becoming prosperous and happy from having learned how to provide a certain and comfortable support for themselves and their families by the cultivation of the soil and other modes of labor. The most marked change, however, when this transition takes place, is in the condition of the females. She who had been the drudge and the slave then begins to assume her true position as an equal; and her labor is transferred from the field to her household—to the care of her family and children. This great change in disposition and condition has taken place, to a greater or less extent, in all the tribes that have been removed and permanently settled west of the Mississippi. It is true, that portions of some of them enjoyed a considerable degree of civilization before they were transplanted; but prior to that event they were retrograding in all respects; while now, they and others who have been colonized and confined within reasonable and fixed limits, are rapidly advancing in intelligence and morality, and in all the means and elements of national and individual prosperity; so that before many years, if we sacredly observe all our obligations towards them, they will have reached a point at which they will be able to compete with a white population, and to sustain themselves under any probable circumstances of contact or connexion with it. If this great end is to be accomplished, however, material changes will soon have to be made in the position of some of the smaller tribes on the frontier, so as to leave an ample outlet for our white population to spread and to pass towards and beyond the Rocky mountains; else, not only will they be run over and extinguished, but all may be materially injured.

It may be said that we have commenced the establishment of two colonies for the Indian tribes that we have been compelled to remove; one north, on the head waters of the Mississippi, and the other south, on the western borders of Missouri and Arkansas, the southern limit of which is the Red river. The northern colony is intended to embrace the Chippewas of Lake Superior and the upper Mississippi, the Winnebagoes, the Menomonies, such of the Sioux, if any, as may choose to remain in that region, and all other northern Indians east of the Mississippi (except those in the State of New York,) who have yet to be removed west of that river. The southern boundary of this colony will be the Watab river, which is the southern limit of the country of the Winnebagoes, who have removed there from Iowa, within the past year. The Menomonies, now residing near Green Bay in Wisconsin, are to be located above and adjoining the Winnebagoes; a treaty having very recently been concluded with them to that effect. Above these, to our northern boundary line, and westward to the Red river of the north, the country is owned by the Chippewas, many of whom now live there, though they still own a large tract east of the Mississippi, computed at 10,743,000 acres, and lying above a line running nearly due east, from opposite the junction of the Crow Wing and Mississippi rivers, to a point about 92°15 west longitude; thence due north to the St. Louis river, and down that river to Lake Superior. Many live north of the above line, but, as stated in my last annual report, a considerable number still remain south of it, on lands heretofore ceded by them, which, for reasons given at that time, they should soon be required to leave for their own country. But with reference to the civilization and welfare of these people, it would be a wise, and even necessary measure, to purchase all the lands they own east of the Mississippi, and concentrate them altogether upon those that would still remain to them west of that river. Until this shall have been done, they will continue in so dispersed a condition that it will be difficult, if not impossible, to do anything effective towards their permanent improvement. You are aware that an effort to effect such a purchase was made last year and failed; but it is believed, that if renewed, in connexion with the removal of those on the ceded lands, and the transfer of the agency to the Mississippi from Lapointe, Lake Superior, where it now is, it would be successful. These people and the Menomonies being removed west of the Mississippi, the remaining Indians east of that river to be sent to this colony, would probably not exceed three thousand six hundred. Of the Sioux it is not probable many will remain for any considerable period in the Mississippi region. Wild and untameable, and scattered over an immense extent of country, no effort could concentrate them; and, living wholly by the chase, they will probably follow the buffalo and other game as it gradually disappears, towards the Rocky mountains; either in the direction of the head waters of the Platte or those of the Missouri river, or both.

If the Kanzas river were made the northern boundary of the southern colony there would be ample space of unoccupied territory below it for all the Indians above it that should be included in this colony. But the Delawares, Pottawatomies, and possibly the Kickapoos, who, or nearly all of whom, are just above that river, it would not probably be necessary to disturb. Above these, and on or adjacent to the frontier, are the band of Sacs and Foxes, known as the "Sacs and Foxes of the Missouri," the Iowas, the Ottoes and Missourias, the Omahas, the Poncas, and the Pawnees. The last mentioned tribe are back some distance from the frontier, on the Platte river, directly on the route to Oregon, and have been the most troublesome Indians to the emigrants to that territory. By the treaty of 1833 they ceded all their lands south of that river, and obligated themselves to remove north of it; but as they are constantly liable to attacks from the Sioux in that direction, those south have never removed. As, however, there will soon be a military force in that region, which can afford them protection from the Sioux, they may properly be compelled at an early day to remove and to keep within their own country; and thus be out of the way of our emigrants. They are so obnoxious to the tribes south that they could not, for the present at least, be colonized with them. They must eventually be driven west or exterminated by the Sioux, who have a strong antipathy to them, unless a better understanding can be effected between them and the southern tribes, which will admit of their being moved down among or in the rear of them. No reasonable amount of military force could prevent their being killed off in detail by the Sioux, if they remain long in their present country. The other tribes mentioned can gradually be removed down to the southern colony, as the convenience of our emigrants and the pressure of our white population may require; which may be the case at no distant day, as the greater portion of the lands they occupy are eligibly located on and near the Missouri river, and from that circumstance, and their superior quality, said to be very desirable. Indeed, it would be a measure of great humanity to purchase out and remove the Omahas and the Ottoes and Missourias at an early period, particularly the former, who are a very interesting people, being mild and tractable in disposition, and much attached to the whites. Were they in a better position, they might, with proper measures, be easily civilized, and be made the instruments of imparting civilization to others. . . .

[*House Executive Document* no. 1, 30th Cong., 2d sess., serial 537, pp. 385-89.]

54. Transfer of Indian Affairs to the Department of the Interior
March 3, 1849

At a time of relative tranquillity on the frontier, responsibility for Indian affairs was transferred from the War Department to the newly created Department of the Interior. Insistent attempts in the post-Civil War decades to return the Indian bureau to the War Department were unsuccessful.

An Act to establish the Home Department, and to provide for the Treasury Department an Assistant Secretary of the Treasury, and a Commissioner of the Customs.

Be it enacted . . . , That, from and after the passage of this act, there shall be created a new executive department of the government of the United States, to be called the Department of the Interior; the head of which department shall be called the Secretary of the Interior, who shall be appointed by the President of the United States, by and with the advice and consent of the Senate, and who shall hold his office by the same tenure, and receive the same salary, as the Secretaries of the other executive departments, and who shall perform all the duties assigned to him by this act. . . .

SEC. 5. *And be it further enacted,* That the Secretary of the Interior shall exercise the supervisory and appellate powers now exercised by the Secretary of the War Department, in relation to all the acts of the Commissioner of Indian Affairs; and shall sign all requisitions for the advance or payment of money out of the treasury, on estimates or accounts, subject to the same adjustment or control now exercised on similiar estimates or accounts by the Second Auditor and Second Comptroller of the Treasury. . . .

[*U.S. Statutes at Large,* 9:395.]

55. Organization of Indian Affairs in Oregon
June 5, 1850

Although the United States acquired exclusive claim to Oregon in 1846 and Oregon Territory was organized in 1848, it was not until 1850 that provision was made for dealing with the Indian tribes of that region. Congress then authorized the negotiation of treaties, provided for a superintendent of Indian affairs and for one or more Indian agents for Oregon, and extended the provisions of the trade and intercourse act to the area.

An Act authorizing the Negotiation of Treaties with the Indian Tribes in the Territory of Oregon, for the Extinguishment of their Claims to Lands lying west of the Cascade Mountains, and for other Purposes.

Be it enacted . . . , That the President be authorized to appoint one or more commissioners to negotiate treaties with the several Indian tribes in the Territory of Oregon, for the extinguishment of their claims to lands lying west of the Cascade Mountains; and, if found expedient and practicable, for their removal east of said mountains; also, for obtaining their assent and submission to the existing laws regulating trade and intercourse with the Indian tribes in the other Territories of the United States, so far as they may be applicable to the tribes in the said Territory of Oregon; the compensation to such commissioner or commissioners not to exceed the rate heretofore allowed for similar services.

SEC. 2. And be it further enacted, That the President be authorized, by and with the advice and consent of the Senate, to appoint a Superintendent of Indian Affairs for the Territory of Oregon, who shall receive an annual salary of twenty-five hundred dollars, and whose duty it shall be to exercise a general superintendence over all the Indian tribes in Oregon, and to exercise and perform all the powers and duties assigned by law to other superintendents of Indian affairs.

SEC. 3. And be it further enacted, That so much of the act to establish the territorial government of Oregon, approved the eleventh [14th] August, 1848, as requires the governor of said Territory to perform the duties of Superintendent of Indian Affairs, and authorizes him to receive a salary therefor, in addition to the salary allowed for his services as governor, be repealed; and that the governor of said Territory shall hereafter receive an annual salary of three thousand dollars.

SEC. 4. And be it further enacted, That the President be authorized, by and with the advice and consent of the Senate, to appoint one or more Indian agents, not exceeding three, as he shall deem expedient, each of whom shall receive an annual salary of fifteen hundred dollars, give bond as now required by law, and perform all the duties of agent to such tribe or tribes of Indians in the Territory of Oregon as shall be assigned to him by the superintendent to be appointed by the provisions of this act, under the direction of the President.

SEC. 5. And be it further enacted, That the law regulating trade and intercourse with the Indian tribes east of the Rocky Mountains, or such provisions of the same as may be applicable, be extended over the Indian tribes in the Territory of Oregon.

SEC. 6. And be it further enacted, That the sum of twenty-five thousand dollars be appropriated, out of any moneys in the treasury not otherwise appropriated, to carry into effect the provisions of this act.

[U.S. Statutes at Large, 9:437.]

56. Indian Commissioner Lea on Reservation Policy
Extract from the Annual Report of the Commissioner of Indian Affairs
November 27, 1850

A reservation policy gradually evolved as the federal government sought to concentrate Indian tribes into restricted areas, where they could be prevented from depredation and where they could be more easily induced to accept an agricultural economy. Commissioner Luke Lea in 1850 recommended such a course for the Sioux and Chippewas and neighboring tribes.

. . . . Among the less remote tribes with which we have fixed and defined relations, and which, to a greater or less extent, have felt the controlling and meliorating effects of the policy and measures of the government for preserving peace among them and improving their condition, an unusual degree of order and quietude has prevailed. It is gratifying to know that amongst this class, comprising a large portion of the red race within our widely extended borders, there probably has never, during the same period of time, been so few occurrences of a painful nature. All have been peaceful towards our

81

citizens; while, with the exception of the Sioux and Chippewas, they have preserved a state of peace and harmony among themselves. These two tribes are hereditary enemies, and scarcely a year passes without scenes of bloody strife between them. From their remoteness and scattered condition, it is difficult to exercise any effective restraint over them while their proximity to each other affords them frequent opportunities for indulging their vengeful and vindictive feelings. Each tribe seems to be constantly on the watch for occasions to attack weaker parties of the other, when an indiscriminate massacre of men, women, and children, is the lamentable result. During the last spring mutual aggressions, of an aggravated character, threatened to involve these tribes in a general war; but the acting superintendent, Governor Ramsey, aided and assisted by the commanding officer at Fort Snelling, promptly interposed, and by timely and judicious efforts prevented such a catastrophe.

Such occurrences are not only revolting to humanity, but they foster that insatiable passion for war, which, in combination with love of the chase, is the prominent characteristic feature of our wilder tribes, and presents a formidable obstacle in the way of their civilization and improvement. We know not yet to what extent these important objects may be accomplished; but the present and improving condition of some of our semi-civilized tribes affords ample encouragement for further and more extended effort. Experience, however, has conclusively shown that there is but one course of policy by which the great work of regenerating the Indian race may be effected.

In the application of this policy to our wilder tribes, it is indispensably necessary that they be placed in positions where they can be controlled, and finally compelled by stern necessity to resort to agricultural labor or starve. Considering, as the untutored Indian does, that labor is a degradation, and there is nothing worthy of his ambition but prowess in war, success in the chase, and eloquence in council, it is only under such circumstances that his haughty pride can be subdued, and his wild energies trained to the more ennobling pursuits of civilized life. There should be assigned to each tribe, for a permanent home, a country adapted to agriculture, of limited extent and well-defined boundaries; within which all, with occasional exceptions, should be compelled constantly to remain until such time as their general improvement and good conduct may supersede the necessity of such restrictions. In the mean time the government should cause them to be supplied with stock, agricultural implements, and useful materials for clothing; encourage and assist them in the erection of comfortable dwellings, and secure to them the means and facilities of education, intellectual, moral, and religious. The application of their own funds to such purposes would be far better for them than the present system of paying their annuities in money, which does substantial good to but few, while to the great majority it only furnishes the means and incentive to vicious and depraving indulgence, terminating in destitution and misery, and too frequently in premature death.

The time is at hand for the practical application of the foregoing views to the Sioux and Chippewas, as well as to some of the more northern tribes on the borders of Missouri and Iowa. . . .

Since the treaties of 1837 and 1842, with the Chippewas, a considerable portion of those Indians have continued, by sufferance, to reside on the ceded lands east of the Mississippi River, in Wisconsin and Minnesota, where they have for some years been brought into injurious contact with our rapidly advancing and increasing population in that quarter. Having ample facilities for procuring ardent spirits, they have become much injured and corrupted by unrestrained indulgence in the use of that accursed element of evil. To remedy this unfortunate state of things, it was determined, at an early period of the present year, to have these Indians removed northward to the country belonging to their tribe. Measures for this purpose were accordingly adopted; but, in consequence of the very late period at which the appropriation requisite to meet the necessary expenses was made, only a small number have, as yet, been removed. Their entire removal, however, will not sufficiently relieve our citizens from annoyance by them, as they will for some time have the disposition, and be near enough, to return with facility to their old haunts and hunting grounds. Nor will the situation of the Chippewas, generally, then be such as their well-being requires. They own a vast extent of territory on each side of the Mississippi, over which they will be scattered, following the chase and indulging in their vagrant habits, until the wild products of the country, on which they depend for a subsistence, are exhausted, and they are brought to a state of destitution and want. Efforts should therefore be made, at as early a period as practicable, to concentrate them within proper limits, where, with some additional means beyond those already provided, effective arrangements could be made to introduce among them a system of education, and the practice of agriculture and the simpler mechanic arts. The best portion of their country for this purpose is west of the Mississippi river; but it is not owned by the whole tribe in common—a considerable part of it being the exclusive property of particular bands, who are not parties to any of our treaties, and receive no annuities or other material aid from the United States. This circumstance not only excites dissatisfaction with the government, but produces much jealousy and bad feeling towards the rest of the tribe, which may hereafter lead to serious difficulty, and, as the game on which they mainly depend for the means of living must soon fail them, the government will be under the necessity of interposing to save them from starvation. A wise forecast and the dictates of a benevolent policy alike suggest that timely measures be taken to avert so disastrous a result. This may easily be done, and at a moderate expense compared with the importance of the objects to be accomplished.

In order to enable the department to carry out these views in reference to the whole Chippewa tribe, I respectfully recommend that Congress be asked for an appropriation at the ensuing session to defray the expense of negotiating a joint treaty with the different bands, for the purpose of acquiring so much of their country on the east side of the Mississippi as we may require for a long time to come; to provide that the whole of their remaining lands, together with their present and future means, shall be the common property of the whole tribe, so that all will be placed upon an equal footing; and that as large a proportion of their funds as practicable shall be set apart and applied in such a manner as will secure their comfort, and most rapidly advance them in civilization and prosperity. With such arrangements for this tribe, and the adoption of a like policy towards the Winnebagoes, now located in their vicinity on the west side of the Mississippi, and the Menomonies, soon to be removed there, the whole face of our Indian relations in that quarter would in a few years present an entire and gratifying change. We should soon witness in this, our northern colony of Indians, those evidences of general improvement now becoming clearly manifest among a number of our colonized tribes in the southwest, and which present to the mind of the philanthropist and the Christian encouraging assurance of the practicability of regenerating the red race of our country, and elevating them to a position, moral and social, similar if not equal to our own. . . .

[*Senate Executive Document* no. 1, 31st Cong., 2d sess., serial 587, pp. 35-37.]

57. Modifications in the Indian Department
February 27, 1851

In 1851 Congress provided a new arrangement of superintendencies and agencies east of the Rockies and north of New Mexico and Texas. It also authorized agents for New Mexico and Utah territories and extended the provisions of the trade and intercourse acts over those regions.

An Act making Appropriations for the current and contingent Expenses of the Indian Department. . . .

. . . . SEC. 2. *And be it further enacted,*

That from and after the thirtieth day of June next, all laws or parts of laws now in force, providing for the appointment or employment of superintendents of Indian affairs, of whatever character, for any of the Indian tribes east of the Rocky Mountains, and north of New Mexico and Texas, shall be, and the same are hereby repealed; and that the President be, and he is hereby, authorized by and with the advice and consent of the Senate, to appoint three superintendents of Indian affairs, for said Indians, who shall receive an annual salary each of two thousand dollars, and whose duty it shall be to exercise a general superintendance over such tribes of Indians as the President of the United States, or the Secretary of the Department of the Interior may direct, and to execute and perform all the powers and duties now assigned by law to superintendents of Indian affairs: *Provided*, That the governor of Minnesota shall continue to be, ex officio, superintendent of Indian affairs, for that Territory until the President shall otherwise direct.

SEC. 3. *And be it further enacted*, That hereafter all Indian treaties shall be negotiated by such officers and agents of the Indian department as the President of the United States may designate for that purpose, and no officer or agent so employed shall receive any additional compensation for such service.

SEC. 4. *And be it further enacted*, That in lieu of the twenty-three agents and subagents, heretofore employed for the Indians east of the Rocky Mountains, and north of New Mexico and Texas, the President be, and he is hereby, authorized by and with the advice and consent of the Senate, to appoint eleven Indian agents, who shall each receive an annual salary of fifteen hundred dollars;

and, also, six other agents, with an annual salary each of one thousand dollars, whose appointments shall take effect from and after the thirtieth day of June next; and the said agents shall execute and perform all the powers and duties now assigned by law to Indian agents.

SEC. 5. *And be it further enacted*, That the President be authorized, by and with the advice and consent of the Senate, to appoint four agents for the Indians in the territory of New Mexico, and one agent for those in the territory of Utah, who shall receive an annual salary each of fifteen hundred and fifty dollars, and perform all the duties of agent to such Indians or tribes, as shall be assigned them by the Superintendents of Indian Affairs for these territories respectively, under the direction of the President, or the Secretary of the Department of the Interior.

SEC. 6. *And be it further enacted*, That the superintendents and agents to be appointed under the provisions of this act, before entering upon the duties of their respective offices, shall give bond in such penalties and with such security, as the President or Secretary of the Interior may require, and shall hold their offices respectively for the term of four years.

SEC. 7. *And be it further enacted*, That all the laws now in force, regulating trade and intercourse with the Indian tribes, or such provisions of the same as may be applicable, shall be, and the same are hereby, extended over the Indian tribes in the Territories of New Mexico and Utah. . . .

[*U.S. Statutes at Large*, 9:586-87.]

58.   Treaty of Fort Laramie

September 17, 1851

As emigrants crossed the plains in large numbers, diplomatic as well as military measures were undertaken to preserve peace with the Indians. A treaty established formal relations with the northern plains tribes at Fort Laramie in 1851 and sought to gain security for the overland travelers. The treaty set boundaries for the various tribes, authorized the United States to build roads and military posts, and provided restitution for damages to white travelers. A similar treaty was signed with the southern plains tribes at Fort Atkinson in July 1853.

Articles of a treaty made and concluded at Fort Laramie, in the Indian Territory, between D. D. Mitchell, superintendent of Indian affairs, and Thomas Fitzpatrick, Indian agent, commissioners specially appointed and authorized by the Presi-

dent of the United States, of the first part, and the chiefs, headmen, and braves of the following Indian nations, residing south of the Missouri River, east of the Rocky Mountains, and north of the lines of Texas and New Mexico, viz, the Sioux or

Dahcotahs, Cheyennes, Arrapahoes, Crows, Assinaboines, Gros-Ventre Mandans, and Arrickaras, parties of the second part, on the seventeenth day of September, A.D. one thousand eight hundred and fifty-one.

ARTICLE 1. The aforesaid nations, parties to this treaty, having assembled for the purpose of establishing and confirming peaceful relations amongst themselves, do hereby convenant and agree to abstain in future from all hostilities whatever against each other, to maintain good faith and friendship in all their mutual intercourse, and to make an effective and lasting peace.

ARTICLE 2. The aforesaid nations do hereby recognize the right of the United States Government to establish roads, military and other posts, within their respective territories.

ARTICLE 3. In consideration of the rights and privileges acknowledged in the preceding article, the United States bind themselves to protect the aforesaid Indian nations against the commission of all depredations by the people of the said United States, after the ratification of this treaty.

ARTICLE 4. The aforesaid Indian nations do hereby agree and bind themselves to make restitution or satisfaction for any wrongs committed, after the ratification of this treaty, by any band or individual of their people, on the people of the United States, whilst lawfully residing in or passing through their respective territories.

ARTICLE 5. The aforesaid Indian nations do hereby recognize and acknowledge the following tracts of country, included within the metes and boundaries hereinafter designated, as their respective territories [descriptions of the boundaries]. . . .

It is, however, understood that, in making this recognition and acknowledgement, the aforesaid Indian nations do not hereby abandon or prejudice any rights or claims they may have to other lands; and further, that they do not surrender the privilege of hunting, fishing, or passing over any of the tracts of country heretofore described.

ARTICLE 6. The parties to the second part of this treaty having selected principals or head-chiefs for their respective nations, through whom all national business will hereafter be conducted, do hereby bind themselves to sustain said chiefs and their successors during good behavior.

ARTICLE 7. In consideration of the treaty stipulations, and for the damages which have or may occur by reason thereof to the Indian nations, parties hereto, and for their maintenance and the improvement of their moral and social customs, the United States bind themselves to deliver to the said Indian nations the sum of fifty thousand dollars per annum for the term of ten years, with the right to continue the same at the discretion of the President of the United States for a period not exceeding five years thereafter, in provisions, merchandise, domestic animals, and agricultural implements, in such proportions as may be deemed best adapted to their condition by the President of the United States, to be distributed in proportion to the population of the aforesaid Indian nations.

ARTICLE 8. It is understood and agreed that should any of the Indian nations, parties to this treaty, violate any of the provisions thereof, the United States may withhold the whole or a portion of the annuities mentioned in the preceding article from the nation so offending, until, in the opinion of the President of the United States, proper satisfaction shall have been made. . . .

[Charles J. Kappler, ed., *Indian Affairs: Laws and Treaties*, 2:594-95.]

59.   Indian Commissioner Lea on the Civilization of the Indians

Extract from the *Annual Report of the Commissioner of Indian Affairs*

November 27, 1851

The United States government's goal of incorporating the Indians into white civilization was expressed by Commissioner Luke Lea at the end of his annual report in 1851.

. . . . The civilization of the Indians within the territory of the United States is a cherished object of the government. It undoubtedly merits all the consideration bestowed upon it, and the employment of all the means necessary for its accomplishment. There are not wanting those, who, judging from the apparently little success which in some instances has attended the instrumentalities employed, doubt the practicability of the measure. It should be remembered, however, that to change a savage people from their barbarous habits to those of civilized life, is, in its nature, a work of time, and the results already attained, as evinced in the improved condition of several of our tribes, are sufficient to silence the most skeptical, and warrant the assurance that perseverance in the cause will achieve success.

The history of the Indian furnishes abundant proof that he possesses all the elements essential to his elevation; all the powers, instincts and sympathies which appertain to his white brother; and which only need the proper development and direction to enable him to tread with equal step and dignity the walks of civilized life. He is intellectual, proud, brave, generous; and in his devotion to his family, his country, and the graves of his fathers, it is clearly shown that the kind affections and the impulses of patriotism animate his heart. That his inferiority is a necessity of his nature, is neither taught by philosophy nor attested by experience. Prejudice against him, originating in error of opinion on this subject, has doubtless been a formidable obstacle in the way of his improvement; while, on the other hand, it is equally certain that his progress has been retarded by ill conceived and misdirected efforts to hasten his advance. It is even questionable whether the immense amounts paid to them in the way of annuities have not been, and are not now, all things considered, a curse to them rather than a blessing. Certain it is, there has not at all times been the most wise and beneficial application of their

funds. To arouse the spirit of enterprise in the Indian, and bring him to realize the necessity of reliance upon himself, in some industrial pursuit, for his support and comfort, is, generally, if not universally, the initiative step to his civilization, which he is often prevented from taking by the debasing influence of the annuity system. But the system is fastened upon us, and its attendant evils must be endured.

On the general subject of the civilization of the Indians, many and diversified opinions have been put forth; but, unfortunately, like the race to which they relate, they are too wild to be of much utility. The great question, How shall the Indians be civilized? yet remains without a satisfactory answer. The magnitude of the subject, and the manifold difficulties inseparably connected with it, seem to have bewildered the minds of those who have attempted to give it the most thorough investigation. The remark of the late Attorney General Legaré, is not more striking than true, that "there is nothing in the whole compass of our laws so anomalous, so hard to bring within any precise definition, or any logical and scientific arrangement of principles, as the relation in which the Indians stand towards this government and those of the States." My own views are not sufficiently matured to justify me in undertaking to present them here. To do so would require elaborate detail, and swell this report beyond its proper limits. I therefore leave the subject for the present, remarking, only, that any plan for the civilization of our Indians will, in my judgment, be fatally defective, if it do not provide, in the most efficient manner, first, for their ultimate incorporation into the great body of our citizen population.

[*House Executive Document* no. 2, 32d Cong., 1st sess., serial 636, pp. 273-74.]

60. Superintendent of Indian Affairs in California

March 3, 1852

Indian affairs in the Far West were regularized little by little. In 1852 Congress authorized a superintendent of Indian affairs for California, with powers similar to those of the superintendent at Saint Louis.

An Act to provide for the Appointment of a Superintendent of Indian Affairs in California.

Be it enacted . . . , That the sixth section

of an act approved May sixth, eighteen hundred and twenty-two, entitled "An act to amend an act entitled An act to regulate trade and intercourse with the Indian tribes, and to preserve peace on the frontiers, approved the thirtieth March, eighteen hundred and two;" also, the fifth section of an act approved May twenty-fifth, eighteen hundred and twenty-four, entitled "An act to enable the President to hold treaties with certain Indian tribes, and for other purposes," be and the same hereby are revived, and extended to the State of California, for the purpose of establishing a superintendency of Indian affairs for said State, and that the President, by and with the advice and consent of the Senate, be, and he hereby is authorized to appoint a superintendent of Indian Affairs to reside in said State, who shall possess the same powers, and be subject to the same duties within his superintendency as belong to the Superintendent of Indian Affairs at St. Louis, in the State of Missouri, with the power also of exercising administrative examination over all claims, and accounts and vouchers for disbursements, connected with Indian affairs in the said State of California, which shall be transmitted to the Commissioner of Indian Affairs for final adjudication, and by him passed to the proper accounting officers of the treasury for settlement.

SEC. 2. *And be it further enacted*, That the said superintendent shall have an annual salary not exceeding four thousand dollars.

SEC. 3. *And be it further enacted*, That the said superintendent shall be allowed a clerk, whose compensation for his services shall not exceed two thousand five hundred dollars per annum.

[*U.S. Statutes at Large*, 10:2.]

61. Treaty with the Oto and Missouri Indians

March 15, 1854

To make room for white settlers in Kansas and Nebraska territories, numerous treaties were negotiated with the Indians of the area by Commissioner of Indian Affairs George W. Manypenny. These treaties were noteworthy because many of them provided for the allotment of reservation land in severalty to individual Indians. The treaty with the Oto and Missouri Indians is an example.

Articles of agreement and convention made and concluded at the city of Washington, this fifteenth day of March, one thousand eight hundred and fifty-four, by George W. Manypenny, as commissioner on the part of the United States, and the following-named Chiefs of the confederate tribes of the Ottoe and Missouria Indians, viz: Ar-ke-kee-tah, or Stay by It; Heb-cah-po, or Kickapoo; Shaw-ka-haw-wa, or Medicine Horse; Mi-ar-ke-tah-hun-she, or Big Soldier; Cha-won-a-ke, or Buffalo Chief; Ah-hah-che-ke-saw-ke, or Missouria Chief; and Maw-thra-ti-ne, or White Water; they being thereto duly authorized by said confederate tribes.

ARTICLE 1. The confederate tribes of Ottoe and Missouria Indians cede to the United States all their country west of the Missouri River, excepting a strip of land on the Waters of the Big Blue River, ten miles in width and bounded as follows: Commencing at a point in the middle of the main branch of the Big Blue River, in a west or southwest direction from Old Fort Kearney, at a place called by the Indians the "Islands;" thence west to the western boundary of the country hereby ceded; thence in a northerly course with said western boundary, ten miles; thence east to a point due north of the starting point and ten miles therefrom; thence to the place of beginning: *Provided*, That in case the said initial point is not within the limits of the country hereby ceded, or that the western boundary of said country is not distant twenty-five miles or more from the initial point, in either case, there shall be assigned by the United States to said Indians, for their future home, a tract of land not less then ten miles wide by twenty-five miles long, the southeast corner of which tract shall be the initial point above named. And such portion of such tract, if any, as shall prove to be outside of the ceded country, shall be and the same is hereby granted and ceded to the confederate tribes of Ottoe and Missouria Indians by the United States, who will have said tract properly set off by durable monuments as soon after the ratification of this instrument as the same can conveniently be done.

87

ARTICLE 2. The said confederate tribes agree, that as soon after the United States shall make the necessary provision for fulfilling the stipulations of this instrument, as they can conveniently arrange their affairs, and not to exceed one year after such provision is made, they will vacate the ceded country, and remove to the lands herein reserved for them.

ARTICLE 3. The said confederate tribes relinquish to the United States, all claims, for money or other thing, under former treaties, and all claim which they may have heretofore, at any time, set up, to any land on the east side of the Missouri River: *Provided*, That said confederate tribes shall receive the unexpended balances of former appropriations now in the United States Treasury, of which, four thousand dollars shall at once be applied for the purchase of provisions and to farming purposes.

ARTICLE 4. In consideration of, and payment for the country herein ceded, and the relinquishments herein made, the United States agree to pay to the said confederate tribes of Ottoe and Missouria Indians the several sums of money following, to wit:

1st. Twenty thousand dollars, per annum, for the term of three years, commencing on the first day of January, one thousand eight hundred and fifty-five.

2d. Thirteen thousand dollars, per annum, for the term of ten years, next succeeding the three years.

3d. Nine thousand dollars, per annum, for the term of fifteen years, next succeeding the ten years.

4th. Five thousand dollars, per annum, for the term of twelve years, next succeeding the fifteen years.

All which several sums of money shall be paid to the said confederate tribes, or expended for their use and benefit under the direction of the President of the United States, who may, from time to time, determine, at his discretion, what proportion of the annual payments, in this article provided for, if any, shall be paid to them in money, and what proportion shall be applied to and expended, for their moral improvement and education; for such beneficial objects as in his judgment will be calculated to advance them in civilization; for buildings, opening farms, fencing, breaking land, providing

stock, agricultural implements, seeds, &c., for clothing, provisions, and merchandise; for iron, steel, arms and ammunition; for mechanics, and tools; and for medical purposes.

ARTICLE 5. In order to enable the said confederate tribes to settle their affairs, and to remove, and subsist themselves for one year at their new home, (and which they agree to do without further expense to the United States,) and to break up and fence one hundred and fifty acres of land at their new home, they shall receive from the United States the further sum of twenty thousand dollars, to be paid out and expended under the direction of the President, and in such manner as he shall approve.

ARTICLE 6. The President may, from time to time, at his discretion, cause the whole of the land herein reserved or appropriated west of the Big Blue River, to be surveyed off into lots, and assign to such Indian or Indians of said confederate tribes, as are willing to avail of the privilege, and who will locate on the same as a permanent home, if a single person over twenty-one years of age, one-eighth of a section; to each family of two, one-quarter section; to each family of three and not exceeding five, one-half section; to each family of six and not exceeding ten, one section; and to each family exceeding ten in number, one quarter section for every additional five members. And he may prescribe such rules and regulations as will secure to the family, in case of the death of the head thereof, the possession and enjoyment of such permanent home and the improvements thereon. And the President may, at any time in his discretion, after such person or family has made a location on the land assigned for a permanent home, issue a patent to such person or family for such assigned land, conditioned that the tract shall not be aliened or leased for a longer term than two years; and shall be exempt from levy, sale, or forfeiture, which conditions shall continue in force, until a State constitution embracing such land within its boundaries shall have been formed, and the legislature of the State shall remove the restrictions. And if any such person or family shall at any time neglect or refuse to occupy and till a portion of the land assigned, and on which they have located, or shall rove from place to place, the President may, if the patent shall have been issued, revoke the same, or, if not issued, cancel the assignment, and may also withhold from such person or family, their proportion of the annuities or other moneys due them, until they shall have returned to such permanent home, and resumed the pursuits of industry; and in default of their return, the tract may be declared abandoned, and thereafter assigned to some other person or family of such confederate tribes, or disposed of as is provided for the disposal of the excess of said land. And the residue of the land hereby reserved, after all the Indian persons or families of such confederate tribes shall have had assigned to them permanent homes, may be sold for their benefit, under such laws, rules, or regulations as may hereafter be prescribed by the Congress or President of the United States. No State legislature shall remove the restriction herein provided for, without the consent of Congress.

ARTICLE 7. The United States will erect for said confederate tribes at their new home a grist and saw mill, and keep the same in repair, and provide a miller for a term of ten years; also erect a good blacksmith shop, supply the same with tools, and keep it in repair for the term of ten years, and provide a good blacksmith for a like period, and employ an experienced farmer, for ten years, to instruct the Indians in agriculture.

ARTICLE 8. The annuities of the Indians shall not be taken to pay the debts of individuals.

ARTICLE 9. The said confederate tribes acknowledge their dependence on the Government of the United States, and promise to be friendly with all the citizens thereof, and pledge themselves to commit no depredations on the property of such citizens. And should any one or more of the Indians violate this pledge, and the fact be satisfactorily proven before the agent, the property taken shall be returned, or in default thereof, or if injured or destroyed, compensation may be made by the Government out of their annuities. Nor will they make war on any other tribe except in self-defence, but will submit all matters of difference between them and other Indians, to the Government of the United States, or its agent, for decision, and abide thereby. And if any of the said Indians commit any depredations on any other Indians, the same rule shall prevail as that prescribed in this article in cases of depredations against citizens.

ARTICLE 10. The Ottoes and Missourias are desirous to exclude from their country the use of ardent spirits, and to prevent their people from drinking the same; and therefore it is provided that any one of them who is guilty of bringing liquor into their country, or who drinks liquor, may have his or her proportion of the annuities withheld from him or her for such time, as the President may determine.

ARTICLE 11. The said confederate tribes agree, that all the necessary roads and highways, and railways, which may be constructed as the country improves, and the lines of which may run through their land west of the Big Blue River, shall have a right of way through the reservation, a just compensation being made therefor in money. . . .

[Charles J. Kappler, ed., *Indian Affairs: Laws and Treaties*, 2:608-10.]

62. Indian Commissioner Manypenny on Indian Affairs

Extract from the *Annual Report of the Commissioner of Indian Affairs*

November 22, 1856

George W. Manypenny, commissioner of Indian affairs from 1853 to 1857, faced the problems that arose from the opening of Kansas and Nebraska to white settlement. In his report of 1856 he discussed the treaties made with the Indians and his general views on Indian policy.

. . . . Since the 4th of March, 1853, fifty-two treaties with various Indian tribes have been entered into. These treaties may, with but few exceptions of a specific character, be separated into three classes: first, treaties of peace and friendship; second, treaties of acquisition, with a view of colonizing the Indians on reservations; and third, treaties of acquisition, and providing for the permanent settlement of the individuals of the tribes, at once or in the future, on separate tracts of lands or homesteads, and for the gradual abolition of the tribal character. The quantity of land acquired by these treaties, either by the extinguishment of the original Indian title, or by the re-acquisition of lands granted to Indian tribes by former treaties, is about one hundred and seventy-four millions of acres. Thirty-two of these treaties have been ratified, and twenty are now before the Senate for its consideration and action. In no former equal period of our history have so many treaties been made, or such vast accessions of land been obtained. Within the same period the jurisdiction of this office and the operations of its agents have been extended over an additional area of from four to six thousand square miles of territory, embracing tribes about which, before that time, but little was known; and by authority of several acts of Congress thirteen new agencies and nine sub-agencies have been established. The increased labor which has been thus devolved on the Commissioner of Indian Affairs and the entire force of the bureau, as well as upon the superintendents and agents, has been very great, and has swelled the business connected with our Indian affairs to an extent almost incredible. The labor of this branch of the service has doubled since 1852, and yet with this extraordinary increase, the permanent clerical force of this office is the same now that it was on the 4th of March, 1853. The permanent force is now insufficient to promptly perform the labor of the bureau; and the classification and arrangement of the business of the office should be modified and improved, but this cannot be done thoroughly without a small permanent increase in the clerical force.

The existing laws for the protection of the persons and property of the Indian wards of the government are sadly defective. New and more stringent statutes are required. The relation which the federal government sustains towards the Indians, and the duties and obligations flowing from it, cannot be faithfully met and discharged without ample legal provisions, and the necessary power and means to enforce them. The rage for speculation and the wonderful desire to obtain choice lands, which seems to possess so many of those who go into our new territories, causes them to lose sight of and entirely overlook the rights of the aboriginal inhabitants. The most dishonorable expedients have, in many cases, been made use of to dispossess the Indian; demoralizing means employed to obtain his property; and, for the want of adequate laws, the department is now often perplexed and embarrassed, because of inability to afford prompt relief and apply the remedy in cases obviously requiring them.

The general disorder so long prevailing in Kansas Territory, and the consequent unsettled state of civil affairs there have been very injurious to the interests of many of the Indian tribes in that Territory. The state of affairs referred to, with the influx of lawless men and speculators incident and introductory thereto, has impeded the surveys and the selections for the homes of the Indians, and otherwise prevented the full establishment and proper efficiency of all the means for civilization and improvement within the scope of the several treaties with them. The schools have not been as fully attended, nor the school buildings, agency houses, and other improvements, as rapidly constructed as they might otherwise have been. Trespasses and depredations of every conceivable kind have been committed on the Indians. They have been personally maltreated, their property stolen, their timber destroyed, their possession encroached upon, and divers other wrongs and injuries done them. Notwithstanding all which they have afforded a praiseworthy example of good conduct, under the most trying circumstances. They have at no time, that I am aware of, attempted to redress their own wrongs, but have patiently submitted to injury, relying on the good faith and justice of the government to indemnify them. In the din and strife between the anti-slavery and pro-slavery parties with reference to the condition of the African race there, and in which the rights and interests of the red man have been completely overlooked and disregarded, the good conduct and patient submission of the latter contrasts favorably with the disorderly and lawless conduct of many of their white brethren, who, while they have quarrelled about the African, have united upon the soil of Kansas in wrong doing toward the Indian!

In relation to the emigrated and partially civilized tribes in Kansas, the circumstances under which they were transplanted to that country, and the pledges of this government that it should be to them and their posterity a permanent home forever; the distrust and doubt under which they assented to the sale of a portion of their respective tracts to the United States for the use and occupation of our own population, I have in former reports treated fully; and have likewise endeavored to impress upon the minds of all persons that the small tracts which these tribes have reserved in Kansas as their permanent homes must be so regarded. They cannot again be removed. They must meet their fate upon their present reservations in that Territory, and there be made a civilized people, or crushed and blotted out. Their condition is critical, simply because their rights and interests seem thus far to have been entirely lost sight of and disregarded by their new neighbors. They may be preserved and civilized, and will be if the guarantees and stipulations of their treaties are faithfully fulfilled and enforced, and the federal government discharges its obligations and redeems its pledged faith towards them. As peace and order seem now to be restored to the Territories, it is to be hoped that the good citizens thereof will make haste to repair the wrong and injury which the red men of Kansas have suffered by the acts of their white neighbors, and that hereafter they will not only treat the Indians fairly, but that all good citizens will set their faces against the conduct of any lawless men who may attempt to trespass upon the rights of, or otherwise injure, the Indian population there.

In reviewing the events of the past year with reference to the improvement of our Indian population, there appears within the reserves of several tribes such unmistakable manifestations of progress as to excite and stimulate our lawgivers and the benevolent and philanthropic of the land to a more lively and active interest in the present condition and future prospects of the race, and to invite an increased effort and energy in the cause of Indian civilization. That the red man can be transformed in his habits, domesticated, and civilized, and made a useful element in society, there is abundant evidence. With reference to his true character, erroneous opinions very generally prevail. He is, indeed, the victim of prejudice. He is only regarded as the irreclaimable, terrible savage, who in war spares neither age nor sex, but with heartless and cruel barbarity subjects the innocent and defenceless to inhuman tortures, committing with exultant delight the most horrible massacres. These are chronicled from year to year, and are, indeed, sad chapters in our annals. But the history of the sufferings of the Indian has never been written; the story of his wrongs never been told. Of these there is not, and never can be, an earthly record.

As a man he has his joys and his sorrows. His love for his offspring is intense. In his friendships he is steadfast and true, and will never be the first to break faith. His courage is undoubted, his perception quick, and his memory of the highest order. His judgment is defective, but by proper training and discipline his intellectual powers are susceptible of culture and can be elevated to a fair standard. He can be taught the arts of peace, and is by no means inapt in learnng to handle agricultural and mechanical implements and applying them to their appropriate uses. With these qualities, although the weaker, he is eminently entitled to the kind consideration of the stronger race.

The wonderful emigration to our newly acquired States and Territories, and its effect upon the wild tribes inhabiting them and the plains and prairies, is well calculated at the present period to attract special attention. Not only are our settlements rapidly advancing westward from the Mississippi river towards the Pacific ocean, and from the shores of the Pacific eastward towards the Mississippi river, but large settlements have been made in Utah and New Mexico between the two. Already the settlements of Texas are extending up to El Paso and spreading into the Gadsden purchase, and those of California have reached into the great valley of the Colorado, whilst the settlers of Minnesota are building cities at the very head of Lake Superior and villages in the remote valley of the Red river of the north, on their way to Puget Sound. Railroads built and building, from the Atlantic and Gulf cities, not only reach the

Mississippi river at about twenty different points, but are extending west across Louisiana, Arkansas, Missouri, and Iowa. Roads of that character have also been commenced in Texas, looking to El Paso, and in Iowa, looking for the great bend of the Minnesota river for a present and for Pembina for a future terminus. The railroad companies of Missouri and Iowa are even now seeking aid from Congress to enable them to extend their roads to New Mexico, Kansas, Nebraska, and Utah, and thence to California, Oregon, and Washington. California has actually commenced the construction of a railroad leading up the Sacramento valley toward Utah.

It is impossible to avoid the conclusion that in a few years, in a very few, the railroads of the east, from New Orleans to the extreme west end of Lake Superior, will be extended westwardly up towards the Rocky mountains, at least as far as good lands can be found, and that roads from the Pacific coast will be built as far east as good lands extend; and that in both cases an active population will keep up with the advance of the railroads—a population that will open farms, erect workshops, and build villages and cities.

When that time arrives, and it is at our very doors, ten years, if our country is favored with peace and prosperity, will witness the most of it; where will be the habitation and what the condition of the rapidly wasting Indian tribes of the plains, the prairies, and of our new States and Territories?

As sure as these great physical changes are impending, so sure will these poor denizens of the forest be blotted out of existence, and their dust be trampled under the foot of rapidly advancing civilization, unless our great nation shall generously determine that the necessary provision shall at once be made, and appropriate steps be taken to designate suitable tracts or reservations of land, in proper localities, for permanent homes for, and provide the means to colonize, them thereon. Such reservations should be selected with great care, and when determined upon and designated the assurances by which they are guarantied to the Indians should be irrevocable, and of such a character as to effectually protect them from encroachments of every kind. . . .

To preserve their property and to give them the blessings of education and Christianity is indispensible to their continuing "long in the land" which God gave to their fathers and to them. I sincerely hope that our government will have the aid of all its good citizens in faithfully executing its high trust and discharging its obligations to the remnants of the Indian tribes now left to its oversight and guardianship, so that they shall be intelligently and generously protected and cared for in all that makes life useful and happy.

[*Senate Executive Document* no. 5, 34th Cong., 3d sess., serial 875, pp. 571-75.]

63. Indian Commissioner Mix on Reservation Policy

Extract from the *Annual Report of the Commissioner of Indian Affairs*

November 6, 1858

Commissioner of Indian Affairs Charles E. Mix in 1858 discussed problems concerning the development of reservation policy in the West.

. . . . From the commencement of the settlement of this country, the principle has been recognised and acted on, that the Indian tribes possessed the occupant or usufruct right to the lands they occupied, and that they were entitled to the peaceful enjoyment of that right until they were fairly and justly divested of it. Hence the numerous treaties with the various tribes, by which, for a stipulated consideration their lands have, been acquired, as our population increased.

Experience has demonstrated that at least three serious, and, to the Indians, fatal errors have, from the beginning, marked our policy towards them, viz: their removal from place to place as our population advanced; the assignment to them of too great an extent of country, to be held in common; and the allowance of large sums of money, as annui-

92

ties, for the lands ceded by them. These errors, far more than the want of capacity on the part of the Indian, have been the cause of the very limited success of our constant efforts to domesticate and civilize him. By their frequent changes of position and the possession of large bodies of land in common, they have been kept in an unsettled condition and prevented from acquiring a knowledge of separate and individual property, while their large annuities, upon which they have relied for a support, have not only tended to foster habits of indolence and profligacy, but constantly made them the victims of the lawless and inhuman sharper and speculator. The very material and marked difference between the northern Indians and those of the principal southern tribes, may be accounted for by the simple fact that the latter were permitted, for long periods, to remain undisturbed in their original locations; where, surrounded by, or in close proximity with a white population, they, to a considerable extent, acquired settled habits and a knowledge of and taste for civilized occupations and pursuits. Our present policy, as you are aware, is entirely the reverse of that heretofore pursued in the three particulars mentioned. It is to permanently locate the different tribes on reservations embracing only sufficient land for their actual occupancy; to divide this among them in severalty, and require them to live upon and cultivate the tracts assigned to them; and in lieu of money annuities, to furnish them with stock animals, agricultural implements, mechanic-shops, tools and materials, and manual labor schools for the industrial and mental education of their youth. Most of the older treaties, however, provide for annuities in money, and the department has, therefore, no authority to commute them even in cases where the Indians may desire, or could be influenced to agree to such a change. In view of this fact, and the better to enable the department to carry out its present and really more benevolent policy, I would respectfully recommend and urge that a law be enacted by Congress, empowering and requiring the department, in all cases where money annuities are provided for by existing treaties, and the assent of the Indians can be obtained, to commute them

for objects and purposes of a beneficial character.

The principle of recognising and respecting the usufruct right of the Indians to the lands occupied by them, has not been so strictly adhered to in the case of the tribes in the Territories of Oregon and Washington. When a territorial government was first provided for Oregon, which then embraced the present Territory of Washington, strong inducements were held out to our people to emigrate and settle there, without the usual arrangements being made, in advance, for the extinguishment of the title of the Indians who occupied and claimed the lands. Intruded upon, ousted of their homes and possessions without any compensation, and deprived, in most cases, of their accustomed means of support, without any arrangement having been made to enable them to establish and maintain themselves in other locations, it is not a matter of surprise that they have committed many depredations upon our citizens, and been exasperated to frequent acts of hostility.

The Indians in Oregon and Washington number about 42,000, and are divided into 35 tribes and bands. The only treaties in force with any of them, are with those who inhabited the valuable sections of country embraced in the Rogue river, Umpqua and Willamette valleys. After repeated acts of hostility and continued depredations upon the white settlers, the Indians in Oregon were removed to, and are now living upon the reservations, one on the western and the other on the eastern side of the coast range of mountains; and the country to which their title was extinguished has rapidly filled up with an enterprising and thrifty population. In the year 1855, treaties were also entered into by the superintendent of Indian affairs for Oregon, and by Governor Stevens, *ex officio* superintendent for Washington Territory, with various other tribes and bands, for the purpose of extinguishing their title to large tracts of country, which were needed for the extension of our settlements, and to provide homes for the Indians in other and more suitable locations, where they could be controlled and domesticated. These treaties not having been ratified, the Indians were sorely disappointed in consequence of the expectations they were led to entertain of benefits and advantages to be derived from them not being realized. Moreover, the whites have gone on to occupy their country without regard to their rights, which has led the Indians to believe that they were to be dispossessed of it without compensation or any provision being made for them. This state of things has naturally had a tendency to exasperate them; and, in the opinion of well informed persons, has been the cause of their recent acts of hostility. The belief is confidently entertained, that, had the treaties referred to been ratified and put in course of execution, the difficulties that have occurred would not have taken place; and there can be but little if any doubt, that the cost of the military operations to subdue the Indians, and the losses sustained by our citizens from their depredations and hostilities, will amount to a far greater sum than would have been required to extinguish their title and establish and maintain them, for the necessary period, on properly selected reservations, had that policy in respect to them been sanctioned and timely measures taken to carry it out.

It cannot be expected that Indians situated like those in Oregon and Washington, occupying extensive sections of country, where, from the game and otherwise, they derive a comfortable support, will quietly and peaceably submit, without any equivalent, to be deprived of their homes and possessions, and to be driven off to some other locality where they cannot find their usual means of subsistence. Such a proceeding is not only contrary to our policy hitherto, but is repugnant alike to the dictates of humanity and the principles of natural justice. In all cases where the necessities of our rapidly increasing population have compelled us to displace the Indian, we have ever regarded it as a sacred and binding obligation to provide him with a home elsewhere, and to contribute liberally to his support until he could re-establish and maintain himself in his new place of residence. The policy, it is true, has been a costly one, but we have been amply repaid its expense by the revenue obtained from the sale of the lands acquired from the Indians, and by the rapid extension of our settlements and the corre-

sponding increase in the resources and prosperity of our country. . . .

The policy of concentrating the Indians on small reservations of land, and of sustaining them there for a limited period, until they can be induced to make the necessary exertions to support themselves, was commenced in 1853, with those in California. It is, in fact, the only course compatible with the obligations of justice and humanity, left to be pursued in regard to all those with which our advancing settlements render new and permanent arrangements necessary. We have no longer distant and extensive sections of country which we can assign them, abounding in game, from which they could derive a ready and comfortable support; a resource which has, in a great measure, failed them where they are, and in consequence of which they must, at times, be subjected to the pangs of hunger, if not actual starvation, or obtain a subsistence by depredations upon our frontier settlements. If it were practicable to prevent such depredations, the alternative to providing for the Indians in the manner indicated, would be to leave them to starve; but as it is impossible, in consequence of the very great extent of our frontier, and our limited military force, to adequately guard against such occurrences, the only alternative, in fact, to making such provision for them, is to exterminate them. . . .

The operations thus far, in carrying out the reservation system, can properly be regarded as only experimental. Time and experience were required to develop any defects connected with it, and to demonstrate the proper remedies therefor. From a careful examination of the subject, and the best information in the possession of the department in regard to it, I am satisfied that serious errors have been committed; that a much larger amount has been expended than was necessary, and with but limited and insufficient results. . . .

No more reservations should be established than are absolutely necessary for such Indians as have been, or it may be necessary to displace, in consequence of the extension of our settlements, and whose resources have thereby been cut off or so diminished that they cannot sustain themselves in their accustomed manner. Great care should be taken in the selection of the reservations, so as to isolate the Indians for a time from contact and interference from the whites. They should embrace good lands, which will well repay the efforts to cultivate them. No white persons should be suffered to go upon the reservations, and after the first year the lands should be divided and assigned to the Indians in severalty, every one being required to remain on his own tract and to cultivate it, no persons being employed for them except the requisite mechanics to keep their tools and implements in repair, and such as may be necessary, for a time, to teach them how to conduct their agricultural operations and to take care of their stock. They should also have the advantage of well conducted manual labor schools for the education of their youth in letters, habits of industry, and a knowledge of agriculture and the simpler mechanic arts. By the adoption of this course, it is believed that the colonies can very soon be made to sustain themselves, or so nearly so that the government will be subjected to but a comparatively trifling annual expense on account of them. But it is essential to the success of the system that there should be a sufficient military force in the vicinity of the reservations to prevent the intrusion of improper persons upon them, to afford protection to the agents, and to aid in controlling the Indians and keeping them within the limits assigned to them.

It would materially aid the department in its efforts to carry out the system successfully, in respect to the Indians in California, if that State would, like Texas, so far relinquish to the general government her jurisdiction over the reservations to be permanently retained there, as to admit of the trade and intercourse laws being put in force within their limits, so as to secure the Indians against improper interference and intercourse, and to prevent the traffic with them in ardent spirits. Much good could also probably be accomplished by the introduction of a judicious system of apprenticeship, by which the orphans and other children of both sexes, could be bound out for a term of years, to upright and humane persons, to be taught suitable trades and occupations: provided the necessary State laws were enacted to authorize and regulate such a system. I would suggest the propriety of an application being made to the proper authorities of California for the requisite State legislation on both these subjects. . . .

[*Senate Executive Document* no. 1, 35th Cong., 2d sess., serial 974, pp. 354-59.]

64. Indian Commissioner Dole on Reservation Policy

Extract from the *Annual Report of the Commissioner of Indian Affairs*

November 26, 1862

Lincoln's commissioner of Indian affairs, William P. Dole, strongly supported the emerging policy of confining the Indians on restricted reservations, as a step toward allotment of lands in severalty and ultimate incorporation of the Indians into full American citizenship.

. . . . Another year has but served to strengthen my conviction that the policy, recently adopted, of confining the Indians to reservations, and, from time to time, as they are gradually taught and become accustomed to the idea of individual property, allotting to them lands to be held in severalty, is the best method yet devised for their reclamation and advancement in civilization. The successful working of this policy is not, however, unattended with difficulties and embarrassments arising chiefly from the contact of the red and white races. This is especially the case in relation to Indians whose reservations are located within the limits of States.

In very many instances the reservation is entirely surrounded by white settlements, and however much the fact is to be regretted, it is, nevertheless, almost invariably true that the tracts of land still remaining in the possession of the Indians, small and insignificant as they are when compared with the broad domain of which they were once the undisputed masters, are the objects of the cupidity of their white neighbors; they are regarded as intruders, and are subject to wrongs, insults, and petty annoyances, which, though they may be trifling in detail, are, in the aggregate, exceedingly onerous and hard to be borne.

They find themselves in the pathway of a race they are wholly unable to stay, and on whose sense of justice they can alone rely for a redress of their real or imaginary grievances. Surrounded by this race, compelled by inevitable necessity to abandon all their former modes of gaining a livelihood, and starting out in pursuits which to them are new and untried experiments, they are brought in active competition with their superiors in intelligence and those acquirements which we consider so essential to success. In addition to these disadvantages, they find themselves amenable to a system of local and federal laws, as well as their treaty stipulations, all of which are to the vast majority of them wholly unintelligible. If a white man does them an injury, redress is often beyond their reach; or, if obtained, is only had after delays and vexations which are themselves cruel injustice. If one of their number commits a crime, punishment is sure and swift, and oftentimes is visited upon the whole tribe. Under these circumstances, it is not surprising that very many of them regard their future prospects as utterly hopeless, and consequently cannot be induced to abandon their vicious and idle habits. It is gratifying that so many of them are steadily and successfully acquiring the arts of civilization, and becoming useful members, and, in some instances, ornaments of society.

Very much of the evil attendant upon the location of Indians within the limits of States might be obviated, if some plan could be devised whereby a more hearty co-operation with government on the part of the States might be secured. It being a demonstrated fact that Indians are capable of attaining a high degree of civilization, it follows that the time will arrive, as in the case of some of the tribes it has doubtless now arrived, when the peculiar relations existing between them and the federal government may cease, without detriment to their interests or those of the community or State in which they are located; in other words, that the time will come when, in justice to them and to ourselves, their relations to the general government should be identical with those of the citizens of the various States. In this view, a more generous legislation on the part of most of the States within whose limits Indians are located, looking to a gradual removal of the disabilities under which they labor, and their ultimate admission to all the rights of citizenship, as from time to time the improvement and advancement made by a given tribe may warrant, is earnestly to be desired, and would, I doubt not, prove a powerful incentive to exertion on the part of the Indians themselves. . . .

[*House Executive Document* no. 1, 37th Cong., 3d sess., serial 1157, pp. 169-70.]

65. Report of the President of the Southern Treaty Commission

October 30, 1865

At the conclusion of the Civil War, the United States government sent to Fort Smith a special commission, headed by Commissioner of Indian Affairs Dennis N. Cooley, to deal with the Indian tribes of the Indian Territory, most of whom had actively supported the Confederacy. Cooley's report indicates the terms that were proposed to the Indian delegates at Fort Smith. The Indians refused to accept the full terms, objecting especially to organization as a regular territory of the United States. Final treaties with the tribes were not signed until the following year.

SIR: As president of the commission designated by the President to negotiate, under your instructions, "a treaty or treaties with all or any of the nations, tribes, or bands of Indians now located in the Indian country or in the State of Kansas, and also with the Indians of the plains west of Kansas and the said Indian country," I have the honor to submit the following: . . . .

The council was called to order by me, as president of the commission; after which the blessing of the Great Spirit over our deliberations was invoked by Rev. Lewis Downing, acting chief of the Cherokee nation. When Mr. Downing had concluded, I addressed the council as follows:

BROTHERS: It is proper that thanks should be returned to the Great Spirit, the creator of us all, that our lives have been preserved to meet upon this occasion. This, as you saw, has been done in our style of addressing the Great Spirit. We have thanked Him for His goodness in keeping us in good health, and for putting it into your minds to meet us at this time. We trust that His wisdom may guide us all in the deliberations on every question that may come before us.

We are glad to meet so many of our brothers in council, and pray the Great Spirit to keep you all in health, and to preserve your wives and children during your absence, and return us all safely to our homes when our council shall terminate.

BROTHERS: You will listen further: your Great Father the President, hearing that the Indians in the southwest desired to meet commissioners sent by him, in council, to renew their allegiance to the United States, and to settle difficulties among themselves which have arisen in consequence of a portion of the several tribes uniting with wicked white men who have engaged in war, has sent the commissioners now before you to hear and consider any matter which you may desire to lay before us, and to make a treaty of peace and amity with all his red children who may desire his favor and protection.

Portions of several tribes and nations have attempted to throw off their allegiance to the United States, and have made treaty stipulations with the enemies of the government, and have been in open war with those who remained loyal and true, and at war with the United States. All such have rightfully forfeited all annuities and interests in the lands in the Indian territory; but with the return of peace, after subduing and punishing severely in battle those who caused the rebellion, the President is willing to hear his erring children in extenuation of their great crime. He has authorized us to make new treaties with such nations and tribes as are willing to be at peace among themselves and with the United States.

The President has been deeply pained by the course of those who have violated their plighted faith and treaty obligations by engaging in war with those in rebellion against the United States.

He directs us to say to those who remain true, and who have aided him in punishing the rebels, he is well pleased with you, and your rights and interests will be protected by the United States.

The President directs us to express to you the hope that your dissensions may soon all be healed, and your people soon again united, prosperous, and happy.

We are now ready to hear anything you may wish to say in reply.

The response and explanations of the different nations and tribes will be found in the proceedings of the council, hereto appended.

On the second day, (Saturday, September 9,) after council met, I addressed the Indians, in which I stated that the commissioners had considered the talks of the Indians on the proceding day, and had authorized me to submit the following statement and propositions, as the basis on which the United States were prepared to negotiate with them:

"BROTHERS: We are instructed by the President to negotiate a treaty or treaties with any or all of the nations, tribes, or bands of Indians in the Indian territory, Kansas, or of the plains west of the Indian territory and Kansas.

"The following named nations and tribes have by their own acts, by making treaties with the enemies of the United States at the dates hereafter named, forfeited all right to annuities, lands, and protection by the United States.

"The different nations and tribes having made treaties with the rebel government are as follows, viz: The Creek nation, July 10, 1861; Choctaws and Chickasaws, July 12, 1861; Seminoles, August 1, 1861; Shawnees, Delawares, Wichitas and affiliated tribes risiding in leased territory, August 12, 1861; the Comanches of the Prairie, August 12, 1861; the Great Osages, October 21, 1861; the Senecas, Senecas and Shawnees, (Neosho agency,) October 4, 1861; the Quapaws, October 4, 1861; the Cherokees, October 7, 1861.

"By these nations having entered into treaties with the so-called Confederate States, and the rebellion being now ended, they are left without any treaty whatever or treaty obligations for protection by the United States.

"Under the terms of the treaties with the United States, and the law of Congress of July 5, 1862, all these nations and tribes forfeited and lost all their rights to annuities and lands. The President, however, does not desire to take advantage of or enforce the penalties for the unwise actions of these nations.

"The President is anxious to renew the relations which existed at the breaking out of the rebellion.

"We, as representatives of the President, are empowered to enter into new treaties with the proper delegates of the tribes located within the so-called Indian territory, and others above named, living west and north of the Indian territory.

"Such treaties must contain substantially the following stipulations:

"1. Each tribe must enter into a treaty for permanent peace and amity with themselves, each nation and tribe, and with the United States.

"2. Those settled in the Indian territory must bind themselves, when called upon by the government, to aid in compelling the Indians of the plains to maintain peaceful relations with each other, with the Indians in the territory, and with the United States.

"3. The institution of slavery, which has existed among several of the tribes, must be forthwith abolished, and measures taken for the unconditional emancipation of all persons held in bondage, and for their incorporation into the tribes on an equal footing with the original members, or suitably provided for.

"4. A stipulation in the treaties that slavery, or involuntary servitude, shall never exist in the tribe or nation, except in punishment of crime.

"5. A portion of the lands hitherto owned and occupied by you must be set apart for the friendly tribes in Kansas and elsewhere, on such terms as may be agreed upon by the parties and approved by government, or such as may be fixed by the government.

"6. It is the policy of the government, unless other arrangement be made, that all the nations and tribes in the Indian territory be formed into one consolidated government after the plan proposed by the Senate of the United States, in a bill for organizing the Indian territory.

"7. No white person, except officers, agents, and employés of the government, or of any internal improvement authorized by the government, will be permitted to reside in the territory, unless formally incorporated with some tribes, according to the usages of the band.

"BROTHERS: You have now heard and understand what are the views and wishes of the President; and the commissioners, as they told you yesterday, will expect definite answers from each of you upon the questions submitted.

"As we said yesterday, we say again, that, in any event, those who have always been loyal, although their nation may have gone over to the enemy, will be liberally provided for and dealt with."

I then caused copies of the statement and propositions to be prepared and furnished to each agent, with instructions that they be fully interpreted and explained to them. . . .

[*House Executive Document* no 1, 39th Cong., 1st sess., serial 1248, pp. 480-83.]

66.   Treaty with the Creeks

June 14, 1866

The treaty with the Creeks, signed in Washington in 1866, was one of the treaties made with the Five Civilized Tribes after the Civil War. It reinstated relations between the United States and the Creek Nation, required the emancipation of Negro slaves and relinquishment of territory by the Creeks for the use of other Indians, and provided for a cenfederated general council.

Treaty of cession and indemnity concluded at the city of Washington on the fourteenth day of June, in the year of our Lord one thousand eight hundred and sixty-six, by and between the United States, represented by Dennis N. Cooley, Commissioner of Indian Affairs, Elija Sells, superintendent of Indian affairs for the southern superintendency, and Col. Ely S. Parker, special commissioner, and the Creek Nation of Indians, represented by Ok-tars-sars-harjo, or Sands; Cow-e-to-me-co and Che-chu-chee, delegates at large, and D. N. McIntosh and James Smith, special delegates of the Southern Creeks.

PREAMBLE.

Whereas existing treaties between the United States and the Creek Nation have become insufficient to meet their mutual necessities; and whereas the Creeks made a treaty with the so-called Confederate States, on the tenth of July, one thousand eight hundred and sixty-one, whereby they ignored their allegiance to the United States, and unsettled the treaty relations existing between the Creeks and the United States, and did so render themselves liable to forfeit to the United States all benefits and advantages enjoyed by them in lands, annuities, protection, and immunities, including their lands and other property held by grant or gift from the United States; and whereas in view of said liabilities the United States require of the Creeks a portion of their land whereon to settle other Indians; and whereas a treaty of peace and amity was entered into between the United States and the Creeks and other tribes at Fort Smith, September *thirteenth* [tenth], eighteen hundred and sixty-five, whereby the Creeks revoked, cancelled, and repudiated the aforesaid treaty made with the so-called Confederate States; and whereas the United States, through its commissioners, in said treaty of peace and amity, promised to enter into treaty with the Creeks to arrange and settle all questions relating to and growing out of said treaty with the so-called Confederate States: Now, therefore, the United States, by its commissioners, and the above-named delegates of the Creek Nation, the day and year above mentioned, mutually stipulate and agree, on behalf of the respective parties, as follows, to wit:

ARTICLE 1. There shall be perpetual peace and friendship between the parties to this treaty, and the Creeks bind themselves to remain firm allies and friends of the United States, and never to take up arms against the United States, but always faithfully to aid in putting down its enemies. They also agree to remain at peace with all other Indian tribes; and, in return, the United States guarantees them quiet possession of their country, and protection against hostilities on the part of other tribes. In the event of hostilities, the United States agree that the tribe commencing and prosecuting the same shall, as far as may be practicable, make just reparation therefor. To insure this protection, the Creeks agree to a military occupation of their country, at any time, by the United States, and the United States agree to station and continue in said country from time to time, at its own expense, such force as may be necessary for that purpose. A general amnesty of all past offenses against the laws of the United States, committed by any member of the Creek Nation, is hereby declared. And the Creeks, anxious for the restoration of kind and friendly feelings among themselves, do hereby declare an amnesty for all past offenses against their government, and no Indian or Indians shall be proscribed, or any act of forfeiture or confiscation passed against those who have remained friendly to, or taken up arms against, the United States, but they shall enjoy equal privileges with other members of said tribe, and all laws heretofore passed inconsistent herewith are hereby declared inoperative.

ARTICLE 2. The Creeks hereby covenant and agree that henceforth neither slavery nor involuntary servitude, otherwise than in the punishment of crimes, whereof the parties shall have been duly convicted in accordance with laws applicable to all members of said tribe, shall ever exist in said nation; and inasmuch as there are among the Creeks many persons of African descent, who have no interest in the soil, it is stipulated that hereafter these persons lawfully residing in said Creek country under their laws and usages, or who have been thus residing in said country, and may return within one year from the ratification of this treaty, and their descendants and such others of the same race as may be permitted by the laws of the said nation to settle within the limits of the jurisdiction of the Creek Nation as citizens [there of,] shall have and enjoy all the rights and privileges of native citizens, including an equal interest in the soil and national funds, and the laws of the said nation shall be equally binding upon and give equal protection to all such persons, and all others, of whatsoever race or color, who may be adopted as citizens or members of said tribe.

ARTICLE 3. In compliance with the desire of the United States to locate other Indians and freedmen thereon, the Creeks hereby cede and convey to the United States, to be sold to and used as homes for such other civilized Indians as the United States may choose to settle thereon, the west half of their entire domain, to be divided by a line running north and south; the eastern half of said Creek lands, being retained by them, shall, except as herein otherwise stipulated, be forever set apart as a home for said Creek Nation; and in consideration of said cession of the west half of their lands, estimated to contain three millions two hundred and fifty thousand five hundred and sixty acres, the United States agree to pay the sum of thirty (30) cents per acre, amounting to nine hundred and seventy-five thousand one hundred and sixty-eight dollars, in the manner hereinafter provided, to wit: two hundred thousand dollars shall be paid per capita in money, unless otherwise directed by the President of the United States, upon the ratification of this treaty, to enable the Creeks to occupy, restore, and improve their farms, and to make their nation independent and self-sustaining, and to pay the damages sustained by the mission schools on the North Fork and the Arkansas Rivers, not to exceed two thousand dollars, and to pay the delegates such per diem as the agent and Creek council may agree upon, as a just and fair compensation, all of which shall be distributed for that purpose by the agent, with the advice of the Creek Council, under the direction of the Secretary of the Interior. One hundred thousand dollars shall be paid in money and divided to soldiers that enlisted in the Federal Army and the loyal refugee Indians and freedmen who were driven from their homes by the rebel

forces, to reimburse them in proportion to their respective losses; four hundred thousand dollars be paid in money and divided per capita to said Creek Nation, unless otherwise directed by the President of the United States, under the direction of the Secretary of the Interior, as the same may accrue from the sale of land to other Indians. The United States agree to pay to said Indians, in such manner and for such purposes as the Secretary of the Interior may direct, interest at the rate of five per cent. per annum from the date of the ratification of this treaty, on the amount hereinbefore agreed upon for said ceded lands, after deducting the said two hundred thousand dollars; the residue, two hundred and seventy-five thousand one hundred and sixty-eight dollars, shall remain in the Treasury of the United States, and the interest thereon, at the rate of five per centum per annum, be annually paid to said Creeks as above stipulated.

ARTICLE 4. [Provision for losses sustained by soldiers, loyal refugee Indians, and freedmen.]

ARTICLE 5. The Creek Nation hereby grant a right of way through their lands, to the Choctaw and Chickasaw country, to any company which shall be duly authorized by Congress, and shall, with the express consent and approbation of the Secretary of the Interior, undertake to construct a railroad from any point north of to any point in or south of the Creek country, and likewise from any point on their eastern to their western or southern boundary, but said railroad company, together with all its agents and employés, shall be subject to the laws of the United States relating to intercourse with Indian tribes, and also to such rules and regulations as may be prescribed by the Secretary of the Interior for that purpose, and the Creeks agree to sell to the United States, or any company duly authorized as aforesaid, such lands not legally owned or occupied by a member or members of the Creek Nation, lying along the line of said contemplated railroad, not exceeding on each side thereof a belt or strip of land three miles in width, at such price per acre as may be eventually agreed upon between said Creek Nation and the party or parties building said road, subject to the approval of the President of the United

100

States: *Provided, however,* That said land thus sold shall not be reconveyed, leased, or rented to, or be occupied by any one not a citizen of the Creek Nation, according to its laws and recognized usages: *Provided, also,* That officers, servants, and employés of said railroad necessary to its construction and management, shall not be excluded from such necessary occupancy, they being subject to the provisions of the Indian intercourse law and such rules and regulations as may be established by the Secretary of the Interior, nor shall any conveyance of any of said lands be made to the party building and managing said road until its completion as a first-class railroad, and its acceptance as such by the Secretary of the Interior. . . .

ARTICLE 7. The Creeks hereby agree that the Seminole tribe of Indians may sell and convey to the United States all or any portion of the Seminole lands, upon such terms as may be mutually agreed upon by and between the Seminoles and the United States.

ARTICLE 8. It is agreed that the Secretary of the Interior forthwith cause the line dividing the Creek country, as provided for by the terms of the sale of Creek lands to the United States in article third of this treaty, to be accurately surveyed under the direction of the Commissioner of Indian Affairs, the expenses of which survey shall be paid by the United States.

ARTICLE 9. Inasmuch as the agency buildings of the Creek tribe have been destroyed during the late war, it is further agreed that the United States shall at their own expense, not exceeding ten thousand dollars, cause to be erected suitable agency buildings, the sites whereof shall be selected by the agent of said tribe, in the reduced Creek reservation, under the direction of the superintendent of Indian affairs.

In consideration whereof, the Creeks hereby cede and relinquish to the United States one section of their lands, to be designated and selected by their agent, under the direction of the superintendent of Indian affairs, upon which said agency buildings shall be erected, which section of land shall revert to the Creek nation when said agency buildings are no longer used by the United States, upon said nation paying a fair and reasonable value for said buildings at the time vacated.

ARTICLE 10. The Creeks agree to such legislation as Congress and the President of the United States may deem necessary for the better administration of justice and the protection of the rights of person and property within the Indian territory: *Provided, however,* [That] said legislation shall not in any manner interfere with or annul their present tribal organization, rights, laws, privileges, and customs. The Creeks also agree that a general council, consisting of delegates elected by each nation or tribe lawfully resident within the Indian territory, may be annually convened in said territory, which council shall be organized in such manner and possess such powers as are hereinafter described. [Detailed provisions for the general council.]

ARTICLE 11. The stipulations of this treaty are to be a full settlement of all claims of said Creek Nation for damages and losses of every kind growing out of the late rebellion and all expenditures by the United States of annuities in clothing and feeding refugee and destitute Indians since the diversion of annuities for that purpose consequent upon the late war with the so-called Confederate States; and the Creeks hereby ratify and confirm all such diversions of annuities heretofore made from the funds of the Creek Nation by the United States, and the United States agree that no annuities shall be diverted from the objects for which they were originally devoted by treaty stipulations with the Creeks, to the use of refugee and destitute Indians other than the Creeks or members of the Creek Nation after the close of the present fiscal year, June thirtieth, eighteen hundred and sixty-six.

ARTICLE 12. The United States re-affirms and re-assumes all obligations of treaty stipulations with the Creek Nation entered into before the treaty of said Creek Nation with the so-called Confederate States, July tenth, eighteen hundred and sixty-one, not inconsistent herewith; and further agrees to renew all payments accruing by force of said treaty stipulations from and after the close of the present fiscal year, June thirtieth, eighteen hundred and sixty-six, except as is provided in article eleventh.

ARTICLE 13. A quantity of land not exceeding one hundred and sixty acres, to be selected according to legal subdivision, in one body, and to include their improvements, is hereby granted to every religious society or denomination, which has erected, or which, with the consent of the Indians, may hereafter erect, buildings within the Creek country for missionary or educational purposes; but no land thus granted, nor the buildings which have been or may be erected thereon, shall ever be sold or otherwise disposed of, except with the consent and approval of the Secretary of the Interior; and whenever any such lands or buildings shall be so sold or disposed of, the proceeds thereof shall be applied, under the direction of the Secretary of the Interior, to the support and maintenance of other similiar establishments for the benefit of the Creeks and such other persons as may be or may hereafter become members of the tribe according to its laws, customs, and usages; and if at any time said improvements shall be abandoned for one year for missionary or educational purposes, all the rights herein granted for missionary and educational purposes shall revert to the said Creek Nation.

ARTICLE 14. It is further agreed that all treaties heretofore entered into between the United States and the Creek Nation which are inconsistent with any of the articles or provisions of this treaty shall be, and are hereby, rescinded and annulled; and it is further agreed that ten thousand dollars shall be paid by the United States, or so much thereof as may be necessary, to pay the expenses incurred in negotiating the foregoing treaty. . . .

[Charles J. Kappler, ed. *Indian Affairs: Laws and Treaties*, 2:931-37.]

67. Report of the Doolittle Committee
January 26, 1867

The Joint Special Committee of Congress, appointed under a joint resolution of March 3, 1865, and chaired by Senator James Doolittle of Wisconsin, submitted its report in January 1867. The report, entitled "Condition of the Indian Tribes," discussed reasons for the decrease in Indian population and made recommendations for ameliorating the conditions.

At its meeting on the 9th of March the following subdivision of labor was made: To Messrs. Doolittle, Foster, and Ross was assigned the duty of inquiring into Indian affairs in the State of Kansas, the Indian Territory, Colorado, New Mexico, and Utah.

To Messrs. Nesmith and Higby the same duty was assigned in the States of California, Oregon, and Nevada, and in the Territories of Washington, Idaho, and Montana.

To Messrs. Windom and Hubbard the same duty was assigned in the State of Minnesota and in the Territories of Nebraska, Dakota, and upper Montana. The result of their inquiries is to be found in the appendix accompanying this report.

The work was immense, covering a continent. While they have gathered a vast amount of testimony and important information bearing upon our Indian affairs, they are still conscious that their explorations have been imperfect.

As it was found impossible for the members of the committee in person to take the testimony or from personal observations to learn all that they deemed necessary to form a correct judgment of the true condition of the Indian tribes, they deemed it wise, by a circular letter addressed to officers of the regular army, experienced Indian agents and superintendents, and to other persons of great knowledge in Indian affairs, to obtain from them a statement of the result of their experience and information; which, with the testimony taken by the various members of the sub-committees, is also to be found in the appendix.

The committee have arrived at the following conclusions:

First. The Indians everywhere, with the exception of the tribes within the Indian Territory, are rapidly decreasing in numbers from various causes: By disease; by intemperance; by wars, among themselves and with the whites; by the steady and resistless emigration of white men into the territories of the west, which, confining the

Indians to still narrower limits, destroys that game which, in their normal state, constitutes their principal means of subsistence; and by the irrepressible conflict between a superior and an inferior race when brought in presence of each other. Upon this subject all the testimony agrees. . . .

INDIAN WARS WITH THE WHITES

Second. The committee are of opinion that in a large majority of cases Indian wars are to be traced to the aggressions of lawless white men, always to be found upon the frontier, or boundary line between savage and civilized life. Such is the statement of the most experienced officers of the army, and of all those who have been long conversant with Indian affairs. . . .

From whatever cause wars may be brought on, either between different Indian tribes or between the Indians and the whites, they are very destructive, not only of the lives of the warriors engaged in it, but of the women and children also, often becoming a war of extermination. Such is the rule of savage warfare, and it is difficult if not impossible to restrain white men, especially white men upon the frontiers, from adopting the same mode of warfare against the Indians. The indiscriminate slaughter of men, women, and children has frequently occurred in the history of Indian wars. But the fact which gives such terrible force to the condemnation of the wholesale massacre of Arrapahoes and Cheyennes, by the Colorado troops under Colonel Chivington, near Fort Lyon, was, that those Indians were there encamped under the direction of our own officers, and believed themselves to be under the protection of our flag. A full account of this bloody affair will be found also in the appendix. To the honor of the government it may be said that a just atonement for this violation of its faith was sought to be made in the late treaty with these tribes.

Third. Another potent cause of their decay is to be found in the loss of their hunting grounds and in the destruction of that game upon which the Indian subsists. This cause, always powerful, has of late greatly increased. Until the white settlements crossed the Mississippi, the Indians could still find hunting grounds without limit and game, especially the buffalo, in great abundance upon the western plains.

But the discovery of gold and silver in California, and in all the mountain territories, poured a flood of hardy and adventurous miners across those plains, and into all the valleys and gorges of the mountains from the east.

Two lines of railroad are rapidly crossing the plains, one by the valley of the Platte, and the other by the Smoky Hill. They will soon reach the Rocky mountains, crossing the centre of the great buffalo range in two lines from east to west. It is to be doubted if the buffalo in his migrations will many times cross a railroad where trains are passing and repassing, and with the disappearance of the buffalo from this immense region, all the powerful tribes of the plains will inevitably disappear, and remain north of the Platte or south of the Arkansas. Another route further north, from Minnesota by the Upper Missouri, and one further south, from Arkansas by the Canadian, are projected, and will soon be pressed forward. These will drive the last vestige of the buffalo from all the region east of the Rocky mountains, and put an end to the wild man's means of life.

On the other hand, the emigration from California and Oregon into the Territories from the west is filling every valley and gorge of the mountains with the most energetic and fearless men in the world. In those wild regions, where no civil law has ever been administered, and where our military forces have scarcely penetrated, these adventurers are practically without any law, except such as they impose upon themselves, viz: the law of necessity and of self-defence.

Even after territorial governments are established over them in form by Congress, the population is so sparse and the administration of the civil law so feeble that the people are practically without any law but their own will. In their eager search for gold or fertile tracts of land, the boundaries of Indian reservations are wholly disregarded; conflicts ensue; exterminating wars follow, in which the Indian is, of course, at the last, overwhelmed if not destroyed.

THE INDIAN BUREAU.

Fourth. The question whether the Indian

103

bureau should be placed under the War Department or retained in the Department of the Interior is one of considerable importance, and both sides have very warm advocates. Military men generally, unite in recommending that change to be made, while civilians, teachers, missionaries, agents and superintendents, and those not in the regular army generally oppose it. The arguments and objections urged by each are not without force.

The argument in favor of it is that in case of hostilities the military forces must assume control of our relations to the hostile tribes, and therefore it is better for the War Department to have the entire control, both in peace and in war; secondly, that the annuity goods and clothing, paid to Indians under treaty stipulations, will be more faithfully and honestly made by officers of the regular army, who hold their places for life, and are subject to military trials for misconduct, than when made by the agents and superintendents appointed under the Interior Department; and thirdly, that it would prevent conflict between different departments in the administration of their affairs.

Upon the other side it is urged with great force that, for the proper administration of Indian affairs, there must be some officer of the government whose duty it is to remain upon the reservations with the tribes and to look after their affairs; that, as their hunting grounds are taken away, the reservation system, which is the only alternative to their extermination, must be adopted. When the Indians are once located upon them, farmers, teachers, and missionaries become essential to any attempt at civilization—are absolutely necessary to take the first step toward changing the wild hunter into a cultivator of the soil—to change the savage into a civilized man. The movement of troops from post to post is, of necessity, sudden and frequent, and, therefore, the officers of the army, however competent, cannot take charge of the affairs and interests of Indians upon reservations any longer than military force is required to compel the Indians to remain upon them, as in the case of the Navajoes in New Mexico, and during that time even proper and competent persons acting as agents, farmers, teachers, and missionaries, devoting their whole time to these

occupations, can serve that purpose much better than officers of the army.

While it is true many agents, teachers, and employés of the government are inefficient, faithless, and even guilty of peculations and fraudulent practices upon the government and upon the Indians, it is equally true that military posts among the Indians have frequently become centres of demoralization and destruction to the Indian tribes, while the blunders and want of discretion of inexperienced officers in command have brought on long and expensive wars, the cost of which, being included in the expenditures of the army, are never seen and realized by the people of the country. . . .

Another strong reason for retaining the Indian Bureau in the Department of the Interior is, that the making of treaties and the disposition of the lands and funds of the Indians is of necessity intimately connected with our public land system, and, with all its important land questions, would seem to fall naturally under the jurisdiction of the Interior Department.

The inconveniences arising from the occasional conflicts and jealousies between officers appointed under the Interior and War Departments are not without some benefits also; to some extent they serve as a check upon each other; neither are slow to point to the mistakes and abuses of the other. It is therefore proper that they should be independent of each other, receive their appointments from and report to different heads of departments. Weighing this matter and all the arguments for and against the proposed change, your committee are unanimously of the opinion that the Indian Bureau should remain where it is.

BOARDS OF INSPECTION.

Fifth. In our Indian system, beyond all doubt, there are evils, growing out of the nature of the case itself, which can never be remedied until the Indian race is civilized or shall entirely disappear.

The committee are satisfied that these evils are sometimes greatly aggravated, not so much by the system adopted by the government in dealing with the Indian tribes, as by the abuses of that system.

As the best means of correcting those

abuses and ameliorating those evils, the committee recommend the subdivision of the Territories and States wherein the Indian tribes remain into five inspection districts, and the appointment of five boards of inspection; and they earnestly recommend the passage of Senate bill 188, now pending before the House. That bill was unanimously recommended by the joint special committee, and also recommended by the committees of both Houses upon Indian Affairs. It is the most certainly efficient mode of preventing these abuses which they have been able to devise. . . .

It is believed that such boards of inspec-

tion thus organized and composed of the men who should be appointed to fill them, would save the country from many useless wars with the Indians, and secure in all branches of the Indian service greater efficiency and fidelity. If such boards should cost the government a hundred and fifty thousand dollars annually, and should avert but one Indian war in ten years, still, upon the score of economy alone, the government would be repaid five hundred per cent.

[*Senate Report* no. 156, 39th Cong., 2d sess., serial 1279, pp. 3-10.]

68.   Creation of an Indian Peace Commission

July 20, 1867

The outbreak of wars on the plains in the mid-1860s convinced Congress that a serious peace offensive was in order. It authorized a Peace Commission, which was to determine the reasons for Indian hostilities and at its discretion to make treaty arrangements and to select reservations for the tribes.

An Act to establish Peace with certain Hostile Indian Tribes.

Be it enacted . . . , That the President of the United States be, and he is hereby, authorized to appoint a commission to consist of three officers of the army not below the rank of brigadier general, who, together with N. G. Taylor, Commissioner of Indian Affairs, John B. Henderson, Chairman of the Committee of Indian Affairs of the Senate, S. F. Tappan, and John B. Sanborn, shall have power and authority to call together the chiefs and headmen of such bands or tribes of Indians as are now waging war against the United States or committing depredations upon the people thereof, to ascertain the alleged reasons for their acts of hostility, and in their discretion, under the direction of the President, to make and conclude with said bands or tribes such treaty stipulations, subject to the action of the Senate, as may remove all just causes of complaint on their part, and at the same time establish security for person and property along the lines of railroad now being constructed to the Pacific and other thoroughfares of travel to the western Territories, and such as will most likely insure civilization for

the Indians and peace and safety for the whites.

SEC. 2. *And be it further enacted,* That said commissioners are required to examine and select a district or districts of country having sufficient area to receive all the Indian tribes now occupying territory east of the Rocky mountains, not now peacefully residing on permanent reservations under treaty stipulations, to which the government has the right of occupation or to which said commissioners can obtain the right of occupation, and in which district or districts there shall be sufficient tillable or grazing land to enable the said tribes, respectively, to support themselves by agricultural and pastoral pursuits. Said district or districts, when so selected, and the selection approved by Congress, shall be and remain permanent homes for said Indians to be located thereon, and no person[s] not members of said tribes shall ever be permitted to enter thereon without the permission of the tribes interested, except officers and employees of the United States: *Provided,* That the district or districts shall be so located as not to interfere with travel on highways located by authority of the United States, nor with the route of the Northern Pacific Railroad, the Union Pacific Railroad, the Union Pacific Railroad

105

Eastern Division, or the proposed route of the Atlantic and Pacific Railroad by the way of Albuquerque.

SEC. 3. *And be it further enacted*, That the following sums of money are hereby appropriated out of any moneys in the treasury, to wit: To carry out the provisions of the preceding sections of this act, one hundred and fifty thousand dollars; to enable the Secretary of the Interior to subsist such friendly Indians as may have separated or may hereafter separate themselves from the hostile bands or tribes and seek the protection of the United States, three hundred thousand dollars.

SEC. 4. *And be it further enacted*, That the Secretary of War be required to furnish transporation, subsistence, and protection to the commissioners herein named during the discharge of their duties.

SEC. 5. *And be it further enacted*, That if said commissioners fail to secure the consent of the Indians to remove to the reservations and fail to secure peace, then the Secretary of War, under the direction of the President, is hereby authorized to accept the services of mounted volunteers from the Governors of the several States and Territories, in organized companies and battalions, not exceeding four thousand men in number, and for such term of service as, in his judgment, may be necessary for the suppression of Indian hostilities.

SEC. 6. *And be it further enacted*, That all volunteers so accepted shall be placed upon the same footing, in respect to pay, clothing, subsistence, and equipment, as the troops of the regular army.

SEC. 7. *And be it further enacted*, That said commissioners report their doings under this act to the President of the United States, including any such treaties and all correspondence as well as evidence by them taken.

[*U.S. Statutes at Large*, 15:17-18.]

69. Report of the Indian Peace Commission

January 7, 1868

The Peace Commission, in its initial report of January 7, 1868, reviewed the causes of Indian hostilities and severely indicted white treatment of the Indians. It urged bringing the Indians into white civilization and made formal recommendations of means to that end.

. . . . In making treaties it was enjoined on us to remove, if possible, the causes of complaint on the part of the Indians. This would be no easy task. We have done the best we could under the circumstances, but it is now rather late in the day to think of obliterating from the minds of the present generation the remembrance of wrong. Among civilized men war usually springs from a sense of injustice. The best possible way then to avoid war is to do no act of injustice. When we learn that the same rule holds good with Indians, the chief difficulty is removed. But, it is said our wars with them have been almost constant. Have we been uniformly unjust? We answer, unhesitatingly, yes! We are aware that the masses of our people have felt kindly toward them, and the legislation of Congress has always been conceived in the best intentions, but it has been erroneous in fact or perverted in execution. Nobody pays any attention to Indian matters. This is a deplorable fact. Members of Congress understand the negro question, and talk learnedly of finance, and other problems of political economy, but when the progress of settlement reaches the Indian's home, the only question considered is, "how best to get his lands." When they are obtained the Indian is lost sight of. While our missionary societies and benevolent associations have annually collected thousands of dollars from the charitable, to be sent to Asia and Africa for purposes of civilization, scarcely a dollar is expended or a thought bestowed on the civilization of Indians at our very doors. Is it because the Indians are not worth the effort at civilization? Or is it because our people, who have grown rich in the occupation of their former lands—too often taken by force or procured in fraud—will not contribute? It would be harsh to insinuate that covetous eyes have possibly been set on their remaining posses-

106

sions, and extermination harbored as a means of accomplishing it. As we know that our legislators and nine-tenths of our people are actuated by no such spirit, would it not be well to so regulate our future conduct in this matter as to exclude the possibility of so unfavorable an inference?

We are aware that it is an easy task to condemn the errors of former times, as well as a very thankless one to criticise those of the present; but the past policy of the government has been so much at variance with our ideas of treating this important subject, that we hope to be indulged in a short allusion to it.

The wave of our population has been from the east to the west. The Indian was found on the Atlantic seaboard, and thence to the Rocky mountains lived numerous distinct tribes, each speaking a language as incomprehensible to the other as was our language to any of them. As our settlements penetrated the interior, the border came in contact with some Indian tribe. The white and Indian must mingle together and jointly occupy the country, or one of them must abandon it. If they could have lived together, the Indian by this contact would soon have become civilized and war would have been impossible. All admit this would have been beneficial to the Indian. Even if we thought it would not have been hurtful to the white man, we would not venture on such an assertion, for we know too well his pride of race. But suppose it had proved a little inconvenient as well as detrimental, it is questionable whether the policy adopted has not been more injurious. What prevented their living together? First. The antipathy of race. Second. The difference of customs and manners arising from their tribal or clannish organization. Third. The difference in language, which, in a great measure, barred intercourse and a proper understanding each of the other's motives and intentions.

Now by educating the children of these tribes in the English language these differences would have disappeared, and civilization would have followed at once. Nothing then would have been left but the antipathy of race, and that too is always softened in the beams of a higher civilization.

Naturally the Indian has many noble qualities. He is the very embodiment of courage. Indeed at times he seems insensible of fear. If he is cruel and revengeful it is because he is outlawed, and his companion is the wild beast. Let civilized man be his companion and the association warms into life virtues of the rarest worth. Civilization has driven him back from the home he loved; it has often tortured and killed him, but it never could make him a slave. As we have had so little respect for those we did enslave, to be consistent this element of Indian character should challenge some admiration.

But suppose, when civilized, our pride had still rejected his association, we could at least have removed the causes of war by giving him a home to himself, where he might, with his own race, have cultivated the arts of peace. Through sameness of language is produced sameness of sentiment and thought; customs and habits are moulded and assimilated in the same way, and thus in process of time the differences producing trouble would have been gradually obliterated. By civilizing one tribe others would have followed. Indians of different tribes associate with each other on terms of equality; they have not the Bible, but their religion, which we call superstition, teaches them that the Great Spirit made us all. In the difference of language to-day lies two-thirds of our trouble. . . .

The next injunction upon us was to make secure our frontier settlements and the building of our railroads to the Pacific. If peace is maintained with the Indian, every obstacle to the spread of our settlements and the rapid construction of the railroads will be removed. To maintain peace with the Indian, let the frontier settler treat him with humanity, and railroad directors see to it that he is not shot down by employés in wanton cruelty. In short, if settlers and railroad men will treat Indians as they would treat whites under similar circumstances, we apprehend but little trouble will exist. They must acquaint themselves with the treaty obligations of the government, and respect them as the highest law of the land. Instead of regarding the Indian as an enemy, let them regard him as a friend, and they will almost surely receive his friendship and es-

107

teem. If they will look upon him as an unfortunate human being, deserving their sympathy and care, instead of a wild beast to be feared and detested, then their own hearts have removed the chief danger.

We were also required to suggest some plan for the civilization of Indians. In our judgment, to civilize is to remove the causes of war, and under that head we suggested a plan for civilizing those east of the mountains. But as it is impracticable to bring within the two districts named all the Indians under our jurisdiction, we beg the privilege to make some general suggestions, which may prove beneficial to the service.

1. We recommend that the intercourse laws with the Indian tribes be thoroughly revised. They were adopted when the Indian bureau was connected with the War Department. Since that time the jurisdiction has been transferred to the Interior Department. This was done by simply declaring that the authority over this subject, once exercised by the Secretary of War, should now be exercised by the Secretary of the Interior. Some of the duties enjoined by these laws are intimately connected with the War Department, and it is questionable whether they were intended to be transferred to the Secretary of the Interior. If they were so transferred, the military officers insist that the command of the army is, *pro tanto*, withdrawn from them. If not transferred, the Indian department insists that its powers are insufficient for its own protection in the administration of its affairs. Hence the necessity of clearly defining the line separating the rights and duties of the two departments.

2. This brings us to consider the much mooted question whether the bureau should belong to the civil or military department of the government. To determine this properly we must first know what is to be the future treatment of the Indians. If we intend to have war with them the bureau should go to the Secretary of War. If we intend to have peace it should be in the civil department. In our judgment, such wars are wholly unnecessary, and hoping that the government and the country will agree with us, we cannot now advise the change. It is possible, however, that, despite our efforts to maintain peace, war may be forced on us by some

tribe or tribes of Indians. In the event of such occurrence it may be well to provide, in the revision of the intercourse laws or elsewhere, at what time the civil jurisdiction shall cease and the military jurisdiction begin. If thought advisable, also, Congress may authorize the President to turn over to the military the exclusive control of such tribes as may be continually hostile or unmanageable. Under the plan which we have suggested the chief duties of the bureau will be to educate and instruct in the peaceful arts—in other words, to civilize the Indians. The military arm of the government is not the most admirably adapted to discharge duties of this character. We have the highest possible appreciation of the officers of the army, and fully recognize their proverbial integrity and honor; but we are satisfied that not one in a thousand would like to teach Indian children to read and write, or Indian men to sow and reap. These are emphatically civil, and not military, occupations. But it is insisted that the present Indian service is corrupt, and this change should be made to get rid of the dishonest. That there are many bad men connected with the service cannot be denied. The records are abundant to show that agents have pocketed the funds appropriated by the government and driven the Indians to starvation. It cannot be doubted that Indian wars have originated from this cause. The Sioux war, in Minnesota, is supposed to have been produced in this way. For a long time these officers have been selected from partisan ranks, not so much on account of honesty and qualification, as for devotion to party interests and their willingness to apply the money of the Indian to promote the selfish schemes of local politicians. We do not doubt that some such men may be in the service of the bureau now, and this leads us to suggest:

3. That Congress pass an act fixing a day (not later than the 1st of February, 1869) when the offices of all superintendents, agents, and special agents shall be vacated. Such persons as have proved themselves competent and faithful may be reappointed. Those who have proved unfit will find themselves removed without an opportunity to divert attention from their own unworthiness by professions of party zeal.

4. We believe the Indian question to be

one of such momentous importance, as it respects both the honor and interests of the nation, as to require for its proper solution an undivided responsibility. The vast and complicated duties now devolved upon the Secretary of the Interior leave him too little time to examine and determine the multiplicity of questions necessarily connected with the government and civilization of a race. The same may be said of the Secretary of War. As things now are, it is difficult to fix responsibility. When errors are committed the civil department blames the military; the military retort by the charge of inefficiency or corruption against the officers of the bureau. The Commissioner of Indian Affairs escapes responsibility by pointing to the Secretary of the Interior, while the Secretary may well respond that, though in theory he may be responsible, practically he is governed by the head of the bureau. We, therefore, recommend that Indian affairs be committed to an independent bureau or department. Whether the head of the department should be made a member of the President's cabinet is a matter for the discretion of Congress and yourself, and may be as well settled without any suggestions from us.

5. We cannot close this report without alluding to another matter calling for the special attention of Congress. Governors of Territories are now *ex officio* superintendents of Indian affairs within their respective jurisdictions. The settlements in the new Territories are generally made on Indian lands before the extinguishment of the Indian title. If difficulties ensue between the whites and Indians, the governor too frequently neglects the rights of the red man, and yields to the demands of those who have votes to promote his political aspirations in the organization of the forthcoming State. Lest any acting governor may suppose himself alluded to, we take occasion to disclaim such intention. We might cite instances of gross outrage in the past, but we prefer to base the recommendation upon general principles, which can be readily understood.

And in this connection we deem it of the highest importance that—

6. No governor or legislature of States or Territories be permitted to call out and equip troops for the purpose of carrying on war against Indians. It was Colorado troops

that involved us in the war of 1864-'65 with the Cheyennes. It was a regiment of hundred-day men that perpetrated the butchery at Sand creek, and took from the treasury millions of money. A regiment of Montana troops, last September, would have involved us in an almost interminable war with the Crows but for the timely intervention of the military authorities. If we must have Indian wars, let them be carried on by the regular army, whose officers are generally actuated by the loftiest principles of humanity, and the honor of whose profession requires them to respect the rules of civilized warfare.

7. In reviewing the intercourse laws it would be well to prescribe anew the conditions upon which persons may be authorized to trade. At present every one trades with or without the authority of the bureau officers, on giving a bond approved by a judge of one of the district courts. Corrupt and dangerous men thus find their way among the Indians, who cheat them in trade, and sow the seeds of dissension and trouble.

8. New provision should be made authorizing and positively directing the military authorities to remove white persons who persist in trespassing on Indian reservations and unceded Indian lands.

9. The Navajo Indians in New Mexico were for several years held as prisoners of war at the Bosque Redondo, at a very great expense to the government. They have now been turned over to the Interior Department, and must be subsisted as long as they remain there. We propose that a treaty be made with them, or their consent in some way obtained, to remove at an early day to the southern district selected by us, where they may soon be made self-supporting.

10. We suggest that the President may, at times, appoint some person or persons in the distant Territories, either civilians or military men, to make inspection of Indian affairs, and report to him.

11. A new commission should be appointed, or the present one be authorized to meet the Sioux next spring, according to our agreement, and also to arrange with the Navajoes for their removal. It might be well, also, in case our suggestions are adopted in regard to selecting Indian territories, to extend the powers of the commission, so as to

enable us to conclude treaties or agreements with tribes confessedly at peace, looking to their concentration upon the reservations indicated. . . .

[*House Executive Document* no. 97, 40th Cong., 2d sess., serial 1337, pp. 15-17, 20-22.]

70. Treaty of Fort Laramie
April 29, 1868

A treaty with the Sioux and their allies was drawn up by the Indian Peace Commission at Fort Laramie in 1868. It recognized hunting rights of the Indians in the Powder River area, closed the Bozeman Trail and withdrew the military posts built to protect it, and established a Sioux reservation west of the Missouri in what became the state of South Dakota.

Articles of a treaty made and concluded by and between Lieutenant-General William T. Sherman, General William S. Harney, General Alfred H. Terry, General C. C. Augur, J.B. Henderson, Nathaniel G. Taylor, John B. Sanborn, and Samuel F. Tappan, duly appointed commissioners on the part of the United States, and the different bands of the Sioux Nation of Indians, by their chiefs and head-men, whose names are hereto subscribed, they being duly authorized to act in the premises.

ARTICLE 1. From this day forward all war between the parties to this agreement shall forever cease. The Government of the United States desires peace, and its honor is hereby pledged to keep it. The Indians desire peace, and they now pledge their honor to maintain it.

If bad men among the whites, or among other people subject to the authority of the United States, shall commit any wrong upon the person or property of the Indians, the United States will, upon proof made to the agent and forwarded to the Commissioner of Indian Affairs at Washington City, proceed at once to cause the offender to be arrested and punished according to the laws of the United States, and also re-imburse the injured person for the loss sustained.

If bad men among the Indians shall commit a wrong or depredation upon the person or property of any one, white, black, or Indian, subject to the authority of the United States, and at peace therewith, the Indians herein named solemnly agree that they will, upon proof made to their agent and notice by him, deliver up the wrong-doer to the United States, to be tried and punished according to its laws; and in case they wil-fully refuse so to do, the person injured shall be re-imbursed for his loss from the annuities or other moneys due or to become due to them under this or other treaties made with the United States. And the President, on advising with the Commissioner of Indian Affairs, shall prescribe such rules and regulations for ascertaining damages under the provisions of this article as in his judgment may be proper. But no one sustaining loss while violating the provisions of this treaty or the laws of the United States shall be re-imbursed therefor.

ARTICLE 2. The United States agrees that the following district of country, to wit, viz: commencing on the east bank of the Missouri River where the forty-sixth parallel of north latitude crosses the same, thence along low-water mark down said east bank to a point opposite where the northern line of the State of Nebraska strikes the river, thence west across said river, and along the northern line of Nebraska to the one hundred and fourth degree of longitude west from Greenwich, thence north on said meridian to a point where the forty-sixth parallel of north latitude intercepts the same, thence due east along said parallel to the place of beginning; and in addition thereto, all existing reservations on the east bank of said river shall be, and the same is, set apart for the absolute and undisturbed use and occupation of the Indians herein named, and for such other friendly tribes or individual Indians as from time to time they may be willing, with the consent of the United States, to admit amongst them; and the United States now solemnly agrees that no persons except those herein designated and authorized so to do, and except such officers,

110

agents, and employés of the Government as may be authorized to enter upon Indian reservations in discharge of duties enjoined by law, shall ever be permitted to pass over, settle upon, or reside in the territory described in this article, or in such territory as may be added to this reservation for the use of said Indians, and henceforth they will and do hereby relinquish all claims or right in and to any portion of the United States or Territories, except such as is embraced within the limits aforesaid, and except as hereinafter provided.

ARTICLE 3. If it should appear from actual survey or other satisfactory examination of said tract of land that it contains less than one hundred and sixty acres of tillable land for each person who, at the time, may be authorized to reside on it under the provisions of this treaty, and a very considerable number of such persons shall be disposed to commence cultivating the soil as farmers, the United States agrees to set apart, for the use of said Indians, as herein provided, such additional quantity of arable land, adjoining to said reservation, or as near to the same as it can be obtained, as may be required to provide the necessary amount.

ARTICLE 4. The United States agrees, at its own proper expense, to construct at some place on the Missouri River, near the center of said reservation, where timber and water may be convenient, the following buildings, to wit: a warehouse, a store-room for the use of the agent in storing goods belonging to the Indians, to cost not less than twenty-five hundred dollars; an agency-building for the residence of the agent, to cost not exceeding three thousand dollars; a residence for the physician, to cost not more than three thousand dollars; and five other buildings, for a carpenter, farmer, blacksmith, miller, and engineer, each to cost not exceeding two thousand dollars; also a school-house or mission-building, so soon as a sufficient number of children can be induced by the agent to attend school, which shall not cost exceeding five thousand dollars.

The United States agrees further to cause to be erected on said reservation, near the other buildings herein authorized, a good steam circular-saw mill, with a grist-mill and shingle-machine attached to the same, to cost not exceeding eight thousand dollars.

ARTICLE 5. The United States agrees that the agent for said Indians shall in the future make his home at the agency-building; that he shall reside among them, and keep an office open at all times for the purpose of prompt and diligent inquiry into such matters of complaint by and against the Indians as may be presented for investigation under the provisions of their treaty stipulations, as also for the faithful discharge of other duties enjoined on him by law. In all cases of depredation on person or property he shall cause the evidence to be taken in writing and forwarded, together with his findings, to the Commissioner of Indian Affairs, whose decision, subject to the revision of the Secretary of the Interior, shall be binding on the parties to this treaty.

ARTICLE 6. If any individual belonging to said tribes of Indians, or legally incorporated with them, being the head of a family, shall desire to commence farming, he shall have the privilege to select, in the presence and with the assistance of the agent then in charge, a tract of land within said reservation, not exceeding three hundred and twenty acres in extent, which tract, when so selected, certified, and recorded in the "land-book," as herein directed, shall cease to be held in common, but the same may be occupied and held in the exclusive possession of the person selecting it, and of his family, so long as he or they may continue to cultivate it.

Any person over eighteen years of age, not being the head of a family, may in like manner select and cause to be certified to him or her, for purposes of cultivation, a quantity of land not exceeding eighty acres in extent, and thereupon be entitled to the exclusive possession of the same as above directed.

For each tract of land so selected a certificate, containing a description thereof and the name of the person selecting it, with a certificate endorsed thereon that the same has been recorded, shall be delivered to the party entitled to it, by the agent, after the same shall have been recorded by him in a book to be kept in his office, subject to inspection, which said book shall be known as the "Sioux Land-Book."

The President may, at any time, order a survey of the reservation, and, when so sur-

111

veyed, Congress shall provide for protecting the rights of said settlers in their improvements, and may fix the character of the title held by each. The United States may pass such laws on the subject of alienation and descent of property between the Indians and their descendants as may be thought proper. And it is further stipulated that any male Indians, over eighteen years of age, of any band or tribe that is or shall hereafter become a party to this treaty, who now is or who shall hereafter become a resident or occupant of any reservation or Territory not included in the tract of country designated and described in this treaty for the permanent home of the Indians, which is not mineral land, nor reserved by the United States for special purposes other than Indian occupation, and who shall have made improvements thereon of the value of two hundred dollars or more, and continuously occupied the same as a homestead for the term of three years, shall be entitled to receive from the United States a patent for one hundred and sixty acres of land including his said improvements, the same to be in the form of the legal subdivisions of the surveys of the public lands. Upon application in writing, sustained by the proof of two disinterested witnesses, made to the register of the local land-office when the land sought to be entered is within a land district, and when the tract sought to be entered is not in any land district, then upon said application and proof being made to the Commissioner of the General Land-Office, and the right of such Indian or Indians to enter such tract or tracts of land shall accrue and be perfect from the date of his first improvements thereon, and shall continue as long as he continues his residence and improvements, and no longer. And any Indian or Indians receiving a patent for land under the foregoing provisions, shall thereby and from thenceforth become and be a citizen of the United States, and be entitled to all the privileges and immunities of such citizens, and shall, at the same time, retain all his rights to benefits accruing to Indians under this treaty.

ARTICLE 7. In order to insure the civilization of the Indians entering into this treaty, the necessity of education is admitted, especially of such of them as are or may be settled on said agricultural reservations, and they therefore pledge themselves to compel their children, male and female, between the ages of six and sixteen years, to attend school; and it is hereby made the duty of the agent for said Indians to see that this stipulation is strictly complied with; and the United States agrees that for every thirty children between said ages who can be induced or compelled to attend school, a house shall be provided and a teacher competent to teach the elementary branches of an English education shall be furnished, who will reside among said Indians, and faithfully discharge his or her duties as a teacher. The provisions of this article to continue for not less than twenty years.

ARTICLE 8. When the head of a family or lodge shall have selected lands and received his certificate as above directed, and the agent shall be satisfied that he intends in good faith to commence cultivating the soil for a living, he shall be entitled to receive seeds and agricultural implements for the first year, not exceeding in value one hundred dollars, and for each succeeding year he shall continue to farm, for a period of three years more, he shall be entitled to receive seeds and implements as aforesaid, not exceeding in value twenty-five dollars.

And it is further stipulated that such persons as commence farming shall receive instruction from the farmer herein provided for, and whenever more than one hundred persons shall enter upon the cultivation of the soil, a second blacksmith shall be provided, with such iron, steel, and other material as may be needed.

ARTICLE 9. At any time after ten years from the making of this treaty, the United States shall have the privilege of withdrawing the physician, farmer, blacksmith, carpenter, engineer, and miller herein provided for, but in case of such withdrawal, an additional sum thereafter of ten thousand dollars per annum shall be devoted to the education of said Indians, and the Commissioner of Indian Affairs shall, upon careful inquiry into their condition, make such rules and regulations for the expenditure of said sum as will best promote the educational and moral improvement of said tribes.

ARTICLE 10. In lieu of all sums of money or other annuities provided to be paid to the

Indians herein named, under any treaty or treaties heretofore made, the United States agrees to deliver at the agency-house on the reservation herein named, on or before the first day of August of each year, for thirty years, the following articles, to wit:

For each male person over fourteen years of age, a suit of good substantial woolen clothing, consisting of coat, pantaloons, flannel shirt, hat, and a pair of home-made socks.

For each female over twelve years of age, a flannel skirt, or the goods necessary to make it, a pair of woolen hose, twelve yards of calico, and twelve yards of cotton domestics.

For the boys and girls under the ages named, such flannel and cotton goods as may be needed to make each a suit as aforesaid, together with a pair of woolen hose for each.

And in order that the Commissioner of Indian Affairs may be able to estimate properly for the articles herein named, it shall be the duty of the agent each year to forward to him a full and exact census of the Indians, on which the estimate from year to year can be based.

And in addition to the clothing herein named, the sum of ten dollars for each person entitled to the beneficial effects of this treaty shall be annually appropriated for a period of thirty years, while such persons roam and hunt, and twenty dollars for each person who engages in farming, to be used by the Secretary of the Interior in the purchase of such articles as from time to time the condition and necessities of the Indians may indicate to be proper. And if within the thirty years, at any time, it shall appear that the amount of money needed for clothing under this article can be appropriated to better uses for the Indians named herein, Congress may, by law, change the appropriation to other purposes; but in no event shall the amount of this appropriation be withdrawn or discontinued for the period named. And the President shall annually detail an officer of the Army to be present and attest the delivery of all the goods herein named to the Indians, and he shall inspect and report on the quantity and quality of the goods and the manner of their delivery. And it is hereby expressly stipulated that each

Indian over the age of four years, who shall have removed to and settled permanently upon said reservation and complied with the stipulations of this treaty, shall be entitled to receive from the United States, for the period of four years after he shall have settled upon said reservation, one pound of meat and one pound of flour per day, provided the Indians cannot furnish their own subsistence at an earlier date. And it is further stipulated that the United States will furnish and deliver to each lodge of Indians or family of persons legally incorporated with them, who shall remove to the reservation herein described and commence farming, one good American cow, and one good well-broken pair of American oxen within sixty days after such lodge or family shall have so settled upon said reservation.

ARTICLE 11. In consideration of the advantages and benefits conferred by this treaty, and the many pledges of friendship by the United States, the tribes who are parties to this agreement hereby stipulate that they will relinquish all right to occupy permanently the territory outside their reservation as herein defined, but yet reserve the right to hunt on any lands north of North Platte, and on the Republican Fork of the Smoky Hill River, so long as the buffalo may range thereon in such numbers as to justify the chase. And they, the said Indians, further expressly agree:

1st. That they will withdraw all opposition to the construction of the railroads now being built on the plains.

2nd. That they will permit the peaceful construction of any railroad not passing over their reservation as herein defined.

3d. That they will not attack any persons at home, or travelling, nor molest or disturb any wagon-trains, coaches, mules, or cattle belonging to the people of the United States, or to persons friendly therewith.

4th. They will never capture, or carry off from the settlements, white women or children.

5th. They will never kill or scalp white men, nor attempt to do them harm.

6th. They withdraw all pretence of opposition to the construction of the railroad now being built along the Platte River and westward to the Pacific Ocean, and they will not in future object to the construction of

113

railroads, wagon-roads, mail-stations, or other works of utility or necessity, which may be ordered or permitted by the laws of the United States. But should such roads or other works be constructed on the lands of their reservation, the Government will pay the tribe whatever amount of damage may be assessed by three disinterested commissioners to be appointed by the President for that purpose, one of said commissioners to be a chief or head-man of the tribe.

7th. They agree to withdraw all opposition to the military posts or roads now established south of the North Platte River, or that may be established, not in violation of treaties heretofore made or hereafter to be made with any of the Indian tribes.

ARTICLE 12. No treaty for the cession of any portion or part of the reservation herein described which may be held in common shall be of any validity or force as against the said Indians, unless executed and signed by at least three-fourths of all the adult male Indians, occupying or interested in the same; and no cession by the tribe shall be understood or construed in such manner as to deprive, without his consent, any individual member of the tribe of his rights to any tract of land selected by him, as provided in article 6 of this treaty.

ARTICLE 13. The United States hereby agrees to furnish annually to the Indians the physician, teachers, carpenter, miller, engineer, farmer, and blacksmiths as herein contemplated, and that such appropriations shall be made from time to time, on the estimates of the Secretary of the Interior, as will be sufficient to employ such persons.

ARTICLE 14. It is agreed that the sum of five hundred dollars annually, for three years from date, shall be expended in presents to the ten persons of said tribe who in the judgment of the agent may grow the most valuable crops for the respective year.

ARTICLE 15. The Indians herein named agree that when the agency-house or other buildings shall be constructed on the reservation named, they will regard said reservation their permanent home, and they will make no permanent settlement elsewhere; but they shall have the right, subject to the conditions and modifications of this treaty, to hunt, as stipulated in Article 11 hereof.

ARTICLE 16. The United States hereby agrees and stipulates that the country north of the North Platte River and east of the summits of the Big Horn Mountains shall be held and considered to be unceded Indian territory, and also stipulates and agrees that no white person or persons shall be permitted to settle upon or occupy any portion of the same; or without the consent of the Indians first had and obtained, to pass through the same; and it is further agreed by the United States that within ninety days after the conclusion of peace with all the bands of the Sioux Nation, the military posts now established in the territory in this article named shall be abandoned, and that the road leading to them and by them to the settlements in the Territory of Montana shall be closed.

ARTICLE 17. It is hereby expressly understood and agreed by and between the respective parties to this treaty that the execution of this treaty and its ratification by the United States Senate shall have the effect, and shall be construed as abrogating and annulling all treaties and agreements heretofore entered into between the respective parties hereto, so far as such treaties and agreements obligate the United States to furnish and provide money, clothing, or other articles of property to such Indians and bands of Indians as become parties to this treaty, but no further. . . .

[Charles J. Kappler, ed., *Indian Affairs: Laws and Treaties*, 2:998-1003.]

71. House Debate on Treaty-Making Power
June 18, 1868

When the commissioner of Indian affairs negotiated a treaty with the Osage Indians in Kansas in 1868, by which a railroad corporation was to receive the lands ceded by the Indians, members of the House of Representatives strongly objected. They argued that such alienation of lands instead of returning them to the public domain was wrong. They further denied that the treaty-making power could be used for such purposes. It was in large part this kind of opposition on the part of the House that led in 1871 to the end of treaty making with the Indians. Debate by Congressmen Sidney Clarke of Kansas and Glenni W. Scofield of Pennsylvania on June 18, 1868, is printed here.

. . . . Mr. CLARKE, of Kansas. Mr. Speaker, this is one of the most remarkable transactions that has ever occurred in the whole history of this Government, one which, in my judgment, demands the earnest, serious consideration of this House. It is neither more nor less than the transfer of eight million acres of land, which properly belong to the public domain of the United States, which belong to the landless millions in all parts of the country, into the hands of a railroad corporation, to be subjected to their supreme and unlimited control.

It will be my purpose, in the brief time I shall occupy the attention of the House, to state, as well as I may, the main facts connected with this proposed speculation. This most remarkable treaty now before the Senate, and being pressed upon their attention by the most remarkable and unjustifiable means, was made and framed in all its details and in all its essential features between the high contracting parties here in the city of Washington long before it was transmitted by the commission appointed by the President to the Indian country; it was so framed several months before it was sent to the Indian country by the commission appointed by the President; in fact, it was not made by the commission at all, but by the parties in interest, who design to absorb eight million acres of land which properly belong to the public domain of the United States. . . .

Sir, the people of Kansas are anxious to have an outlet upon the Gulf of Mexico. In this anxiety I fully share. But, sir, notwithstanding that, I have abundant evidence in extracts from newspapers and letters that they earnestly protest against this treaty in its present obnoxious form. My constituents demand protection from all systems of land monopoly. They protest against injustice in all its forms. They ask, if this land is to be used for the benefit of railroads, that provision be made to open it to immediate settlement at a stated price per acre, and that the profits accruing be used to construct at least eight hundred miles of different railroads, instead of one hundred and fifty miles, as provided in this treaty . . . .

Mr. Speaker, aside from all this, aside from the great injustice the treaty perpetrates upon the people of my State, it is wrong in principle, wrong in fact, and ought to be earnestly and sternly resisted by the Congress of the United States. I pass, then, to the consideration of the power of this House over this question. Perhaps if we act in accordance with the past policy of the Government in reference to the transfer of these Indian reservations to individuals and private corporations we have little power in connection with this question; but, sir, representing the people of the United States, representing the interests of the whole country, it appears to me it is within the province, and within the just prerogatives and powers, of this House to enter its protest, having the facts before it, on an examination into the case by one of the legally constituted committees of the House. It is clearly within our power to enter a protest against the ratification of this treaty on behalf of the United States; and to say to the Senate that if that remarkable treaty is ratified by that body we will not make the appropriation to carry it out, and will not recognize its validity. . . .

Mr. SCOFIELD. The committee, as I understand, do not undertake to decide the question whether the Indians have a possessory right to the land or a right in fee-simple. But it is conceded on all hands that they

115

cannot alienate the land, whatever title they may have to it, except to the United States. That is the stipulation. The question now is whether a few worthless Indians may be brought to Washington or some men not much more deserving sent out there to treat with them, and a treaty may be made with them in this way, by which the United States are made to consent to the alienation of this land to a body of speculators that may happen to fall in with the Indians and get control of their agent. The committee were of opinion, I believe all who were present—at all events I was of that opinion—that the consent to be given by the United States was not within the treaty-making power; that the President and the Senate could not give that consent to the alienation of this large body of land belonging to the public; that we could not carve out a tract of eight million acres of land, as large as the States of Massachusetts, Connecticut, and Rhode Island all together, and put it under the control of a few speculators. They may be very good men, and we have no objection to their making a fortune legitimately, but we do object to putting this land beyond the control of the United States and closing it to the right of settlement. The question now is, will the House consent that the control over this vast domain shall, under a wrong interpretation of the treaty-making power, be confined to the hands of a few men, who have in the first place got the consent of the Indian department and of the President, then the consent of a committee of the Senate, and lastly, the consent of the Senate itself. Shall this land belong to the nation or to these men?

Sir, for myself I intend never to give my consent to allowing the treaty-making power to add to or diminish the domain of this country. It has no power either to cede away the State of Maine to Great Britain or to acquire new territory on the Northwest, or to exercise exclusive control of the House of Representatives over the limits of this country either to contract or enlarge them. . . .

Mr. CLARKE, of Kansas. . . . Now, sir, it seems to me that the action proposed by the Committee on Indian Affairs, to whom this subject has been referred, is just and proper. It seems to me that the House ought not to sit idly by and see eight million acres of the public domain of the United States transferred by treaty into the hands of a corporation or of one individual, this House, representing the people, exercising no control or supervision over the matter whatever. The time has come here and now for us to exercise the prerogatives which properly belong to us, to put a stop to this outrage, this wrong, which is being inflicted upon the people of this country by transactions of this character, which of late have been far too frequent.

This treaty is not alone involved in a proper decision of this question. There are other treaties at this moment pending in the Senate proposing to transfer other Indian reserves—in fact other Indian reserves have been transferred into the hands of railway companies and private parties to the detriment of the interests of the people. And if this House shall, by refusing to exercise its power, by refusing to express its opinion, sanction this course of proceeding, how long will it be before the whole public domain of the United States will be absorbed by these unjustifiable means, and it will be beyond our reach to arrest this great wrong.

The Committee on Indian Affairs have thought proper to report these resolutions and to ask for them the favorable consideration of this House to assert the power which we properly possess in this matter, expressing our opinion as one of the coördinate branches of Congress, presuming that the Senate will respect that opinion, and hesitate before they give their sanction to this flagrant injustice. . . .

[*Congressional Globe*, 40th Cong., 2d sess., pp. 3261-64.]

72. Resolutions of the Indian Peace Commission

October 9, 1868

After a renewal of hostilities on the plains in the summer of 1868, the Peace Commission met again in Chicago in October. It took a strong stand against the hostile Indians and, in a reversal of its earlier position, now recommended the transfer of the Bureau of Indian Affairs to the War Department.

116

The PRESIDENT *of the United States:*

At a meeting of the Indian peace commission held this day the following resolutions, embodying the views of the commission, were adopted, to wit:

Resolved, That this commission recommend to the President of the United States and Congress that full provisions be at once made to feed, clothe, and protect all Indians of the Crow, Blackfeet, Piegan, Gros Ventres, Sioux, Ponca, Cheyenne, Arapahoe, Apache, Kiowa, and Comanche nations of Indians, who now have located or may hereafter locate permanently on their respective agricultural reservations.

Resolved, That the treaties of said tribes with United States, whether ratified or not, should be considered to be and remain in full force as to all Indians of such tribes as now have or may hereafter have their homes upon the agricultural reservations described in their respective treaties, and no others.

Resolved, That in the opinion of this commission the time has come when the government should cease to recognize the Indian tribes as "domestic dependent nations," except so far as it may be required to recognize them as such by existing treaties, and by treaties made but not yet ratified; that hereafter all Indians should be considered and held to be individually subject to the laws of the United States, except where and while it is otherwise provided in said treaties, and that they should be entitled to the same protection from said laws as other persons owing allegiance to the government enjoy.

Resolved, That the recent outrages and depredations committed by the Indians of the plains justify the government in abrogating those clauses of the treaties made in October, 1867, at Medicine Lodge creek, which secure to them the right to roam and hunt outside their reservations; that all said Indians should be requested to remove at once to said reservations and remain within them, except that after peace shall have been restored, hunting parties may be permitted to cross their boundaries with written authority from their agent or superintendent. And

Resolved further, That military force should be used to compel the removal into said reservations of all such Indians as may refuse to go, after due notice has been given to them that provision has been made to feed and protect them within the same.

Resolved, That in the opinion of this commission the Bureau of Indian Affairs should be transferred from the Department of the Interior to the Department of War. . . .

[*House Executive Document* no. 1, 40th Cong., 3d sess., serial 1366, pp. 831-32.]

73. Secretary of War Schofield on Transfer of the Indian Bureau

Extract from the *Annual Report of the Secretary of War*

November 20, 1868

The arguments of military men in favor of transferring the Bureau of Indian Affairs from the Department of the Interior to the War Department were well stated by Secretary of War J. M. Schofield in his annual report for 1868.

. . . . I believe it manifest that an important change should be made in our mode of dealing with the Indians. While good faith and sound policy alike require us to strictly observe existing treaties so long as the Indians maintain like good faith, when any tribe has violated its treaty it should no longer be regarded as a nation with which to treat, but as a *dependent uncivilized people*, to be cared for, fed when necessary, and governed.

It is manifest that any branch of the public service cannot be efficiently and economically managed by *two* departments of the government. If the Interior Department can alone manage Indian affairs, and thus save the large expense of the army in the Indian country, very well. But if the army must be kept there for the protection of railroads and frontier settlements, why not require the army officers to act as Indian agents, and thus save all the expense of the civilians so employed. Besides, an army officer has his military reputation and commission at stake, and is subject to trial by court-martial for any misconduct in office. Thus is afforded the strongest possible security the government can have for an honest administration of Indian affairs by officers of the army; while the civilian agent, being only a temporary officer of the government, and practically exempt from trial and punishment for misconduct, gives the government the *least* possible security for honest administration.

For the sake of economy to the government, for the sake of more efficient protection to the frontier settlements, and for the sake of justice to the Indians, I recommend that the management of Indian affairs be restored to the War Department, with authority to make regulations for their government and for their protection against lawless whites. . . .

[*House Executive Document* no. 1, 40th Cong., 3d sess., serial 1367, pp. xvii-xviii.]

74. Indian Commissioner Taylor on Transfer of the Indian Bureau

Extract from the *Annual Report of the Commissioner of Indian Affairs*

November 23, 1868

The proposal, advanced strongly in the late 1860s and again a decade later, to transfer the Bureau of Indian Affairs from civilian control under the Interior Department to military control under the War Department brought a spirited attack from Commissioner Nathaniel G. Taylor. He admitted, however, that affairs had not been well handled under the Interior Department, and he recommended the creation of a separate department of Indian affairs.

THE QUESTION OF THE TRANSFER OF THE INDIAN BUREAU TO THE WAR DEPARTMENT

It will be seen, by recurring to the proceedings of the peace commission at its late meeting at Chicago, that a resolution was adopted recommending to Congress the transfer of the Indian Bureau to the War Department. In view of probable action upon that recommendation, and impelled by solemn convictions of duty, I feel called upon to offer some facts and arguments, for the consideration of Congress, in opposition to the proposed transfer, and to give some views, suggested by nearly two years' intimate official connection with the Indian service, with regard to the best method for the future conduct of Indian affairs.

In 1849, Congress, upon the creation of the Department of the Interior, incorporated the Bureau of Indian Affairs in that department, giving to its head the supervisory and appellate powers theretofore exercised over Indian affairs by the Secretary of War. It is now proposed to re-transfer the bureau to the War Office.

It is presumed the question for legislative solution will be three-fold: Shall the bureau be transferred to the War Department; or shall it remain under the direction of the Secretary of the Interior; or shall it be erected into an independent department, upon an equal footing in all respects with the other departments, as recommended, unanimously, by the peace commission in their report to the President of 7th January last.

I shall endeavor to present some reasons against the transfer. These I proceed to offer, assuming all the time that the transfer means that in future all our Indian affairs are to be administered by the army, under the direction of the War Office.

My reasons in opposition are—

1. *That the prompt, efficient, and successful management and direction of our Indian affairs is too large, onerous, and important a burden to be added to the existing duties of the Secretary of War.*

There is a limit to human capacity and endurance, and when either is taxed beyond that limit, it must fail in the performance of its functions, and the result must be disappointment, and most probably disaster, to the service.

The business of the War Department, in all its varied and complex ramifications, is sufficient already, if properly transacted, to employ all the faculties of the most accomplished head, even with all the aids he may summon to his assistance; and there are few men living, if any, who can give the requisite attention to its demands, and at the same time discharge properly and with requisite promptness the delicate, important, and numerous duties the care of Indian affairs would superadd.

118

None can deny that the safe and successful management of the military affairs of a republic of 40,000,000 of people, demands the constant and exclusive exercise of all the powers of an accomplished and experienced statesman.

A little investigation, and even a superficial knowledge and a little reflection, will convince every candid mind that there is no branch of the public service more intricate and difficult, and involving more varied and larger public and private interests, than our "Indian affairs;" none requiring in their control and direction a larger brain, or a more sensitive and charitable heart.

If these things be true, the conclusion is irresistible that the proposed "transfer" is unreasonable and wrong.

If the argument applies as well to the Interior as to the War Department, let it be so; its force is not abated by the admission.

2. *The "transfer," in my judgment, will create a necessity for maintaining a large standing army in the field.*

I yield to none in admiration and love of the gallant officers and soldiers of our army. They are the hope of the nation in times of public danger, when the honor, integrity, or the existence of the republic is threatened by foreign or domestic foes. But "there is a time for all things," and I submit that a time of peace is *not* the time for a large standing army. In time of war, the army is our wall of defence. In peace, large armies exhaust the national resources without advantage to the country. The safety of the country in peace is not to be sought in a magnificent array of bayonets; but in the virtue, intelligence, industry, and patriotism of the citizens. With the restoration of all the States to their peaceful relations to the federal government, and the return of their population to industrial avocations and prosperity, if peace is maintained, as at the present, with all foreign powers, our military establishment should soon be reduced to a peace footing, its material returned to industrial and producing employments, and the people, to the extent of many millions of dollars, annually relieved of taxes now expended in the support and pay of the army.

Surely Congress is not prepared to transfer the Indian Bureau to the War Department merely to create a necessity to keep up the army, and with it the taxes.

3. *Our true policy towards the Indian tribes is peace, and the proposed transfer is tantamount, in my judgment, to perpetual war.*

Everybody knows that the presence of troops, with the avowed purpose of regulating affairs by force, arouses feelings of hostility and begets sentiments of resistance and war even in the most civilized and peaceful communities. How much more intense and bitter are the feelings of hostility engendered in the bosoms of barbarians and semi-civilized Indians by the presence of soldiers, who they know are sent to force them into subjection and keep them so. To their ears the sounds of the camp and the boom of the morning and evening gun are the infallible signs of oppression and war; and the very sight of armed and uniformed soldiers in their haunts and hunting grounds provokes and inflames the profoundest feelings of hostility and hate.

If a chronic war, with additional annual expenses of $50,000,000 to $150,000,000 annually on account of Indian affairs, is desired, the transfer, it seems to me, is a logical way to the result. . . .

Now if, as I think, I have shown military interference has been prolific of war, even since the bureau has been in civil control, what of peace and tranquillity can be expected if it be placed entirely in military hands?

4. *Military management of Indian affairs has been tried for seventeen years and has proved a failure, and must, in my judgment, in the very nature of things, always prove a failure.*

Soldiers are educated and trained in the science of war and in the arts of arms. Civilians are taught in the sciences and arts of peaceful civilization. In lifting up races from the degradation of savage barbarism and leading them into the sunlight of a higher life, in unveiling to their benighted vision the benefits of civilization and the blessings of a peaceful Christianity, I cannot for the life of me perceive the propriety or the efficacy of employing the military instead of the civil departments, unless it is intended to adopt the Mohammedan motto, and proclaim to these people "Death or the Koran."

If the mass of our people desire peaceful

relations with our Indian tribes, mean to continue to recognize their natural rights, as our fathers have done, and do not desire their violent extermination, then I submit the peaceful and therefore the civil and not the military agencies of the government are better adapted to secure the desired ends.

Blight follows the sword as surely as desolation sits in the track of the hurricane or the conflagration.

Has not military management essentially failed in civilizing the Indians? When and where did it turn their minds from war and the chase and fix them upon agriculture or pastoral life? When and where did it reduce the cost of Indian affairs? It has only succeeded in illuminating our Indian history with bloody pictures, in surcharging the hearts of our tribes with hatred and revenge, and spending the money of the people by the fifty million dollars, oft repeated. . . .

5. *It is inhuman and unchristian, in my opinion, leaving the question of economy out of view, to destroy a whole race by such demoralization and disease as military government is sure to entail upon our tribes.*

I know no exception to the rule that the presence of military posts in the Indian country is speedily subversive of even the sternest ideas of Indian domestic morals. Female chastity, the abandonment of which in some tribes is punished with death, yields to bribery or fear; marital rights are generally disregarded, and shameless concubinage, with its disgusting concomitants, spreads its pestiferous stench through camp and lodge. The most loathsome, lingering, and fatal diseases, which reach many generations in their ruinous effects, are spread broadcast, and the seeds of moral and physical death are planted among the miserable creatures.

If you wish to see some of the results of establishing military posts in the Indian country, I call your attention to the 600 or 800 half-breeds till recently loafing around Fort Laramie; to the posts along the Missouri; to Fort Sumner in New Mexico, before the Navajoe exodus, and *to all our military posts in the Indian country, with no known exception.* If you wish to exterminate the race, pursue them with the ball and blade; if you please, massacre them wholesale, as we sometimes have done; or, to make it cheap, call them to a peaceful feast, and feed them on beef salted with wolf bane; but, for humanity's sake, save them from the lingering syphilitic poisons, so sure to be contracted about military posts.

6. *The conduct of Indian affairs is, in my judgment, incompatible with the nature and objects of the military department.*

The policy of our government has always been to secure and maintain peaceful and friendly relations with all the Indian tribes, and to advance their interests, by offering them inducements to abandon nomadic habits and the chase, and to learn to adopt the habits and methods of civilized life. To carry this benevolent and humane policy into practical effect, we have stipulated to settle them upon ample reserves of good land, adapted to pastoral and agricultural pursuits; to subsist them as long as requisite; to supply them with all necessary stock and implements, and teachers to instruct them in letters, in the arts of civilization, and in our holy religion. But all these things pertain properly, as all will admit, to civil affairs, not military. Military officers will doubtless display wonderful skill in the erection of forts; in the handling of arms and armies, and in the management of campaigns, but who would not prefer a practical civilian in the erection of corn cribs or hay racks; in the manoeuvering of ox teams, and the successful management of reapers and mowers? A well-trained lieutenant will doubtless perform admirably in drilling a squad in the manual of arms, but I doubt his capacity, as well as inclination, to teach Indians the profitable and efficient use of the hoe or the mattock, or to successfully instruct naked young Indians. . . how to shoot in a mechanical, literary, or scientific direction. You wish to make your son a farmer, a mechanic, a minister; you do not send him to be educated at West Point, but somewhere else to be taught as a civilian. Will you send professional soldiers, sword in one hand, musket in the other, and tactics on the brain, to teach the wards of the nation agriculture, the mechanic arts, theology, and peace? You would civilize the Indian! Will you send him the sword? You would inspire him with the peaceful principles of Christianity! Is the bayonet their symbol? You would invite him to the sanctuary! Will you herald his approach with the clangor of arms and the thunder of artillery?

The nation thinks of the War Department as the channel through which the chief executive directs the movements of our armies and manages all the military business and interests of the nation, not as the overseer, guardian, teacher, and missionary of the Indian tribes; it regards our officers and soldiers as its sword to repel and punish its enemies in war, to guard and secure its honor and interests, whenever necessary, in peace; but not as its superintendents, agents, agricultural and mechanical teachers of peaceful Indian tribes.

7. *The transfer to the War Office will be offensive to the Indians, and in the same proportion injurious to the whites.*

Let it be remembered that the demoralization resulting from the presence of military posts is not confined to the Indian, but reacts, with accumulated power, upon the soldier.

The nature and objects of the War Department, as indicated by its very name, WAR, are essentially military, while the nature of our relations with the Indians ought to be, and the objects aimed at in their conduct are, essentially civil. . . .

As a rule, with rare exceptions, if any, Indian tribes never break the peace without powerful provocation or actual wrong perpetrated against them first; if they are properly treated, their rights regarded, and our promises faithfully kept to them, our treaty engagements promptly fulfilled, and their wants of subsistence liberally supplied, there is seldom, if ever, the slightest danger of a breach of the peace on their part.

If for want of appropriations the Indians now at war had not had their supplies of subsistence unfortunately stopped this spring, in my judgment the Cheyennes and their allies would have been at peace with us to-day. Respect then their wishes; keep them well fed, and there will be no need of armies among them. But violate our pledges; postpone, neglect, or refuse the fulfilment of our treaty engagements with them; permit them to get hungry and half-starved, and the presence of armies will not restrain them from war.

8. *In the report, 7th January last, of the peace commission, after full examination of the whole*

question, the commission unanimously recommended that the Indian affairs should be placed, not in the War Office, but upon the footing of an independent department or bureau.*

Then their facts were correct, their reasoning and conclusion sound, and to go back now upon that report and repudiate their own deliberate and unanimous recommendation, it seems to me, will subject the commission to severe criticism.

I have no reflections to cast upon those gentlemen of the commission who have changed front, for reasons doubtless satisfactory to themselves; but as no such reasons have addressed themselves to my mind, I adhere to the unanimous recommendation of our January report.

I think I can readily understand, however, why my colleagues of the army might desire the transfer. It is but natural they should desire it. It is the history of power to seek more power, and the dispensation of patronage is power. Besides, it is but natural that gentlemen educated to arms, and of the army, should desire to see the aggrandizement of the army.

9. *The methods of military management are utterly irreconcilable with the relation of guardian and ward.*

The self assumed guardianship of our government over these unlettered children of the wilderness, carries with it all the obligations that grow out of that relation. These can neither be shaken off nor disregarded without national crime as well as disgrace.

Guardianship is a most sacred and responsible trust, and as a nation we must answer to the God of nations for its faithful administration.

The paramount duty growing out of the trust is to teach, to enlighten, to civilize our wards. If teaching means the instruction given to the Aztecs by Cortez and Pizarro; if enlightening signifies the conflagration of Indian villages; if civilization means peace, and peace means massacre *a la* Sand creek, then by all means let us have the transfer. To every unprejudiced mind the mere mention of the military in connection with the relation of guardian and ward discloses the absurdity of the association.

10. *The transfer will in my opinion entail*

upon the treasury a large increase of annual expenditure.

It is clearly demonstrable that the war policy in conducting our Indian affairs is infinitely more expensive than the peace policy; and if the transfer is made, as a matter of course the former will prevail. If so, it seems to me, our legislators would do well to investigate the question of comparative cost. It will not surprise me if an examination will show that in the last 40 years the war policy and management of Indian affairs have cost the nation little if any less than $500,000,000, and also that the civil management or peace policy has cost less than $60,000,000, including annuities, presents, payments for immense bodies of land, and everything else. . . .

If economy is desirable in our present financial situation, the proposed transfer will, in my judgment, be disastrous.

11. *The presence in peaceful times of a large military establishment in a republic always endangers the supremacy of civil authority and the liberties of the people.*

History is so replete with striking illustrations of the truth of this proposition that argument to sustain it would be simply attempting to prove an axiom. I therefore close the argument by merely announcing it.

This brings me to the question, *whether the bureau ought not to be erected into an independent department?*

In whatever management Indian affairs are placed, there should be division of neither duties, powers nor responsibilities, but these should all, by all means, be concentrated in the same hands.

But I have already shown that the War Department should not be intrusted with these affairs, and I am of the opinion that the Interior Department should not have charge of them except in the alternative between the two; if for no other reason, from the fact that the head of that department, like the Secretary of War, has already as many duties as he can perform well without superadding the all-important business of Indian affairs.

I reach the conclusion, therefore, that the only wise and proper answer to the question is that Congress ought immediately to create a department exclusively for the management of Indian affairs.

If, however, Congress should think differently and make the transfer, it seems to me in that event the transfer should consist in a change of jurisdiction from the Interior Secretary to the Secretary of War, while all the functions of the bureau should still be performed by civilians.

If the management of Indian affairs by the bureau under the department of war was a failure, and if, as is admitted, it has been not fully satisfactory under the Interior, it is clear that the mere transfer of the bureau from one to the other will leave the management still a failure.

Why talk of the transfer as if the simple turning over of a bureau from one department to another would magically cure all the defects of this branch of the public service. To me the proposition seems absurd. What is the "transfer?" Only a change, and, in my opinion, from bad enough to worse—that's all. The War Office operated the bureau 17 years and it did not give satisfaction. In 1849 it was transferred to the Interior Department, where it has remained ever since, and still its conduct of affairs is assailed. Each department in turn, with ample time for trial, has failed to manage Indian affairs with popular approbation. If either department is to blame, both are, for both in the public mind have failed. What is the remedy? To know this we must first ascertain the cause. In my judgment, the cause lies on the surface and is simply this: there is too much cargo for the capacity of the vessel, and too much vessel and freight for the power of the machinery. We have crammed into a bureau, which under the supervisory and appellate power is a mere clerkship, all the large, complex, difficult and delicate affairs that ought to employ every function of a first-class department. Now, with the cause of failure before our eyes, what is the remedy? Surely not merely to put the old bureau under another crew and commander! Why, such a transfer can give neither more capacity to the vessel nor more strength to the machinery. There is but one reasonable answer, and that is: If you would have all prosperous and safe in any sea and any weather, adapt your vessel to her cargo, and your machinery to your vessel and tonnage. In other words, launch a new Department of Indian Affairs, freight it with the vast and complicated reciprocal interests of both races, and the experiment must, I believe, prove a grand success.

Can it be that the civil departments of this great government have become so degenerate and weak, or the military so exalted and so potent, that the functions of the one are to be laid at the feet of the other, and the congenial sway of the republican statesman to be replaced by the mailed hand of the military tribune?

I believe there is ingenuity and wisdom enough in the American Congress to devise civil remedies for supposed bureau mismanagement; to strengthen where there is weakness; to purge and purify if there is rottenness; to punish if there is crime; to concentrate power for promptness and efficiency; and to make responsibility answerable in proportion to power, without transferring the functions of civil government to the military organization. . . .

[*House Executive Document* no. 1, 40th Cong., 3d sess., serial 1366, pp. 467-74]

75. Indian Commissioner Taylor on Indian Civilization

Extract from the *Annual Report of the Commissioner of Indian Affairs*

November 23, 1868

Commissioner of Indian Affairs Nathaniel G. Taylor was an ardent promoter of civilian control of Indian affairs and of programs for the civilization of the Indians. In his annual report of 1868 he included a forthright statement of his belief in the feasibility of such programs.

SHALL OUR INDIANS BE CIVILIZED? AND HOW?

How can our Indian tribes be civilized?—Assuming that the government has a right, and that it is its duty to solve the Indian question definitely and decisively, it becomes necessary that it determine at once the best and speediest method of its solution, and then, armed with right, to act in the interest of both races.

If might makes right, we are the strong and they the weak; and we would do no wrong to proceed by the cheapest and nearest route to the desired end, and could, therefore, justify ourselves in ignoring the natural as well as the conventional rights of the Indians, if they stand in the way, and, as their lawful masters, assign them their status and their tasks, or put them out of their own way and ours by extermination with the sword, starvation, or by any other method.

If, however, they have rights as well as we, then clearly it is our duty as well as sound policy to so solve the question of their future relations to us and each other, as to secure their rights and promote their highest interest, in the simplest, easiest, and most economical way possible.

But to assume they have no rights is to deny the fundamental principles of Christianity, as well as to contradict the whole theory upon which the government has uniformly acted towards them; we are therefore bound to respect their rights, and, if possible, make our interest harmonize with them. This brings us to the consideration of the question:

How can the Indian problem be solved so as best to protect and secure the rights of the Indians, and at the same time promote the highest interests of both races?—This question has long trembled in the hearts of philanthropists, and perplexed the brains of statesmen. It is one that forces itself at this moment upon Congress and the country, for an immediate practical answer.

The time for speculation and delay has passed; action must be had, and that promptly. History and experience have laid the key to its solution in our hands, at the proper moment, and all we need to do is to use it, and we at once reach the desired answer. It so happens that under the silent and seemingly slow operation of efficient causes, certain tribes of our Indians have already emerged from a state of pagan barbarism, and are to-day clothed in the garments of civilization, and sitting under the vine and fig tree of an intelligent scriptural Christianity.

Within the present century their blanketed fathers struggled in deadly conflict with our pioneer ancestors in the lovely valleys of Georgia, Alabama, and Mississippi; among

123

the mountain gorges and along the banks of the beautiful streams of western North Carolina and East Tennessee, and in the everglades of Florida; and made classic the fields of Talladega, Emuckfau, and the Horse-shoe, which gave to history and fame the illustrious name of Andrew Jackson.

Within the memory of living men, their tomahawks reflected the light of the burning cabins of white settlers on the Nolachucky and French Broad, the Hiawassee and the Tennessee rivers and their tributaries; their scalping-knives dripped with the blood of our border settlers, and their defiant battle-yells woke the echoes among the green savannahs and vine-tangled forests of the south.

But behold the contrast which greets the world to-day! The blanket and the bow are discarded; the spear is broken, and the hatchet and war-club lie buried; the skin lodge and primitive tepe have given place to the cottage and the mansion; the buckskin robe, the paint and beads have vanished, and are now replaced with the tasteful fabrics of civilization. Medicine lodges and their orgies, and heathen offerings, are mingling with the dust of a forgotten idolatry. School-houses abound, and the feet of many thousand little Indian children—children intelligent and thirsting after knowledge—are seen every day entering these vestibules of science; while churches dedicated to the Christian's God, and vocal with His praise from the lips of redeemed thousands, reflect from their domes and spires the earliest rays and latest beams of that sun whose daily light now blesses them as five Christian and enlightened nations so recently heathen savages.

The Cherokees, Choctaws, Chickasaws, Creeks, and Seminoles are the tribes to which I refer. They are to-day civilized and Christian peoples. True, there are portions of each tribe still carrying with them the leaven of their ancestral paganism and superstition, but their average intelligence is very nearly up to the standard of like communities of whites. If any doubt this statement, I respectfully make profert of the delegates of these tribes to be found in this city.

As a body, the men representing all these tribes in Washington will compare favorably with any like number of representative men in our State legislatures and in our national Congress, as respects breadth and vigor of native intellect, thoroughness of cultivation, and propriety and refinement of manners.

I could refer to other tribes and parts of tribes, but those mentioned already will serve the purpose in view.

Thus the fact stands out clear, well-defined, and indisputable, that Indians, not only as individuals but as tribes, are capable of civilization and of christianization.

Now if like causes under similar circumstances always produce like effects—which no sensible person will deny—it is clear that the application of the same causes, that have resulted in civilizing these tribes, to other tribes under similar circumstances, must produce their civilization.

What leading or essential causes, then, operated in civilizing the Cherokees and these other tribes? The Cherokees lived on the borders of the white settlements for a great while, with a boundless wilderness behind them, to which they retired after each successive advance of the whites, until at length they reached the mountainous regions of North Carolina, South Carolina, Georgia, Alabama, and what is now known as East Tennessee. Here they remained for many years, until the enterprise of the whites surrounded their possessions on all sides, and began to press heavily upon their borders. Down to this period the Cherokees had made but small advance in civilization. They were still dependent largely on the chase—still clung to the habits and customs of their savage ancestors—and little change will be found to have taken place in their habits of thought and life until the pressure of immigration on all sides compelled them to so reduce the area of their territory by successive cessions of land, and so destroyed and drove away their game as to compel them to resort to agriculture and pastoral pursuits to save themselves from famine. Agriculture and stock-breeding brought with them the important idea of individual rights or of personal property, and the notion of fixed local habitations, of sale and barter, profit and loss, &c.

Contact with the white settlements all around confirmed and fastened this new class of ideas upon them, and soon resulted in a corresponding change of habits, customs, and manners.

With this change of ideas and habits, when the ancient was struggling more and more feebly with the modern, when darkness was more and more fading away before advancing light, Christianity, under the labors of godly missionaries who had exiled themselves from society and home for the love of God and souls, began to lay its foundations upon the ruins of a crumbling heathenism. These faithful men went forth "bearing precious seed," struggled and toiled, endured severe privations, afflictions, and trials, and sowed in tears the germs of light, truth, and hope, which have ripened into a glorious harvest of intelligence and Christian civilization. This tribe are not only civilized and self-supporting, but before the fearful disasters of the great rebellion fell upon them, were perhaps the richest people, per capita, in the world.

This historical sketch demonstrates beyond question that the mainsprings of Cherokee civilization were, first, the circumscribing of their territorial domain; this resulted in, second, the localization of the members of the tribe, and consequently in, third, the necessity of agriculture and pastoral pursuits instead of the chase as a means of existence; and as a logical sequence, fourth, the introduction of ideas of property in things, of sale and barter, &c.; and hence, fifth, of course, a corresponding change from the ideas, habits, and customs of savages to those of civilized life; and, sixth, the great coadjutor in the whole work in all its progress, the Christian teacher and missionary, moving *pari passu* with every other cause.

Unless history is a fable, and the observation and the experience of living men a delusion or a lie, I have demonstrated that an Indian tribe may become civilized. I think the causes also operating that result are clearly shown, so that they are patent and palpable to every observer. And I might close the argument here with, "It is demonstrated."

But truth must not only be demonstrated, it is necessary also to impress it with fact upon fact; argument must not only be conclusive, but it must be made weighty by cumulative truths.

To make the logic of the argument and the conclusions irresistible, let it be remembered that the history of the civilization of each of the other tribes I have named is in all its leading features the same. The necessities imposed by diminished territory, of individual localization and permanent habitation, of abandonment of the chase, of resorting to the herd, the flock, the field, the plough, the loom, and the anvil, of embracing ideas of property in things, of a change of habits, customs, laws, &c., to suit new ideas and new methods of life, and of imbibing corresponding ideas of morals and religion, operated alike in all these tribes, and led them each through the same pathway into the broad sunlight of our civilization.

Now, if the laws of God are immutable, the application of similar causes to each of the other tribes under our jurisdiction must produce a like effect upon each. If the Cherokees, Choctaws, Chickasaws, Creeks, and Seminoles are civilized and advancing in development, so will be the Cheyennes, Arapahoes, Apaches, Kiowas, Comanches, Sioux, and all our other tribes, if we will only use the means in their cases that have been so wonderfully successful in the first named tribe.

It may be objected that some of our tribes have long been under the action of kindred causes, but have not advanced in numbers, knowledge, or civilization. This I emphatically deny.

If tribes long under the care of the government have failed to improve and advance, the causes of the failure lie on the surface and are easily seen by those who will take the trouble to look.

Our course has generally been to circumscribe, but not to localize them in the proper sense, and thus give them the certainty of fixed and permanent homes, but to hold them as pilgrims resting a year or two on this reservation, and then removing them to a new one on the outer verge of civilization, there to linger awhile in sad suspense till the remorseless rapacity of our race requires them to move farther back into darkness again.

These miserable wanderers after rest in their new reservations, which are always assured to *them and their children forever* by our government *in the treaty*, meet with a fearful drawback upon their prospects at every remove. Beyond the tide of emigration, and hanging like the froth of the billows upon its very edge, is generally a host of law-defying white men, who introduce among the Indians every form of demoralization and disease with which depraved humanity in its most degrading forms is ever afflicted. These are by far the most numerous examples of civilization, except the military, these creatures ever see; and just when better people begin to appear in the advance of emigration around and among them, away they are required to move again. It is no wonder that the philosophic chief of the Arapahoes, Little Raven, laughed heartily in my face when, having told him something of hell and heaven, I remarked that all good men, white and red, would go to heaven, and all bad ones to hell. Inquiring the cause of his merriment, when he had recovered his breath, he said, "I was much pleased with what you say of heaven and hell and the characters that will go to each after death; it's a good notion—heap good—for if all the whites are like the ones I know, when Indian gets to heaven but few whites will trouble him there—pretty much all go to t'other place." Thus while we have been puzzling our brains to find a solution of the problem of Indian civilization and christianization, the fact of their capability for both and of the manner of achieving both is demonstrated to us so clearly that there is no possibility of being deceived.

What, then, is our duty as the guardian of all the Indians under our jurisdiction? To outlaw, to pursue, to hunt down like wolves, and slay? Must we drive and exterminate them as if void of reason, and without souls? Surely, no.

It is beyond question our most solemn duty to protect and care for, to elevate and civilize them. We have taken their heritage, and it is a grand and magnificent heritage. Now is it too much that we carve for them liberal reservations out of their own lands and guarantee them homes forever? Is it too much that we supply them with agricultural implements, mechanical tools, domestic animals, instructors in the useful arts, teachers, physicians, and Christian missionaries? If we find them fierce, hostile and revengeful; if they are cruel, and if they sometimes turn upon us and burn, pillage, and desolate our frontiers, and perpetrate atrocities that sicken the soul and paralyze us with horror, let us remember that two hundred and fifty years of injustice, oppression and wrong, heaped upon them by our race with cold, calculating and relentless perseverance, have filled them with the passion of revenge, and made them desperate.

It remains for us, if we would not hold their lands with their blighting curse, and the curse of a just God, who holds nations to a strict accountability upon it, to do justice, and more than justice, to the remnant; to hide our past injustice under the mantle of present and future mercy, and to blot out their remembrance of wrongs and oppressions by deeds of God-like love and benevolence.

That they can be elevated and enlightened to the proud stature of civilized manhood is demonstrated. We know the process by which this result is accomplished. Our duty is plain; let us enter upon its discharge without delay; end the war policy; create a new department of Indian affairs; give it a competent head; clothe him with adequate powers for the performance of all his duties, define those duties clearly, and hold him to a strict accountability. . . .

[*House Executive Document* no. 1, 40th Cong., 3d sess., serial 1366, pp. 476-79.]

76. Authorization of the Board of Indian Commissioners

April 10, 1869

Part of the change in Indian policy known as Grant's "peace policy" rested upon the Board of Indian Commissioners, a body of unpaid philanthropists appointed to aid the secretary of the interior in Indian affairs. The board was authorized by a section of the Indian appropriation act of April 10, 1869.

An Act making Appropriations for the current and contingent Expenses of the Indian Department. . . .

. . . . SEC. 4. *And be it further enacted,* That there be appropriated the further sum of two millions of dollars, or so much thereof

126

as may be necessary, to enable the President to maintain the peace among and with the various tribes, bands, and parties of Indians, and to promote civilization among said Indians, bring them, where practicable, upon reservations, relieve their necessities, and encourage their efforts at self-support; a report of all expenditures under this appropriation to be made in detail to Congress in December next; and for the purpose of enabling the President to execute the powers conferred by this act he is hereby authorized, at his discretion, to organize a board of commissioners, to consist of not more than ten persons, to be selected by him from men eminent for their intelligence and philanthropy, to serve without pecuniary compensation, who may, under his direction, exercise joint control with the Secretary of the Interior over the disbursement of the appropriations made by this act or any part thereof that the President may designate; and to pay the necessary expenses of transportation, subsistence, and clerk hire of said commissioners while actually engaged in said service, there is hereby appropriated, out of any money in the treasury not otherwise appropriated, the sum of twenty-five thousand dollars, or so much thereof as may be necessary. . . .

[*U.S. Statutes at Large*, 16:40.]

77. Instructions to the Board of Indian Commissioners

1869

Both President Grant and his commissioner of Indian affairs, Ely S. Parker, sent instructions to the members of the Board of Indian Commissioners, appointed in 1869. The board was given broad responsibilities to investigate Indian affairs and to advise the commissioner of Indian affairs and the secretary of the interior.

DEPARTMENT OF THE INTERIOR,
OFFICE OF INDIAN AFFAIRS,
Washington, May 26, 1869.

GENTLEMEN: You have been solicited by the President, under the provision of the fourth section of the act of Congress, approved April 10, 1869, entitled "An act making appropriation for the current and contingent expenses of the Indian Department," &c., for the year ending June 30, 1870, for the purpose of enabling the President to exercise the power conferred by said act, and being authorized by the same to exercise, under the direction of the President, joint control with the Secretary of the Interior over the disbursement of the appropriations made by said act, or any part thereof that the President may designate, and having been convened in the city for the purpose of organizing for the execution of your duties, and believing that, in common with the President and other officers of the government, you desire the humanization, civilization, and Christianization of the Indians, I very respectfully, after consultation with the honorable Secretary of the Interior, submit the following questions, which, with a view to proper and intelligent action in the future relation of the government with the Indians, I deem it important should receive your early consideration and suggestion, viz: A determination or settlement of what should be the legal status of the Indians; a definition of their rights and obligations under the laws of the United States, of the States and Territories and treaty stipulations; whether any more treaties shall be stipulated with the Indians, and if not, what legislation is necessary for those with whom there are existing treaty stipulations, and what for those with whom no such stipulations exist; should the Indians be placed upon reservations, and what is the best method to accomplish this object; should not legislation discriminate between the civilized and localized Indians, and the united roving tribes of the plains and mountains; what changes are necessary in existing laws relating to purchasing goods and provisions for the Indians, in order to prevent fraud, &c.; should any change be made in the method of paying the money annuities; and if so, what. Great mischief, evils, and frequently serious results follow from friendly Indians leaving the reservations, producing conflicts between the citizens, soldiers, and Indians. At what time and point shall the civil rule cease and the military begin? Is any change required in the

127

intercourse laws by reason of the present and changed condition of the country? I respectfully suggest that inspection should be made by your commission of as many Indian tribes, especially the wild and roving ones, as the time of the honorable commissioners will permit, and their conditions and wants be reported on, with any suggestions that each case may seem to require. Also, the accounts of superintendents and agents should be examined, and the efficiency or inefficiency of those officers should be reported upon. All suggestions, recommendations, and reports from the commission should be made to the honorable Secretary of the Interior, to be by him submitted, when necessary, to the President and Congress.

Very respectfully, your obedient servant,
E. S. PARKER,
Commissioner.
Addressed to Hon. Wm. Welsh, John V. Farwell, George H. Stuart, Robert Campbell, Wm. E. Dodge, E. S. Tobey, Felix R. Brunot, Nathan Bishop, Henry S. Lane.

EXECUTIVE MANSION
Washington, D.C., June 3, 1869.
A commission of citizens having been appointed, under the authority of law, to co-operate with the administrative departments in the management of Indian affairs, consisting of Wm. Welsh, of Philadelphia; John V. Farwell, Chicago; George H. Stuart, Philadelphia; Robert Campbell, St. Louis; W. E. Dodge, New York; E. S. Tobey, Boston; Felix R. Brunot, Pittsburg; Nathan Bishop, New York; and Henry S. Lane, Indiana—the following regulations will, till further directions, control the action of said commission and of the Bureau of Indian Affairs in matters coming under their joint supervision:

1. The commission will make its own organization, and employ its own clerical assistants, keeping its "necessary expenses of transportation, subsistence, and clerk-hire, when actually engaged in said service," within the amount appropriated therefor by Congress.

2. The commission shall be furnished with full opportunity to inspect the records of the Indian Office, and to obtain full information as to the conduct of all parts of the affairs thereof.

3. They shall have full power to inspect, in person or by sub-committee, the various Indian superintendencies and agencies in the Indian country; to be present at payment of annuities, at consultations or councils with the Indians; and when on the ground, to advise superintendents and agents in the performance of their duties.

4. They are authorized to be present, in person or by sub-committee, at purchases of goods for Indian purposes, and inspect said purchases, advising with the Commissioner of Indian Affairs in regard thereto.

5. Whenever they shall deem it necessary or advisable that instructions of superintendents or agents be changed or modified, they will communicate such advice, through the office of the Commissioner of Indian Affairs, to the Secretary of the Interior; and, in like manner, their advice as to changes in modes of purchasing goods, or conducting the affairs of the Indian Bureau proper. Complaints against superintendents, or agents, or other officers, will, in the same manner, be forwarded to the Indian Bureau or Department of the Interior for action.

6. The commission will, at their board meetings, determine upon the recommendations to be made as to the plans of civilizing or dealing with the Indians, and submit the same for action in the manner above indicated; and all plans involving the expenditure of public money will be acted upon by the Executive or the Secretary of the Interior before expenditure is made under the same.

7. The usual modes of accounting with the Treasury cannot be changed; and all the expenditures, therefore, must be subject to the approvals now required by law and by the regulations of the Treasury Department, and all vouchers must conform to the same laws and requirements, and pass through the ordinary channels.

8. All the officers of the government connected with the Indian service are enjoined to afford every facility and opportunity to said commission and their sub-committees in the performance of their duties, and to give the most respectful heed to their advice within the limits of such officers'

positive instructions from their superiors; to allow such commissioners full access to their records and accounts; and to co-operate with them in the most earnest manner, to the extent of their proper powers, in the general work of civilizing the Indians, protecting them in their legal rights, and stimulating them to become industrious citizens in permanent homes, instead of following a roving and savage life.

9. The commission will keep such records or minutes of their proceedings as may be necessary to afford evidence of their action, and will provide for the manner in which their communications with, and advice to, the government shall be made and authenticated.

U. S. GRANT.

[*Annual Report of the Board of Indian Commissioners, 1869*, pp. 3-5.]

78. Secretary of the Interior Cox on Reservations and on the Peace Policy

Extract from the *Annual Report of the Secretary of the Interior*

November 15, 1869

Jacob D. Cox, first secretary of the interior in Grant's administration, supported the policy of settling the Indians within reservations. In his annual report of 1869 he also spoke favorably of the Board of Indian Commissioners and of the policy of assigning Indians agencies to the Quakers—two elements of Grant's "peace policy."

. . . . The problems presented by our relations to the Indian tribes which still inhabit portions of the western States and Territories are every year making more imperative demands for a fixed general policy that shall give some reasonable probability of an early and satisfactory solution.

The completion of one of the great lines of railway to the Pacific coast has totally changed the conditions under which the civilized population of the country come in contact with the wild tribes. Instead of a slowly advancing tide of migration, making its gradual inroads upon the circumference of the great interior wilderness, the very center of the desert has been pierced. Every station upon the railway has become a nucleus for a civilized settlement, and a base from which lines of exploration for both mineral and agricultural wealth are pushed in every direction. Daily trains are carrying thousands of our citizens and untold values of merchandise across the continent, and must be protected from the danger of having hostile tribes on either side of the route. The range of the buffalo is being rapidly restricted, and the chase is becoming an uncertain reliance to the Indian for the sustenance of his family. If he is in want he will rob, as white men do in the like circumstances, and robbery is but the beginning of war, in which savage barbarities and retaliations

soon cause a cry of extermination to be raised along the whole frontier.

It has long been the policy of the government to require of the tribes most nearly in contact with white settlements that they should fix their abode upon definite reservations and abandon the wandering life to which they had been accustomed. To encourage them in civilization, large expenditures have been made in furnishing them with the means of agriculture and with clothing adapted to their new mode of life.

A new policy is not so much needed as an enlarged and more enlightened application of the general principles of the old one. We are now in contact with all the aboriginal tribes within our borders, and can no longer assume that we may, even for a time, leave a large part of them out of the operation of our system.

I understand this policy to look to two objects: First, the location of the Indians upon fixed reservations, so that the pioneers and settlers may be freed from the terrors of wandering hostile tribes; and second, an earnest effort at their civilization, so that they may themselves be elevated in the scale of humanity, and our obligation to them as fellow-men be discharged.

In carrying out this policy a great practical difficulty has arisen from the fact that in most instances a separate reservation was

129

given to each tribe. These reservations have been surrounded and gradually invaded by the white settlers, and the Indians crowded out of their homes and forced to negotiate for a new settlement, because their presence, their habits, and their manners were distasteful to their new and more powerful neighbors.

It is believed that the only remedy for this condition of things is to encourage the Indians to assemble upon larger reservations, where their numbers will be aggregated, and where the more civilized of them will influence the others in striving to progress in the arts of peace. Congress has already passed an act to enable the civilized Indians of the Indian Territory, properly so called, to form a general organization, with most of the elements of a territorial government; but the requisite appropriations of money have not been made to carry the plan into effect. I would earnestly recommend that no further delay be made in this matter. The associated tribes, of which the Cherokees have taken the lead, are those best fitted for a fuller experiment in self-government. They are already familiar with most of the forms of executive, legislative, and judicial action in use among us, and I believe them well prepared to dispense with the tutelage of our agents, if they may have a delegate of their own upon the floor of the House of Representatives to speak for them. Both they and we are suffering for the lack of such direct representation. The white constituencies which are nearest to them are the ones of all the nation whose interests are most in opposition, and whose personal tendencies are most hostile to theirs. The representatives of such constituencies would be more than human if they were not influenced by this fact. Representation chosen by the tribes themselves, and responsible to themselves, is the only mode of making the country acquainted with their condition and with our obligations to them. In such a territory the tribal organization would easily merge into the county, and the territorial legislature would not be very different from the grand councils at present in vogue among them. . . .

In the organization of the Indian Bureau itself, at the beginning of your administration, it was deemed advisable to depart from the usual mode of selecting and appointing the superintendents and agents. The tribes in Nebraska and Kansas, and some of those most recently placed upon reservations in the Indian territory, were placed under control of members of the Society of Friends; the others were given in charge of military officers, who were given in charge of military officers, who were waiting orders under the laws for the reduction of the army.

These sweeping changes were made because it was believed that the public opinion of the country demanded a radical re-organization of this branch of the service. The selection of the officers of the army was made partly for economical reasons, as they were on pay though not on duty, and the salaries of many civil officers could thus be saved, and partly because it was believed they furnished a corps of public servants whose integrity and faithfulness could be relied upon, and in whom the public were prepared to have confidence.

The Friends were appointed not because they were believed to have any monopoly of honesty or of good will toward the Indians, but because their selection would of itself be understood by the country to indicate the policy adopted, namely, the sincere cultivation of peaceful relations with the tribes, and the choice of agents who did not, for personal profit, seek the service, but were sought for it because they were at least deemed fit for its duties. The two yearly meetings of "Friends" were asked to select men in whom they had confidence, and who might become at once the business agents of the government and zealous missionaries of civilization. The persons so selected were appointed by you by and with the advice and consent of the Senate, and although it was somewhat late in the season when they were sent to their posts, enough has been seen of their labors to make it certain that the mode of selection was not a mistake. It is due to these societies to say that they have at their own cost sent officers of their own body to inspect the work of the agents as far as it aimed at the civilization and instruction of the Indians. The moral support and encouragement thus given to the agents must be valuable.

In accordance with the same general plan of bringing moral influences to bear upon the conduct of Indian affairs, the present

130

Congress authorized you to appoint a commission of philanthropic citizens, to serve without pay, in such supervisory and visitorial duty as might be assigned to them. No difficulty was found in securing the services of men of the highest character and known benevolence. By an executive order they were authorized to inspect all the accounts and records of the Bureau, to be present at the purchases of Indian goods and advise as to the conduct of the same, and to visit and inspect the tribes in their reservations and examine the business of all the agencies. The officers of the department were also directed to give respectful heed to the suggestions and reports of the commission. No direct responsibility, either pecuniary or administrative, was put upon this commission, because it was believed that their usefulness would not be increased thereby. They now constitute an entirely disinterested body of intelligent advisers, with full power to throw the light of the most searching scrutiny upon the conduct of our relations with the Indians, and to give the public, through their reports, the most reliable knowledge of the condition and progress of the several tribes. It is believed, also, that their efforts cannot fail to stimulate the public conscience, and to give greater unity and vigor to the voluntary efforts made throughout the country in the cause of Indian civilization—a result desirable in itself, and certain to make easier and more satisfactory the duties of the officers of the bureau. . . .

[*House Executive Document* no. 1, 41st Cong., 2d sess., serial 1414, pp. vii-xi.]

79. Report of the Board of Indian Commissioners
November 23, 1869

The first report of the Board of Indian Commissioners shows how seriously they took their responsibilities. They presented a startling indictment of past dealings with the Indians and then offered recommendations for changes in Indian policy which foreshadowed most of the reforms proposed through the rest of the century.

SIR: The commission of citizens appointed by the President under the act of Congress of April 10, 1869, to co-operate with the administration in the management of Indian affairs, respectfully report: . . . .

It is not proposed to make this report either final or in any degree exhaustive. In its moral and political, as well as economic aspects, the Indian question is one of the gravest importance. The difficulties which surround it are of a practical nature, as are also the duties of the commission with reference to them. We cannot offer recommendations as the result of theorizing, but must reach our conclusions through personal observation and knowledge, as well as testimony. The comparatively short period of the existence of the commission, and the preventing causes already mentioned, compel the board to pass over, for the present, some of the important points which have occupied their attention. Should the commission be continued, it is hoped that visits of inspection to the reservations will, in each case, be productive of benefits, and the aggregate of the information acquired will enable the board to make important suggestions, for which it is not now prepared. Should the commission be discontinued, it is hoped some other permanent supervisory body will be created, which, in its material, office, and powers, shall be as far as possible beyond suspicion of selfish motives or personal profits in connection with its duties.

While it cannot be denied that the government of the United States, in the general terms and temper of its legislation, has evinced a desire to deal generously with the Indians, it must be admitted that the actual treatment they have received has been unjust and iniquitous beyond the power of words to express.

Taught by the government that they had rights entitled to respect; when those rights have been assailed by the rapacity of the white man, the arm which should have been raised to protect them has been ever ready to sustain the aggressor.

The history of the government connections with the Indians is a shameful record of broken treaties and unfulfilled promises.

The history of the border white man's

131

connection with the Indians is a sickening record of murder, outrage, robbery, and wrongs committed by the former as the rule, and occasional savage outbreaks and unspeakably barbarous deeds of retaliation by the latter as the exception.

The class of hardy men on the frontier who represent the highest type of the energy and enterprise of the American people, and are just and honorable in their sense of moral obligation and their appreciations of the rights of others, have been powerless to prevent these wrongs, and have been too often the innocent sufferers from the Indians' revenge. That there are many good men on the border is a subject of congratulation, and the files of the Indian Bureau attest that among them are found some of the most earnest remonstrants against the evils we are compelled so strongly to condemn.

The testimony of some of the highest military officers of the United States is on record to the effect that, in our Indian wars, almost without exception, the first aggressions have been made by the white man, and the assertion is supported by every civilian of reputation who has studied the subject. In addition to the class of robbers and outlaws who find impunity in their nefarious pursuits upon the frontiers, there is a large class of professedly reputable men who use every means in their power to bring on Indian wars, for the sake of the profit to be realized from the presence of troops and the expenditure of government funds in their midst. They proclaim death to the Indians at all times, in words and publications, making no distinction between the innocent and the guilty. They incite the lowest class of men to the perpetration of the darkest deeds against their victims, and, as judges and jurymen, shield them from the justice due to their crimes. Every crime committed by a white man against an Indian is concealed or palliated; every offense committed by an Indian against a white man is borne on the wings of the post or the telegraph to the remotest corner of the land, clothed with all the horrors which the reality or imagination can throw around it. Against such influences as these the people of the United States need to be warned. The murders, robberies, drunken riots and outrages perpetrated by Indians in time of peace—taking into consideration

the relative population of the races on the frontier—do not amount to a tithe of the number of like crimes committed by white men in the border settlements and towns. Against the inhuman idea that the Indian is only fit to be exterminated, and the influence of the men who propagate it, the military arm of the government cannot be too strongly guarded. It is hardly to be wondered at that inexperienced officers, ambitious for distinction, when surrounded by such influences, have been incited to attack Indian bands without adequate cause, and involve the nation in an injust war. It should, at least, be understood that in the future such blunders should cost the officer his commission, and that such distinction is infamy.

Paradoxical as it may seem, the white man has been the chief obstacle in the way of Indian civilization. The benevolent measures attempted by the government for their advancement have been almost uniformly thwarted by the agencies employed to carry them out. The soldiers, sent for their protection, too often carried demoralization and disease into their midst. The agent, appointed to be their friend and counsellor, business manager, and the almoner of the government bounties, frequently went among them only to enrich himself in the shortest possible time, at the cost of the Indians, and spend the largest available sum of the government money with the least ostensible beneficial result. The general interest of the trader was opposed to their enlightenment as tending to lessen his profits. Any increase of intelligence would render them less liable to his impositions; and, if occupied in agricultural pursuits, their product of furs would be proportionally decreased. The contractor's and transporter's interests were opposed to it, for the reason that the production of agricultural products on the spot would measurably cut off their profits in furnishing army supplies. The interpreter knew that if they were taught, his occupation would be gone. The more submissive and patient the tribe, the greater the number of outlaws infesting their vicinity; and all these were the missionaries teaching them the most degrading vices of which humanity is capable. If in spite of these obstacles a tribe made some progress in agriculture, or their lands be-

132

came valuable from any cause, the process of civilization was summarily ended by driving them away from their homes with fire and sword, to undergo similar experiences in some new locality.

Whatever may have been the original character of the aborigines, many of them are now precisely what the course of treatment received from the whites must necessarily have made them—suspicious, revengeful, and cruel in their retaliation. In war they know no distinction between the innocent and the guilty. In his most savage vices the worst Indian is but the imitator of bad white men on the border. To assume that all of them, or even a majority of them, may be so characterized with any degree of truthfulness, would be no more just than to assume the same of all the white people upon the frontier. Some of the tribes, as a whole, are peaceful and industrious to the extent of their knowledge, needing only protection, and a reasonable amount of aid and Christian instruction, to insure the rapid attainment of habits of industry, and a satisfactory advance toward civilization. Even among the wildest of the nomadic tribes there are large bands, and many individuals in other bands, who are anxious to remain quietly upon their reservation, and are patiently awaiting the fulfillment of the government promise that they and their children shall be taught to "live like the white man."

To assert that "the Indian will not work" is as true as it would be to say that the white man will not work. In all countries there are non-working classes. The chiefs and warriors are the Indian aristocracy. They need only to be given incentives to induce them to work. Why should the Indian be expected to plant corn, fence lands, build houses, or do anything but get food from day to day, when experience has taught him that the product of his labor will be seized by the white man to-morrow? The most industrious white man would become a drone under similar circumstances. Nevertheless, many of the Indians are already at work, and furnish ample refutation of the assertion that "the Indian will not work." There is no escape from the inexorable logic of facts. . . .

The policy of collecting the Indian tribes upon small reservations contiguous to each other, and within the limits of a large reser-

vation, eventually to become a State of the Union, and of which the small reservations will probably be the counties, seems to be the best that can be devised. Many tribes may thus be collected in the present Indian territory. The larger the number that can be thus concentrated the better for the success of the plan; care being taken to separate hereditary enemies from each other. When upon the reservation they should be taught as soon as possible the advantage of individual ownership of property; and should be given land in severalty as soon as it is desired by any of them, and the tribal relations should be discouraged. To facilitate the future allotment of the land the agricultural portions of the reservations should be surveyed as soon as it can be done without too much exciting their apprehensions. The titles should be inalienable from the family of the holder for at least two or three generations. The civilized tribes now in the Indian territory should be taxed, and made citizens of the United States as soon as possible.

The treaty system should be abandoned, and as soon as any just method can be devised to accomplish it, existing treaties should be abrogated.

The legal status of the uncivilized Indians should be that of wards of the government; the duty of the latter being to protect them, to educate them in industry, the arts of civilization, and the principles of Christianity; elevate them to the rights of citizenship, and to sustain and clothe them until they can support themselves.

The payment of money annuities to the Indians should be abandoned, for the reason that such payments encourage idleness and vice, to the injury of those whom it is intended to benefit. Schools should be established, and teachers employed by the government to introduce the English language in every tribe. It is believed that many of the difficulties with Indians occur from misunderstanding as to the meaning and intention of either party. The teachers employed should be nominated by some religious body having a mission nearest to the location of the school. The establishment of Christian missions should be encouraged, and their schools fostered. The pupils should at least receive the rations and clothing they would get if remaining with their families. The religion of our blessed Saviour is believed to be the most effective agent for the civilization of any people.

A reversal of the policy which has heretofore prevailed, of taking the goods of the peaceable and industrious and giving them to the vicious and unruly, should be insisted on. Every means in the power of the government and its agents should be employed to render settlement and industrious habits on the reservation attractive and certain in its rewards. Experience has already shown that this is the best mode of inducing the Indians to settle upon their reservations.

The honest and prompt performance of all the treaty obligations to the reservation Indians is absolutely necessary to success in the benevolent designs of the administration. There should be no further delay in the erection of the promised dwellings, schoolhouses, mills, &c., and the opening of the farms and furnishing instructors. There can be no question or doubt as to the wisdom of the President in selecting Indian superintendents and agents with a view to their moral as well as business qualifications, and aside from any political considerations. There should be some judicial tribunal constituted within the Indian territory competent to the prompt punishment of crime, whether committed by white man, Indian, or negro. The agent upon the reservation in which the offense is committed, the agent of the next nearest reservation, and the nearest post commander might constitute a court, all the agents being clothed with the necessary powers. The Indian treaties we have examined provide, in effect, that proof of any offense committed by a white man against an Indian shall be made before the agent, who shall transmit the same to the Commissioner of Indian Affairs, who shall proceed to cause the offender to be arrested and tried by the laws of the United States. If the Indian commits an offense, he shall be given up to be tried by the laws of the United States. It is a long process to get a white man tried; a shorter one for the Indian, in proportion to the difference in distance between the agency and the nearest white settlement and that to Washington City; and in the trials the Indian never escapes punishment; the white man rarely fails to be acquitted. . . .

[*Annual Report of the Board of Indian Commissioners, 1869*, pp. 5-11.]

80. Indian Commissioner Parker on the Treaty System

Extract from the *Annual Report of the Commissioner of Indian Affairs*

December 23, 1869

The treaty system of dealing with the Indians had long been under attack because of the inequality of the two contracting parties. After the Civil War such criticisms came to a head and contributed to the abolition of treaty making in 1871. One strong statement against negotiating treaties with the Indians was made by Commissioner Ely S. Parker, who was himself a Seneca Indian, in his annual report of 1869.

. . . . Arrangements now, as heretofore, will doubtless be required with tribes desiring to be settled upon reservations for the relinquishment of their rights to the lands claimed by them and for assistance in sustaining themselves in a new position, but I am of the opinion that *they should not be of a treaty nature*. It has become a matter of serious import whether the treaty system in use ought longer to be continued. In my judgment it should not. A treaty involves the idea of a compact between two or more sovereign powers, each possessing sufficient authority and force to compel a compliance with the obligations incurred. The Indian tribes of the United States are not sovereign nations, capable of making treaties, as none of them have an organized government of such inherent strength as would secure a faithful obedience of its people in the observance of compacts of this character. They are held to be the wards of the government, and the only title the law concedes to them to the lands they occupy or claim is a mere possessory one. But, because treaties have been made with them, generally for the extinguishment of their supposed absolute title to land inhabited by them, or over which they roam, they have become falsely impressed with the notion of national independence. It

134

is time that this idea should be dispelled, and the government cease the cruel farce of thus dealing with its helpless and ignorant wards. Many good men, looking at this matter only from a Christian point of view, will perhaps say that the poor Indian has been greatly wronged and ill treated; that this whole country was once his, of which he has been despoiled, and that he has been driven from place to place until he has hardly left to him a spot where to lay his head. This indeed may be philanthropic and humane, but the stern letter of the law admits of no such conclusion, and great injury has been done by the government in deluding this people into the belief of their being independent sovereignties, while they were at the same time recognized only as its dependents and wards. As civilization advances and their possessions of land are required for settlement, such legislation should be granted to them as a wise, liberal, and just government ought to extend to subjects holding their dependent relation. In regard to treaties now in force, justice and humanity require that they be promptly and faithfully executed, so that the Indians may not have cause of complaint, or reason to violate their obligations by acts of violence and robbery.

While it may not be expedient to negotiate treaties with any of the tribes hereafter, it is no doubt just that those made within the past year, and now pending before the United States Senate, should be definitely acted upon. Some of the parties are anxiously waiting for the fulfillment of the stipulations of these compacts and manifest dissatisfaction at the delay. . . .

[*House Executive Document* no. 1, 41st Cong., 2d sess., serial 1414, p. 448.]

81. President Grant's Peace Policy
Extract from Grant's Second Annual Message to Congress
December 5, 1870

In an attempt to eliminate abuses in the Indian service occasioned by political appointments, President Grant authorized the assignment of the Indian agencies to religious denominations, who would select the agents and other personnel. Grant explained and justified the action in his message to Congress in 1870.

. . . . Reform in the management of Indian affairs has received the special attention of the Administration from its inauguration to the present day. The experiment of making it a missionary work was tried with a few agencies given to the denomination of Friends, and has been found to work most advantageously. All agencies and superintendencies not so disposed of were given to officers of the Army. The act of Congress reducing the Army renders army officers ineligible for civil positions. Indian agencies being civil offices, I determined to give all the agencies to such religious denominations as had heretofore established missionaries among the Indians, and perhaps to some other denominations who would undertake the work on the same terms—*i.e.*, as a missionary work. The societies selected are allowed to name their own agents, subject to the approval of the Executive, and are expected to watch over them and aid them as missionaries, to Christianize and civilize the Indian, and to train him in the arts of peace. The Government watches over the official acts of these agents, and requires of them as strict an accountability as if they were appointed in any other manner. I entertain the confident hope that the policy now pursued will in a few years bring all the Indians upon reservations, where they will live in houses, and have schoolhouses and churches, and will be pursuing peaceful and self-sustaining avocations, and where they may be visited by the law-abiding white man with the same impunity that he now visits the civilized white settlements. I call your special attention to the report of the Commissioner of Indian Affairs for full information on this subject. . . .

[James D. Richardson, comp., *Messages and Papers of the Presidents*, 7:109-10.]

82. Cherokee Tobacco Case
December, 1870

Cherokees Elias C. Boudinot and Stand Watie refused to pay taxes required by the Internal Revenue Act of 1868 on tobacco manufactured in the Cherokee Nation because they claimed the Cherokee treaty of 1866 exempted them from such taxation. The Supreme Court decided against them on the grounds that a law of Congress can supersede the provisions of a treaty.

. . . . The second section of the fourth article of the Constitution of the United States declares that "this Constitution and the laws of the United States which shall be made in pursuance thereof, and all treaties which shall be made under the authority of the United States, shall be the supreme law of the land."

It need hardly be said that a treaty cannot change the Constitution or be held valid if it be in violation of that instrument. This results from the nature and fundamental principles of our government. The effect of treaties and acts of Congress, when in conflict, is not settled by the Constitution. But the question is not involved in any doubt as to its proper solution. A treaty may supersede a prior act of Congress, and an act of Congress may supersede a prior treaty. In the cases referred to these principles were applied to treaties with foreign nations. Treaties with

Indian nations within the jurisdiction of the United States, whatever considerations of humanity and good faith may be involved and require their faithful observance, cannot be more obligatory. They have no higher sanctity; and no greater inviolability or immunity from legislative invasion can be claimed for them. The consequences in all such cases give rise to questions which must be met by the political department of the government. They are beyond the sphere of judicial cognizance. In the case under consideration the act of Congress must prevail as if the treaty were not an element to be considered. If a wrong has been done the power of redress is with Congress not with the judiciary, and that body, upon being applied to, it is to be presumed, will promptly give the proper relief. . . .

[11 *Wallace*, 616, 620-21.]

83. Abolition of Treaty Making
March 3, 1871

Because of humanitarian attacks upon the treaty system and the objections of the House of Representatives to the concentration of authority for dealing with the Indians in the hands of the Senate through its treaty-making power, Congress in 1871, in an obscure rider to the Indian appropriation bill, outlawed further treaty making with Indian tribes.

An Act making Appropriations for the current and contingent Expenses of the Indian Department. . . .

. . . *Yankton Tribe of Sioux.*— . . . For insurance and transportation of goods for the Yanktons, one thousand five hundred dollars: *Provided,* That hereafter no Indian nation or tribe within the territory of the Unit-

ed States shall be acknowledged or recognized as an independent nation, tribe, or power with whom the United States may contract by treaty: *Provided, further,* That nothing herein contained shall be construed to invalidate or impair the obligation of any treaty heretofore lawfully made and ratified with any such Indian nation or tribe. . . .

[*U.S. Statutes at Large*, 16:566.]

84. Indian Commissioner Walker on Indian Policy
Extract from the *Annual Report of the Commissioner of Indian Affairs*
November 1, 1872

Commissioner of Indian Affairs Francis A. Walker spoke bluntly in his report of 1872 about the relationship of the federal government to the Indians. It was a harsh, practical statement, made by a man who later won renown as a statistician, economist, and educator.

THE INDIAN POLICY

The Indian policy, so called, of the Government, is a policy, and it is not a policy, or rather it consists of two policies, entirely distinct, seeming, indeed, to be mutually inconsistent and to reflect each upon the other: the one regulating the treatment of the tribes which are potentially hostile, that is, whose hostility is only repressed just so long as, and so far as, they are supported in idleness by the Government; the other regulating the treatment of those tribes which, from traditional friendship, from numerical weakness, or by the force of their location, are either indisposed toward, or incapable of, resistance to the demands of the Government. The treatment of the feeble Poncas, and of the friendly Arrickarees, Mandans, and Gros Ventres of the north is an example of the latter; while the treatment of their insolent and semi-hostile neighbors, the Sioux, furnishes an example of the former. In the same way at the south, the treatment of the well-intentioned Papagoes of Arizona contrasts just as strongly with the dealings of the Government by their traditional enemies, the treacherous and vindictive Apaches. This want of completeness and consistency in the treatment of the Indian tribes by the Government has been made the occasion of much ridicule and partisan abuse; and it is indeed calculated to provoke criticism and to afford scope for satire; but it is none the less compatible with the highest expediency of the situation. It is, of course, hopelessly illogical that the expenditures of the Government should be proportioned not to the good but to the ill desert of the several tribes; that large bodies of Indians should be supported in entire indolence by the bounty of the Government simply because they are audacious and insolent, while well-disposed Indians are only assisted to self-maintenance, since it is known they will not fight.

It is hardly less than absurd, on the first view of it, that delegations from tribes that have frequently defied our authority and fought our troops, and have never yielded more than a partial and grudging obedience to the most reasonable requirements of the Government, should be entertained at the national capital, feasted, and loaded with presents. There could be no better subject for the lively paragraphist in his best estate, or for the heavy editorial writer on a dull news day, than such a course on the part of the Government. These things can be made to appear vastly amusing, and the unreflecting are undoubtedly influenced in a great degree to the prejudice of the Indian policy by the incessant small-arms fire of squibs and epigrams, even more perhaps than by the ponderous artillery of argument and invective directed against it. And yet, for all this, the Government is right and its critics wrong; and the "Indian policy" is sound, sensible, and beneficent, because it reduces to the minimum the loss of life and property upon our frontier, and allows the freest development of our settlements and railways possible under the circumstances.

The mistake of those who oppose the present Indian policy is not in erroneously applying to the course of the Government the standard they have taken, but in taking an altogether false standard for the purpose. It is not a whit more unreasonable that the Government should do much for hostile Indians and little for friendly Indians than it is that a private citizen should, to save his life, surrender all the contents of his purse to a highwayman; while on another occasion, to a distressed and deserving applicant for charity, he would measure his contribution by his means and disposition at the time. There is precisely the same justification for the course of the Government in feeding saucy and mischievous Indians to repletion, while permitting more tractable and peace-

137

ful tribes to gather a bare subsistence by hard work, or what to an Indian is hard work. It is not, of course, to be understood that the Government of the United States is at the mercy of Indians; but thousands of its citizens are, even thousands of families. Their exposed situation on the extreme verge of settlement affords a sufficient justification to the Government for buying off the hostility of the savages, excited and exasperated as they are, and most naturally so, by the invasion of their hunting-grounds and the threatened extinction of game. It would require one hundred thousand troops at least to form a *cordon* behind which our settlements could advance with the extent of range, and unrestrained choice of location, the security of feeling, and the freedom of movement which have characterized the growth of the past three or four years. Indeed, the presence of no military force could give that confidence to pioneer enterprise which the general cessation of Indian hostilities has engendered. Men of an adventurous cast will live and work behind a line of troops with, it is possible, some exhilaration of feeling on that account; but, as a rule, men will not place women and children in situations of even possible peril, nor will they put money into permanent improvements under such circumstances. Especially has the absence of Indian hostilities been of the highest value, within the last few years, in directing and determining to the extreme frontier the immigrants arriving in such vast numbers on our shores. Americans habituated to the contemplation of this species of danger as one of the features of pioneer life, will scarcely comprehend the reluctance with which men accustomed to the absolute security of person and property in the settled countries of Europe expose themselves and their families to perils of this kind. I was informed by the late president of the Northern Pacific Railroad that it was found almost impossible to hire Swedes and Norwegians to work upon the line of that road, then under construction from the Red River to the Missouri, on account of the vague apprehension of Indian attack which prevailed in connection with the progress of the road through the past summer. As a matter of fact, no well informed person believed that the savages would undertake any offensive operations whatever until after the Missouri had been crossed and passed at least one hundred miles. But these people, unaccustomed to regard possible torture and murder as one of the conditions of a contract to labor, would refuse high wages rather than subject themselves to the slightest risk. The fact that Americans are more daring and adventurous in the presence of a danger more familiar to them, only constitutes a stronger reason for maintaining the immunity which has, for three years now, been secured by the feeding system. There are innumerable little rifts of agricultural or mining settlements all over the western country which, if unmolested, will in a few years become self-protecting communities, but which, in the event of a general Indian war occurring at the present time, would utterly and instantly disappear, either by abandonment or massacre. The first month of hostilities would see fifty valleys, up which population is now slowly but steadily creeping under cover of the feeding system, swept bare by the horrid atrocities of Indian warfare, or deserted by their affrighted inhabitants, hastily driving before them what of their stock could be gathered at a moment's notice, and bearing away what of their household goods could be carried in their single wagons. Such would be the result even with the most favorable issue of military operations. It is right that those who criticise the policy of the Government toward the Indians, and ridicule it as undignified in its concessions and unstatesman-like in its temporizing with a recognized evil, should fairly face the one alternative which is presented. There is no question of national dignity, be it remembered, involved in the treatment of savages by a civilized power. With wild men, as with wild beasts, the question whether in a given situation one shall fight, coax, or run, is a question merely of what is easiest and safest.

THE USE OF THE MILITARY ARM.

The system now pursued in dealing with the roving tribes dangerous to our frontier population and obstructing our industrial progress, is entirely consistent with, and, indeed, requires the occasional use of the military arm, in restraining or chastising refractory individuals and bands. Such a use of the military constitutes no abandonment of the "peace policy," and involves no disparagement of it. It was not to be expected—it was not in the nature of things—that the entire body of wild Indians should submit to be restrained in their Ishmaelitish proclivities without a struggle on the part of the more audacious to maintain their traditional freedom. In the first announcement made of the reservation system, it was expressly declared that the Indians should be made as comfortable on, and as uncomfortable off, their reservations as it was in the power of the Government to make them; that such of them as went right should be protected and fed, and such as went wrong should be harassed and scourged without intermission. It was not anticipated that the first proclamation of this policy to the tribes concerned would effect the entire cessation of existing evils; but it was believed that persistence in the course marked out would steadily reduce the number of the refractory, both by the losses sustained in actual conflict and by the desertion of individuals as they should become weary of a profitless and hopeless struggle, until, in the near result, the system adopted should apply without exception to all the then roving and hostile tribes. Such a use of the strong arm of the Government is not war, but discipline. . . .

It will be sufficient, perhaps, to mark the distinction, to say that a general Indian war could not be carried on with the present military force of the United States, or anything like it. Regiments would be needed where now are only companies, and long lines of posts would have to be established for the protection of regions which, under the safeguard of the feeding system, are now left wholly uncovered. On the other hand, by the reservation system and the feeding system combined, the occasions for collision are so reduced by lessening the points of contact, and the number of Indians available for hostile expeditions involving exposure, hardship, and danger is so diminished through the appeal made to their indolence and self-indulgence, that the Army in its present force is able to deal effectively with the few marauding bands which refuse to accept the terms of the Government.

It is unquestionably true that the Government has seemed somewhat tardy in proceeding under the second half of the reservation policy, and in applying the scourge to individuals and bands leaving their prescribed limits without authority, or for hostile purposes. This has been partly from a legitimate deference to the conviction of the great body of citizens that the Indians have been in the past unjustly and cruelly treated, and that great patience and long forbearance ought to be exercised in bringing them around to submission to the present reasonable requirements of the Government, and partly from the knowledge on the part of the officers of the Government charged with administering Indian affairs, that, from the natural jealousy of these people, their sense of wrongs suffered in the past, and their suspiciousness arising from repeated acts of treachery on the part of the whites; from the great distance of many bands and individuals from points of personal communication with the agents of the Government, and the absence of all means of written communication with them; from the efforts of abandoned and degraded whites, living among the Indians and exerting much influence over them, to misrepresent the policy of the Government, and to keep alive the hostility and suspicion of the savages; and, lastly, from the extreme untrustworthiness of many of the interpreters on whom the Government is obliged to rely for bringing its intentions to the knowledge of the Indians: that by the joint effect of all these obstacles, many tribes and bands could come very slowly to hear, comprehend, and trust the professions and promises of the Government. . . .

The patience and forbearance exercised have been fully justified in their fruits. The main body of the roving Indians have, with good grace or with ill grace, submitted to the reservation system. Of those who still remain away from the assigned limits, by far the greater part are careful to do so with as little offense as possible; and when their range is such as for the present not to bring them into annoying or dangerous contact with the whites, this Office, has, from the motive of economy, generally been disposed

139

to allow them to pick up their own living still by hunting and fishing, in preference to tying them up at agencies where they would require to be fed mainly or wholly at the expense of the Government. . . .

THE BEGINNING OF THE END.

It belongs not to a sanguine, but to a sober view of the situation, that three years will see the alternative of war eliminated from the Indian question, and the most powerful and hostile bands of to-day thrown in entire helplessness on the mercy of the Government. Indeed, the progress of two years more, if not of another summer, on the Northern Pacific Railroad will of itself completely solve the great Sioux problem, and leave the ninety thousand Indians ranging between the two trans-continental lines as incapable of resisting the Government as are the Indians of New York or Massachusetts. Columns moving north from the Union Pacific, and south from the Northern Pacific, would crush the Sioux and their confederates as between the upper and the nether millstone; while the rapid movement of troops along the northern line would prevent the escape of the savages, when hard pressed, into the British Possessions, which have heretofore afforded a convenient refuge on the approach of a military expedition.

Toward the south the day of deliverance from the fear of Indian hostility is more distant, yet it is not too much to expect that three summers of peaceful progress will forever put it out of the power of the tribes and bands which at present disturb Colorado, Utah, Arizona, and New Mexico to claim consideration of the country in any other attitude than as pensioners upon the national bounty. The railroads now under construction, or projected with a reasonable assurance of early completion, will multiply fourfold the striking force of the Army in that section; the little rifts of mining settlement, now found all through the mountains of the southern Territories will have become self-protecting communities; the feeble, wavering line of agricultural occupation, now sensitive to the faintest breath of Indian hostility, will then have grown to be the powerful "reserve" to lines still more closely advanced upon the last range of the intractable tribes.

SUBMISSION THE ONLY HOPE OF THE INDIANS.

No one certainly will rejoice more heartily than the present Commissioner when the Indians of this country cease to be in a position to dictate, in any form or degree, to the Government; when, in fact, the last hostile tribe becomes reduced to the condition of suppliants for charity. This is, indeed, the only hope of salvation for the aborigines of the continent. If they stand up against the progress of civilization and industry, they must be relentlessly crushed. The westward course of population is neither to be denied nor delayed for the sake of all the Indians that ever called this country their home. They must yield or perish; and there is something that savors of providential mercy in the rapidity with which their fate advances upon them, leaving them scarcely the chance to resist before they shall be surrounded and disarmed. It is not feebly and futilely to attempt to stay this tide, whose depth and strength can hardly be measured, but to snatch the remnants of the Indian race from destruction from before it, that the friends of humanity should exert themselves in this jucture, and lose no time. And it is because the present system allows the freest extension of settlement and industry possible under the circumstances, while affording space and time for humane endeavors to rescue the Indian tribes from a position altogether barbarous and incompatible with civilization and social progress, that this system must be approved by all enlightened citizens. . . .

THE CLAIMS OF THE INDIAN.

The people of the United States can never without dishonor refuse to respect these two considerations: 1st. That this continent was originally owned and occupied by the Indians, who have on this account a claim somewhat larger than the privilege of one hundred and sixty acres of land, and "find himself" in tools and stock, which is granted as a matter of course to any newly-arrived foreigner who declares his intention to become a citizen; that something in the nature of an endowment, either capitalized or in the form of annual expenditures for a series of years for the benefit of the Indians, though at the discretion of the Government as to the specific objects, should be provided for every tribe or band which is deprived of its roaming privilege and confined to a diminished reservation: such an endowment being not in the nature of a gratuity, but in common honesty the right of the Indian on account of his original interest in the soil. 2d. That inasmuch as the progress of our industrial enterprise has cut these people off from modes of livelihood entirely sufficient for their wants, and for which they were qualified, in a degree which has been the wonder of more civilized races, by inherited aptitudes and by long pursuit, and has left them utterly without resource, they have a claim on this account again to temporary support and to such assistance as may be necessary to place them in a position to obtain a livelihood by means which shall be compatible with civilization.

Had the settlements of the United States not been extended beyond the frontier of 1867, all the Indians of the continent would to the end of time have found upon the plains an inexhaustible supply of food and clothing. Were the westward course of population to be stayed at the barriers of to-day, notwithstanding the tremendous inroads made upon their hunting-grounds since 1867, the Indians would still have hope of life. But another such five years will see the Indians of Dakota and Montana as poor as the Indians of Nevada and Southern California; that is, reduced to an habitual condition of suffering from want of food.

The freedom of expansion which is work-ing these results is to us of incalculable value. To the Indian it is of incalculable cost. Every year's advance of our frontier takes in a territory as large as some of the kingdoms of Europe. We are richer by hundreds of millions; the Indian is poorer by a large part of the little that he has. This growth is bringing imperial greatness to the nation; to the Indian it brings wretchedness, destitution, beggary. Surely there is obligation found in considerations like these, requiring us in some way, and in the best way, to make good to these original owners of the soil the loss by which we so greatly gain.

Can any principle of national morality be clearer than that, when the expansion and development of a civilized race involve the rapid destruction of the only means of subsistence possessed by the members of a less fortunate race, the higher is bound as of simple right to provide for the lower some substitute for the means of subsistence which it has destroyed? That substitute is, of course, best realized, not by systematic gratuities of food and clothing continued beyond a present emergency, but by directing these people to new pursuits which shall be consistent with the progress of civilization upon the continent; helping them over the first rough places on "the white man's road," and, meanwhile, supplying such subsistence as is absolutely necessary during the period of initiation and experiment. . . .

[*House Executive Document* no. 1, 42d Cong., 3d sess., serial 1560, pp. 391-99.]

85. Assignment of Indian Agencies to Religious Societies

Extract from the *Annual Report of the Commissioner of Indian Affairs*

November 1, 1872

The apportionment of the Indian agencies among missionary societies of the several religious denominations, begun with the Quakers in 1869, was in full operation by 1872, when Commissioner of Indian Affairs Francis A. Walker included a tabulation of the agency assignments in his annual report.

THE INDIAN SERVICE AND THE RELIGIOUS SOCIETIES.

For the year preceding the passage of the act of July 15, 1870, all superintendents of Indian affairs and Indian agents, with the exception of those for the States of Kansas and Nebraska, were officers of the Army assigned to duty under the orders of the Indian Office. In the two States named, however, the superintendents of Indian affairs and Indian agents had been for somewhat more than a year appointed by the Executive upon the recommendation of the two Societies of Friends, the appointees being in all cases recognized members of one

141

or the other of those religious bodies, and, while duly subordinate and responsible in all official respects to the Indian Office, maintaining close correspondence with committees of their respective societies appointed for that purpose. So fortunate were the results of this system of appointment in Kansas and Nebraska considered, that when under the provisions of the 18th section of the act of July 15, 1870, it became necessary to relieve officers of the Army from this service, it was decided by the Executive that all the agencies thus vacated in the remaining States and the Territories should be filled by appointment upon the recommendation of some religious body; and to this end the agencies were, so to speak, apportioned among the prominent denominational associations of the country, or the missionary societies representing such denominational views; and these associations or societies were thereupon requested to place themselves in communication with the Department of the Interior, to make nominations to the position of agent whenever a vacancy should occur within the list of the agencies assigned them respectively, and in and through this extra-official relationship to assume charge of the intellectual and moral education of the Indians thus brought within the reach of their influence. The reason formally announced for this somewhat anomalous order of appointment was the desirableness of securing harmony between agents and missionaries, complaints having become general that, in the frequent change of agents, no missionary efforts could long be carried on at any specified agency without encountering, sooner or later, from some agent of different religious views or of no religious views, a degree of opposition to or persecution which would necessarily extinguish such missionary enterprise and even destroy the fruits of past labors. When it is remembered that efforts of this kind must, to achieve valuable results, be continued for many years, confidence being a plant of slow growth in savage breasts, and the hope of the missionary being almost universally founded on the education of the rising generation, while, in fact, Indian agents were under the old political *régime* changed every few months, or every two or three years at the longest, it will readily be seen that the

chances of missionary enterprises being cut off in the flower were far greater than the chances of continuance and success. Such indeed had been in general history of these efforts among the Indians of North America, and it may fairly be said that almost the only enterprises of this kind which have secured a permanent footing are those which preceded the Government control of the Indians, and which had founded themselves on the confidence and sympathies of the natives too strongly to be shaken by official hostility or neglect.

While, however, the importance of securing harmony of feeling and concert of action between the agents of the Government and the missionaries at the several agencies, in the matter of the moral and religious advancement of the Indians, was the single reason formally given for placing the nominations to Indian agencies in the hands of the denominational societies, it is, perhaps, not improper to say that the Executive was also influenced by the consideration that the general character of the Indian service might be distinctly improved by taking the nomination to the office of agent out of the domain of politics and placing it where no motives but those of disinterested benevolence could be presumed to prevail.

The following schedule exhibits the present apportionment of Indian agencies among the several religious associations and missionary societies. The figures refer to the number of Indians embraced in the several agencies:

Friends, (Hicksite,) the Northern superintendency and the agencies therein, viz: Great Nemaha, 313; Omaha, 969; Winnebago, 1,440; Pawnee, 2,447; Otoe, 464; and Santee Sioux, 965; all located within the State of Nebraska.

Friends, (Orthodox,) the Central superintendency and the agencies therein, viz: Pottawatomie, 400; Kaw, 290; Kickapoo, 598; all located in Kansas; and Quapaw, 1,070; Osage, 4,000; Sac and Fox, 463; Shawnee, 663; Wichita, 1,250; Kiowa, 5,490; and Upper Arkansas, 3,500; all located in the Indian Territory.

Baptist, the Cherokee, 18,000; Creek, 12,300, in the Indian Territory; Walker River, 6,000 and Pi-Ute, 2,500, in Nevada; and Special, 3,000, in Utah.

142

Presbyterian, the Choctaw, 16,000; and Seminoles, 2,398, in the Indian Territory; Abiquiu or Tierra Amarilla, 1,920; Navajo, 9,114; Mescalero Apache, 830; Tularosa, or Southern Apache, 1,200, in New Mexico Territory; Moquis Pueblo, 3,000, in Arizona Territory; Nez Percé, 2,807, in Idaho Territory; and Uintah Valley, 800, in Utah Territory.

Christian, the Pueblo, 7,683, in New Mexico; Neeah Bay, 604, in Washington Territory.

Methodist, Hoopa Valley, 725; Round Valley, 1,700; and Tule River, 374, in California; Yakama, 3,000; Skokomish, 919; Quinaielt, 520, in Washington Territory; Warm Springs, 626; Siletz, 2,500; and Klamath, 4,000, in Oregon; Blackfeet, 7,500; Crow, 2,700; and Milk River, 19,755 in Montana Territory; Fort Hall, 1,037, in Idaho Territory; and Michigan, 9,117, in Michigan.

Catholic, Tulalip, 3,600; and Colville, 3,349, in Washington Territory; Grand Ronde, 870; Umatilla, 837, in Oregon; Flathead, 1,780, in Montana Territory; Grand River, 6,700; and Devil's Lake, 720, in Dakota Territory.

Reformed Dutch, Colorado River, 828; Pima and Maricopa, 4,342; Camp Grant, 900; Camp Verde, 748; and White Mountain, or Camp Apache, 1,300, in Arizona Territory.

Congregational, Green Bay, 2,871; and Chippewas of Lake Superior, 5,150, in Wisconsin; and Chippewas of the Mississippi, 6,455, in Minnesota.

Protestant Episcopal, Whetstone, 5,000; Ponca, 735; Upper Missouri, 2,547; Fort Berthold, 2,700; Cheyenne River, 6,000; Yankton, 1,947; and Red Cloud, 7,000, in Dakota Territory; and Shoshone, 1,000, in Wyoming Territory.

American Board of Commissioners for Foreign Missions, Sisseton, 1,496, in Dakota Territory.

Unitarian, Los Pinos, 3,000; and White River, 800, in Colorado Territory.

Lutheran, Sac and Fox, 273, in Iowa.

Recapitulation.

The Hicksite Friends have in their charge 6 agencies, with 6,598 Indians; Orthodox Friends, 10 agencies, with 17,724 Indians; Baptists, 5 agencies, with 40,800 Indians; Presbyterians, 9 agencies, with 38,069 Indians; Christians, 2 agencies, with 8,287 Indians; Methodists, 14 agencies, with 54,473 Indians; Catholics, 7 agencies, with 17,856 Indians; Reformed Dutch, 5 agencies, with 8,118 Indians; Congregationalists, 3 agencies, with 14,476 Indians; Episcopalians, 8 agencies, with 26,929 Indians; the American Board of Commissioners for Foreign Missions, 1 agency, with 1,496 Indians; Unitarians, 2 agencies, with 3,800 Indians; Lutherans, 1 agency, with 273 Indians.

[*House Executive Document* no. 1, 42d Cong., 3d sess., serial 1560, pp. 460-62.]

86. Establishment of a Reservation by Executive Order
May 29, 1873

Although Indian reservations initially were set aside by treaty stipulations, reservations were also designated by executive order of the president of the United States. An example of such creation of a reservation is that of the Mescalero Apaches in New Mexico.

DEPARTMENT OF THE INTERIOR, *Office of Indian Affairs, May 23, 1873.*
The above diagram is intended to show a proposed reservation for the Mescalero band of Apache Indians in New Mexico; said proposed reservation is indicated on the diagram by the red lines bordered with yellow, and is described as follows, viz:

Commencing at the southwest corner of the Fort Stanton reduced military reserva-tion, and running thence due south to a point on the hills near the north bank of the Rio Rindoso; thence along said hills to a point above the settlements; thence across said river to a point on the opposite hills, and thence to the same line upon which we start from Fort Stanton; and thence due south to the thirty-third degree north latitude; thence to the top of the Sacramento Mountains, and along the top of said mountains to the top of

143

the White Mountains; thence along the top of said mountains to the headwaters of the Rio Nogal, to a point opposite the starting point, and thence to the starting point.

I respectfully recommend that the President be requested to order that the land comprised within the above-described limits be withheld from entry and settlement as public lands, and that the same be set apart as an Indian reservation, as indicated in my report to the Department of this date.

EDW. P. SMITH, *Commissioner.*

DEPARTMENT OF THE INTERIOR,
May 26, 1873.

Respectfully presented to the President, with the recommendation that he make the order above proposed by the Commissioner of Indian Affairs.

C. DELANO, *Secretary.*

EXECUTIVE MANSION, *May 29, 1873.*

It is hereby ordered that the tract of country above described be withheld from entry and settlement as public lands, and that the same be set apart as a reservation for the Mescalero Apache Indians, as recommended by the Secretary of the Interior and Commissioner of Indian Affairs.

U.S. GRANT.

[Charles J. Kappler, ed., *Indian Affairs: Laws and Treaties, 1:870-71.*]

87. Indian Commissioner Smith on Indian Citizenship

Extract from the *Annual Report of the Commissioner of Indian Affairs*

November 1, 1874

Changing relationships between the Indians and the United States called for new legislation. One detailed proposal, which showed the direction taken by official thinking in the Indian Office, was that of Commissioner Edward P. Smith in his annual report of 1874.

LEGISLATION FOR INDIANS ON A NEW BASIS

Frequent mention has been made in this report of the necessity for additional legislation on behalf of the Indians. This necessity is apparent from the fact that the only statutes under which Indians are managed and controlled are substantially those enacted in 1834, known as the trade and intercourse laws, whose main purpose was to regulate traffic in furs, and prevent sale of ammunition and intoxicating drinks, and intrusion upon an Indian reservation. This meager legislation was in accord with the theory then prevailing, that the Indian tribes were related to the American Government only as sovereignties who naturally would provide their own laws; and that the red men, being a people essentially wild and untamable, needed only to be kept as remotely as possible from all settlements, to be assisted as hunters, to be forcibly precluded from an undue supply of gunpowder and rum, and to be made as peaceable as possible by the presence of an agent and the distribution of a few annuities in cash and blankets.

In my judgment, whatever of failure has attended the management of Indian affairs in the past has been largely attributable to this fundamental failure to recognize and treat the Indian as a man capable of civilization, and, therefore, a proper subject of the Government and amenable to its laws. A judge in Idaho, who is also a United States commissioner, has decided that he had no jurisdiction, either as a territorial or Federal officer, in a case where one Indian had killed another, though the murder was committed in his own county and outside of any reserve. Thus it has come to pass that we have within our borders at the present time 75,000 wild Indians who need legislation appropriate to a people passing rapidly out from a savage tribal government into a degree of control by the United States Government; and 200,000 other Indians who might be readily brought within the protection and restraint of ordinary law, and yet are practically without the benefit of any suitable government, a majority of them being property-holders, living upon their farms, having their schools and churches, and scarcely differing in their mode of life from the pioneer settlers of the country.

144

The damage which is inevitable to the Indians from this anomalous state of things, will be more apparent if we keep in mind that no officer of the Government has authority by law for punishing an Indian for crime, or restraining him in any degree; that the only means of enforcing law and order among the tribes is found in the use of the bayonet by the military, or such arbitrary force as the agent may have at command. Among the Indians themselves, all tribal government has been virtually broken down by their contact with the Government. The chiefs hold a nominal headship, depending for its continuance on the consent of the most turbulent and factious portion of the tribe. If a white man commits depredations upon the Indians in their own country no penalty is provided beyond that of putting him out of the country, a penalty which he readily takes upon himself when escaping with his booty.

Neither is there any provision of law by which an Indian can begin to live for himself as an American citizen. Being by the fiction of sovereignty, which has come into our Indian relations, citizens of a "domestic dependent nation," contrary to the American doctrine upon this subject he is not allowed to change his nationality at will, but required first to obtain consent of both parties to his tribal treaty. As a result of this restriction, many Indians are kept with the mass of their tribe who otherwise would strike out for themselves. The case of the Flandreaus, a small band of Sioux in Dakota, hereafter detailed, who availed themselves of a special provision to this effect in their treaty, is interesting as illustrating the advantage of a privilege which should be provided for all Indians.

Neither is there any provision under existing law by which an Indian desiring to continue his relations with his tribe is allowed to receive an allotment of his portion of the land owned in common; thus individual enterprise and self-support are materially repressed.

Many of the appropriations, in accordance with treaty stipulations, provide that annuities should be paid cash in hand, or in goods distributed per capita, to be accounted for to the Government on the receipts of the chief. All bounty of the Government bestowed in this form is worse than wasted, tending to perpetual poverty by providing for idleness and unthrift.

QUALIFIED CITIZENSHIP.

I therefore respectfully recommend that the attention of Congress be called to this subject, and that such legislation be requested as will secure—

First. A suitable government of Indians:

(1.) By providing that the criminal laws of the United States shall be in force upon Indian reservations, and shall apply to all offenses, including offenses of Indians against Indians, and extending the jurisdiction of the United States courts to enforce the same.

(2.) By declaring Indians amenable to the police laws of the State or Territory for any act committed outside a reservation.

(3.) By conferring upon the President authority, at his discretion, to extend the jurisdiction of the State courts, or any portion of them, to any reservation, whenever, in his judgment, any tribe is prepared for such control.

(4.) By providing a sufficient force of deputy marshals to enforce law and order both among and in behalf of Indians.

(5.) By giving authority to the Secretary of the Interior to prescribe for all tribes prepared, in his judgment, to adopt the same, an elective government, through which shall be administered all necessary police regulations of a reservation.

(6.) By providing a distinct territorial government, or United States court, wherever Indians are in numbers sufficient to justify it.

Second. Legislation for the encouragement of individual improvement:

(1.) By providing a way into citizenship for such as desire it.

(2.) By providing for holding lands in severalty by allotment for occupation, and for patents with an ultimate fee, but inalienable for a term of years.

(3.) By providing that wherever per capita distribution provided by treaty has proved injurious or without benefit to its recipients, a distribution of the same may, in the discretion of the President, be made only in return for labor of some sort.

In concluding these general statements

145

respecting the Indian service, I desire to reiterate my conviction of the entire feasibility of Indian civilization, and that the difficulty of its problem is not so inherent in the race-character and disposition of the Indian—great as these obstacles are—as in his anomalous relation to the Government, and in his surroundings affected by the influence and interest of the white people. The main difficulty, so far as the Government is concerned, lies in the fact that the Indian's deepest need is that which the Government, through its political organization and operations, cannot well bestow. The first help which a man in barbarism requires is not that which can be afforded through a political party, but that which is offered by a fellow-man, wiser than himself, coming personally and extending a hand of sympathy and truth. No amount of appropriations and no governmental machinery can do much toward lifting an ignorant and degraded people, except as it works through the willing hands of men made strong and constant by their love for their fellow-men.

If, therefore, it shall be possible to continue the sympathy and aid of the religious people of the land in this work, and to rally for its prosecution the enthusiasm and zeal which belong to religion, and also if it shall be possible to procure the enactment of such laws as will recognize the essential manhood and consequent capabilities and necessities of the Indian, and to provide reasonably adequate appropriations which shall be expended both honestly and wisely for their benefit, and to hold steadily to well-defined and carefully prepared methods of treatment, every year will witness a steady decrease of barbarism and its consequent danger and annoyance, and a constant accession to the number of peaceful and intelligent Indians who shall take their place and part as subjects of the United States. Surely this cannot be too much to ask and expect of the people of the great republic. The record of the past cannot be rewritten, and it is not pleasant to recall. Much of administrative mistake, neglect, and injustice is beyond repair. But for Indians now living much of protection and elevation and salvation is still not only possible, but feasible and highly promising; and well will it be if we are wise enough to make the most of the opportunity left to deal justly and humanely with these remnants of the first American people.

[*House Executive Document* no. 1, 43d Cong., 2d sess., serial 1639, pp. 324-27.]

88. General Sherman on Transfer of the Indian Bureau
January 19, 1876

General William T. Sherman, in a letter to W. A. J. Sparks, chairman of the House Subcommittee on Indian Affairs, spoke in favor of transferring the Bureau of Indian Affairs to the War Department and of substituting military personnel for the civilian agents and superintendents.

. . . . The great mass of the Indians of our country are now located on reservations, and are entitled to receive annuities, goods, and food, according to treaties made long ago, and for the faithful execution of which treaties the faith of the Government is pledged. These Indians vary widely in their habits, and should be dealt with accordingly. The present Army is now stationed in small detachments at military posts, chiefly at or near these reservations, to keep the peace between these Indians and their white neighbors, between whom there has always existed a conflict of interest and natural hostility. Now, as the military authorities are already charged with the duty of keeping the peace, I am sure they will be the better able to accomplish this end if intrusted with the issue of the annuities, whether of money, food, or clothing. Each military post has its quartermaster and commissary, who can, without additional cost, make the issues directly to the Indians, and account for them; and the commanding officer can exercise all the supervision now required of the civil agent, in a better manner, because he has soldiers to support his authority, and can easily anticipate and prevent the minor causes which have so often resulted in Indian wars. In like manner, our country is divided

146

into military departments and divisions, commanded by experienced general officers named by the President, who can fulfill all the functions now committed to Indian superintendents; and these, too, have near them inspectors who can promptly investigate and prevent the incipient steps that are so apt to result in conflict and war.

Therefore, I firmly believe that the Army now occupies the positions and relations to the great mass of the Indian tribes that will better enable the Government to execute any line of policy it may deem wise and proper, than by any possible system that can be devised with civil agents. The Indians, more especially those who occupy the vast region west of the Mississippi, from the Rio Grande to the British line, are natural warriors, and have always looked to the military rather than to the civil agents of Government for protection or punishment; and, were the troops to be withdrawn, instant war would result. If it be the policy of the Government, as I believe it is, to save the remnant of these tribes, it can only be accomplished by and through military authority. These will obey orders, and *enforce* any line of policy that may be prescribed for them by law or regulation. Sooner or later these Indians, say the Sioux, Cheyennes, Arapahoes, Kioways, and Comanches, must be made self-supporting. Farming and the mechanic arts are so obnoxious to their nature and traditions, that any hope of their becoming an agricultural people can hardly be expected in our day, though there are many individual exceptions; but the Indians themselves see that the buffalo, elk, antelope, deer, and large game are rapidly disappearing, and that they must raise cattle and sheep, or starve. This, in my judgment, is the proper direction in which to turn their attention, and an excellent beginning has been made with the tribes in New Mexico, and more recently with the Kioways and Comanches, near Fort Sill. This has been done by the influence of the Army stationed in their midst, who are, in my opinion, now and have always been the best friends the Indians have had. The idea which prevails with some, that the Army wants war with the Indians, is not true. Such wars bring exposure, toil, risk, and privations, with no honor. Therefore, it (the Army) naturally wants peace, and very often has prevented wars by its mere presence; and if intrusted with the exclusive management and control of the annuities and supplies, as well as force, I think Indian wars will cease, and the habits of the Indians will be gradually molded into a most necessary and useful branch of industry—the rearing of sheep, cattle, horses, &c. In some localities they may possibly be made farmers.

The present laws bearing on this Indian problem were wise in their day, but the extension of States and Territories, with their governments, over the whole domain of the United States, has entirely changed the condition of facts; and I think you will find that these will need revision and change.

I do not profess to know anything of the practical workings of the Indian Bureau as now organized; but if transferred to the War Department, I suppose it will be made subject to such changes as the Secretary of War may recommend.

If, as I conceive, the present military machinery already in existence be used, viz, the commanding generals of departments be made supervisors of Indian affairs in their commands, and commanding officers of posts be constituted "agents," the Bureau will need a military head, resident in the War Department.

[*House Report* no. 354, 44th Cong., 1st sess., serial 1709, p. 9.]

89.   Indian Commissioner Smith on Principles of Indian Policy

Extract from the *Annual Report of the Commissioner of Indian Affairs*

October 30, 1876

Commissioner John Q. Smith, in his annual report of 1876, discussed three principles which he believed essential for the welfare and progress of the Indians. Although the first (concentration of all Indians on a few reservations) was later abandoned, the other two (allotment of land in severalty and extension of United States law over the Indians) became established parts of federal Indian policy.

.... In considering whether modifications of existing methods may not be desirable, I have arrived at the conviction that the welfare and progress of the Indians require the adoption of three principles of policy:

First. Concentration of all Indians on a few reservations.

Second. Allotment to them of lands in severalty.

Third. Extension over them of United States law and the jurisdiction of United States courts.

The reservations upon which, in my opinion, the Indians should be consolidated, are the Indian Territory, the White Earth reservation in Northern Minnesota, and a reservation in the southern part of Washington Territory, probably the Yakama reservation. If it should be found impracticable to remove the Indians of Colorado, Utah, New Mexico, and Arizona, to the Indian Territory, they might be concentrated on some suitable reservation either in Colorado or Arizona.

I am well aware that it will take a long time, much patient effort, and considerable expense, to effect this proposed consolidation; but after consulting with many gentlemen thoroughly acquainted with Indian questions and Indian character, I am satisfied that the undertaking can be accomplished. If legislation were secured giving the President authority to remove any tribe or band, or any portion of a tribe or band, whenever in his judgment it was practicable, to any one of the reservations named, and if Congress would appropriate, from year to year, a sum sufficient to enable him to take advantage of every favorable opportunity to make such removals, I am confident that a few years' trial would conclusively demonstrate the entire feasibility of the plan. I believe that all the Indians in Kansas, Nebraska, and Dakota, and a part at least of those in Wyoming and Montana, could be induced to remove to the Indian Territory. There is also ground for the belief that the Colorado, Arizona, and New Mexico Indians, and a part if not all of those in Nevada, could also be taken to that Territory.

Many of these Indians are now located on lands utterly unfit for cultivation, where starvation or perpetual support by the Government are the only alternatives. It is doubtful whether even white people could cultivate profitably the greater part of the Sioux reservation in Dakota. In the Indian Territory, on the other hand, are fertile land, a genial climate, and room for more Indians than there are in the whole Union.

That the Indian sentiment is opposed to such removal is true. Difficulties were experienced in bringing to the Territory its present inhabitants from east of the Mississippi; but the obstacles were overcome, and experience shows that there the race can thrive. With a fair degree of persistence the removal thither of other Indians can also be secured. The Pawnees have recently gone there, and seem content with their new home. The Poncas, and even the Red Cloud and Spotted Tail Sioux, give evidence that they are ready for the change; and if Congress will make a liberal appropriation to effect the removal of these Sioux, it is quite likely that within a year or two, other bands now on the Missouri River may also be induced to remove. If the Sioux are given a suitable reservation in that Territory for a permanent home, and are aided by the Government for a few years in their efforts at agriculture and stock-raising, I know of no reason why they may not, in one generation, become as far advanced as are the Cherokees and Choctaws now.

It is to be regretted that all the Indians in the United States cannot be removed to the Indian Territory; but it is doubtful whether, at least for many years, it will be best to attempt to remove Indians thither from the region of the great lakes or from the Pacific coast. I would therefore suggest that, for the tribes of Wisconsin and Minnesota, and the wandering Pembinas in Dakota, the White Earth reservation is best adapted as a permanent home. Containing thirty-six townships of well-watered timber and wheat lands, it offers far better agricultural facilities than do other reservations in those States, and is in about the same latitude with them.

My information in regard to the proper reservation for the Indians on the Pacific coast is less definite, and I have suggested the Yakama reservation, mainly because it is well known that the Indians there, under the

148

direction of Agent Wilbur, have made remarkable progress. A commission now visiting the Indians in that region has been requested to make such suggestions on the subject as they may deem wise.

The importance of reducing the number of reservations is shown by the following considerations:

Many of the present reserves are almost worthless for agricultural purposes; others are rich in soil, mineral wealth, and timber. Nearly all are too small to subsist the Indians by hunting, and too large for them to occupy in agricultural and civilized pursuits. Many are so remote and difficult of access, that needed supplies can be furnished only at great expense. Nearly all are surrounded by white settlers, more or less numerous. Wherever an Indian reservation has on it good land, or timber, or minerals, the cupidity of the white man is excited, and a constant struggle is inaugurated to dispossess the Indian, in which the avarice and determination of the white man usually prevails. The length of the boundary-line between the reservations and the contiguous white settlements amounts in the aggregate to thousands of miles, every mile being a point of contact and difficulty. This aggregate boundary is so extensive as to render almost impossible the prevention of illicit trade in arms and whisky. As now constituted, these reservations are a refuge to the most lawless and desperate white men in America. There the vagabonds, the outcasts, the criminals, the most immoral and licentious of the population of the western portion of the country take up their abode, because there they are practically beyond the reach and operation of law, and can live lives of crime and debauchery with impunity and without reproach. Such men seriously obstruct, if they do not render nugatory, every effort to give assistance to the Indians.

By the concentration of Indians on a few reservations, it is obvious that much of the difficulty now surrounding the Indian question will vanish. Many agencies now conducted at large expense could be abolished. The aggregate boundary-lines between the reservations and country occupied by white people would be greatly reduced, and the danger of violence, bloodshed, and mutual wrong materially lessened. The sale of liquors and arms could be more effectually prevented; bad white men could more easily be kept out of the Indian country; necessary supplies could be more cheaply furnished; a far smaller military force would be required to keep the peace; and generally, the Indians, being more compact, could be more efficiently aided and controlled by the officers of the Government. Moreover, large bodies of land would be thrown open to settlement, proceeds of whose sale would be ample to defray all expense of the removals.

ALLOTMENTS IN SEVERALTY.

It is doubtful whether any high degree of civilization is possible without individual ownership of land. The records of the past and the experience of the present testify that the soil should be made secure to the individual by all the guarantees which law can devise, and that nothing less will induce men to put forth their best exertions. No general law exists which provides that Indians shall select allotments in severalty, and it seems to me a matter of great moment that provision should be made not only permitting, but requiring, the head of each Indian family, to accept the allotment of a reasonable amount of land, to be the property of himself and his lawful heirs, in lieu of any interest in any common tribal possession. Such allotments should be inalienable for at least twenty, perhaps fifty years, and if situated in a permanent Indian reservation, should be transferable only among Indians.

I am not unaware that this proposition will meet with strenuous opposition from the Indians themselves. Like the whites, they have ambitious men, who will resist to the utmost of their power any change tending to reduce the authority which they have acquired by personal effort or by inheritance; but it is essential that these men and their claims should be pushed aside and that each individual should feel that his home is his own; that he owes no allegiance to any great man or to any faction; that he has a direct personal interest in the soil on which he lives, and that that interest will be faithfully protected for him and for his children by the Government.

149

My predecessors have frequently called attention to the startling fact that we have within out midst 275,000 people, the least intelligent portion of our population, for whom we provide no law, either for their protection or for the punishment of crime committed among themselves. Civilization even among white men could not long exist without the guarantees which law alone affords; yet our Indians are remitted by a great civilized government to the control, if control it can be called, of the rude regulations of petty, ignorant tribes. Year after year we expend millions of dollars for these people in the faint hope that, without law, we can civilize them. That hope has been, to a great degree, a long disappointment; and year after year we repeat the folly of the past. That the benevolent efforts and purposes of the Government have proved so largely fruitless, is, in my judgment, due more to its failure to make these people amenable to our laws than to any other cause, or to all other causes combined.

I believe it to be the duty of Congress at once to extend over Indian reservations the jurisdiction of United States courts, and to declare that each Indian in the United States shall occupy the same relation to law that a white man does. An Indian should be given to understand that no ancient custom, no tribal regulation, will shield him from just punishment for crime; and also that he will be effectually protected, by the authority and power of the Government, in his life, liberty, property, and character, as certainly as if he were a white man. There can be no doubt of the power of Congress to do this, and surely the intelligent Committees on Indian Affairs of the Senate and House can readily propose legislation which will accomplish this most desirable result. I regard this suggestion as by far the most important which I have to make in this report.

Since our Government was organized two questions, or rather two classes of questions, have transcended all others in importance and difficulty, viz, the relations of the Government and the white people to the negroes and to the Indians. The negro question has doubtless absorbed more of public attention, aroused more intense feeling, and

cost our people more blood and treasure than any other question, if not all others combined. That question, it is to be hoped, is settled forever in the only way in which its settlement was possible—by the full admission of the negro to all the rights and privileges of citizenship. Next in importance comes the Indian question, and there can be no doubt that our Indian wars have cost us more than all the foreign wars in which our Government has been engaged. It is time that some solution of this whole Indian problem, decisive, satisfactory, just, and final, should be found. In my judgment it can be reached only by a process similar to that pursued with the negroes.

In the three propositions above stated, will, I believe, be found the true and final settlement of this perplexing subject. However efficient may be the administration of the Indian Office, and however faithful the labors of its agents and their subordinates, I have little hope of any marked degree of success until the above suggestions are substantially adopted as a permanent Indian policy. If Congress concludes to act on these suggestions, laws should be passed at the coming session to extend the jurisdiction of the courts over all Indians, and to provide for the allotment of lands in severalty in the Indian Territory, and on such other reservations as may be selected as permanent; and an appropriation should be made with which to begin the removal of Indians to their permanent homes.

I trust I may be pardoned for stating that it appears to me that the fundamental difficulty in our relations hitherto with Indians has been the want of a well-defined, clearly-understood, persistent purpose on the part of the Government. Indian affairs have heretofore been managed largely by the application of mere temporary expedients in a fragmentary and disjointed manner. For a hundred years the United States has been wrestling with the "Indian question," but has never had an Indian policy. The only thing yet to be done by the Government in regard to the Indians which seems to have been permanent and far-reaching in its scope and purpose, is the dedication of the Indian Territory as the final home for the race. Surely it is time that a policy should be determined on, which shall be fully understood by the Government, the people, and the Indians. We cannot afford to allow this race to perish without making an honest effort to save it. We cannot afford to keep them in our midst as vagabonds and paupers.

I appeal to the statesmen of the country to give to this subject their earnest attention; the sooner it is settled on some wise and comprehensive principle the better for all concerned. We have despoiled the Indians of their rich hunting-grounds, thereby depriving them of their ancient means of support. Ought we not and shall we not give them at least a secure home, and the cheap but priceless benefit of just and equitable laws? . . .

[*House Executive Document* no. 1, 44th Cong., 2d sess., serial 1749, pp. vii-xi.]

90. Indian Commissioner Hayt on Indian Police

Extract from the *Annual Report of the Commissioner of Indian Affairs*

November 1, 1877

The use of Indians to police the reservations had been tried with success by John Clum, agent of the Apaches on the San Carlos Reservation, and by other agents. Commissioner Ezra A. Hayt recommended the general adoption of an Indian police force in his annual report of 1877. Congress authorized pay for 430 privates and 50 officers in 1878 and raised the number to 800 privates and 100 officers in 1879 (U.S. Statutes at Large, 20:86, 315).

. . . . The preservation of order is as necessary to the promotion of civilization as is the enactment of wise laws. Both are essential to the peace and happiness of any people. As a means of preserving order upon an Indian reservation, an Indian police has been found to be of prime importance. I have recommended an additional outlay of money to enable the government to extend the usefulness of a police system now in its infancy with us. In Canada, the entire body of Indians are kept in order by such force. In this country, as far as it has been tried, it works admirably. I would recommend that the force be composed of Indians, properly officered and drilled by white men, and where capable Indians can be found, that they be promoted to command, as reward for faithful service. The Army has used Indians for scouts with great success, and wherever employed the Indian has been found faithful to the trust confided to him. I would also recommend that the police force be supplied with a uniform similar to the style of clothing which I shall hereafter suggest to be furnished for all Indians, with the addition of a few brass buttons by way of distinction. The employment of such a force, properly officered and handled, would, in great measure, relieve the Army from doing police duty on Indian reservations. I am thoroughly satisfied that the saving in life and property by the employment of such a force would be very large, and that it would materially aid in placing the entire Indian population of the country on the road to civilization. . . .

[*House Executive Document* no. 1, 45th Cong., 2d sess., serial 1800, pp. 398-99.]

91. Standing Bear v. Crook

May 12, 1879

In 1877 the United States government forced members of the Ponca tribe to move to the Indian Territory from their reservation in Dakota, which had inadvertently been assigned also to the Sioux. One group of Poncas, led by Standing Bear, unable to endure their new condition, fled back to their old homeland. When arrested by General George Crook, Standing Bear sought a writ of habeas corpus for his release. The case in the United States Circuit Court, District of Nebraska, was heard by Judge Elmer S. Dundy, who decided in the Indians' favor.

DUNDY, District Judge. During the fifteen years in which I have been engaged in administering the laws of my country, I have never been called upon to hear or decide a case that appealed so strongly to my sympathy as the one now under consideration. On the one side, we have a few of the remnants of a once numerous and powerful, but now weak, insignificant, unlettered, and generally despised race; on the other, we have the representative of one of the most powerful, most enlightened, and most Christianized nations of modern times. On the one side, we have the representatives of this wasted race coming into this national tribunal of ours, asking for justice and liberty to enable them to adopt our boasted civilization, and to pursue the arts of peace, which have made us great and happy as a nation; on the other side, we have this magnificent, if not magnanimous, government, resisting this application with the determination of sending these people back to the country which is to them less desirable than perpetual imprisonment in their own native land. But I think it is creditable to the heart and mind of the brave and distinguished officer who is made respondent herein to say that he has no sort of sympathy in the business in which he is forced by his position to bear a part so conspicuous; and, so far as I am individually concerned, I think it not improper to say that, if the strongest possible sympathy could give the relators title to freedom, they would have been restored to liberty the moment the arguments in their behalf were closed. No examination or further thought would then have been necessary or expedient. But in a country where liberty is regulated by law, something more satisfactory and enduring than mere sympathy must furnish and constitute the rule and basis of judicial action. It follows that this case must be examined and decided on principles of law, and that unless the relators are entitled to their discharge under the constitution or laws of the United States, or some treaty made pursuant thereto, they must be remanded to the custody of the officer who caused their arrest, to be returned to the Indian Territory, which they left without the consent of the government. . . .

Every "person" who comes within our jurisdiction, whether he be European, Asiatic, African, or "native to the manor born," must obey the laws of the United States. Every one who violates them incurs the penalty provided thereby. When a "person" is charged, in a proper way, with the commission of crime, we do not inquire upon the trial in what country the accused was born, nor to what sovereign or government allegiance is due, nor to what race he belongs. The questions of guilt and innocence only form the subjects of inquiry. An Indian, then, especially off from his reservation, is amenable to the criminal laws of the United States, the same as all other persons. They being subject to arrest for the violation of our criminal laws, and being "persons" such as the law contemplates and includes in the description of parties who may sue out the writ, it would indeed be a sad commentary on the justice and impartiality of our laws to hold that Indians, though natives of our own country, cannot test the validity of an alleged illegal imprisonment in this manner, as well as a subject of a foreign government who may happen to be sojourning in this country, but owing it no sort of allegiance. I cannot doubt that congress intended to give to every person who might be unlawfully restrained of liberty under color of authority of the United States, the right to the writ and a discharge thereon. I conclude, then, that, so far as the issuing of the writ is concerned, it was properly issued, and that the relators are within the jurisdiction conferred by the habeas corpus act. . . .

I have searched in vain for the semblance of any authority justifying the commissioner in attempting to remove by force any Indians, whether belonging to a tribe or not, to any place, or for any other purpose than what has been stated. Certainly, without some specific authority found in an act of congress, or in a treaty with the Ponca tribe of Indians, he could not lawfully force the relators back to the Indian Territory, to remain and die in that country, against their will. In the absence of all treaty stipulations or laws of the United States authorizing such removal, I must conclude that no such arbitrary authority exists. It is true, if the relators are to be regarded as a part of the great nation of Ponca Indians, the government might, in time of war, remove them to any place of safety so long as the war should last,

152

but perhaps no longer, unless they were charged with the commission of some crime. This is a war power merely, and exists in time of war only. Every nation exercises the right to arrest and detain an alien enemy during the existence of a war, and all subjects or citizens of the hostile nations are subject to be dealt with under this rule.

But it is not claimed that the Ponca tribe of Indians are at war with the United States, so that this war power might be used against them; in fact, they are amongst the most peaceable and friendly of all the Indian tribes, and have at times received from the government unmistakable and substantial recognition of their long-continued friendship for the whites. In time of peace the war power remains in abeyance, and must be subservient to the civil authority of the government until something occurs to justify its exercise. No fact exists, and nothing has occurred, so far as the relators are concerned, to make it necessary or lawful to exercise such an authority over them. If they could be removed to the Indian Territory by force, and kept there in the same way, I can see no good reason why they might not be taken and kept by force in the penitentiary at Lincoln, or Leavenworth, or Jefferson City, or any other place which the commander of the forces might, in his judgment, see proper to designate. I cannot think that any such arbitrary authority exists in this country.

The reasoning advanced in support of my views, leads me to conclude:

1. That an Indian is a "person" within the meaning of the laws of the United States, and has, therefore, the right to sue out a writ of habeas corpus in a federal court, or before a federal judge, in all cases where he may be confined or in custody under color of authority of the United States, or where he is restrained of liberty in violation of the constitution or laws of the United States.

2. That General George Crook, the respondent, being commander of the military department of the Platte, has the custody of the relators, under color of authority of the United States, and in violation of the laws thereof.

3. That no rightful authority exists for removing by force any of the relators to the Indian Territory, as the respondent has been directed to do.

4. That the Indians possess the inherent right of expatriation, as well as the more fortunate white race, and have the inalienable right to "life, liberty, and the pursuit of happiness," so long as they obey the laws and do not trespass on forbidden ground. And,

5. Being restrained of liberty under color of authority of the United States, and in violation of the laws thereof, the relators must be discharged from custody, and it is so ordered.

[25 *Federal Cases*, 695, 697, 700-01.]

92. Secretary of the Interior Schurz on Reservation Policy

Extract from the *Annual Report of the Secretary of the Interior*

November 1, 1880

Secretary of the Interior Carl Schurz took a strong interest in Indian affairs. He made it his business to eliminate corruption and abuses within the Indian Office, but he also vigorously promoted elements of Indian policy. In his annual report for 1880, he indicated a reversal of the policy of removing Indians from their homelands in order to concentrate them on a few large reservations. He also argued in favor of allotting reservation lands in severalty to individual Indians.

. . . When I took charge of this department the opinion seemed to be generally prevailing that it were best for the Indians to be gathered together upon a few large reservations where they could be kept out of contact with the white population, and where their peaceful and orderly conduct might be enforced by a few strong military posts. It was, perhaps, natural that, with limited knowledge of the character and needs of the Indians, and no experience in their management, I should at first accept that opinion, for the very reason that it was entertained by many who might have been regarded as competent authorities upon the subject. This view had already been acted

153

upon to some extent before this administration came into office. It involved the removal of Indian tribes and bands from the lands they occupied, with their consent freely or reluctantly and doubtfully given, and in some cases the breaking up of beginnings of civilized occupations in their old homes. It was believed that this policy would be apt to keep the Indians out of hostile collision with their white neighbors, and in exclusive and congenial contact with their own kind, and thus prevent disturbances on the part of the Indians themselves and encroachments by the whites. Some measures of this nature had been carried out, and others were, indeed, not initiated, but executed during the early part of this administration. I refer especially to the removal to the Indian Territory of the Pawnees, of the Northern Cheyennes, and the Poncas, which I have found good reason very much to regret.

More extensive observation and study of the matter gradually convinced me that this was a mistaken policy; that it would be vastly better for the Indians and more in accordance with justice as well as wise expediency to respect their home attachments, to leave them upon the lands they occupied, provided such lands were capable of yielding them a sustenance by agriculture or pastoral pursuits, and to begin and follow up the practice of introducing among them the habits and occupations of civilized life on the ground they inhabited. It became also clear to me that the maintenance of the system of large reservations against the pressure of white immigration and settlement would in the course of time become impracticable. The policy of changing, shifting, and consolidating reservations for the purpose above stated was therefore abandoned, except in cases where the lands held by the Indians were not capable of useful development, and other lands better adapted to their advancement could be assigned to them.

The policy which, during the larger part of this administrative period, was pursued as a fixed line of conduct is the following: to respect such rights as the Indians have in the land they occupy; to make changes only where such lands were found to be unsuitable for agriculture and herding; to acquaint the Indians with the requirements of civilized life by education; to introduce among them various kinds of work, by practical impulse and instruction; gradually to inspire them with a sense of responsibility through the ownership of private property and a growing dependence for their support upon their own efforts; to afford to them all facilities of trade consistent with their safety, as to the disposition of the products of their labor and industry for their own advantage; to allot to them lands in severalty with individual ownership, and a fee simple title inalienable for a certain period; then, with their consent and for their benefit, to dispose of such lands as they cannot cultivate and use themselves, to the white settlers; to dissolve, by gradual steps, their tribal cohesion, and merge them in the body politic as independent and self-relying men invested with all the rights which other inhabitants of the country possess.

Having thus fixed the ultimate end to be accomplished as well as indicated in general terms the means by which it is to be reached, in the shape of a clearly-defined policy, the department proceeded not only to continue the promotion of those civilizing influences which already had been set to work, but also to add others which so far had not been adopted. . . .

LAND TITLES IN SEVERALTY.

I mentioned before that the feeling of uncertainty which prevails among the Indians as to the permanency of their possession of the lands they occupy has proved in many cases a serious impediment to their improvement and progress. From all quarters we receive expressions of a desire on the part of the Indians to have the land they occupy and cultivate secured to them by the "white man's paper," that is, a patent equal in legal force to that by which white men hold title to their land. Bills have been submitted to Congress for two sessions providing for the division of farm tracts among the Indians in severalty on their respective reservations; the issuance of patents to them individually and their investment with a fee-simple title to their farms inalienable for a certain number of years until they may be presumed to have overcome the improvident habits in which a large part of the present generation have grown up; and, this being accomplished, for

154

the disposition of the residue of the reservations not occupied and used by the Indians, with their consent and for their benefit, to white settlers. It was hoped that this measure would pass before the adjournment of the last session. Had it become a law a very large number of Indians would have been so settled by this time. In this expectation the issuance of patents not containing the important clause of temporary inalienability, which is authorized by a few Indian treaties, has been withheld until a general law should insure to all titles of greater security. It is to be hoped that this important measure will now receive the earliest possible consideration and action by Congress. I look upon it as the most essential step in the solution of the Indian problem. It will inspire the Indians with a feeling of assurance as to the permanency of their ownership of the lands they occupy and cultivate; it will give them a clear and legal standing as landed proprietors in the courts of law; it will secure to them for the first time fixed homes under the protection of the same law under which white men own theirs; it will eventually open to settlement by white men the large tracts of land now belonging to the reservations, but not used by the Indians. It will thus put the relations between the Indians and their white neighbors in the Western country upon a new basis, by gradually doing away with the system of large reservations, which has so frequently provoked those encroachments which in the past have led to so much cruel injustice and so many disastrous collisions. It will also by the sale, with their consent, of reservation lands not used by the Indians, create for the benefit of the Indians a fund, which will gradually relieve the government of those expenditures which have now to be provided for by appropriations. It will be the most effective measure to place Indians and white men upon an equal footing as to the protection and restraints of laws common to both. I desire also to call attention once more to the bill repeatedly introduced in Congress, extending over Indian reservations the government of the laws of the States or Territories in which such reservations are located, giving the Indians standing in the courts and securing to them the full benefit of the laws. I venture to express the hope that Congress may not adjourn again without having taken action upon these important measures, so essential to the progress and security of our Indian wards. . . .

[*House Executive Document* no. 1, 46th Cong., 3d sess., serial 1959, pp. 3-4, 11-13.]

93. Indian Commissioner Price on Civilizing the Indians

Extract from the *Annual Report of the Commissioner of Indian Affairs*

October 24, 1881

The 1880s marked a new drive to solve the "Indian problem." Typical arguments in favor of making the Indians support themselves on individual homesteads were advanced by Commissioner Hiram Price in his annual report of 1881. His goal was to make the Indians a happy and prosperous people according to white modes of life.

. . . . It is claimed and admitted by all that the great object of the government is to civilize the Indians and render them such assistance in kind and degree as will make them self-supporting, and yet I think no one will deny that one part of our policy is calculated to produce the very opposite result. It must be apparent to the most casual observer that the system of gathering the Indians in bands or tribes on reservations and carrying to them victuals and clothes, thus relieving them of the necessity of labor, never will and never can civilize them. Labor is an essential element in producing civilization. If white men were treated as we treat the Indians the result would certainly be a race of worthless vagabonds. The greatest kindness the government can bestow upon the Indian is to teach him to labor for his own support, thus developing his true manhood, and, as a consequence, making him self-relying and self-supporting.

We are expending annually over one million dollars in feeding and clothing Indians where no treaty obligation exists for so doing. This is simply a gratuity, and it is

155

presumed no one will question the expediency or the right of the government, if it bestows gratuities upon Indians, to make labor of some useful sort a condition precedent to such gift, especially when all of the products of such labor go to the Indian. To domesticate and civilize wild Indians is a noble work, the accomplishment of which should be a crown of glory to any nation. But to allow them to drag along year after year, and generation after generation, in their old superstitions, laziness, and filth, when we have the power to elevate them in the scale of humanity, would be a lasting disgrace to our government. The past experience of this government with its Indians has clearly established some points which ought to be useful as guides in the future.

There is no one who has been a close observer of Indian history and the effect of contact of Indians with civilization, who is not well satisfied that one of two things must eventually take place, to wit, either civilization or extermination of the Indian. Savage and civilized life cannot live and prosper on the same ground. One of the two must die. If the Indians are to be civilized and become a happy and prosperous people, which is certainly the object and intention of our government, they must learn our language and adopt our modes of life. We are fifty millions of people, and they are only one-fourth of one million. The few must yield to the many. We cannot reasonably expect them to abandon their habits of life and modes of living, and adopt ours, with any hope of speedy success as long as we feed and clothe them without any effort on their part.

In this connection I wish to call attention to the fact that in almost every case it is only the non-laboring tribes that go upon the war-path, and the stubborn facts of history compel me to say that the government is largely to blame for this.

The peaceable and industrious Indian has had less consideration than the turbulent and vicious. One instance in proof of this can be found at this moment in the case of the White River Utes (the murderers of Meeker) and the Utes on the Uintah Reservation. The White River Utes have just been moved to the Uintah Reservation alongside of the peaceable Uintah Utes. We feed the White River murderers and compel the peaceable Uintahs to largely care for themselves. This course induces the Indians to believe that if they are to get favors from the government they must refuse to work, refuse to be orderly and peaceable, and must commit some depredations or murder, and then a commission will be appointed to treat with them, and pay them in goods, provisions, and money to behave themselves. This looks to an Indian very much like rewarding enemies and punishing friends, and gives him a singular idea of our Christian civilization and our manner of administering justice, which has so much the appearance of rewarding vice and punishing virtue.

Another cause of the unsatisfactory condition of our Indian affairs is the failure of the government to give the Indian land in severalty, and to give it to him in such a way that he will know that it is his. He has learned by painful experience that a small piece of paper called scrip is not good for much as a title to land. He has again and again earnestly solicited the government to give him a title to a piece of land, that he might make for himself a home. These requests have, in a great many instances, been neglected or refused, and this is true even in cases where, by treaty stipulations, the government agreed to give the Indian a patent for his land. Under this state of facts, it is not to be wondered at that the Indian is slow to cultivate the soil. He says, when urged to do so, that he has no heart to do it, when in a month or a year he may be moved, and some white man be allowed to enjoy the fruit of his labor. That is the way the Indian talks, and that is the way a white man would talk under similar circumstances.

Another just cause of complaint which the Indians have is that in our treaties with them, in some instances, we agree to give them so many pounds of beef, flour, coffee, sugar, &c., and then a certain sum of money is appropriated for the purpose of fulfilling the promise, which sum so appropriated (as is the case the present year, because of the increased price of beef, &c.) will not buy the *pounds*; consequently, the Indians do not get what was promised them. This they construe as bad faith on the part of the government, and use it as an excuse for doing something wrong themselves; and thus troubles of a serious and extensive nature frequently arise. This would all be avoided if appropriations were sufficiently large to cover all contingencies, and such appropriations would not interfere with or violate the rules of strict economy; for any surplus (if there should be any) would be turned into the Treasury, as is always done, at the end of the fiscal year, when an unexpended balance remains of any particular appropriation. This would be keeping our contracts to the letter and would inspire confidence and respect on the part of the Indian for our government, and give him no excuse for wrong-doing.

But I am very decidedly of opinion that ultimate and final success never can be reached without adding to all other means and appliances the location of each family, or adult Indian who has no family, on a certain number of acres of land which they may call their own and hold by a title as good and strong as a United States patent can make it. Let it be inalienable for, say, twenty years; give the Indian teams, implements, and tools amply sufficient for farming purposes; give him seed, food, and clothes for at least one year; in short, give him every facility for making a comfortable living, and then *compel* him to depend upon his own exertions for a livelihood. Let the laws that govern a white man govern the Indian. The Indian must be made to understand that if he expects to live and prosper in this country he must learn the English language, and learn to *work*. The language will enable him to transact his business understandingly with his white neighbors, and his labor will enable him to provide the necessaries and comforts of life for himself and family. The policy thus indicated will in a few years rid the government of this vexed "Indian question," making the Indian a blessing instead of a curse to himself and country, which, judging the future by the past, will never be done by the present policy. . . .

[*House Executive Document* no. 1, 47th Cong., 1st sess., serial 2018, pp. 1-3.]

94. Indian Commissioner Price on Cooperation with Religious Societies

Extract from the *Annual Report of the Commissioner of Indian Affairs*

October 10, 1882

Indicative of the important influence of Christian sentiment on government officials was the praise of Christian educators and missionaries in the annual report of Commissioner Hiram Price in 1882. Price was a prominent Methodist layman.

. . . . One very important auxiliary in transforming men from savage to civilized life is the influence brought to bear upon them through the labors of Christian men and women as educators and missionaries. This I think, has been forcibly illustrated and clearly demonstrated among the different Indian tribes by the missionary labors of the various religious societies in the last few years. Civilization is a plant of exceeding slow growth, unless supplemented by Christian teaching and influences. I am decidedly of the opinion that a liberal encouragement by the government to all religious denominations to extend their educational missionary operations among the Indians would be of immense benefit. I find that during the year there has been expended in cash by the different religious societies for regular educational and missionary purposes among the Indians the sum of $216,680, and doubtless much more which was not reported through the regular channels. This is just so much money saved to the government, which is an item of some importance, but insignificant in comparison with the healthy influences created by the men and women who have gone among the Indians, not for personal pecuniary benefit, but for the higher and nobler purpose of helping these untutored and uncivilized people to a higher plane of existence. In no other manner and by no other means, in my judgment, can our Indian population be so speedily and permanently reclaimed from the barbarism, idolatry, and savage life, as by the educational and missionary operations of the Christian people of our country. This kind

157

of teaching will educate them to be sober, industrious, self-reliant, and to respect the rights of others; and my deliberate opinion is, that it is not only the interest but the duty of the government to aid and encourage these efforts in the most liberal manner. No money spent for the civilization of the Indian will return a better dividend than that spent in this way. In urging this point I do not wish to be understood as claiming that all the good people are inside the churches and all the bad ones outside; but a little observation, I think, will convince any one that a very large proportion of those who sacrifice time and money for the good of others is found inside of some Christian organization. If we expect

to stop sun dances, snake worship, and other debasing forms of superstition and idolatry among Indians, we must teach them some better way. This, with liberal appropriations by the government for the establishment of industrial schools, where the thousands of Indian children now roaming wild shall be taught to speak the English language and earn their own living, will accomplish what is so much desired, to wit, the conversion of the wild roving Indian into an industrious, peaceable, and law-abiding citizen. . . .

[*House Executive Document* no. 1, 47th Cong., 2d sess., serial 2100, pp. 3-4.]

95. Report on the Mission Indians of California

Extract from the *Annual Report of the Commissioner of Indian Affairs*

October 10, 1883

The pitiable condition of the Mission Indians in California was called to public attention by a report submitted in 1883 by Helen Hunt Jackson and Abbot Kinney. Commissioner Hiram Price provided a succinct summary of their findings and recommendations in his annual report of 1883. The plight of the Indians was further dramatized in Mrs. Jackson's novel Ramona *(1884).*

. . . . The injustice done the Mission Indians, and their deplorable condition, have been set forth by several commissions and have been treated of at length in various annual reports of this office, especially in those of 1875 and 1880, and Congress has repeatedly been solicited to interfere in their behalf, but without avail.

The situation of these people is peculiar. It is probable that they are entitled to all the rights and immunities of citizens of the United States, by virtue of the treaty of Guadalupe Hidalgo, yet from poverty and ignorance and unwillingness to abandon their custom of dwelling together in villages, under a tribal or village government, they have failed to secure individual titles to their lands, under the public land laws, or under the Indian homestead act. Many of these Indians have been driven from lands occupied and cultivated by them for years, to which they had at least a color of title from the Spanish government, and the ejectments have often been made with force and violence.

After nearly all desirable land had been wrested from them or "taken up" by settlers

a few small tracts remaining were set aside by Executive order for their permanent use and occupation, and entries unlawfully made by white men upon such lands have been held for cancellation. The few little villages left to them in the cañons of the mountains, from long years of cultivation have become extremely fertile, and are looked upon with longing eyes by the surrounding white settlers.

In accordance with authority granted by the Department, Mrs. Helen Jackson, of Colorado, was instructed, under date of July 7, 1882, to visit the Mission Indians in California, and ascertain the location and condition of the various bands; whether suitable land in their vicinity, belonging to the public domain, could be made available as a permanent home for such of those Indians as were not established upon reservations, and what, if any lands should be purchased for their use. At her request Mr. Abbot Kinney, of California, was authorized to assist in the work. Their final report gives, with great particularity, the condition of each village, recites in detail the wrongs that have been inflicted upon

158

these Indians, and contains numerous and important recommendations for their improvement.

They recommend as the first and most essential step, the resurveying, rounding out, and distinctly marking of reservations already existing.

2d. The removal of all white settlers now on such reservations.

3d. In cases where their villages are included in confirmed grants that other provision be made for the Indians, or that they be upheld and defended in their right to remain where they are.

4th. That all the reservations be patented to the several bands occupying them; the United States to hold the patents in trust for twenty-five years; a provision to be incorporated in the patent for allotments in severalty from time to time, as they may appear desirable.

5th. The establishment of at least two or more schools in addition to the five already in operation at the various villages.

6th. That it be made the duty of the agent to make a round of inspection at least twice a year.

7th. The appointment of a law firm as special attorneys in all cases affecting the interests of the Indians.

This recommendation has already been carried out, Messrs. Brunson & Wells, of Los Angeles, having been appointed assistants to the United States district attorney in such cases, the appointment taking effect on the 1st of July last.

8th. A judicious distribution of agricultural implements among these Indians.

9th. A small fund for the purchase of food and clothing for the very old and sick in time of special destitution.

10th. The purchase of certain tracts of land.

The necessity for the action recommended is given with great clearness and force in each case. With these recommendations, with the possible exception of the last, I fully agree, and will hereafter submit a draft of the necessary legislation. With the measures already taken and with those herein recommended, it is believed that these poor and persecuted people may be protected from further encroachments, and enjoy in some measure the prosperity to which their peaceful conduct under all their wrongs entitles them. . . .

[*House Executive Document* no. 1, 48th Cong., 1st sess.', serial 2191, pp. 36-37.]

96. General Sherman on the End of the Indian Problem
October 27, 1883

In his final report as General of the Army, William T. Sherman noted the end of the Indian wars and the settlement of the Indian question.

. . . . I now regard the Indians as substantially eliminated from the problem of the Army. There may be spasmodic and temporary alarms, but such Indian wars as have hitherto disturbed the public peace and tranquillity are not probable. The Army has been a large factor in producing this result, but it is not the only one. Immigration and the occupation by industrious farmers and miners of land vacated by the aborigines have been largely instrumental to that end, but the *railroad* which used to follow in the rear now goes forward with the picket-line in the great battle of civilization with barbarism, and has become the *greater* cause. I have in former reports, for the past fifteen years, treated of this matter, and now, on the eve of withdrawing from active participation in public affairs, I beg to emphasize much which I have spoken and written heretofore. The recent completion of the last of the four great transcontinental lines of railway has settled forever the Indian question, the Army question, and many others which have hitherto troubled the country. . . .

[*House Executive Document* no. 1, 48th Cong., 1st sess., serial 2182, pp. 45-46.]

97. Courts of Indian Offenses
Extract from the *Annual Report of the Secretary of the Interior*
November 1, 1883

Secretary of the Interior Henry M. Teller instigated the establishment on Indian reservations of so-called courts of Indian offenses. His goal was to eliminate "heathenish practices" among the Indians, but the courts came to be general tribunals for handling minor offenses on the reservations. His directions to the commissioner of Indian affairs in regard to the courts were given in his annual report of 1883.

. . . . Many of the agencies are without law of any kind, and the necessity for some rule of government on the reservations grows more and more apparent each day. If it is the purpose of the Government to civilize the Indians, they must be compelled to desist from the savage and barbarous practices that are calculated to continue them in savagery, no matter what exterior influences are brought to bear on them. Very many of the progressive Indians have become fully alive to the pernicious influences of these heathenish practices indulged in by their people, and have sought to abolish them; in such efforts they have been aided by their missionaries, teachers, and agents, but this has been found impossible even with the aid thus given. The Government furnishes the teachers, and the charitable people contribute to the support of missionaries, and much time, labor, and money is yearly expended for their elevation, and yet a few non-progressive, degraded Indians are allowed to exhibit before the young and susceptible children all the debauchery, diabolism, and savagery of the worst state of the Indian race. Every man familiar with Indian life will bear witness to the pernicious influence of these savage rites and heathenish customs.

On the 2d of December last, with the view of as soon as possible putting an end to these heathenish practices, I addressed a letter to the Commissioner of Indian Affairs, which I here quote as expressive of my ideas on this subject:

I desire to call your attention to what I regard as a great hindrance to the civilization of the Indians, viz, the continuance of the old heathenish dances, such as the sun-dance, scalp-dance, &c. These dances, or feasts, as they are sometimes called, ought, in my judgment, to be discontinued, and if the Indians now supported by the Government are not willing to discontinue them, the agents should be instructed to compel such discontinuance. These feasts or dances are not social gatherings for the amusement of these people, but, on the contrary, are intended and calculated to stimulate the warlike passions of the young warriors of the tribe. At such feasts the warrior recounts his deeds of daring, boasts of his inhumanity in the destruction of his enemies, and his treatment of the female captives, in language that ought to shock even a savage ear. The audience assents approvingly to his boasts of falsehood, deceit, theft, murder, and rape, and the young listener is informed that this and this only is the road to fame and renown. The result is the demoralization of the young, who are incited to emulate the wicked conduct of their elders, without a thought that in so doing they violate any law, but, on the contrary, with the conviction that in so doing they are securing for themselves an enduring and deserved fame among their people. Active measures should be taken to discourage all feasts and dances of the character I have mentioned.

The marriage relation is also one requiring the immediate attention of the agents. While the Indians were in a state of at least semi-independence, there did not seem to be any great necessity for interference, even if such interference was practicable (which it doubtless was not). While dependent on the chase the Indian did not take many wives, and the great mass found themselves too poor to support more than one; but since the Government supports them this objection no longer exists, and the more numerous the family the greater the number of the rations allowed. I would not advise any interference with plural marriages now existing; but I would by all possible methods discourage future marriages of that character. The marriage relation, if it may be said to exist at all among the Indians, is exceedingly lax in its character, and it will be found impossible, for some time yet, to impress them with our idea of this important relation.

The marriage state, existing only by the consent of both parties, is easily and readily dissolved, the man not recognizing any obligation on his part to care for his offspring. As far as practicable, the Indian having taken to himself a wife should be compelled to continue that relation with her, unless dissolved by some recognized tribunal on the reservation or by the courts. Some system of marriage should be adopted, and the Indian compelled to conform to it. The Indian should also be instructed that he is under obligations to care for and support, not only his wife, but his children, and on his failure, without proper cause, to continue as the head of such family, he ought in some manner to be punished, which should be either by confinement in the guard-house or agency prison, or by a reduction of his rations.

Another great hindrance to the civilization of the Indians is the influence of the medicine men, who are always found with the anti-progressive party. The medicine men resort to various artifices and devices to keep the people under their influence, and are especially active in preventing the attendance of the children at the public schools, using their conjurers' arts to prevent the people from abandoning their heathenish rites and customs. While they profess to cure diseases by the administering of a few simple remedies, still they rely mainly on their art of conjuring. Their services are not required even for the administration of the few simple remedies they are competent to recommend, for the Government supplies the several agencies with skillful physicians, who practice among the Indians without charge to them. Steps should be taken to compel these impostors to abandon this deception and discontinue their practices, which are not only without benefit to the Indians but positively injurious to them.

The value of property as an agent of civilization ought not to be overlooked. When an Indian acquires property, with a disposition to retain the same free from tribal or individual interference, he has made a step forward in the road to civilization. One great obstacle to the acquirement of property by the Indian is the very general custom of destroying or distributing his property on the death of a member of his family. Frequently on the death of an important member of the family all the property accumulated by its head is destroyed or carried off by the "mourners," and his family left in desolation and want. While in their independent state but little inconvenience was felt in such a case, on account of the general community of interest and property, in their present condition

not only real inconvenience is felt, but disastrous consequences follow. I am informed by reliable authority that frequently the head of a family, finding himself thus despoiled of his property, becomes discouraged, and makes no further attempt to become a property owner. Fear of being considered mean, and attachment to the dead, frequently prevents the owner from interfering to save his property while it is being destroyed in his presence and contrary to his wishes.

It will be extremely difficult to accomplish much towards the civilization of the Indians while these adverse influences are allowed to exist.

The Government having attempted to support the Indians until such time as they shall become self-supporting, the interest of the Government as well as that of the Indians demands that every possible effort should be made to induce them to become self-supporting at as early a day as possible. I therefore suggest whether it is not practicable to formulate certain rules for the government of the Indians on the reservations that shall restrict and ultimately abolish the practices I have mentioned. I am not ignorant of the difficulties that will be encountered in this effort; yet I believe in all the tribes there will be found many Indians who will aid the Government in its efforts to abolish rites and customs so injurious to the Indians and so contrary to the civilization that they earnestly desire.

In accordance with the suggestions of this letter, the Commissioner of Indian Affairs established a tribunal at all agencies, except among the civilized Indians, consisting of three Indians, to be known as the court of Indian offenses. The members of this tribunal consist of the first three officers in rank of the police force, if such selection is approved by the agent; otherwise, the agent may select from among the members of the tribe three suitable persons to constitute such tribunal.

The Commissioner of Indian Affairs, with the approval of the Secretary of the Interior, promulgated certain rules for the government of this tribunal, defining offenses of which it was to take cognizance. It is believed that such a tribunal, composed as it is of Indians, will not be objectionable to the Indians and will be a step in the direction of bringing the Indians under the civilizing influence of law. Since the creation of this tribunal the time has not been sufficient to give it a fair trial, but so far it promises to

161

accomplish all that was hoped for at the time of its creation. The Commissioner recommends an appropriation for the support of this tribunal, and in such recommendation I concur. . . .

[*House Executive Document* no. 1, 48th Cong., 1st sess., serial 2190, pp. x-xiii.]

98. Ex Parte Crow Dog
December 17, 1883

When the Brulé Sioux chief Crow Dog was sentenced to death by the First Judicial District Court of Dakota for the murder of Spotted Tail, he brought suit for release on the grounds that the federal courts had no jurisdiction over crimes committed in the Indian country by one Indian against another. The Supreme Court upheld his petition and released him.

. . . . The petitioner is in the custody of the marshal of the United States for the Territory of Dakota, imprisoned in the jail of Lawrence County, in the First Judicial District of that Territory, under sentence of death, adjudged against him by the district court for that district, to be carried into execution January 14th, 1884. That judgment was rendered upon a conviction for the murder of an Indian of the Brulé Sioux band of the Sioux Nation of Indians, by the name of Sin-ta-ge-le-Scka, or in English, Spotted Tail, the prisoner also being an Indian, of the same band and nation, and the homicide having occurred as alleged in the indictment, in the Indian country, within a place and district of country under the exclusive jurisdiction of the United States and within the said judicial district. The judgment was affirmed, on a writ of error, by the Supreme Court of the Territory. It is claimed on behalf of the prisoner that the crime charged against him, and of which he stands convicted, is not an offence under the laws of the United States; that the district court had no jurisdiction to try him, and that its judgment and sentence are void. He therefore prays for a writ of habeas corpus, that he may be delivered from an imprisonment which he asserts to be illegal. . . .

It must be remembered that the question before us is whether the express letter of § 2146 of the Revised Statutes, which excludes from the jurisdiction of the United States the case of a crime committed in the Indian country by one Indian against the person or property of another Indian, has been repealed. If not, it is in force and applies to the present case. The treaty of 1868 and the agreement and act of Congress of 1877, it is admitted, do not repeal it by any express words. What we have said is sufficient at least to show that they do not work a repeal by necessary implication. . . .

. . . It is a case involving the judgment of a court of special and limited jurisdiction, not to be assumed without clear warrant of law. It is a case of life and death. It is a case where, against an express exception in the law itself, that law, by argument and inference only, is sought to be extended over aliens and strangers; over the members of a community separated by race, by tradition, by the instincts of a free though savage life, from the authority and power which seeks to impose upon them the restraints of an external and unknown code, and to subject them to the responsibilities of civil conduct, according to rules and penalties of which they could have no previous warning; which judges them by a standard made by others and not for them, which takes no account of the conditions which should except them from its exactions, and makes no allowance for their inability to understand it. It tries them, not by their peers, nor by the customs of their people, nor the law of their land, but by superiors of a different race, according to the law of a social state of which they have an imperfect conception, and which is opposed to the traditions of their history, to the habits of their lives, to the strongest prejudices of their savage nature; one which measures the red man's revenge by the maxims of the white man's morality. It is a case, too, of first impression, so far as we are advised, for, if the question has been mooted heretofore in any courts of the United States, the jurisdiction has never before been practically assert-

162

ed as in the present instance. . . .

To give to the clauses in the treaty of 1868 and the agreement of 1877 effect, so as to uphold the jurisdiction exercised in this case, would be to reverse in this instance the general policy of the government towards the Indians, as declared in many statutes and treaties, and recognized in many decisions of this court, from the beginning to the present time. To justify such a departure, in such a case, requires a clear expression of the inten-

tion of Congress, and that we have not been able to find.

It results that the First District Court of Dakota was without jurisdiction to find or try the indictment against the prisoner, that the conviction and sentence are void, and that his imprisonment is illegal.

The writs of habeas corpus and certiorari prayed for will accordingly be issued.

[109 *U.S. Reports*, 557, 571-72.]

99. Program of the Lake Mohonk Conference
September 1884

Reformers interested in Indian affairs met each year from 1883 to 1916 at Lake Mohonk, New York, to discuss Indian matters and to make recommendations. These Lake Mohonk Conferences of Friends of the Indian had tremendous impact on the formulation of federal policy. In 1884, in a series of resolutions, the conference gave a preview of the topics that would concern it during the following decades.

. . . . The motive, therefore, which has urged the members of the Mohonk Conference to issue their address to the public is twofold:

1st. To inform the people of the United States as to the most direct practicable way in which the Indian question may be solved.

2d. To stimulate the thoughtful and right-minded citizens of the country to take immediate steps toward the solution of the problem.

It was felt by all those who took part in the work of the Conference that a calm, definite, and earnest appeal made to the conscience and intelligence of the country in behalf of a poor and helpless people, and for the righting of a national wrong, would not be uttered in vain. . . .

WHAT IS NECESSARY TO SECURE INDIAN CITIZENSHIP

1st. *Resolved,* That the organization of the Indians in tribes is, and has been, one of the most serious hindrances to the advancement of the Indian toward civilization, and that every effort should be made to secure the disintegration of all tribal organizations; that to accomplish this result the Government should, except where it is clearly necessary either for the fulfillment of treaty stipulations or for some other binding rea-

son, cease to recognize the Indians as political bodies or organized tribes.

2d. *Resolved,* That to all Indians who desire to hold their land in severalty allotments should be made without delay; and that to all other Indians like allotments should be made so soon as practicable.

3d. *Resolved,* That lands allotted and granted in severalty to Indians should be made inalienable for a period of not less than ten or more than twenty-five years.

4th. *Resolved,* That all adult male Indians should be admitted to the full privileges of citizenship by a process analogous to naturalization, upon evidence presented before the proper court of record of adequate intellectual and moral qualifications. . . .

5th. *Resolved,* That we earnestly and heartily approve of the Senate Bill No. 48, generally known as the Coke Bill, as the best practicable measure yet brought before Congress for the preservation of the Indian from aggression, for the disintegration of the tribal organizations, and for the ultimate breaking up of the reservation system; that we tender our hearty thanks and the thanks of the constituency which we represent to those members of the Senate who have framed this bill and secured its passage. We respectfully urge upon the House of Representatives the early adoption of this bill, that its beneficent provisions for rendering the Indian self-supporting and his land productive may be carried out with the least possible delay. . . .

EDUCATION.

a. Industrial.
b. Intellectual.
c. Moral and religious.

6th. *Resolved*, That from testimony laid before the Conference, our confidence in the good results flowing from the education of Indians has been confirmed, and that we regard with great satisfaction the increasing appropriations made by Congress for Indian schools, for instruction in farming and trades, for supplies of cattle, for irrigation, and for other means to promote self-supporting industries. That our conviction has been strengthened as to the importance of taking Indian youth from the reservations to be trained in industrial schools placed among communities of white citizens, and we favor the use of a larger proportion of the funds appropriated for Indian education for the maintenance of such schools. The placing of the pupils of these schools in the families of farmers or artisans where they may learn the trades and home habits of their employers has proved very useful and should be encouraged by the Government.

Resolved, That from evidence brought before the Conference it is apparent that the plan carried out to a small extent at Hampton and elsewhere, of bringing young men and their wives to industrial schools and there furnishing them with small houses so that they may be instructed in work and a proper home life, has been successful and should be carried out more largely.

Resolved, That while we approve the methods of Indian education pursued at Hampton and Carlisle, we do not fail to recognize that the schools and other methods of instruction, industrial, intellectual, moral, and religious, as carried on within or near the reservations by Christian missionaries for the last fifty years, have lifted up tribe after tribe to civilization and fitted them to take lands in severalty, and the good already achieved should stimulate and encourage Christian people to continued efforts in the same direction.

7th. *Resolved*, That education is essential to civilization. The Indian must have a knowledge of the English language, that he may associate with his white neighbors and transact business as they do. He must have practical industrial training to fit him to compete with others in the struggle for life. He must have a Christian education to enable him to perform duties of the family, the State, and the Church. Such an education can be best acquired apart from his reservation and amid the influences of Christian and civilized society. Such Government industrial training schools as those at Carlisle, Hampton, Forest Grove, Lawrence, Chiloco, and Genoa should be sustained and their number increased. The Government should continue to avail itself of institutions such as the training schools at Albuquerque, New Mexico; Lincoln Institute, Pennsylvania, and others conducted by religious or philanthropic associations, and promote the placing of pupils educated in all these schools in the families of farmers and artisans. But since the great majority of the Indians cannot be educated away from their homes, it is a matter of the highest importance that the Government should provide and liberally sustain good manual labor and day schools on the reservations. These should be established in sufficient number to accommodate all Indian children of school age. The Christian people of the country should exert through the Indian schools a strong moral and religious influence. This the Government cannot do, but without this the true civilization of the Indian is impossible.

HOW TO SECURE THESE THINGS.

a. Public sentiment.
b. Legislation.

8th. *Resolved*, That since legislation in Congress and the benevolent work of the Christian people on behalf of the Indian is dependent upon public sentiment, every effort should be made to further the development of such sentiment. To this end we commend to the sympathy and support of the public the Indian Rights Association and the Woman's National Indian Association. We urge the organization of branches of these Societies in the principal cities and towns of the country. We think it extremely desirable that the press be enlisted in bringing the Indian cause to public attention, and we also rejoice in the efforts of the many benevolent societies belonging to the various religious bodies to diffuse information concerning the Indians and to arouse public interest in their behalf.

SECOND TOPIC.

1st.   Treaties.

9th. *Resolved,* That we are bound by many treaties with various Indian tribes. These treaties are the bases of our relations with them, and yet are in some instances prejudicial to the best interests of both the Government and the Indians. Nevertheless, the treaties are binding upon the Government and the tribes until they can be modified by mutual agreement. The only way, therefore, to escape their evils is to persuade the Indians to agree to some modification of their provisions.

We rejoice that since March 3d, 1871, it has been the policy of the Government to make no fresh treaties with the Indians. We trust that this policy may be strictly adhered to, and that the Government will have no dealings with chiefs alone as the representatives of tribal organizations.

2d.   Reservations.

10th. *Resolved,* That careful observation has conclusively proved that the removal of Indians from reservations which they have long occupied, to other reservations far distant from the former and possessing different soil and climate, is attended by great suffering and loss of life. Such removals destroy the fruits of past industry and discourage the Indians from further effort in the habits of civilized life. These removals are usually made, not for wise reasons, but are instigated by the covetousness of the whites, who desire possession of the Indian lands or wish to rid themselves of the Indians' presence. We, therefore, earnestly protest against such Indian removals in the future, excepting in those cases where they shall be justified by full and sufficient reasons, and shall not be detrimental to the welfare of the Indians. When the removal of an Indian tribe becomes a necessity, individual Indians belonging to the tribe who have formed settled homes should have the privilege of taking homesteads upon the lands they occupy prior to the opening of the reservation and before white men are permitted to make land-entries thereon.

11th. *Resolved,* That the Conference gives its hearty approval to Senate bill No. 1755, providing for the division of the Sioux Reservation, which passed the Senate at the last session; that we record our gratitude to Senator Dawes and his colleagues upon the Select Committee for the skill and care with which they have embodied in this bill the important points agreed upon by the first Mohonk Conference; that we heartily commend the bill to the support of all friends of the Indians, and hope that it may be considered and passed by Congress at its next session.

Resolved, That the bill be referred to the Committee appointed to advocate the bill on lands in severalty, and that this Committee bring it to the attention of the Committees of Congress on Indian Affairs soon after that body shall have met. . . .

3d.   Government aid.

12th. *Resolved,* That the Conference hereby calls attention to the fact that Government aid extended to Indians in the form of rations, implements, clothing, etc., is in many instances not a gratuity, but is given simply in fulfillment of treaty stipulations and in payment for land ceded by the Indians to the United States.

In cases where Indians have been rendered destitute by the sudden destruction of the game on which they subsisted, as in the case of many Indians in Montana, they should be supplied with rations until time has been given them and opportunity afforded them to become self-supporting.

4th.   Agencies.

13th. *Resolved,* That since Indian agents are obliged to live, in many instances, at a distance from the conveniences of civilized life, and where, owing to difficulties of transportation, the cost of living is extreme, and that as they are, furthermore, cut off from all means of self-support beyond the salary paid to them by the Government, this salary should in some cases be much larger than it is at present. Such an increase of salary would not be more than just compensation for the difficult and laborious duties of

Indian agent, nor more than sufficient to secure the services of a high grade of men.

From personal observation and the testimony of competent judges, we are convinced that in many instances the agency buildings on reservations are unsuited to serve as homes for agents and their employees. In such cases suitable buildings should be provided.

We desire emphatically to reaffirm our conviction, expressed in the address of the first annual Conference, that the success of the Government in its effort to elevate the Indians depends on the ability, integrity, and energy of Indian agents and their employees, and we protest against any return to a system by which agents and their employees are appointed on the ground of political or personal favoritism.

5th. Law.

14th. *Resolved,* That immediate efforts should be made to place the Indian in the same position before the law as that held by the rest of the population, but that if it is not advisable, under existing circumstances, to subject the Indian at once to our entire body of law, the friends of the Indian should promptly endeavor: *First,* to provide for him some method of admission to citizenship so soon as he has prepared himself for its privileges and responsibilities; *second,* to give him at once the right to sue in our courts, and, *third,* to provide some system for the administration of certain laws on the reservations. We believe that the laws relating to marriage and inheritance and the criminal law affecting person and property should be extended over the reservations immediately.

As may be seen from the above resolutions, the Conference unites in urging that plain and sensible policy the main points of which have been so long and patiently recommended to Congress by men of practical experience in Indian affairs.

As these resolutions show, the Conference recognized that to permanently keep Indians as tribes, under the control of agents on reservations set apart for them, is both impossible and undesirable.

They recognized that the Indian must be forced out into the current of ordinary life; that to make him a citizen is the solution of the Indian problem.

Yet the resolutions express with equal strength the conviction that Indians should not be at once made citizens in a mass. The *preparation* for citizenship should be general, vigorous, and immediate. The Indian is to be prepared for citizenship by giving him his land in severalty in the manner provided for by the Coke Bill, by larger appropriations for Indian education and the careful use of such appropriations in the establishment and support of schools, industrial and otherwise, and by the *education* of the race in the broadest and largest sense of the word.

By adequate provision for the administration of law among the Indians, and by giving the Indian the right to sue.

By Christian teaching and the establishing and support of churches.

By the gradual reduction of rations given to Indians, the systematic instruction in farming, and the encouragement in self-support.

By the appointment and support of agents of ability and integrity, uninfluenced by political preference, the only standard being that of individual fitness.

By proper provision for the immediate admission to citizenship of such Indians as are fitted for its duties and responsibilities.

These are substantially the recommendations which the Conference respectfully urges upon Congress and the people of the United States, as the just, obvious, and practical answer to the Indian question.

[*Second Annual Address to the Public of the Lake Mohonk Conference* (Philadelphia: Indian Rights Association, 1884), pp. 3-4, 6-7, 13-16, 20-22.]

100. Elk v. Wilkins

November 3, 1884

John Elk, an Indian who had voluntarily separated himself from his tribe and taken up residence among the whites, was denied the right to vote in Omaha, Nebraska, on the ground that he was not a citizen. The Supreme Court considered the question of whether Elk had been made a citizen by the Fourteenth Amendment and decided against him.

. . . . The plaintiff, in support of his action, relies on the first clause of the first section of the Fourteenth Article of Amendment of the Constitution of the United States, by which "all persons born or naturalized in the United States, and subject to the jurisdiction thereof, are citizens of the United States and of the State wherein they reside;" and on the Fifteenth Article of Amendment, which provides that "the right of citizens of the United States to vote shall not be denied or abridged by the United States or by any State on account of race, color, or previous condition of servitude." . . .

The petition, while it does not show of what Indian tribe the plaintiff was a member, yet, by the allegations that he "is an Indian, and was born within the United States," and that "he had severed his tribal relation to the Indian tribes," clearly implies that he was born a member of one of the Indian tribes within the limits of the United States, which still exists and is recognized as a tribe by the government of the United States. Though the plaintiff alleges that he "had fully and completely surrendered himself to the jurisdiction of the United States," he does not allege that the United States accepted his surrender, or that he has ever been naturalized, or taxed, or in any way recognized or treated as a citizen, by the State or by the United States. Nor is it contended by his counsel that there is any statute or treaty that makes him a citizen.

The question then is, whether an Indian, born a member of one of the Indian tribes within the United States, is, merely by reason of his birth within the United States, and of his afterwards voluntarily separating himself from his tribe and taking up his residence among white citizens, a citizen of the United States, within the meaning of the first section of the Fourteenth Amendment of the Constitution. . . .

Indians born within the territorial limits of the United States, members of, and owing immediate allegiance to, one of the Indian tribes (an alien, though dependent, power), although in a geographical sense born in the United States, are no more "born in the United States and subject to the jurisdiction thereof," within the meaning of the first section of the Fourteenth Amendment, than the children of subjects of any foreign government born within the domain of that government, or the children born within the United States, of ambassadors or other public ministers of foreign nations.

This view is confirmed by the second section of the Fourteenth Amendment, which provides that "representatives shall be apportioned among the several States according to their respective numbers, counting the whole number of persons in each State, excluding Indians not taxed." Slavery having been abolished, and the persons formerly held as slaves made citizens, this clause fixing the apportionment of representatives has abrogated so much of the corresponding clause of the original Constitution as counted only three-fifths of such persons. But Indians not taxed are still excluded from the count, for the reason that they are not citizens. Their absolute exclusion from the basis of representation, in which all other persons are now included, is wholly inconsistent with their being considered citizens. . . .

The plaintiff, not being a citizen of the United States under the Fourteenth Amendment of the Constitution, has been deprived of no right secured by the Fifteenth Amendment, and cannot maintain this action.

[112 *U.S. Reports*, 98-99, 102, 109.]

101. Major Crimes Act

March 3, 1885

To prevent a recurrence of cases like the murder of Spotted Tail by Crow Dog, in which the murderer was freed because the federal courts had no jurisdiction over crimes committed by one Indian against another within the Indian country, Congress declared that seven major crimes committed by Indians on the reservations would fall under the jurisdiction of United States courts. This was a major encroachment upon traditional tribal autonomy.

An Act making appropriations for the current and contingent expenses of the Indian Department. . . .

. . . .Sec. 9. That immediately upon and after the date of the passage of this act all Indians, committing against the person or property of another Indian or other person any of the following crimes, namely, murder, manslaughter, rape, assault with intent to kill, arson, burglary, and larceny within any Territory of the United States, and either within or without an Indian reservation, shall be subject therefor to the laws of such Territory relating to said crimes, and shall be tried therefor in the same courts and in the same manner and shall be subject to the same penalties as are all other persons charged with the commission of said crimes, respectively; and the said courts are hereby given jurisdiction in all such cases; and all such Indians committing any of the above crimes against the person or property of another Indian or other person within the boundaries of any State of the United States, and within the limits of any Indian reservation, shall be subject to the same laws, tried in the same courts and in the same manner, and subject to the same penalties as are all other persons committing any of the above crimes within the exclusive jurisdiction of the United States.

[*U.S. Statutes at Large*, 23:385.]

102. United States v. Kagama
May 10, 1886

The constitutionality of the Major Crimes Act (section 9 of the act of March 3, 1885) was tested in 1886 in a case involving two Indians who committed murder on the Hoopa Valley Indian Reservation in California. The Supreme Court upheld the law.

. . . . The case of *Crow Dog*, 109 U.S. 556, in which an agreement with the Sioux Indians, ratified by an act of Congress, was supposed to extend over them the laws of the United States and the jurisdiction of its courts, covering murder and other grave crimes, shows the purpose of Congress in this new departure. The decision in that case admits that if the intention of Congress had been to punish, by the United States courts, the murder of one Indian by another, the law would have been valid. But the court could not see, in the agreement with the Indians sanctioned by Congress, a purpose to repeal § 2146 of the Revised Statutes, which expressly excludes from that jurisdiction the case of a crime committed by one Indian against another in the Indian country. The passage of the act now under consideration was designed to remove that objection, and to go further by including such crimes on reservations lying within a State.

Is this latter fact a fatal objection to the law? The statute itself contains no express limitation upon the powers of a State or the jurisdiction of its courts. If there be any limitation in either of these, it grows out of the implication arising from the fact that

Congress has defined a crime committed within the State, and made it punishable in the courts of the United States. But Congress *has* done this, and *can* do it, with regard to all offences relating to matters to which the Federal authority extends. Does that authority extend to this case?

It will be seen at once that the nature of the offence (murder) is one which in almost all cases of its commission is punishable by the laws of the States, and within the jurisdiction of their courts. The distinction is claimed to be that the offence under the statute is committed by an Indian, that it is committed on a reservation set apart within the State for residence of the tribe of Indians by the United States, and the fair inference is that the offending Indian shall belong to that or some other tribe. It does not interfere with the process of the State courts within the reservation, nor with the operation of State laws upon white people found there. Its effect is confined to the acts of an Indian of some tribe, of a criminal character, committed within the limits of the reservation.

It seems to us that this is within the competency of Congress. These Indian tribes *are* the wards of the nation. They are

168

communities *dependent* on the United States. Dependent largely for their daily food. Dependent for their political rights. They owe no allegiance to the States, and receive from them no protection. Because of the local ill feeling, the people of the States where they are found are often their deadliest enemies. From their very weakness and helplessness, so largely due to the course of dealing of the Federal Government with them and the treaties in which it has been promised, there arises the duty of protection, and with it the power. This has always been recognized by the Executive and by Congress, and by this court, whenever the question has arisen. . . .

The power of the General Government over these remnants of a race once powerful, now weak and diminished in numbers, is necessary to their protection, as well as to the safety of those among whom they dwell. It must exist in that government, because it never has existed anywhere else, because the theatre of its exercise is within the geographical limits of the United States, because it has never been denied, and because it alone can enforce its laws on all the tribes.

We answer the questions propounded to us, that the 9th section of the act of March, 1885, is a valid law in both its branches, and that the Circuit Court of the United States for the District of California has jurisdiction of the offence charged in the indictment in this case.

[118 *U.S. Reports*, 375, 382-85.]

103.   Indian Commissioner Atkins on the Five Civilized Tribes

Extract from the *Annual Report of the Commissioner of Indian Affairs*

September 28, 1886

Proposals following the Civil War to create a regular territorial government for the Indian nations in the Indian Territory were successfully beaten down by the Indians. As the reform movement to absorb the Indians as citizens into white society gained headway in the 1880s, new attention was paid to the Five Civilized Tribes. Arguments in favor of changing their status were advanced by Commissioner J. D. C. Atkins in his annual report for 1886.

. . . . In view of this policy of protection for the Indians, it is reasonable that the Indian Bureau and the country should look to the five civilized tribes of the Indian Territory about whom so much has been said by orators and statesmen, and of whom so much is expected by the friends of the Indian, to set freely and promptly such an example as shall advance the civilization of their savage brethren of other tribes. The influence of their example upon the semicivilized and savage tribes makes the study of their condition and methods a matter not only of great interest but also of first importance.

The treaties of 1866, and other treaties also, guarantee to the five civilized tribes the possession of their lands; but, without the moral and physical power which is represented by the Army of the United States, what are these treaties worth as a protection against the rapacious greed of the homeless people of the States who seek homesteads within the borders of the Indian Territory? If the protecting power of this Government were withdrawn for thirty days, where

would the treaties be, and the laws of the Indians and the Indians themselves? The history of Payne and Couch and their followers, and the determined effort of both Republican and Democratic administrations to resist their unlawful claims and demands, is too recent not to be still fresh in the memory of these Indians. It is not reasonable to expect that the Government will never tire of menacing its own people with its own Army. Therefore it becomes vastly important that these five civilized tribes, who have among them men competent to be Representatives and Senators in Congress, governors of States, and judges on the bench, should cordially, and in a spirit of friendly gratitude for what has been done for them, co-operate with the Government in bringing about such a change of affairs in their midst as will bring peace and quiet to their borders, settle existing agitations as to their rights and interests, and dispose of disquieting questions which will surely grow out of the present alarming condition of things in the whole Indian Territory.

At present the rich Indians who cultivate

169

tribal lands pay no rent to the poorer and more unfortunate of their race, although they are equal owners of the soil. The rich men have too large homesteads and control many times more than their share of the land. It will not do to say, as the wealthy and influential leaders of the nations contend, that their system of laws gives to every individual member of the tribe equal facilities to be independent and equal opportunity to possess himself of a homestead. Already the rich and choice lands are appropriated by those most enterprising and self seeking. A considerable number of Indians have in cultivation farms exceeding 1,000 acres in extent, and a still larger number are cultivating between 500 and 1,000 acres. Now, think of one Indian having a farm fenced in of 1,000 acres, with the right, according to their system (as I understand the fact to be), of adding nearly 1,000 acres more by excluding all others from the use or occupancy of a quarter of a mile in width all around the tract fenced. What a baronial estate! In theory the lands are held in common under the tribal relation, and are equally owned by each member of the tribe, but in point of fact they are simply held in the grasping hand of moneyed monopolists and powerful and influential leaders and politicians, who pay no rental to the other members of the tribe, who, under their tribal ownership in common, have equal rights with the occupants. . . .

I am not recommending that Congress shall undertake to do anything with reference to these five civilized tribes which is inhibited by the treaties. But I do advise the nations themselves to awake to a true appreciation of their own situation, and to have respect for that public opinion in this country which makes laws and forms States and which has thus far protected them in their treaty rights. I do advise our red brothers, whose interests I desire to see promoted, to advise with each other and to act wisely by passing just and equal laws for the division of lands in severalty, allotting to each member of the tribe his own birthright. The treaties I hope to see observed. But where the continued observance of those treaty obligations works an injury to the Indians by alienating from them the mass of the people of the United States, who are by

instinct opposed to all monopoly, or where it does great injury to the Indians themselves, it seems to me it is the duty of the Indians to agree among themselves to a modification of those treaties—to remodel all such laws and customs as give a monopoly to a few (or even to many), and to place themselves abreast the times and in accord with the ideas of free and equal citizenship which prevail in this great country.

Territorial government.—If the Indians of the five civilized tribes would then put away tribal relations, and adopt the institutions common to our Territories or States, they would no longer be subjected to the jealousy, contention, and selfish greed of adventurous land-grabbers who now seem to regard the Indian a legitimate object of prey and plunder. These adventurers do not attempt to dislodge and drive from their domiciles the peaceful white settlers in their distant homes. Let these Indians once assume all the responsibilities of citizens of the United States, with its laws extended as a protecting aegis over them, and the day of their fear and apprehension of marauding whites will be forever ended. When this is done then will the five civilized tribes, and perhaps other tribes of the Indian Territory, be ready to form a territorial government and pass, as other Territories, under the protection of our Constitution and laws and be represented in Congress by their own delegate.

The great objection that is urged by the Indians to dissolving their tribal relations, alloting their lands, and merging their political form of government into an organized Territory of the United States, arises out of their excessive attachment to Indian tradition and nationality. I have great respect for those sentiments. They are patriotic and noble impulses and principles. But is it not asking too much of the American people to permit a political paradox to exist within their midst—nay, more, to ask and demand that the people of this country shall forever burden themselves with the responsibility and expense of maintaining and extending over these Indians its military arm, simply to gratify this sentimentality about a separate nationality? No such exclusive privilege was granted the Pueblos of New Mexico, nor the inhabitants of California, Utah, and Arizona, or any of the more northern Territories, including Alaska.

It is alleged that Congress has no power, in view of the treaties with those Indians, to do away with their present form of government and institute in its stead a Territorial government similar to those now existing in the eight organized Territories. While I greatly prefer that these people should voluntarily change their form of government, yet it is perfectly plain to my mind that the treaties never contemplated the un-American and absurd idea of a separate nationality in our midst, with power as they may choose to organize a government of their own, or not to organize any government nor allow one to be organized, for the one proposition contains the other. These Indians have no right to obstruct civilization and commerce and set up an exclusive claim to self-government, establishing a government within a government, and then expect and claim that the United States shall protect them from all harm, while insisting that it shall not be the ultimate judge as to what is best to be done for them in a political point of view. I repeat, to maintain any such view is to acknowledge a foreign sovereignty, with the right of eminent domain, upon American soil—a theory utterly repugnant to the spirit and genius of our laws, and wholly unwarranted by the Constitution of the United States.

Congress and the Executive of the United States are the supreme guardians of these mere wards, and can administer their affairs as any other guardian can. Of course it must be done in a just and enlightened way. It must be done in a spirit of protection and not of oppression and robbery. Congress can sell their surplus lands and distribute the proceeds equally among the owners for the purposes of civilization and the education of their children, and the protection of the infirm, and the establishment of the poor upon homesteads with stock and implements of husbandry. Congress cannot consistently or justly or honestly take their lands from them and give or sell them to others except as above referred to, and for those objects alone. The sentiment is rapidly growing among these five nations that all existing forms of Indian government which have produced an unsatisfactory and dangerous condition of things, menacing the peace of the Indians and irritating their white neighbors, should be replaced by a regularly organized Territorial form of government, the territory thus constituted to be admitted at some future time as a State into the Union on an equal footing with other States, thereby securing all the protection, sympathy, and guarantees of this great and beneficent nation. The sooner this sentiment becomes universal the better for all concerned. . . .

[*House Executive Document* no. 1, 49th Cong., 2d sess., serial 2467, pp. 81-82, 86-88.]

104. General Allotment Act (Dawes Act)
February 8, 1887

The demand of reformers that Indian reservations be allotted in severalty to individual Indians and that tribal relations be broken up was fulfilled by the Dawes Act of 1887. The law authorized the president of the United States to proceed with allotment and declared Indians who received allotments to be citizens of the United States.

An act to provide for the allotment of lands in severalty to Indians on the various reservations, and to extend the protection of the laws of the United States and the Territories over the Indians, and for other purposes.

Be it enacted . . . . , That in all cases where any tribe or band of Indians has been, or shall hereafter be, located upon any reservation created for their use, either by treaty stipulation or by virtue of an act of Congress or executive order setting apart the same for their use, the President of the United States be, and he hereby is, authorized, whenever in his opinion any reservation or any part thereof of such Indians is advantageous for agricultural and grazing purposes, to cause said reservation, or any part thereof, to be

171

surveyed, or resurveyed if necessary, and to allot the lands in said reservation in severalty to any Indian located thereon in quantities as follows:

To each head of a family, one-quarter of a section;

To each single person over eighteen years of age, one-eighth of a section;

To each orphan child under eighteen years of age, one-eighth of a section; and

To each other single person under eighteen years now living, or who may be born prior to the date of the order of the President directing an allotment of the lands embraced in any reservation, one-sixteenth of a section: *Provided*, That in case there is not sufficient land in any of said reservations to allot lands to each individual of the classes above named in quantities as above provided, the lands embraced in such reservation or reservations shall be allotted to each individual of each of said classes pro rata in accordance with the provisions of this act: *And provided further*, That where the treaty or act of Congress setting apart such reservation provides for the allotment of lands in severalty in quantities in excess of those herein provided, the President, in making allotments upon such reservation, shall allot the lands to each individual Indian belonging thereon in quantity as specified in such treaty or act: *And provided further*, That when the lands allotted are only valuable for grazing purposes, an additional allotment of such grazing lands, in quantities as above provided, shall be made to each individual.

SEC. 2. That all allotments set apart under the provisions of this act shall be selected by the Indians, heads of families selecting for their minor children, and the agents shall select for each orphan child, and in such manner as to embrace the improvements of the Indians making the selection. Where the improvements of two or more Indians have been made on the same legal subdivision of land, unless they shall otherwise agree, a provisional line may be run dividing said lands between them, and the amount to which each is entitled shall be equalized in the assignment of the remainder of the land to which they are entitled under this act: *Provided*, That if any one entitled to an allotment shall fail to make a selection within four years after the President shall direct that allotments may be made on a particular reservation, the Secretary of the Interior may direct the agent of such tribe or band, if such there be, and if there be no agent, then a special agent appointed for that purpose, to make a selection for such Indian, which selection shall be allotted as in cases where selections are made by the Indians, and patents shall issue in like manner.

SEC. 3. That the allotments provided for in this act shall be made by special agents appointed by the President for such purpose, and the agents in charge of the respective reservations on which the allotments are directed to be made, under such rules and regulations as the Secretary of the Interior may from time to time prescribe, and shall be certified by such agents to the Commissioner of Indian Affairs, in duplicate, one copy to be retained in the Indian Office and the other to be transmitted to the Secretary of the Interior for his action, and to be deposited in the General Land Office.

SEC. 4. That where any Indian not residing upon a reservation, or for whose tribe no reservation has been provided by treaty, act of Congress, or executive order, shall make settlement upon any surveyed or unsurveyed lands of the United States not otherwise appropriated, he or she shall be entitled, upon application to the local land-office for the district in which the lands are located, to have the same allotted to him or her, and to his or her children, in quantities and manner as provided in this act for Indians residing upon reservations; and when such settlement is made upon unsurveyed lands, the grant to such Indians shall be adjusted upon the survey of the lands so as to conform thereto; and patents shall be issued to them for such lands in the manner and with the restrictions as herein provided. And the fees to which the officers of such local land-office would have been entitled had such lands been entered under the general laws for the disposition of the public lands shall be paid to them, from any moneys in the Treasury of the United States not otherwise appropriated, upon a statement of an account in their behalf for such fees by the Commissioner of the General Land Office, and a certification of such account to the Secretary of the Treasury by the Secretary of the Interior.

SEC. 5. That upon the approval of the allotments provided for in this act by the

Secretary of the Interior, he shall cause patents to issue therefor in the name of the allottees, which patents shall be of the legal effect, and declare that the United States does and will hold the land thus allotted, for the period of twenty-five years, in trust for the sole use and benefit of the Indian to whom such allotment shall have been made, or, in case of his decease, of his heirs according to the laws of the State or Territory where such land is located, and that at the expiration of said period the United States will convey the same by patent to said Indian, or his heirs as aforesaid, in fee, discharged of said trust and free of all charge or incumbrance whatsoever: *Provided*, That the President of the United States may in any case in his discretion extend the period. And if any conveyance shall be made of the lands set apart and allotted as herein provided, or any contract made touching the same, before the expiration of the time above mentioned, such conveyance or contract shall be absolutely null and void: *Provided*, That the law of descent and partition in force in the State or Territory where such lands are situate shall apply thereto after patents therefor have been executed and delivered, except as herein otherwise provided; and the laws of the State of Kansas regulating the descent and partition of real estate shall, so far as practicable, apply to all lands in the Indian Territory which may be allotted in severalty under the provisions of this act: *And provided further*, That at any time after lands have been allotted to all the Indians of any tribe as herein provided, or sooner if in the opinion of the President it shall be for the best interests of said tribe, it shall be lawful for the Secretary of the Interior to negotiate with such Indian tribe for the purchase and release by said tribe, in conformity with the treaty or statute under which such reservation is held, of such portions of its reservation not allotted as such tribe shall, from time to time, consent to sell, on such terms and conditions as shall be considered just and equitable between the United States and said tribe of Indians, which purchase shall not be complete until ratified by Congress, and the form and manner of executing such release shall also be prescribed by Congress: *Provided however*, That all lands adapted to agriculture, with or without irrigation so sold or released to the United States by any

Indian tribe shall be held by the United States for the sole purpose of securing homes to actual settlers and shall be disposed of by the United States to actual and bona fide settlers only in tracts not exceeding one hundred and sixty acres to any one person, on such terms as Congress shall prescribe, subject to grants which Congress may make in aid of education: *And provided further*, That no patents shall issue therefor except to the person so taking the same as and for a homestead, or his heirs, and after the expiration of five years occupancy thereof as such homestead; and any conveyance of said lands so taken as a homestead, or any contract touching the same, or lien thereon, created prior to the date of such patent, shall be null and void. And the sums agreed to be paid by the United States as purchase money for any portion of any such reservation shall be held in the Treasury of the United States for the sole use of the tribe or tribes of Indians; to whom such reservations belonged; and the same, with interest thereon at three per cent per annum, shall be at all times subject to appropriation by Congress for the education and civilization of such tribe or tribes of Indians or the members thereof. The patents aforesaid shall be recorded in the General Land Office, and afterward delivered, free of charge, to the allottee entitled thereto. And if any religious society or other organization is now occupying any of the public lands to which this act is applicable, for religious or educational work among the Indians, the Secretary of the Interior is hereby authorized to confirm such occupation to such society or organization, in quantity not exceeding one hundred and sixty acres in any one tract, so long as the same shall be so occupied, on such terms as he shall deem just; but nothing herein contained shall change or alter any claim of such society for religious or educational purposes heretofore granted by law. And hereafter in the employment of Indian police, or any other employes in the public service among any of the Indian tribes or bands affected by this act, and where Indians can perform the duties required, those Indians who have availed themselves of the provisions of this act and become citizens of the United States shall be preferred.

SEC. 6. That upon the completion of said allotments and the patenting of the

173

lands to said allottees, each and every member of the respective bands or tribes of Indians to whom allotments have been made shall have the benefit of and be subject to the laws, both civil and criminal, of the State or Territory in which they may reside; and no Territory shall pass or enforce any law denying any such Indian within its jurisdiction the equal protection of the law. And every Indian born within the territorial limits of the United States to whom allotments shall have been made under the provisions of this act, or under any law or treaty, and every Indian born within the territorial limits of the United States who has voluntarily taken up, within said limits, his residence separate and apart from any tribe of Indians therein, and has adopted the habits of civilized life, is hereby declared to be a citizen of the United States, and is entitled to all the rights, privileges, and immunities of such citizens, whether said Indian has been or not, by birth or otherwise, a member of any tribe of Indians within the territorial limits of the United States without in any manner impairing or otherwise affecting the right of any such Indian to tribal or other property.

Sec. 7. That in cases where the use of water for irrigation is necessary to render the lands within any Indian reservation available for agricultural purposes, the Secretary of the Interior be, and he is hereby, authorized to prescribe such rules and regulations as he may deem necessary to secure a just and equal distribution thereof among the Indians residing upon any such reservations; and no other appropriation or grant of water by any riparian proprietor shall be author-

ized or permitted to the damage of any other riparian proprietor.

Sec. 8. That the provision of this act shall not extend to the territory occupied by the Cherokees, Creeks, Choctaws, Chickasaws, Seminoles, and Osage, Miamies and Peorias, and Sacs and Foxes, in the Indian Territory, nor to any of the reservations of the Seneca Nation of New York Indians in the State of New York, nor to that strip of territory in the State of Nebraska adjoining the Sioux Nation on the south added by executive order.

Sec. 9. That for the purpose of making the surveys and resurveys mentioned in section two of this act, there be, and hereby is, appropriated, out of any moneys in the Treasury not otherwise appropriated, the sum of one hundred thousand dollars, to be repaid proportionately out of the proceeds of the sales of such land as may be acquired from the Indians under the provisions of this act.

Sec. 10. That nothing in this act contained shall be so construed as to affect the right and power of Congress to grant the right of way through any lands granted to an Indian, or a tribe of Indians, for railroads or other highways, or telegraph lines, for the public use, or to condemn such lands to public uses, upon making just compensation.

Sec. 11. That nothing in this act shall be so construed as to prevent the removal of the Southern Ute Indians from their present reservation in Southwestern Colorado to a new reservation by and with the consent of a majority of the adult male members of said tribe.

[*U.S. Statutes at Large*, 24:388-91.]

105.   Use of English in Indian Schools
Extract from the *Annual Report of the Commissioner of Indian Affairs*
September 21, 1887

One of the chief tools in bringing white civilization to the Indians was the English language. Commissioner J.D.C. Atkins, in his annual report of 1887, argued for the exclusive use of English at all Indian schools and reprinted some of his directives.

. . . . Longer and closer consideration of the subject has only deepened my conviction that it is a matter not only of importance, but of necessity that the Indians acquire the English language as rapidly as possible. The

Government has entered upon the great work of educating and citizenizing the Indians and establishing them upon homesteads. The adults are expected to assume the role of citizens, and of course the rising generation

174

will be expected and required more nearly to fill the measure of citizenship, and the main purpose of educating them is to enable them to read, write, and speak the English language and to transact business with English-speaking people. When they take upon themselves the responsibilities and privileges of citizenship their vernacular will be of no advantage. Only through the medium of the English tongue can they acquire a knowledge of the Constitution of the country and their rights and duties thereunder.

Every nation is jealous of its own language, and no nation ought to be more so than ours, which approaches nearer than any other nationality to the perfect protection of its people. True Americans all feel that the Constitution, laws, and institutions of the United States, in their adaptation to the wants and requirements of man, are superior to those of any other country; and they should understand that by the spread of the English language will these laws and institutions be more firmly established and widely disseminated. Nothing so surely and perfectly stamps upon an individual a national characteristic as language. So manifest and important is this that nations the world over, in both ancient and modern times, have ever imposed the strictest requirements upon their public schools as to the teaching of the national tongue. Only English has been allowed to be taught in the public schools in the territory acquired by this country from Spain, Mexico, and Russia, although the native populations spoke another tongue. All are familiar with the recent prohibitory order of the German Empire forbidding the teaching of the French language in either public or private schools in Alsace and Lorraine. Although the population is almost universally opposed to German rule, they are firmly held to German political allegiance by the military hand of the Iron Chancellor. If the Indians were in Germany or France or any other civilized country, they should be instructed in the language there used. As they are in an English-speaking country, they must be taught the language which they must use in transacting business with the people of this country. No unity or community of feeling can be established among different peoples unless they are brought to speak the same language, and thus become imbued with like ideas of duty.

Deeming it for the very best interest of the Indian, both as an individual and as an embryo citizen, to have this policy strictly enforced among the various schools on Indian reservations, orders have been issued accordingly to Indian agents, and the texts of the orders and of some explanations made thereof are given below:

DECEMBER 14, 1886.

In all schools conducted by missionary organizations it is required that all instructions shall be given in the English language.

FEBRUARY 2, 1887.

In reply I have to advise you that the rule applies to all schools on Indian reservations, whether they be Government or mission schools. The instruction of the Indians in the vernacular is not only of no use to them, but is detrimental to the cause of their education and civilization, and no school will be permitted on the reservation in which the English language is not exclusively taught.

JULY 16, 1887.

Your attention is called to the regulation of this office which forbids instruction in schools in any Indian language. This rule applies to all schools on an Indian reservation, whether Government or mission schools. The education of Indians in the vernacular is not only of no use to them, but is detrimental to their education and civilization.

You are instructed to see that this rule is rigidly enforced in all schools upon the reservation under your charge.

No mission school will be allowed upon the reservation which does not comply with the regulation.

The following was sent to representatives of all societies having contracts with this bureau for the conduct of Indian schools:

JULY 16, 1887.

Your attention is called to the provisions of the contracts for educating Indian pupils, which provides that the schools shall "teach the ordinary branches of an English education." This provision must be faithfully adhered to, and no

175

books in any Indian language must be used or instruction given in that language to Indian pupils in any school where this office has entered into contract for the education of Indians. The same rule prevails in all Government Indian schools and will be strictly enforced in all contract and other Indian schools.

The instruction of Indians in the vernacular is not only of no use to them, but is detrimental to the cause of their education and civilization, and it will not be permitted in any Indian school over which the Government has any control, or in which it has any interest whatever.

This circular has been sent to all parties who have contracted to educate Indian pupils during the present fiscal year.

You will see that this regulation is rigidly enforced in the schools under your direction where Indians are placed under contract.

I have given the text of these orders in detail because various misrepresentations and complaints in regard to them have been made, and various misunderstandings seem to have arisen. They do not, as has been urged, touch the question of the preaching of the Gospel in the churches nor in any wise hamper or hinder the efforts of missionaries to bring the various tribes to a knowledge of the Christian religion. Preaching of the Gospel to Indians in the vernacular is, of course, not prohibited. In fact, the question of the effect of this policy upon any missionary body was not considered. All the office insists upon is that in the schools established for the rising generation of Indians shall be taught the language of the Republic of which they are to become citizens.

It is believed that if any Indian vernacular is allowed to be taught by the missionaries in schools on Indian reservations, it will prejudice the youthful pupil as well as his untutored and uncivilized or semi-civilized parent against the English language, and, to some extent at least, against Government schools in which the English language exclusively has always been taught. To teach Indian school children their native tongue is practically to exclude English, and to prevent them from acquiring it. This language, which is good enough for a white man and a black man, ought to be good enough for the red man. It is also believed that teaching an Indian youth in his own barbarous dialect is a positive detriment to him. The first step to be taken toward civilization, toward teaching the Indians the mischief and folly of continuing in their barbarous practices, is to teach them the English language. The impracticability, if not impossibility, of civilizing the Indians of this country in any other tongue than our own would seem to be obvious, especially in view of the fact that the number of Indian vernaculars is even greater than the number of tribes. Bands of the same tribes inhabiting different localities have different dialects, and sometimes can not communicate with each other except by the sign language. If we expect to infuse into the rising generation the leaven of American citizenship, we must remove the stumbling blocks of hereditary customs and manners, and of these language is one of the most important elements. . . .

[*House Executive Document* no. 1, 50th Cong., 1st sess., serial 2542, pp. 19-21.]

106. Marriage Between White Men and Indian Women
August 9, 1888

The effects of marriage between white men and Indian women were regulated in this law of 1888.

An act in relation to marriage between white men and Indian women.

Be it enacted . . . , That no white man, not otherwise a member of any tribe of Indians, who may hereafter marry, an Indian woman, member of any Indian tribe in the United States, or any of its Territories except the five civilized tribes in the Indian

Territory, shall by such marriage hereafter acquire any right to any tribal property, privilege, or interest whatever to which any member of such tribe is entitled.

Sec. 2. That every Indian woman, member of any such tribe of Indians, who may hereafter be married to any citizen of the United States, is hereby declared to become by such marriage a citizen of the

176

United States, with all the rights, privileges, and immunities of any such citizen, being a married woman: *Provided,* That nothing in this act contained shall impair or in any way affect the right or title of such married woman to any tribal property or any interest therein.

SEC. 3. That whenever the marriage of any white man with any Indian woman, a member of any such tribe of Indians, is re-quired or offered to be proved in any judicial proceeding, evidence of the admission of such fact by the party against whom the proceeding is had, or evidence of general repute, or of cohabitation as married persons, or any other circumstantial or presumptive evidence from which the fact may be inferred, shall be competent.

[*U.S. Statutes at Large,* 25:392.]

107. Indian Commissioner Morgan on Indian Policy

Extract from the *Annual Report of the Commissioner of Indian Affairs*

October 1, 1889

Thomas J. Morgan, appointed commissioner of Indian affairs in 1889, was a man of strong convictions about the need to Americanize the Indians and absorb them into white society. In his first annual report he set forth his general views.

. . . . Unexpectedly called to this responsible position, I entered upon the discharge of its duties with a few simple, well-defined, and strongly-cherished convictions:

First.—The anomalous position heretofore occupied by the Indians in this country can not much longer be maintained. The reservation system belongs to a "vanishing state of things" and must soon cease to exist.

Second.—The logic of events demands the absorption of the Indians into our national life, not as Indians, but as American citizens.

Third.—As soon as a wise conservatism will warrant it, the relations of the Indians to the Government must rest solely upon the full recognition of their individuality. Each Indian must be treated as a man, be allowed a man's rights and privileges, and be held to the performance of a man's obligations. Each Indian is entitled to his proper share of the inherited wealth of the tribe, and to the protection of the courts in his "life, liberty, and pursuit of happiness." He is not entitled to be supported in idleness.

Fourth.—The Indians must conform to "the white man's ways," peaceably if they will, forcibly if they must. They must adjust themselves to their environment, and conform their mode of living substantially to our civilization. This civilization may not be the best possible, but it is the best the Indians can get. They can not escape it, and must either conform to it or be crushed by it.

Fifth.—The paramount duty of the hour is to prepare the rising generation of Indians for the new order of things thus forced upon them. A comprehensive system of education modeled after the American public-school system, but adapted to the special exigencies of the Indian youth, embracing all persons of school age, compulsory in its demands and uniformly administered, should be developed as rapidly as possible.

Sixth.—The tribal relations should be broken up, socialism destroyed, and the family and the autonomy of the individual substituted. The allotment of lands in severalty, the establishment of local courts and police, the development of a personal sense of independence, and the universal adoption of the English language are means to this end.

Seventh.—In the administration of Indian affairs there is need and opportunity for the exercise of the same qualities demanded in any other great administration—integrity, justice, patience, and good sense. Dishonesty, injustice, favoritism, and incompetency have no place here any more than elsewhere in the Government.

Eighth.—The chief thing to be considered in the administration of this office is the character of the men and women employed to carry out the designs of the Government. The best system may be perverted to bad

177

ends by incompetent or dishonest persons employed to carry it into execution, while a very bad system may yield good results if wisely and honestly administered. . . .

[*House Executive Document* no. 1, 51st Cong., 1st sess., serial 2725, pp. 3-4.]

108. Supplemental Report on Indian Education
December 1, 1889

In October 1889, Commissioner Thomas J. Morgan presented at the Lake Mohonk Conference a detailed plan for a national system of Indian schools, modeled on the public school system of the states. Having received the support of the reformers at the conference, he submitted the plan to the secretary of the interior as a "Supplemental Report on Indian Education." After presenting the general principles that are reprinted here, he outlined provisions for high schools, grammar schools, and day schools.

A SYSTEM OF EDUCATION FOR INDIANS.

GENERAL PRINCIPLES.

The American Indians, not including the so-called Indians of Alaska, are supposed to number about 250,000, and to have a school population (six to sixteen years) of perhaps 50,000. If we exclude the five civilized tribes which provide for the education of their own children and the New York Indians, who are provided for by that State, the number of Indians of school age to be educated by the Government does not exceed 36,000, of whom 15,000 were enrolled in schools last year, leaving but 21,000 to be provided with school privileges.

These people are separated into numerous tribes, and differ very widely in their language, religion, native characteristics, and modes of life. Some are very ignorant and degraded, living an indolent and brutish sort of life, while others have attained to a high degree of civilization, scarcely inferior to that of their white neighbors. Any generalizations regarding these people must, therefore, be considered as applicable to any particular tribe with such modifications as its peculiar place in the scale of civilization warrants. It is certainly true, however, that as a mass the Indians are far below the whites of this country in their general intelligence and mode of living. They enjoy very few of the comforts, and almost none of the luxuries, which are the pride and boast of their more fortunate neighbors.

When we speak of the education of the Indians, we mean that comprehensive system of training and instruction which will convert them into American citizens, put within their reach the blessings which the rest of us enjoy, and enable them to compete successfully with the white man on his own ground and with his own methods. Education is to be the medium through which the rising generation of Indians are to be brought into fraternal and harmonious relationship with their white fellow-citizens, and with them enjoy the sweets of refined homes, the delight of social intercourse, the emoluments of commerce and trade, the advantages of travel, together with the pleasures that come from literature, science, and philosophy, and the solace and stimulus afforded by a true religion.

That such a great revolution for these people is possible is becoming more and more evident to those who have watched with an intelligent interest the work which, notwithstanding all its hindrances and discouragements, has been accomplished for them during the last few years. It is no longer doubtful that, under a wise system of education, carefully administered, the condition of this whole people can be radically improved in a single generation.

Under the peculiar relations which the Indians sustain to the Government of the United States, the responsibility for their education rests primarily and almost wholly upon the nation. This grave responsibility, which has now been practically assumed by the Government, must be borne by it alone. It can not safely or honorably either shirk it or delegate it to any other party. The task is not by any means an herculean one. The entire Indian school population is less than that of Rhode Island. The Government of the United States, now one of the richest on the face of the earth, with an overflowing Treasury, has at its command unlimited means, and can undertake and complete this work without feeling it to be in any degree a burden. Although very imperfect in its details, and needing to be modified and improved in many particulars, the present system of schools is capable, under wise direction, of accomplishing all that can be desired.

In order that the Government shall be able to secure the best results in the education of the Indians, certain things are desirable, indeed, I might say necessary, viz:

First. Ample provision should be made at an early day for the accommodation of the entire mass of Indian school children and youth. To resist successfully and overcome the tremendous downward pressure of inherited prejudice and the stubborn conservatism of centuries, nothing less than universal education should be attempted.

Second. Whatever steps are necessary should be taken to place these children under proper educational influences. If, under any circumstances, compulsory education is justifiable, it certainly is in this case. Education, in the broad sense in which it is here used, is the Indians only salvation. With it they will become honorable, useful, happy citizens of a great republic, sharing on equal terms in all its blessings. Without it they are doomed either to destruction or to hopeless degradation.

Third. The work of Indian education should be completely systematized. The camp schools, agency boarding schools, and the great industrial schools should be related to each other so as to form a connected and complete whole. So far as possible there should be a uniform course of study, similar methods of instruction, the same textbooks, and a carefully organized and well-understood system of industrial training.

Fourth. The system should be conformed, so far as practicable, to the common-school system now universally adopted in all the States. It should be non-partisan, non-sectarian. The teachers and employés should be appointed only after the most rigid

scrutiny into their qualifications for their work. They should have a stable tenure of office, being removed only for cause. They should receive for their service wages corresponding to those paid for similar service in the public schools. They should be carefully inspected and supervised by a sufficient number of properly qualified superintendents.

Fifth. While, for the present, special stress should be laid upon that kind of industrial training which will fit the Indians to earn an honest living in the various occupations which may be open to them, ample provision should also be made for that general literary culture which the experience of the white race has shown to be the very essence of education. Especial attention should be directed toward giving them a ready command of the English language. To this end, only English should be allowed to be spoken, and only English-speaking teachers should be employed in schools supported wholly or in part by the Government.

Sixth. The scheme should make ample provision for the higher education of the few who are endowed with special capacity or ambition, and are destined to leadership. There is an imperative necessity for this, if the Indians are to be assimilated into the national life.

Seventh. That which is fundamental in all this is the recognition of the complete manhood of the Indians, their individuality, their right to be recognized as citizens of the United States, with the same rights and privileges which we accord to any other class of people. They should be free to make for themselves homes wherever they will. The reservation system is an anachronism which has no place in our modern civilization. The Indian youth should be instructed in their rights, privileges, and duties as American citizens; should be taught to love the American flag; should be imbued with a genuine patriotism, and made to feel that the United States, and not some paltry reservation, is their home. Those charged with their education should constantly strive to awaken in them a sense of independence, self-reliance, and self-respect.

Eighth. Those educated in the large industrial boarding-schools should not be returned to the camps against their will, but should be not only allowed, but encouraged to choose their own vocations, and contend for the prizes of life wherever the opportunities are most favorable. Education should seek the disintegration of the tribes, and not their segregation. They should be educated, not as Indians, but as Americans. In short, the public school should do for them what it is so successfully doing for all the other races in this country, assimilate them.

Ninth. The work of education should begin with them while they are young and susceptible, and should continue until habits of industry and love of learning have taken the place of indolence and indifference. One of the chief defects which have heretofore characterized the efforts made for their education has been the failure to carry them far enough, so that they might compete successfully with the white youth, who have enjoyed the far greater advantages of our own system of education. Higher education is even more essential to them than it is for white children.

Tenth. Special pains should be taken to bring together in the large boarding-schools members of as many different tribes as possible, in order to destroy the tribal antagonism and to generate in them a feeling of common brotherhood and mutual respect. Wherever practicable, they should be admitted on terms of equality into the public schools, where, by daily contact with white children, they may learn to respect them and become respected in turn. Indeed, it is reasonable to expect that at no distant day, when the Indians shall have all taken up their lands in severalty and have become American citizens, there will cease to be any necessity for Indian schools maintained by the Government. The Indians, where it is impracticable for them to unite with their white neighbors, will maintain their own schools.

Eleventh. Co-education of the sexes is the surest and perhaps only way in which the Indian women can be lifted out of that position of servility and degradation which most of them now occupy, on to a plane where their husbands and the men generally will treat them with the same gallantry and respect which is accorded to their more favored white sisters.

Twelfth. The happy results already achieved at Carlisle, Hampton, and elsewhere, by the so-called "outing system," which consists in placing Indian pupils in white families where they are taught the ordinary routine of housekeeping, farming, etc., and are brought into intimate relationship with the highest type of American rural life, suggests the wisdom of a large extension of the system. By this means they acquire habits of industry, a practical acquaintance with civilized life, a sense of independence, enthusiasm for home, and the practical ability to earn their own living. This system has in it the "promise and the potency" of their complete emancipation.

Thirteenth. Of course, it is to be understood that, in addition to all of the work here outlined as belonging to the Government for the education and civilization of the Indians, there will be requisite the influence of the home, the Sabbath-school, the church, and religious institutions of learning. There will be urgent need of consecrated missionary work and liberal expenditure of money on the part of individuals and religious organizations in behalf of these people. Christian schools and colleges have already been established for them by missionary zeal, and others will doubtless follow. But just as the work of the public schools is supplemented in the States by Christian agencies, so will the work of Indian education by the Government be supplemented by the same agencies. There need be no conflict and no unseemly rivalry. The Indians, like any other class of citizens, will be free to patronize those schools which they believe to be best adapted to their purpose. . . .

[*House Executive Document* no. 1, 51st Cong., 1st sess., serial 2725, pp. 93-97.]

109.   Inculcation of Patriotism in Indian Schools

December 10, 1889

The effort to train the Indian children as American citizens was well illustrated by the "Instructions to Indian Agents in Regard to Inculcation of Patriotism in Indian Schools," issued by Commissioner of Indian Affairs Thomas J. Morgan in December 1889.

To Indian Agents and Superintendents of Indian Schools:

The great purpose which the Government has in view in providng an ample system of common school education for all Indian youth of school age, is the preparation of them for American citizenship. The Indians are destined to become absorbed into the national life, not as Indians, but as Americans. They are to share with their fellow-citizens in all the rights and privileges and are likewise to be called upon to bear fully their share of all the duties and responsibilities involved in American citizenship.

It is in the highest degree important, therefore, that special attention should be paid, particularly in the higher grades of the schools, to the instruction of Indian youth in the elements of American history, acquainting them especially with the leading facts in the lives of the most notable and worthy historical characters. While in such study the wrongs of their ancestors can not be ignored, the injustice which their race has suffered can be contrasted with the larger future open to them, and their duties and opportunities rather than their wrongs will most profitably engage their attention.

Pupils should also be made acquainted with the elementary principles of the Government under which they live, and with their duties and privileges as citizens. To this end, regular instructions should be given them in the form of familiar talks, or by means of the use of some elementary text-book in civics. Debating societies should be organized in which may be learned the practical rules of procedure which govern public assemblies. Some simple manual of rules of order should be put into the hands of the more advanced students, and they should be carefully instructed in its use.

On the campus of all the more important schools there should be erected a flagstaff, from which should float constantly, in suitable weather, the American flag. In all schools of whatever size and character, supported wholly or in part by the Government, the "Stars and Stripes" should be a familiar object, and students should be taught to reverence the flag as a symbol of their nation's power and protection.

Patriotic songs should be taught to the pupils, and they should sing them frequently until they acquire complete familiarity with them. Patriotic selections should be committed and recited publicly, and should constitute a portion of the reading exercises.

National holidays—Washington's birthday, Decoration Day, Fourth of July, Thanksgiving, and Christmas—should be observed with appropriate exercises in all Indian schools. It will also be well to observe the anniversary of the day upon which the "Dawes bill" for giving to Indians allotments of land in severalty became a law, viz, February 8, 1887, and to use that occasion to impress upon Indian youth the enlarged scope and opportunity given them by this law and the new obligations which it imposes.

In all proper ways, teachers in the Indian schools should endeavor to appeal to the highest elements of manhood and womanhood in their pupils, exciting in them an ambition after excellence in character and dignity of surroundings, and they should carefully avoid any unnecessary reference to the fact that they are Indians.

They should point out to their pupils the provisions which the Government has made for their education, and the opportunities which it affords them for earning a livelihood, and for achieving for themselves honorable places in life, and should endeavor to awaken reverence for the nation's power, gratitude for its beneficence, pride in its history, and a laudable ambition to contribute to its prosperity.

Agents and school superintendents are specially charged with the duty of putting these suggestions into practical operation.

[*House Executive Document* no. 1, 51st Cong., 2d sess., serial 2841, p. clxvii.]

110.   The Board of Indian Commissioners on Civil Service Reform

January 10, 1891

The need for competent administration of Indian affairs led to a demand on the part of reformers for application of civil service rules to the Indian service. An early example of such proposals was a letter of the Board of Indian Commissioners to President Benjamin Harrison on January 10, 1891.

BOARD OF INDIAN COMMISSIONERS,
Washington, D.C., January 10, 1891.
The President of the United States:
   Sir: As the United States Board of Indian Commissioners, we wish to express to you our conviction, based upon close observation of Indian affairs and now for several years expressed in our reports, that for many of the greatest evils of the Indian service a remedy can be found only by securing permanence in the service for capable, efficient, and honest men and women.
   Recognizing your steadfast purpose to secure justice for the Indians and to advance their preparation for American citizenship, and believing that upon the whole the Indian service is now in better condition than ever before, we respectfully call your attention to the fact that a single executive act on your part can at once secure permanence in the service for the greater part of the officers and employés.
   And we respectfully request, and in the name of the most intelligent opinion of the wisest friends of the Indian throughout the country we strongly urge, that the civil-service rules and regulations be at this time extended over all that part of the Indian service which can be reached by executive action to that effect.

By vote of the Board.
   MERRILL C. GATES, *Chairman.*
   E. WHITTLESEY, *Secretary.*

[*Annual Report of the Board of Indian Commissioners, 1890,* pp. 4-5.]

111.   Relief of the Mission Indians

January 12, 1891

After long neglect of the rights of the Mission Indians of California to their lands, Congress established reservations for these Indians. The law provided also for allotment of land in severalty.

An Act for the relief of the Mission Indians in the State of California.

   Be it enacted . . . , That immediately after the passage of this act the Secretary of the Interior shall appoint three disinterested persons as commissioners to arrange a just and satisfactory settlement of the Mission Indians residing in the State of California, upon reservations which shall be secured to them as hereinafter provided.
   SEC. 2.   That it shall be the duty of said commissioners to select a reservation for each band or village of the Mission Indians residing within said State, which reservation shall include, as far as practicable, the lands and villages which have been in the actual occupation and possession of said Indians, and which shall be sufficient in extent to meet their just requirements, which selection shall be valid when approved by the President and Secretary of the Interior. They shall also appraise the value of the improvements belonging to any person to whom valid existing rights have attached under the public-land laws of the United States, or to the assignee of such person, where such improvements are situated within the limits of any reservation selected and defined by said commissioners subject in each case to the approval of the Secretary of the Interior. In cases where the Indians are in occupation of lands within the limits of confirmed private grants, the commissioners shall determine and define the boundaries of such lands, and shall ascertain whether there are vacant public lands in the vicinity to which they may be removed. And the said commission is hereby authorized to employ a competent surveyor and the necessary assistants.
   SEC. 3.   That the commissioners, upon

182

the completion of their duties, shall report the result to the Secretary of the Interior, who, if no valid objection exists, shall cause a patent to issue for each of the reservations selected by the commission and approved by him in favor of each band or village of Indians occupying any such reservation, which patents shall be of the legal effect, and declare that the United States does and will hold the land thus patented, subject to the provisions of section four of this act, for the period of twenty-five years, in trust, for the sole use and benefit of the band or village to which it is issued, and that at the expiration of said period the United States will convey the same or the remaining portion not previously patented in severalty by patent to said band or village, discharged of said trust, and free of all charge or incumbrance whatsoever: *Provided*, That no patent shall embrace any tract or tracts to which existing valid rights have attached in favor of any person under any of the United States laws providing for the disposition of the public domain, unless such person shall acquiesce in and accept the appraisal provided for in the preceding section in all respects and shall thereafter, upon demand and payment of said appraised value, execute a release of all title and claim thereto; and a separate patent, in similar form, may be issued for any such tract or tracts, at any time thereafter. Any such person shall be permitted to exercise the same right to take land under the public-land laws of the United States as though he had not made settlement on the lands embraced in said reservation; and a separate patent, in similar form, may be issued for any tract or tracts at any time after the appraised value of the improvements thereon shall have been paid: *And provided further*, That in case any land shall be selected under this act to which any railroad company is or shall hereafter be entitled to receive a patent, such railroad company shall, upon releasing all claim and title thereto, and on the approval of the President and Secretary of the Interior, be allowed to select an equal quantity of other land of like value in lieu thereof, at such place as the Secretary of the Interior shall determine: *And provided further*, That said patents declaring such lands to be held in trust as aforesaid shall be retained and kept in the

Interior Department, and certified copies of the same shall be forwarded to and kept at the agency by the agent having charge of the Indians for whom such lands are to be held in trust, and said copies shall be open to inspection at such agency.

SEC. 4. That whenever any of the Indians residing upon any reservation patented under the provisions of this act shall, in the opinion of the Secretary of the Interior, be so advanced in civilization as to be capable of owning and managing land in severalty, the Secretary of the Interior may cause allotments to be made to such Indians, out of the land of such reservation, in quantity as follows: To each head of a family not more than six hundred and forty acres nor less than one hundred and sixty acres of pasture or grazing land, and in addition thereto not exceeding twenty acres, as he shall deem for the best interest of the allottee, of arable land in some suitable locality; to each single person over twenty-one years of age not less than eighty nor more than six hundred and forty acres of pasture or grazing land and not exceeding ten acres of such arable land.

SEC. 5. That upon the approval of the allotments provided for in the preceding section by the Secretary of the Interior he shall cause patents to issue therefor in the name of the allottees, which shall be of the legal effect and declare that the United States does and will hold the land thus allotted for the period of twenty-five years, in trust for the sole use and benefit of the Indian to whom such allotment shall have been made, or, in the case of his decease, of his heirs according to the laws of the State of California, and that at the expiration of said period the United States will convey the same by patent to the said Indian, or his heirs as aforesaid, in fee, discharged of said trust and free of all charge or incumbrance whatsoever. And if any conveyance shall be made of the lands set apart and allotted as herein provided, or any contract made touching the same, before the expiration of the time above mentioned, such conveyance or contract shall be absolutely null and void: *Provided*, That these patents, when issued, shall override the patent authorized to be issued to the band or village as aforesaid, and shall separate the individual allotment from the lands held in common, which proviso shall be incorporated in each of the village patents.

SEC. 6. That in cases where the lands occupied by any band or village of Indians are wholly or in part within the limits of any confirmed private grant or grants, it shall be the duty of the Attorney-General of the United States, upon request of the Secretary of the Interior, through special counsel or otherwise, to defend such Indians in the rights secured to them in the original grants from the Mexican Government, and in an act for the government and protection of Indians passed by the legislature of the State of California April twenty-second, eighteen hundred and fifty, or to bring any suit, in the name of the United States, in the Circuit Court of the United States for California, that may be found necessary to the full protection of the legal or equitable rights of any Indian or tribe of Indians in any of such lands.

SEC. 7. [Pay of commissioners.]

SEC. 8. [Authorizaton for irrigation systems and railroad rights of way.]

[*U.S. Statutes at Large*, 26:712-14.]

112. Amendment to the Dawes Act
February 28, 1891

Four years after its passage, the Dawes Act was amended to provide for equal allotments to all Indians and for the leasing of allotments under certain conditions.

An act to amend and further extend the benefits of the act approved February eighth, eighteen hundred and eighty-seven, entitled "An act to provide for the allotment of land in severalty to Indians on the various reservations, and to extend the protection of the laws of the United States over the Indians, and for other purposes."

Be it enacted . . . , That section one of the act entitled "An act to provide for the allotment of lands in severalty to Indians on the various reservations, and to extend the protection of the laws of the United States and the Territories over the Indians, and for other purposes," approved February eighth, eighteen hundred and eighty-seven, be, and the same is hereby, amended so as to read as follows:

"SEC. 1. That in all cases where any tribe or band of Indians has been, or shall hereafter be, located upon any reservation created for their use, either by treaty stipulation or by virtue of an Act of Congress or Executive order setting apart the same for their use, the President of the United States be, and he hereby is, authorized, whenever in his opinion any reservation, or any part thereof, of such Indians is advantageous for agricultural or grazing purposes, to cause said reservation, or any part thereof, to be surveyed, or resurveyed, if necessary, and to allot to each Indian located thereon one-eighth of a section of land: *Provided*, That in case there is not sufficient land in any of said reservations to allot lands to each individual in quantity as above provided the land in such reservation or reservations shall be allotted to each individual pro rata, as near as may be, according to legal subdivisions: *Provided further*, That where the treaty or act of Congress setting apart such reservation provides for the allotment of lands in severalty to certain classes in quantity in excess of that herein provided the President, in making allotments upon such reservation, shall allot the land to each individual Indian of said classes belonging thereon in quantity as specified in such treaty or act, and to other Indians belonging thereon in quantity as herein provided: *Provided further*, That where existing agreements or laws provide for allotments in accordance with the provisions of said act of February eighth, eighteen hundred and eighty-seven, or in quantities substantially as therein provided, allotments may be made in quantity as specified in this act, with the consent of the Indians, expressed in such manner as the President, his discretion, may require: *And provided further*, That when the lands allotted, or any legal subdivision thereof, are only valuable for grazing purposes, such lands shall be allotted in double quantities."

SEC. 2. That where allotments have been made in whole or in part upon any reservation under the provisions of said act of February eighth, eighteen hundred and eighty-seven, and the quantity of land in such reservation is sufficient to give each member of the tribe eighty acres, such allotments shall be revised and equalized under the provisions of this act: *Provided*, That no allotment heretofore approved by the Secretary of the Interior shall be reduced in quantity.

SEC. 3. That whenever it shall be made to appear to the Secretary of the Interior that, by reason of age or other disability, any allottee under the provisions of said act, or any other act or treaty can not personally and with benefit to himself occupy or improve his allotment or any part thereof the same may be leased upon such terms, regulations and conditions as shall be prescribed by such Secretary, for a term not exceeding three years for farming or grazing, or ten years for mining purposes: *Provided*, That where lands are occupied by Indians who have bought and paid for the same, and which lands are not needed for farming or agricultural purposes, and are not desired for individual allotments, the same may be leased by authority of the Council speaking for such Indians, for a period not to exceed five years for grazing, or ten years for mining purposes in such quantities and upon such terms and conditions as the agent in charge of such reservation may recommend, subject to the approval of the Secretary of the Interior.

SEC. 4. That where any Indian entitled to allotment under existing laws shall make settlement upon any surveyed or unsurveyed lands of the United States not otherwise appropriated, he or she shall be entitled, upon application to the local land office for the district in which the lands are located, to have the same allotted to him or her and to his or her children, in quantities and manner as provided in the foregoing section of this amending act for Indians residing upon reservations; and when such settlement is made upon unsurveyed lands the grant to such Indians shall be adjusted upon the survey of the lands so as to conform thereto; and patents shall be issued to them for such lands in the manner and with the restrictions provided in the act to which this is an amendment. And the fees to which the officers of such local land office would have been entitled had such lands been entered upon the general laws for the disposition of the public lands shall be paid to them from any moneys in the Treasury of the United States not otherwise appropriated, upon a statement of an account in their behalf for such fees by the Commissioner of the General Land Office, and a certification of such account to the Secretary of the Treasury by the Secretary of the Interior.

SEC. 5. That for the purpose of determining the descent of land to the heirs of any deceased Indian under the provisions of the fifth section of said act, whenever any male and female Indian shall have co-habited together as husband and wife according to the custom and manner of Indian life the issue of such co-habitation shall be, for the purpose aforesaid, taken and deemed to be the legitimate issue of the Indians so living together, and every Indian child, otherwise illegitimate, shall for such purpose be taken and deemed to be the legitimate issue of the father of such child. . . .

[*U.S. Statutes at Large*, 26:794-96.]

113. Civil Service Classifications in the Indian Service

April 13, 1891

The application of civil service rules to the Indian service began with the classification of four groups of employees in 1891.

DEPARTMENT OF THE INTERIOR,
Washington, April 13, 1891.

By direction of the President of the United States and in accordance with the third clause of section 6 of an act entitled "An act to regulate and improve the civil service of the United States," approved January 16, 1883—

It is ordered, That all physicians, school superintendents and assistant superintendents, school-teachers, and matrons in the Indian service be, and they are hereby, arranged in the following classes, without regard to salary or compensation:

Class 1. Physicians.

185

Class 2. School superintendents and assistant superintendents.
Class 3. School-teachers.
Class 4. Matrons.
Provided, That no person who may be required by law to be appointed to an office by and with the advice and consent of the Senate, and that no person who may be employed merely as a laborer or workman or in connection with any contract schools, shall be considered as within this classification, and no person so employed shall be assigned to the duties of a classified place.

It is further ordered, That no person shall be admitted to any place not excepted from examination by the civil-service rules in any of the classes above designated until he or she shall have passed an appropriate examination under the United States Civil Service Commission and his or her eligibility has been certified to by said Commission or the appropriate board of examiners.

JOHN W. NOBLE, *Secretary.*

EXECUTIVE MANSION, *April 13, 1891.*
The SECRETARY OF THE INTERIOR:
I approve of the within classification, and if you see no reason to suggest any further modification you will please put it in force.

BENJ. HARRISON.

[James D. Richardson, comp., *Messages and Papers of the Presidents,* 9:173.]

114. Army Officers as Indian Agents
July 13, 1892

One way around political appointment of Indian agents was the use of army officers as agents. This was directed in 1892 by the Indian appropriation act.

An Act making appropriations for the current and contingent expenses of the Indian Department . . . .

. . . . *Provided,* That from and after the passage of this act the President shall detail officers of the United States Army to act as Indian agents at all Agencies where vacancies from any cause may hereafter occur, who, while acting as such agents, shall be under the orders and direction of the Secretary of the Interior, except at agencies where, in the opinion of the President, the public service would be better promoted by the appointment of a civilian. . . .

[*U.S. Statutes at Large,* 27:120-21.]

115. Rules for Indian Courts
August 27, 1892

Rules for the courts of Indian offenses drawn up in 1883, when the courts were instituted, were reissued with some modifications in 1892 by Commissioner of Indian Affairs Thomas J. Morgan.

1. *Districting reservation.*—Whenever it shall appear to the Commissioner of Indian Affairs that the best interests of the Indians on any Indian reservation will be subserved thereby, such reservation shall be divided into three or more districts, each of which shall be given a name by which it shall thereafter be designated and known. As far as practicable the county lines established by the laws of the State or Territory within which the reservation is located shall be observed in making the division, provided that each district shall include, as nearly as can be, an equal proportion of the total Indian population on the reservation. All mixed bloods and white persons who are actually and lawfully members, whether by birth or adoption, of any tribe residing on the reservation shall be counted as Indians. Where the lands of the reservation have not been surveyed, or where it is not practicable to observe the State or Territory county lines on the reservation, the lines of the district shall be defined by such natural boundaries as will enable the Indians to readily ascertain the district in which they reside.

2. *Appointment of judges.*—There shall be appointed by the Commissioner of Indian Affairs for each district a person from among the Indians of the reservation who shall be

186

styled "judge of the Indian court." The judges must be men of intelligence, integrity, and good moral character, and preference shall be given to Indians who read and write English readily, wear citizens' dress, and engage in civilized pursuits, and no person shall be eligible to such appointment who is a polygamist.

Each judge shall be appointed for the term of one year, subject, however, to earlier removal from office for cause by the Commissioner of Indian Affairs; but no judge shall be removed before the expiration of his term of office until the charges against him, with proofs, shall have been presented in writing to the Commissioner of Indian Affairs, and until he shall have been furnished a copy thereof and given opportunity to reply in his own defense, which reply shall also be in writing and be accompanied by such counter proofs as he may desire to submit.

3. *District courts.*—Each judge shall reside within the district to which he may be assigned and shall keep an office open at some convenient point to be designated by the Commissioner of Indian Affairs; and he shall hold court at least one day in each week for the purpose of investigating and trying any charge of offense or misdemeanor over which the judges of the Indian court have jurisdiction as provided in these regulations: *Provided,* That appeals from his judgment or decision may be taken to the Indian court in general term, at which all the judges on the reservation shall sit together.

4. *Offenses.*—For the purpose of these regulations the following shall be deemed to constitute *offenses,* and the judges of the Indian court shall severally have jurisdiction to try and punish for the same when committed within their respective districts.

(a) Dances, etc.—Any Indian who shall engage in the sun dance, scalp dance, or war dance, or any other similar feast, so called, shall be deemed guilty of an offense, and upon conviction thereof shall be punished for the first offense by the withholding of his rations for not exceeding ten days or by imprisonment for not exceeding ten days; and for any subsequent offense under this clause he shall be punished by withholding his rations for not less than ten nor more than thirty days, or by imprisonment for not less than ten nor more than thirty days.

(b) Plural or polygamous marriages.—Any Indian under the supervision of a United States Indian agent who shall hereafter contract or enter into any plural or polygamous marriage shall be deemed guilty of an offense, and upon conviction thereof shall pay a fine of not less than twenty nor more than fifty dollars, or work at hard labor for not less than twenty nor more than sixty days, or both, at the discretion of the court; and so long as the person shall continue in such unlawful relation he shall forfeit all right to receive rations from the Government.

(c) Practices of medicine men.—Any Indian who shall engage in the practices of so-called medicine men, or who shall resort to any artifice or device to keep the Indians of the reservation from adopting and following civilized habits and pursuits, or shall adopt any means to prevent the attendance of children at school, or shall use any arts of a conjurer to prevent Indians from abandoning their barbarous rites and customs, shall be deemed to be guilty of an offense, and upon conviction thereof, for the first offense shall be imprisoned for not less than ten nor more than thirty days: *Provided,* That for any subsequent conviction for such offense the maximum term or imprisonment shall not exceed six months.

(d) Destroying property of other Indians.—Any Indian who shall willfully or wantonly destroy or injure, or, with intent to destroy or injure or appropriate, shall take and carry away any property of any other Indian or Indians, shall, without reference to its value, be deemed guilty of an offense, and upon conviction shall be compelled to return the property to the owner or owners, or, in case the property shall have been lost, injured, or destroyed, the estimated full value of the same; and in addition he shall be imprisoned for not exceeding thirty days; and the plea that the person convicted or the owner of the property in question was at the time a "mourner," and that thereby the taking, destroying, or injuring of the property was justified by the customs or rites of the tribe, shall not be accepted as a sufficient defense.

(e) Immorality.—Any Indian who shall pay, or offer to pay, money or other thing of value to any female Indian, or to her friends or relatives, or to any other persons, for the purpose of living or cohabiting with any such female Indian not his wife, shall be deemed guilty of an offense, and upon conviction thereof shall forfeit all right to Government rations for not exceeding ninety days, or be imprisoned for not exceeding ninety days, or both, in the discretion of the court. And any Indian who shall receive, or offer to receive money or other valuable things in consideration for allowing, consenting to, or practicing such immorality, shall be punished in the same manner as provided for the punishment of the party paying, or offering to pay, said consideration.

(f) Intoxication and the introduction of intoxicants.—Any Indian who shall become intoxicated, or who shall sell, exchange, give, barter, or dispose of any spirituous, vinous, fermented, or other intoxicating liquors to any other member of an Indian tribe, or who shall introduce, or attempt to introduce, under any pretense whatever, any spirituous, vinous, fermented, or other intoxicating liquors on an Indian reservation, shall be deemed guilty of an offense, and upon conviction thereof shall be punishable by imprisonment for not less than thirty nor more than ninety days, or by a fine of not less than twenty nor more than one hundred dollars, or both, in the discretion of the court.

5. *Misdemeanors.*—The judges of the Indian courts shall also have jurisdiction within their respective districts to try and punish any Indian belonging upon the reservation for any misdemeanor committed thereon, as defined in the laws of the State or Territory within which the reservation may be located; and the punishment for such misdemeanors shall be such as may be prescribed by such State or Territorial laws: *Provided,* That if an Indian who is subject to road duty shall refuse or neglect to work the roads the required number of days each year, or to furnish a proper substitute therefor, he shall be deemed guilty of a misdemeanor, and shall be liable to a fine of one dollar and fifty cents for every day that he fails to perform road duty, or to imprisonment for not more than five days: *And provided further,* That if an Indian refuses or neglects to adopt habits of industry, or to engage in civilized pursuits

or employments, but habitually spends his time in idleness and loafing, he shall be deemed a vagrant and guilty of a misdemeanor, and shall, upon the first conviction thereof, be liable to a fine of not more than five dollars, or to imprisonment for not more than ten days, and for any subsequent conviction thereof to a fine of not more than ten dollars, or to imprisonment for not more than thirty days, in the discretion of the court.

6. *Judges to solemnize marriages.*—The said judges shall have power also to solemnize marriages between Indians. They shall keep a record of all marriages solemnized by them, respectively, and shall issue certificates of marriage in duplicate, one certificate to be delivered to the parties thereto and the duplicate to be forwarded to the clerk of the court in general term, hereinafter provided for, to be kept among the records of that court; and for each marriage solemnized the judge may charge a fee not to exceed one dollar.

7. *Indian court in general term.*—The judges of the Indian court shall sit together at some convenient place on the reservation, to be designated by the Commissioner of Indian Affairs, at least once in every month, at which sitting they shall constitute the Indian court in general term. A majority of the judges appointed for the reservation shall constitute a quorum of the court and shall have power to try and finally determine any suit or charge that may be properly brought before it; but no judgment or decision by said court shall be valid unless it is concurred in by a majority of all the judges appointed for the reservation, and in case of a failure of a majority of the judges to agree in any cause, the same shall be continued, to be again tried at a subsequent term of the court. The court in general term shall be presided over by the senior judge in point of service on the reservation, and in case there be no such senior judge, the Commissioner of Indian Affairs shall designate one of the judges to preside. . . .

11. *Agents to compel attendance of witnesses and enforce orders of the court.*—That the orders of the court in general term and of the judges of the several districts may be carried into full effect, the United States Indian agent for the agency under which the reser-

vation may be is hereby authorized, empowered, and required to compel the attendance of witnesses at any session of the court, or before any judge within his proper district, and to enforce all orders that may be passed by said court, or a majority thereof, or by any judge within his proper district; and for this purpose he may use the Indian police of his agency.

[*House Executive Document* no. 1, 52d Cong., 2d sess., serial 3088, pp. 28-31.]

116. Indian School Superintendents as Indian Agents
March 3, 1893

As the work at the Indian agencies became increasingly educational, it was argued that the school superintendent could assume the duties of agent. Since the superintendents were classified under civil service rules, such a policy would help to eliminate politically appointed agents. Congress in 1893 authorized such assignment of superintendents.

An Act making appropriations for current and contingent expenses . . . .

. . . . The Commissioner of Indian Affairs, with the approval of the Secretary of the Interior, may devolve the duties of any Indian agency upon the superintendent of the Indian training school located at such agency, whenever in his judgment such superintendent can properly perform the duties of such agency.

The superintendent of the Indian Training School at Cherokee, North Carolina, shall, in addition to his duties as superintendent, perform the duties heretofore required of the agent at said Cherokee Agency, and receive in addition to his salary as superintendent two hundred dollars per annum, and shall give bond as other Indian agents, and that the office of agent be, and the same is hereby abolished at that place. . . .

[*U.S. Statutes at Large*, 27:614.]

117. Commission to the Five Civilized Tribes (Dawes Commission)
March 3, 1893

The Five Civilized Tribes of the Indian Territory were excluded from the provisions of the Dawes Act and formed an important enclave of communally held lands. In order to force these Indians into conformity with the policy that called for allotment of Indian lands in severalty, Congress authorized a special commission to negotiate with the tribes for allotment of their lands. This Commission to the Five Civilized Tribes was generally known as the Dawes Commission, since Henry L. Dawes served as its first chairman.

An Act making appropriations for current and contingent expenses . . . .

. . . SEC. 16. The President shall nominate and, by and with the advice and consent of the Senate, shall appoint three commissioners to enter into negotiations with the Cherokee Nation, the Choctaw Nation, the Chickasaw Nation, the Muscogee (or Creek) Nation; the Seminole Nation, for the purpose of the extinguishment of the national or tribal title to any lands within that Territory now held by any and all of such nations or tribes, either by cession of the same or some part thereof to the United States, or by the allotment and division of the same in severalty among the Indians of such nations or tribes, respectively, as may be entitled to the same, or by such other method as may be agreed upon between the several nations and tribes aforesaid, or each of them, with the United States, with a view to such an adjustment, upon the basis of justice and equity, as may, with the consent of such nations or tribes of Indians, so far as may be necessary, be requisite and suitable to enable the ultimate creation of a State or States of the Union which shall embrace the lands within said Indian Territory.

The commissioners so appointed shall each receive a salary, to be paid during such time as they may be actually employed,

189

under direction of the President, in the duties enjoined by this act, at the rate of five thousand dollars per annum, and shall also be paid their reasonable and proper expenses incurred in prosecution of the objects of this act, upon accounts therefor to be rendered to and allowed by the Secretary of the Interior from time to time. That such commissioners shall have power to employ a secretary, a stenographer, and such interpreter or interpreters as may be found necessary to the performance of their duties, and by order to fix their compensation, which shall be paid, upon the approval of the Secretary of the Interior, from time to time, with their reasonable and necessary expenses, upon accounts to be rendered as aforesaid; and may also employ, in like manner and with the like approval, a surveyor or other assistant or agent, which they shall certify in writing to be necessary to the performance of any part of their duties.

Such commissioners shall, under such regulations and directions as shall be prescribed by the President, through the Secretary of the Interior, enter upon negotiation with the several nations, of Indians as aforesaid in the Indian Territory, and shall endeavor to procure, first, such allotment of lands in severalty to the Indians belonging to each such nation, tribe, or band, respectively, as may be agreed upon as just and proper to provide for each such Indian a sufficient quantity of land for his or her needs, in such equal distribution and apportionment as may be found just and suited to the circumstances; for which purpose, after the terms of such an agreement shall have been arrived at, the said commissioners shall cause the lands of any such nation or tribe or band to be surveyed and the proper allotment to be designated; and, secondly, to procure the cession, for such price and upon such terms as shall be agreed upon, of any lands not found necessary to be so allotted or divided,

to the United States; and to make proper agreements for the investment or holding by the United States of such moneys as may be paid or agreed to be paid to such nation or tribes or bands, or to any of the Indians thereof, for the extinguishment of their [titles] therein. But said commissioners shall, however, have power to negotiate any and all such agreements as, in view of all the circumstances affecting the subject, shall be found requisite and suitable to such an arrangement of the rights and interests and affairs of such nations, tribes, bands, or Indians, or any of them, to enable the ultimate creation of a Territory of the United States with a view to the admission of the same as a state in the Union.

The commissioners shall at any time, or from time to time, report to the Secretary of the Interior their transactions and the progress of their negotiations, and shall at any time, or from time to time, if separate agreements shall be made by them with any nation, tribe or band, in pursuance of the authority hereby conferred, report the same to the Secretary of the Interior for submission to Congress for its consideration and ratification.

For the purpose aforesaid there is hereby appropriated, out of any money in the Treasury of the United States, the sum of fifty thousand dollars, to be immediately available.

Neither the provisions of this section nor the negotiations or agreements which may be had or made thereunder shall be held in any way to waive or impair any right of sovereignty which the Government of the United States has over or respecting said Indian Territory or the people thereof, or any other right of the Government relating to said Territory, its lands, or the people thereof.

[*U.S. Statutes at Large*, 27:645-46.]

118.   Report of the Dawes Commission

November 20, 1894

The Dawes Commission met little support for its work among the Five Civilized Tribes. Its report of 1894 contained severe criticism of conditions in the Indian Territory and expressed the views and attitudes of those who wished to destroy the national existence of the Five Civilized Tribes.

. . . . The barrier opposed at all times by those in authority in the tribes, and assuming to speak for them as to any change in existing conditions, is what they claim to be "the treaty situation." They mean by this term that the United States is under treaty obligations not to interfere in their internal policy, but has guaranteed to them self-government and absolute exclusion of white citizens from any abode among them; that the United States is bound to isolate them absolutely. It can not be doubted that this was substantially the original governing idea in establishing the Five Tribes in the Indian Territory, more or less clearly expressed in the treaties, which are the basis of whatever title and authority they at present have in the possession of that Territory, over which they now claim this exclusive jurisdiction. To that end the United States, in different treaties and patents executed in pursuance of such treaties, conveyed to the several tribes the country originally known as the "Indian Territory," of which their present possessions are a part only, and agreed to the establishment by them therein of governments of their own. The United States also agreed to exclude all white persons from their borders.

These treaties, however, embraced stipulations equally clear, that these tribes were to hold this territory for the use and enjoyment of all Indians belonging to their respective tribes, so that every Indian, as is expressed in some of the treaties, "shall have an equal right with every other Indian in each and every portion of the territory," and the further stipulation that their laws should not conflict with the Constitution of the United States. These were executory provisions to be observed in the future by both sides. Without regard to any observance of them on their part, the Indians claim that these treaties are irrevocably binding on the United States. These stipulations naturally grew out of the situation of the country at the time they were made, and of the character of the Indians with whom they were made. The present growth of the country and its present relations to this territory were not thought of or even dreamed of by either party when they entered into these stipulations. These Indians were then at a considerably advanced stage of civilization, and were

thought capable of self-government, in conformity with the spirit if not the forms of the National Government, within whose limits they were to remain. It was not altogether unreasonable, therefore, to conclude that it would be possible, as it was by them desirable, that these Indians could have set apart to them a tract of country so far remote from white civilization and so isolated that they could work out the problem of their own preservation under a government of their own, and that not only with safety to the Union but with altogether desirable results to themselves.

For quite a number of years after the institution of this project it seemed successful, and the Indians under it made favorable advance toward its realization. But within the last few years all the conditions under which it was inaugurated have undergone so complete a change that it has become no longer possible. It is hardly necessary to call attention to the contrast between the present conditions surrounding this Territory and those under which it was set apart. Large and populous States of the Union are now on all sides of it, and one-half of it has been constituted a Territory of the United States. These States and this Territory are teeming with population and increasing in numbers at a marvelous rate. The resources of the Territory itself have been developed to such a degree and are of such immense and tempting value that they are attracting to it an irresistible pressure from enterprising citizens. The executory conditions contained in the treaties have become impossible of execution. It is no longer possible for the United States to keep its citizens out of the Territory. Nor is is now possible for the Indians to secure to each individual Indian his full enjoyment in common with other Indians of the common property of the Territory.

The impossibility of enforcing these executory provisions has arisen from a neglect on both sides to enforce them. This neglect is largely the result of outside considerations for which neither is responsible and of the influence of forces which neither can control. These executory conditions are not only impossible of execution, but have ceased to be applicable or desirable. It has been demonstrated that isolation is an impossibility, and that if possible, it could never result in the elevation or civilization of the Indian. It has been made clear that under its operations, imperfectly as it has been carried out, its effect has been to retard rather than to promote civilization, to impair rather than strengthen the observance of law and order and regard for human life and human rights or the protection or promotion of a virtuous life. To such a degree has this sad deterioration become evident that to-day a most deplorable and dangerous condition of affairs exist in the Territory, causing widespread alarm and demanding most serious consideration.

All the functions of the so-called governments of these five tribes have become powerless to protect the life or property rights of the citizen. The courts of justice have become helpless and paralized. Violence, robbery, and murder are almost of daily occurrence, and no effective measures of restraint or punishment are put forth to suppress crime. Railroad trains are stopped and their passengers robbed within a few miles of populous towns and the plunder carried off with impunity in the very presence of those in authority. A reign of terror exists, and barbarous outrages, almost impossible of belief, are enacted, and the perpetrators hardly find it necessary to shun daily intercourse with their victims. We are now informed that, within the territory of one of these tribes, there were 53 murders during the month of September and the first twenty-four days of October last, and not a single person brought to trial.

In every respect the present condition of affairs demonstrates that the permission to govern themselves, under the Constitution of the United States, which was originally embraced in the treaty, has proved a failure. So, likewise, has the provision that requires the United States to exclude white citizens from the Territory. The course of procedure by the governments of the Five Tribes has largely contributed to this result, and they are quite as much responsible as the United States for the fact that there are 250,000 white people residing in the Territory. These citizens of the United States have been induced to go there in various ways and by various methods by the Indian governments themselves. These governments consented to the construction of a number of railways through the Territory, and thereby consented that they bring into the Territory all that is necessary in the building and operation of such railroads—the necessary depots, stations, and the inevitable towns which their traffic was sure to build up, and the large building which white men alone could develop and which these railroads were sure to stimulate and make profitable.

Besides these, they have, by their laws, invited men from the border States to become their employés in the Territory, receiving into their treasuries a monthly tax for the privilege of such employment. They have also provided by law for the intermarriage of white persons with their citizens and adopted them into their tribes. By operation of these laws large numbers of white people have become adopted citizens, participating in the benefits of citizenship. A single instance of such marriage has enabled one white man under the laws to appropriate to his exclusive use 50,000 acres of valuable land. They have, by their legislation, induced citizens of the United States to come in from all sides and under leases and other agreements with private citizens, sanctioned by their own laws, farmed out to them large ranges of their domain, as well as inexhaustible coal deposits within their respective borders, and other material interests which civilized white men alone could turn to profit. In some sections of the Territory the production of cotton has proved so feasible and profitable that white men have been permitted to come in by thousands and cultivate it and build trading marts and populous towns for the successful operation of this branch of trade alone.

In a single town of 5,000 white inhabitants, built there by their permission and also for the profit of the Indian, there were during last year marketed 40,000 bales of cotton. They have also sold off to the United States one-half of their original territory, to be opened up to white settlement on their western borders, in which, with their consent thus obtained, 300,000 white citizens have made their homes, and a Territorial government by this means has been erected in the midst of their own territory, which is forbidden by one of the executory provisions of the treaty. The day of isolation has passed. Not less regardless have they been of the stipulations in their title that they should hold their territory for the common and equal use of all their citizens. Corruption of the grossest kind, openly and unblushingly practiced, has found its way into every branch of the service of the tribal governments. All branches of the governments are reeking with it, and so common has it become that no attempt at concealment is thought necessary. The governments have fallen into the hands of a few able and energetic Indian citizens, nearly all mixed blood and adopted whites, who have so administered their affairs and have enacted such laws that they are enabled to appropriate to their own exclusive use almost the entire property of the Territory of any kind that can be rendered profitable and available.

In one of these tribes, whose whole territory consists of but 3,040,000 acres of land, within the last few years laws have been enacted under the operation of which 61 citizens have appropriated to themselves and are now holding for pasturage and cultivation 1,237,000 acres. This comprises the arable and greater part of the valuable grazing lands belonging to that tribe. The remainder of that people, largely the full-bloods who do not speak the English language, are excluded from the enjoyment of any portion of this land, and many of them occupy the poor and hilly country where they get a scanty living from such portions as they are able to turn to any account. This class of persons in the Territory are making little if any progress in civilization. They are largely dependent on those in control of public affairs, whose will they register at the polls and with whose bidding, in a large measure, they comply without question. Those holding power by these means oppose any change and ask only to be let alone.

In another of these tribes, under similar legislation, vast and rich deposits of coal of incalculable value have been appropriated by the few, to the exclusion of the rest of the tribe and to the great profit of those who operate them and appropriate their products to their individual use. Large and valuable plants for mining coal have been established by capitalists under leases by which, together with "discoverer's claims" authorized by the tribal governments, these coal lands are covered, and under the workings of which the rightful owners are being despoiled of this valuable property with very little or no profit to them; and it is clear that this property should be restored to the common domain and protected to the common people, and the mines worked under a system just and equitable to all who have rights therein.

The vast pine forests heretofore spoken of, which are of incalculable value, if not indispensable, in the future development of the country and the building up of homes and improvements of the agricultural lands, are being spoliated and laid waste by attempts, under laws enacted for that purpose, to grant to a few, mostly adopted white citizens, the right to cut and market for their own use whatever timber they can turn to their own profit. This is an irreparable destruction of one of the most essential elements of the progress of the country in the future and should be at once arrested.

Towns of considerable importance have been built by white persons under leases obtained from Indians claiming the right to appropriate the common property to these uses. Permanent improvements of great value have thus been made by white citizens of the United States, induced and encouraged thereto by the tribal governments themselves, and have become immovable fixtures which can not be taken away. However difficult the problem of adjusting rights thus involved, nothing can be more clear than that the step can not be retraced. Towns built under such inducements can not be removed nor their structures razed to the ground, nor can the places they occupy be restored to the conditions originally contemplated by the treaties. Ruinous as any such attempt would be to those thus induced to expend their money in building these towns, it would not be less ruinous to the Indians themselves to be, by any such attempt, forced back to the methods of life existing before the coming of these white men. The original idea of a community of property has been entirely lost sight of and disregarded in every branch of the administration of their affairs by the governments which have been permitted to control this Territory under the treaty stipulations which are now being invoked, by those who

193

are in this manner administering them, as a protection for their personal holdings and enterprises.

The large payments of moneys to the Indians of these tribes within the last few years have been attended by many and apparently well-authenticated complaints of fraud, and those making such payments, with others associated with them in the business, have, by unfair means and improper use of the advantages thus afforded them, acquired large fortunes, and in many instances private persons entitled to payments have received but little benefit therefrom. And worse still is the fact that the places of payments were thronged with evil characters of every possible caste, by whom the people were swindled, defrauded, robbed, and grossly debauched and demoralized. And in case of further payments of money to them the Government should make such disbursements to the people directly, through one of its own officers.

We feel it our duty to here suggest that any measures looking to any change of affairs in this Territory should embrace special, strict, and effective provisions for protection of the Indian and other citizens from the introduction, manufacture, or sale of intoxicants of any kind in the Territory, with penalties therefor and for failure by officers to enforce same, sufficiently severe to cause their perfect execution. A failure to thus protect these Indians will, in a measure, work their extinction at no distant day.

It is a deplorable fact, which should not be overlooked by the Government, that there are thousands of white children in this territory who are almost wholly without the means of education, and are consequently growing up with no fitting preparation for useful citizenship. A matter of so much concern to the country should not be disregarded.

When the treaties were reaffirmed in 1866, a provision was made for the adoption and equality of rights of the freedmen, who had theretofore been slaves in the tribes, upon terms provided in the treaties. The Cherokees and Choctaws have appeared to comply with the letter of the prescribed terms, although very inadequately and tardily, and the Chickasaws at one time took some steps toward complying with these terms, but now deny that they ever adopted the freedmen, and are endeavoring to retrace the steps originally taken. They now treat the whole class as aliens without any legal right to abide among them, or to claim any protection under their laws. They are shut out of the schools of the tribe, and from their courts, and are granted no privileges of occupancy of any part of the land for a home, and are helplessly exposed to the hostilities of the citizen Indian and the personal animosity of the former master. Peaceable, law-abiding, and hard-working, they have sought in vain to be regarded as a part of the people to whose wealth their industry is daily contributing a very essential portion. They number in that tribe about 4,000, while the Chickasaws number 3,500. The United States is bound by solemn treaty to place these freedmen securely in the enjoyment of their rights as Chickasaw Indians, and can not with honor ignore the obligation. . . .

The condition of the freedmen in the Choctaw and Cherokee tribes is little better than that of those among the Chickasaws, although they have been adopted according to the requirements of the treaties. They are yet very far from the enjoyment of all the rights, privileges, and immunities to which they are entitled under the treaties. In the Choctaw tribe, the 40 acres to which they are entitled for a home has not been set apart to them and no one has any title to a single foot of land he may improve or occupy. Whenever his occupancy of land is in the way of any citizen Indian he is at once, by means sufficiently severe and threatening, compelled to leave his improvements. He consequently has no abiding place, and what he is enabled to get from the soil for his support, he is compelled to gather either furtively or by the most absolute subserviency to the will, caprices, or exactions of his former master. But meager provision is made for the schooling of his children, and but little participation in the management of the government of which he is a citizen is permitted him. He is nevertheless moral, industrious, and frugal, peaceable, orderly, and obedient to the laws, taking no part in the crimes which have of late filled the country with alarm and put in peril the lives and property of law-abiding citizens. A number of these sought an interview with us on one occasion, but were, as we were informed, warned by a prominent Indian citizen that if they called upon us they would be killed, which warning they heeded.

In the Cherokee tribe the schools provided for the freedmen are of very inferior and inefficient character, and practically their children are growing up in deplorable ignorance. They are excluded from participation in the per capita distribution of all funds, and are ignored in almost all respects as a factor in the government of a people of whose citizenship they are by the treaties in all respects made a part. Yet in this tribe the freedmen are conspicuous for their morality, industrial and frugal habits, and for peaceable and orderly lives.

Justice has been utterly perverted in the hands of those who have thus laid hold of the forms of its administration in this Territory and who have inflicted irreparable wrongs and outrages upon a helpless people for their own gain. The United States put the title to a domain of countless wealth and unmeasured resources in these several tribes or nationalities, but it was a conveyance in trust for specific uses, clearly indicated in the treaties themselves, and for no other purpose. It was for the use and enjoyment in common by each and every citizen of his tribe, of each and every part of the Territory, thus tersely expressed in one of the treaties: "To be held in common, so that each and every member of either tribe shall have an equal undivided interest in the whole." The tribes can make no other use of it. They have no power to grant it to anyone, or to grant to anyone an exclusive use of any portion of it. These tribal governments have wholly perverted their high trusts, and it is the plain duty of the United States to enforce the trust it has so created and recover for its original uses the domain and all the gains derived from the perversions of the trust or discharge the trustee.

The United States also granted to these tribes the power of self-government, not to conflict with the Constitution. They have demonstrated their incapacity to so govern themselves, and no higher duty can rest upon the Government that granted this authority than to revoke it when it has so lamentably failed.

In closing this report we may be permitted to add that we have observed with pain and deep regret that the praiseworthy efforts of the Christian church, and of benevolent associations from different parts of the country, so long continued among the tribes, are being counteracted and rendered in a large measure nugatory by the untoward influences and methods now in force among them tending directly to destroy and obliterate the beneficial effects of their good work.

[*Senate Miscellaneous Document* no. 24, 53d Cong., 3d sess., serial 3281, pp. 8-12.]

119. Extension of Civil Service Rules

Extract from the *Annual Report of the Commissioner of Indian Affairs*

September 15, 1896

In 1896 most employees of the Indian service were placed under civil service rules, leaving only the agents and a few others outside the system. Commissioner Daniel M. Browning reported on the status of the service in his annual report for 1896.

. . . . The classified service has been extended over almost every branch of the Indian work.

By direction of the President, in accordance with the third clause of section 6 of the civil-service act of January 16, 1883, the Department, March 30, 1896, amended the classification of the employees of the Department of the Interior so as to include therein "all clerks, assistant clerks, issue clerks, property clerks, and other clerical positions and storekeepers at Indian agencies and Indian schools."

Another Department order of same date amended the classification of the Indian service so as to include therein "all physicians, school superintendents, assistant superintendents, supervisors of schools, day school inspectors, school-teachers, assistant teachers, industrial teachers, teachers of industries, disciplinarians, kindergarten teachers, matrons, assistant matrons, farmers, seam-

195

stresses and nurses * * * without regard to salary or compensation, all subject to competitive examination for original appointment." Physicians, superintendents, teachers, and matrons were already in the classified service; but all persons employed in any of the other positions named were on March 30 also brought within its limits.

May 6, 1896, the President still further enlarged the scope of the classified service by including therein "all officers and employees, of whatever designation, except persons merely employed as laborers or workmen and persons who have been nominated for confirmation by the Senate, however or for whatever purpose employed, whether compensated by fixed salary or otherwise, who are serving in or are on detail from * * * the Indian service."

Recognizing the disadvantage under which the Indian labors in competing with his more favored white brother, permission was given for the appointment of Indians, without examination or certification by the Civil Service Commission, to all positions except those of superintendent, teacher, teacher of industries, kindergartner, and physician; and for those positions Indians could be selected upon noncompetitive examination, which should consist of such tests of fitness as should be approved by the Department and not disapproved by the Commission.

An abstract of all persons in the field in the Indian service June 30, 1896, except school employees, arranged with reference to their relations to the civil-service classification, gives the following items:

White persons in the classified service:

Agency employees classified by compensation—
Salary less than $720 per annum .. 80
Salary $720 or less than $840 164
Salary $840 or less than $900 29
Salary $900 or less than $1,000 ...112
Salary $1,000 or less than $1,200 .. 58
Salary $1,200 or less than $1,400 .. 74
Salary $1,400 or less than $1,600 .. 2
Salary $1,600 or less than $1,800 .. 1
Salary $1,800 or less than $2,000 .. 2
Salary $2,000 or less than $2,500 .. 3
Salary $2,500 and over 2
                                    527

Special agents, commissioners, surveying engineers, and physician to L'Anse Indians 14
Presidential appointments 11
Total white persons in the classified service 552

White persons in the unclassified service:

Confirmed by the Senate: 38 agents, 5 inspectors, 5 commissioners to Five Civilized Tribes 48
Military officers acting as agents 17
Physicians paid for occasional services 3
Transportation agents 3
Employed at agencies at compensation below classification 12
Total white persons in the unclassified service 83
Total white persons 635

Indians in excepted places 1,356
Indians in positions having salaries below classification 78
Total Indian employees 1,434

The total of salaries paid to white persons employed at agencies was $546,670; to officials, such as inspectors, special agents, commissioners, etc., not located at agencies, $104,815. Salaries paid to Indians aggregated $258,140, nearly half the amount paid to white employees at agencies.

Whenever it has been found practicable to employ Indians it has been the policy of this office to give them the preference, and in the large majority of cases they have been found faithful and earnest, entering heartily into the work of advancing their own people. There are Indian employees at every agency except two; one of these is a very small agency and the other has only two employees. One agency has 107 Indians employed, one has 76, another 72, two have 51, twenty-two have over 20, and nineteen have from 10 to 20 Indians on their employee rolls. Of course a large number are policemen and judges of the courts of Indian offenses, but the number holding other positions is not small, and steadily increases.

As stated, none of the above figures refer to employees in schools. Under the orders referred to the entire school service was classified, thus bringing under the operation of civil-service rules 2,070 superintendents, teachers, etc., employed in the various schools, whose aggregate salaries amounted last year to nearly one million dollars. This included 705 Indians, about 34 per cent of the total number of school employees. The statement in detail is as follows:

Whites in the classified service:

Salary less than $720 979
Salary $720 or less than $840 206
Salary $840 or less than $900 39
Salary $900 or less than $1,000 . . . 44
Salary $1,000 or less than $1,200 . . 42
Salary $1,200 or less than $1,400 . . 26
Salary $1,400 or less than $1,600 . . 27
Salary $1,800 or less than $2,000 . . 1
                                       1,364

Whites in the unclassified service:

Confirmed by Senate 1
Total white persons 1,365
Indians in excepted places 705

The salaries paid white school employees amounted to $849,645. Those paid Indians amounted to $148,766. The classes graduating from the various nonreservation schools are fast furnishing material with which to fill school positions of importance and responsibility which require special training as well as aptitude. The first normal class, which was graduated last June, will be referred to hereafter.

The recognition of the merit system in the Indian service is a long step forward, and will undoubtedly elevate its standard, improve its morale, and promote its efficiency. The removal of all partisan influence from appointments will give added dignity to the positions and increase the zeal of those engaged in the work. . . .

[*House Document* no. 5, 54th Cong., 2d sess., serial 3489, pp. 3-5.]

120. Curtis Act
June 28, 1898

With the Curtis Act, Congress accomplished by legislation what the Dawes Commission has been unable to do by negotiation–effectively destroy the tribal governments in the Indian Territory. This long and detailed act provided for establishment and regulation of townsites, for management of leases of mineral rights, and for other technical matters. Printed here are several key sections, which authorized the Dawes Commission to draw up rolls and allot the lands to Indians on the rolls, prohibited aggrandizement of lands, and abolished the tribal courts.

An Act for the protection of the people of the Indian Territory, and for other purposes.

. . . . SEC. 11. That when the roll of citizenship of any one of said nations or tribes is fully completed as provided by law, and the survey of the lands of said nation or tribe is also completed, the commission heretofore appointed under Acts of Congress, and known as the "Dawes Commission," shall proceed to allot the exclusive use and occupancy of the surface of all the lands of said nation or tribe susceptible of allotment among the citizens thereof, as shown by said roll, giving to each, so far as possible, his fair and equal share thereof, considering the nature and fertility of the soil, location, and

value of same; but all oil, coal, asphalt, and mineral deposits in the lands of any tribe are reserved to such tribe, and no allotment of such lands shall carry the title to such oil, coal, asphalt, or mineral deposits; and all town sites shall also be reserved to the several tribes, and shall be set apart by the commission heretofore mentioned as incapable of allotment. There shall also be reserved from allotment a sufficient amount of lands now occupied by churches, schools, parsonages, charitable institutions, and other public buildings for their present actual and necessary use, and no more, not to exceed five acres for each school and one acre for each church and each parsonage, and for such new schools as may be needed; also

197

sufficient land for burial grounds where necessary. When such allotment of the lands of any tribe has been by them completed, said commission shall make full report thereof to the Secretary of the Interior for his approval. . . .

SEC. 17. That it shall be unlawful for any citizen of any one of said tribes to inclose or in any manner, by himself or through another, directly or indirectly, to hold possession of any greater amount of lands or other property belonging to any such nation or tribe than that which would be his approximate share of the lands belonging to such nation or tribe and that of his wife and his minor children as per allotment herein provided; and any person found in such possession of lands or other property in excess of his share and that of his family, as aforesaid, or having the same in any manner inclosed, at the expiration of nine months after the passage of this Act, shall be deemed guilty of a misdemeanor. . . .

SEC. 19. That no payment of any moneys on any account whatever shall hereafter be made by the United States to any of the tribal governments or to any officer thereof for disbursement, but payments of all sums to members of said tribes shall be made under direction of the Secretary of the Interior by an officer appointed by him; and per capita payments shall be made direct to each individual in lawful money of the United States, and the same shall not be liable to the payment of any previously contracted obligation. . . .

SEC. 26. That on and after the passage of this Act the laws of the various tribes or nations of Indians shall not be enforced at law or in equity by the courts of the United States in the Indian Territory. . . .

SEC. 28. That on the first day of July, eighteen hundred and ninety-eight, all tribal courts of Indian Territory shall be abolished, and no officer of said courts shall thereafter have any authority whatever to do or perform any act theretofore authorized by any law in connection with said courts, or to receive any pay for same; and all civil and criminal causes then pending in any such court shall be transferred to the United States court in said Territory by filing with the clerk of the court the original papers in the suit: *Provided,* That this section shall not be in force as to the Chickasaw, Choctaw, and Creek tribes or nations until the first day of October, eighteen hundred and ninety-eight. . . .

[*U.S. Statutes at Large,* 30:497-98, 502, 504-05.]

121. Stephens v. Cherokee Nation

May 15, 1899

Suits brought against the determination of property rights by the Dawes Commission tested the constitutionality of the Curtis Act. The Supreme Court upheld the act in all its provisions.

. . . . We repeat that in view of the paramount authority of Congress over the Indian tribes, and of the duties imposed on the Government by their condition of dependency, we cannot say that Congress could not empower the Dawes Commission to determine, in the manner provided, who were entitled to citizenship in each of the tribes and make out correct rolls of such citizens, an essential preliminary to effective action in promotion of the best interests of the tribes. It may be remarked that the legislation seems to recognize, especially the act of June 28, 1898, a distinction between admission to citizenship merely and the distribution of property to be subsequently made, as if there might be circumstances under which the right to a share in the latter would not necessarily follow from the concession of the former. But in any aspect, we are of opinion that the constitutionality of these acts in respect of the determination of citizenship cannot be successfully assailed on the ground of the impairment or destruction of vested rights. The lands and moneys of these tribes are public lands and public moneys, and are not held in individual ownership, and the assertion by any particular applicant that his right therein is so vested as to preclude inquiry into his status involves a contradiction in terms.

The judgments in these cases were rendered before the passage of the act of June 28, 1898, commonly known as the Curtis Act, and necessarily the effect of that act was not considered. As, however, the provision for an appeal to this court was made after the passage of the act, some observations upon it are required, and, indeed, the inference is not unreasonable that a principal object intended to be secured by an appeal was the testing of the constitutionality of this act, and that may have had controlling weight in inducing the granting of the right to such appeal.

The act is comprehensive and sweeping in its character, and notwithstanding the abstract of it in the statement prefixed to this opinion, we again call attention to its provisions. The act gave jurisdiction to the United States courts in the Indian Territory in their respective districts to try cases against those who claimed to hold lands and tenements as members of a tribe and whose membership was denied by the tribe, and authorized their removal from the same if the claim was disallowed; and provided for the allotment of lands by the Dawes Com-

mission among the citizens of any one of the tribes as shown by the roll of citizenship when fully completed as provided by law, and according to a survey also fully completed; and "that if the person to whom an allotment shall have been made shall be declared, upon appeal as herein provided for, by any of the courts of the United States in or for the aforesaid Territory, to have been illegally accorded rights of citizenship, and for that or any other reason declared to be not entitled to any allotment, he shall be ousted and ejected from said lands." . . .

For reasons already given we regard this act in general as not obnoxious to constitutional objection, but in so holding we do not intend to intimate any opinion as to the effect that changes made thereby, or by the agreements referred to, may have, if any, on the status of the several applicants, who are parties to these appeals. . . .

As we hold the entire legislation constitutional, the result is that all the *Judgments must be affirmed.*

[*174 U.S. Reports*, 445, 488-89, 491-92.]

122. Citizenship for Indians in the Indian Territory
March 3, 1901

Since the Dawes Act excluded the Five Civilized Tribes and other groups in the Indian Territory, those Indians did not fall under the citizenship provisions of that law. In 1901 Congress granted citizenship to all Indians in the Indian Territory by an amendment to the Dawes Act.

An Act to amend section six, chapter one hundred and nineteen, United States Statutes at Large numbered twenty-four.

Be it enacted . . . , That section six of chapter one hundred and nineteen of the United States Statutes at Large numbered

twenty-four, page three hundred and ninety, is hereby amended as follows, to wit: After the words "civilized life," in line thirteen of said section six, insert the words "and every Indian in Indian Territory."

[*U.S. Statutes at Large*, 31:1447.]

123. Indian Commissioner Jones on Indian Self-Support
Extract from the *Annual Report of the Commissioner of Indian Affairs*
October 15, 1901

In the first two decades of the twentieth century much attention was paid to moving the Indians toward self-support. The annual report of Commissioner William A. Jones in 1901 included a clear statement of this interest.

. . . . In the last annual report some attention was given to the obstacles in the way of the Indian toward independence and self-

support, and three of the most important were pointed out and made the subject of discussion. It was shown that the indiscriminate issue of rations was an effectual barrier to civilization; that the periodical distribution of large sums of money was demoralizing in the extreme; and that the general leasing of allotments instead of benefiting the Indians, as originally intended, only contributed to their demoralization.

Further observation and reflection leads to the unwelcome conviction that another obstacle may be added to these already named, and that is education. It is to be distinctly understood that it is not meant by this to condemn education in the abstract—far from it; its advantages are too many and too apparent to need any demonstration here. Neither is it meant as a criticism upon the conduct or management of any particular school or schools now in operation. What is meant is that the present Indian educational system, taken as a whole, is not calculated to produce the results so earnestly claimed for it and so hopefully anticipated when it was begun.

No doubt this idea will be received with some surprise, and expressions of dissent will doubtless spring at once to the lips of many of those engaged or interested in Indian work. Nevertheless, a brief view of the plan in vogue will, it is believed, convince the most skeptical that the idea is correct.

There are in operation at the present time 113 boarding schools, with an average attendance of something over 16,000 pupils, ranging from 5 to 21 years old. These pupils are gathered from the cabin, the wickiup, and the tepee. Partly by cajolery and partly by threats; partly by bribery and partly by fraud; partly by persuasion and partly by force, they are induced to leave their homes and their kindred to enter these schools and take upon themselves the outward semblance of civilized life. They are chosen not on account of any particular merit of their own, not by reason of mental fitness, but solely because they have Indian blood in their veins. Without regard to their worldly condition; without any previous training; without any preparation whatever, they are transported to the schools—sometimes thousands of miles away—without the slightest expense or trouble to themselves or their people.

The Indian youth finds himself at once, as if by magic, translated from a state of poverty to one of affluence. He is well fed and clothed and lodged. Books and all the accessories of learning are given him and teachers provided to instruct him. He is educated in the industrial arts on the one hand, and not only in the rudiments but in the liberal arts on the other. Beyond "the three r's" he is instructed in geography, grammar, and history; he is taught drawing, algebra and geometry, music, and astronomy, and receives lessons in physiology, botany, and entomology. Matrons wait on him while he is well and physicians and nurses attend him when he is sick. A steam laundry does his washing and the latest modern appliances do his cooking. A library affords him relaxation for his leisure hours, athletic sports and the gymnasium furnish him exercise and recreation, while music entertains him in the evening. He has hot and cold baths, and steam heat and electric light, and all the modern conveniences. All of the necessities of life are given him and many of the luxuries. All of this without money and without price, or the contribution of a single effort of his own or of his people. His wants are all supplied almost for the wish. The child of the wigwam becomes a modern Aladdin, who has only to rub the Government lamp to gratify his desires.

Here he remains until his education is finished, when he is returned to his home—which by contrast must seem squalid indeed—to the parents whom his education must make it difficult to honor, and left to make his way against the ignorance and bigotry of his tribe. Is it any wonder he fails? Is it surprising if he lapses into barbarism? Not having earned his education, it is not appreciated; having made no sacrifice to obtain it, it is not valued. It is looked upon as a right and not as a privilege; it is accepted as a favor to the Government and not to the recipient, and the almost inevitable tendency is to encourage dependence, foster pride, and create a spirit of arrogance and selfishness. The testimony on this point of those closely connected with the Indian employees of the service would, it is believed, be interesting. . . .

What, then, shall be done? And this inquiry brings into prominence at once the whole Indian question.

It may be well first to take a glance at

what has been done. For about a generation the Government has been taking a very active interest in the welfare of the Indian. In that time he has been located on reservations and fed and clothed; he has been supplied lavishly with utensils and means to earn his living, with materials for his dwelling and articles to furnish it; his children have been educated and money has been paid him; farmers and mechanics have been supplied him, and he has received aid in a multitude of different ways. In the last thirty-three years over $240,000,000 have been spent upon an Indian population not exceeding 180,000, enough, if equitably divided, to build each one a house suitable to his condition and furnish it throughout; to fence his land and build him a barn; to buy him a wagon and team and harness; to furnish him plows and the other implements necessary to cultivate the ground, and to give him something besides to embellish and beautify his home. It is not pretended that this amount is exact, but it is sufficiently so for the purposes of this discussion.

What is his condition to-day? He is still on his reservation; he is still being fed; his children are still being educated and money is still being paid him; he is still dependent upon the Government for existence; mechanics wait on him and farmers still aid him; he is little, if any, nearer the goal of independence than he was thirty years ago, and if the present policy is continued he will get little, if any, nearer in thirty years to come. It is not denied that under this, as under the school system, there has been some progress, but it has not been commensurate with the money spent and effort made.

THROWING THE INDIAN ON HIS OWN RESOURCES

It is easy to point out difficulties, but it is not so easy to overcome them. Nevertheless, an attempt will now be made to indicate a policy which, if steadfastly adhered to, will not only relieve the Government of an enormous burden, but, it is believed, will practically settle the entire Indian question within the space usually allotted to a generation. Certainly it is time to make a move toward terminating the guardianship which has so long been exercised over the Indians and putting them upon equal footing with the white man so far as their relations with Government are concerned. Under the present system the Indian ward never attains his majority. The guardianship goes on in an unbroken line from father to son, and generation after generation the Indian lives and dies a ward.

To begin at the beginning, then, it is freely admitted that education is essential. But it must be remembered that there is a vital difference between white and Indian education. When a white youth goes away to school or college his moral character and habits are already formed and well defined. In his home, at his mother's knee, from his earliest moments he has imbibed those elements of civilization which developing as he grows up distinguish him from the savage. He goes to school not to acquire a moral character, but to prepare himself for some business or profession by which he can make his way in after life.

With the Indian youth it is quite different. Born a savage and raised in an atmosphere of superstition and ignorance, he lacks at the outset those advantages which are inherited by his white brother and enjoyed from the cradle. His moral character has yet to be formed. If he is to rise from his low estate the germs of a nobler existence must be implanted in him and cultivated. He must be taught to lay aside his savage customs like a garment and take upon himself the habits of civilized life.

In a word, the primary object of a white school is to educate the mind; the primary essential of Indian education is to enlighten the soul. Under our system of government the latter is not the function of the state.

What, then, is the function of the state? Briefly this: To see that the Indian has the opportunity for self-support, and that he is afforded the same protection of his person and property as is given to others. That being done, he should be thrown entirely upon his own resources to become a useful member of the community in which he lives, or not, according as he exerts himself or fails to make an effort. He should be located where the conditions are such that by the exercise of ordinary industry and prudence he can support himself and family. He must be made to realize that in the sweat of his face he shall eat his bread. He must be brought to recognize the dignity of labor and the importance of building and maintaining a home. He must understand that the more useful he is there the more useful he will be to society. It is there he must find the incentive to work, and from it must come the uplifting of his race. . . .

CUTTING OFF RATIONS.

In pursuance of the policy of the Department to cut off rations from all Indians except those who are incapacitated in some way from earning a support, this office issued an order in June last to the 'six great Sioux agencies directing the agents to erase from the ration rolls all Indians who had become self-supporting and had therefore complied with the Black Hills treaty of 1877. And further, to issue rations to other Indians only in accord with their actual needs and to inaugurate, wherever it is possible, the policy of giving rations only in return for labor performed, either for themselves or for the benefit of the tribe.

While a sufficient lapse of time has not taken place to determine the great benefit this action will have on the industrial and educational progress of these Indians, the results obtained so far have been very gratifying, as well as surprising. At one agency 870 persons were declared entirely self-supporting and were dropped from the ration rolls; at another, 400; at another, 300. Of course a large number of these were "squaw men" and their families. Some were not only self-supporting, but able to live in comparative affluence; some had grown wealthy through the ration system. At first the order caused considerable dissatisfaction among those it affected, as naturally it would, but it was well received by the majority of the Indians. It would seem rather a sad commentary on the ration system to see Indians driving into the agency regularly in buggies and carriages to receive a gratuitous distribution of supplies from an indulgent Government "to keep them from starving."

Since the issuance of the above order to the Sioux a somewhat similar order has been issued to all other ration agencies. These agencies receive rations under a somewhat different arrangement, as in almost every instance the ration is a gratuity and not stipulated by any treaty, as in the case of Sioux. Here the order has been better received and the result has been equally surprising. The office feels that a great stride has been taken toward the advancement, civilization, and independence of the race; a step, that if followed up, will lead to the discontinuance of the ration system as far as it applies to able-bodied Indians, the abolition of the reservation, and ultimately to the absorption of the Indian into our body politic. . . .

[Annual Reports of the Department of the Interior, 1901, pp. 1-6.]

124. Lone Wolf v. Hitchcock
January 5, 1903

The Treaty of Medicine Lodge (1867) in Article 12 provided that no part of the Kiowa-Comanche Reservation could be ceded without the approval of three-fourths of the adult males. When Congress, after allotment of the reservation in severalty, approved the sale of excess tribal lands without the three-fourths approval, action was taken to enjoin the implementation of the act. The Supreme Court declared that Congress had plenary authority over Indian relations and that it had power to pass laws abrogating treaty stipulations.

. . . . The contention in effect ignores the status of the contracting Indians and the relation of dependency they bore and continue to bear towards the government of the United States. To uphold the claim would be to adjudge that the indirect operation of the treaty was to materially limit and qualify the controlling authority of Congress in respect to the care and protection of the Indians, and to deprive Congress, in a possible emergency, when the necessity might be urgent for a partition and disposal of tribal lands, of all power to act, if the assent of the Indians could not be obtained.

Now, it is true that in decisions of this court, the Indian right of occupancy of tribal lands, whether declared in a treaty or otherwise created, has been stated to be sacred, or, as sometimes expressed, as sacred as the fee of the United States in the same lands. . . . But in none of these cases was there involved a controversy between Indians and the government respecting the power of Congress to administer the property of the Indians. The questions considered in the cases referred to, which either directly or indirectly had relation to the nature of the property rights of the Indians, concerned the character and extent of such rights as respected States or individuals. In one of the cited cases it was clearly pointed out that Congress possessed a paramount power over the property of the Indians, by reason of its exercise of guardianship over their interests, and that such authority might be implied. . . .

Plenary authority over the tribal relations of the Indians has been exercised by Congress from the beginning, and the power has always been deemed a political one, not subject to be controlled by the judicial department of the government. Until the year 1871 the policy was pursued of dealing with the Indian tribes by means of treaties, and, of course, a moral obligation rested upon Congress to act in good faith in performing the stipulations entered into on its behalf. But, as with treaties made with foreign nations, *Chinese Exclusion Case*, 130 U.S. 581, 600, the legislative power might pass laws in conflict with treaties made with the Indians. . . .

The power exists to abrogate the provisions of an Indian treaty, though presumably such power will be exercised only when circumstances arise which will not only justify the government in disregarding the stipulations of the treaty, but may demand, in the interest of the country and the Indians themselves, that it should do so. When, therefore, treaties were entered into between the United States and a tribe of Indians it was never doubted that the *power* to abrogate existed in Congress, and that in a contingency such power might be availed of from considerations of governmental policy, particularly if consistent with perfect good faith towards the Indians. . . .

In view of the legislative power possessed by Congress over treaties with the Indians and Indian tribal property, we may not specially consider the contentions pressed upon our notice that the signing by the Indians of the agreement of October 6, 1892, was obtained by fraudulent misrepresentations and concealment, that the requisite three-fourths of adult male Indians had not signed, as required by the twelfth article of the treaty of 1867, and that the treaty as signed had been amended by Congress without submitting such amendments to the action of the Indians, since all these matters, in any event, were solely within the domain of the legislative authority and its action is conclusive upon the courts. . . .

[187 *U.S. Reports*, 553, 564-68.]

125. Indian Commissioner Leupp on Indian Policy

Extract from the *Annual Report of the Commissioner of Indian Affairs*

September 30, 1905

Commissioner Francis E. Leupp, in his first annual report, outlined his views on a proper Indian policy. While stressing the concept of self-support advanced by his predecessor, he also recommended preservation of elements of Indian culture.

. . . . Assuming the responsibilities of the commissionership in the very middle of the fiscal year, I have endeavored to gather up the threads of the work of my immediate predecessor and weave them into a consistent fabric, with only such new features of design as changeful passing conditions seemed to demand. For whatever in this report bears the stamp of novelty, but has not yet earned the seal of accomplishment, I shall crave your indulgence on the plea that the field of Indian affairs is presenting every day fresh problems for solution, and that, there being no precedents to guide us in solving these, we are necessarily driven to experiment. But in order that the general end toward which my efforts are directed may be the more clearly understood, I beg

203

respectfully to lay before you one of the fruits of my twenty years' study of the Indian face to face and in his own home, as well as of his past and present environment, in the form of a few

OUTLINES OF AN INDIAN POLICY.

The commonest mistake made by his white wellwishers in dealing with the Indian is the assumption that he is simply a white man with a red skin. The next commonest is the assumption that because he is a non-Caucasian he is to be classed indiscriminately with other non-Caucasians, like the negro, for instance. The truth is that the Indian has as distinct an individuality as any type of man who ever lived, and he will never be judged aright till we learn to measure him by his own standards, as we whites would wish to be measured if some more powerful race were to usurp dominion over us.

Suppose, a few centuries ago, an absolutely alien people like the Chinese had invaded our shores and driven the white colonists before them to districts more and more isolated, destroyed the industries on which they had always subsisted, and crowned all by disarming them and penning them on various tracts of land where they could be fed and clothed and cared for at no cost to themselves, to what condition would the white Americans of today have been reduced? In spite of their vigorous ancestry they would surely have lapsed into barbarism and become pauperized. No race on earth could overcome, with forces evolved from within themselves, the effect of such treatment. That our red brethren have not been wholly ruined by it is the best proof we could ask of the sturdy traits of character inherent in them. But though not ruined, they have suffered serious deterioration, and the chief problem now before us is to prevent its going any further. To that end we must reckon with several facts.

First, little can be done to change the Indian who has already passed middle life. By virtue of that very quality of steadfastness which we admire in him when well applied, he is likely to remain an Indian of the old school to the last. With the younger adults we can do something here and there, where we find one who is not too conserva-

tive; but our main hope lies with the youthful generation, who are still measurably plastic. The picture which rises in the minds of most Eastern white persons when they read petitions in which Indians pathetically describe themselves as "ignorant" and "poor," is that of a group of red men hungry for knowledge and eager for a chance to work and earn their living like white men. In actual life and in his natural state, however, the Indian is suspicious of the white race—we can hardly blame him for that—and wants nothing to do with us; he clings to the ways of his ancestors, insisting that they are better than ours; and he resents every effort of the Government either to educate his children or to show him how he can turn an honest dollar for himself by other means than his grandfathers used—or an appropriation from the Treasury. That is the plain truth of the situation, strive as we may to gloss it with poetic fancies or hide it under statistical reports of progress. The task we must set ourselves is to win over the Indian children by sympathetic interest and unobtrusive guidance. It is a great mistake to try, as many good persons of bad judgment have tried, to start the little ones in the path of civilization by snapping all the ties of affection between them and their parents, and teaching them to despise the aged and nonprogressive members of their families. The sensible as well as the humane plan is to nourish their love of father and mother and home—a wholesome instinct which nature planted in them for a wise end—and then to utilize this affection as a means of reaching through them, the hearts of the elders.

Again, in dealing with these boys and girls it is of the utmost importance not only that we start them aright, but that our efforts be directed to educating rather than merely instructing them. The foundation of everything must be the development of character. Learning is a secondary consideration. When we get to that, our duty is to adapt it to the Indian's immediate and practical needs. Of the 30,000 or 40,000 Indian children of school age in the United States, probably at least three-fourths will settle down in that part of the West which we still style the frontier. Most of these will try to draw a living out of the soil; a less—though, let us hope, an ever increasing—part will enter the

204

general labor market as lumbermen, ditchers, miners, railroad hands, or what not. Now, if anyone can show me what advantage will come to this large body of manual workers from being able to reel off the names of the mountains in Asia, or extract the cube root of 123456789, I shall be deeply grateful. To my notion, the ordinary Indian boy is better equipped for his life struggle on a frontier ranch when he can read the simple English of the local newspaper, can write a short letter which is intelligible though maybe ill-spelled, and knows enough of figures to discover whether the storekeeper is cheating him. Beyond these scholastic acquirements his time could be put to its best use by learning how to repair a broken harness, how to straighten a sprung tire on his wagon wheel, how to fasten a loose horseshoe without breaking the hoof, and how to do the hundred other bits of handy tinkering which are so necessary to the farmer who lives 30 miles from a town. The girl who has learned only the rudiments of reading, writing and ciphering, but knows also how to make and mend her clothing, to wash and iron, and to cook her husband's dinner will be worth vastly more as mistress of a log cabin than one who has given years of study to the ornamental branches alone.

Moreover, as fast as an Indian of either mixed or full blood is capable of taking care of himself, it is our duty to set him upon his feet and sever forever the ties which bind him either to his tribe, in the communal sense, or to the Government. This principle must become operative in respect to both land and money. We must end the un-American absurdity of keeping one class of our people in the condition of so many undivided portions of a common lump. Each Indian must be recognized as an individual and so treated, just as each white man is. Suppose we were to enact a law every year, one paragraph of which should be applicable solely to persons with red hair, another solely to persons with round chins, another solely to persons with Roman noses? Yet this would be no more illogical in principle than our annual Indian legislation making one sweeping provision for all Osages, another for all Pawnees, another for all Yankton Sioux, as if these several tribes were not composed of men and women and children with as diverse human characteristics as any equal groups of Germans or Italians. Thanks to the late Senator Henry L. Dawes of Massachusetts, we have for eighteen years been individualizing the Indian as an owner of real estate by breaking up, one at a time, the reservations set apart for whole tribes and establishing each Indian as a separate landholder on his own account. Thanks to Representative John F. Lacey of Iowa, I hope that we shall soon be making the same sort of division of the tribal funds. At first, of course, the Government must keep its protecting hand on every Indian's property after it has been assigned to him by book and deed; then, as one or another shows himself capable of passing out from under this tutelage he should be set fully free and given "the white man's chance," with the white man's obligations to balance it.

Finally, we must strive in every way possible to make the Indian an active factor in the upbuilding of the community in which he is going to live. The theory, too commonly cherished on the frontier, that he is a sort of necessary nuisance surviving from a remote period, like the sagebrush and the giant cactus, must be dispelled, and the way to dispel it is to turn him into a positive benefit. To this end I would, for instance, teach him to transact all of his financial business that he can in his nearest market town, instead of looking to the United States Treasury as the only source of material blessings. Any money of his which he can not use or is not using for his own current profit I should prefer to deposit for him, in reasonably small parcels, in local banks which will bond themselves sufficiently for its safe-keeping, so that the industries of the neighborhood will have the use of it, and everybody thereabout will be the better off for such prosperity as may come to an Indian depositor. On like grounds of reasoning I should encourage every proper measure which points toward absolving the Indian from his obsolete relation to the licensed trader and teaches him to make his purchases from those merchants who will ask of him the fairest price, whether near the agency or at a distance. In short, our aim ought to be to keep him moving steadily down the path which leads from his close domain of artificial restraints and artifical protection toward the broad area of individual liberty enjoyed by the ordinary citizen.

Incidentally to this programme, I should seek to make of the Indian an independent laborer as distinguished from one for whom the Government is continually straining itself to find something to do. He can penetrate a humbug, even a benevolent humbug, as promptly as the next man; and when he sees the Government inventing purely fictitious needs to be supplied and making excuses of one kind and another to create a means of employment for him, he despises the whole thing as a fraud, like the white man whom some philanthropist hires to carry a pile of bricks from one side of the road to the other and then back again. The employment bureau recently organized for the Indians in the Southwest is designed to gather up all the able-bodied Indians who, through the pinch of hunger it may be, have been moved to think that they would like to earn some money, and plant them upon ranches, upon railroads, in mines—wherever in the outer world, in short, there is an opening for a dollar to be got for a day's work. The clerk who has been placed in charge of the bureau is to supervise their contracts with their employers, see that their wages are paid them when due, and look out for them if they fall ill. For the rest, the Indians engaged are to be required to stand on their own feet like other men, and to understand that for what comes to them hereafter they will have themselves to thank.

Some one has styled this a policy of shrinkage, because every Indian whose name is stricken from a tribal roll by virtue of his emancipation reduces the dimensions of our red-race problem by a fraction—very small, it may be, but not negligible. If we can thus gradually watch our body of dependent Indians shrink, even by one member at a time, we may congratulate ourselves that the final solution is indeed only a question of a few years.

The process of general readjustment must be gradual, but it should be carried forward as fast as it can be with presumptive security for the Indian's little possessions; and I should not let its educative value be obscured for a moment. The leading strings which have tied the Indian to the Treasury ever since he began to own anything of value have been a curse to him. They have kept him an economic nursling long past the time when he ought to have been able to take a few steps alone. The tendency of whatever crude training in money matters he has had for the last half century has been toward making him an easy victim to such waves of civic heresy as swept over the country in the early nineties. That is not the sort of politics into which we wish the Indian to plunge as he assumes the responsibilities of citizenship. . . .

I like the Indian for what is Indian in him. I want to see his splendid inherited physique kept up, because he glories, like his ancestors, in fresh air, in freedom, in activity, in feats of strength. I want him to retain all his old contempt for hunger, thirst, cold, and danger when he has anything to do. I love the spirit of manly independence which moved a copper-colored sage once to beg that I would intercede with the Great Father and throttle a proposal to send rations to his people, because it would pauperize their young men and make them slaves to the whites. I have no sympathy with the sentiment which would throw the squaw's bead bag into the rubbish heap and set her to making lace. Teach her lace making, by all means, just as you would teach her bread making, as an addition to her stock of profitable accomplishments; but don't set down her beaded moccasins as merely barbarous, while holding up her lace handkerchief as a symbol of advanced civilization.

The Indian is a natural warrior, a natural logician, a natural artist. We have room for all three in our highly organized social system. Let us not make the mistake, in the process of absorbing them, of washing out of them whatever is distinctly Indian. Our aboriginal brother brings, as his contribution to the common store of character, a great deal which is admirable, and which needs only to be developed along the right line. Our proper work with him is improvement, not transformation. . . .

[*Report of the Commissioner of Indian Affairs, 1905*, pp. 1-5, 12.]

126. Burke Act
May 8, 1906

The Dawes Act was significantly amended in 1906. Discretion was authorized in the length of the trust period for allotments and citizenship was to be granted at the end, rather than at the beginning, of the trust period.

An Act To amend section six of an Act approved February eighth, eighteen hundred and eighty-seven, entitled *"An Act to provide for the allotment of lands in severalty to Indians on the various reservations, and to extend the protection of the laws of the United States and the Territories over the Indians, and for other purposes."*

Be it enacted . . . . , That section six of an Act approved February eighth, eighteen hundred and eighty-seven, entitled "An Act to provide for the allotment of lands in severalty to Indians on the various reservations, and to extend the protection of the laws of the United States and the Territories over the Indians, and for other purposes," be amended to read as follows:

"SEC. 6. That at the expiration of the trust period and when the lands have been conveyed to the Indians by patent in fee, as provided in section five of this Act, then each and every allottee shall have the benefit of and be subject to the laws, both civil and criminal, of the State or Territory in which they may reside; and no Territory shall pass or enforce any law denying any such Indian within its jurisdiction the equal protection of the law. And every Indian born within the territorial limits of the United States to whom allotments shall have been made and who has received a patent in fee simple under the provisions of this Act, or under any law or treaty, and every Indian born within the territorial limits of the United States who has voluntarily taken up within said limits his residence, separate and apart from any tribe of Indians therein, and has adopted the habits of civilized life, is hereby declared to be a citizen of the United States, and is entitled to all the rights, privileges, and immunities of such citizens, whether said Indian has been or not, by birth or otherwise, a member of any tribe of Indians within the territorial limits of the United States without in any manner impairing or otherwise affecting the right of any such Indian to tribal or other property: *Provided,* That the Secretary of the Interior may, in his discretion, and he is hereby authorized, whenever he shall be satisfied that any Indian allottee is competent and capable of managing his or her affairs at any time to cause to be issued to such allottee a patent in fee simple, and thereafter all restrictions as to sale, incumbrance, or taxation of said land shall be removed and said land shall not be liable to the satisfaction of any debt contracted prior to the issuing of such patent: *Provided further,* That until the issuance of fee-simple patents all allottees to whom trust patents shall hereafter be issued shall be subject to the exclusive jurisdiction of the United States: *And provided further,* That the provisions of this Act shall not extend to any Indians in the Indian Territory."

That hereafter when an allotment of land is made to any Indian, and any such Indian dies before the expiration of the trust period, said allotment shall be cancelled and the land shall revert to the United States, and the Secretary of the Interior shall ascertain the legal heirs of such Indian, and shall cause to be issued to said heirs and in their names, a patent in fee simple for said land, or he may cause the land to be sold as provided by law and issue a patent therefor to the purchaser or purchasers, and pay the net proceeds to the heirs, or their legal representatives, of such deceased Indian. The action of the Secretary of the Interior in determining the legal heirs of any deceased Indian, as provided herein, shall in all respects be conclusive and final.

[*U.S. Statutes at Large*, 34:182-83.]

Extract from the *Annual Report of the Commissioner of Indian Affairs*
September 30, 1906

Praise of the Burke Act and arguments in its favor appeared in the annual report of Commissioner Francis E. Leupp in 1906.

. . . . The general allotment act of February 8, 1887 (24 Stat. L., 388), better known as the Dawes law, was the crystallization of the resolve of our Government that the tribal relations of the Indian should cease. The power conferred by it to segregate the lands occupied by the Indians and have them taken in severalty has been exercised to as great an extent as conditions have seemed to warrant. By its provisions the lands allotted in severalty were to be held in trust for twenty-five years, and the Indians were to become citizens of the United States and of the several States at the instant of the approval of their allotments.

The citizenship provision is in the sixth section of the act; and as many allotments were made under treaties and special acts the terms of this section were so drawn as to include all allotments under any law or treaty. Thus a large number of Indians were made citizens, and a still larger number have since that time been placed theoretically on the same footing with their white neighbors. . . .

Like his white neighbor, the Indian is of more than one sort, ranging from good degrees of intelligence, industry, and thrift to the depths of helplessness, ignorance, and vice. Experience has proved that Indians of the former class do better when allowed to run their own business than when the Government tries to run it for them, but that citizenship and the jurisdiction of the local courts are of no advantage to Indians of the latter class, because the community, as a rule, does not interest itself to compel the proper exercise of police or judicial powers in behalf of these poor people. The very cost of resorting to law for the enforcement of a right or the redress of a wrong is in some places prohibitive as far as they are concerned.

Such conditions made plain the need of some law which would enable the Indian Office to manage the affairs of the helpless class with undisputed authority, but, on the other hand, to remove from the roll of wards and dependants the large and increasing number of Indians who no longer need any supervision from a bureau in Washington. To this need came a response from Representative Charles H. Burke, of South Dakota, who last winter introduced in the Congress a measure which, with some modification, became law on May 8. . . .

The Burke law materially modifies the Dawes law. It postpones the acquisition of citizenship until the termination of the trust as to all allotments made after May 8, 1906, and declares that the allottees shall be subject to the exclusive jurisdiction of the United States until they acquire citizenship. To nullify the injustice which such a general provision might inflict upon Indians capable of taking their places in the State as citizens, a very comprehensive proviso confers authority on the Secretary of the Interior to terminate the trust period by issuing a patent in fee whenever he is satisfied of the competency of an allottee to manage his own affairs. Fortunately this power is broad enough to cover all allotments, no matter when made. . . .

The important points in the Burke law are those relating to citizenship and fee-simple patents. Twenty-five years is not too long a time for most Indians to serve their apprenticeship in civic responsibilities. Meanwhile, also, the new community amid which he is thrown will presumptively have become more settled and better fitted for enlightened local self-government. The police powers of the Indian establishment are ample to control the Indian wards of the Government as long as no question of jurisdiction can be raised, and the noncitizen Indian can be better protected thereby from the class who make prey of the helpless, ignorant, or vicious. . . .

The power vested in the Secretary of the Interior to end the trust period by issuing patents in fee simple, thereby making citizens of the allottees, is a very important one, if not the most important relating to Indians that has been vested in the Department; and it is logically correct and in harmony with the spirit of the body of our law. The only way in which an intelligent and self-dependent Indian could obtain relief from the shackles of wardship before the enactment of the Burke law was by special legislation, and the evils of encouraging that practice in any direction are too obvious to call for rehearsal here. The usual accompaniment of graft and blackmail is enough to condemn a resort to such procedure for any purpose which it is practicable to effect by other means.

While on this subject, I trust I may be pardoned if I volunteer a few thoughts as to the policy to be pursued in exercising the power to issue patents in fee. Any Indian who is earning a livelihood at any honorable occupation, if he wishes to own his lands in fee, should have the privilege at once, because a man who has worked for his own support for any length of time will generally have some idea of the value of his land. Under ordinary conditions I would rather see an Indian who is working as a section hand on a railroad get his land free from governmental control than one who has no fixed calling, no matter what may be the relative scholastic education of the two. I know full-blood Indians who can not speak or write a word of English, but are making their way creditably as farmers or freighters or boatmen, who would better deserve their patents in fee than one who takes a job as interpreter at $10 per month rather than cultivate his allotment. It is no sign of an Indian's fitness to manage his own affairs that he employs some one to get his patent issued; if he does not know that the agent or superintendent is paid by the Government to do such work for him, it is open to question whether he knows enough to conduct his everyday business.

In short, I would make industry the primary test and use this as a lever to force Indians to earn their bread by labor. There is no danger of proceeding too slowly; the spirit of the times will not permit any stagnation. The legislation of recent years shows conclusively that the country is demanding an end of the Indian question and it is right. The Burke law, wisely administered, will accomplish more in this direction than any other single factor developed in a generation of progress. When it is supplemented by other legislation which will enable their pro rata shares of the tribal moneys to be paid, principal and interest, to competent Indians, the beginning of the end will be at hand. Such Indians, owning their land in fee, and receiving their portions of the tribal property without restriction can not by any course of action maintain a claim for further consideration. Through such measures the grand total of the nation's wards will be diminished daily and at a growing ratio.

The various agents and superintendents have been advised of the provisions of the Burke Act and instructed how to proceed under it. On receipt of an application they are to post a notice of it as conspicuously as possible, giving the allottee's name and the description of the land, announcing that at the expiration of thirty days the Indian Office will consider the application with a view of recommending to the Secretary of the Interior the issue of the patent desired, and urging that any person acquainted with the applicant and aware of any fact which would tend to show that the patent ought not to issue will make it known forthwith.

Experience may show that other safeguards are necessary. Many applications have already been received, and doubtless a large number of patents will be distributed during the coming year. . . .

[*House Document* no. 5, 59th Cong., 2d sess., serial 5118, pp. 27-31.]

128. Lacey Act

March 2, 1907

The Dawes Act and the Burke Act provided for the allotment of reservation lands to individual Indians, but they did not affect communally owned trust funds. In 1907, in a bill introduced by Congressman John F. Lacey of Iowa, Congress made provision for the allotment of tribal funds to certain classes of Indians.

An Act Providing for the allotment and distribution of Indian tribal funds.

Be it enacted . . . , That the Secretary of the Interior is hereby authorized, in his discretion, from time to time, to designate any individual Indian belonging to any tribe or tribes whom he may deem to be capable of managing his or her affairs, and he may cause to be apportioned and allotted to any such Indian his or her pro rata share of any tribal or trust funds on deposit in the Treasury of the United States to the credit of the tribe or tribes of which said Indian is a member, and 'the amount so apportioned and allotted shall be placed to the credit of such Indian upon the books of the Treasury, and the same shall thereupon be subject to the order of such Indian: *Provided*, That no apportionment or allotment shall be made to any Indian until such Indian has first made an application therefor: *Provided further*, That the Secretaries of the Interior and of the Treasury are hereby directed to withhold from such apportionment and allotment a sufficient sum of the said Indian funds as may be necessary or required to pay any existing claims against said Indians that may be pending for settlement by judicial determination in the Court of Claims or in the Executive Departments of the Government, at time of such apportionment and allotment.

SEC. 2. That the Secretary of the Interior is hereby authorized to pay any Indian who is blind, crippled, decrepit, or helpless from old age, disease, or accident, his or her share, or any portion thereof, of the tribal trust funds in the United States Treasury belonging to the tribe of which such Indian is a member, and of any other money which may hereafter be placed in the Treasury for the credit of such tribe and susceptible of division among its members, under such rules, regulations, and conditions as he may prescribe.

[*U.S. Statutes at Large*, 34:1221-22.]

129. Indian Commissioner Leupp on Reservation Schools

Extract from the *Annual Report of the Commissioner of Indian Affairs*

September 30, 1907

Nonreservation Indian schools like that at Carlisle, Pennsylvania, operated on the principle of taking the Indian child out of his reservation environment and training him for the white man's world. The principle won the support of many reformers, but it was directly challenged by Commissioner Francis E. Leupp, who urged instead the enlarging of the system of day schools on the reservations.

. . . . To the attentive reader of my reports for the last two years it must have been plain that their argument pointed toward a marked change in the Indian educational establishment, always in the direction of greater simplicity and a more logical fitness to the end for which it was designed. Such a change must be almost as slow in its complete accomplishment as the upbuilding of the structure whose plans are to be modified. No one hand can bring it all about; the official term, the powers and the resources of no one commissioner are extensive enough to do more than set the machinery in motion and point out to his successors, the Congress, and the public the reasons for his course, trusting that such an appeal to the national common sense will bear fruit in the continuation at least of the general features of his policy.

I entered office with a purpose, which I have kept steadily in view, to enlarge the system of day-school instruction as opposed to the increase of the boarding schools, and among the boarding schools the preference of those on the reservations to those at a distance. The subject has been so fully discussed that no elaborate rehearsal of the argument is called for here. Briefly stated, it pivots on the question whether we are to carry civilization to the Indian or carry the Indian to civilization, and the former seems to me infinitely the wiser plan. To plant our schools among the Indians means to bring the older members of the race within the sphere of influence of which every school is a

210

center. This certainly must be the basis of any practical effort to uplift a whole people. For its demonstration we do not have to look beyond the border line of our experience with Caucasian communities, where it is obvious that the effect upon the character as well as the intelligence of any neighborhood of having abundant school facilities close at hand is by no means confined to the generation actually under the teachers' daily care.

Though the day-school system is the ideal mechanism for the uplifting of the Indians, we can not yet wholly dispense with boarding schools, because so many tribes still continue the nomadic or semi-nomadic habits which would require the continual moving of the day schools from place to place in order to keep near a sufficient number of families for their support. In other cases a tribe which has had its lands allotted to its members individually has become so scattered over a large area that the distances the pupils would have to come and go would be prohibitive of their regular daily attendance at any school or schools, no matter how carefully located with regard to the convenience of the greatest number of possible patrons. In such instances the difficulties of the situation are reduced to a minimum by a resort to the reservation boarding school, where the children are within easy enough reach of their parents to enable the latter to see them at rather frequent intervals.

But boarding schools, conducted on the basis on which the Government conducts those established for the benefit of the Indians, are an anomaly in our American scheme of popular instruction. They furnish gratuitously not only tuition—the prime object of their existence—but food, clothing, and permanent shelter during the whole period of a pupil's attendance. In plain English, they are simply educational almshouses, with the unfortunate feature, from the point of view of our ostensible purpose of cultivating a spirit of independence in the Indians, that the charitable phase is obtrusively pushed forward as an attraction instead of wearing the stamp which makes the almshouse wholesomely repugnant to Caucasian sentiment. This tends steadily to foster in the Indian an ignoble willingness to accept unearned privileges; nay, more, from learning

to accept them he presently comes, by a perfectly natural evolutionary process, to demand them as rights and to heap demand upon demand. The result is that in certain parts of the West the only conception his white neighbors entertain of an Indian is that of a beggar as aggressive as he is shameless.

Was ever a worse wrong perpetrated upon a weaker by a stronger race? If so, history has failed to record it. Scores of books have been written within the last generation assailing our white civilization for its disregard of the rights of the Indian, seeking their illustrations in the unjustifiable wars opened upon him; in the frauds practiced upon him by unscrupulous traders, contractors, and Government functionaries; in the absorption of his lands, a few thousand acres at a time, at prices which look small indeed beside the valuations at which the same lands have been held since white enterprise has developed them; and yet the authors of these works have been so hypnotized by their abhorrence of such merely physical iniquities that they have overlooked entirely the vastly greater moral damage wrought upon the same victim under the guise of a benevolent desire to civilize him—at long range. As if self-reliance were not at the very foundation of our own civilization! The evils of war, of graft, big and little, of business frauds and all other forms of bad faith are capable of remedy in the same monetary terms in which we measure and remedy evils among our own race; but what compensation can we offer him for undermining his character, and doing it by a method so insidious and unfair?

Unhappily our generation can not go back and make over from the start the conditions which have come down to us by inheritance. We can, however, do the next best thing, and avoid extending or perpetuating the errors for which we are not responsible, and we can improve every available opportunity for reducing their burden. Just as we have undertaken to free the Indian from the shackles which the reservation system has imposed upon his manhood, so we should recognize it as a duty to free him from the un-American and pauperizing influences which still invest his path to civilization through the schools. The rudiments of an education, such as can be given his children in the little day school, should remain within their reach, just as they are within the reach of the white children who must be neighbors and competitors of the Indian children in their joint struggle for a livelihood. Indeed, this being a reciprocal obligation—the right of the child, red or white, to enough instruction to enable him to hold his own as a citizen, and the right of the Government to demand that every person who handles a ballot shall have his intelligence trained to the point that reading, writing, and simple ciphering will train it—I believe in compelling the Indian parent, whether he wishes to or not, to give his offspring this advantage. My interpretation of the duty laid upon me by the statute in this regard has carried me even to the use of physical force and arms in the few instances where reasoning and persuasion failed and the Indians have defied the Government.

For a little while still, as I have said, the reservation boarding schools must stay for lack of something adequate to take their places; but as fast as one of these can be replaced with day schools the change should be made, and I am pleased to have been able, in my short term of office, to give this movement its start. For the continuance of our 25 nonreservation schools there is no longer any excuse. We spend on these now nearly $2,000,000 a year, which is taken bodily out of the United States Treasury and is, in my judgment, for the most part a mere robbery of the taxladen Peter to pay the non-taxladen Paul and train him in false, undemocratic, and demoralizing ideas. The same money, spent for the same number of years on expanding and strengthening the Indians' home schools, would have accomplished a hundredfold more good, unaccompanied by any of the harmful effects upon the character of the race. . . .

[*Reports of the Department of the Interior, Administrative Reports, 1907*, 2:17-20.]

130. Indian Commissioner Valentine on Indian Health
Extract from the *Annual Report of the Commissioner of Indian Affairs*
November 1, 1910

In the twentieth century the Indian Office became increasingly aware of the serious health conditions existing among the Indians. Commissioner Robert Valentine in his annual report of 1910 indicated some of the problems and a method of attacking them.

. . . . The Indian Service in its health work is not aiming merely to more effectively care for and cure those that are sick. The reduction of the death rate is not its primary interest. It is working rather to increase the vitality of the Indian race and to establish for it a new standard of physical well-being. The work is being scientifically developed along lines which have already been successfully tried out by modern preventive medicine. The principal features of this work as it is now organized are: (1) An intensive attack upon the two diseases that most seriously menace the health of the Indians—trachoma and tuberculosis; (2) preventive work on a large scale, by means of popular education along health lines and more effective sanitary inspection; (3) increased attention to the physical welfare of the children in the schools, so that the physi-cal stamina of the coming generation may be conserved and increased. . . .

Systematic efforts are being made to educate the Indians in the schools and on the reservations as to the best methods of treating and preventing the spread of tuberculosis, trachoma, and other infectious and contagious diseases. A manual on tuberculosis, its cause, prevention, and treatment has been published by the medical supervisor and distributed throughout the service. A series of illustrated lectures for a traveling health exhibit are being prepared. A special physician and photographer are in the field securing photographs from which these stereopticon slides and moving pictures can be made. This exhibit will be sent to the different schools and reservations. One of the most important results of this educational work will be that it will instruct the employees at the schools and agencies of the Indian Service as to the methods of preventing disease, and in this way unite the entire service in the health campaign.

Increased attention is being given to sanitary inspection. It is planned, wherever possible, to have a house-to-house inspection by a physician of all Indian homes on a reservation. This will make it possible not only to accurately learn the extent of disease and provide for proper treatment, but it will also make it possible for instruction to be given the Indians as to how they may improve the sanitary conditions of their homes, and thereby prevent disease in future. A beginning in this work was made last year on the White Earth Reservation, where the need was pressing. Two special physicians were authorized to carry on the work. More than 200 homes were visited and 1,266 persons examined. Of this number 690 had trachoma and 164 tuberculosis in its various forms. Only 25 per cent of the homes visited were considered sanitary. This work will be vigorously followed up during the present year until the whole reservation is covered. Arrangements have been made with the Bureau of Animal Industry to make an inspection and test for tuberculosis of all of the dairy

herds in the service. The sanitary inspection of the equipment and methods for the production and handling of the milk supply is included. This work is now in progress.

The medical supervisor is having the schools in the service systematically inspected with special attention to ventilation, disinfection, and personal hygiene. He has recommended, where practicable, the construction of screened porches for sleeping quarters for pupils whose physical condition is not up to the standard. All pupils presented for admission to a boarding school are given a thorough physical examination. If a child is found to be affected with any disease that would probably be made worse by attending school or that would endanger the health of the other pupils he is not admitted. Three of the reservations where the greater number of day schools are located, namely, Cheyenne River, Pine Ridge, and Rosebud, have a day-school physician, who makes regular visits to each of the day schools under his supervision to look after the health of the pupils and to see that proper hygienic and sanitary conditions are maintained in the schools. . . .

[*Reports of the Department of the Interior, Administrative Reports, 1910*, 2:9-11.]

131.   Indian Commissioner Sells, A Declaration of Policy

Extract from the *Annual Report of the Commissioner of Indian Affairs*

October 15, 1917

Commissioner Cato Sells worked to free the Indians from federal guardianship. In 1917 he issued a new statement of policy, which would speed up declarations of competence for individual Indians and force them out into the white man's society.

A DECLARATION OF POLICY.

A careful study of the practical effects of governmental policies for determining the wardship of the Indians of this country is convincing that the solution is individual and not collective. Each individual must be considered in the light of his own environment and capacity for larger responsibilities and privileges.

While ethnologically a preponderance of white blood has not heretofore been a criterion of competency, nor even now is it always a safe standard, it is almost an axiom that an Indian who has a larger proportion of white blood than Indian partakes more of the

characteristics of the former than of the latter. In thought and action, so far as the business world is concerned, he approximates more closely to the white blood ancestry.

On April 17, 1917, there was announced a declaration of policy for Indian affairs, as follows:

DECLARATION OF POLICY IN THE
ADMINISTRATION OF INDIAN AFFAIRS.

During the past four years the efforts of the administration of Indian affairs have been largely concentrated on the following fundamental activities—the betterment of

213

health conditions of Indians, the suppression of the liquor traffic among them, the improvement of their industrial conditions, the further development of vocational training in their schools, and the protection of the Indians' property. Rapid progress has been made along all these lines, and the work thus reorganized and revitalized will go on with increased energy. With these activities and accomplishments well under way, we are now ready to take the next step in our administrative program.

The time has come for discontinuing guardianship of all competent Indians and giving even closer attention to the incompetent that they may more speedily achieve competency.

Broadly speaking, a policy of greater liberalism will henceforth prevail in Indian administration to the end that every Indian, as soon as he has been determined to be as competent to transact his own business as the average white man, shall be given full control of his property and have all his lands and moneys turned over to him, after which he will no longer be a ward of the Government.

Pursuant to this policy, the following rules shall be observed:

1. *Patents in fee.*—To all able-bodied adult Indians of less than one-half Indian blood, there will be given as far as may be under the law full and complete control of all their property. Patents in fee shall be issued to all adult Indians of one-half or more Indian blood who may, after careful investigation, be found competent, provided, that where deemed advisable patents in fee shall be withheld for not to exceed 40 acres as a home.

Indian students, when they are 21 years of age, or over, who complete the full course of instruction in the Government schools, receive diplomas and have demonstrated competency will be so declared.

2. *Sale of lands.*—A liberal ruling will be adopted in the matter of passing upon applications for the sale of inherited Indian lands where the applicants retain other lands and the proceeds are to be used to improve the homesteads or for other equally good purposes. A more liberal ruling than has hither-

to prevailed will hereafter be followed with regard to the applications of noncompetent Indians for the sale of their lands where they are old and feeble and need the proceeds for their support.

3. *Certificates of competency.*—The rules which are made to apply in the granting of patents in fee and the sale of lands will be made equally applicable in the matter of issuing certificates of competency.

4. *Individual Indian moneys.*—Indians will be given unrestricted control of all their individual Indian moneys upon issuance of patents in fee or certificates of competency. Strict limitations will not be placed upon the use of funds of the old, the indigent, and the invalid.

5. *Pro-rata shares–trust funds.*—As speedily as possible their pro rata shares in tribal trust or other funds shall be paid to all Indians who have been declared competent, unless the legal status of such funds prevents. Where practicable the pro rata shares of incompetent Indians will be withdrawn from the Treasury and placed in banks to their individual credit.

6. *Elimination of ineligible pupils from the Government Indian schools.*—In many of our boarding schools Indian children are being educated at Government expense whose parents are amply able to pay for their education and have public school facilities at or near their homes. Such children shall not hereafter be enrolled in Government Indian schools supported by gratuity appropriations, except on payment of actual per capita cost and transportation.

These rules are hereby made effective, and all Indian Bureau administrative officers at Washington and in the field will be governed accordingly.

This is a new and far-reaching declaration of policy. It means the dawn of a new era in Indian administration. It means that the competent Indian will no longer be treated as half ward and half citizen. It means reduced appropriations by the Government and more self-respect and independence for the Indian. It means the ultimate absorption of the Indian race into the body politic of the

Nation. It means, in short, the beginning of the end of the Indian problem.

In carrying out this policy, I cherish the hope that all real friends of the Indian race will lend their aid and hearty cooperation.

CATO SELLS,
Commissioner.
Approved:
FRANKLIN K. LANE,
Secretary.

The cardinal principle of this declaration revolves around this central thought—that an Indian who is as competent as an ordinary white man to transact the ordinary affairs of life should be given untrammeled control of his property and assured his personal rights in every particular so that he may have the opportunity of working out his own destiny. The practical application of this principle will relieve from the guardianship of the Government a very large number of Indians who are qualified to mingle on a plane of business equality with the white people. It will also begin the reduction of expenditures, and afford a better opportunity for closer attention to those who will need our protecting care for some years longer.

A vitally important result also will be obtained in placing a true ideal before those Indians remaining under guardianship. It will be a strong motive for endeavoring to reach the goal of competency, and prove a material incentive to a sincere effort for that end.

This new declaration of policy is calculated to release practically all Indians who have one-half or more white blood, although there will be exceptions in the case of those who are manifestly incompetent. It will also give like freedom from guardianship to those having more than one-half Indian blood when, after careful investigation, it is determined that they are capable of handling their own affairs. This latter class, however, will be much more limited since only about 40 per cent of the Indians of the country speak the English language and the large majority of this latter class still greatly need the protecting arm of the Government. . . .

[*Annual Report of the Commissioner of Indian Affairs, 1917*, pp. 3-5.]

132. Citizenship for World War I Veterans

November 6, 1919

Indians who served in the military or naval establishments during World War I could be granted citizenship at their request.

An Act Granting citizenship to certain Indians.

Be it enacted. . . , That every American Indian who served in the Military or Naval Establishments of the United States during the war against the Imperial German Government, and who has received or who shall hereafter receive an honorable discharge, if not now a citizen and if he so desires, shall, on proof of such discharge and after proper identification before a court of competent jurisdiction, and without other examination except as prescribed by said court, be granted full citizenship with all the privileges pertaining thereto, without in any manner impairing or otherwise affecting the property rights, individual or tribal, of any such Indian or his interest in tribal or other Indian property.

[*U.S. Statutes at Large*, 41:350.]

133. Bursum Bill

1922

In 1922 Senator Holm O. Bursum of New Mexico introduced a bill to quiet title to lands within the Pueblo Indian land grants. The bill would have given strong advantage to the whites in their disputes over land title with the Pueblos. The bill was passed by the Senate on September 11, 1922, but violent opposition to it by the Indians and their friends led to the ultimate defeat of the bill.

215

Be it enacted . . . [Jurisdiction of the District Court of the United States for the District of New Mexico over criminal and civil cases involving the Pueblos] . . . .

SEC. 7. That all persons or corporations who, prior to and since the date of the ratification and proclamation of the treaty of Guadalupe Hidalgo, July 4, 1848, either in person or through their predecessors, in claim of interest, grantors, privies, or agents, have had actual, open, notorious, exclusive, and continuous possession, under color of title, of, in, or to any lands included within the exterior boundaries of any grant of land confirmed or patented to any of the pueblos hereinbefore named by the United States of America, shall be entitled to a decree in their respective favor for all of the lands so possessed, and the district court shall, by its decree, segregate the said land from the said pueblo grant, and shall ascertain and adjudicate the true boundaries and extent thereof, in the proof of which character of possession and of the boundaries and extent thereof secondary evidence shall be admissible and competent. Upon the entry of any decree segregating any of the lands of any pueblo grant pursuant to the provisions and requirements of this paragraph, the clerk of the said court shall forthwith send to the Secretary of the Interior of the United States a certified copy of said decree, and the said tract of land so segregated having been surveyed by or under his direction, according to the boundaries and extent as set forth in said decree, said Secretary of the Interior shall cause patent therefor to be issued to said person, his heirs or assigns, or to such corporation or its successors in interest. In all cases arising under the provisions of this act wherein the original title and the adverse possession thereunder antedates the dates of ratification and proclamation of the treaty of Guadalupe Hidalgo, the remedy, relief, and procedure in this paragraph provided shall be exclusive and either party to any suit brought pursuant to the provisions of this act may make proof of date and source of title and the possession thereunder.

SEC. 8. That all persons who, or corporations which, for more than 10 years prior to June 20, 1910, either in person or through their respective predecessors in claim of interest, grantors, privies, or agents, have had actual, open, notorious, exclusive and continuous possession, with or without color of title, of any lands falling or included within the exterior boundaries of any grant confirmed or patented to any of the pueblos in this act specified, and all persons who or corporations which in person or through their respective predecessors in claim of interest or grantors claim any such lands lying within the exterior boundaries of any of said pueblo grants under valid grant from the Governments of Spain or Mexico, or under any grant, act of confirmation or patent of the United States of America, shall be entitled to a decree in their favor respectively for the whole of the lands so claimed, and the district court shall in its decree segregate the said land from the said pueblo grant and shall ascertain and adjudicate the area and extent thereof and the value of the said lands without improvement if any there shall be thereon, as of the date of the decree, and upon the entry of any decree provided for in this paragraph segregating any of the lands of any pueblo grant therefrom, the clerk of the district court shall forthwith send to the Secretary of the Interior of the United States of America a certified copy of the final decree, and, thereupon, the Secretary of the Interior shall cause to be surveyed from the public lands of the United States of America a tract or tracts of land as nearly adjacent to the said pueblo as possible, equal in area and value or equal in value to the lands so segregated in said final decree and shall cause patent therefor to be issued to the pueblo entitled thereto: but if it be found that such lands are not available then the Secretary of the Interior shall place to the credit of the said pueblo the value of the said land so segregated in cash as provided in said adjudication, and shall disburse the same to the best advantage and interest of the said pueblo.

SEC. 9. That the Secretary of the Interior shall promulgate all necessary rules and regulations relative to the selection of such lieu lands to be patented to any pueblo as in this act provided, and all necessary surveys, field notes, and plats made or necessary in ascertaining the extent and area of any land to be segregated from any pueblo shall be made under the direction of the surveyor general of the United States for New Mexico

216

upon instructions to that effect from the Secretary of the Interior, without cost to litigants.

SEC. 10. That whenever upon, through, or over, in whole or in part, any lands of any pueblo grant sought to be segregated, or segregated, from any Indian pueblo under the provisions of this act, there shall be located any river, creek, lake, pond, spring, reservoir, dam, irrigating ditch, canal, or other watercourse or source of water supply used for the irrigation and cultivation of any lands of any Indian pueblo not included within the areas so segregated, or sought to be segregated, the right of the pueblo to the use and benefit of any waters existing or found in any such river, creek, lake, pond, spring, reservoir, dam, irrigating ditch, canal, or other watercourse shall, in case of suit brought therefor, be decreed to the said pueblo according to its appropriation thereof for the irrigation of the lands of the pueblo as irrigated and cultivated at the time of the passage and approval hereof, and any further and additional use of such waters and the appropriation thereof shall be acquired, determined, and adjudicated according to the laws of the State of New Mexico governing the appropriation and use of waters for irrigation purposes.

SEC. 11. That all proceedings under this act in the said district court shall be without costs to parties.

SEC. 12. That any party aggrieved by any final judgment or decree of the district court in any of the foregoing cases, either civil or criminal, shall have the right to an appeal or writ of error as in other civil and criminal cases.

SEC. 13. That in any action brought under the provisions of this act in which the segregation of any lands of any pueblo is sought the United States of America, in its capacity of guardian of the said Pueblo Indians, shall appear and shall be represented by some person learned in the law, who shall be named and designated by the Attorney General of the United States for that purpose, with such assistants, legal and clerical, and with such compensation as to the Attorney General shall seem meet and proper.

SEC. 14. That all suits which may be brought by persons or corporations other than the pueblos hereinbefore named and the inhabitants thereof, commonly known and accepted by the pueblo as Pueblo Indians, involving any right, title, interest, benefit, use, possession, or right of possession, of any such person or corporation, to any lands falling or included within the exterior boundary lines of any of the pueblo grants in this act enumerated and specified shall be commenced within five years from the date of the passage and approval of this act; otherwise the same shall be forever barred, and said persons or corporations shall lose all rights and benefits by this act provided.

SEC. 15. That surveys of lands within pueblo grants and reservations held and occupied by persons not Indian, or corporations, as heretofore made under the supervision of the surveyor general for New Mexico, and plats and field notes of which have been filed in his office, shall be accepted as prima facie evidence of the boundaries of lands therein described.

SEC. 16. That in cases where lands within such grants, or any part or parcel thereof, shall at the trial be shown not to have been held and occupied by the claimants, non-Indian, for the period fixed by section 8 of this act for the acquiring of title under the provisions hereof, but have been purchased, or acquired by inheritance, used and cultivated, or purchased, or acquired by inheritance, held, occupied, or otherwise used for pastoral purposes under fence, in good faith by the claimant, the court shall make a special finding determining the boundaries of the tract so purchased, acquired, held and occupied, used and cultivated, in good faith, as well as also the value of the land without improvement, and shall report such finding to the Secretary of the Interior, and the claimant, if the Secretary of the Interior shall approve an application made by the claimant for said land, may purchase the same at the value found by the court, and the purchase price shall be held in trust and expended for the pueblo under such rules and regulations as shall be from time to time prescribed for the benefit of the pueblo within whose grant any such tract of land shall be situated.

[*Congressional Record*, 62:12324-25.]

134.   Indian Citizenship Act
June 2, 1924

In 1924 Congress granted citizenship to all Indians born within the United States who were not yet citizens.

An Act To authorize the Secretary of the Interior to issue certificates of citizenship to Indians.

Be it enacted . . . , That all non-citizen Indians born within the territorial limits of the United States be, and they are hereby, declared to be citizens of the United States: *Provided*, That the granting of such citizenship shall not in any manner impair or otherwise affect the right of any Indian to tribal or other property.

[*U.S. Statutes at Large*, 43:253.]

135.   Pueblo Lands Board
June 7, 1924

The vigorous opposition of reformers to the Bursum Bill of 1922 led to the creation of a special board to adjudicate the land controversies in New Mexico between the whites and the Pueblo Indians.

An Act To quiet the title to lands within Pueblo Indian land grants, and for other purposes.

Be it enacted . . . , That in order to quiet title to various lots, parcels, and tracts of land of the State of New Mexico for which claim shall be made by or on behalf of the Pueblo Indians of said State as hereinafter provided, the United States of America, in its sovereign capacity as guardian of said Pueblo Indians shall by its Attorney General, file in the District Court of the United States for the District of New Mexico, its bill or bills of complaint with a prayer for discovery of the nature of any claim or claims of any kind whatsoever adverse to the claim of said Pueblo Indians, as hereinafter determined.

SEC. 2. That there shall be, and hereby is, established a board to be known as "Pueblo Lands Board" to consist of the Secretary of the Interior, the Attorney General, each of whom may act through an assistant in all hearings, investigations, and deliberations in New Mexico, and a third member to be appointed by the President of the United States. The board shall be provided with suitable quarters in the city of Santa Fe, New Mexico, and shall have power to require the presence of witnesses and the production of documents of subpoena, to employ a clerk who shall be empowered to administer oaths and take acknowledgements, shall employ such clerical assistance, interpreters, and stenographers with such compensation as the Attorney General shall deem adequate, and it shall be provided with such necessary supplies and equipment as it may require on requisitions to the Department of Justice. The compensation and allowance for travel and expenses of the member appointed by the President shall be fixed by the Attorney General.

It shall be the duty of said board to investigate, determine, and report and set forth by metes and bounds, illustrated where necessary by field notes and plats, the lands within the exterior boundaries of any land granted or confirmed to the Pueblo Indians of New Mexico by any authority of the United States of America, or any prior sovereignty, or acquired by said Indians as a community by purchase or otherwise, title to which the said board shall find not to have been extinguished in accordance with the provisions of this Act, and the board shall not include in their report any claims of non-Indian claimants who, in the opinion of said board after investigation, hold and occupy such claims of which they have had adverse possession, in accordance with the provisions of section 4 of this Act: *Provided, however*, That the board shall be unanimous in all decisions whereby it shall be determined that the Indian title has been extinguished.

The board shall report upon each pueblo

as a separate unit and upon the completion of each report one copy shall be filed with the United States District Court for the District of New Mexico, one with the Attorney General of the United States, one with the Secretary of the Interior, and one with the Board of Indian Commissioners.

[Details of procedures and bases of land rights.]

[*U.S. Statutes at Large,* 43:636-37.]

136. Meriam Report
1928

In 1928 the Institute for Government Research (Brookings Institution) published The Problem of Indian Administration. *This large volume was the report of a survey made at the request of Secretary of the Interior Hubert Work and was popularly known as the Meriam Report, or Meriam Survey, from Lewis Meriam, who directed the survey staff. It was a monumental work, which set forth the economic and social conditions of the Indians and presented detailed recommendations for solutions to the problems discovered. It became a guide for governmental action in regard to the Indians for more than twenty years.*

. . . . The fundamental requirement is that the task of the Indian Service be recognized as primarily educational, in the broadest sense of that word, and that it be made an efficient educational agency, devoting its main energies to the social and economic advancement of the Indians, so that they may be absorbed into the prevailing civilization or be fitted to live in the presence of that civilization at least in accordance with a minimum standard of health and decency.

To achieve this end the Service must have a comprehensive, well-rounded educational program, adequately supported, which will place it at the forefront of organizations devoted to the advancement of a people. This program must provide for the promotion of health, the advancement of productive efficiency, the acquisition of reasonable ability in the utilization of income and property, guarding against exploitation, and the maintenance of reasonably high standards of family and community life. It must extend to adults as well as to children and must place special emphasis on the family and the community. Since the great majority of the Indians are ultimately to merge into the general population, it should cover the transitional period and should endeavor to instruct Indians in the utilization of the services provided by public and quasi public agencies for the people at large in exercising the privileges of citizenship and in making their contribution in service and in taxes for the maintenance of the government. It should also be directed toward preparing the white communities to receive the Indian. By improving the health of the Indian, increasing his productive efficiency, raising his standard of living, and teaching him the necessity for paying taxes, it will remove the main objections now advanced against permitting Indians to receive the full benefit of services rendered by progressive states and local governments for their populations. By actively seeking coöperation with state and local governments and by making a fair contribution in payment for services rendered by them to untaxed Indians, the national government can expedite the transition and hasten the day when there will no longer be a distinctive Indian problem and when the necessary governmental services are rendered alike to whites and Indians by the same organization without discrimination.

In the execution of this program scrupulous care must be exercised to respect the rights of the Indian. This phrase "rights of the Indian" is often used solely to apply to his property rights. Here it is used in a much broader sense to cover his rights as a human being living in a free country. Indians are entitled to unfailing courtesy and consideration from all government employees. They should not be subjected to arbitrary action. Recognition of the educational nature of the whole task of dealing with them will result in taking the time to discuss with them in detail their own affairs and to lead rather than force them to sound conclusions. The effort to substitute educational leadership for the more dictatorial methods now used in some places will necessitate more understanding of and sympathy for the Indian point of view. Leadership will recognize the good in the economic and social life of the Indians in their religion and ethics, and will seek to develop it and build on it rather than to crush out all that is Indian. The Indians have much to contribute to the dominant civilization, and the effort should be made to secure this contribution, in part because of the good it will do the Indians in stimulating a proper race pride and self respect. . . .

At the outset of this report the effort will be made to state briefly the position taken by the survey staff with respect to certain fundamental matters of general policy in Indian affairs. Subsequent sections will deal fairly minutely with the subjects of organization and management, health, education, economic condition, family and community life, and legal aspects of the problem. Each of these sections rests on substantially the same assumptions regarding the general policies which should govern in the conduct of Indian affairs. If these assumptions are sound, as the survey staff believes they are, the findings and recommendations in these detailed sections follow logically and more or less inevitably. If these fundamental statements of policy are acceptable, one may differ here and there with respect to matters of detail but not with general principles. The best course therefore seems to be to present these assumptions as clearly as possible at the outset, so that they may be definitely understood, in order that those who wish to take issue on fundamentals may do so at the beginning. In this way it is hoped that thinking and discussion may be considered as fundamentals and the details of practice and procedure as details, highly important though they are and vital in giving effect to general policies.

The Object of Work with or for the Indians. The object of work with or for the Indians is to fit them either to merge into the social and economic life of the prevailing civilization as developed by the whites or to live in the presence of that civilization at least in accordance with a minimum standard of health and decency. The first of these alternatives is apparently so clear on its face as to require no further explanation. The second, however, demands some further explanation.

Some Indians proud of their race and devoted to their culture and their mode of life have no desire to be as the white man is. They wish to remain Indians, to preserve what they have inherited from their fathers, and insofar as possible to escape from the ever increasing contact with and pressure from the white civilization. In this desire they are supported by intelligent, liberal whites who find real merit in their art, music, religion, form of government, and other things which may be covered by the broad term culture. Some of these whites would even go so far, metaphorically speaking, as to enclose these Indians in a glass case to preserve them as museum specimens for future generations to study and enjoy, because of the value of their culture and its picturesqueness in a world rapidly advancing in high organization and mass production. With this view as a whole if not in its extremities, the survey staff has great sympathy. It would not recommend the disastrous attempt to force individual Indians or groups of Indians to be what they do not want to be, to break their pride in themselves and their Indian race, or to deprive them of their Indian culture. Such efforts may break down the good in the old without replacing it with compensating good from the new.

The fact remains, however, that the hands of the clock cannot be turned backward. These Indians are face to face with the predominating civilization of the whites. This advancing tide of white civilization has as a rule largely destroyed the economic foundation upon which the Indian culture rested. This economic foundation cannot be restored as it was. The Indians cannot be set apart away from contacts with the whites. The glass case policy is impracticable.

Even among the Rio Grande Pueblos, the Hopis, and the Zunis, where more of the old culture apparently remains than among any other group, the Indians are by no means unanimous in their desire for the preservation of every detail of the old. Some pueblos, notably Laguna, taken as a whole seem to be seeking and finding the white man's path. Even in the most conservative pueblos individual Indians will be found who have no desire for a glass case existence, who want to take their place in the white civilization, to make their living in a distinctly white industrial pursuit, to dwell in a house with modern sanitary conveniences, to dress like a white man, to have their wives in childbirth attended by skilled physicians in a hospital, to have the doctor in illness as the white man does, to have for their children the educational equipment needful for advance in the white civilization, and to spend their earnings for automobiles and other things made possible by the white man's mass production. These Indians are as much entitled to direct their lives according to their desires as are the conservative Indians. It would be as unjust and as unwise to attempt to force them back to the old or to withhold guidance in the achievement of the new ends they seek as it would be to attempt to force the ones who love the old into the new.

The position taken, therefore, is that the work with and for the Indians must give consideration to the desires of the individual Indians. He who wishes to merge into the social and economic life of the prevailing civilization of this country should be given all practicable aid and advice in making the necessary adjustments. He who wants to remain an Indian and live according to his old culture should be aided in doing so. The question may be raised "Why aided? Just leave him alone and he will take care of himself." The fact is, however, as has been pointed out, that the old economic basis of his culture has been to a considerable extent destroyed and new problems have been forced upon him by contacts with the whites. Adjustments have to be made, economic, social and legal. Under social is included health. The advent of white civilization has forced on the Indians new problems of health and sanitation that they, unaided, can no more solve than can a few city individuals solve municipal problems. The presence of their villages in close proximity to white settlements make the health and sanitary conditions in those villages public questions of concern to the entire section. Both the Indians and their white neighbors are concerned in having those Indians who want to stay Indians and preserve their culture, live according to at least a minimum standard of health and decency. Less than that means not only that they themselves will go through a long drawn out and painful process of vanishing. They must be aided for the preservation of themselves.

Whichever way the individual Indian may elect to face, work in his behalf must be designed not to do for him but to help him to do for himself. The whole problem must be regarded as fundamentally educational. However much the early policy of rationing may have been necessary as a defensive, preventive war measure on the part of the whites, it worked untold harm to the Indians because it was pauperizing and lacked any appreciable educational value. Anything else done for them in a way that neglects educating them to do for themselves will work in the same direction. Controlling the expenditure of individual Indian money, for example, is pauperizing unless the work is so done that the Indian is being educated to control his own. In every activity of the Indian Service the primary question should be, how is the Indian to be trained so that he will do this for himself. Unless this question can be clearly and definitely answered by an affirmative showing of distinct educational purpose and method the chances are that the activity is impeding rather than helping the advancement of the Indian. . . .

[Lewis Meriam et al., *The Problem of Indian Administration* (Baltimore: Johns Hopkins Press, 1928), pp. 21-22, 86-89.]

137. Johnson-O'Malley Act

April 16, 1934

Congress in 1934 authorized contracts with states whereby the federal government would pay for educational, medical, and other services provided Indians by the states.

An Act Authorizing the Secretary of the Interior to arrange with States or Territories for the education, medical attention, relief of distress, and social welfare of Indians, and for other purposes.

Be it enacted . . . , That the Secretary of the Interior is hereby authorized, in his discretion, to enter into a contract or contracts with any State or Territory having legal authority so to do, for the education, medical attention, agricultural assistance, and social welfare, including relief of distress, of Indians in such State or Territory, through the qualified agencies of such State or Territory, and to expend under such contract or contracts moneys appropriated by Congress for the education, medical attention, agricultural assistance, and social welfare, including relief of distress, of Indians in such State.

SEC. 2. That the Secretary of the Interior, in making any contract herein authorized with any State or Territory, may permit such State or Territory to utilize for the purpose of this Act, existing school buildings, hospitals, and other facilities, and all equipment therein or appertaining thereto, including livestock and other personal property owned by the Government, under such terms and conditions as may be agreed upon for their use and maintenance.

SEC. 3. That the Secretary of the Interior is hereby authorized to perform any and all acts and to make such rules and regulations, including minimum standards of service, as may be necessary and proper for the purpose of carrying the provisions of this Act into effect: *Provided*, That such minimum standards of service are not less than the highest maintained by the States or Territories with which said contract or contracts, as herein provided, are executed.

SEC. 4. That the Secretary of the Interior shall report annually to the Congress any contract or contracts made under the provisions of this Act, and the moneys expended thereunder.

SEC. 5. That the provisions of this Act shall not apply to the State of Oklahoma.

[*U.S. Statutes at Large*, 48:596.]

138. Wheeler-Howard Act (Indian Reorganization Act)

June 18, 1934

The culmination of the reform movement of the 1920s led by John Collier was the Wheeler-Howard Act of 1934. This important legislation reversed the policy of allotment and encouraged tribal organization.

An Act to conserve and develop Indian lands and resources; to extend to Indians the right to form business and other organizations; to establish a credit system for Indians; to grant certain rights of home rule to Indians; to provide for vocational education for Indians; and for other purposes.

Be it enacted . . . , That hereafter no land of any Indian reservation, created or set apart by treaty or agreement with the Indians, Act of Congress, Executive order, purchase, or otherwise, shall be allotted in severalty to any Indian.

SEC. 2. The existing periods of trust placed upon any Indian lands and any restriction on alienation thereof are hereby extended and continued until otherwise directed by Congress.

SEC. 3. The Secretary of the Interior, if he shall find it to be in the public interest, is hereby authorized to restore to tribal ownership the remaining surplus lands of any Indian reservation heretofore opened, or authorized to be opened, to sale, or any other form of disposal by Presidential proclamation, or by any of the public land laws of the United States: *Provided, however*, That valid rights or claims of any persons to any lands so withdrawn existing on the date of the withdrawal shall not be affected by this Act: . . . .

SEC. 4. Except as herein provided, no sale, devise, gift, exchange or other transfer of restricted Indian lands or of shares in the assets of any Indian tribe or corporation organized hereunder, shall be made or approved: *Provided, however*, That such lands or interests may, with the approval of the Secretary of the Interior, be sold, devised, or otherwise transferred to the Indian tribe in which the lands or shares are located or from which the shares were derived or to a successor corporation; and in all instances such lands or interests shall descend or be devised, in accordance with the then existing laws of the State, or Federal laws where applicable, in which said lands are located or in which the subject matter of the corporation is located, to any member of such tribe or of such corporation or any heirs of such member: *Provided further*, That the Secretary of the Interior may authorize voluntary exchanges of lands of equal value and the voluntary exchange of shares of equal value whenever such exchange, in his judgment, is expedient and beneficial for or compatible with the proper consolidation of Indian lands and for the benefit of cooperative organizations.

SEC. 5. The Secretary of the Interior is hereby authorized, in his discretion, to acquire through purchase, relinquishment, gift, exchange, or assignment, any interest in lands, water rights or surface rights to lands, within or without existing reservations, including trust or otherwise restricted allotments whether the allottee be living or deceased, for the purpose of providing land for Indians.

For the acquisition of such lands, interests in lands, water rights, and surface rights, and for expenses incident to such acquisition, there is hereby authorized to be appropriated, out of any funds in the Treasury not otherwise appropriated, a sum not to exceed $2,000,000 in any one fiscal year: . . . .

The unexpended balances of any appropriations made pursuant to this section shall remain available until expended.

Title to any lands or rights acquired pursuant to this Act shall be taken in the name of the United States in trust for the Indian tribe or individual Indian for which the land is acquired, and such lands or rights shall be exempt from State and local taxation.

SEC. 6. The Secretary of the Interior is directed to make rules and regulations for the operation and management of Indian forestry units on the principle of sustained-yield management, to restrict the number of livestock grazed on Indian range units to the estimated carrying capacity of such ranges, and to promulgate such other rules and regulations as may be necessary to protect the range from deterioration, to prevent soil erosion, to assure full utilization of the range, and like purposes.

SEC. 7. The Secretary of the Interior is hereby authorized to proclaim new Indian reservations on lands acquired pursuant to any authority conferred by this Act, or to add such lands to existing reservations: *Provided*, That lands added to existing reserva-tions shall be designated for the exclusive use of Indians entitled by enrollment or by tribal membership to residence at such reservations.

SEC. 8. Nothing contained in this Act shall be construed to relate to Indian holdings of allotments or homesteads upon the public domain outside of the geographic boundaries of any Indian reservation now existing or established hereafter.

SEC. 9. There is hereby authorized to be appropriated, out of any funds in the Treasury not otherwise appropriated, such sums as may be necessary, but not to exceed $250,000 in any fiscal year, to be expended at the order of the Secretary of the Interior, in defraying the expenses of organizing Indian chartered corporations or other organizations created under this Act.

SEC. 10. There is hereby authorized to be appropriated, out of any funds in the Treasury not otherwise appropriated, the sum of $10,000,000 to be established as a revolving fund from which the Secretary of the Interior, under such rules and regulations as he may prescribe, may make loans to Indian chartered corporations for the purpose of promoting the economic development of such tribes and of their members, and may defray the expenses of administering such loans. Repayment of amounts loaned under this authorization shall be credited to the revolving fund and shall be available for the purposes for which the fund is established. A report shall be made annually to Congress of transactions under this authorization.

SEC. 11. There is hereby authorized to be appropriated, out of any funds in the United States Treasury not otherwise appropriated, a sum not to exceed $250,000 annually, together with any unexpended balances of previous appropriations made pursuant to this section, for loans to Indians for the payment of tuition and other expenses in recognized vocational and trade schools: *Provided*, That not more than $50,000 of such sum shall be available for loans to Indian students in high schools and colleges. Such loans shall be reimbursable under rules established by the Commissioner of Indian Affairs.

SEC. 12. The Secretary of the Interior is directed to establish standards of health, age, character, experience, knowledge, and ability for Indians who may be appointed, without regard to civil-service laws, to the various positions maintained, now or hereafter, by the Indian Office, in the administration of functions or services affecting any Indian tribe. Such qualified Indians shall hereafter have the preference to appointment to vacancies in any such positions.

SEC. 13. The provisions of this Act shall not apply to any of the Territories, colonies, or insular possessions of the United States, except that sections 9, 10, 11, 12, and 16, shall apply to the Territory of Alaska: *Provided*, That Sections 2, 4, 7, 16, 17, and 18 of this Act shall not apply to the following-named Indian tribes, the members of such Indian tribes, together with members of other tribes affiliated with such named tribes located in the State of Oklahoma, as follows: Cheyenne, Arapaho, Apache, Comanche, Kiowa, Caddo, Delaware, Wichita, Osage, Kaw, Otoe, Tonkawa, Pawnee, Ponca, Shawnee, Ottawa, Quapaw, Seneca, Wyandotte, Iowa, Sac and Fox, Kickapoo, Pottawatomi, Cherokee, Chickasaw, Choctaw, Creek, and Seminole. Section 4 of this Act shall not apply to the Indians of the Klamath Reservation in Oregon.

SEC. 14. [Special provisions regarding Sioux allotments.]

SEC. 15. Nothing in this Act shall be construed to impair or prejudice any claim or suit of any Indian tribe against the United States. It is hereby declared to be the intent of Congress that no expenditures for the benefit of Indians made out of appropriations authorized by this Act shall be considered as offsets in any suit brought to recover upon any claim of such Indians against the United States.

SEC. 16. Any Indian tribe, or tribes, residing on the same reservation, shall have the right to organize for its common welfare, and may adopt an appropriate constitution and bylaws, which shall become effective when ratified by a majority vote of the adult members of the tribe, or of the adult Indians residing on such reservation, as the case may be, at a special election authorized and called by the Secretary of the Interior under such rules and regulations as he may prescribe. Such constitution and bylaws when ratified as aforesaid and approved by the Secretary of the Interior shall be revocable by an election open to the same voters and conducted in the same manner as hereinabove provided. Amendments to the constitution and bylaws may be ratified and approved by the Secretary in the same manner as the original constitution and bylaws.

In addition to all powers vested in any Indian tribe or tribal council by existing law, the constitution adopted by said tribe shall also vest in such tribe or its tribal council the following rights and powers: To employ legal counsel, the choice of counsel and fixing of fees to be subject to the approval of the Secretary of the Interior; to prevent the sale, disposition, lease, or encumbrance of tribal lands, interests in lands, or other tribal assets without the consent of the tribe; and to negotiate with the Federal, State, and local Governments. The Secretary of the Interior shall advise such tribe or its tribal council of all appropriation estimates or Federal projects for the benefit of the tribe prior to the submission of such estimates to the Bureau of the Budget and the Congress.

SEC. 17. The Secretary of the Interior may, upon petition by at least one-third of the adult Indians, issue a charter of incorporation to such tribe: *Provided*, That such charter shall not become operative until ratified at a special election by a majority vote of the adult Indians living on the reservation. Such charter may convey to the incorporated tribe the power to purchase, take by gift, or bequest, or otherwise, own, hold, manage, operate, and dispose of property of every description, real and personal, including the power to purchase restricted Indian lands and to issue in exchange therefor interests in corporate property, and such further powers as may be incidental to the conduct of corporate business, not inconsistent with law, but no authority shall be granted to sell, mortgage, or lease for a period exceeding ten years any of the land included in the limits of the reservation. Any charter so issued shall not be revoked or surrendered except by Act of Congress.

SEC. 18. This Act shall not apply to any reservation wherein a majority of the adult Indians, voting at a special election duly called by the Secretary of the Interior, shall vote against its application. It shall be the duty of the Secretary of the Interior, within one year after the passage and approval of this Act, to call such an election which election shall be held by secret ballot upon thirty days' notice.

SEC. 19. The term "Indian" as used in this Act shall include all persons of Indian descent who are members of any recognized Indian tribe now under Federal jurisdiction, and all persons who are descendants of such members who were, on June 1, 1934, residing within the present boundaries of any Indian reservation and shall further include all other persons of one-half or more Indian blood. For the purposes of this Act, Eskimos and other aboriginal peoples of Alaska shall be considered Indians. The term "tribe" wherever used in this Act shall be construed to refer to any Indian tribe, organized band, pueblo, or the Indians residing on one reservation. The words "adult Indians" wherever used in this Act shall be construed to refer to Indians who have attained the age of twenty-one years.

[*U.S. Statutes at Large*, 48:984-88.]

139.   Indian Commissioner Collier on the Wheeler-Howard Act

Extract from the *Annual Report of the Commissioner of Indian Affairs*

1934

Commissioner John Collier, the architect of the policy embodied in the Wheeler-Howard Act, described and praised the act in his annual report of 1934.

. . . In the last paragraph of the Commissioner's annual report for 1933 it was stated:

If we can relieve the Indian of the unrealistic and fatal allotment system, if we can provide him with land and the means to work the land; if, through group organization and tribal incorporation, we can give him a real share in the management of his own affairs, he can develop normally in his own natural environment. The Indian problem as it exists today, including the heaviest and most unproductive administration costs of public service, has largely grown out of the allotment system which has destroyed the economic integrity of the Indian estate and deprived the Indians of normal economic and human activity.

The allotment system with its train of evil consequences was definitely abandoned as the backbone of the national Indian policy when Congress adopted and the President approved the Wheeler-Howard bill. The first section of this act in effect repeals the General Allotment Act of 1887. During numerous committee hearings, during several redrafts and modifications affecting every other part of the measure, this first section was never questioned or revised. It reached the President's desk in its original form without the change of a word or a comma, indicating that Congress was thoroughly convinced of the allotment system's complete failure and was eager to abandon it as the governing policy.

THE ACT'S TWOFOLD AIM

The Wheeler-Howard Act, the most important piece of Indian legislation since the eighties, not only ends the long, painful, futile effort to speed up the normal rate of Indian assimilation by individualizing tribal land and other capital assets, but it also endeavors to provide the means, statutory and financial, to repair as far as possible, the incalculable damage done by the allotment policy and its corollaries. Unfortunately, the beginning of the repair work had to be in large part postponed because the authorized appropriations could not be made by Congress after the passage of the act during the closing days of the session.

The repair work authorized by Congress under the terms of the act aims at both the economic and the spiritual rehabilitation of the Indian race. Congress and the President recognized that the cumulative loss of land brought about by the allotment system, a loss reaching 90,000,000 acres—two-thirds of the land heritage of the Indian race in 1887—had robbed the Indians in large part of the necessary basis for self-support. They clearly saw that this loss and the companion effort to break up all Indian tribal relations had condemned large numbers of Indians to become chronic recipients of charity; that the system of leasing individualized holdings had created many thousands of petty landlords unfitted to support themselves when their rental income vanished; that a major proportion of the red race was, therefore, ruined economically and pauperized spiritually.

ECONOMIC REHABILITATION–LAND PURCHASES

To meet this situation, the act authorized a maximum annual appropriation of $2,000,000 for the purchase of land for landless Indians. This maximum appropriation, even if continued over a term of years, will meet only the most pressing emergency-land needs of the Indians. It must be remembered that since 1887 the Indian race has lost the use of 90,000,000 acres, the cream of its land holding. With an annual appropriation of $2,000,000 and an average base price of $20 per acre, it would require 20 years to restore 2,000,000 acres for Indian use.

While Congress did not specifically direct the consolidation of Indian lands broken up and checkerboarded with white holdings in the allotment process, it authorized such consolidation and set up the machinery for it. Congress also authorized the establishment of new reservations for now completely landless and homeless Indians and directed that title to all newly purchased land should be taken in the name of the United States in trust for the Indian tribe or individual Indian, who will have the use and occupancy of the land. Thus the policy of common ownership of land enunciated in section 1 of the Wheeler-Howard Act is reaffirmed and implemented throughout the body of the statute.

Part of the effort at economic rehabilitation is the indefinite extension of all restrictions on the alienation of Indian trust lands as prescribed by section 2. However, this section merely locks the door out of which passed the valuable team of work horses, leaving the decrepit plug behind.

THE REVOLVING CREDIT-FUND

The sponsors of the General Allotment Act of 1887 believed that the division of the tribal land among the members of the tribe would create in the Indian the pride of individual ownership and induce him to make use of his own land for the support of his family. Overlooked entirely was the cold fact that capital in some form is needed to transform even a piece of the best raw land into a productive farm. Since the Indian's newly acquired private land could not legally be pledged as security for bank or private loans, it was the duty of the Federal Government to place at the disposal of its wards, credit in sufficient volume to meet their need for operating capital.

This imperative duty the Federal Government never recognized. Instead, it chose the easier road. It rapidly relaxed its restrictions on leasing. Lacking equipment for farming, the average Indian family proceeded to lease its land to white farmers or stockmen for cash. The leasing system, demoralizing to the Indians and contributing to the surplus of commercial farm products, spread like the Russian thistle. To this day the Indians who rely on the shrinking volume of lease money for their main support far outnumber those who farm their own allotted land.

What was true 50 years ago is true today. Without a reasonable amount of capital for permanent improvements, livestock, seed, implements, etc., the Indian owner of a piece of land cannot hope to make his living from the cultivation of the soil. To meet this pressing need, the Wheeler-Howard Act authorizes a revolving credit fund of $10,000,000.

This fund is to supply the long-term and short-term credit requirements of some 250,000 persons. Much of it must be tied up in long-term loans for sawmills, homes, and other improvements. Yet there is a huge demand for short-term loans to finance seasonal farm operations. The new lands to be bought for landless Indians must be improved and fenced, homes must be built, implements and seed acquired for the settlers, almost solely out of the revolving credit fund. In all probability the demands of the forthcoming year will demonstrate that it is inadequate.

THE HEIRSHIP-LAND PROBLEM

In the natural course of events, privately

226

owned Indian lands must on the death of the owner be divided among his heirs and, in turn, among the heirs of the heirs. This result of the allotment system brings about the forced sale of Indian heirship lands, usually to white buyers. If there are no buyers, the heirship land must be leased and the proceeds distributed among the numerous heirs at an expense out of all proportion to the size of the gross revenue.

The Wheeler-Howard Act is taking the first hesitant step toward the solution of this problem. The new law, while allowing Indian owners to leave or devise their restricted land to any member of the tribe or to their heirs regardless of tribal affiliations in accordance with applicable State or Federal laws, bars the owners or heirs from selling restricted Indian lands to anyone except the tribe or the tribal corporation in the jurisdiction of which the land is located.

Obviously this negative provision, inapplicable in Oklahoma and on the Klamath Reservation, does not solve the problem. Some 7,000,000 acres are now in the heirship status; the acreage is increasing every month. The tribes have not the money with which to purchase this land. At only $5 per acre, it would require $35,000,000 to reacquire this land; the maximum authorized appropriation for 17½ years would be needed to return the land now in the heirship status for tribal use.

If the problem is to be solved within a reasonable time, the cooperation of the allottees and heirs must be had. They must learn that for the sake of their race and of their children they should voluntarily transfer the title to their individual holdings to the tribe or to the tribal corporation, receiving in return the same rights as they enjoy now; namely, the right to use and occupy the land and its improvements, to receive the income from the land and to leave the same rights to their children, except that the children and other heirs could not cut up the land into small, unusable pieces.

Where the land in process of inheritance has already been so divided among numerous heirs, they will have the opportunity to return the small parcels to the tribe or tribal corporation, receiving interests in the corporate property in exchange. Thus the tribe would acquire title to now unusable land which, after consolidation, could be assigned for the use of interest-holders in tracts of usable size.

SPIRITUAL REHABILITATION

Through 50 years of "individualization", coupled with an ever-increasing amount of arbitrary supervision over the affairs of individuals and tribes so long as these individuals and tribes had any assets left, the Indians have been robbed of initiative, their spirit has been broken, their health undermined, and their native pride ground into the dust. The efforts at economic rehabilitation cannot and will not be more than partially successful unless they are accompanied by a determined simultaneous effort to rebuild the shattered morale of a subjugated people that has been taught to believe in its racial inferiority.

The Wheeler-Howard Act provides the means of destroying this inferiority complex, through those features which authorize and legalize tribal organization and incorporation, which give these tribal organizations and corporations limited but real power, and authority over their own affairs, which broaden the educational opportunities for Indians, and which give Indians a better chance to enter the Indian Service.

Even before the passage of the Wheeler-Howard bill a great spiritual stirring had become noticeable throughout the Indian country. That awakening of the racial spirit must be sustained, if the rehabilitation of the Indian people is to be successfully carried through. It is necessary to face the fact that pauperization, as the result of a century of spoliation, suppression, and paternalism, has made deep inroads. Of necessity it will take time, patience, and intelligent, sympathetic help to rebuild the Indian character where it has been broken down.

The first step in this rebuilding process must be the reorganization of the tribes, authorized by the Wheeler-Howard Act. In the past they managed their own affairs effectively whenever there was no white interference for selfish ends. They can learn to do it again under present conditions with the aid of modern organization methods, once they realize that these organizations will be permanent and will not be subject to the whims of changing administrations. These organizations, both tribal and corporate, will make many initial mistakes; there will be many complaints against shouldering the load of responsibility that accompanies authority. The task of organizing and incorporating the tribes will be difficult and laborious, calling for the maximum amount of skill, tact, firmness, and understanding on the part of the organizers. But the result should be the development of Indian leadership capable of making the Indian tribal organizations and corporations function effectively with a minimum of governmental interference.

OKLAHOMA TRIBES PENALIZED

It is to be regretted that the Oklahoma tribes, containing almost one-third of the Indians of the United States, should have been excluded by Congress from many of the important provisions of the Wheeler-Howard Act. Through this exclusion the Oklahoma Indians lose the benefit of section 2, which automatically extends the protective trust period on all restricted land; no new reservations can be established in Oklahoma; Oklahoma tribes cannot organize under the new act, nor can they form tribal corporations. Because they are denied the incorporation privilege, they cannot receive loans from the revolving credit fund, which loans can be made only to tribal corporations. It is hoped that Congress will amend the act so as to extend all of the

benefits of the legislation to all Oklahoma Indians.

LAW AND ORDER

The entire title creating a special court of Indian affairs was omitted and consideration of this subject adjourned until the next Congress. In view of the chaotic state of Indian law enforcement, it is important that this subject be given adequate consideration and that early remedial action be had.

INDIAN CLAIMS

Section 15 of the Wheeler-Howard Act declares that nothing in the statute shall prejudice or impair any Indian claim or suit against the United States. But this declaration does not cure the situation created by the snail-like pace of the hundreds of suits and claims by Indians against the Government. While these suits and claims remain unsettled, they will be used by designing white persons to prejudice the Indian mind against the Government, to raise false hopes of recovering fabulous sums, and by these hopes to make more difficult the task of getting the Indians to face reality and to strive in earnest to help themselves. It is hoped that the next Congress will enact legislation designed finally to settle all Indian claims in the shortest possible time. . . .

[*Annual Report of the Secretary of the Interior, 1934*, pp. 78-83.]

140.   Indian Arts and Crafts Board
August 27, 1935

Congress in 1935 authorized a special board to promote the development of Indian arts and crafts. This was an action urged by John Collier.

An Act To promote the development of Indian arts and crafts and to create a board to assist therein, and for other purposes.

Be it enacted . . . , That a board is hereby created in the Department of the Interior to be known as "Indian Arts and Crafts Board," and hereinafter referred to as the Board. The Board shall be composed of five commissioners, who shall be appointed by the Secretary of the Interior as soon as pos-

sible after the passage of this Act and shall continue in office, two for a term of two years, one for a term of three years, and two for a term of four years from the date of their appointment, the term of each to be designated by the Secretary of the Interior, but their successors shall be appointed for a term of four years except that any person chosen to fill a vacancy shall be appointed for the unexpired term of the commissioner whom he succeeds. Both public officers and private citizens shall be eligible for membership on the Board. The Board shall elect one of the commissioners as chairman. One or two vacancies on the Board shall not impair the right of the remaining commissioners to exercise all the powers of the Board.

The commissioners shall serve without compensation: *Provided,* That each Commissioner shall be reimbursed for all actual expenses, including travel expenses, subsistence and office overhead, which the Board shall certify to have been incurred as properly incidental to the performance of his duties as a member of the Board.

SEC. 2. It shall be the function and the duty of the Board to promote the economic welfare of the Indian tribes and the Indian wards of the Government through the development of Indian arts and crafts and the expansion of the market for the products of Indian art and craftsmanship. In the execution of this function the Board shall have the following powers: (a) To undertake market research to determine the best opportunity for the sale of various products; (b) to engage in technical research and give technical advice and assistance; (c) to engage in experimentation directly or through selected agencies; (d) to correlate and encourage the activities of the various governmental and private agencies in the field; (e) to offer assistance in the management of operating groups for the furtherance of specific projects; (f) to make recommendations to appropriate agencies for loans in furtherance of the production and sale of Indian products; (g) to create Government trade marks of genuineness and quality for Indian products and the products of particular Indian tribes or groups; to establish standards and regulations for the use of such trade marks; to license corporations, associations, or individuals to use them; and to charge a fee for their use; to register them in the United States Patent Office without charge; (h) to employ executive officers, including a general manager, and such other permanent and temporary personnel as may be found necessary, and prescribe the authorities, duties, responsibilities, and tenure and fix the compensation of such officers and other employ-ees . . . ; (i) as a Government agency to negotiate and execute in its own name contracts with operating groups to supply management, personnel, and supervision at cost, and to negotiate and execute in its own name such other contracts and to carry on such other business as may be necessary for the accomplishment of the duties and purposes of the Board: *Provided,* That nothing in the foregoing enumeration of powers shall be construed to authorize the Board to borrow or lend money or to deal in Indian goods. . . .

SEC. 5. Any person who shall counterfeit or colorably imitate any Government trade mark used or devised by the Board as provided in section 2 of this Act, or shall, except as authorized by the Board, affix any such Government trade mark, or shall knowingly, willfully, and corruptly affix any reproduction, counterfeit, copy, or colorable imitation thereof upon any products, Indian or otherwise, or to any labels, signs, prints, packages, wrappers, or receptacles intended to be used upon or in connection with the sale of such products, or any person who shall knowingly make any false statement for the purpose of obtaining the use of any such Government trade mark, shall be guilty of a misdemeanor, and upon conviction thereof shall be enjoined from further carrying on the act or acts complained of and shall be subject to a fine not exceeding $2,000, or imprisonment not exceeding six months, or both such fine and imprisonment.

SEC. 6. Any person who shall willfully offer or display for sale any goods, with or without any Government trade mark, as Indian products or Indian products of a particular Indian tribe or group, resident within the United States or the Territory of Alaska, when such person knows such goods are not Indian products or are not Indian products of the particular Indian tribe or group, shall be guilty of a misdemeanor and be subject to a fine not exceeding $2,000 or imprisonment not exceeding six months, or both such fine and imprisonment. . . .

[*U.S. Statutes at Large,* 49:891-93.]

229

141. Oklahoma Indian Welfare Act
June 26, 1936

In 1936 Congress extended the principles of the Wheeler-Howard Act to the Indians living in Oklahoma.

An Act To promote the general welfare of the Indians of the State of Oklahoma, and for other purposes.

Be it enacted . . . , That the Secretary of the Interior is hereby authorized, in his discretion, to acquire by purchase, relinquishment, gift, exchange, or assignment, any interest in lands, water rights, or surface rights to lands, within or without existing Indian reservations, including trust or otherwise restricted lands now in Indian ownership: *Provided*, That such lands shall be agricultural and grazing lands of good character and quality in proportion to the respective needs of the particular Indian or Indians for whom such purchases are made. Title to all lands so acquired shall be taken in the name of the United States, in trust for the tribe, band, group, or individual Indian for whose benefit such land is so acquired, and while the title thereto is held by the United States said lands shall be free from any and all taxes, save that the State of Oklahoma is authorized to levy and collect a gross-production tax, not in excess of the rate applied to production from lands in private ownership, upon all oil and gas produced from said lands, which said tax the Secretary of the Interior is hereby authorized and directed to cause to be paid.

SEC. 2. Whenever any restricted Indian land or interests in land, other than sales or leases of oil, gas, or other minerals therein, are offered for sale, pursuant to the terms of this or any other Act of Congress, the Secretary of the Interior shall have a preference right, in his discretion, to purchase the same for or in behalf of any other Indian or Indians of the same or any other tribe, at a fair valuation to be fixed by the appraisement satisfactory to the Indian owner or owners, or if offered for sale at auction said Secretary shall have a preference right, in his discretion, to purchase the same for or in behalf of any other Indian or Indians by meeting the highest bid otherwise offered therefor.

SEC. 3. Any recognized tribe or band of Indians residing in Oklahoma shall have the right to organize for its common welfare and to adopt a constitution and bylaws, under such rules and regulations as the Secretary of the Interior may prescribe. The Secretary of the Interior may issue to any such organized group a charter of incorporation, which shall become operative when ratified by a majority vote of the adult members of the organization voting: *Provided, however*, That such election shall be void unless the total vote cast be at least 30 per centum of those entitled to vote. Such charter may convey to the incorporated group, in addition to any powers which may properly be vested in a body corporate under the laws of the State of Oklahoma, the right to participate in the revolving credit fund and to enjoy any other rights or privileges secured to an organized Indian tribe under the Act of June 18, 1934 (48 Stat. 984): *Provided*, That the corporate funds of any such chartered group may be deposited in any national bank within the State of Oklahoma or otherwise invested, utilized, or disbursed in accordance with the terms of the corporate charter.

SEC. 4. Any ten or more Indians, as determined by the official tribal rolls, or Indian descendants of such enrolled members, or Indians as defined in the Act of June 18, 1934 (48 Stat. 984), who reside within the State of Oklahoma in convenient proximity to each other may receive from the Secretary of the Interior a charter as a local cooperative association for any one or more of the following purposes: Credit administration, production, marketing, consumers' protection, or land management. The provisions of this Act, the regulations of the Secretary of the Interior, and the charters of the cooperative associations issued pursuant thereto shall govern such cooperative associations: *Provided*, That in those matters not covered by said Act, regulations, or charters, the laws of the State of Oklahoma, if applicable, shall govern. In any stock or nonstock cooperative association no one member shall have more than one vote, and membership therein shall be open to all Indians residing within the prescribed district.

SEC. 5. [Regulations concerning suits involving such cooperative associations]

SEC. 6. The Secretary is authorized to make loans to individual Indians and to associations or corporate groups organized pursuant to this Act. For the making of such loans and for expenses of the cooperative associations organized pursuant to this Act, there shall be appropriated, out of the Treasury of the United States, the sum of $2,000,000.

SEC. 7. All funds appropriated under the several grants of authority contained in the Act of June 18, 1934 (48 Stat. 984), are hereby made available for use under the provisions of this Act, and Oklahoma Indians shall be accorded and allocated a fair and just share of any and all funds hereafter appropriated under the authorization herein set forth: *Provided*, That any royalties, bonuses, or other revenues derived from mineral deposits underlying lands purchased in Oklahoma under the authority granted by this Act, or by the Act of June 18, 1934, shall be deposited in the Treasury of the United States, and such revenues are hereby made available for expenditure by the Secretary of the Interior for the acquisition of lands and for loans to Indians in Oklahoma as authorized by this Act and by the Act of June 18, 1934 (48 Stat. 984).

SEC. 8. This Act shall not relate to or affect Osage County, Oklahoma. . . .

[*U.S. Statutes at Large*, 49:1967-68.]

142. Indian Claims Commission Act
August 13, 1946

The difficulty encountered by Indian tribes seeking suits against the United States in the Court of Claims led eventually to the formation of the Indian Claims Commission, a special tribunal to handle Indian claims. Originally established for ten years, the commission's life has been periodically extended.

An Act To create an Indian Claims Commission, to provide for the powers, duties, and functions thereof, and for other purposes.

Be it enacted . . . , That there is hereby created and established an Indian Claims Commission, hereafter referred to as the Commission.

SEC. 2. The Commission shall hear and determine the following claims against the United States on behalf of any Indian tribe, band, or other identifiable group of American Indians residing within the territorial limits of the United States or Alaska: (1) claims in law or equity arising under the Constitution, laws, treaties of the United States, and Executive orders of the President; (2) all other claims in law or equity, including those sounding in tort, with respect to which the claimant would have been entitled to sue in a court of the United States if the United States was subject to suit; (3) claims which would result if the treaties, contracts, and agreements between the claimant and the United States were revised on the ground of fraud, duress, unconscionable consideration, mutual or unilateral mistake, whether of law or fact, or any other ground cognizable by a court of equity; (4) claims arising from the taking by the United States, whether as the result of a treaty of cession or otherwise, of lands owned or occupied by the claimant without the payment for such lands of compensation agreed to by the claimant; and (5) claims based upon fair and honorable dealings that are not recognized by any existing rule of law or equity. No claim accruing after the date of the approval of this Act shall be considered by the Commission.

All claims hereunder may be heard and determined by the Commission notwithstanding any statute of limitations or laches, but all other defenses shall be available to the United States.

In determining the quantum of relief the Commission shall make appropriate deductions for all payments made by the United States on the claim, and for all other offsets, counterclaims, and demands that would be allowable in a suit brought in the Court of Claims under section 145 of the Judicial Code (36 Stat. 1136; 28 U.S.C. sec. 250), as amended; the Commission may also inquire

231

into and consider all money or property given to or funds expended gratuitously for the benefit of the claimant and if it finds that the nature of the claim and the entire course of dealings and accounts between the United States and the claimant in good conscience warrants such action, may set off all or part of such expenditures against any award made to the claimant, except that it is hereby declared to be the policy of Congress that monies spent for the removal of the claimant from one place to another at the request of the United States, or for agency or other administrative, educational, health or highway purposes, or for expenditures made prior to the date of the law, treaty or Executive Order under which the claim arose, or for expenditures made pursuant to the Act of June 18, 1934 (48 Stat. 984), save expenditures made under section 5 of that Act, or for expenditures under any emergency appropriation or allotment made subsequent to March 4, 1933, and generally applicable throughout the United States for relief in stricken agricultural areas, relief from distress caused by unemployment and conditions resulting therefrom, the prosecution of public work and public projects for the relief of unemployment or to increase employment, and for work relief (including the Civil Works Program) shall not be a proper offset against any award. . . .

SEC. 10. Any claim within the provisions of this Act may be presented to the Commission by any member of an Indian tribe, band, or other identifiable group of Indians as the representative of all its members; but wherever any tribal organization exists, recognized by the Secretary of the Interior as having authority to represent such tribe, band, or group, such organization shall be accorded the exclusive privilege of representing such Indians, unless fraud, collusion, or laches on the part of such organization be shown to the satisfaction of the Commission. . . .

SEC. 13. (a) As soon as practicable the Commission shall send a written explanation of the provisions of this Act to the recognized head of each Indian tribe and band, and to any other identifiable groups of American Indians existing as distinct entities, residing within the territorial limits of the United States and Alaska, and to the superintendents of all Indian agencies, who shall promulgate the same, and shall request that a detailed statement of all claims be sent to the Commission, together with the names of aged or invalid Indians from whom depositions should be taken immediately and a summary of their proposed testimonies. . . .

SEC. 14. The Commission shall have the power to call upon any of the departments of the Government for any information it may deem necessary, and shall have the use of all records, hearings, and reports made by the committees of each House of Congress, when deemed necessary in the prosecution of its business.

At any hearing held hereunder, any official letter, paper, document, map, or record in the possession of any officer or department, or court of the United States or committee of Congress (or a certified copy thereof), may be used in evidence insofar as relevant and material, including any deposition or other testimony of record in any suit or proceeding in any court of the United States to which an Indian or Indian tribe or group was a party, and the appropriate department of the Government of the United States shall give to the attorneys for all tribes or groups full and free access to such letters, papers, documents, maps, or records as may be useful to said attorneys in the preparation of any claim instituted hereunder, and shall afford facilities for the examination of the same and, upon written request by said attorneys, shall furnish certified copies thereof.

SEC. 15. Each such tribe, band, or other identifiable group of Indians may retain to represent its interests in the presentation of claims before the Commission an attorney or attorneys at law, of its own selection, whose practice before the Commission shall be regulated by its adopted procedure. The fees of such attorney or attorneys for all services rendered in prosecuting the claim in question, whether before the Commission or otherwise, shall, unless the amount of such fees is stipulated in the approved contract between the attorney or attorneys and the claimant, be fixed by the Commission at such amount as the Commission, in accordance with standards obtaining for prosecuting similar contingent claims in courts of law, finds to be adequate compensation for services rendered and results obtained, considering the contingent nature of the case, plus all reasonable expenses incurred in the prosecution of the claim; but the amount so fixed by the Commission, exclusive of reimbursements for actual expenses, shall not exceed 10 per centum of the amount recovered in any case. . . .

The Attorney General or his assistants shall represent the United States in all claims presented to the Commission. . . .

[*U.S. Statutes at Large*, 60:1049-56.]

143. House Concurrent Resolution 108
August 1, 1953

In the Eighty-third Congress a fundamental change was made in Indian policy. House Concurrent Resolution 108 declared it to be the policy of the United States to abolish federal supervision over the tribes as soon as possible and to subject the Indians to the same laws, privileges, and responsibilities as other citizens of the United States. As a result of this resolution the government began the process of "termination," which aroused strong opposition on the part of the Indians.

Whereas it is the policy of Congress, as rapidly as possible, to make the Indians within the territorial limits of the United States subject to the same laws and entitled to the same privileges and responsibilities as are applicable to other citizens of the United States, to end their status as wards of the United States, and to grant them all of the rights and prerogatives pertaining to American citizenship; and Whereas the Indians within the territorial limits of the United States should assume their full responsibilities as American citizens: Now, therefore, be it

Resolved by the House of Representatives (the Senate concurring),

That it is declared to be the sense of Congress that, at the earliest possible time, all of the Indian tribes and the individual members thereof located within the States of California, Florida, New York, and Texas, and all of the following named Indian tribes and individual members thereof, should be freed from Federal supervision and control and from all disabilities and limitations spe-cially applicable to Indians: The Flathead Tribe of Montana, the Klamath Tribe of Oregon, the Menominee Tribe of Wisconsin, the Potowatamie Tribe of Kansas and Nebraska, and those members of the Chippewa Tribe who are on the Turtle Mountain Reservation, North Dakota. It is further declared to be the sense of Congress that, upon the release of such tribes and individual members thereof from such disabilities and limitations, all offices of the Bureau of Indian Affairs in the States of California, Florida, New York, and Texas and all other offices of the Bureau of Indian Affairs whose primary purpose was to serve any Indian tribe or individual Indian freed from Federal supervision should be abolished. It is further declared to be the sense of Congress that the Secretary of the Interior should examine all existing legislation dealing with such Indians, and treaties between the Government of the United States and each such tribe, and report to Congress at the earliest practicable date, but not later than January 1, 1954, his recommendations for such legislation as, in his judgment, may be necessary to accomplish the purposes of this resolution.

[*U.S. Statutes at Large*, 67:B132.]

144. Public Law 280
August 15, 1953

Tribal self-determination and tribal relations with the federal government were significantly changed by Public Law 280 of the Eighty-third Congress, which extended state jurisdiction over offenses committed by or against Indians in the Indian country.

233

An Act To confer jurisdiction on the States of California, Minnesota, Nebraska, Oregon, and Wisconsin, with respect to criminal offenses and civil causes of action committed or arising on Indian reservations within such States, and for other purposes.

. . . . SEC. 2. Title 18, United States Code, is hereby amended by inserting in chapter 53 thereof immediately after section 1161 a new section, to be designated as section 1162, as follows:

"§1162. State jurisdiction over offenses committed by or against Indians in the Indian country

"(a) Each of the States listed in the following table shall have jurisdiction over offenses committed by or against Indians in the areas of Indian country listed opposite the name of the State to the same extent that such State has jurisdiction over offenses committed elsewhere within the State, and the criminal laws of such State shall have the same force and effect within such Indian country as they have elsewhere within the State:

"State of	Indian country affected
California	. . . . . All Indian country within the State
Minnesota	. . . . All Indian country within the State, except the Red Lake Reservation
Nebraska	. . . . . . All Indian country within the State
Oregon	. . . . All Indian country within the State, except the Warm Springs Reservation
Wisconsin	. . . . All Indian country within the State, except the Menominee Reservation

"(b) Nothing in this section shall authorize the alienation, encumbrance, or taxation of any real or personal property, including water rights, belonging to any Indian or any Indian tribe, band, or community that is held in trust by the United States or is subject to a restriction against alienation imposed by the United States; or shall authorize regulation of the use of such property in a manner inconsistent with any Federal treaty, agreement, or statute or with any regulation made pursuant thereto; or shall deprive any Indian or any Indian tribe, band, or community of any right, privilege, or immunity afforded under Federal treaty, agreement, or statute with respect to hunting, trapping, or fishing or the control, licensing, or regulation thereof. . . ."

[U.S. Statutes at Large, 67:588-90.]

145. Termination of the Menominee Indians

June 17, 1954

The Menominee Indians of Wisconsin were one of the tribes to feel the effects of the termination policy. In 1954 Congress provided for the withdrawal of federal jurisdiction from the tribe, although the law did not take final effect until 1961. After tremendous outcry against the termination policy, the Menominee action was reversed in 1973.

An Act To provide for a per capita distribution of Menominee tribal funds and authorize the withdrawal of the Menominee Tribe from Federal jurisdiction.

Be it enacted . . . , That the purpose of this Act is to provide for orderly termination of Federal supervision over the property and members of the Menominee Indian Tribe of Wisconsin.

SEC. 2. For the purposes of the Act—
(a) "Tribe" means the Menominee Indian Tribe of Wisconsin;

(b) "Secretary" means the Secretary of the Interior.

SEC. 3. At midnight of the date of enactment of this Act the roll of the tribe maintained pursuant to the Act of June 15, 1934 (48 Stat. 965), as amended by the Act of July 14, 1939 (53 Stat. 1003), shall be closed and no child born thereafter shall be eligible for enrollment: *Provided*, That applicants for enrollment in the tribe shall have three months from the date the roll is closed in which to submit applications for enrollment: *Provided*

234

further, That the tribe shall have three months thereafter in which to approve or disapprove any application for enrollment: *Provided further*, That any applicant whose application is not approved by the tribe within six months from the date of enactment of this Act may, within three months thereafter, file with the Secretary an appeal from the failure of the tribe to approve his application or from the disapproval of his application, as the case may be. The decision of the Secretary on such appeal shall be final and conclusive. When the Secretary has made decisions on all appeals, he shall issue and publish in the Federal Register a Proclamation of Final Closure of the roll of the tribe and the final roll of the members. Effective upon the date of such proclamation, the rights or beneficial interests of each person whose name appears on the roll shall constitute personal property and shall be evidenced by a certificate of beneficial interest which shall be issued by the tribe. Such interests shall be distributable in accordance with the laws of the State of Wisconsin. Such interests shall be alienable only in accordance with such regulations as may be adopted by the tribe.

SEC. 4. Section 6 of the Act of June 15, 1934 (48 Stat. 965, 966) is hereby repealed.

SEC. 5. The Secretary is authorized and directed, as soon as practicable after the passage of this Act, to pay from such funds as are deposited to the credit of the tribe in the Treasury of the United States $1,500 to each member of the tribe on the rolls of the tribe on the date of the Act. Any other person whose application for enrollment on the rolls of the tribe is subsequently approved, pursuant to the terms of section 3 hereof, shall, after enrollment, be paid a like sum of $1,500: *Provided*, That such payments shall be made first from any funds on deposit in the Treasury of the United States to the credit of the Menominee Indian Tribe drawing interest at the rate of 5 per centum, and thereafter from the Menominee judgment fund, symbol 14X7142.

SEC. 6. The tribe is authorized to select and retain the services of qualified management specialists, including tax consultants, for the purpose of studying industrial programs on the Menominee Reservation and making such reports or recommendations, including appraisals of Menominee tribal property, as may be desired by the tribe, and to make other studies and reports as may be deemed necessary and desirable by the tribe in connection with the termination of Federal supervision as provided for hereinafter. Such reports shall be completed not later than December 31, 1957. Such specialists are to be retained under contracts entered into between them and authorized representatives of the tribe, subject to approval by the Secretary. Such amounts of Menominee tribal funds as may be required for this purpose shall be made available by the Secretary.

SEC. 7. The tribe shall formulate and submit to the Secretary a plan or plans for the future control of the tribal property and service functions now conducted by or under the supervision of the United States, including, but not limited to, services in the fields of health, education, welfare, credit, roads, and law and order. The Secretary is authorized to provide such reasonable assistance as may be requested by officials of the tribe in the formulation of the plan or plans heretofore referred to, including necessary consultations with representatives of Federal departments and agencies, officials of the State of Wisconsin and political subdivisions thereof, and members of the tribe: *Provided*, That the responsibility of the United States to furnish all such supervision and services to the tribe and to the members thereof, because of their status as Indians, shall cease on December 31, 1958, or on such earlier date as may be agreed upon by the tribe and the Secretary.

SEC. 8. The Secretary is hereby authorized and directed to transfer to the tribe, on December 31, 1958, or on such earlier date as may be agreed upon by the tribe and the Secretary, the title to all property, real and personal, held in trust by the United States for the tribe: *Provided, however*, That if the tribe obtains a charter for a corporation or otherwise organizes under the laws of a State or of the District of Columbia for the purpose, among any others, of taking title to all tribal lands and assets and enterprises owned by the tribe or held in trust by the United States for the tribe, and requests such transfer to be made to such corporation or organization, the Secretary shall make such transfer to such corporation or organization.

SEC. 9. No distribution of the assets made under the provisions of this Act shall be subject to any Federal or State income tax: *Provided,* That so much of any cash distribution made hereunder as consists of a share of any interest earned on funds deposited in the Treasury of the United States pursuant to the Supplemental Appropriation Act, 1952 (65 Stat. 736, 754), shall not by virtue of this Act be exempt from individual income tax in the hands of the recipients for the year in which paid. Following any distribution of assets made under the provisions of this Act, such assets and any income derived therefrom in the hands of any individual, or any corporation or organization as provided in section 8 of this Act, shall be subject to the same taxes, State and Federal, as in the case of non-Indians, except that any valuation for purposes of Federal income tax on gains or losses shall take as the basis of the particular taxpayer the value of the property on the date title is transferred by the United States pursuant to section 8 of this Act.

SEC. 10. When title to the property of the tribe has been transferred, as provided in section 8 of this Act, the Secretary shall publish in the Federal Register an appropriate proclamation of that fact. Thereafter individual members of the tribe shall not be entitled to any of the services performed by the United States for Indians because of their status as Indians, all statutes of the United States which affect Indians because of their status as Indians shall no longer be applicable to the members of the tribe, and the laws of the several States shall apply to the tribe and its members in the same manner as they apply to other citizens or persons within their jurisdiction. Nothing in this Act shall affect the status of the members of the tribe as citizens of the United States.

SEC. 11. Prior to the transfer pursuant to section 8 of this Act, the Secretary shall protect the rights of members of the tribe who are less than eighteen years of age, non compos mentis, or in the opinion of the Secretary in need of assistance in conducting their affairs, by causing the appointment of guardians for such members in courts of competent jurisdiction, or by such other means as he may deem adequate.

SEC. 12. The Secretary is authorized and directed to promulgate such rules and regulations as are necessary to effectuate the purposes of this Act.

SEC. 13. If any provision of this Act, or the application thereof to any person or circumstance, is held invalid, the remainder of the Act and the application of such provision to other persons or circumstances shall not be affected thereby.

[*U.S. Statutes at Large,* 68:250-52.]

146. Transfer of Indian Health Services

August 5, 1954

In order to provide better health facilities for the Indians, hospitals and health care were transferred from the Bureau of Indian Affairs to the Public Health Service of the Department of Health, Education, and Welfare.

An Act To transfer the maintenance and operation of hospital and health facilities for Indians to the Public Health Service, and for other purposes.

Be it enacted . . . , That all functions, responsibilities, authorities, and duties of the Department of the Interior, the Bureau of Indian Affairs, Secretary of the Interior, and the Commissioner of Indian Affairs relating to the maintenance and operation of hospital and health facilities for Indians, and the conservation of the health of Indians, are hereby transferred to, and shall be administered by, the Surgeon General of the United States Public Health Service, under the supervision and direction of the Secretary of Health, Education, and Welfare: *Provided,* That hospitals now in operation for a specific tribe or tribes of Indians shall not be closed prior to July 1, 1956, without the consent of the governing body of the tribe or its organized council.

SEC. 2. Whenever the health needs of the Indians can be better met thereby, the Secretary of Health, Education, and Wel-

236

fare is authorized in his discretion to enter into contracts with any State, Territory, or political subdivision thereof, or any private nonprofit corporation, agency or institution providing for the transfer by the United States Public Health Service of Indian hospitals or health facilities, including initial operating equipment and supplies.

It shall be a condition of such transfer that all facilities transferred shall be available to meet the health needs of the Indians and that such health needs shall be given priority over those of the non-Indian population. No hospital or health facility that has been constructed or maintained for a specific tribe of Indians, or for a specific group of tribes, shall be transferred by the Secretary of Health, Education, and Welfare to a non-Indian entity or organization under this Act unless such action has been approved by the governing body of the tribe, or by the governing bodies of a majority of the tribes, for which such hospital or health facility has been constructed or maintained: *Provided,* That if, following such transfer by the United States Public Health Service, the Secretary of Health, Education, and Welfare finds the hospital or health facility transferred under this section is not thereafter serving the need of the Indians, the Secretary of Health, Education, and Welfare shall notify those charged with management thereof, setting forth needed improvements, and in the event such improvements are not made within a time to be specified, shall immediately assume management and operation of such hospital or health facility.

SEC. 3. The Secretary of Health, Education, and Welfare is also authorized to make such other regulations as he deems desirable to carry out the provisions of this Act. . . .

[*U.S. Statutes at Large*, 68:674.]

147. Relocation of Indians in Urban Areas
Extract from the *Annual Report of the Commissioner of Indian Affairs*
1954

The progress of the relocation policy, initiated in the 1950s to move Indians from the reservations to urban areas, was described optimistically by Commissioner of Indian Affairs Glenn L. Emmons in 1954.

. . . . During the 1954 fiscal year, 2,163 Indians were directly assisted to relocate under the Bureau's relocation program. This included 1,649 persons in over 400 family groups, and 514 unattached men and women. In addition, over 300 Indians left reservations without assistance to join relatives and friends who had been assisted to relocate. At their destination, Bureau Relocation Offices assisted this group also to adjust to the new community. The total number of relocations represented a substantial increase over relocations during previous fiscal year.

Of the 2,163 Indians assisted to relocate, financial assistance, to cover all or part of the costs of transportation to the place of relocation and short-term temporary subsistence, were provided to 1,637 Indians, in addition to relocation services. This number included 1,329 persons in over 300 family groups, and 308 unattached men and women. An additional 526 Indians, including 320 in approximately 100 family groups and 206 unattached men and women, were assisted to relocate without financial assistance, but were provided relocation services only. These services included counseling and guidance prior to relocation, and assistance in establishing residence and securing permanent employment in the new community.

In addition to the above-mentioned persons who were assisted to relocate, Bureau Relocation Offices assisted a number of Indian workers to secure employment which did not involve relocation, and cooperated with public employment offices and the Railroad Retirement Board in recruitment of Indians for temporary and seasonal work. However, in order to concentrate on providing relocation services, placement activities which do not involve relocation have been progressively decreased and responsibility for such placement activities has been largely left to established employment agencies.

237

In recognition of this emphasis, and following the recommendation of the survey team for the Bureau of Indian Affairs, the name of the former Branch of Placement and Relocation was changed during the year to the Branch of Relocation.

Approximately 54 percent of the Indians assisted to relocate came from 3 northern areas (Aberdeen, Billings, and Minneapolis), and 46 percent came from 4 southern areas (Anadarko, Gallup, Muskogee, and Phoenix). They went to 20 different States. The Los Angeles and Chicago metropolitan areas continued to be the chief centers of relocation.

On the reservations there was continued interest in relocation throughout the year. Relocation assistance funds were used up in almost every area, and at the end of the year there was a backlog of applications for relocation. Letters from relocated Indians to friends and relatives back on the reservation, describing their experiences and new standards of living, served to stimulate interest as did a decrease in employment opportunities in the vicinity of some of the reservations and a marked decrease in railroad employment.

There was a slight tightening of the labor market during part of the year. However, through intensive efforts on the part of field relocation offices, it was still possible to assure permanent types of employment to almost all qualified workers who requested assistance in settling away from reservations. Field relocation offices followed a policy of securing employment for Indians in diversified industries and with a large number of employers. This policy proved of great benefit when industrial disputes developed in certain industries on the west coast.

To adjust to changes in the labor market which reduced employment in military installations and certain Government projects, the field relocation office formerly located in Salt Lake City was transferred to Oakland, Calif., effective June 1.

The Chicago Field Relocation Office, in recognition of the needs of the growing number of relocatees in that city and in accordance with the Bureau policy of encouraging the development of non-Bureau facilities for Indians, assisted in the establishment of an All-Tribes American Indian Center in Chicago. This center raised its own funds, and under the directorship of a board composed almost entirely of Indians, began providing opportunities for Indian relocatees to meet, engage in social and recreational programs, exchange experiences, and assist each other. Its operations were completely independent of the Bureau. . . .

[*Annual Report of the Secretary of the Interior, 1954*, pp. 242-43.]

148. Senator Watkins on Termination Policy

May 1957

The principal congressional promoter of the termination policy was Senator Arthur V. Watkins of Utah. In an article published in 1957 he gave a clear statement of the policy and of the arguments for it.

Virtually since the first decade of our national life the Indian, as tribesman and individual, was accorded a status apart. Now, however, we think constructively and affirmatively of the Indian as a fellow American. We seek to assure that in health, education, and welfare, in social, political, economic, and cultural opportunity, he or she stands as one with us in the enjoyment and responsibilities of our national citizenship. It is particularly gratifying to know that recent years of united effort, mutual planning, and Indian self-appraisal truly have begun to bear increasing fruit.

One facet of this over-all development concerns the freeing of the Indians from special federal restrictions on the property and the person of the tribes and their members. This is not a novel development, but a natural outgrowth of our relationship with the Indians. Congress is fully agreed upon its accomplishment. By unanimous vote in both the Senate and the House of Representatives termination of such special federal supervision has been called for as soon as possible. . . .

A little more than two years ago—June 17, 1954—President Dwight D. Eisenhower signed a bill approved by the Eighty-third Congress that signified a landmark in Indian legislative history. By this measure's terms an Indian tribe and its members, the Menominee of Wisconsin, were assured that after a brief transition period they would at last have full control of their own affairs and would possess all of the attributes of complete American citizenship. This was a most worthy moment in our history. We should all dwell upon its deep meaning. Considering the lengthy span of our Indian relationship, the recency of this event is significant. Obviously, such affirmative action for the great majority of Indians has just begun. Moreover, it should be noted that the foundations laid are solid.

Philosophically speaking, the Indian wardship problem brings up basically the questionable merit of treating the Indian of today as an Indian, rather than as a fellow American citizen. Now, doing away with restrictive federal supervision over Indians, as such, does *not* affect the retention of those cultural and racial qualities which people of Indian descent would wish to retain; many of us are proud of our ancestral heritage, but that does not nor should it alter our status as American citizens. The distinction between abolishment of wardship and abandonment of the Indian heritage is vitally important. . . .

Unfortunately, the major and continuing Congressional movement toward full freedom was delayed for a time by the Indian Reorganization Act of 1934, the Wheeler-Howard Act. Amid the deep social concern of the depression years, Congress deviated from its accustomed policy under the concept of promoting the general Indian welfare. In the postdepression years Congress—realizing this change of policy—sought to return to the historic principles of much earlier decades. Indeed, one of the original authors of the Act was desirous of its repeal. We should recall, however, that war years soon followed in which Congress found itself engrossed in problems first of national defense and then of mutual security. As with many other major projects, action was thus delayed. . . .

We may admit the it-takes-time view, but we should not allow it to lull us into inaction.

Freedom of action for the Indian as a full-fledged citizen—that is the continuing aim. Toward this end Congress and the Administration, state and local governments, Indian tribes and members, interested private agencies, and individual Americans as responsible citizens should all be united and work constantly. The legislatively set target dates for Indian freedom serve as significant spurs to accomplishment. Congress steadily continues to inform itself, to seek out, delimit, and assist those Indians most able to profit immediately by freedom from special supervision, and it acts primarily to speed the day for all Indian tribes and members to be relieved of their wardship status. A basic purpose of Congress in setting up the Indian Claims Commission was to clear the way toward complete freedom of the Indians by assuring a final settlement of all obligations—real or purported—of the federal government to the Indian tribes and other groups. . . .

The basic principle enunciated so clearly and approved unanimously by the Senate and House in House Concurrent Resolution 108 of the Eighty-third Congress continues to be the over-all guiding policy of Congress in Indian affairs. In view of the historic policy of Congress favoring freedom for the Indians, we may well expect future Congresses to continue to indorse the principle that "as rapidly as possible" we should end the status of Indians as wards of the government and grant them all of the rights and prerogatives pertaining to American citizenship.

With the aim of "equality before the law" in mind our course should rightly be no other. Firm and constant consideration for those of Indian ancestry should lead us all to work diligently and carefully for the full realization of their national citizenship with all other Americans. Following in the footsteps of the Emancipation Proclamation of ninety-four years ago, I see the following words emblazoned in letters of fire above the heads of the Indians—*THESE PEOPLE SHALL BE FREE!*

[*Annals of the American Academy of Political and Social Science* 311 (May 1957): 47-50, 55. Reprinted with permission.]

149. Secretary of the Interior Seaton on Termination Policy
September 18, 1958

The first significant break in the termination policy of the federal government came in a radio speech made by Secretary of the Interior Fred A. Seaton in Flagstaff, Arizona, September 18, 1958. Seaton rejected termination without full consent of the Indians concerned.

. . . . On August 1, 1953, House Concurrent Resolution No. 108 was adopted expressing the sense of the Congress of the United States to be that of ending the wardship status of Indian tribes as rapidly as possible. Certain additional provisions applied to Indian tribes located in the States of California, Florida, New York, and Texas, and to some other tribes in other States, with relation to the earliest possible elimination of Federal control over their persons and properties.

This stands as the most recent congressional declaration upon the subject.

Since that time—that is since 1953—the pros and cons of public opinion relative to congressional policy on Indian affairs have been given wide expression in the press and in other media throughout the country. Some people have interpreted these statements to mean that it is the intention of Congress and the Department of the Interior to abandon Indian groups regardless of their ability to fend for themselves.

In my opinion, the stated intentions of the Congress to free Indian tribes from Federal supervision, and to eliminate the need for the special services rendered by the Bureau of Indian Affairs to Indian citizens, is more than adequately counterbalanced in the congressional resolution itself. I now refer you to such qualifying phrases as, and I quote, "at the earliest possible time," and "at the earliest practicable date." The intent is clear, I believe. What the Congress intended was to state an objective, not an immediate goal.

Just today I discussed that matter with Senator BARRY GOLDWATER, of Arizona, who tells me that his memory of the debate is very clear and that what I have said to you was, in his opinion, the intent of the Congress. If the resolution in any way lent itself to varied interpretation, and evidently it did in the minds of some people, the subsequently expressed policies of the Department of the Interior and the Bureau of Indian Affairs, as well as the actions of Congress itself since 1953, should place the national policy statement on Indian affairs in a clear perspective.

To be specific, my own position is this: no Indian tribe or group should end its relationship with the Federal Government unless such tribe or group has clearly demonstrated—first, that it understands the plan under which such a program would go forward, and second, that the tribe or group affected concurs in and supports the plan proposed.

Now, ladies and gentlemen, it is absolutely unthinkable to me as your Secretary of the Interior that consideration would be given to forcing upon an Indian tribe a so-called termination plan which did not have the understanding and acceptance of a clear majority of the members affected. Those tribes which have thus far sought to end their Federal wardship status have, in each instance, demonstrated their acceptance of the plan prior to action by the Congress. I shall continue to insist this be the case and I hope and believe that Congress and its leaders will pursue the same course. To make my position perfectly clear, as long as I am Secretary of the Interior, I shall be dedicated to preserving the principle which I have just enunciated.

I further believe the Commissioner of Indian Affairs tried to make the position of the Congress and the Department of the Interior clear when in the fall of 1953, he stated, and I quote, "We want to give the Indians the same opportunities for advancement—the same freedom and responsibility for the management of their properties—as have other American citizens." Then Mr. Emmons continued, "I know that there are some tribes which are ready and anxious to take over full responsibility for their own affairs at the earliest possible time, and that others will have to move along toward that objective much more slowly and gradually." He then added he recognized that in many areas there is a real need for a continuation of the trusteeship and will be for a span of years. And so it seems to me the intent has never been one of precipitating Indian groups into a position for which they were unprepared.

True enough, Indian groups can continue to exist as cultural islands in the midst of our national populations, isolated from the main group by language and custom, and living at standards far below those of the average American citizen. They can do this. In fact, many of them have done so for many years. But let me put this question to you: "Does the majority of the population of such tribes prefer to live in that manner, or does it do so because there seems to be no other choice? Or does it do so because there is no general awareness of the alternatives?" I believe the majority of our Indian citizens are as desirous and capable of exercising all of the duties and responsibilities of citizenship as are the rest of us, provided they have equal opportunities with their fellow citizens. And having said that, I want to add this: under no circumstances could I bring myself to recommend the termination of the Federal relationship with any Indian tribe in this country until the members of that tribe have been given the opportunity of a sound and effective education. To me it would be incredible, even criminal, to send any Indian tribe out into the stream of American life until and unless the educational level of that tribe was one which was equal to the responsibilities which it was shouldering. . . .

[*Congressional Record*, 105:3105.]

150. Native American Church v. Navajo Tribal Council
November 17, 1959

The Native American Church undertook action to enjoin enforcement of an ordinance of the Navajo tribal council which made it an offense to use peyote. The plaintiff argued that the ordinance violated the freedom of religion clause of the First Amendment. The United States Court of Appeals, Tenth Circuit, held that the First Amendment did not bind the tribal council even though its laws had an impact on forms of religious worship.

. . . . No law is cited and none has been found which undertakes to subject the Navajo tribe to the laws of the United States with respect to their internal affairs, such as police powers and ordinances passed for the purposes of regulating the conduct of the members of the tribe on the reservation. It follows that the Federal courts are without jurisdiction over matters involving purely penal ordinances passed by the Navajo legislative body for the regulation of life on the reservation.

But it is contended that the First Amendment to the United States Constitution applies to Indian nations and tribes as it does to the United States and to the States. It is, accordingly, argued that the ordinance in question violates the Indians' rights of religious freedom and freedom of worship guaranteed by the First Amendment. No case is cited and none has been found where the impact of the First Amendment, with respect to religious freedom and freedom of worship by members of the Indian tribes, has been before the court. . . .

The First Amendment applies only to Congress. It limits the powers of Congress to interfere with religious freedom or religious worship. It is made applicable to the States only by the Fourteenth Amendment. Thus construed, the First Amendment places limitations upon the action of Congress and of the States. But as declared in the decisions hereinbefore discussed, Indian tribes are not states. They have a status higher than that of states. They are subordinate and dependent nations possessed of all powers as such only to the extent that they have expressly been required to surrender them by the superior sovereign, the United States. The Constitution is, of course, the supreme law of the land, but it is nonetheless a part of the laws of the United States. Under the philosophy of the decisions, it, as any other law, is binding upon Indian nations only where it expressly binds them, or is made binding by treaty or some act of Congress. No provision in the Constitution makes the First Amendment applicable to Indian nations nor is there any law of Congress doing so. It follows that neither, under the Constitution or the laws of Congress, do the Federal courts have jurisdiction of tribal laws or regulations, even though they may have an impact to some extent on forms of religious worship.

[272 *Federal Reports*, 2d series, 131, 134-35.]

151. A Program for Indian Citizens
January 1961

The private Commission on the Rights, Liberties, and Responsibilities of the American Indian, established in 1957 by the Fund for the Republic, published a summary report in 1961. The report was one of a number of prominent statements urging new attention to Indian wishes. The first section, printed here, dealt with Indian values. Other sections discussed termination, economic development, tribal government, education, health, and the Bureau of Indian Affairs. A final report was published in 1966, entitled The Indian: America's Unfinished Business.

INDIAN VALUES AND ATTITUDES

INTRODUCTION

The Indian himself should be the focus of all government policy affecting him. Money, land, education, and technical assistance are to be considered only as means to an end: on the one hand, that of restoring the Indian's pride of origin and faith in himself—a faith undermined by years of political and economic dependence on the Federal government; on the other, the arousing of a desire to share in the benefits of modern civilization. These are deeply human considerations. If neglected, they will defeat the best-intentioned of government plans.

To encourage pride in Indianness is not to turn back the clock. On the contrary, it is to recognize that the United States policy has hitherto failed to use this vital factor effectively as a force for assimilation and for enriching American culture. As a result, Indians who have already entered the dominant society have generally disdained their historic background, drawing away from it as though ashamed. Instead of serving as a bridge to enable others to move freely between the two worlds, they have too often interpreted their heritage imperfectly to the majority race and have proved useless in explaining their adopted culture to their own people. Only men who have a foot in each way of life and an appreciation of both can effectively lessen the gap which divides the two and thus cross-fertilize both.

No program imposed from above can serve as a substitute for one willed by Indians themselves. Nor is their mere consent to a plan to be taken as sufficient. Such "consent" may be wholly passive, representing a submission to the inevitable, or it may be obtained without their full understanding or before they are either able or willing to shoulder unfamiliar responsibilities. What is essential is to elicit their own initiative and intelligent cooperation.

While emphasis should as hitherto be put on fitting Indian youth for its new opportunities and responsibilities, we yet must not dismiss the old Indian culture as being necessarily a barrier to change. In their society and in their religion, Indians believe they have values worth preserving. These are sometimes stated in mystical terms and, if related to the Supreme Being, are sometimes kept secret. Nonetheless they exist. Two examples out of many involve their idea of unity and their reverence for Mother Earth.

Unity is evidenced by the individual's voluntarily working with the community of which he is a part. He gives his strength and help to perpetuate the traditional culture. Cohesion is also furthered in many tribes by a veneration for elders and reliance on their wisdom. Status as well as personal security is often gained by service. Conversely, the pattern of sinking self into the group tends to discourage competitiveness or a pride in the possession of material objects for their monetary value. This complex of attitudes is perhaps one of the reasons for the improvidence of many Indians. Since ideals, however, are not consistently achieved, exceptions to the norm are found in every group.

The spiritual attachment to nature, an essential aspect of many pre-Columbian cultures, has brought the Indian into an intimate accord with the elements. This appears strikingly evident in the Indian attitude toward land. Land is believed to be part of a benevolent mother and, like her, vital to life. Among Indian tribes it was generally considered to be not a merchantable product but one the user had the natural right to enjoy. These attitudes and the attachment to their ancient religion and customs still tend to persist.

These and related ideas, if given due weight as part of the Indian's heritage, will prevent the confusion brought about in both races by the assumption that assimilation may be achieved through Indians' adopting a few simple attitudes of their white neighbors. For example, it is often said that the Indian *needs to be thrifty, to acquire habits of diligence, and to learn the importance of punctuality.*

Yet in their own culture, where the goals were understood, Indians were economical, were hard-working, and possessed a keen appreciation of time. Thrift was shown in their utilization of every part of animals killed in the chase, as well as by their gathering and drying of berries and edible roots. Hunting or tilling the soil with wooden sticks to grow enough food for the family demanded a high order of perseverance. The element of time for the agriculturists was determined by the planting and harvesting seasons, and for the hunter by the habits of the animals he stalked down. In each case, time was a vital factor, though not in the white man's sense of hours and minutes marked on the clock.

In occupations which appeal to the established Indian ideals, such as those calling for facing danger, for careful craftsmanship, or for common effort, Indians have not only found satisfaction but have achieved national recognition. Teams of Iroquois are outstanding structural steelworkers on high bridges and skyscrapers; groups of Apache and Pueblo "Red-Hats," flown to fight fires in the western forests, have excelled at this perilous work; and the demand for Navajos in factories which require delicate precision work is well known.

Nor should it be overlooked that Indian values are not unique. "Honour thy father and thy mother" is a commandment found among many peoples. The importance of any set of values does not arise from their origin, existence, uniqueness, or validity. What is of paramount concern is that we recognize those of the Indian in making plans for the race.

The matter of government aid also requires a new look. Sine 1933 the dominant society has been meeting its human needs in ways similar to those traditional to Indian tribes. "Sharing" was with them a means of helping the helpless. The United States has supplied comparable relief through Social Security, and aid to the old, the blind, and dependent, crippled children, and the unemployed as well as by free distribution of surplus commodities. In other respects also, it has been extending to the entire population the kind of help formerly given only to Indians. Such things as Federal financial assistance for public schools, scholarships, the construction of highways and hospitals, and medical aid to the elderly are now benefits available to or planned for all Americans. These services have come as a consequence of Acts of Congress. The Indians through the years have received theirs as the result of bargains set forth in treaties, agreements, statutes, and policies.

As the outlook of two civilizations converges and the services to the rest of the people, financed partially or largely by the United States, actually outstrip those once given only to Indians, the movement of Indians into the broader society will be facilitated. What the members of this underprivileged race need is more and better education, improved economic assistance, a better state of health, and a more carefully designed preparation for the responsibilities of the white man's way of life. Provided that they can avail themselves of the services enjoyed by the rest of us, and also that they find material opportunities appropriate to their abilities, Indians can only benefit from a merging of the two cultures.

RECOMMENDATIONS

An objective which should undergird all Indian policy is that the Indian individual, the Indian family, and the Indian community be motivated to participate in solving their own problems. The Indian must be given responsibility, must be afforded an opportunity he can utilize, and must develop faith in himself.

Indian-made plans should receive preferential treatment, and, when workable, should be adopted.

Government programs would be more effective if plans for education, health and economic development drew on those parts of the Indian heritage which are important not only to the Indians but also to the cultural enrichment of modern America. . . .

[*A Program for Indian Citizens: A Summary Report* (Albuquerque, N. Mex.: Commission on the Rights, Liberties, and Responsibilities of the American Indian, 1961), pp. 1-4.]

152. Declaration of Indian Purpose

June 1961

A notable conference of Indians from many tribes met at the University of Chicago in June 1961. It drew up a declaration of purpose, including proposals and recommendations on economic development, health, welfare, housing, education, law, and other topics. Printed here are the initial creed and the concluding statement, as well as legislative and regulatory proposals.

CREED

WE BELIEVE in the inherent right of all people to retain spiritual and cultural values, and that the free exercise of these values is necessary to the normal development of any people. Indians exercised this inherent right to live their own lives for thousands of years before the white man came and took their lands. It is a more complex world in which Indians live today, but the Indian people who first settled the New World and built the great civilizations which only now are being dug out of the past, long ago demonstrated that they could master complexity.

WE BELIEVE that the history and development of America show that the Indian has been subjected to duress, undue influence, unwarranted pressures, and policies which have produced uncertainty, frustration, and despair. Only when the public understands these conditions and is moved to take action toward the formulation and adoption of sound and consistent policies and programs will these destroying factors be removed and the Indian resume his normal growth and make his maximum contribution to modern society.

WE BELIEVE in the future of a greater America, an America which we were first to love, where life, liberty, and the pursuit of happiness will be a reality. In such a future, with Indians and all other Americans cooperating, a cultural climate will be created in which the Indian people will grow and develop as members of a free society.

LEGISLATIVE AND REGULATORY PROPOSALS

In order that basic objectives may be restated and that action to accomplish these objectives may be continuous and may be pursued in a spirit of public dedication, it is proposed that recommendations be adopted to strengthen the principles of the Indian Reorganization Act and to accomplish other purposes. These recommendations would be comparable in scope and purpose to the Indian Trade and Intercourse Act of June 30, 1834, the Act of the same date establishing the Bureau of Indian Affairs, and the Indian Reorganization Act of June 18, 1934, which recognized the inherent powers of Indian Tribes.

The recommendations we propose would redefine the responsibilities of the United States toward the Indian people in terms of a positive national obligation to modify or remove the conditions which produce the poverty and lack of social adjustment as these prevail as the outstanding attributes of Indian life today. Specifically, the recommendations would:

244

(1) Abandon the so-called termination policy of the last administration by revoking House Concurrent Resolution 108 of the 83rd Congress.

(2) Adopt as official policy the principle of broad educational process as the procedure best calculated to remove the disabilities which have prevented Indians from making full use of their resources.

It has been long recognized that one Commissioner cannot give the personal attention to all tribal matters which they deserve. He cannot meet all callers to his office, make necessary visits to the field, and give full attention to the review of tribal programs and supporting budget requests. In view of these conditions, we most urgently recommend that the present organization of the Bureau of Indian Affairs be reviewed and that certain principles be considered no matter what the organizational change might be.

The basic principle involves the desire on the part of Indians to participate in developing their own programs with help and guidance as needed and requested, from a local decentralized technical and administrative staff, preferably located conveniently to the people it serves. Also in recent years certain technical and professional people of Indian descent are becoming better qualified and available to work with and for their own people in determining their own programs and needs. The Indians as responsible individual citizens, as responsible tribal representatives, and as responsible Tribal Councils want to participate, want to contribute to their own personal and tribal improvements and want to cooperate with their Government on how best to solve the many problems in a business-like, efficient and economical manner as rapidly as possible.

It is, therefore, recommended that:

1. Area offices be abolished and their authority be given to the agency superintendents.

2. The position of reservation Superintendent be strengthened to permit broader exercise of responsibility and authority to act on significant and important matters of daily operations of Indian problems, preventing undue delays.

3. Position qualifications require the employment of Superintendents with courage and determination, among other qualities, to help with local problems and be willing to make without further referral to higher levels, decisions commensurate with the delegated authorities.

4. The Superintendent be charged with the responsibilities of cooperating with the local tribal governing bodies in developing the Federal Program and Budget for that particular tribe or reservation. . . .

CONCLUDING STATEMENT

To complete our Declaration, we point out that in the beginning the people of the New World, called Indians by accident of geography, were possessed of a continent and a way of life. In the course of many lifetimes, our people had adjusted to every climate and condition from the Arctic to the torrid zones. In their livelihood and family relationships, their ceremonial observances, they reflected the diversity of the physical world they occupied.

The conditions in which Indians live today reflect a world in which every basic aspect of life has been transformed. Even the physical world is no longer the controlling factor in determining where and under what conditions men may live. In region after region, Indian groups found their means of existence either totally destroyed or materially modified. Newly introduced diseases swept away or reduced regional populations. These changes were followed by major shifts in the internal life of tribe and family.

The time came when the Indian people were no longer the masters of their situation. Their life ways survived subject to the will of a dominant sovereign power. This is said, not in a spirit of complaint; we understand that in the lives of all nations of people, there are times of plenty and times of famine. But we do speak out in a plea for understanding.

When we go before the American people, as we do in this Declaration, and ask for material assistance in developing our resources and developing our opportunities, we pose a moral problem which cannot be left unanswered. For the problem we raise

245

affects the standing which our nation sustains before world opinion.

Our situation cannot be relieved by appropriated funds alone, though it is equally obvious that without capital investment and funded services, solutions will be delayed. Nor will the passage of time lessen the complexities which beset a people moving toward new meaning and purpose.

The answers we seek are not commodities to be purchased, neither are they evolved automatically through the passing of time.

The effort to place social adjustment on a money-time interval scale which has characterized Indian administration, has resulted in unwanted pressure and frustration.

When Indians speak of the continent they yielded, they are not referring only to the loss of some millions of acres in real estate. They have in mind that the land supported a universe of things they knew, valued, and loved.

With that continent gone, except for the few poor parcels they still retain, the basis of life is precariously held, but they mean to hold the scraps and parcels as earnestly as any small nation or ethnic group was ever determined to hold to identity and survival.

What we ask of America is not charity, not paternalism, even when benevolent. We ask only that the nature of our situation be recognized and made the basis of policy and action.

In short, the Indians ask for assistance, technical and financial, for the time needed, however long that may be, to regain in the America of the space age some measure of the adjustment they enjoyed as the original possessors of their native land.

[*Declaration of Indian Purpose* (Chicago: American Indian Chicago Conference, University of Chicago, 1961), pp. 5-6, 19-20.]

153. Task Force on Indian Affairs
Extract from the *Annual Report of the Commissioner of Indian Affairs*
1961

Secretary of the Interior Stewart Udall in February 1961 appointed a special Task Force on Indian Affairs, which submitted a report on Indian conditions on July 10, 1961. The recommendations of the Task Force were summarized by Commissioner of Indian Affairs Philleo Nash in his report for 1961.

A "New Trail" for Indians leading to equal citizenship rights and benefits, maximum self-sufficiency and full participation in American life became the keynote for administration of the program of the Bureau of Indian Affairs of the Department of the Interior shortly after the close of the 1961 fiscal year.

This keynote was provided in a 77-page report submitted to Secretary Udall by a special Task Force on Indian Affairs which he appointed in February 1961. The report was presented shortly after the end of the fiscal year, and its major recommendations were at that time accepted and endorsed by the Secretary.

Probably the most important single recommendation was for a shift in program emphasis away from termination of Federal trust relationships toward greater development of the human and natural resources on Indian reservations.

This was coupled, however, with a recommendation that eligibility for special Federal service be withdrawn from "Indians with substantial incomes and superior educational experience, who are as competent as most non-Indians to look after their own affairs." Emphasis was also given to the beneficial nature of Federal programs—such as those under the Social Security Act and the Area Redevelopment Act—which treat Indians and non-Indians alike.

In addition, the report recommend (1) more vigorous efforts to attract industries to reservation areas, (2) an expanded program of vocational training and placement, (3) creation of a special Reservation Development Loan Fund and enlargement of the present Revolving Loan Fund, (4) establishment of a statutory Advisory Board on Indian Affairs, (5) negotiation with States and counties, and resort to the courts where necessary, to make certain that off-reservation Indians are accorded the same rights and privileges as other citizens of their areas, (6) collaboration with States and tribes to bring tribal law and order codes into conformity with those of the States and counties where reservations are located, (7) acceleration in the adjudication of cases pending before the Indian Claims Commission, and (8) more active and widespread efforts to inform the public about the status of the Indian people and the nature of their problems.

Calling attention to the complex problem of "heirship" land allotments owned by numerous Indians who either cannot be located or cannot agree on use of the property, the report advocated transferring these fractionated holdings to the tribe and permitting the latter to compensate the owners through some system of deferred payment.

As a step toward transferring the responsibility for Indian education to local school districts, the Task Force urged renovation of present Federal school buildings, construction of new plants, and road improvements so that more Indian children can be bussed to classes. It also called for greater efforts to involve Indian parents in school planning and parent-teacher activities. As a measure to relieve overcrowding of present facilities, the report suggested that consideration be given to keeping them in use throughout the entire year. During the summer months, it added, some of these facilities could also be used for programs to help Indian youngsters make constructive use of their leisure time.

The Task Force was headed by W. W. Keeler, principal chief of the Oklahoma Cherokees and oil company executive. The other members were Philleo Nash, longtime student of Indian affairs and former lieutenant governor of Wisconsin; William Zimmerman, Jr., assistant commissioner of the Bureau from 1933 to 1950; and James Officer, a University of Arizona anthropologist. Acting Commissioner John O. Crow consulted with the Task Force and accompanied it on field trips.

The Task Force study extended over a period of about 5 months and included consultations both in Washington and the West with numerous tribal leaders and non-Indian experts in the field. . . .

[*Annual Report of the Secretary of the Interior, 1961*, pp. 277-79.]

154. Colliflower v. Garland

February 4, 1965

Madeline Colliflower, an Indian on the Fort Belknap Reservation, was imprisoned for failing to obey an order of the court of Indian offenses. She sought a writ of habeas corpus, claiming that her imprisonment was illegal and violated her constitutional rights. The United States Court of Appeals, Ninth Circuit, held that the tribal courts were in effect a part of the federal system and that the federal court had jurisdiction to issue a writ of habeas corpus for the purpose of determining the validity of detention of an Indian committed by a tribal court.

. . . . In spite of the theory that for some purposes an Indian tribe is an independent sovereignty, we think that, in the light of their history, it is pure fiction to say that the Indian courts functioning in the Fort Belknap Indian community are not in part, at least, arms of the federal government. Originally they were created by the federal executive and imposed upon the Indian community, and to this day the federal government still maintains a partial control over them. . . .

Under these circumstances, we think that these courts function in part as a federal agency and in part as a tribal agency, and that consequently it is competent for a federal court in a habeas corpus proceeding to inquire into the legality of the detention of an Indian pursuant to an order of an Indian court. We confine our decision to the courts of the Fort Belknap reservation. The history of other Indian courts may call for a different ruling, a question which is not before us.

The writ of habeas corpus lies on behalf of anyone who is "in custody under or by color of the authority of the United States"

247

or "in violation of the Constitution * * * of the United States." . . . We think that this covers Mrs. Colliflower's case.

It may well be that one hundred years ago it would have been held that a federal court lacked jurisdiction to issue a writ of habeas corpus at the instance of an Indian imprisoned in a tribal jail, pursuant to the judgment of a tribal court. We think, however, that the status of the Indians today is such, and particularly that the history and status of the tribal court at the Fort Belknap Reservation is such, that we should uphold the jurisdiction of a federal court in this habeas corpus proceeding.

We do not pass upon the merits of Mrs. Colliflower's claims, because the district court did not reach them. It does not follow from our decision that the tribal court must comply with every constitutional restriction that is applicable to federal or state courts. Nor does it follow that the Fourteenth Amendment applies to tribal courts at all; some of the cases cited above indicate that it does not. . . .

[342 *Federal Reporter*, 2d series, 369, 378-79.]

155. President Johnson, Special Message To Congress
March 6, 1968

A forceful statement of a new direction in Indian policy which recognized Indian self-determination was made by President Lyndon B. Johnson in a "Special Message to Congress on the Problems of the American Indian: 'The Forgotten American,' " on March 6, 1968.

. . . . I propose a new goal for our Indian programs: A goal that ends the old debate about "termination" of Indian programs and stresses self-determination; a goal that erases old attitudes of paternalism and promotes partnership self-help.
  Our goal must be:
  —*A standard of living for the Indians equal to that of the country as a whole.*
  —*Freedom of Choice: An opportunity to remain in their homelands, if they choose, without surrendering their dignity; an opportunity to move to the towns and cities of America, if they choose, equipped with the skills to live in equality and dignity.*
  —*Full participation in the life of modern America, with a full share of economic opportunity and social justice.*
  I propose, in short, a policy of maximum choice for the American Indian: a policy expressed in programs of self-help, self-development, self-determination.
  To start toward our goal in Fiscal 1969, I recommend that the Congress appropriate one-half a billion dollars for programs targeted at the American Indian—about 10 percent more than Fiscal 1968.

STRENGTHENED FEDERAL LEADERSHIP

In the past four years, with the advent of major new programs, several agencies have undertaken independent efforts to help the American Indian. Too often, there has been too little coordination between agencies; and no clear, unified policy which applied to all.
  To launch an undivided, Government-wide effort in this area, I am today issuing an Executive Order to establish a National Council on Indian Opportunity.
  The Chairman of the Council will be the Vice President who will bring the problems of the Indians to the highest levels of Government. The Council will include a cross section of Indian leaders, and high government officials who have programs in this field:
  —The Secretary of the Interior, who has primary responsibility for Indian Affairs.
  —The Secretary of Agriculture, whose programs affect thousands of Indians.
  —The Secretary of Commerce, who can help promote economic development of Indian lands.
  —The Secretary of Labor, whose manpower programs can train more Indians for more useful employment.
  —The Secretary of Health, Education, and Welfare, who can help Indian communities with two of their most pressing needs—health and education.

—The Secretary of Housing and Urban Development, who can bring better housing to Indian lands.

—The Director of the Office of Economic Opportunity, whose programs are already operating in several Indian communities.

The Council will review Federal programs for Indians, make broad policy recommendations, and ensure that programs reflect the needs and desires of the Indian people. Most important, I have asked the Vice President, as Chairman of the Council, to make certain that the American Indian shares fully in all our federal programs.

SELF-HELP AND SELF-DETERMINATION

The greatest hope for Indian progress lies in the emergence of Indian leadership and initiative in solving Indian problems. Indians must have a voice in making the plans and decisions in programs which are important to their daily life.

Within the last few months we have seen a new concept of community development—a concept based on self-help—work successfully among Indians. Many tribes have begun to administer activities which Federal agencies had long performed in their behalf. . . .

Passive acceptance of Federal service is giving way to Indian involvement. More than ever before, Indian needs are being identified from the Indian viewpoint—as they should be.

This principle is the key to progress for Indians—just as it has been for other Americans. If we base our programs upon it, the day will come when the relationship between Indians and the Government will be one of full partnership—not dependency. . . .

[Sections on education, health and medical care, jobs and economic development,

community services, civil rights, off-reservation Indians, and Alaska Natives claims.]

THE FIRST AMERICANS

The program I propose seeks to promote Indian development by improving health and education, encouraging long-term economic growth, and strengthening community institutions.

Underlying this program is the assumption that the Federal government can best be a responsible partner in Indian progress by treating the Indian himself as a full citizen, responsible for the pace and direction of his development.

But there can be no question that the government and the people of the United States have a responsibility to the Indians.

In our efforts to meet that responsibility, we must pledge to respect fully the dignity and the uniqueness of the Indian citizen.

That means partnership—not paternalism.

We must affirm the right of the first Americans to remain Indians while exercising their rights as Americans.

We must affirm their right to freedom of choice and self-determination.

We must seek new ways to provide Federal assistance to Indians—with new emphasis on Indian self-help and with respect for Indian culture.

And we must assure the Indian people that it is our desire and intention that the special relationship between the Indian and his government grow and flourish.

For, the first among us must not be last.

I urge the Congress to affirm this policy and to enact this program.

[*Public Papers of the Presidents of the United States: Lyndon B. Johnson, 1968-69*, 1:336-37, 343-44.]

156. Civil Rights Act of 1968

April 11, 1968

Titles II-VII of the Civil Rights Act of 1968 dealt with Indian matters. Most significant was the application of the provisions of the Bill of Rights to Indians in their relations with the tribal governments, the authorization of a model code for courts of Indian offenses, and the requirement that Indian consent be given to assumption by states of jurisdiction over Indian country.

An Act To prescribe penalties for certain acts of violence or intimidation, and for other purposes.

TITLE II—RIGHTS OF INDIANS

DEFINITIONS

Sec. 201. For purposes of this title, the term—

(1) "Indian tribe" means any tribe, band, or other group of Indians subject to the jurisdiction of the United States and recognized as possessing powers of self-government;

(2) "powers of self-government" means and includes all governmental powers possessed by an Indian tribe, executive, legislative, and judicial, and all offices, bodies, and tribunals by and through which they are executed, including courts of Indian offenses; and

(3) "Indian court" means any Indian tribal court or court of Indian offense.

INDIAN RIGHTS

Sec. 202. No Indian tribe in exercising powers of self-government shall—

(1) make or enforce any law prohibiting the free exercise of religion, or abridging the freedom of speech, or of the press, or the right of the people peaceably to assemble and to petition for a redress of grievances;

(2) violate the right of the people to be secure in their persons, houses, papers, and effects against unreasonable search and seizures, nor issue warrants, but upon probable cause, supported by oath or affirmation, and particularly describing the place to be searched and the person or thing to be seized;

(3) subject any person for the same offense to be twice put in jeopardy;

(4) compel any person in any criminal case to be a witness against himself;

(5) take any private property for a public use without just compensation;

(6) deny to any person in a criminal proceeding the right to a speedy and public trial, to be informed of the nature and cause of the accusation, to be confronted with the witnesses against him, to have compulsory process for obtaining witnesses in his favor, and at his own expense to have the assistance of counsel for his defense;

(7) require excessive bail, impose excessive fines, inflict cruel and unusual punishments, and in no event impose for conviction of any one offense any penalty or punishment greater than imprisonment for a term of six months or a fine of $500, or both;

(8) deny to any person within its jurisdiction the equal protection of its laws or deprive any person of liberty or property without due process of law;

(9) pass any bill of attainder or ex post facto law; or

(10) deny to any person accused of an offense punishable by imprisonment the right, upon request, to a trial by jury of not less than six persons.

HABEAS CORPUS

Sec. 203. The privilege of the writ of habeas corpus shall be available to any person, in a court of the United States, to test the legality of his detention by order of an Indian tribe.

TITLE III— MODEL CODE GOVERNING COURTS OF INDIAN OFFENSES

Sec. 301. The Secretary of the Interior is authorized and directed to recommend to the Congress, on or before July 1, 1968, a model code to govern the administration of justice by courts of Indian offenses on Indian reservations. Such code shall include provisions which will (1) assure that any individual being tried for an offense by a court of Indian offenses shall have the same rights, privileges, and immunities under the United States Constitution as would be guaranteed any citizen of the United States being tried in a Federal court for any similar offense, (2) assure that any individual being tried for an offense by a court of Indian offenses will be advised and made aware of his rights under the United States Constitution, and under any tribal constitution applicable to such individual, (3) establish proper qualifications for the office of judge of the courts of Indian offenses, and (4) provide for the establishing of educational classes for the training of judges of courts of Indian offenses. In carrying out the provisions of this title, the Secretary of the Interior shall consult with the Indians, Indian tribes, and interested agencies of the United States.

SEC. 302. There is hereby authorized to be appropriated such sum as may be necessary to carry out the provisions of this title.

TITLE IV—JURISDICTION OVER CRIMINAL AND CIVIL ACTIONS

ASSUMPTION BY STATE

SEC. 401. (a) The consent of the United States is hereby given to any State not having jurisdiction over criminal offenses committed by or against Indians in the areas of Indian country situated within such State to assume, with the consent of the Indian tribe occupying the particular Indian country or part thereof which could be affected by such assumption, such measure of jurisdiction over any or all of such offenses committed within such Indian country or any part thereof as may be determined by such State to the same extent that such State has jurisdiction over any such offense committed elsewhere within the State, and the criminal laws of such State shall have the same force and effect within such Indian country or part thereof as they have elsewhere within that State.

(b) Nothing in this section shall authorize the alienation, encumbrance, or taxation of any real or personal property, including water rights, belonging to any Indian or any Indian tribe, band, or community that is held in trust by the United States or is subject to a restriction against alienation imposed by the United States; or shall authorize regulation of the use of such property in a manner inconsistent with any Federal treaty, agreement, or statute or with any regulation made pursuant thereto; or shall deprive any Indian or any Indian tribe, band, or community of any right, privilege, or immunity afforded under Federal treaty, agreement, or statute with respect to hunting, trapping, or fishing or the control, licensing, or regulation thereof.

ASSUMPTION BY STATE OF CIVIL JURISDICTION

SEC. 402. (a) The consent of the United States is hereby given to any State not having jurisdiction over civil causes of action between Indians or to which Indians are parties which arise in the areas of Indian country situated within such State to assume, with the consent of the tribe occupying the particular Indian country or part thereof which would be affected by such assumption, such measure of jurisdiction over any or all such civil causes of action arising within such Indian country or any part thereof as may be determined by such State to the same extent that such State has jurisdiction over other civil causes of action, and those civil laws of such State that are of general application to private persons or private property shall have the same force and effect within such Indian country or part thereof as they have elsewhere within that State.

(b) Nothing in this section shall authorize the alienation, encumbrance, or taxation of any real or personal property, including water rights, belonging to any Indian or any Indian tribe, band, or community that is held in trust by the United States or is subject to a restriction against alienation imposed by the United States; or shall authorize regulation of the use of such property in a manner inconsistent with any Federal treaty, agreement, or statute, or with any regulation made pursuant thereto; or shall confer jurisdiction upon the State to adjudicate, in probate proceedings or otherwise, the ownership or right to possession of such property or any interest therein.

(c) Any tribal ordinance or custom heretofore or hereafter adopted by an Indian tribe, band, or community in the exercise of any authority which it may possess shall, if not inconsistent with any applicable civil law of the State, be given full force and effect in the determination of civil causes of action pursuant to this section.

RETROCESSION OF JURISDICTION BY STATE

SEC. 403. (a) The United States is authorized to accept a retrocession by any State of all or any measure of the criminal or civil jurisdiction, or both, acquired by such State pursuant to the provisions of section 1162 of title 18 of the United States Code, section 1360 of title 28 of the United States

Code, or section 7 of the Act of August 15, 1953 (67 Stat. 588), as it was in effect prior to its repeal by subsection (b) of this section.

(b) Section 7 of the Act of August 15, 1953 (67 Stat. 588), is hereby repealed, but such repeal shall not affect any cession of jurisdiction made pursuant to such section prior to its repeal. . . .

SEC. 406. State jurisdiction acquired pursuant to this title with respect to criminal offenses or civil causes of action, or with respect to both, shall be applicable in Indian country only where the enrolled Indians within the affected area of such Indian country accept such jurisdiction by a majority vote of the adult Indians voting at a special election held for that purpose. The Secretary of the Interior shall call such special election under such rules and regulations as he may prescribe, when requested to do so by the tribal council or other governing body, or by 20 per centum of such enrolled adults.

TITLE V—OFFENSES WITHIN INDIAN COUNTRY

AMENDMENT

SEC. 501. Section 1153 of title 18 of the United States Code is amended by inserting immediately after "weapon,", the following: "assault resulting in serious bodily injury,".

TITLE VI—EMPLOYMENT OF LEGAL COUNSEL

APPROVAL

SEC. 601. Notwithstanding any other provision of law, if any application made by an Indian, Indian tribe, Indian council, or any band or group of Indians under any law requiring the approval of the Secretary of the Interior or the Commissioner of Indian Affairs of contracts or agreements relating to the employment of legal counsel (including the choice of counsel and the fixing of fees) by any such Indians, tribe, council, band, or

group is neither granted nor denied within ninety days following the making of such application, such approval shall be deemed to have been granted.

TITLE VII—MATERIALS RELATING TO CONSTITUTIONAL RIGHTS OF INDIANS

SECRETARY OF INTERIOR TO PREPARE

SEC. 701. (a) In order that the constitutional rights of Indians might be fully protected, the Secretary of the Interior is authorized and directed to—

(1) have the document entitled "Indian Affairs, Laws and Treaties" (Senate Document Numbered 319, volumes 1 and 2, Fifty-eighth Congress), revised and extended to include all treaties, laws, Executive orders, and regulations relating to Indian affairs in force on September 1, 1967, and to have such revised document printed at the Government Printing Office;

(2) have revised and republished the treatise entitled "Federal Indian Law"; and

(3) have prepared, to the extent determined by the Secretary of the Interior to be feasible, an accurate compilation of the official opinions, published and unpublished, of the Solicitor of the Department of the Interior relating to Indian affairs rendered by the Solicitor prior to September 1, 1967, and to have such compilation printed as a Government publication at the Government Printing Office.

(b) With respect to the document entitled "Indian Affairs, Laws and Treaties" as revised and extended in accordance with paragraph (1) of subsection (a), and the compilation prepared in accordance with paragraph (3) of such subsection, the Secretary of the Interior shall take such action as may be necessary to keep such document and compilation current on an annual basis.

(c) There is authorized to be appropriated for carrying out the provisions of this title, with respect to the preparation but not including printing, such sum as may be necessary.

[*U.S. Statutes at Large*, 82:77-81.]

157. Report on Indian Education
November 3, 1969

A Special Subcommittee on Indian Education, of the Senate Committee on Labor and Public Welfare, submitted a stinging critique of Indian education. Chaired first by Senator Robert Kennedy and after his death by Senator Edward Kennedy, the subcommittee made extensive recommendations. Printed here is the introductory "Summary" of the lengthy report.

For more than 2 years the members of this subcommittee have been gaging how well American Indians are educated. We have traveled to all parts of the country; we have visited Indians in their homes and in their schools; we have listened to Indians, to Government officials, and to experts; and we have looked closely into every aspect of the educational opportunities this Nation offers its Indian citizens.

Our work fills 4,077 pages in seven volumes of hearings and 450 pages in five volumes of committee prints. This report is the distillate of this work.

We are shocked at what we discovered.

Others before us were shocked. They recommended and made changes. Others after us will likely be shocked, too—despite our recommendations and efforts at reform. For there is so much to do—wrongs to right, omissions to fill, untruths to correct—that our own recommendations, concerned as they are with education alone, need supplementation across the whole board of Indian life.

We have developed page after page of statistics. These cold figures mark a stain on our national conscience, a stain which has spread slowly for hundreds of years. They tell a story, to be sure. But they cannot tell the whole story. They cannot, for example, tell of the despair, the frustration, the hopelessness, the poignancy, of children who want to learn but are not taught; of adults who try to read but have no one to teach them; of families which want to stay together but are forced apart; or of 9-year-old children who want neighborhood school but are sent thousands of miles away to remote and alien boarding schools.

We have seen what these conditions do to Indian children and Indian families. The sights are not pleasant.

We have concluded that our national policies for educating American Indians are a failure of major proportions. They have not offered Indian children—either in years past or today—an educational opportunity anywhere near equal to that offered the great bulk of American children. Past generations of lawmakers and administrators have failed the American Indian. Our own generation thus faces a challenge—we can continue the unacceptable policies and programs of the past or we can recognize our failures, renew our commitments, and reinvest our efforts with new energy.

It is this latter course that the subcommittee chooses. We have made 60 separate recommendations. If they are all carried into force and effect, then we believe that all American Indians, children and adults, will have the unfettered opportunity to grow to their full potential. Decent education has been denied Indians in the past, and they have fallen far short of matching their promise with performance. But this need not always be so. Creative, imaginative, and above all, relevant educational experiences can blot the stain on our national conscience. This is the challenge the subcommittee believes faces our own generation.

This Nation's 600,000 American Indians are a diverse ethnic group. They live in all 50 States and speak some 300 separate languages. Four hundred thousand Indians live on reservations, and 200,000 live off reservations. The tribes have different customs and mores, and different wants and needs. The urban Indian has a world different from that of the rural Indian.

Indian children attend Federal, public, private, and mission schools. In the early days of this republic, what little formal education there was available to Indians was under the control of the church. Gradually, however, as the Nation expanded westward and Indian nations were conquered, the treaties between the conquering United States and the defeated Indian nation pro-

253

vided for the establishment of schools for Indian children. In 1842, for example, there were 37 Indian schools run by the U.S. Government. This number had increased to 106 in 1881, and to 226 in 1968.

This pattern of Federal responsibility for Indian education has been slowly changing. In 1968, for example, the education of Indian children in California, Idaho, Michigan, Minnesota, Nebraska, Oregon, Texas, Washington, and Wisconsin was the total responsibility of the State and not the Federal Government.

In 1968, there were 152,088 Indian children between the ages of 6 and 18. 142,630 attended one type of school or another. Most of these—61.3 percent—attended public, non-Federal schools with non-Indian children. Another 32.7 percent were enrolled in Federal schools, and 6.0 percent attended mission and other schools. Some 6,616 school-age Indian children were not in school at all. The Bureau of Indian Affairs in the Department of the Interior, the Federal agency charged with managing Indian affairs for the United States, was unable to determine the educational status of some 2,842 Indian children.

The Bureau of Indian Affairs operates 77 boarding schools and 147 day schools. There are 35,309 school-age Indian children in these boarding schools, and 16,139 in the day schools. Nearly 9,000 of the boarding-school children are under 9 years old.

In its investigation of "any and all matters pertaining to the education of Indian children" (S. Res. 165, August 31, 1967), the subcommittee thus was compelled to examine not only the Federal schools, but the State and local public schools and the mission schools as well.

What concerned us most deeply, as we carried out our mandate, was the low quality of virtually every aspect of the schooling available to Indian children. The school buildings themselves; the course materials and books; the attitude of teachers and administrative personnel; the accessibility of school buildings—all these are of shocking quality.

A few of the statistics we developed:

Forty thousand Navajo Indians, nearly a third of the entire tribe, are functional illiterates in English;

The average educational level for all Indians under Federal supervision is 5 school years;

More than one out of every five Indian men have less than 5 years of schooling;

Dropout rates for Indians are twice the national average;

In New Mexico, some Indian high school students walk 2 miles to the bus every day and then ride 50 miles to school;

The average age of top level BIA education administrators is 58 years;

In 1953 the BIA began a crash program to improve education for Navajo children. Between then and 1967, supervisory positions in BIA headquarters increased 113 percent; supervisory positions in BIA schools increased 144 percent; administrative and clerical positions in the BIA schools increased 94 percent. Yet, teaching positions increased only 20 percent;

In one school in Oklahoma the student body is 100-percent Indian; yet it is controlled by a three-man, non-Indian school board.

Only 18 percent of the students in Federal Indian schools go on to college; the national average is 50 percent;

Only 3 percent of Indian students who enroll in college graduate; the national average is 32 percent;

The BIA spends only $18 per year per child on textbooks and supplies, compared to a national average of $40;

Only one of every 100 Indian college graduates will receive a masters degree; and

despite a Presidential directive 2 years ago, only one of the 226 BIA schools is governed by an elective school board.

These are only a few of the statistics which tell the story of how poor the quality of education is that American Indians have available to them. Running all through this report are many others, which are some measure of the depth of the tragedy. There are, too, specific examples of visits we made to various facilities in the Indian education system. These are too lengthy to summarize; however, the subcommittee believes that their cumulative effect is chilling.

We reacted to our findings by making a

long series of specific recommendations. These recommendations embrace legislative changes; administrative changes; policy changes; structural changes—all of which are geared to making Indian education programs into models of excellence, not of bureaucratic calcification.

We have recommended that the Nation adopt as national policy a commitment to achieving educational excellence for American Indians. We have recommended that the Nation adopt as national goals a series of specific objectives relating to educational opportunities for American Indians. Taken together, this policy and these goals are a framework for a program of action. Clearly, this action program needs legislative and executive support if it is to meet its promise. Most of all, however, it needs dedicated and imaginative management by those Federal officials, and State and local officials as well, who have the principal responsibilities for educating American Indians.

We have recommended that there be convened a White House Conference on American Indian Affairs. We have recommended—although not unanimously—that there be established a Senate Select Committee on the Human Needs of American Indians. We have recommended the enactment of a comprehensive Indian education statute, to replace the fragmented and inadequate education legislation now extant. We have recommended that the funds available for Indian education programs be markedly increased.

One theme running through all our recommendations is increased Indian participation and control of their own education programs. For far too long, the Nation has paid only token heed to the notion that Indians should have a strong voice in their own destiny. We have made a number of recommendations to correct this historic, anomalous paternalism. We have, for example, recommended that the Commissioner of the BIA be raised to the level of Assistant Secretary of the Department of Interior; that there be established a National Indian Board of Indian Education with authority to set standards and criteria for the Federal Indian schools; that local Indian boards of education be established for Indian school districts; and that Indian parental and commu-

nity involvement be increased. These reforms, taken together, can—at last—make education of American Indians relevant to the lives of American Indians.

We have recommended programs to meet special, unmet needs in the Indian education field. Culturally-sensitive curriculum materials, for example, are seriously lacking; so are bi-lingual education efforts. Little educational material is available to Indians concerning nutrition and alcoholism. We have developed proposals in all these fields, and made strong recommendations to rectify their presently unacceptable status.

The subcommittee spent much time and devoted considerable effort to the "organization problem," a problem of long and high concern to those seeking reform of our policies toward American Indians. It is, in fact, two problems bound up as one—the internal organization of the Bureau of Indian Affairs, and the location of the Bureau within the Federal establishment. We made no final recommendation on this most serious issue. Instead, because we believe it critically important that the Indians themselves express their voices on this matter, we have suggested that it be put high on the agenda of the White House Conference on American Indian Affairs. Because, as we conceive it, this White House Conference will be organized by the Indians themselves, with the support of the National Council on Indian Opportunity, it is entirely appropriate that this organization problem be left for the conference.

In this report, we have compared the size and scope of the effort we believe must be mounted to the Marshall plan which revitalized postwar Europe. We believe that we have, as a Nation, as great a moral and legal obligation to our Indian citizens today as we did after World War II to our European allies and adversaries.

The scope of this subcommittee's work was limited by its authorizing resolution to education. But as we traveled, and listened, and saw, we learned that education cannot be isolated from the other aspects of Indian life. These aspects, too, have much room for improvement. This lies in part behind the recommendation for a Senate Select Committee on the Human Needs of American Indians. Economic development, job training, legal representation in water rights and oil lease matters—these are only a few of the correlative problems sorely in need of attention.

In conclusion, it is sufficient to restate our basic finding: that our Nation's policies and programs for educating American Indians are a national tragedy. They present us with a national challenge of no small proportions. We believe that this report recom- mends the proper steps to meet this challenge. But we know that it will not be met without strong leadership and dedicated work. We believe that with this leadership for the Congress and the executive branch of the Government, the Nation can and will meet this challenge.

[*Indian Education: A National Tragedy—A National Challenge*, Senate Report no. 501, 91st Cong., 1st sess., serial 12836-1, pp. xi-xiv.]

158. President Nixon, Special Message on Indian Affairs

July 8, 1970

The new direction of Indian policy which aimed at Indian self-determination was set forth by President Richard Nixon in a special message to Congress in July 1950. Nixon condemned forced termination and proposed recommendations for specific action. His introduction and conclusion are printed here.

To the Congress of the United States:

The first Americans—the Indians—are the most deprived and most isolated minority group in our nation. On virtually every scale of measurement—employment, income, education, health—the condition of the Indian people ranks at the bottom.

This condition is the heritage of centuries of injustice. From the time of their first contact with European settlers, the American Indians have been oppressed and bru- talized, deprived of their ancestral lands and denied the opportunity to control their own destiny. Even the Federal programs which are intended to meet their needs have fre- quently proven to be ineffective and demeaning.

But the story of the Indian in America is something more than the record of the white man's frequent aggression, broken agree- ments, intermittent remorse and prolonged failure. It is a record also of endurance, of survival, of adaptation and creativity in the face of overwhelming obstacles. It is a record of enormous contributions to this country—to its art and culture, to its strength and spirit, to its sense of history and its sense of purpose.

It is long past time that the Indian policies of the Federal government began to recog- nize and build upon the capacities and in- sights of the Indian people. Both as a matter of justice and as a matter of enlightened social policy, we must begin to act on the basis of what the Indians themselves have long been telling us. The time has come to break decisively with the past and to create the conditions for a new era in which the Indian future is determined by Indian acts and Indian decisions.

SELF-DETERMINATION WITHOUT TERMINATION

The first and most basic question that must be answered with respect to Indian policy concerns the historic and legal rela- tionship between the Federal government and Indian communities. In the past, this relationship has oscillated between two equally harsh and unacceptable extremes.

On the one hand, it has—at various times during previous Administrations—been the stated policy objective of both the Executive and Legislative branches of the Federal gov- ernment eventually to terminate the trustee- ship relationship between the Federal gov- ernment and the Indian people. As recently as August of 1953, in House Concurrent Resolution 108, the Congress declared that termination was the long-range goal of its Indian policies. This would mean that Indi- an tribes would eventually lose any special standing they had under Federal law: the tax exempt status of their lands would be dis- continued; Federal responsibility for their economic and social well-being would be repudiated; and the tribes themselves would be effectively dismantled. Tribal property would be divided among individual members who would then be assimilated into the society at large.

This policy of forced termination is wrong, in my judgment, for a number of reasons. First, the premises on which it rests are wrong. Termination implies that the Federal government has taken on a trusteeship responsibility for Indian communities as an act of generosity toward a disadvantaged people and that it can therefore discontinue this responsibility on a unilateral basis whenever it sees fit. But the unique status of Indian tribes does not rest on any premise such as this. The special relationship between Indians and the Federal government is the result instead of solemn obligations which have been entered into by the United States Government. Down through the years, through written treaties and through formal and informal agreements, our government has made specific commitments to the Indian people. For their part, the Indians have often surrendered claims to vast tracts of land and have accepted life on government reservations. In exchange, the government has agreed to provide community services such as health, education and public safety, services which would presumably allow Indian communities to enjoy a standard of living comparable to that of other Americans.

This goal, of course, has never been achieved. But the special relationship between the Indian tribes and the Federal government which arises from these agreements continues to carry immense moral and legal force. To terminate this relationship would be no more appropriate than to terminate the citizenship rights of any other American.

The second reason for rejecting forced termination is that the practical results have been clearly harmful in the few instances in which termination actually has been tried. The removal of Federal trusteeship responsibility has produced considerable disorientation among the affected Indians and has left them unable to relate to a myriad of Federal, State and local assistance efforts. Their economic and social condition has often been worse after termination than it was before.

The third argument I would make against forced termination concerns the effect it has had upon the overwhelming majority of tribes which still enjoy a special relationship with the Federal government. The very threat that this relationship may someday be ended has created a great deal of apprehension among Indian groups and this apprehension, in turn, has had a blighting effect on tribal progress. Any step that might result in greater social, economic or political autonomy is regarded with suspicion by many Indians who fear that it will only bring them closer to the day when the Federal government will disavow its responsibility and cut them adrift.

In short, the fear of one extreme policy, forced termination, has often worked to produce the opposite extreme: excessive dependence on the Federal government. In many cases this dependence is so great that the Indian community is almost entirely run by outsiders who are responsible and responsive to Federal officials in Washington, D.C., rather than to the communities they are supposed to be serving. This is the second of the two harsh approaches which have long plagued our Indian policies. Of the Department of the Interior's programs directly serving Indians, for example, only 1.5 percent are presently under Indian control. Only 2.4 percent of HEW's Indian health programs are run by Indians. The result is a burgeoning Federal bureaucracy, programs which are far less effective than they ought to be, and an erosion of Indian initiative and morale.

I believe that both of these policy extremes are wrong. Federal termination errs in one direction, Federal paternalism errs in the other. Only by clearly rejecting both of these extremes can we achieve a policy which truly serves the best interests of the Indian people. Self-determination among the Indian people can and must be encouraged without the threat of eventual termination. In my view, in fact, that is the only way that self-determination can effectively be fostered.

This, then, must be the goal of any new national policy toward the Indian people: to strengthen the Indian's sense of autonomy without threatening his sense of community. We must assure the Indian that he can assume control of his own life without being separated involuntarily from the tribal group. And we must make it clear that Indians can become independent of Federal control without being cut off from Federal concern and Federal support. My specific recommendations to the Congress are designed to carry out this policy. . . .

The recommendations of this Administration represent an historic step forward in Indian policy. We are proposing to break sharply with past approaches to Indian problems. In place of a long series of piecemeal reforms, we suggest a new and coherent strategy. In place of policies which simply call for more spending, we suggest policies which call for wiser spending. In place of policies which oscillate between the deadly extremes of forced termination and constant paternalism, we suggest a policy in which the Federal government and the Indian community play complementary roles.

But most importantly, we have turned from the question of *whether* the Federal government has a responsibility to Indians to the question of *how* that responsibility can

best be fulfilled. We have concluded that the Indians will get better programs and that public monies will be more effectively expended if the people who are most affected by these programs are responsible for operating them.

The Indians of America need Federal assistance—this much has long been clear. What has not always been clear, however, is that the Federal government needs Indian energies and Indian leadership if its assistance is to be effective in improving the conditions of Indian life. It is a new and balanced relationship between the United States government and the first Americans that is at the heart of our approach to Indian problems. And that is why we now approach these problems with new confidence that they will successfully be overcome.

[*Public Papers of the Presidents of the United States: Richard Nixon, 1970*, pp. 564-67, 575-76.]

159. Return of Blue Lake Lands to Taos Pueblo

1970

In 1906 President Theodore Roosevelt proclaimed the Blue Lake lands of the Taos Pueblo part of what is now Carson National Forest, thus restricting the exclusive Indian use of the lands. For sixty-four years the Indians struggled to regain the lands, which were sacred to them and used for religious ceremonies. Finally Congress in 1970 authorized the return of the lands. The significance of this action was emphasized by President Richard Nixon in his remarks on signing the bill.

1. Return of the Lands

December 15, 1970

An Act To amend section 4 of the Act of May 31, 1933 (48 Stat. 108).

Be it enacted . . . , That section 4 of the Act of May 31, 1933 (48 Stat. 108), providing for the protection of the watershed within the Carson National Forest for the Pueblo de Taos Indians in New Mexico, be and hereby is amended to read as follows:

"SEC. 4. (a) That, for the purpose of safeguarding the interests and welfare of the tribe of Indians known as the Pueblo de Taos of New Mexico, the following described lands and improvements thereon, upon which said Indians depend and have depended since time immemorial for water supply, forage for their domestic livestock, wood and timber for their personal use, and

as the scene of certain religious ceremonials, are hereby declared to be held by the United States in trust for the Pueblo de Taos: [Description of boundaries.]

"(b) The lands held in trust pursuant to this section shall be a part of the Pueblo de Taos Reservation, and shall be administered under the laws and regulations applicable to other trust Indian lands: *Provided*, That the Pueblo de Taos Indians shall use the lands for traditional purposes only, such as religious cermonials, hunting and fishing, a source of water, forage for their domestic livestock, and wood, timber, and other natural resources for their personal use, all subject to such regulations for conservation purposes as the Secretary of the Interior may prescribe. Except for such uses, the lands shall remain forever wild and shall be maintained as a wilderness as defined in section

258

2(c) of the Act of September 3, 1964 (78 Stat. 890). With the consent of the tribe, but not otherwise, nonmembers of the tribe may be permitted to enter the lands for purposes compatible with their preservation as a wilderness. The Secretary of the Interior shall be responsible for the establishment and maintenance of conservation measures for these lands, including, without limitation, protection of forests from fire, disease, insects or trespass; prevention or elimination of erosion, damaging land use, or stream polution; and maintenance of streamflow and sanitary conditions; and the Secretary is authorized to contract with the Secretary of Agriculture for any services or materials deemed necessary to institute or carry out any of such measures.

"(c) Lessees or permittees of lands described in subsection (a) which are not included in the lands described in the Act of May 31, 1933, shall be given the opportunity to renew their leases of permits under rules and regulations of the Secretary of the Interior to the same extent and in the same manner that such leases or permits could have been renewed if this Act had not been enacted; but the Pueblo de Taos may obtain the relinquishment of any or all of such leases or permits from the lessees or permittees under such terms and conditions as may be mutually agreeable. The Secretary of the Interior is authorized to disburse, from the tribal funds in the Treasury of the United States to the credit of said tribe, so much thereof as may be necessary to pay for such relinquishments and for the purchase of any rights or improvements on said lands owned by non-Indians. The authority to pay for the relinquishment of a permit pursuant to this subsection shall not be regarded as a recognition of any property right of the permittee in the land or its resources.

"(d) The Indian Claims Commission is directed to determine in accordance with the provisions of section 2 of the Act of August 13, 1946 (60 Stat. 1049, 1050), the extent to which the value of the interest in land conveyed by this Act should be credited to the United States or should be set off against any claim of the Taos Indians against the United States.

"(e) Nothing in this section shall impair any vested water right."
[*U.S. Statutes at Large*, 84:1437-39.]

2. Remarks of President Nixon
December 15, 1970

Ladies and gentlemen:

I want to welcome all of you here on this very special occasion during the Christmas season, and particularly our guests from the western part of the United States who have come from a long way to be with us.

We are here for a bill signing ceremony that has very special significance—the Taos-Blue Lake bill. It is a bill that has bipartisan support. Both Democrats and Republicans joined together to get it through the Congress so that the President could have the honor of signing it today.

And it is a bill which could be interpreted particularly in the Christmas season as one where a gift was being made by the United States to the Indian population of the United States.

That is not the case.

This is a bill that represents justice, because in 1906 an injustice was done in which land involved in this bill, 48,000 acres, was taken from the Indians involved, the Taos Pueblo Indians. And now, after all those years, the Congress of the United States returns that land to whom it belongs.

This bill also involves respect for religion. Those of us who know something about the background of the first Americans realize that long before any organized religion came to the United States, for 700 years the Taos Pueblo Indians worshiped in this place.

We restore this place of worship to them for all the years to come.

And finally, this bill indicates a new direction in Indian affairs in this country, a new direction in which we will have the cooperation of both Democrats and Republicans, one in which there will be more of an attitude of cooperation rather than paternalism, one of self-determination rather than termination, one of mutual respect.

I can only say that in signing the bill I trust that this will mark one of those periods in American history where, after a very, very long time, and at times a very sad

259

history of injustice, that we started on a new road—a new road which leads us to justice in the treatment of those who were the first Americans, of our working together for the better nation that we want this great and good country of ours to become. . . .

[*Public Papers of the Presidents of the United States: Richard Nixon, 1970*, pp. 1131-32.]

160. Alaska Native Claims Settlement Act

December 18, 1971

After long negotiations with the Alaska natives, the United States provided for settlement of native land claims in Alaska. The act provided for enrollment of natives, the organization of regional corporations of natives, conveyance of lands to the corporations, and deposit of moneys in an Alaska Native Fund. The claims asserted by the natives of Alaska as original owners of the soil had been honored.

An Act To provide for the settlement of certain land claims of Alaska Natives, and for other purposes.

Be it enacted . . . , That this Act may be cited as the "Alaska Native Claims Settlement Act."

DECLARATION OF POLICY

SEC. 2. Congress finds and declares that—

(a) there is an immediate need for a fair and just settlement of all claims by Natives and Native groups of Alaska, based on aboriginal land claims;

(b) the settlement should be accomplished rapidly, with certainty, in conformity with the real economic and social needs of Natives, without litigation, with maximum participation by Natives in decisions affecting their rights and property, without establishing any permanent racially defined institutions, rights, privileges, or obligations, without creating a reservation system or lengthy wardship or trusteeship, and without adding to the categories of property and institutions enjoying special tax privileges or to the legislation establishing special relationships between the United States Government and the State of Alaska;

(c) no provision of this Act shall replace or diminish any right, privilege, or obligation of Natives as citizens of the United States or of Alaska, or relieve, replace, or diminish any obligation of the United States or of the State of Alaska to protect and promote the rights or welfare of Natives as citizens of the United States or of Alaska; the Secretary is authorized and directed, to-

gether with other appropriate agencies of the United States Government, to make a study of all Federal programs primarily designed to benefit Native people and to report back to the Congress with his recommendations for the future management and operation of these programs within three years of the date of enactment of this Act;

(d) no provision of this Act shall constitute a precedent for reopening, renegotiating, or legislating upon any past settlement involving land claims or other matters with any Native organization, or any tribe, band, or identifiable group of American Indians;

(e) no provision of this Act shall effect a change or changes in the petroleum reserve policy reflected in sections 7421 through 7438 of title 10 of the United States Code except as specifically provided in this Act;

(f) no provision of this Act shall be construed to constitute a jurisdictional act, to confer jurisdiction to sue, nor to grant implied consent to Natives to sue the United States or any of its officers with respect to the claims extinguished by the operation of this Act; and

(g) no provision of this Act shall be construed to terminate or otherwise curtail the activities of the Economic Development Administration or other Federal agencies conducting loan or loan and grant programs in Alaska. For this purpose only, the terms "Indian reservation" and "trust or restricted Indian-owned land areas" in Public Law 89-136, the Public Works and Economic Development Act of 1965, as amended, shall be interpreted to include lands granted to Natives under this Act as long as such lands remain in the ownership of the Native villages or the Regional Corporations. . . .

DECLARATION OF SETTLEMENT

SEC. 4. (a) All prior conveyances of public land and water areas in Alaska, or any interest therein, pursuant to Federal law, and all tentative approvals pursuant to section 6 (g) of the Alaska Statehood Act, shall be regarded as an extinguishment of the aboriginal title thereto, if any.

(b) All aboriginal titles, if any, and claims of aboriginal title in Alaska based on use and occupancy, including submerged land underneath all water areas, both inland and offshore, and including any aboriginal hunting or fishing rights that may exist, are hereby extinguished.

(c) All claims against the United States, the State, and all other persons that are based on claims of aboriginal right, title, use, or occupancy of land or water areas in Alaska, or that are based on any statute or treaty of the United States relating to Native use and occupancy, or that are based on the laws of any other nation, including any such claims that are pending before any Federal or state court or the Indian Claims Commission, are hereby extinguished.

ENROLLMENT

SEC. 5. (a) The Secretary shall prepare within two years from the date of enactment of this Act a roll of all Natives who were born on or before, and who are living on, the date of enactment of this Act. Any decision of the Secretary regarding eligibility for enrollment shall be final.

(b) The roll prepared by the Secretary shall show for each Native, among other things, the region and the village or other place in which he resided on the date of the 1970 census enumeration, and he shall be enrolled according to such residence. Except as provided in subsection (c), a Native eligible for enrollment who is not, when the roll is prepared, a permanent resident of one of the twelve regions established pursuant to subsection 7(a) shall be enrolled by the Secretary in one of the twelve regions, giving priority in the following order to—

(1) the region where the Native resided on the 1970 census date if he had resided there without substantial interruption for two or more years;

(2) the region where the Native pre-

viously resided for an aggregate of ten years or more;

(3) the region where the Native was born; and

(4) the region from which an ancestor of the Native came.

The Secretary may enroll a Native in a different region when necessary to avoid enrolling members of the same family in different regions or otherwise avoid hardship.

(c) A Native eligible for enrollment who is eighteen years of age or older and is not a permanent resident of one of the twelve regions may, on the date he files an application for enrollment, elect to be enrolled in a thirteenth region for Natives who are nonresidents of Alaska, if such region is established pursuant to subsection 7(c). If such region is not established, he shall be enrolled as provided in subsection (b). His election shall apply to all dependent members of his household who are less than eighteen years of age, but shall not affect the enrollment of anyone else.

ALASKA NATIVE FUND

SEC. 6. (a) There is hereby established in the United States Treasury an Alaska Native Fund into which the following moneys shall be deposited:

(1) $462,500,000 from the general fund of the Treasury, which are authorized to be appropriated according to the following schedule:

(A) $12,500,000 during the fiscal year in which this Act becomes effective;

(B) $50,000,000 during the second fiscal year;

(C) $70,000,000 during each of the third, fourth, and fifth fiscal years;

(D) $40,000,000 during the sixth fiscal year; and

(E) $30,000,000 during each of the next five fiscal years.

(2) Four percent interest per annum, which is authorized to be appropriated, on any amount authorized to be appropriated by this paragraph that is not appropriated within six months after the fiscal year in which payable.

(3) $500,000,000 pursuant to the revenue sharing provisions of section 9. . . .

REGIONAL CORPORATIONS

Sec. 7. (a) For purposes of this Act, the State of Alaska shall be divided by the Secretary within one year after the date of enactment of this Act into twelve geographic regions, with each region composed as far as practicable of Natives having a common heritage and sharing common interests. In the absence of good cause shown to the contrary, such regions shall approximate the areas covered by the operations of the following existing Native associations:

(1) Arctic Slope Native Association (Barrow, Point Hope);

(2) Bering Straits Association (Seward Peninsula, Unalakleet, Saint Lawrence Island);

(3) Northwest Alaska Native Association (Kotzebue);

(4) Association of Village Council Presidents (southwest coast, all villages in the Bethel area, including all villages on the Lower Yukon River and the Lower Kuskokwim River);

(5) Tanana Chiefs' Conference (Koyukuk, Middle and Upper Yukon Rivers, Upper Kuskokwim, Tanana River);

(6) Cook Inlet Association (Kenai, Tyonek, Eklutna, Iliamna);

(7) Bristol Bay Native Association (Dillingham, Upper Alaska Peninsula);

(8) Aleut League (Aleutian Islands, Pribilof Islands and that part of the Alaska Peninsula which is in the Aleut League);

(9) Chugach Native Association (Cordova, Tatitlek, Port Graham, English Bay, Valdez, and Seward);

(10) Tlingit-Haida Central Council (southeastern Alaska, including Metlakatla);

(11) Kodiak Area Native Association (all villages on and around Kodiak Island); and

(12) Copper River Native Association (Copper Center, Glennallen, Chitina, Mentasta).

Any dispute over the boundaries of a region or regions shall be resolved by a board of arbitrators consisting of one person selected by each of the Native associations involved, and an additional one or two persons, whichever is needed to make an odd number of arbitrators, such additional person or persons to be selected by the arbitrators selected by the Native associations involved.

(b) The Secretary may, on request made within one year of the date of enactment of this Act, by representative and responsible leaders of the Native associations listed in subsection (a), merge two or more of the twelve regions: *Provided*, That the twelve regions may not be reduced to less than seven, and there may be no fewer than seven Regional Corporations. . . .

CONVEYANCE OF LANDS

Sec. 14. (a) Immediately after selection by a Village Corporation for a Native village listed in section 11 which the Secretary finds is qualified for land benefits under this Act, the Secretary shall issue to the Village Corporation a patent to the surface estate in the number of acres shown in the following table:

If the village had on the 1970 census enumeration date a Native population between—	It shall be entitled to a patent to an area of public lands equal to—
25 and 99	69,120 acres.
100 and 199	92,160 acres.
200 and 399	115,200 acres.
400 and 599	138,240 acres.
600 or more	161,280 acres.

The lands patented shall be those selected by the Village Corporation pursuant to subsection 12(a). In addition, the Secretary shall issue to the Village Corporation a patent to the surface estate in the lands selected pursuant to subsection 12(b).

(b) Immediately after selection by any Village Corporation for a Native village listed in section 16 which the Secretary finds is qualified for land benefits under this Act, the Secretary shall issue to the Village Corporation a patent to the surface estate to 23,040 acres. The lands patented shall be the lands within the township or townships that enclose the Native village, and any additional lands selected by the Village Corporation from the surrounding townships withdrawn for the Native village by subsection 16 (a). . . .

[*U.S. Statutes at Large*, 85:688-92, 702-3.]

262

161. Indian Education Act
June 23, 1972

The severe criticism of Indian education in the 1969 report of the Senate Special Subcommittee on Indian Education elicited a substantial response from Congress. In the Education Amendments Act of 1972, a special title provided extensive support for the education of Indians and established new administrative structures in the Department of Health, Education, and Welfare to carry out the work.

An Act to amend the Higher Education Act of 1965 . . . and related Acts, and for other purposes (P.L. 92–318).

TITLE IV—INDIAN EDUCATION
. . . .

DECLARATION OF POLICY

Sec. 302. (a) In recognition of the special educational needs of Indian students in the United States, Congress hereby declares it to be the policy of the United States to provide financial assistance to local educational agencies to develop and carry out elementary and secondary school programs specially designed to meet these special educational needs.

(b) The Commissioner [of Education] shall, in order to effectuate the policy set forth in subsection (a), carry out a program of making grants to local educational agencies which are entitled to payments under this title and which have submitted, and had approved, applications therefor, in accordance with the provisions of this title. . . .

IMPROVEMENT OF EDUCATIONAL
OPPORTUNITIES FOR INDIAN CHILDREN

Sec. 810. (a) The Commissioner shall carry out a program of making grants for the improvement of educational opportunities for Indian children. . . .

(b) The Commissioner is authorized to make grants to State and local educational agencies, federally supported elementary and secondary schools for Indian children and to Indian tribes, organizations, and institutions to support planning, pilot, and demonstration projects which are designed to plan for, and test and demonstrate the effectiveness of, programs for improving educational opportunities for Indian children. . . .

(c) The Commissioner is also authorized to make grants to State and local educational agencies and to tribal and other Indian community organizations to assist and stimulate them in developing and establishing educational services and programs specifically designed to improve educational opportunities for Indian children. . . .

(d) The Commissioner is also authorized to make grants to institutions of higher education and to State and local educational agencies, in combination with institutions of higher education, for carrying out programs and projects—

(1) to prepare persons to serve Indian children as teachers, teacher aides, social workers, and ancillary educational personnel; and

(2) to improve the qualifications of such persons who are serving Indian children in such capacities.

Grants for the purposes of this subsection may be used for the establishment of fellowship programs leading to an advanced degree, for institutes and, as part of a continuing program, for seminars, symposia, workshops, and conferences. In carrying out the programs authorized by this subsection, preference shall be given to the training of Indians . . . .

IMPROVEMENT OF EDUCATIONAL
OPPORTUNITIES FOR ADULT INDIANS

Sec. 314. (a) The Commissioner shall carry out a program of making grants to State and local educational agencies, and to Indian tribes, institutions, and organizations, to support planning, pilot, and demonstration projects which are designed to plan for, and test and demonstrate the effectiveness of, programs for providing adult education for Indians. . . .

OFFICE OF INDIAN EDUCATION

Sec. 441. (a) There is hereby established, in the Office of Education, a bureau to be

263

known as the "Office of Indian Education". . . . The Office shall be headed by a Deputy Commissioner of Indian Education, who shall be appointed by the Commissioner of Education from a list of nominees submitted to him by the National Advisory Council on Indian Education. . . .

NATIONAL ADVISORY COUNCIL ON INDIAN EDUCATION

Sec. 442. (a) There is hereby established the National Advisory Council on Indian Education . . . , which shall consist of fifteen members who are Indians and Alaska Natives appointed by the President of the United States. Such appointments shall be made by the President from lists of nominees furnished, from time to time, by Indian tribes and organizations, and shall represent diverse geographic areas of the country. . . .

[*U.S. Statutes at Large*, 86:335, 339–43.]

162. Extension of Indian Preference in Employment

June 26, 1972

The Indian Reorganization Act of 1934 authorized Indian preference in employing personnel for the Bureau of Indian Affairs without regard for civil service regulations, but that authority was generally applied only to original hiring. Commissioner of Indian Affairs Louis R. Bruce extended the practice to cover all vacancies. His action was upheld in Morton v. Mancari *(1974).*

The Secretary of the Interior announced today he has approved the Bureau's policy to extend Indian Preference to training and to filling vacancies by original appointment, reinstatement and promotions. The new policy was discussed with the National President of the National Federation of Federal Employees under National Consultation Rights NFFE has with the Department. Secretary Morton and I jointly stress that careful attention must be given to protecting the rights of non-Indian employees. The new policy provides as follows: Where two or more candidates who meet the established qualification requirements are available for filling a vacancy, if one of them is an Indian, he shall be given preference in filling the vacancy. This new policy is effective immediately, and is incorporated into all existing programs such as the Promotion Program. . . . You should take immediate steps to notify all employees and recognized unions of this policy.

[Bureau of Indian Affairs, Personnel Management Letter no. 72–12, printed in *Morton* v. *Mancari*, 417 *U.S. Reports* 538n.]

163. Menominee Restoration Act

December 22, 1973

The deleterious effects of termination on the Menominee Indians of Wisconsin led to agitation for repeal of the termination act of June 17, 1954. This repeal was accomplished on December 22, 1973, and the Menominee tribe was restored to federal status.

An Act to repeal the Act terminating Federal supervision over the property and members of the Menominee Indian Tribe of Wisconsin; to reinstitute the Menominee Indian Tribe of Wisconsin as a federally recognized sovereign Indian tribe; and to restore to the Menominee Tribe of Wisconsin those Federal services furnished to American Indians because of their status as American Indians; and for other purposes.
Be it enacted. . . , *That:*

This Act may be cited as the "Menominee Restoration Act".

Sec. 2. For the purposes of this Act—
(1) The term "tribe" means the Menominee Indian Tribe of Wisconsin.
(2) The term "Secretary" means the Secretary of the Interior.
(3) The term "Menominee Restoration Committee" means that committee of nine Menominee Indians who shall be elected

pursuant to subsections 4(a) and 4(b) of this Act.

SEC. 3. (a) Notwithstanding the provisions of the Act of June 17, 1954 (68 Stat. 250; 25 U.S.C. 891-902), as amended, or any other law, Federal recognition is hereby extended to the Menominee Indian Tribe of Wisconsin and the provisions of the Act of June 18, 1934 (48 Stat. 984; 25 U.S.C. 461 et seq.), as amended, are made applicable to it.

(b) The Act of June 17, 1954 (68 Stat. 250; 25 U.S.C. 891-902), as amended, is hereby repealed and there are hereby reinstated all rights and privileges of the tribe or its members under Federal treaty, statute, or otherwise which may have been diminished or lost pursuant to such Act.

(c) Nothing contained in this Act shall diminish any rights or privileges enjoyed by the tribe or its members now or prior to June 17, 1954, under Federal treaty, statute, or otherwise, which are not inconsistent with the provisions of this Act.

(d) Except as specifically provided in this Act, nothing contained in this Act shall alter any property rights or obligations, any contractual rights or obligations, including existing fishing rights, or any obligations for taxes already levied.

(e) In providing to the tribe such services to which it may be entitled upon its recognition pursuant to subsection (a) of this section, the Secretary of the Interior and the Secretary of Health, Education, and Welfare, as appropriate, are authorized from funds appropriated pursuant to the Act of November 2, 1921 (42 Stat. 208; 25 U.S.C. 13), the Act of August 5, 1954 (68 Stat. 674), as amended, or any other Act authorizing appropriations for the administration of Indian affairs, upon the request of the tribe and subject to such terms and conditions as may be mutually agreed to, to make grants and contract to make grants which will accomplish the general purposes for which the funds were appropriated. The Menominee Restoration Committee shall have full authority and capacity to be a party to receive such grants, to make such contracts, and to bind the tribal governing body as the successor in interest to the Menominee Restoration Committee: *Provided, however,* That the Menominee Restoration Committee shall have no authority to bind the tribe for a period of more than six

months after the date on which the tribal governing body takes office.

SEC. 4. (a) Within fifteen days after the enactment of this Act, the Secretary shall announce the date of a general council meeting of the tribe to nominate candidates for election to the Menominee Restoration Committee. Such general council meeting shall be held within thirty days of the date of enactment of this Act. Within forty-five days of the general council meeting provided for herein, the Secretary shall hold an election by secret ballot, absentee balloting to be permitted, to elect the membership of the Menominee Restoration Committee from among the nominees submitted to him from the general council meeting provided for herein. The ballots shall provide for write-in votes. The Secretary shall approve the Menominee Restoration Committee elected pursuant to this section if he is satisfied that the requirements of this section relating to the nominating and election process have been met. The Menominee Restoration Committee shall represent the Menominee people in the implementation of this Act and shall have no powers other than those given to it in accordance with this Act. The Menominee Restoration Committee shall have no power or authority under this Act after the time which the duly-elected tribal governing body takes office: *Provided, however,* That this provision shall in no way invalidate or affect grants or contracts made pursuant to the provisions of subsection 3 (e) of this Act.

(b) In the absence of a completed tribal roll prepared pursuant to subsection (c) hereof and solely for the purposes of the general council meeting and the election provided for in subsection (a) hereof, all living persons on the final roll of the tribe published under section 3 of the Act of June 17, 1954 (25 U.S.C. 893), and all descendants, who are at least eighteen years of age and who possess at least one-quarter degree of Menominee Indian blood, of persons on such roll shall be entitled to attend, participate, and vote at such general council meeting and such election. Verification of descendancy, age, and blood quantum shall be made upon oath before the Secretary or his authorized representative and his determination thereon shall be conclusive and final. The Secretary shall assure that adequate notice of such meeting and election shall be provided eligible voters.

SEC. 5. (a) Upon request from the Menominee Restoration Committee, the Secretary shall condict an election by secret ballot, pursuant to the provisions of the Act of June 18, 1934, as amended, for the purpose of determining the tribe's constitution and bylaws. The election shall be held within sixty days after final certification of the tribal roll.

(b) The Menominee Restoration Committee shall distribute to all enrolled persons who are entitled to vote in the election, at least thirty days before the election, a copy of the constitution and bylaws as drafted by the Menominee Restoration Committee which will be presented at the election, along with a brief impartial description of the constitution and bylaws. The Menominee Restoration Committee shall freely consult with persons entitled to vote in the election concerning the text and description of the constitution and bylaws. Such consultation shall not be carried on within fifty feet of the polling places on the date of the election.

(c) Within one hundred and twenty days after the tribe adopts a constitution and by-laws, the Menominee Restoration Committee shall conduct an election by secret ballot for the purpose of determining the individuals who will serve as tribal officials as provided in the tribal constitution and bylaws. For the purpose of this initial election and notwithstanding any provision in the tribal constitution and bylaws to the contrary, absentee balloting shall be permitted and all tribal members who are eighteen years of age or over shall be entitled to vote in the election. All further elections of tribal officers shall be as provided in the tribal constitution and bylaws and ordinances adopted thereunder.

(d) In any election held pursuant to this section, the vote of a majority of those actually voting shall be necessary and sufficient to effectuate the adoption of a tribal constitution and bylaws and the initial election of the tribe's governing body, so long as, in each such election, the total vote cast is at least 30 per centum of those entitled to vote. . . .

SEC. 6. [Provisions concerning transfer of assets and arrangements with the State of Wisconsin.]

[*U.S. Statutes at Large*, 87:700 ff.]

164. Comprehensive Employment and Training Act
December 28, 1973

Congress in 1973 provided job training and employment opportunities for unemployed and underemployed persons. A special section of the law pertained to Indians, who had special needs. The legislation reflected the new emphasis on Indian participation in running the programs.

An Act to assure opportunities for employment and training to unemployed and underemployed persons.

. . . .

STATEMENT OF PURPOSE

SEC. 2. It is the purpose of this Act to provide job training and employment opportunities for economically disadvantaged, unemployed, and underemployed persons, and to assure that training and other services lead to maximum employment opportunities and enhance self-sufficiency by establishing a flexible and decentralized system of Federal, State, and local programs. . . .

INDIAN MANPOWER PROGRAMS

SEC. 302. (a) The Congress finds that (1) serious unemployment and economic disadvantage exist among members of Indian and Alaskan native communities; (2) there is a compelling need for the establishment of comprehensive manpower training and employment programs for members of those communities; (3) such programs are essential to the reduction of economic disadvantage among individual members of those communities and to the advancement of economic and social development in these communities consistent with their goals and life styles.

(b) The Congress therefore declares that,

because of the special relationship between the Federal Government and most of those to be served by the provisions of this section, (1) such programs can best be administered at the national level; (2) such programs shall be available to federally recognized Indian tribes, bands, and individuals and to other groups and individuals of native American descent such as, but not limited to, the Lummis in Washington, the Menominees in Wisconsin, the Klamaths in Oregon, the Oklahoma Indians, the Passamaquoddys and Penobscots in Maine, and Eskimos and Aleuts in Alaska; (3) such programs shall be administered in such a manner as to maximize the Federal commitment to support growth and development as determined by representatives of the communities and groups served by this part.

(c) (1) In carrying out his responsibilities under this section, the Secretary [of the Interior] shall, wherever possible, utilize Indian tribes, bands or groups (including Alaska Native villages or groups . . .) having a gov-

erning body, for the provision of manpower services under this title. . . .

(2) In carrying out his responsibilities under this section the Secretary shall make arrangements with prime sponsors and organizations (meeting requirements prescribed by the Secretary) serving non-reservation Indians for programs and projects designed to meet the needs of such Indians for employment and training and related services.

(d) Whenever the Secretary determines not to utilize Indian tribes, bands, or groups for the provisions of manpower services under this section, he shall, to the maximum extent feasible, enter into arrangements for the provision of such services with public or private non-profit agencies which meet with the approval of the tribes, bands, or groups to be served. . . .

(h) No provision of this section shall abrogate in any way the trust responsibilities of the Federal Government to Indian bands or tribes. . . .

[U.S. Statutes at Large 87:839, 858–59.]

165. United States v. State of Washington
March 22, 1974

The vital question of Indian fishing rights in the Pacific Northwest was decided in the landmark decision by Judge George Boldt of the Federal District Court for the Western District of Washington. After a long analysis of treaties, fish migratory patterns, Indian fishing customs, and state regulations, this "Boldt Decision" set forth a series of principles to govern Indian fishing rights. The most controversial was the decision that Indians were entitled to one-half the harvestable fish. On July 2, 1979, the Supreme Court upheld with minor changes Judge Boldt's decision (Washington v. Washington State Commericial Passenger Fishing Vessel Association, 443 U.S. Reports, 658–708).

. . . . Since tribal on reservation treaty right fishing is exclusive, fish taken on reservation shall not be included in any allocation of fish between treaty and non-treaty fishermen. Therefore, the *amount* or *quantity* of any species of fish that may be taken off reservation by treaty right fishing during a particular fishing period can only be limited by either:

(a) The number of fish required for spawning escapement and any other requirements established to be reasonable and necessary for conservation, and

(b) The number of harvestable fish non-treaty fishermen may take at the

tribes' "usual and accustomed grounds and stations" while fishing "in common with" treaty right fishermen.

As used above, "harvestable" means the number of fish remaining to be taken by any and all fishermen, at usual and accustomed grounds and stations, after deducting the number of fish required for spawning escapement and tribal needs. . . .

By dictionary definition and as intended and used in the Indian treaties and in this decision "in common with" means *sharing equally* the opportunity to take fish at "usual and accustomed grounds and stations"; therefore, non-treaty fishermen shall have the opportunity to take up to 50% of the harvestable number of fish that may be taken by all fishermen at usual and accustomed grounds and stations and treaty right fishermen shall have the opportunity to take up to the same percentage of harvestable fish, as stated above. . . .

11. The right of a Treaty Tribe to harvest anadromous fish outside reservation boundaries arises from a provision which appears in each of the Stevens' treaties and which, with immaterial variations, states:

The right of taking fish, at all usual and accustomed grounds and stations, is further secured to said Indians, in common with all citizens of the Territory. . . .

12. It is the responsibility of all citizens to see that the terms of the Stevens' treaties are carried out, so far as possible, in accordance with the meaning they were understood to have by the tribal representatives at the councils, and in a spirit which generously recognizes the full obligation of this nation to protect the interests of a dependent people.

13. From the earliest known times, up to and beyond the time of the Stevens' treaties, the Indians comprising each of the treating tribes and bands were primarily a fishing, hunting and gathering people dependent almost entirely upon the natural animal and vegetative resources of the region for their subsistence and culture. They were heavily dependent upon anadromous fish for their subsistence and for trade with other tribes and later with the settlers. Anadromous fish was the great staple of their diet and livelihood. They cured and dried large quantities for year around use, both for themselves and for others through sale, trade, barter and employment. With the advent of canning technology in the latter half of the 19th Century the commercial exploitation of the anadromous fish resources by non-Indians increased tremendously. Indians, fishing under their treaty-secured rights, also participated

in this expanded commercial fishery and sold many fish to non-Indian packers and dealers.

14. The taking of anadromous fish from usual and accustomed places, the right to which was secured to the Treaty Tribes in the Stevens' treaties, constituted both the means of economic livelihood and the foundation of native culture. Reservation of the right to gather food in this fashion protected the Indians' right to maintain essential elements of their way of life, as a complement to the life defined by the permanent homes, allotted farm lands, compulsory education, technical assistance and pecuniary rewards offered in the treaties. Settlement of the West and the rise of industrial America have significantly circumscribed the opportunities of members of the Treaty Tribes to fish for subsistence and commerce and to maintain tribal traditions. But the mere passage of time has not eroded, and cannot erode, the rights guaranteed by solemn treaties that both sides pledged on their honor to uphold.

15. The treaty-secured rights to resort to the usual and accustomed places to fish were a part of larger rights possessed by the treating Indians, upon the exercise of which there was not a shadow of impediment, and which were not much less necessary to their existence than the atmosphere they breathed. The treaty was not a grant of rights to the treating Indians, but a grant of rights from them, and a reservation of those not granted. In the Stevens' treaties, such reservations were not of particular parcels of land, and could not be expressed in deeds, as dealings between private individuals. The reservations were in large areas of territory, and the negotiations were with the tribes. The treaties reserved rights, however, to every individual Indian, as though described therein. There was an exclusive right of fishing reserved within certain boundaries. There was a right outside of those boundaries reserved for exercise "in common with citizens of the Territory". . . .

[384 *Federal Supplement* 343, 406–7.]

166. Indian Financing Act
April 12, 1974

In order to encourage Indian economic development and self-sufficiency, Congress provided special credit sources, loan guarantees, and business grants to Indian groups and individuals. The law is in line with other self-determination legislation.

An Act to provide for financing the economic development of Indians and Indian organizations, and for other purposes.
. . . .

DECLARATION OF POLICY

SEC. 2. It is hereby declared to be the policy of Congress to provide capital on a reimbursable basis to help develop and utilize Indian resources, both physical and human, to a point where the Indians will fully exercise responsibility for the utilization and management of their own resources and where they will enjoy a standard of living from their own productive efforts comparable to that enjoyed by non-Indians in neighboring communities. . . .

TITLE I—INDIAN REVOLVING LOAN FUND

SEC. 101. In order to provide credit that is not available from private money markets, all funds that are now or hereafter a part of the revolving fund authorized by the Act of June 18, 1934 (48 Stat. 986), the Act of June 26, 1936 (49 Stat. 1968), and the Act of April 19, 1950 (64 Stat. 44), as amended and supplemented, including sums received in settlement of debts of livestock pursuant to the Act of May 4, 1950 (64 Stat. 190), and sums collected in repayment of loans heretofore made, and as interest or other charges on loans, shall hereafter be administered as a single Indian Revolving Loan Fund. The fund shall be available for loans to Indians having a form of organization that is satisfactory to the Secretary [of the Interior] and for loans to individual Indians who are not members of or eligible for membership in an organization which is making loans to its members: *Provided*, That, where the Secretary determines a rejection of a loan application from a member of an organization making loans to its membership from moneys borrowed from the fund is unwarranted, he may, in his discretion, make a direct loan to

such individual from the fund. The fund shall also be available for administrative expenses incurred in connection therewith.

SEC. 102. Loans may be made for any purpose which will promote the economic development of (a) the individual Indian borrower, including loans for educational purposes, and (b) the Indian organization and its members including loans by such organizations to other organizations and investments in other organizations regardless of whether they are organizations of Indians: *Provided*, That not more than 50 per centum of loan made to an organization shall be used by such organization for the purpose of making loans to or investments in non-Indian organizations.

SEC. 103. Loans may be made only when, in the judgment of the Secretary, there is a reasonable prospect of repayment, and only to applicants who in the opinion of the Secretary are unable to obtain financing from other sources on reasonable terms and conditions.
. . .

TITLE IV—INDIAN BUSINESS GRANTS

SEC. 401. There is established within the Department of the Interior the Indian Business Development Program whose purpose is to stimulate and increase Indian entrepreneurship and employment by providing equity capital through nonreimbursable grants made by the Secretary of the Interior to Indians and Indian tribes to establish and expand profit-making Indian-owned economic enterprises on or near reservations.

SEC. 402. (a) No grant in excess of $50,000, or such lower amount as the Secretary may determine to be appropriate, may be made to an Indian or Indian tribe.

(b) A grant may be made only to an applicant who, in the opinion of the Secretary, is unable to obtain adequate financing for its economic enterprise from other sources: *Provided*, That prior to making any grant under this title, the Secretary shall assure that, where practical, the applicant has reasonably made available for the economic enterprise funds from the applicant's own financial resources.

(c) No grant may be made to an applicant who is unable to obtain at least 60 per centum of the necessary funds for the economic enterprise from other sources. . . .

[*U.S. Statutes at Large*, 88:77–79, 82–83.]

167. Morton v. Mancari
June 17, 1974

The preferential hiring of Indians for BIA positions was challenged by non-Indian employees, who claimed that the Indian preference law of 1934 had been repealed by the Equal Employment Opportunity Act of 1972. The Supreme Court, overturning a district court decision, supported the preference policy and declared that the preference was based not on "racial discrimination" but on the special legal status of the Indians.

. . . . The federal policy of according some hiring preference to Indians in the Indian service dates at least as far back as 1834. Since that time, Congress repeatedly has enacted various preferences of the general type here at issue. The purpose of these preferences, as variously expressed in the legislative history, has been to give Indians a greater participation in their own self-government; to further the Government's trust obligation toward the Indian tribes; and to reduce the negative effect of having non-Indians administer matters that affect Indian tribal life.

The preference directly at issue here was enacted as an important part of the sweeping Indian Reorganization Act of 1934. The overriding purpose of that particular Act was to establish machinery whereby Indian tribes would be able to assume a greater degree of self-government, both politically and economically. Congress was seeking to modify the then-existing situation whereby primarily non-Indian-staffed BIA had plenary control, for all practical purposes, over the lives and destinies of the federally recognized Indian tribes. . . .

One of the primary means by which self-government would be fostered and the Bureau made more responsive was to increase the participation of tribal Indians in the BIA operations. In order to achieve this end, it was recognized that some kind of preference and exemption from otherwise prevailing civil service requirements was necessary. . . .

Congress was well aware that the proposed preference would result in employment disadvantages within the BIA for non-Indians. Not only was this displacement unavoidable if room were to be made for

Indians, but it was explicitly determined that gradual replacement of non-Indians with Indians within the Bureau was a desirable feature of the entire program for self-government. . . . The Commissioner's extension of the preference in 1972 to promotions within the BIA was designed to bring more Indians into positions of responsibility and, in that regard, appears to be a logical extension of the congressional intent. . . .

A provision aimed at furthering Indian self-government by according an employment preference within the BIA for qualified members of the governed group can readily co-exist with a general rule prohibiting employment discrimination on the basis of race. Any other conclusion can be reached only by formalistic reasoning that ignores both the history and purposes of the preference and the unique legal relationship between the Federal Government and tribal Indians.

Furthermore, the Indian preference statute is a specific provision applying to a very specific situation. The 1972 [Equal Employment Opportunity] Act, on the other hand, is of general application. Where there is no clear intention otherwise, a specific statute will not be controlled or nullified by a general one, regardless of the priority of enactment. . . .

The courts are not at liberty to pick and choose among congressional enactments, and when two statutes are capable of co-existence, it is the duty of the courts, absent a clearly expressed congressional intention to the contrary, to regard each as effective. . . . In light of the factors indicating no repeal, we simply cannot conclude that Congress consciously abandoned its policy of furthering

270

Indian self-government when it passed the 1972 amendments.

We therefore hold that the District Court erred in ruling that the Indian preference was repealed by the 1972 Act. . . .

Literally every piece of legislation dealing with Indian tribes and reservations, and certainly all legislation dealing with the BIA, single out for special treatment a constituency of tribal Indians living on or near reservations. If these laws, derived from historical relationships and explicitly designed to help only Indians, were deemed invidious racial discrimination, an entire Title of the United States Code (25 U.S.C.) would be effectively erased and the solemn commitment of the Government toward the Indians would be jeopardized. . . .

Contrary to the characterization made by appellees, this preference does not constitute "racial discrimination." Indeed, it is not even a "racial" preference. Rather, it is an employment criterion reasonably designed to further the cause of Indian self-government and to make the BIA more responsive to the needs of its constituent groups. It is directed to participation by the governed in the governing agency. The preference is similar in kind to the constitutional requirement that a United States Senator, when elected, be "an Inhabitant of the State for which he shall be chosen," Art. I, §3, cl. 3, or that a member of a city council reside within the city governed by the council. Congress has sought only to enable the BIA to draw more heavily from among the constituent group in staffing its projects, all of which, either directly or indirectly, affect the lives of tribal Indians. The preference, as applied, is granted to Indians not as a discrete racial group, but, rather, as members of quasi-sovereign tribal entities whose lives and activities are governed by the BIA in a unique fashion. . . . In the sense that there is no other group of people favored in this manner, the legal status of the BIA is truly *sui generis*. . . .

On numerous occasions this Court specifically has upheld legislation that singles out Indians for particular and special treatment. . . . As long as the special treatment can be tied rationally to the fulfillment of Congress' unique obligation toward the Indians, such legislative judgments will not be disturbed. Here, where the preference is reasonable and rationally designed to further Indian self-government, we cannot say that Congress' classification violates due process. . . .

[417 *U.S. Reports* 541–45, 550–55.]

168. Student Rights and Due Process Procedures
October 11, 1974

Concern for Indian rights in education extended to the fundamental rights of students in the schools. The statement of rights set forth in these regulations was a far cry from the dictatorial and repressive control of the students that once marked the Indian boarding schools.

Purpose.

The regulations in this part govern establishing programs of student rights and due process procedures in Bureau of Indian Affairs schools and in schools that are operating under contract with the Bureau of Indian Affairs.

Application to Bureau schools.

All Bureau of Indian Affairs schools shall be governed by the regulations set forth in this part and said regulations shall be expressly included as a part of the local school regulations of each Bureau of Indian Affairs school. Upon admission, all students of Bureau of Indian Affairs schools shall be given a copy of the school regulations governing the conduct of students and shall be notified of any amendments thereto.

Rights of the individual student.

Individual students at Bureau of Indian Affairs schools have, and shall be accorded, the following rights:

(a) The right to an education.

(b) The right to be free from unreasonable search and seizure of their person and property, to a reasonable degree of privacy, and to a safe and secure environment.

(c) The right to make his or her own decisions where applicable.

(d) The right to freedom of religion and culture.

(e) The right to freedom of speech and

271

expression, including symbolic expression, such as display of buttons, posters, choice of dress, and length of hair, so long as the symbolic expression does not unreasonably and in fact disrupt the educational process or endanger the health and safety of the student or others.

(f) The right to freedom of the press, except where material in student publications is libelous, slanderous, or obscene.

(g) The right to peaceably assemble and to petition the redress of grievances.

(h) The right to freedom from discrimination.

(i) The right to due process. Every student is entitled to due process in every instance of disciplinary action for alleged violation of school regulations for which the student may be subjected to penalties of suspension, expulsion, or transfer.

Due Process.
[Due process procedures are spelled out in detail.]

Application to schools under Bureau contract.

Non-Bureau of Indian Affairs schools which are funded under contract with the Bureau of Indian Affairs must also recognize these student rights.

[*Federal Register*, 39:32741–42 (September 11, 1974); codified in 25 *Code of Federal Regulations* 35.]

169. Establishment of the American Indian Policy
Review Commission
January 2, 1975

The confused state of Indian affairs in the early 1970s led Senator James Abourezk of South Dakota to promote the establishment of a commission to study the historical and legal status of the Indians and to recommend new legislation. Such a commission was authorized by this joint resolution.

Joint Resolution to provide for the establishment of the American Indian Policy Review Commission.

CONGRESSIONAL FINDINGS

The Congress, after careful review of the Federal Government's historical and special legal relationship with American Indian people, finds that—

(a) the policy implementing this relationship has shifted and changed with changing administrations and passing years, without apparent rational design and without a consistent goal to achieve Indian self-sufficiency;

(b) there has been no general comprehensive review of conduct of Indian affairs by the United States nor a coherent investigation of the many problems and issues involved in the conduct of Indian affairs since the 1928 Meriam Report conducted by the Institute for Government Research; and

(c) in carrying out its responsibilities under its plenary power over Indian affairs, it is imperative that the Congress now cause such a compre-hensive review of Indian affairs to be conducted.

DECLARATION OF PURPOSE

Congress declares that it is timely and essential to conduct a comprehensive review of the historical and legal developments underlying the Indians' unique relationship with the Federal Government in order to determine the nature and scope of necessary revisions in the formulation of policies and programs for the benefit of Indians.

Resolved by the Senate and House of Representatives of the United States of America in Congress assembled, That—

(a) In order to carry out the purposes described in the preamble hereof and as further set out herein, there is hereby created the American Indian Policy Review Commission, hereinafter referred to as the "Commission."

(b) The Commission shall be composed of eleven members, as follows:

(1) three Members of the Senate appointed by the President pro tempore of the Senate, two from the majority party

and one from the minority party;

(2) three Members of the House of Representatives appointed by the Speaker of the House of Representatives, two from the majority party and one from the minority party; and

(3) five Indian members as provided in subsection (c) of this section.

(c) At its organization meeting, the members of the Commission appointed pursuant to section (b)(1) and (b)(2) of this section shall elect from among their members a Chairman and a Vice Chairman. Immediately thereafter, such members shall select, by majority vote, five Indian members of the Commission from the Indian community, as follows:

(1) three members shall be selected from Indian tribes that are recognized by the Federal Government;

(2) one member shall be selected to represent urban Indians; and

(3) one member shall be selected who is a member of an Indian group not recognized by the Federal Government. . . .

SEC. 2. It shall be the duty of the Commission to make a comprehensive investigation and study of Indian affairs and the scope of such duty shall include, but shall not be limited to—

(1) a study and analysis of the Constitution, treaties, statutes, judicial interpretations, and Executive orders to determine the attributes of the unique relationship between the Federal Government and Indian tribes and the land and other resources they possess;

(2) a review of the policies, practices, and structure of the Federal agencies charged with protecting Indian resources and providing services to Indians: *Provided*, That such review shall include a management study of the Bureau of Indian Affairs utilizing experts from the public and private sector;

(3) an examination of the statutes and procedures for granting Federal recognition and extending services to Indian communities and individuals;

(4) the collection and compilation of data necessary to understand the extent of Indian needs which presently exist or will exist in the near future;

(5) an exploration of the feasibility of alternative elective bodies which could

fully represent Indians at the national level of Government to provide Indians with maximum participation in policy formation and program development;

(6) a consideration of alternative methods to strengthen tribal government so that the tribes might fully represent their members and, at the same time, guarantee the fundamental rights of individual Indians; and

(7) the recommendation of such modification of existing laws, procedures, regulations, policies, and practices as will, in the judgment of the Commission, best serve to carry out the policy and declaration of purposes as set out above. . . .

INVESTIGATING TASK FORCES

SEC. 4. (a) As soon as practicable after the organization of the Commission, the Commission shall, for the purpose of gathering facts and other information necessary to carry out its responsibilities pursuant to section 2 of this resolution, appoint investigating task forces to be composed of three persons, a majority of whom shall be of Indian descent. Such task forces shall be appointed and directed to make preliminary investigations and studies in the various areas of Indian affairs, including, but not limited to—

(1) trust responsibility and Federal-Indian relationship, including treaty review;

(2) tribal government;

(3) Federal administration and structure of Indian affairs;

(4) Federal, State, and tribal jurisdiction;

(5) Indian education;

(6) Indian health;

(7) reservation development;

(8) urban, rural nonreservation, terminated, and nonfederally recognized Indians; and

(9) Indian law revision, consolidation, and codification. . . .

REPORT OF THE COMMISSION

SEC. 5. (a) Upon the report of the task forces made pursuant to section 4 hereof, the Commission shall review and compile such reports, together with its independent find-

273

ings, into a final report. Within six months after the reports of the investigating task forces, the Commission shall submit its final report, together with the recommendations thereon, to the President of the Senate and the Speaker of the House of Representatives. The Commission shall cease to exist six months after submission of said final report but not later than June 30, 1977. All records and papers of the Commission shall thereupon be delivered to the Administrator of the General Services Administration for deposit in the Archives of the United States.

(b) Any recommendation of the Commission involving the enactment of legislation shall be referred by the President of the Senate or the Speaker of the House of Representatives to the appropriate standing committee of the Senate and House of Representatives, respectively, and such committees shall make a report thereon to the respective house within two years of such referral.

[*U.S. Statutes at Large*, 88:1910–13.]

170. Indian Self-Determination and Education Assistance Act

January 4, 1975

One result of the drive for Indian participation in federal programs affecting Indians was this act, which provided that tribes could contract to run education and health programs themselves. The second part of the act provided more Indian control of schools educating Indian children.

An Act to provide maximum Indian participation in the Government and education of Indian people; to provide for the full participation of Indian tribes in programs and services conducted by the Federal Government for Indians and to encourage the development of human resources of the Indian people; to establish a program of assistance to upgrade Indian education; to support the right of Indian citizens to control their own educational activities; and for other purposes (P.L. 93–638).
. . . .

CONGRESSIONAL FINDINGS

SEC. 2. (a) The Congress, after careful review of the Federal Government's historical and special legal relationship with, and resulting responsibilities to, American Indian people, finds that—

(1) the prolonged Federal domination of Indian service programs has served to retard rather than enhance the progress of Indian people and their communities by depriving Indians of the full opportunity to develop leadership skills crucial to the realization of self-government, and has denied to the Indian people an effective voice in the planning and implementation of programs for the benefit of Indians which are responsive to the true needs of Indian communities; and

(2) the Indian people will never surrender their desire to control their rela-

tionships both among themselves and with non-Indian governments, organizations, and persons.

(b) The Congress further finds that—

(1) true self-determination in any society of people is dependent upon an educational process which will insure the development of qualified people to fulfill meaningful leadership roles;

(2) the Federal responsibility for and assistance to education of Indian children has not effected the desired level of educational achievement or created the diverse opportunities and personal satisfaction which education can and should provide; and

(3) parental and community control of the educational process is of crucial importance to the Indian people.

DECLARATION OF POLICY

SEC. 3. (a) The Congress hereby recognizes the obligation of the United States to respond to the strong expression of the Indian people for self-determination by assuring maximum Indian participation in the direction of educational as well as other Federal services to Indian communities so as to render such services more responsive to the needs and desires of those communities.

(b) The Congress declares its commitment to the maintenance of the Federal Government's unique and continuing relationship with and responsibility to the Indian people through the establishment of a meaningful Indian self-determination policy which will permit an orderly transition from Federal domination of programs for and services to Indians to effective and meaningful participation by the Indian people in the planning, conduct, and administration of those programs and services.

(c) The Congress declares that a major national goal of the United States is to provide the quantity and quality of educational services and opportunities which will permit Indian children to compete and excel in the life areas of their choice, and to achieve the measure of self-determination essential to their social and economic well-being. . . .

TITLE I—INDIAN SELF-DETERMINATION ACT

SEC. 101. This title may be cited as the "Indian Self-Determination Act."

CONTRACTS BY THE SECRETARY OF THE INTERIOR

SEC. 102. (a) The Secretary of the Interior is directed, upon the request of any Indian tribe, to enter into a contract or contracts with any tribal organization of any such Indian tribe to plan, conduct, and administer programs, or portions thereof, provided for in the Act of April 16, 1934 (48 Stat. 596), as amended by this Act, any other program or portion thereof which the Secretary of the Interior is authorized to administer for the benefit of Indians under the Act of November 2, 1921 (42 Stat. 208), and any Act subsequent thereto: *Provided, however,* That the Secretary may initially decline to enter into any contract requested by an Indian tribe if he finds that: (1) the service to be rendered to the Indian beneficiaries of the particular program or function to be contracted will not be satisfactory; (2) adequate protection of trust resources is not assured, or (3) the proposed project or function to be contracted for cannot be properly completed or maintained by the proposed contract: *Provided further,* That in arriving at his finding, the Secretary shall consider whether the tribe or tribal organization would be deficient in performance under

the contract with respect to (A) equipment, (B) bookkeeping and accounting procedures, (C) substantive knowledge of the program to be contracted for, (D) community support for the contract, (E) adequately trained personnel, or (F) other necessary components of contract performance.

(b) Whenever the Secretary declines to enter into a contract or contracts pursuant to subsection (a) of this section, he shall (1) state his objections in writing to the tribe within sixty days, (2) provide to the extent practicable assistance to the tribe or tribal organization to overcome his stated objections, and (3) provide the tribe with a hearing, under such rules and regulations as he may promulgate, and the opportunity for appeal on the objections raised. . . .

CONTRACTS BY THE SECRETARY OF HEALTH, EDUCATION, AND WELFARE

SEC. 103. (a) The Secretary of Health, Education, and Welfare is directed, upon the request of any Indian tribe, to enter into a contract or contracts with any tribal organization of any such Indian tribe to carry out any or all of his functions, authorities, and responsibilities under the Act of August 5, 1954 (68 Stat. 674), as amended. . . .

GRANTS TO INDIAN TRIBAL ORGANIZATIONS

SEC. 104. (a) The Secretary of the Interior is authorized, upon the request of any Indian tribe (from funds appropriated for the benefit of Indians pursuant to the Act of November 2, 1921 (42 Stat. 208), and any Act subsequent thereto) to contract with or make a grant or grants to any tribal organization for—

(1) the strengthening or improvement of tribal government (including, but not limited to, the development, improvement, and administration of planning, financial management, or merit personnel systems; the improvement of tribally funded programs or activities; or the development, construction, improvement, maintenance, preservation, or operation of tribal facilities or resources);

(2) the planning, training, evaluation of other activities designed to improve the capacity of a tribal organization to enter

into a contract or contracts pursuant to section 102 of this Act and the additional costs associated with the initial years of operation under such a contract or contracts;

(3) the acquisition of land in connection with items (1) and (2) above: *Provided*, That in the case of land within reservation boundaries or which adjoins on at least two sides lands held in trust by the United States for the tribe or for individual Indians, the Secretary of Interior may (upon request of the tribe) acquire such land in trust for the tribe; or

(4) the planning, designing, monitoring, and evaluating of Federal programs serving the tribe.

(b) The Secretary of Health, Education, and Welfare may, in accordance with regulations adopted pursuant to section 107 of this Act, make grants to any Indian tribe or tribal organization for—

(1) the development, construction, operation, provision, or maintenance of adequate health facilities or services including the training of personnel for such work, from funds appropriated to the Indian Health Service for Indian health services or Indian health facilities; or

(2) planning, training, evaluation or other activities designed to improve the capacity of a tribal organization to enter into a contract or contracts pursuant to section 103 of this Act. . . .

EFFECT ON EXISTING RIGHTS

SEC. 110. Nothing in this Act shall be construed as—

(1) affecting, modifying, diminishing, or otherwise impairing the sovereign immunity from suit enjoyed by an Indian tribe; or

(2) authorizing or requiring the termination of any existing trust responsibility of the United States with respect to the Indian people.

TITLE II—THE INDIAN EDUCATION ASSISTANCE ACT

SEC. 201. This title may be cited as the "Indian Education Assistance Act."

PART A—EDUCATION OF INDIANS IN PUBLIC SCHOOLS

SEC. 202. The Act of April 16, 1934 (48 Stat. 596), as amended, is further amended by adding at the end thereof the following new sections:

"SEC. 4. The Secretary of the Interior shall not enter into any contract for the education of Indians unless the prospective contractor has submitted to, and has had approved by the Secretary of the Interior, an education plan, which plan, in the determination of the Secretary, contains educational objectives which adequately address the educational needs of the Indian students who are to be beneficiaries of the contract and assures that the contract is capable of meeting such objectives: *Provided*, That where students other than Indian students participate in such programs, money expended under such contract shall be prorated to cover the participation of only the Indian students.

"SEC. 5 (a) Whenever a school district affected by a contract or contracts for the education of Indians pursuant to this Act has a local school board not composed of a majority of Indians, the parents of the Indian children enrolled in the school or schools affected by such contract or contracts shall elect a local committee from among their number. Such committee shall fully participate in the development of, and shall have the authority to approve or disapprove programs to be conducted under such contract or contracts, and shall carry out such other duties, and be so structured, as the Secretary of the Interior shall by regulation provide. . . .

"SEC. 6. Any school district educating Indian students who are members of recognized Indian tribes, who do not normally reside in the State in which such school district is located, and who are residing in Federal boarding facilities for the purposes of attending public schools within such district may, in the discretion of the Secretary of the Interior, be reimbursed by him for the full per capita costs of educating such Indian students." . . .

[*U.S. Statutes at Large*, 88:2203–14.]

276

171. Passamaquoddy Tribe v. Morton
January 20, 1975

A major issue in the claims of Indians in the eastern states was whether section 4 of the Indian Trade and Intercourse Act of 1790 (often mistakenly called the Nonintercourse Act), which prohibited cessions of Indian lands except under a federal treaty, applied to them. If it did, then land cessions made to eastern states after 1790 were invalid. When the Department of the Interior refused to take up the Passamaquoddies' case because it claimed it had no trust responsibility toward the tribe, the Indians sued Secretary Morton. The decision of Judge Edward T. Gignaux, which supported the Indian position, began a new period in the history of the eastern tribes.

. . . . [The plaintiffs'] basic position is that the Nonintercourse Act applies to all Indian tribes in the United States, including the Passamaquoddies, and that the Act establishes a trust relationship between the United States and the Indian tribes to which it applies, including the Passamaquoddies. Therefore, they say, defendants may not deny plaintiffs' request for litigation on the sole ground that there is no trust relationship between the United States and the Tribe. In opposition, defendants and intervenor [the State of Maine] contend that only those Indian tribes which have been "recognized" by the Federal Government by treaty, statute or a consistent course of conduct are entitled to the protection of the Nonintercourse Act and, since the Passamaquoddies have not been "federally recognized," the Act is not applicable to them. Defendants and intervenor also deny that the Nonintercourse Act creates any trust relationship between the United States and the Indian tribes to which it applies. . . .

The rules of statutory interpretation by which this Court must be guided in determining the applicability of the Nonintercourse Act to the Passamaquoddies are summarized in United States v. New England Coal and Coke Co., 318 F. 2d 138 (1st Cir. 1963), as follows:

In matters of statutory construction the duty of this court is to give effect to the intent of Congress, and in doing so our first reference is of course to the literal meaning of words employed. Unless the contrary appears, it is presumed that statutory words are used in their ordinary sense. . . .

Defendants have rejected plaintiffs' request for assistance on the ground that no trust relationship exists between the United States and the Passamaquoddies. The Court disagrees. In the only decided cases to treat this issue, the Court of Claims has, in a series of decisions during the last ten years, definitively held that the Nonintercourse Act imposes a trust or fiduciary obligation on United States to protect land owned by all Indian tribes covered by the statute. . . .

These Court of Claims decisions are consistent with an unbroken line of Supreme Court decisions which, from the beginning, have defined the fiduciary relationship between the Federal Government and the Indian tribes as imposing a distinctive obligation of trust upon the Government in its dealings with the Indians. . . .

In view of the foregoing, the conclusion must be that the Nonintercourse Act establishes a trust relationship between the United States and the Indian tribes, including the Passamaquoddies, to which it applies. The Court holds that the defendants erred in denying plaintiffs' request for litigation on the sole ground that no trust relationship exists between the United States and the Passamaquoddy Indian Tribe.

[388 *Federal Supplement* 654–55, 660, 662–63.]

172. Indian Crimes Act of 1976
May 29, 1976

The Major Crimes Act of March 3, 1885, declared that seven major crimes committed by Indians on the reservations would fall under federal jurisdiction. This act of 1976 extended the number of crimes to fourteen.

An Act to provide for the definition and punishment of certain crimes in accordance with the Federal laws in force within the special maritime and territorial jurisdiction of the United States when said crimes are committed by an Indian in order to insure equal treatment for Indian and non-Indian offenders.

. . . .

SEC. 2. Section 1153, title 18, United States Code, is amended to read as follows:

"§1153. *Offenses committed within Indian country*

"Any Indian who commits against the person or property of another Indian or other person any of the following offenses, namely, murder, manslaughter, kidnaping, rape, carnal knowledge of any female, not his wife, who has not attained the age of sixteen years, assault with intent to commit rape, incest, assault with intent to commit murder, assault with a dangerous weapon, assault resulting in serious bodily injury, arson, burglary, robbery, and larceny within the Indian country, shall be subject to the same laws and penalties as all other persons committing any of the above offenses, within the exclusive jurisdiction of the United States.

"As used in this section, the offenses of burglary and incest shall be defined and punished in accordance with the laws of the State in which such offense was committed as are in force at the time of such offense.

"In addition to the offenses of burglary and incest, any other of the above offenses which are not defined and punished by Federal law in force within the exclusive jurisdiction of the United States shall be defined and punished in accordance with the laws of the State in which such offense was committed as are in force at the time of such offense." . . .

SEC. 4. Section 3242, title 18, United States Code, is amended to read as follows:

"§3242. *Indians committing certain offenses; acts on reservations*

"All Indians committing any offense listed in the first paragraph of and punishable under section 1153 (relating to offenses committed within Indian country) of this title shall be tried in the same courts and in the same manner as are all other persons committing such offense within the exclusive jurisdiction of the United States."

[*U.S. Statutes at Large*, 90:585–86.]

173. Indian Health Care Improvement Act
September 30, 1976

In order to lessen or remove the gap between Indian health conditions and those of the total population, Congress provided incremental funding for health services and health facilities over a seven-year period. The law also provided funds for urban health centers and for a feasibility study for an Indian medical school.

An Act to implement the Federal responsibility for the care and education of the Indian people by improving the services and facilities of Federal Indian health programs and encouraging maximum participation of Indians in such programs, and for other purposes (P.L. 94–437).

. . . .

FINDINGS

SEC. 2. The Congress finds that—

(a) Federal health services to maintain and improve the health of the Indians are consonant with and required by the Federal Government's historical and unique legal relationship with, and resulting responsibility to, the American Indian people.

(b) A major national goal of the United States is to provide the quantity and quality of health services which will permit the health status of Indians to be raised to the highest possible level and to encourage the maximum participation of Indians in the planning and management of those services.

(c) Federal health services to Indians have resulted in a reduction in the prevalence and incidence of preventable illnesses among, and unnecessary and premature deaths of, Indians.

(d) Despite such services, the unmet health needs of the American Indian people are severe and the health status of the Indians is far below that of the general population of the United States. . . .

(e) All other Federal services and programs in fulfillment of the Federal responsibility to Indians are jeopardized by the low health status of the American Indian people.

(f) Further improvement in Indian health is imperiled by—

(1) inadequate, outdated, inefficient, and undermanned facilities. . . .

(2) shortage of personnel. . . .

(3) insufficient services in such areas as laboratory, hospital inpatient and outpatient, eye care and mental health services, and services available through contracts with private physicians, clinics, and agencies. . . .

(4) related support factors. . . .

(5) lack of access of Indians to health services due to remote residences, undeveloped or underdeveloped communication and transportation systems, and difficult, sometimes severe, climate conditions; and

(6) lack of safe water and sanitary waste disposal services. . . .

(g) The Indian people's growth of confidence in Federal Indian health services is revealed by their increasingly heavy use of such services. Progress toward the goal of better Indian health is dependent on this continued growth of confidence. Both such progress and such confidence are dependent on improved Federal Indian health services.

SEC. 3. The Congress hereby declares that it is the policy of this Nation, in fulfillment of its special responsibilities and legal obligation to the American Indian people, to meet the national goal of providing the highest possible health status to Indians and to provide existing Indian health services with all resources necessary to effect that policy. . . .

TITLE I—INDIAN HEALTH MANPOWER

PURPOSE

SEC. 101. The purpose of this title is to augment the inadequate number of health professionals serving Indians and remove the multiple barriers to the entrance of health professionals into the Service and private practice among Indians.

HEALTH PROFESSIONS RECRUITMENT PROGRAM FOR INDIANS

SEC. 102. (a) The Secretary [of Health, Education and Welfare], acting through the Service, shall make grants to public or nonprofit private health or educational entities or Indian tribes or tribal organizations to assist such entities in meeting the costs of—

(1) identifying Indians with a potential for education or training in the health professions and encouraging and assisting them (A) to enroll in schools of medicine, osteopathy, dentistry, veterinary medicine, optometry, podiatry, pharmacy, public health, nursing, or allied health professions; or (B), if they are not qualified to enroll in any such school, to undertake such post-secondary education or training as may be required to qualify them for enrollment;

(2) publicizing existing sources of financial aid available to Indians enrolled in any school referred to in clause (1)(A) of this subsection or who are undertaking training necessary to qualify them to enroll in any such school; or

(3) establishing other programs which the Secretary determines will enhance and facilitate the enrollment of Indians, and the subsequent pursuit and completion by them of courses of study, in any school referred to in clause (1)(A) of this subsection. . . .

HEALTH PROFESSIONS PREPARATORY SCHOLARSHIP PROGRAM FOR INDIANS

SEC. 103. (a) The Secretary, acting through the Service, shall make scholarship grants to Indians. . . .

(b) Each scholarship grant made under

this section shall be for a period not to exceed two academic years, which years shall be for compensatory pre-professional education of any grantee.

(c) Scholarship grants made under this section may cover costs of tuition, books, transportation, board, and other necessary related expenses. . . .

TITLE II—HEALTH SERVICES

HEALTH SERVICES

SEC. 201. (a) For the purpose of eliminating backlogs in Indian health care services and to supply known, unmet medical, surgical, dental, optometrical, and other Indian health needs, the Secretary is authorized to expend, through the Service, over the seven-fiscal-year period beginning after the date of the enactment of this Act the amounts authorized to be appropriated by subsection (c). . . .

(b) The Secretary, acting through the Service, is authorized to employ persons to implement the provisions of this section during the seven-fiscal-year period in accordance with the schedule provided in subsection (c). . . .

TITLE III—HEALTH FACILITIES

CONSTRUCTION AND RENOVATION OF SERVICE FACILITIES

SEC. 301. (a) The Secretary, acting through the Service, is authorized to expend over the seven-fiscal-year period beginning after the date of the enactment of this Act the sums authorized by subsection (b) for the construction and renovation of hospitals, health centers, health stations, and other facilities of the Service. . . .

CONSTRUCTION OF SAFE WATER AND SANITARY WASTE DISPOSAL FACILITIES

SEC. 302. (a) During the seven-fiscal-year period beginning after the date of the enactment of this Act, the Secretary is authorized to expend under section 7 of the Act of August 5, 1954 (42 U.S.C. 2004a), the sums authorized under subsection (b) to supply unmet needs for safe water and sanitary waste disposal facilities in existing and new Indian homes and communities. . . .

PREFERENCE TO INDIANS AND INDIAN FIRMS

SEC. 303. (a) The Secretary, acting through the Service, may utilize the negotiating authority of the Act of June 25, 1910 (25 U.S.C. 47), to give preference to any Indian or any enterprise, partnership, corporation, or other type of business organization owned and controlled by an Indian or Indians including former or currently federally recognized Indian tribes in the State of New York . . . in the construction and renovation of Service facilities pursuant to section 301 and in the construction of safe water and sanitary waste disposal facilities pursuant to section 302. . . .

TITLE V—HEALTH SERVICES FOR URBAN INDIANS

PURPOSE

SEC. 501. The purpose of this title is to encourage the establishment of programs in urban areas to make health services more accessible to the urban Indian population.

CONTRACTS WITH URBAN INDIAN ORGANIZATIONS

SEC. 502. The Secretary, acting through the Service, shall enter into contracts with urban Indian organizations to assist such organizations to establish and administer, in the urban centers in which such organizations are situated, programs which meet the requirements set forth in sections 503 and 504. . . .

TITLE VI—AMERICAN INDIAN SCHOOL OF MEDICINE; FEASIBILITY STUDY

FEASIBILITY STUDY

SEC. 601. The Secretary, in consultation with Indian tribes and appropriate Indian organizations, shall conduct a study to determine the need for, and the feasibility of, establishing a school of medicine to train Indians to provide health services for Indians. Within one year of the date of the enactment of this Act the Secretary shall complete such study and shall report to the Congress findings and recommendations based on such study. . . .

[*U.S. Statutes at Large*, 90:1400–1407, 1410–12.]

174. Final Report of the American Indian Policy
Review Commission
May 17, 1977

The American Indian Policy Review Commission in 1976 and 1977 published the reports of its task forces and a final summary report of the whole commission. The report adopted controversial views favoring Indian sovereignty and an expanded federal trust responsibility, which in turn elicited a vigorous dissenting opinion from the vice chairman, Representative Lloyd Meeds. There were 206 specific recommendations in the report, but in the end the commission's work was largely ineffective.

A POLICY FOR THE FUTURE

This final report of the American Indian Policy Review Commission represents 2 years of intensive investigative work encompassing the entire field of Federal-Indian relations. The last such investigation occurred almost 50 years ago. The conclusions of that investigation and its condemnation of the policies which had governed Federal administration over the preceding 50 years brought an abrupt shift in the statutory policies governing the Federal-Indian relations, a complete repudiation of the policies which had controlled from the late 1800's to the mid-1930's. And yet the American Indian today finds himself in a position little better than that which he enjoyed in 1928 when the Meriam Report was issued.

It has been the fortune of this Commission to be the first in the long history of this Nation to listen attentively to the voice of the Indian rather than the Indian expert. The findings and recommendations which appear in this report are founded on that Indian voice. It can only be hoped that this Commission will be seen as a watershed in the long and often tarnished history of this country's treatment of its original people.

What are the explanations for the circumstances in which the Indian finds himself today? First and foremost are the consistently damaging Federal policies of the past—policies which sought through the first three-quarters of the 19th century to remove the Indian people from the midst of the European settlers by isolating them on reservations; and policies which after accomplishing isolation were then directed toward breaking down their social and governmental structures and throwing their land, water, timber and mineral resources open to exploitation by non-Indians. These policies were repudiated by Congress with passage of the Indian Reorganization Act of 1934, but by this time severe damage had been done.

It is the legacy of these policies with which the Indian people attempt to cope today; it is the legacy of these policies which this Commission examines in this report; and it is the legacy of these policies which the people of the United States must resolve over the next years.

One of the greatest obstacles faced by the Indian today in his drive for self-determination and a place in this Nation is the American public's ignorance of the historical relationship of the United States with Indian tribes and the lack of general awareness of the status of the American Indian in our society today. To adequately formulate a future Indian policy it is necessary to understand the policies of the past. For this reason the Commission has included extensive discussions of law and history in order to provide a foundation for understanding matters which affect Indian people.

FOUNDATIONS OF FEDERAL INDIAN LAW

The relationship of the American Indian tribes to the United States is founded on principles of international law. It is a political relation: a relation of a weak people to a strong people; a relation of weak governments to a strong government; a relationship founded on treaties in which the Indian tribes placed themselves under the protection of the United States and the United States assumed the obligation of supplying such protection. It is a relationship recognized in the law of this Nation as that of a domestic, dependent sovereign.

It is a relationship which has sometimes in

281

the past been honored but more frequently violated and at times even terminated. It is a relationship which can and should be nurtured and cherished by this Nation. The fact that the United States has not chosen to disavow this relationship, has not chosen to simply abrogate its treaty commitments, has not chosen to withdraw its recognition of Indians as separate and distinct peoples with cultures, lands and governments of their own— these facts set the United States above other nations in its treatment of its native people, and provide a moral and legal setting from which a forward-looking policy of Federal-Indian relations must progress. No other course will do honor to this Nation; no other course can hold any future for the Indian people.

The fundamental concepts which must guide future policy determination are:

1. That Indian tribes are sovereign political bodies, having the power to determine their own membership and power to enact laws and enforce them within the boundaries of their reservations, and

2. That the relationship which exists between the tribes and the United States is premised on a special trust that must govern the conduct of the stronger toward the weaker.

The concept of sovereignty and the concept of trust are imperative to the continuation of the Federal-Indian relationship. These form the foundation upon which our entire legal relationship with the Indian tribes stands. These are not new precepts— they are old, dating from the origins of this Nation. It can only be said that if they had been consistently honored in spirit as well as in name, it would not have been necessary to convene this Commission. Without recognition of these fundamental concepts acknowledging Indian rights, the work of this Commission will have been in vain, for without these concepts there is no future Indian policy—only Federal policy.

The Commission recognizes that there is substantial controversy surrounding the concept of tribal sovereignty and the exercise of governmental authority by the tribes within their reservations. The Commission has devoted a significant portion of this report to analysis of judicial decisions relating to the power of Indian tribes. The trend of these

decisions has favored the tribes in their efforts to achieve good government within the reservations. We approve of the judicial decisions which have thus far been rendered. But we caution that the powers exercised by tribes must bear a reasonable relationship to legitimate tribal interests such as protection of trust resources, maintenance of law and order, delivery of services, and protection of tribal government. . . .

SEPARATE DISSENTING VIEWS OF
REPRESENTATIVE LLOYD MEEDS,
VICE CHAIRMAN OF THE COMMISSION

With the creation of this Commission it was hoped that Congress would have before it an objective statement of past and current American Indian law and policy so that it could exercise its powers wisely in legislating a coherent and lasting policy toward American Indians.

Unfortunately, the majority report of this Commission is the product of one-sided advocacy in favor of American Indian tribes. The interests of the United States, the States, and non-Indian citizens, if considered at all, were largely ignored. . . .

With due regard to those who worked on the task forces, the reports were often based on what the members wished the law to be. Their findings and conclusions were often poorly documented. . . .

In addition, the Commission's staff interpreted the enabling legislation as a charter to produce a document in favor of tribal positions. In support of its one-sided advocacy, the Commission's staff relied on language in the enabling legislation ordering a review of Federal Indian law and policy "in order to determine the nature and scope of necessary revisions in the formation of policies and programs for the benefit of Indians." . . . But, clearly, the formation of policies and programs for the benefit of Indians did not require this Commission to prepare a document encompassing a tribal view of the future of American Indian law and policy. For Congress to realistically find this report of any utility, the report should have been an objective consideration of existing Indian law and policy, a consideration of the views of the United States, the States, non-Indian citizens, the tribes, and Indian citizens. This the Commission did not do. Instead, the Commission saw its role as an opportunity to represent to the Congress the position of some American Indian tribes and their non-Indian advocates.

This Commission failed to consider the fundamental and controversial issues in contemporary Indian law. Instead, it assumed as first principles, the resolution of all contemporary legal and policy issues in favor of Indian tribes. Hence, the report is advocacy and cannot be relied upon as a statement of existing law nor as a statement of what future policy should be. The report's utility, then, is limited to informing the Congress of the special interests of some American Indian tribes and their non-Indian advocates. Congress will either have to authorize another Commission to ascertain the views of non-Indians, the States, and the United States or perform that function on its own. . . .

The fundamental error of this report is that it perceives the American Indian tribe as a body politic in the nature of a sovereign as that word is used to describe the United States and the States, rather than as a body politic which the United States, through its sovereign power, permits to govern itself and order its *internal* affairs, but not the affairs of others. The report seeks to convert a political notion into a legal doctrine. . . .

In sum, the Commission has converted the doctrine of tribal self-government into a doctrine of general tribal government by taking a quantum leap forward without any adequate legal foundation. And, I might add, prescinding now from the legal issues involved, the Commission has not even explained why, for policy reasons, it would be a good thing for Indian tribes to exercise general governmental powers over the lands they occupy. The Commission has just assumed that because Indian tribes would like to exercise governmental powers over their territory, it would be wise to let them. There is no adequate discussion in the Commission report of the detriments of such a course of action, much less any weighing of the advantages and disadvantages. . . .

Finally, there is no adequate theoretical basis for the assertion of inherent tribal sovereignty. The assertion of inherent tribal sovereignty proves too much. It would mean that whenever there is a group of American Indians living together on land which was allocated to them by the Federal Government, they would have the power to exercise general governmental powers. The source of those powers would then be some magical combination of their Indianness and their ownership of land. Governmental powers do not have as their source such magic. Governmental powers in these United States have as their source the State and Federal constitutions. It is clear that Indian tribes do not govern themselves under State power. It is equally clear, however, that they govern themselves under the Federal power, and like all Federal power, their powers are specifically limited and the limitation with respect to tribes is one of self-government rather than the government of others. It is one thing for the Congress to permit tribal Indians to make their own laws and be ruled by them without State interference. It is quite another for the Congress to permit tribes to exercise general governmental powers without general Federal supervision. War, conquest, treaties, statutes, cases, and history have extinguished the tribe as a general governmental entity. All that remains is a policy. And, that policy is that American Indian tribes may govern their own internal relations by the grace of Congress. General governmental powers exist in this country only in the United States and the States.

Having missed this point, the Commission has missed the opportunity to address some of the major issues arising out of American Indian law and policy. What does it mean to be a citizen of a State and yet be immune to its laws? What is the basis for asserting that reservation Indians shall have representation in State government, but without taxation? On the other hand, what is the basis for asserting that non-Indian residents of Indian country shall not be represented in tribal government, yet be subject to tribal law, courts, and taxation? Is this obvious dual standard bothersome? And, if not, why not? What does it mean for a reservation to be within the boundaries of a State? . . .

[American Indian Policy Review Commission, *Final Report* (Washington: Government Printing Office, 1977), pp. 3–4, 571–73, 579–81.]

175. Establishment of Assistant Secretary—Indian Affairs

September 26, 1977

Because the commissioner of Indian affairs did not report directly to the secretary of the interior, there was agitation to raise the administration of Indian affairs to the level of an assistant secretary. President Nixon urged specific legislation, but the move was finally accomplished under President Carter by a department order.

. . . . SEC. 2. *Establishment of Position.* An Assistant Secretary—Indian Affairs is hereby established to administer the laws, functions, responsibilities, and authorities related in Indian affairs matters. In addition to serving as an Assistant Secretary of the Department, the Assistant Secretary—Indian Affairs will assume all the authorities and responsibilities of the Commissioner of Indian Affairs pending subsequent organization and position realignments. . . .

[*Federal Register,* 42:53682 (October 3, 1977).]

176. Oliphant v. Suquamish Indian Tribe

March 6, 1978

Mark Oliphant, a non-Indian residing on the Port Madison Reservation in the State of Washington, was arrested by tribal police and charged with assaulting a tribal officer and resisting arrest. He claimed that he was not subject to tribal authority, and the Supreme Court upheld his claim. The case was considered by Indians as a damaging blow to the revival of their sovereignty.

. . . . While not conclusive on the issue before us, the commonly shared presumption of Congress, the Executive Branch, and lower federal courts that tribal courts do not have the power to try non-Indians carries considerable weight. . . . "Indian law" draws principally upon the treaties drawn and executed by the Executive Branch and legislation passed by Congress. These instruments, which beyond their actual text form the backdrop for the intricate web of judicially made Indian law, cannot be interpreted in isolation but must be read in light of the common notions of the day and the assumptions of those who drafted them.

While in isolation the Treaty of Point Elliott, 12 Stat. 927 (1855), would appear to be silent as to tribal criminal jurisdiction over non-Indians, the addition of historical perspective casts substantial doubt upon the existence of such jurisdiction. . . .

By themselves, these treaty provisions would probably not be sufficient to remove criminal jurisdiction over non-Indians if the Tribe otherwise retained such jurisdiction. But an examination of our earlier precedents satisfies us that, even ignoring treaty provisions and congressional policy, Indians do not have criminal jurisdiction over non-

Indians absent affirmative delegation of such power by Congress. Indian tribes do retain elements of "quasi-sovereign" authority after ceding their lands to the United States and announcing their dependence on the Federal Government. . . . But the tribes' retained powers are not such that they are limited only by specific restrictions in treaties or congressional enactments. As the Court of Appeals recognized, Indian tribes are prohibited from exercising both those powers of autonomous states that are expressly terminated by Congress *and* those powers *"inconsistent with their status."* . . .

Indian reservations are "part of the territory of the United States." . . . Upon incorporation into the territory of the United States, the Indian tribes thereby come under the territorial sovereignty of the United States and their exercise of separate power is constrained so as not to conflict with the interests of this overriding sovereignty. . . .

We have already described some of the inherent limitations on tribal powers that stem from their incorporation into the United States. In *Johnson* v. *M'Intosh* . . . we noted that the Indian tribes' "power to dispose of the soil at their own will, to whomsoever they pleased," was inherently lost to the

284

overriding sovereignty of the United States. And in *Cherokee Nation* v. *Georgia* . . . the Chief Justice observed that since Indian tribes are "completely under the sovereignty and dominion of the United States . . . any attempt [by foreign nations] to acquire their lands, or to form a political connexion with them, would be considered by all as an invasion of our territory, and an act of hostility." . . .

Nor are the intrinsic limitations on Indian tribal authority restricted to limitations on the tribes' power to transfer lands or exercise external political sovereignty. . . . Protection of territory within its external political boundaries is, of course, as central to the sovereign interests of the United States as it is to any other sovereign nation. But from the formation of the Union and the adoption of the Bill of Rights, the United States has manifested an equally great solicitude that its citizens be protected by the United States from unwarranted intrusions on their personal liberty. The power of the United States to try and criminally punish is an important manifestation of the power to restrict personal liberty. By submitting to the overriding sovereignty of the United States, Indian

tribes therefore necessarily give up their power to try non-Indian citizens of the United States except in a manner acceptable to Congress. . . .

We recognize that some Indian tribal court systems have become increasingly sophisticated and resemble in many respects their state counterparts. We also acknowledge that with the passage of the Indian Civil Rights Act of 1968, which extends certain basic procedural rights to *anyone* tried in Indian tribal court, many of the dangers that might have accompanied the exercise by tribal courts of criminal jurisdiction over non-Indians only a few decades ago have disappeared. Finally, we are not unaware of the prevalence of non-Indian crime on today's reservations which the tribes forcefully argue requires the ability to try non-Indians. But these are considerations for Congress to weigh in deciding whether Indian tribes should finally be authorized to try non-Indians. They have little relevance to the principles which lead us to conclude that Indian tribes do not have inherent jurisdiction to try and to punish non-Indians. . . .

[435 *U.S. Reports*, 206–12.]

177. United States v. Wheeler

March 22, 1978

The inherent sovereignty of an Indian tribe was affirmed by the Supreme Court in a case involving double jeopardy. A Navajo Indian prosecuted in a federal court had previously been convicted in a tribal court of a lesser included offense arising out of the same incident. The court found no double jeopardy because the tribal court and the federal court were arms of separate sovereigns.

. . . . It is undisputed that Indian tribes have power to enforce their criminal laws against tribe members. Although physically within the territory of the United States and subject to ultimate federal control, they nonetheless remain "a separate people, with the power of regulating their internal and social relations." . . . Their right of internal self-government includes the right to prescribe laws applicable to tribe members and to enforce those laws by criminal sanctions. . . . The controlling question in this case is the source of this power to punish tribal offenders: Is it a part of inherent tribal sovereignty, or an aspect of the sovereignty of the Federal Government which has been delegated to the tribes by Congress?

A

The powers of Indian tribes are, in general, "*inherent powers of a limited sovereignty which has never been extinguished.*" F. Cohen, Handbook of Federal Indian Law 122 (1945) (emphasis in original). Before the coming of the Europeans, the tribes were self-governing sovereign political communities. . . . Like all sovereign bodies, they then had the inherent power to prescribe laws for their members and to punish infractions of those laws.

Indian tribes are, of course, no longer "possessed of the full attributes of sovereignty." . . . Their incorporation within the territory of the United States, and their acceptance of its protection, necessarily di-

285

vested them of some aspects of the sovereignty which they had previously exercised. By specific treaty provision they yielded up other sovereign powers; by statute, in the exercise of its plenary control, Congress has removed still others.

But our cases recognize that the Indian tribes have not given up their full sovereignty. . . . The sovereignty that the Indian tribes retain is of a unique and limited character. It exists only at the sufferance of Congress and is subject to complete defeasance. But until Congress acts, the tribes retain their existing sovereign powers. In sum, Indian tribes still possess those aspects of sovereignty not withdrawn by treaty or statute, or by implication as a necessary result of their dependent status. . . .

B

It is evident that the sovereign power to punish tribal offenders has never been given up by the Navajo Tribe and that tribal exercise of that power today is therefore the continued exercise of retained tribal sovereignty. Although both of the treaties executed by the Tribe with the United States provided for punishment by the United States of Navajos who commit crimes against non-Indians, nothing in either of them deprived the Tribe of its *own* jurisdiction to charge, try, and punish members of the Tribe for violations of tribal law. On the contrary, we have said that "[i]mplicit in these treaty terms. . . was the understanding that the internal affairs of the Indians remained exclusively within the jurisdiction of whatever tribal government existed." . . .

Similarly, statutes establishing federal criminal jurisdiction over crimes involving Indians have recognized an Indian tribe's jurisdiction over its members. . . . Thus, far from depriving Indian tribes of their sovereign power to punish offenses against tribal law by members of a tribe, Congress has repeatedly recognized that power and declined to disturb it.

Moreover, the sovereign power of a tribe to prosecute its members for tribal offenses clearly does not fall within that part of sovereignty which the Indians implicitly lost by virtue of their dependent status. The areas in which such implicit divestiture of sovereignty has been held to have occurred are those involving the relations between an Indian tribe and nonmembers of the tribe. . . .

These limitations rest on the fact that the dependent status of Indian tribes within our territorial jurisdiction is necessarily inconsistent with their freedom independently to determine their external relations. But the powers of self-government, including the power to prescribe and enforce internal criminal laws, are of a different type. They involve only the relations among members of a tribe. Thus, they are not such powers as would necessarily be lost by virtue of a tribe's dependent status. . . .

C

That the Navajo Tribe's power to punish offenses against tribal law committed by its members is an aspect of its retained sovereignty is further supported by the absence of any federal grant of such power. If Navajo self-government were merely the exercise of delegated federal sovereignty, such a delegation should logically appear somewhere. But no provision in the relevant treaties or statutes confers the right of self-government in general, or the power to punish crimes in particular, upon the Tribe. . . .

In sum, the power to punish offenses against tribal law committed by Tribe members, which was part of the Navajos' primeval sovereignty, has never been taken away from them, either explicitly or implicitly, and is attributable in no way to any delegation to them of federal authority. It follows that when the Navajo Tribe exercises this power, it does so as part of its retained sovereignty and not as an arm of the Federal Government. . . .

Thus, tribal courts are important mechanisms for protecting significant tribal interests. Federal pre-emption of a tribe's jurisdiction to punish its members for infractions of tribal law would detract substantially from tribal self-government, just as federal pre-emption of state criminal jurisdiction would trench upon important state interests. . . .

[435 *U.S. Reports*, 322–28, 332.]

178. Santa Clara Pueblo v. Martinez
May 15, 1978

When Santa Clara Pueblo denied tribal membership to a child of a female member who married outside the tribe, the tribe was charged with violation of the Indian Civil Rights Act of 1968. The court held that Congress did not provide remedies other than habeas corpus for enforcement of the Indian Civil Rights Act and that suits against the tribe were barred by the tribe's sovereign immunity from suit.

. . . . As separate sovereigns pre-existing the Constitution, tribes have historically been regarded as unconstrained by those constitutional provisions framed specifically as limitations on federal or state authority. Thus, in *Talton* v. *Mayes*, 163 U.S. 376 (1896), this Court held that the Fifth Amendment did not "operat[e] upon" "the powers of local self-government enjoyed" by the tribes. . . .

As the Court in *Talton* recognized, however, Congress has plenary authority to limit, modify or eliminate the powers of local self-government which the tribes otherwise possess. . . . In 25 U.S.C. §1302 [Indian Civil Rights Act], Congress acted to modify the effect of *Talton* and its progeny by imposing certain restrictions upon tribal governments similar, but not identical, to those contained in the Bill of Rights and the Fourteenth Amendment. . . .

Indian tribes have long been recognized as possessing the common-law immunity from suit traditionally enjoyed by sovereign powers. . . . This aspect of tribal sovereignty, like all others, is subject to the superior and plenary control of Congress. But "without congressional authorization," the "Indian Nations are exempt from suit." . . .

It is settled that a waiver of sovereign immunity "cannot be implied but must be unequivocally expressed." . . . Nothing on the face of Title I of the ICRA purports to subject tribes to the jurisdiction of the federal courts in civil actions for injunctive or declaratory relief. Moreover, since the respondent in a habeas corpus action is the individual custodian of the prisoner, see, *e.g.* 28 U.S.C. §2243, the provisions of §1303 can hardly be read as a general waiver of the tribe's sovereign immunity. In the absence here of any unequivocal expression of contrary legislative intent, we conclude that suits against the tribe under the ICRA are barred by its sovereign immunity from suit. . . .

Two distinct and competing purposes are manifest in the provisions of the ICRA: In addition to its objective of strengthening the position of individual tribal members vis-à-vis the tribe, Congress also intended to promote the well-established federal "policy of furthering Indian self-government." . . . This commitment to the goal of tribal self-determination is demonstrated by the provisions of Title I itself. Section 1302, rather than providing in wholesale fashion for the extension of constitutional requirements to tribal governments, as had been initially proposed, selectively incorporated and in some instances modified the safeguards of the Bill of Rights to fit the unique political, cultural, and economic needs of tribal governments. . . . Thus, for example, the statute does not prohibit the establishment of religion, nor does it require jury trials in civil cases, or appointment of counsel for indigents in criminal cases. . . .

The other Titles of the ICRA also manifest a congressional purpose to protect tribal sovereignty from undue interference. For instance, Title III, 25 U.S.C. §§1321–1326, hailed by some of the ICRA's supporters as the most important part of the Act, provides that States may not assume civil or criminal jurisdiction over "Indian country" without the prior consent of the tribe, thereby abrogating prior law to the contrary. Other Titles of the ICRA provide for strengthening certain tribal courts through training of Indian judges, and for minimizing interference by the Federal Bureau of Indian Affairs in tribal litigation.

When Congress seeks to promote dual objectives in a single statute, courts must be more than usually hesitant to infer from its silence a cause of action that, while serving one legislative purpose, will disserve the other. Creation of a federal cause of action for the enforcement of rights created in Title I, however useful it might be in securing compliance with §1302, plainly would be at odds with the congressional goal of protecting tribal self-government. Not only would it undermine the authority of tribal forums . . . but it would also impose serious financial burdens on already "financially disadvantaged" tribes. . . .

As we have repeatedly emphasized, Congress' authority over Indian matters is extraordinarily broad, and the role of courts in adjusting relations between and among tribes and their members correspondingly restrained. See *Lone Wolf* v. *Hitchcock*, 187 U.S. 553, 565 (1903). Congress retains au-

thority expressly to authorize civil actions for injunctive or other relief to redress violations of §1302, in the event that the tribes themselves prove deficient in applying and enforcing its substantive provisions. But unless and until Congress makes clear its intention to permit the additional intrusion on tribal sovereignty that adjudication of such actions in a federal forum would represent, we are constrained to find that §1302 does not impliedly authorize actions for declaratory or injunctive relief against either the tribe or its officers. . . .

[436 *U.S. Reports*, 56–59, 62–64, 72.]

179. American Indian Religious Freedom

August 11, 1978

This broad statement of policy about Indian religious freedom, in the form of a joint resolution, was a significant congressional action in support of Indian cultural autonomy. It placed the responsibility for implementing it on federal departments and agencies.

Whereas the freedom of religion for all people is an inherent right, fundamental to the democratic structure of the United States and is guaranteed by the First Amendment of the United States Constitution;

Whereas the United States has traditionally rejected the concept of a government denying individuals the right to practice their religion and, as a result, has benefited from a rich variety of religious heritages in this country;

Whereas the religious practices of the American Indian (as well as Native Alaskan and Hawaiian) are an integral part of their culture, tradition and heritage, such practices forming the basis of Indian identity and value systems;

Whereas the traditional American Indian religions, as an integral part of Indian life, are indispensable and irreplaceable;

Whereas the lack of a clear, comprehensive, and consistent Federal policy has often resulted in the abridgment of religious freedom for traditional American Indians;

Whereas such religious infringements result from the lack of knowledge or the insensitive and inflexible enforcement of Federal policies and regulations premised on a variety of laws;

Whereas such laws were designed for such worthwhile purposes as conservation and preservation of natural species and resources but were never intended to relate to Indian religious practices and, therefore, were passed without consideration of their effect on traditional American Indian religions;

Whereas such laws and policies often deny American Indians access to sacred sites required in their religions, including cemeteries;

Whereas such laws at times prohibit the use and possession of sacred objects necessary to the exercise of religious rites and ceremonies;

Whereas traditional American Indian ceremonies have been intruded upon, interfered with, and in a few instances banned: Now, therefore, be it

Resolved by the Senate and House of Representatives of the United States of America in Congress assembled, That henceforth it shall be the policy of the United States to protect and preserve for American Indians their inherent right of freedom to believe, express, and exercise the traditional religions of the American Indian, Eskimo, Aleut, and Native Hawaiians, including but not limited to access to sites, use and possession of sacred objects, and the freedom to worship through ceremonials and traditional rites.

SEC. 2. The President shall direct the various Federal departments, agencies, and other instrumentalities responsible for administering relevant laws to evaluate their policies and procedures in consultation with native traditional religious leaders in order to determine appropriate changes necessary to protect and preserve Native American religious cultural rights and practices. Twelve months after approval of this resolution, the President shall report back to the Congress the results of his evaluation, including any changes which were made in administrative policies and procedures, and any recommendations he may have for legislative action.

[*U.S. Statutes at Large*, 92:469–70.]

180. Federal Acknowledgment of Indian Tribes
October 2, 1978

The movement for self-determination of Indians was reflected in agitation by nonrecognized groups for acknowledgment of their tribal status by the federal government. In order to provide guidelines for such recognition, the Bureau of Indian Affairs issued "procedures for establishing that an American Indian group exists as an Indian tribe."

. . . .

Purpose.

The purpose of this part is to establish a departmental procedure and policy for acknowledging that certain American Indian tribes exist. Such acknowledgment of tribal existence by the Department [of the Interior] is a prerequisite to the protection, services, and benefits from the Federal Government available to Indian tribes. Such acknowledgment shall also mean that the tribe is entitled to the immunities and privileges available to other federally acknowledged Indian tribes by virtue of their status as Indian tribes as well as the responsibilities and obligations of such tribes. Acknowledgment shall subject the Indian tribe to the same authority of Congress and the United States to which other federally acknowledged tribes are subjected.

Scope.

(a) This part is intended to cover only those American Indian groups indigenous to the continental United States which are ethnically and culturally identifiable, but which are not currently acknowledged as Indian tribes by the Department. It is intended to apply to groups which can establish a substantially continuous tribal existence and which have functioned as autonomous entities throughout history until the present. . . .

Form and content of the petition.

The petition may be in any readable form which clearly indicates that it is a petition requesting the Secretary [of the Interior] to acknowledge tribal existence. All the criteria in paragraphs (a)–(g) of this section are mandatory in order for tribal existence to be acknowledged and must be included in the petition.

(a) A statement of facts establishing that the petitioner has been identified from historical times until the present on a substantially continuous basis, as "American Indian," or "aboriginal." A petitioner shall not fail to satisfy any criteria herein merely because of fluctuations of tribal activity during various years. Evidence to be relied upon in determining the group's substantially continuous Indian identity shall include one or more of the following:

(1) Repeated identification by Federal authorities;

(2) Longstanding relationships with State governments based on identification of the group as Indian;

(3) Repeated dealings with a county, parish, or other local government in a relationship based on the group's Indian identity;

(4) Identification as an Indian entity by records in courthouses, churches, or schools;

(5) Identification as an Indian entity by anthropologists, historians, or other scholars;

(6) Repeated identification as an Indian entity in newspapers and books;

(7) Repeated identification and dealings as an Indian entity with recognized Indian tribes or national Indian organizations.

289

(b) Evidence that a substantial portion of the petitioning group inhabits a specific area or lives in a community viewed as American Indian and distinct from other populations in the area, and that its members are descendants of an Indian tribe which historically inhabited a specific area.

(c) A statement of facts which establishes that the petitioner has maintained tribal political influence or other authority over its members an an autonomous entity throughout history until the present.

(d) A copy of the group's present governing document, or in the absence of a written document, a statement describing in full the membership criteria and the procedures through which the group currently governs its affairs and its members.

(e) A list of all known current members of the group and a copy of each available former list of members based on the tribe's own defined criteria. The membership must consist of individuals who have established, using evidence acceptable to the Secretary, descendancy from a tribe which existed historically or from historical tribes which combined and functioned as a single autonomous entity. . . .

(f) The membership of the petitioning group is composed principally of persons who are not members of any other North American Indian tribe.

(g) The petitioner is not, nor are its members, the subject of congressional legislation which has expressly terminated or forbidden the Federal relationship. . . .

Implementation of decisions.

(a) Upon final determination that the petitioner is an Indian tribe, the tribe shall be eligible for services and benefits from the Federal Government available to other federally recognized tribes and entitled to the privileges and immunities available to other federally recognized tribes by virtue of their status as Indian tribes with a government-to-government relationship to the United States as well as having the responsibilities and obligations of such tribes. Acknowledgment shall subject such Indian tribes to the same authority of Congress and the United States to which other federally acknowledged tribes are subject. . . .

[*Federal Register*, 43:39362–64 (September 5, 1978); codified in 25 *Code of Federal Regulations* 54.]

181. Tribally Controlled Community College Assistance Act

October 17, 1978

The success of the Navajo Community College (established 1968) led Congress to provide funds for other similar institutions, colleges clearly attuned to Indian needs. Title II of this act deals with the Navajo college, which is excluded from the general provisions of the law.

An Act to provide for grants to tribally controlled community colleges, and for other purposes. . . .

TITLE I—TRIBALLY CONTROLLED COMMUNITY COLLEGES

PURPOSE

SEC. 101. It is the purpose of this title to provide grants for the operation and improvement of tribally controlled community colleges to insure continued and expanded educational opportunities for Indian students.

GRANTS AUTHORIZED

SEC. 102 (a) The Secretary [of the Interior] is authorized to make grants pursuant to

this title to tribally controlled community colleges to aid in the post-secondary education of Indian students.

(b) Grants made pursuant to this title shall go into the general operating funds of the institution to defray the expense of activities related to education programs for Indian students. Funds provided pursuant to this title shall not be used in connection with religious worship or sectarian instruction.

ELIGIBLE GRANT RECIPIENTS

SEC. 103. To be eligible for assistance under this title, a tribally controlled community college must be one which—

(1) is governed by a board of directors or board of trustees a majority of which are Indians;

(2) demonstrates adherence to stated goals, a philosophy, or a plan of operation which is directed to meet the needs of Indians; and

(3) if in operation for more than one year, has students a majority of whom are Indians. . . .

GRANTS TO TRIBALLY CONTROLLED
COMMUNITY COLLEGES

SEC. 106 (a) Grants shall be made under this title only in response to applications by tribally controlled community colleges. Such applications shall be submitted at such time, in such manner, and will contain or be accompanied by such information as the Secretary may reasonably require pursuant to regulations. The Secretary shall not consider any grant application unless a feasibility study has been conducted under section 105 and it has been found that the applying community college will service a reasonable student population.

(b) The Secretary shall consult with the Assistant Secretary of Education of the Department of Health, Education, and Welfare to determine the reasonable number of students required to support a tribally controlled community college. Consideration shall be given to such factors as tribal and cultural differences, isolation, the presence of alternate education sources, and proposed curriculum. . . .

(d) In making grants pursuant to this section, the Secretary shall, to the extent practicable, consult with national Indian organizations and with tribal governments chartering the institutions being considered. . . .

[*U.S. Statutes at Large*, 92:1325–27.]

182. Education Amendments Act of 1978 (P.L. 95–561)

Title XI—Indian Education

November 1, 1978

To provide set standards for Indian schools, Congress directed the secretary of the interior to draw up such standards for basic education of Indian children, for dormitories, and for construction of school facilities. The same act reorganized the administration of Indian education and withdrew personnel in Indian schools from civil service regulations.

. . . .

PART B—BUREAU OF INDIAN AFFAIRS
PROGRAMS

STANDARDS FOR THE BASIC EDUCATION OF
INDIAN CHILDREN
IN BUREAU OF INDIAN AFFAIRS SCHOOLS

SEC. 1121. (a) The Secretary [of the Interior], in consultation with the Assistant Secretary of Health, Education, and Welfare for Education, and in consultation with Indian organizations and tribes, shall carry out or cause to be carried out by contract with an Indian organization such studies and surveys, making the fullest use possible of other existing studies, surveys, and plans, as are necessary to establish and revise standards for the basic education of Indian children attending Bureau schools and Indian controlled contract schools. . . . Such studies and surveys shall take into account factors such as academic needs, local cultural differences, type and level of language skills, geographical isolation and appropriate teacher-student ratios for such children, and shall be directed toward the attainment of equal educational opportunity for such children. . . .

NATIONAL CRITERIA FOR DORMITORY
SITUATIONS

SEC. 1122. (a) The Secretary, in consultation with the Assistant Secretary for Health, Education, and Welfare for Education, and in consultation with Indian organizations and tribes, shall conduct or cause to be conducted by contract with an Indian organization, a study of the costs applicable to boarding arrangements for Indian students provided in Bureau and contract schools, for the purpose of establishing national criteria for such dormitory situations. Such criteria shall include adult-child ratios, needs for counselors (including special needs related to

291

off-reservation boarding arrangements), space, and privacy. . . .

FACILITIES CONSTRUCTION

SEC. 1125. (a) The Secretary shall immediately begin to bring all schools, dormitories, and other facilities operated by the Bureau or under contract with the Bureau in connection with the education of Indian children into compliance with all applicable Federal, tribal, or State health and safety standards, whichever provide greater protection (except that the tribal standards to be applied shall be no greater than any otherwise applicable Federal or State standards), and with section 504 of the Rehabilitation Act of 1973 (29 U.S.C. 794), except that nothing in this section shall require termination of the operations of any facility which does not comply with such provisions and which is in use on the date of enactment of this Act. . . .

BUREAU OF INDIAN AFFAIRS EDUCATION FUNCTIONS

SEC. 1126. (a) The Secretary shall vest in the Assistant Secretary for Indian Affairs all functions with respect to formulation and establishment of policy and procedure, and supervision of programs and expenditures of Federal funds for the purpose of Indian education administered by the Bureau. The Assistant Secretary shall carry out such functions through the Director of the Office of Indian Education Programs within the Bureau (hereinafter referred to as the "Office"), which shall be governed by the provisions of this Act, any other provision of law to the contrary notwithstanding.

(b) The Director of the Office shall direct and supervise the operations of all personnel directly and substantially involved with provision of education services by the Bureau. The Assistant Secretary for Indian Affairs shall provide for the adequate coordination between the affected Bureau offices and the Office in order to facilitate the expeditious consideration of all contract functions relating to education. Nothing in this Act shall be construed to require the provision of separate support services for Indian education. . . .

ALLOTMENT FORMULA

SEC. 1128. (a) The Secretary shall establish, by regulation adopted in accordance with section 1138, a formula for determining the minimum annual amount of funds necessary to sustain each Bureau or contract school. In establishing such formula, the Secretary shall consider—

(1) the number of Indian students served and size of the school;

(2) the special cost factors, such as—

(A) isolation of the school;

(B) need for special staffing, transportation, or educational programs;

(C) food and housing costs;

(D) overhead costs associated with administering contracted education functions; and

(E) maintenance and repair costs associated with the physical condition of the educational facilities;

(3) the cost of providing academic services which are at least equivalent to those provided by public schools in the State in which the school is located;

(4) the cost of bringing the school up to the level of the standards established under sections 1121 and 1122; and

(5) such other relevant factors as the Secretary determines are appropriate. . . .

POLICY FOR INDIAN CONTROL OF INDIAN EDUCATION

SEC. 1130. It shall be the policy of the Bureau, in carrying out the functions of the Bureau, to facilitate Indian control of Indian affairs in all matters relating to education.

EDUCATION PERSONNEL

SEC. 1131. (a) (1) Chapter 51, subchapter III of chapter 53, and chapter 63 of title 5, United States Code, relating to leave, pay, and classification, and the sections relating to the appointment, promotion and removal of civil service employees, shall not apply to educators or to education positions. . . .

RECRUITMENT OF INDIAN EDUCATORS

SEC. 1135. The Secretary shall institute a policy for the recruitment of qualified Indian educators and a detailed plan to promote employees from within the Bureau. Such plan shall include opportunities for acquiring work experience prior to actual work assignment. . . .

SEC. 1137. Within six months of the date of enactment of this Act, the Secretary shall prescribe such rules and regulations as are necessary to insure the constitutional and civil rights of Indian students attending Bureau schools, including, but not limited to, their right to privacy under the laws of the United States, their right to freedom of religion and expression and their right to due process in connection with disciplinary actions, suspensions, and expulsions. . . .

[*U.S. Statutes at Large*, 92:2316–22, 2327.]

183. Indian Child Welfare Act
November 8, 1978

The increasing placement of Indian children in white foster or adoptive homes led to a strong reaction about such breaking up of Indian families. The result was this law, which directed the placement of children in Indian surroundings and authorized funds for family service programs.

An Act to establish standards for the placement of Indian children in foster or adoptive homes, to prevent the breakup of Indian families, and for other purposes.
. . . .

SEC. 2. Recognizing the special relationship between the United States and the Indian tribes and their members and the Federal responsibility to Indian people, the Congress finds—

(1) that clause 3, section 8, article I of the United States Constitution provides that "The Congress shall have Power * * * To regulate Commerce * * * with Indian tribes" and, through this and other constitutional authority, Congress has plenary power over Indian affairs;

(2) that Congress, through statutes, treaties, and the general course of dealing with Indian tribes, has assumed the responsibility for the protection and preservation of Indian tribes and their resources;

(3) that there is no resource that is more vital to the continued existence and integrity of Indian tribes than their children and that the United States has a direct interest, as trustee, in protecting Indian children who are members of or are eligible for membership in an Indian tribe;

(4) that an alarmingly high percentage of Indian families are broken up by the removal, often unwarranted, of their children from them by nontribal public and private agencies and that an alarmingly high percentage of such children are placed in non-Indian foster and adoptive homes and institutions; and

(5) that the States, exercising their recognized jurisdiction over Indian child custody proceedings through administrative and judicial bodies, have often failed to recognize the essential tribal relations of Indian people and the cultural and social standards prevailing in Indian communities and families.

SEC. 3. The Congress hereby declares that it is the policy of this Nation to protect the best interests of Indian children and to promote the stability and security of Indian tribes and families by the establishment of minimum Federal standards for the removal of Indian children from their families and the placement of such children in foster or adoptive homes which will reflect the unique values of Indian culture, and by providing for assistance to Indian tribes in the operation of child and family service programs. . . .

TITLE I—CHILD CUSTODY PROCEEDINGS

SEC. 101. (a) An Indian tribe shall have jurisdiction exclusive as to any State over any child custody proceeding involving an Indian child who resides or is domiciled within the reservation of such tribe, except where such jurisdiction is otherwise vested in the State by existing Federal law. Where an Indian child is a ward of a tribal court, the Indian tribe shall retain exclusive jurisdiction, notwithstanding the residence or domicile of the child.

(b) In any State court proceeding for the foster care placement of, or termination of parental rights to, an Indian child not domiciled or residing within the reservation of the Indian child's tribe, the court, in the absence of good cause to the contrary, shall transfer such proceeding to the jurisdiction of the tribe, absent objection by either parent, upon the petition of either parent or the Indian custodian or the Indian child's tribe: *Provided*, That such transfer shall be subject to declination by the tribal court of such tribe. . . .

SEC. 103. (a) Where any parent or Indian custodian voluntarily consents to a foster care placement or to termination of parental rights, such consent shall not be valid unless executed in writing and recorded before a judge of a court of competent jurisdiction and accompanied by the presiding judge's certificate that the terms and consequences of the consent were fully explained in detail and were fully understood by the parent or Indian custodian. The court shall also certify that either the parent or Indian custodian fully understood the explanation in English or that it was interpreted into a language that the parent or Indian custodian understood. Any consent given prior to, or within ten days after, birth of the Indian child shall not be valid. . . .

SEC. 105. (a) In any adoptive placement of an Indian child under State law, a preference shall be given, in the absence of good cause to the contrary, to a placement with (1) a member of the child's extended family; (2) other members of the Indian child's tribe; or (3) other Indian families.

(b) Any child accepted for foster care or preadoptive placement shall be placed in the least restrictive setting which most approximates a family and in which his special needs, if any, may be met. The child shall also be placed within reasonable proximity to his or her home, taking into account any special needs of the child. In any foster care or preadoptive placement, a preference shall be given, in the absence of good cause to the contrary, to a placement with—

(i) a member of the Indian child's extended family;

(ii) a foster home licensed, approved, or specified by the Indian child's tribe;

(iii) an Indian foster home licensed or approved by an authorized non-Indian licensing authority; or

(iv) an institution for children approved by an Indian tribe or operated by an Indian organization which has a program suitable to meet the Indian child's needs. . . .

TITLE II—INDIAN CHILD AND FAMILY PROGRAMS

SEC. 201. (a) The Secretary [of the Interior] is authorized to make grants to Indian tribes and organizations in the establishment and operation of Indian child and family service programs on or near reservations and in the preparation and implementation of child welfare codes. The objective of every Indian child and family service program shall be to prevent the breakup of Indian families and, in particular, to insure that the permanent removal of an Indian child from the custody of his parent or Indian custodian shall be a last resort. . . .

SEC. 202. The Secretary is also authorized to make grants to Indian organizations to establish and operate off-reservation Indian child and family service programs. . . .

[*U.S. Statutes at Large*, 92:3069, 3071–73, 3075–76.]

184. Archaeological Resources Protection Act

October 31, 1979

Indian religious and cultural rights were recognized by this law, which required consent of Indian tribes for the issuing of permits to do archaeological exploration on Indian lands.

An Act to protect archaeological resources on public lands and Indian lands, and for other purposes.

....

FINDINGS AND PURPOSE

Sec. 2. (a) The Congress finds that—

(1) archaeological resources on public lands and Indian lands are an accessible and irreplaceable part of the Nation's heritage;

(2) these resources are increasingly endangered because of their commercial attractiveness;

(3) existing Federal laws do not provide adequate protection to prevent the loss and destruction of these archaeological resources and sites resulting from uncontrolled excavations and pillage; and

(4) there is a wealth of archaeological information which has been legally obtained by private individuals for noncommercial purposes and which could voluntarily be made available to professional archaeologists and institutions.

(b) The purpose of this Act is to secure, for the present and future benefit of the American people, the protection of archaeological resources and sites which are on public lands and Indian lands, and to foster increased cooperation and exchange of information between governmental authorities, the professional archaeological community, and private individuals having collections of archaeological resources and data which were obtained before the date of the enactment of this Act. . . .

EXCAVATION AND REMOVAL

Sec. 4 (a) Any person may apply to the Federal land manager for a permit to excavate or remove any archaeological resource located on public lands or Indian lands and to carry out activities associated with such excavation or removal. The application shall be required, under uniform regulations under this Act, to contain such information as the Federal land manager deems necessary, including information concerning the time, scope, and location and specific purpose of the proposed work. . . .

(c) If a permit issued under this section may result in harm to, or destruction of, any religious or cultural site, as determined by the Federal land manager, before issuing such permit, the Federal land manager shall notify any Indian tribe which may consider the site as having religious or cultural importance. . . .

(g)(1) No permit shall be required under this section or under the Act of June 8, 1906 (16 U.S.C. 431), for the excavation or removal by any Indian tribe or member thereof of any archaeological resource located on Indian lands of such Indian tribe, except that in the absence of tribal law regulating the excavation or removal of archaeological resources on Indian lands, an individual tribal member shall be required to obtain a permit under this section.

(2) In the case of any permits for the excavation or removal of any archaeological resource located on Indian lands, the permit may be granted only after obtaining the consent of the Indian or Indian tribe owning or having jurisdiction over such lands. The permit shall include such terms and conditions as may be requested by such Indian or Indian tribe. . . .

[*U.S. Statutes at Large*, 93:721–23.]

185. United States v. Sioux Nation of Indians
June 30, 1980

In the Treaty of Fort Laramie (1868) the United States guaranteed a large reservation to the Sioux and declared that no further cessions would be valid without the consent of three-fourths of the adult males. But in 1877 the land of the Black Hills was confiscated by the United States. For many years the Sioux sought court action to rectify that action. The Court of Claims finally decided that the 1877 law constituted an illegal taking of the land and that the Indians were due compensation with interest, for a total of more than $100 million. The Supreme Court upheld that decision, thus weakening or discrediting the presumption of congressional good faith asserted in Lone Wolf v. Hitchcock *(1903).*

This case concerns the Black Hills of South Dakota, the Great Sioux Reservation, and a colorful, and in many respects tragic, chapter in the history of the Nation's West. Although the litigation comes down to a claim of interest since 1877 on an award of over $17 million, it is necessary, in order to understand the controversy, to review at some length the chronology of the case and its factual setting. . . .

[Discussion of the history of the case and of the Court of Claims judgment.]

In sum, we conclude that the legal analysis and factual findings of the Court of Claims fully support its conclusion that the terms of the 1877 Act did not effect "a mere change in the form of investment of Indian tribal property." *Lone Wolf* v. *Hitchcock*, 187 U.S. at 568. Rather, the 1877 Act effected a taking of tribal property, property which had been set aside for the exclusive occupation of the Sioux by the Fort Laramie Treaty of 1868. That taking implied an obligation on the part of the Government to make just compensation to the Sioux Nation and that obligation, including an award of interest, must now, at last, be paid.

[448 *U.S. Reports*, 374, 423–24.]

186. Maine Indian Claims Settlement Act
October 10, 1980

Indian tribes in Maine laid claim to a large part of the state on the grounds that land cessions made after 1790 were invalid. In order to prevent long litigation over land titles, which would have caused economic turmoil in Maine, a settlement was reached in 1980. Congress recognized the federal status of the tribes and provided funds in return for a relinquishment of all Indian claims.

An Act to provide for the settlement of land claims of Indians, Indian nations and tribes and bands of Indians in the State of Maine, including the Passamaquoddy Tribe, the Penobscot Nation, and the Houlton Band of Maliseet Indians, and for other purposes.

. . . .

CONGRESSIONAL FINDINGS AND DECLARATION
OF POLICY

SEC. 2. (a) Congress hereby finds and declares that:

(1) The Passamaquoddy Tribe, the Penobscot Nation, and the Maliseet Tribe are asserting claims for possession of lands within the State of Maine and for damages on the ground that the lands in question were originally transferred in violation of law, including, but without limitation, the Trade and Intercourse Act of 1790 (1 Stat. 137), or subsequent reenactments or versions thereof.

(2) The Indians, Indian nations, and tribes and bands of Indians, other than the Passamaquoddy Tribe, the Penobscot Nation, and the Houlton Band of Maliseet Indians, that once may have held aboriginal title to lands within the State of Maine long ago abandoned their aboriginal holdings. . . .

(6) Substantial economic and social hardship to a large number of landowners, citizens, and communities in the State of Maine, and therefore to the economy of the State of Maine as a whole, will result if the aforementioned claims are not resolved promptly.

(7) This Act represents a good faith effort on the part of Congress to provide the Passamaquoddy Tribe, the Penobscot Nation, and the Houlton Band of Maliseet Indians with a fair and just settlement of their land claims. In the absence of congressional action, these land claims would be pursued through the courts, a process which in all likelihood would consume many years and thereby promote hostility and uncertainty in the State of Maine to the ultimate detriment of the Passamaquoddy Tribe, the Penobscot Nation, the Houlton Band of Maliseet Indians, their members, and all other citizens of the State of Maine.

(8) The State of Maine, with the agreement of the Passamaquoddy Tribe and the Penobscot Nation, has enacted legislation defining the relationship between

the Passamaquoddy Tribe, the Penobscot Nation, and their members, and the State of Maine.

(9) Since 1820, the State of Maine has provided special services to the Indians residing within its borders, including the members of the Passamaquoddy Tribe, the Penobscot Nation, and the Houlton Band of Maliseet Indians. During this same period, the United States provided few special services to the respective tribe, nation, or band, and repeatedly denied that it had jurisdiction over or responsibility for the said tribe, nation, and band. In view of this provision of special services by the State of Maine, requiring substantial expenditures by the State of Maine and made by the State of Maine without being required to do so by Federal law, it is the intent of Congress that the State of Maine not be required further to contribute directly to this claims settlement.

(b) It is the purpose of this Act—

(1) to remove the cloud on the titles to land in the State of Maine resulting from Indian claims;

(2) to clarify the status of other land and natural resources in the State of Maine;

(3) to ratify the Maine Implementing Act, which defines the relationship between the State of Maine and the Passamaquoddy Tribe, and the Penobscot Nation, and

(4) to confirm that all other Indians, Indian nations and tribes and bands of Indians now or hereafter existing or recognized in the State of Maine are and shall be subject to all laws of the State of Maine, as provided herein. . . .

SEC. 4. (a) (1) Any transfer of land or natural resources located anywhere within the United States from, by, or on behalf of the Passamaquoddy Tribe, the Penobscot Nation, the Houlton Band of Maliseet Indians, or any of their members, and any transfer of land or natural resources located anywhere within the State of Maine, from, by, or on behalf of any Indian, Indian nation, or tribe or band of Indians, including but without limitation any transfer pursuant to any treaty, compact, or statute of any State, shall be deemed to have been made in accor-

dance with the Constitution and all laws of the United States, including but without limitation the Trade and Intercourse Act of 1790, Act of July 22, 1790 . . . and all amendments thereto and all subsequent reenactments and versions thereof, and Congress hereby does approve and ratify any such transfer effective as of the date of said transfer: *Provided however*, That nothing in this section shall be construed to affect or eliminate the personal claim of any individual Indian (except for any Federal common law fraud claim) which is pursued under any law of general applicability that protects non-Indians as well as Indians. . . .

(b) To the extent that any transfer of land or natural resources described in subsection (a)(1) of this section may involve land or natural resources to which the Passamaquoddy Tribe, the Penobscot Nation, the Houlton Band of Maliseet Indians, or any of their members, or any other Indian, Indian nation, or tribe or band of Indians had aboriginal title, such subsection (a)(1) shall be regarded as an extinguishment of said aboriginal title as of the date of such transfer.

(c) By virtue of the approval and ratification of a transfer of land or natural resources effected by this section, or the extinguishment of aboriginal title effected thereby, all claims against the United States, any State or subdivision thereof, or any other person or entity, by the Passamaquoddy Tribe, the Penobscot Nation, the Houlton Band of Maliseet Indians or any of their members or by any other Indian, Indian nation, tribe or band of Indians, or any predecessors or successors in interest thereof, arising at the time of or subsequent to the transfer and based on any interest in or right involving such land or natural resources, including but without limitation claims for trespass damages or claims for use and occupancy, shall be deemed extinguished as of the date of the transfer. . . .

SEC. 5. (a) There is hereby established in the United States Treasury a fund to be known as the Maine Indian Claims Settlement Fund in which $27,000,000 shall be deposited following the appropriation of sums authorized by section 14 of this Act.

(b)(1) One-half of the principal of the settlement fund shall be held in trust by the Secretary [of the Interior] for the benefit of the Passamaquoddy Tribe, and the other half of the settlement fund shall be held in trust for the benefit of the Penobscot Nation. Each portion of the settlement fund shall be administered by the Secretary in accordance with reasonable terms established by the Passamaquoddy Tribe or the Penobscot Nation, respectively, and agreed to by the Secretary. . . .

(c) There is hereby established in the United States Treasury a fund to be known as the Maine Indian Claims Land Acquisition Fund in which $54,500,000 shall be deposited following the appropriation of sums authorized by section 14 of this Act.

(d) The principal of the land acquisition fund shall be apportioned as follows:

(1) $900,000 to be held in trust for the Houlton Band of Maliseet Indians;

(2) $26,800,000 to be held in trust for the Passamaquoddy Tribe; and

(3) $26,800,000 to be held in trust for the Penobscot Nation.

The Secretary is authorized and directed to expend, at the request of the affected tribe, nation or band, the principal and any income accruing to the respective portions of the land acquisition fund for the purpose of acquiring land or natural resources for the Passamaquoddy Tribe, the Penobscot Nation, and the Houlton Band of Maliseet Indians and for no other purpose. . . .

Sec. 6. (h) Except as otherwise provided in this Act, the laws and regulations of the United States which are generally applicable to Indians, Indian nations, or tribes or bands of Indians or to lands owned by or held in trust for Indians, Indian nations, or tribes or bands of Indians shall be applicable in the State of Maine, except that no law or regulation of the United States (1) which accords or relates to a special status or right of or to any Indian, Indian nation, tribe or band of Indians, Indian lands, Indian reservations, Indian country, Indian territory or land held in trust for Indians, and also (2) which affects or preempts the civil, criminal, or regulatory jurisdiction of the State of Maine, including, without limitation, laws of the State relating to land use or environmental matters, shall apply within the State.

(i) As federally recognized Indian tribes, the Passamaquoddy Tribe, the Penobscot Nation, and the Houlton Band of Maliseet Indians shall be eligible to receive all of the financial benefits which the United States provides to Indians, Indian nations, or tribes or bands of Indians to the same extent and subject to the same eligibility criteria generally applicable to other Indians, Indian nations or tribes or bands of Indians. The Passamaquoddy Tribe, the Penobscot Nation, and the Houlton Band of Maliseet Indians shall be treated in the same manner as other federally recognized tribes for the purposes of Federal taxation and any lands which are held by the respective tribe, nation, or band subject to a restriction against alienation or which are held in trust for the benefit of the respective tribe, nation, or band shall be considered Federal Indian reservations for purposes of Federal taxation.

Sec. 7. (a) The Passamaquoddy Tribe, the Penobscot Nation, and the Houlton Band of Maliseet Indians may each organize for its common welfare and adopt an appropriate instrument in writing to govern the affairs of the tribe, nation, or band when each is acting in its governmental capacity. . . .

[*U.S. Statutes at Large*, 94:1785–89, 1793–95.]

---

187. Statement on Indian Health Programs

March 2, 1981

Indian health continued to be a vital concern of the federal government. The advances made by special legislation and by ongoing programs were described by Dr. Emery A. Johnson, director of the Indian Health Service, in appropriation hearings.

I am pleased to appear before you today to discuss the programs of the Indian Health Service (IHS).

As you know, the IHS is a constituent agency of the Department of Health and Human Services (DHHS) and the Public Health Service and is charged with administering the principal Federal health programs for Indian and Alaska Native citizens. Although this Department has within its purview a variety of health programs, funding mechanisms, and health care payment mechanisms which impact on Indian and Alaska Native people, it has a special and unique responsibility to our Indian citizens.

When reviewing the legislative and programmatic events of the past decade or so, we may fail to see that these events are actually a part of a pattern and if one examines this pattern, it becomes readily apparent that the present Federal Indian policy did not happen by fiat but is the logical outgrowth of a growing awareness of Indian needs.

The decade of the seventies was to witness significant change in the structure of programs designed to provide health services to Indian people. Two significant pieces of legislation, the Indian Self-Determination and Education Assistance Act (Public Law 93–638) signed on January 4, 1975, and the Indian Health Care Improvement Act (Public Law 94–437) signed on September 30, 1976, were passed in this period.

Public Law 93–638 codified in law the desires of Indian people to have a voice in the operation of health programs designed and operated for their benefit. It made self-determination by tribes the keystone of a new relationship, in which Indian people acting through their tribal governments, would determine the control and operation of their health programs. This law states that should a tribe wish to exercise control of all or part of its health programs, the Secretary of DHHS must accede to these wishes except in the case of certain closely prescribed restrictions, which then must be accompanied by Federal technical assistance and guidance.

The Federal government established its philosophy of self-determination for Indian people in Public Law 93–638. Public Law 94–437 authorizes activities to carry out the mandate for self-determination expressed in Public Law 93–638. Further, it defined in law types of programs and levels of service that could be expected by Indian people; in other words the national goal for programs providing services to Indian people. It also requires the Secretary of DHHS to report to the Congress periodically on accomplishments made in implementing these programs and to report on the need for additional resources to accomplish the goals defined in the Act. This latter requirement was accomplished with the submission of a National Plan for the improvement of health care to Indian people, to Congress in April, 1980.

There now exists a Federal health program for Indians in which services are now delivered by tribes and tribal organizations as well as the IHS. Thus, tribes and the IHS are now both components of a system designed to provide needed health services to Indian people.

The rate of participation by tribes in the management of their own health programs is accelerating. Although as expected, a few tribes have exercised their option not to participate, most tribes have chosen to exercise their options to operate parts of their health systems and a few have taken over major portions of their health care systems. Most tribes view their participation as an incremental phasing of increasing responsibility for the operation of health programs as meaningful experience is gained, and qualified Indian people become available to staff programs. A review of the current situation indicates that significant health services formerly provided solely by the IHS are now being provided by tribal organizations. . . . Currently, about 10 percent of the tribes are delivering all of their own health services with another 33 percent delivering major portions of their services. Many tribes are operating smaller or single elements of their health services programs. Altogether, 89 percent of eligible tribes are operating some portion of their health program themselves.

Paralleling the increasing provision of health services by tribes, the IHS continues to operate its health care system providing services to those Indians not served by tribal programs. This system consists of the Hospital and Health Clinic Program, Preventive Health Program, Contract Care Program, Emergency Medical Services, Urban Health Projects, Manpower Development, Tribal Management Programs, Health Facilities and Sanitation Facilities Construction Programs, and Program Management activities.

The passage of Public Law 94–437 is a key element in the operations aspect of IHS programs. Not only did it define just what services Indian people could expect, it authorized activities to improve services and facilities and provided new authorities for training, alcoholism, Medicare and Medicaid reimbursement, and established the basis for limited programs to be provided to Indians living in urban locations. . . .

The National Plan, submitted in April, 1980, is based on 216 tribal and 34 urban specific health plans representing 280 tribes and 41 urban Indian health groups. A significant effort went into clearly and accurately identifying tribal and urban health needs. The IHS is committed to using this Plan in the development of its future programs and resource allocation. . . .

["Department of the Interior and Related Agencies Appropriations for 1982," *Hearings before a Subcommittee of the Committee on Appropriations, House of Representatives, 97th Congress, lst Session, Subcommittee on the Department of the Interior and Related Agencies (1981)*, part 9, pp. 1–3.]

188. Indian Land Consolidation Act

January 12, 1983

The problem of heirship lands, in which subdivision resulted in plots too small to use efficiently, was attacked by this law, which provided for a start toward consolidation of fractionalized land.

An Act to authorize the purchase, sale, and exchange of lands by Indian tribes and by the Devils Lake Sioux Tribe of the Devils Lake Sioux Reservation of North Dakota specifically, and for other purposes.
. . . .

TITLE II

SEC. 201. This title may be cited as the "Indian Land Consolidation Act." . . .

SEC. 204. (a) Notwithstanding any other provision of law, any tribe, acting through its governing body, is authorized, with the approval of the Secretary [of the Interior] to adopt a land consolidation plan providing for the sale or exchange of any tribal lands or interest in lands for the purpose of eliminating undivided fractional interests in Indian trust or restricted lands or consolidating its tribal landholdings.

SEC. 205. Any Indian tribe may purchase at no less than the fair market value all of the interests in any tract of trust or restricted land within that tribe's reservation or otherwise subjected to that tribe's jurisdiction with the consent of over 50 per centum of the owners or with the consent of the owners of over 50 per centum of the undivided interests in such tract: *Provided*, That—

(1) no such tract shall be acquired by any Indian or Indian tribe over the objection of three or less owners owning 50 per centum or more of the total interests in such tract;

(2) any Indian owning any undivided interest in, and in actual use and possession of such tract, may purchase such tract by matching the tribal offer;

(3) this section shall not apply to any tract of land owned by less than fifteen persons; and

(4) all purchases and sales initiated under this section shall be approved by the Secretary. . . .

SEC. 207. No undivided fractional interest in any tract of trust or restricted land within a tribe's reservation or otherwise subjected to a tribe's jurisdiction shall descend by intestacy or devise but shall escheat to that tribe if such interest represents 2 per centum or less of the total acreage in such tract and has earned to its owner less than $100 in the preceding year before it is due to escheat. . . .

SEC. 210. Title to any land acquired under this title by an Indian or Indian tribe shall be taken in trust by the United States for that Indian or Indian tribe.

SEC. 211. All lands or interests in land acquired by the United States for an Indian or Indian tribe under authority of this title shall be exempt from Federal, State and local taxation.

[*U.S. Statutes at Large*, 96:2515–19.]

300

189. Indian Policy: Statement of Ronald Reagan
January 24, 1983

President Reagan's statement on Indian policy reflected his fundamental principles of reducing reliance on federal programs while placing greater responsibility on local units and the private sector. Cuts in federal aid during his administration, however, severely affected Indian communities.

This administration believes that responsibilities and resources should be restored to the governments which are closest to the people served. This philosophy applies not only to State and local governments but also to federally recognized American Indian tribes.

When European colonial powers began to explore and colonize this land, they entered into treaties with sovereign Indian nations. Our new nation continued to make treaties and to deal with Indian tribes on a government-to-government basis. Throughout our history, despite periods of conflict and shifting national policies in Indian affairs, the government-to-government relationship between the United States and Indian tribes has endured. The Constitution, treaties, laws, and court decisions have consistently recognized a unique political relationship between Indian tribes and the United States which this administration pledges to uphold.

In 1970 President Nixon announced a national policy of self-determination for Indian tribes. At the heart of the new policy was a commitment by the Federal Government to foster and encourage tribal self-government. That commitment was signed into law in 1975 as the Indian Self-Determination and Education Assistance Act.

The principle of self-government set forth in this act was a good starting point. However, since 1975 there has been more rhetoric than action. Instead of fostering and encouraging self-government, Federal policies have by and large inhibited the political and economic development of the tribes. Excessive regulation and self-perpetuating bureaucracy have stifled local decisionmaking, thwarted Indian control of Indian resources, and promoted dependency rather than self-sufficiency.

This administration intends to reverse this trend by removing the obstacles to self-government and by creating a more favorable environment for the development of healthy reservation economies. Tribal governments, the Federal Government, and the private sector will all have a role. This administration will take a flexible approach which recognizes the diversity among tribes and the right of each tribe to set its own priorities and goals. Change will not happen overnight. Development will be charted by the tribes, not the Federal Government.

This administration honors the commitment this nation made in 1970 and 1975 to strengthen tribal governments and lessen Federal control over tribal governmental affairs. This administration is determined to turn these goals into reality. Our policy is to reaffirm dealing with Indian tribes on a government-to-government basis and to pursue the policy of self-government for Indian tribes without threatening termination.

In support of our policy, we shall continue to fulfill the Federal trust responsibility for the physical and financial resources we hold in trust for the tribes and their members. The fulfillment of this unique responsibility will be accomplished in accordance with the highest standards.

Tribal Self-Government

Tribal governments, like State and local governments, are more aware of the needs and desires of their citizens than is the Federal Government and should, therefore, have the primary responsibility for meeting those needs. The only effective way for Indian reservations to develop is through tribal governments which are responsive and accountable to their members.

Early in this nation's dealings with Indian tribes, Federal employees began to perform Indian tribal government functions. Despite the Indian Self-Determination Act, major tribal government functions—enforcing tribal laws, developing and managing tribal resources, providing health and social services, educating children—are frequently still carried on by Federal employees. The Federal Government must move away from this surrogate role which undermines the concept of self-government.

301

It is important to the concept of self-government that tribes reduce their dependence on Federal funds by providing a greater percentage of the cost of their self-government. Some tribes are already moving in this direction. This administration pledges to assist tribes in strengthening their governments by removing the Federal impediments to tribal self-government and tribal resource development. Necessary Federal funds will continue to be available. This administration affirms the right of tribes to determine the best way to meet the needs of their members and to establish and run programs which best meet those needs. . . .

In addition, this administration calls upon Congress to replace House Concurrent Resolution 108 of the 83d Congress, the resolution which established the now discredited policy of terminating the Federal-tribal relationship. Congress has implicitly rejected the termination policy by enacting the Indian Self-Determination and Education Assistance Act of 1975. However, because the termination policy declared in H. Con. Res. 108 has not been expressly and formally repudiated by a concurrent resolution of Congress, it continues to create among the Indian people an apprehension that the United States may not in the future honor the unique relationship between the Indian people and the Federal Government. A lingering threat of termination has no place in this administration's policy of self-government for Indian tribes, and I ask Congress to again express its support of self-government.

These actions are but the first steps in restoring control to tribal governments. Much more needs to be done. Without sound reservation economies, the concept of self-government has little meaning. In the past, despite good intentions, the Federal Government has been one of the major obstacles to economic progress. This administration intends to remove the impediments to economic development and to encourage cooperative efforts among the tribes, the Federal Government, and the private sector in developing reservation economies.

Development of Reservation Economies

The economies of American Indian reservations are extremely depressed, with unemployment rates among the highest in the country. Indian leaders have told this administration that the development of reservation economies is their number one priority. Growing economies provide jobs, promote self-sufficiency, and provide revenue for essential services. Past attempts to stimulate growth have been fragmented and largely ineffective. As a result, involvement of private industry has been limited, with only infrequent success. Developing reservation economies offers a special challenge: devising investment procedures consistent with the trust status, removing legal barriers which restrict the type of contracts tribes can enter into, and reducing the numerous and complex regulations which hinder economic growth.

Tribes have had limited opportunities to invest in their own economies, because often there has been no established resource base for community investment and development. Many reservations lack a developed physical infrastructure, including utilities, transportation, and other public services. They also often lack the regulatory, adjudicatory, and enforcement mechanisms necessary to interact with the private sector for reservation economic development. Development on the reservation offers potential for tribes and individual entrepreneurs in manufacturing, agribusiness, and modern technology, as well as fishing, livestock, arts and crafts, and other traditional livelihoods. . . .

[*Public Papers of the Presidents of the United States: Ronald Reagan, 1983*, 1:96–98.]

190. Federal Acknowledgement of Narragansett Indian Tribe of Rhode Island
February 2, 1983

A large number of Indian communities not officially recognized as tribes by the federal government have petitioned for recognition. The Bureau of Indian Affairs Acknowledgement Branch investigates each case; those that meet the criteria set forth in the directives issued on October 2, 1978, are recognized. One successful tribe was the Narragansett Indian Tribe of Rhode Island.

This notice is published in the exercise of authority delegated by the Secretary of the Interior to the Assistant Secretary—Indian Affairs by 209 DM 8. Pursuant to 25 CFR 83.9(h) notice is hereby given that the Assistant Secretary acknowledges that the Narragansett Indian Tribe, c/o Mr. George Watson, Route 2, Charlestown, Rhode Island 02813, exists as an Indian tribe. This notice is based on a determination that the group satisfies the criteria set forth in 25 CFR 83.7.

The Narragansett Indian Tribe is the modern successor of the Narragansett and Niantic tribes which, in aboriginal times, inhabited the area which is today the state of Rhode Island. Members of the tribe are lineal descendants of the aboriginal Niantic and Narragansett Indians. The Narragansetts, once a large and powerful tribe, and the smaller Niantics, were culturally very similar and generally closely allied in historic times. Political structure was organized around leaders, referred to as sachems, who were drawn from high-ranking families.

Evidence indicates that the Narragansett community and its predecessors have existed autonomously since first contact, despite undergoing many modifications. A series of leaders and then tribal councils represented the tribe or its predecessors in its dealings with outside organizations and governmental bodies. These leaders and councils both responded to and influenced the group in matters of importance.

The tribe has a documented history dating from 1614. It was dealt with as an independent nation after 1622 by England and the Rhode Island colony. The Niantics and Narragansetts came increasingly under the authority of the English Crown in the 17th century, and its size and influence decreased steadily. After the Narragansett nation was essentially destroyed in 1675 in King Philip's War, the Niantics combined with the remnants of the Narragansetts. The tribe was placed under a form of guardianship by the colony of Rhode Island in 1709, a relationship which continued until 1880, when the state legislature of Rhode Island enacted a so-called "detribalization" act. This ended the state's relationship with the tribe except for retention of two acres surrounding the Narragansett Indian church which con-

tinued to be held in special status.

After 1880, there continued to be a Narragansett community on or near the former state reservation in southern Rhode Island. There continued to be both identified leaders who had standing as community leaders and, for some periods, a tribal council. The Narragansett Church organization was an important focus of community organization in this period. In 1934, the group created a new formal organization, which was incorporated under the state of Rhode Island. The state again effectively recognized the group beginning in 1934.

No evidence was found that members of the group are members of any other Indian tribes or that the group or its members have been forbidden the Federal relationship by an Act of Congress.

Essentially all of the current membership are believed to be able to trace to at least one ancestor on the membership lists of the Narragansett community prepared after the 1880 Rhode Island "detribalization" act. Most members are in fact expected to be able to trace to several ancestors. These lists are source documents currently used to determine eligibility for membership.

Proposed findings that the Narragansett Indian Tribe exists as an Indian tribe were published on page 35347 of the *Federal Register* on August 13, 1982. Interested parties were given 120 days in which to submit factual and legal arguments to rebut the evidence used to support the findings that the Narragansett Indian tribe exists as an Indian tribe. During this period only two comments were received, both opposing the findings and both from the same party. This individual expressed the opinion that the Narragansetts could not meet a blood degree requirement. While eligibility for benefits under some Federal statutes is limited to tribal members with a certain blood degree, and the right of non-tribal Indians to organize is limited to those with ½ or more degree Indian blood, Federal law imposes no general blood degree requirement for tribal membership. Moreover, under the Federal regulations for determining eligibility as a tribe, a blood quantum requirement is not included in the criteria. While blood degree may be some evidence of social and cultural cohesion and maintenance of tribal relations, it is most definitely not conclusive as to the existence of tribal relations. Accordingly, the opinions submitted were given limited consideration. The findings focused instead on the larger and more important question of maintenance of tribal relations. No factual evidence not already considered was provided in these comments, and they were considered to have no effect on the findings of fact and the decision to recommend the tribe for Federal acknowledgement. . . .

[*Federal Register*, 48:6177–78 (February 10, 1983).]

191. Bureau of Indian Affairs Statement of Policy
1984

From time to time the Bureau of Indian Affairs has issued booklets on the work and policies of the Bureau. One such publication was BIA Profile: The Bureau of Indian Affairs and American Indians, *issued in 1981. Another, prepared by the Public Affairs staff and published in 1984, was called simply* American Indians. *The extract from it printed here states the objectives and policy of the Bureau.*

. . . . *The principal objectives of the Bureau of Indian Affairs are to actively encourage Indian and Alaska Native people to manage their own affairs through the contracting of programs and other means under a trust relationship with the federal government; to facilitate, with maximum involvement of Indian and Alaska Native people, full development of their human and natural resource potentials; to mobilize all public and private aids to the advancement of Indian and Alaska Native people for use by them; and to utilize the skill and capabilities of Indian and Alaska Native people in the direction and management of programs for their benefit.*

───────

In spite of its visibility in working with Indian tribes and Alaska Natives, there remains confusion in the minds of many people concerning just what the Bureau of Indian Affairs actually does. Years of criticism and complaint have colored the image of the Bureau and a general misunderstanding of the mission and goals of the organization continues to surface.

In discharging its duties, the Bureau does not attempt to manage the affairs of the 488 federally-recognized tribes served by the organization. The era of paternalism is dead. Instead, a viable policy of Indian self-determination, emphasized by President Reagan's January 24, 1983, Indian policy statement, keys the direction of the Bureau.

In little more than a decade, self-determination has altered the thrust of Bureau of Indian Affairs activities, shifting the focus from that of a program services organization to one that assists tribes in taking control of their own affairs. Accepting the challenge of this federal policy, tribal governments have established a record of unparalleled progress. To speed the process, the Bureau spends a great deal of time, money and effort in developing tribal administrative skills to operate Indian programs.

Contracting of Bureau programs is one of the principal means for tribes to take control, and Bureau officials are encouraging its use. Instead of the Bureau operating a school or, say, a social services program on a reservation, the tribe operates it under a contract with the Bureau.

Assistant Secretary Kenneth Smith has made it one of his prime objectives to increase dollar volume of programs under contract and the trend is upward. Contracting by tribes to operate programs totalled $241 million in fiscal 1983, and is expected to increase to $245 million in fiscal 1984 and $250 million in fiscal 1985.

It is estimated in fiscal 1985 the Bureau will contract with 325 tribes and tribal groups, entering into some 1,275 separate contracts. The $250 million amount for these contracts represents 27 percent of the total Bureau budget. These figures become even more impressive when compared with fiscal 1976, the first year of the Indian self-determination services program, when around 200 tribes contracted for 800 programs.

Contracting—coupled with the self-determination grants program, which has the same aim—clearly defines the path ahead for the Bureau and federally-recognized Indians and Alaska Natives. Tribes are assuming greater responsibilities in such areas as social services, law enforcement and developing and managing their resources. As tribes accept control of these areas, the presence of the Bureau of Indian Affairs will lessen. But some things will remain the same.

The three major areas of responsibility from which the goals and budget of the Bureau of Indian Affairs are derived include support of the government-to-government relationship, carrying out the trust responsibility, and administrative support required in the conduct of federal operations.

These responsibilities will remain constant in the face of change. Also, the Bureau will continue to staff and support programs for tribes while the transition to self-determination and self-efficiency is being made.

While the Bureau of Indian Affairs supports tribal efforts to reach self-determination and control of their own affairs, it also has a solemn obligation to meet the dictates of the trust responsibility. And when self-determination and the trust face off in a head-to-head confrontation, as they sometimes do, the trust obligation under law take precedence....

[*American Indians* (Washington: Bureau of Indian Affairs, 1984), 11–12.]

192. Report of the Task Force on Indian Economic Development

July 1986

Economic development is a major concern on Indian reservations, and over the years repeated studies have been made of the issue. A special task force, made up of staff members of the Office of the Assistant Secretary for Policy, Budget and Administration (Interior Department) or of the Bureau of Indian Affairs and organized in 1985, issued its report of findings and recommendations in the summer of 1986. While not intended to convey official policy, the report highlighted problems and made recommendations. It relied to some extent on an earlier report issued in November 1984 by the Presidential Commission on Indian Reservations Economies.

. . . .

I. Summary of Task Force Findings
[tables omitted]

Indian Socioeconomic Status

The 1980 U.S. Census identified 1.37 million Indians living in the United States. Of this total, about 25 percent were living on reservations. Of the 1.03 million Indians living off reservations, about 11 percent were residing in the Oklahoma historic areas, 23 percent in counties adjacent to reservations, and 66 percent in areas more distant from reservations (in many cases far from reservations in major urban centers). Indians living on reservations constituted less than 50 percent of the BIA service population and about 40 percent of total enrolled tribal members.

As shown by the 1980 census . . . thirty-two percent, or almost a third of all reservation Indians, were living on the Navajo reservation. Fully 57 percent of reservation Indians were living in the Southwest region (consisting of Arizona, Southern California, New Mexico, Nevada and Utah). The region with the second largest reservation population was the Northern Great Plains, where 16 percent of reservation Indians were living. Reservation Indians in the East constituted 11 percent of all Indians living on reservations. The Northwest, Rocky Mountain and Southern Great Plains regions all had less than 10 percent of the reservation Indian population.

As is widely known, Indians living on many reservations have suffered from relatively low incomes, high unemployment, high poverty rates and other adverse socioeconomic circumstances, compared with the U.S. population as a whole. . . .

Indians living off reservations have a significantly higher socioeconomic status than reservation Indians—at least by standard socioeconomic measures. . . . The 1980 census found the poverty rate for off-reservation Indians to be 22 percent. This was much higher than the 12 percent poverty rate for the U.S. as a whole, but also much lower than the 41 percent poverty rate for reservation Indians.

The total unemployment rate for all Indian males ages 20 to 64 and living off reservation was 26 percent. Again, this was much higher than the corresponding figure for U.S. males (18 percent), but much lower than the corresponding figure for reservation males (58 percent).

Federal Economic Development Programs

The economic problems of Indian reservations began to receive significantly greater national attention under the poverty programs begun in the mid 1960s. . . . Three agencies—the Office of Economic Opportunity (and its successor the Administration for Native Americans), the Economic Development Administration, and the Labor Department under the CETA (and now JTPA) programs—made significant expenditures for Indian programs in the past two decades. Cumulatively, the Indian expenditures of these three agencies rose from $42.3 million in 1969 to $264.6 million in 1980. However, with budget cuts of the 1980s, total Indian expenditures of these agencies fell to $116.7 million in 1984.

The anti-poverty efforts of the 1960s and 1970s generally had a major impact on the circumstances of Indian reservations. Besides significantly increasing the level of Federal funds being spent, anti-poverty programs provided jobs for large numbers of Indians. Many Indians learned how to seek grants, administer programs and generally participate more actively and effectively in the nonIndian world beyond the reservation. Increases in education expenditures since the 1960s sharply increased the numbers of Indians attending college, helping to create a new generation of Indians much better informed and more knowledgeable in science, economics, law and other professional areas. The poverty programs of the 1960s and 1970s also contributed significantly to giving tribal governments a new independence from the Bureau of Indian Affairs, a greater opportunity to administer Federal programs on the reservation, and greater control over outside forces affecting the reservation. Partly as a result, since the 1960s many tribal governments have changed from being largely creations of the BIA without wide Indian support to legitimate governing bodies and voices for Indian people. . . .

The anti-poverty programs and other increased expenditures to promote Indian economic development had a major impact on Indian reservations, but they generally failed to achieve one of their basic purposes. Already in the early and mid 1970s, reviewers were finding that little progress was being made in developing viable Indian reservation economies that could stand on their own feet without continuing infusions of Federal funds. Considerable effort and attention then shifted to a new strategy, development of Indian natural resources as a basis for promoting Indian reservation economic development.

Natural Resources Development

. . . . Total Indian mineral revenues have increased sharply over the past 30 years, most notably following the oil price increases of 1973–74. Indian oil and gas revenues rose from $18.2 million in 1973 to $146.9 million in 1982 (a figure which does not include Osage tribal revenues). Coal revenues, although far lower in absolute magnitude, also rose sharply, from $1.8 million in 1973 to $8.5 million in 1982. Indian oil and gas revenues fell from 1982 to 1983, the first such fall after many years of increase, and then fell more sharply in 1984. Moreover, with further significant reductions in international oil prices since 1984, declining oil and gas revenues are likely to have a major impact on the economic circumstances of Indian reservations for the remainder of the 1980s. . . .

Besides minerals, timber is a major natural resource asset for some Indian tribes. Total Indian timber revenues rose from $11.7 million in 1955 to $50.9 million in 1975, and then reached an all time high of $117.2 million in 1979, at that point rivaling the levels of Indian mineral revenues. However, sharply declining timber prices—a forerunner of declining oil prices—led to a drastic fall in Indian timber revenues to $39.7 million in 1982. Revenues then recovered somewhat to $58.7 million in 1983. . . .

Indians received $48.4 million in revenue from leasing of agricultural land in 1981 (the most recent year for which such figures are available). Traditionally, agriculture has been a main source of revenue for many tribes, playing an especially important role for those tribes not fortunate enough to have significant mineral or timber resources.

Indian natural resources are distributed unequally among Indian tribes. Few tribes receive enough natural resource revenue that those revenues alone can provide a comfortable standard of living for tribal members. . . . [In 1981] only 14.2 percent of Indians were living on reservations receiving natural resource revenues equal to more than $500 per reservation resident.

The 1980s have been a period of declining minerals, timber, agricultural and other natural resource prices. As a result, the earlier promise of major new infusions of natural resource revenue to Indian reservations has faded. Indeed, the Indians have experienced declines in most natural resource revenues since the early 1980s. Moreover, the future prospect is little better, at least for the short term. These circumstances have prompted Indians to look to other means of promoting reservation economic development. The private business sector has become a major focus of attention as the most promising prospect for future reservation development.

The Reservation Business Sector

There is little tradition of private business activity on most Indian reservations. . . .

There are many reasons for the absence of a larger business sector on Indian reservations. Reservations are often isolated, have poor quality land, and have harsh climates. In many tribes individual entrepreneurship and the pursuit of private profit have not been a valued and encouraged form of behavior. Because of the lack of previous economic development, the labor force on many reservations is not highly trained and sometimes lacks the experience that would instill work habits sought by modern industry. If individual Indians find the motivation and discipline to overcome these obstacles, they face major difficulties in obtaining investment capital from sources other than the Federal government.

Tribal governments have made great strides since the 1960s. Yet, the development of Indian political institutions is still in a formative period for many tribes. While the absence of a perfected political system is understandable, it creates a problem in attracting business to reservations. Business seeks well defined groundrules and a secure business environment. . . .

The result has been that few outside businesses have chosen to locate on reservations. The majority of businesses that are located on Indian reservations fall in one of the following categories: (1) tribal businesses established with Federal government and/or tribal funds; (2) businesses engaged in natural resource development with no choice as to location; (3) joint ventures of private business with Indian tribes that benefit from Department of Defense or other preferential contracting; and (4) stores, gas stations, repair shops and other small businesses that service a local population.

A Federal Assistance Strategy

The most important long run actions that the Federal government can take to promote Indian economic development may well involve improvements in Indian education. Beyond education the most critical initiatives must come from Indian tribes and from individual Indian entrepreneurs. Nevertheless, the Federal government still has important roles to play in promoting economic development on Indian reservations.

Tax incentives offer an attractive mechanism for luring business to reservations. Tax advantages are automatic and do not require administrative selection among a pool of eligible candidates, avoiding the extensive politicizing of economic development assistance that often results when many applicants must apply for a limited amount of administratively granted funds or other support. Tax advantages also promote the private profit-making sector, because tax reductions are of benefit only to parties that have some tax obligations. . . .

Besides tax advantages, another potential incentive for business to locate on reservations consists of provision of regulatory relief. Indian bingo, for example, reflects a special form of regulatory relief—an exemption from some of the normal state regulations controlling gambling. Tribes may find that they could gain from providing other forms of regulatory relief—from Federal as well as state rules—in exchange for the employment and income benefits realized.

Preferential contracting is another potentially important means of promoting economic development on reservations. Under such contracting mechanisms Indian owned firms may be able to receive contracts without going through the normal requirements for competitive bidding and other provisions of regulations that control the government procurement process. . . .

Federal assistance to Indians in obtaining loans and capital is another important and traditional government role. The lack of Indian financial institutions, the frequent reluctance of nonIndian financial institutions to loan to Indians, and the financing problems created by trust status and sovereign immunity, all tend to create a need for Federal assistance in obtaining investment capital. The final key function for the Federal government is the provision of technical assistance. The Federal government may provide such assistance directly, or may provide funding to obtain it by contract.

II. Recommendations of the Task Force [Forty-two detailed recommendations under the following headings]

Indian Enterprise Zones. . . .
Preference Contracting. . . .
Financing of Investments. . . .
The Trust Role, Technical Assistance and Contracting. . . .
BIA Organization for Economic Development. . . .
Economic Statistics and Other Items. . . .
[*Report of the Task Force on Indian Economic Development*, July 1986 (Washington: Government Printing Office, 1986), 3–25 passim.]

193. Amendments to the Alaska Native Claims Settlement Act

February 3, 1988

The Alaska Native Claims Settlement Act of 1971 was hailed at the time of its passage as a revolutionary solution to native land claims in Alaska. As the years passed, however, dissatisfactions were voiced, and there was fear that the end of restrictions on alienating land to non-Natives in 1991 would mean loss of the land. The amendments passed did not quiet all fears, but they were a significant step toward resolving problems arising from the original legislation.

An Act to amend the Alaska Native Claims Settlement Act to provide Alaska Natives with certain options for the continued ownership of lands and corporate shares received pursuant to the Act, and for other purposes.

. . . .

CONGRESSIONAL FINDINGS AND DECLARATION
OF POLICY

SEC. 2. The Congress finds and declares that—

(1) the Alaska Native Claims Settlement Act was enacted in 1971 to achieve a fair and just settlement of all aboriginal land and hunting and fishing claims by Natives and Native groups of Alaska with maximum participation by Natives in decisions affecting their rights and property.

(2) the settlement enabled Natives to participate in the subsequent expansion of Alaska's economy, encouraged efforts to address serious health and welfare problems in Native villages, and sparked a resurgence of interest in the cultural heritage of the Native peoples of Alaska;

(3) despite these achievements and Congress's desire that the settlement be accomplished rapidly without litigation and in conformity with the real economic and social needs of Natives, the complexity of the land conveyance process and frequent and costly litigation have delayed implementation of the settlement and diminished its value;

(4) Natives have differing opinions as to whether the Native Corporation, as originally structured by the Alaska Native Claims Settlement Act, is well adapted to the reality of life in Native villages and to the continuation of traditional Native cultural values;

(5) to ensure the continued success of the settlement and to guarantee Natives continued participation in decisions affecting their rights and property, the Alaska Native Claims Settlement Act must be amended to enable the share-

holders of each Native Corporation to structure the further implementation of the settlement in light of their particular circumstances and needs;

(6) among other things, the shareholders of each Native Corporation must be permitted to decide—

(A) when restrictions on alienation of stock issued as part of the settlement should be terminated, and

(B) whether Natives born after December 18, 1971, should participate in the settlement;

(7) by granting the shareholders of each Native Corporation options to structure the further implementation of the settlement, Congress is not expressing an opinion on the manner in which such shareholders choose to balance individual rights and communal rights;

(8) no provision of this Act shall—

(A) unless specifically provided, constitute a repeal or modification, implied or otherwise, of any provision of the Alaska Native Claims Settlement Act;

(B) confer on, or deny to, any Native organization any degree of sovereign governmental authority over lands (including management, or regulation of the taking, of fish and wildlife) or persons in Alaska; and

(9) the Alaska Native Claims Settlement Act and this Act are Indian legislation enacted by Congress pursuant to its plenary authority under the Constitution of the United States to regulate Indian affairs. . . .

DURATION OF ALIENABILITY RESTRICTIONS

SEC. 8. The Alaska Native Claims Settlement Act is further amended by adding the following new section after section 36:

"DURATION OF ALIENABILITY RESTRICTIONS

"SEC. 37. (a) General Rule.— Alienability restrictions shall continue until terminated in accordance with the procedures established by this section. No such termination shall take effect until after December 18, 1991". . . .

[U.S. Statutes at Large, 101:1788–89, 1797.]

194. Report on BIA Education
March 1988

Provision of educational facilities for Indians continued to be a major activity of the Bureau of Indian Affairs, even though students enrolled in BIA-funded schools in 1986 were less than 10 percent of all Indian students in the United States. This "final review draft" of the report produced by the BIA's Office of Indian Education Programs focused on broad policy questions affecting all of BIA education and was a step toward establishing a Comprehensive Education Plan.

SUMMARY
[tables omitted]

. . . . Since the 1960s, the Federal government has adopted a policy of Indian self-determination. This policy was applied in a new legislative framework for Indian education built by Congress in the 1970s (Indian Education Act of 1972; Indian Self-Determination and Education Assistance Act of 1975; and Title XI of the Education Amendments Act of 1978). The cornerstone of this framework has been the promotion of the assumption by tribes and other Indian groups of direct responsibility for the education of Indian children. Following this objective, Indian groups have contracted for the operation of many elementary and secondary schools formerly operated by the BIA. Where schools continue to be run by the BIA, Congress has required the creation of Indian school boards and various other measures to ensure a major role for parents and other tribal members in the operation of the school. For all Indian schools funded by the Federal government, the aim today is to provide Indian students with an effective educational program that offers an environment in which each student can maximize his or her learning and that serves the educational goals and aspirations as they are identified and defined by the local Indian community.

The self-determination policies of the Federal government today generally prescribe that Indians should assume control of their own political affairs and should develop viable reservation economies capable of relieving Indians from their past dependence on Federal assistance. Both these objectives depend heavily on the quality of future Indian education. Better informed and more knowledgeable Indian voters hold the key to a tribal government that serves the best social and economic interests of the full community of tribal members. Successful economic development of Indian reservations depends no less on higher levels of education of reservation workers, managers and entrepreneurs. The future of contract and BIA-operated schools will in significant part determine whether the current Indian policies of the Federal government are successful in introducing a new, more lasting and more satisfactory era in the relations between the Federal government and the Indian tribes.

BIA-Funded Education Today

For the purposes of this report, tribally-operated schools are called "contract schools." Schools that continue to be administered by the BIA are called "BIA-operated." Some of the BIA-operated schools have established cooperative agreements with nearby public schools and are called "cooperative schools." All these schools taken together make up the system of "BIA-funded" schools.

In the early 1980s, more than 3,000 students in BIA-operated schools in Alaska became part of the public school system of Alaska. Excluding Alaska schools, total recorded enrollment in BIA-funded schools has risen by about 2,600 students since 1965. . . . Total enrollment outside Alaska reached a peak of 40,280 in 1978. Since then, there has been a small decline in enrollment to 37,917 students in 1987–1988.

The comparative stability of enrollments has been maintained despite an increasing number of contract schools and contract school enrollments. Total contract school enrollment rose from 2,299 students in 1973 to 11,202 students in 1988. At the same time,

enrollment in BIA-operated schools declined from 33,532 students to 26,715 students.

Boarding schools include significant numbers of day attendees, as well as actual boarders. Counting only the latter, total boarding enrollment has declined sharply, from 24,051 boarding students in 1965 to 11,264 boarding students in 1988, as boarding schools were closed outright or transformed into day schools. A moderate increase in contract school boarding attendance (from 500 boarding students in 1973 to 2,138 boarding students in 1988) has been overwhelmed by the decline in boarding students attending BIA-operated schools. However, enrollment in day schools operated by the BIA has risen from 11,235 students in 1965 to 17,589 students in 1988—an indication of the strength of tribal support for converting boarding schools to day schools.

Over time, BIA-funded schools have educated a smaller percentage of the total number of Indian students attending elementary and secondary schools in the United States. Within BIA areas of service responsibility the percentage of students attending BIA-funded schools fell from 39 percent in 1930 to 23 percent in 1977 (the last year BIA reported this statistic), due partly to the movement of some Indian families off reservation to seek employment. By 1977, more than two-thirds of Indian students within BIA areas of service responsibility were attending public schools.

Many Indian students live in urban areas where they have no connection with BIA or its services. Nationwide there were 391,937 Indian students enrolled in schools of all kinds in 1986. However, students enrolled in BIA-funded schools were slightly less than 10 percent of all Indian students in the United States.

As part of the preparation of this report, the principals of selected BIA-funded schools were requested to develop a statement of the current status and problems of their school. . . .

The principals writing of their BIA-funded schools did agree on one element that is found throughout BIA education. The students of BIA-funded schools face major obstacles in reaching a high level of educational achievement. Besides the primary speaking of languages other than English, many students come from social environments where poverty and joblessness are pervasive. The parents of many Indian children are not well educated themselves and often find it difficult to help their children in school. Some of the poorer families find it difficult to provide their children attending day schools with proper nutrition at home (which contributes to the parents' decision to send their children to BIA boarding schools where students are served three meals a day). Unfortunately, social breakdown reflected in alcoholism, divorce, violence and other problems are found in many Indian families. Indian children are asked in school to make the large jump from a home environment that is distinctly Indian to the values and attitudes of mainstream American society, as they are taught in school. All these and other factors contribute to the poor performance of the students of BIA-funded schools, at least as this performance is measured by scores on nationally standardized tests. . . .

BIA education includes not only the operation of elementary and secondary schools, but also support for higher education, adult education, assistance to Indian students in public schools, and other program elements. Total annual appropriations for the various programs of BIA education rose from $226.5 million in 1975 to $259.3 million in 1986. In constant dollars, however, this represented a significant decrease in funding. In 1987, the largest element of educational expenditure was school operations, receiving $196.0 million. Other major education areas were the Johnson-O'Malley program of assistance to Indian students in public schools ($22.8 million), funding of BIA higher education ($31.2 million), and assistance to tribal community colleges ($12.9 million). . . .

In 1986, BIA-funded schools received a grant total of $318.9 million, equal to $7,917 per student attending BIA-funded schools. By comparison, total spending in U.S. public schools equalled $4,051 per student in 1986. . . .

The higher cost per student in BIA-funded schools reflects a number of special high-cost factors in BIA education. Transportation costs per student are higher because students must often be bused long distances to school over difficult roads. Small BIA day schools—many containing fewer than 100 students—involve high costs of operation. The single most important high-cost factor is the need to provide dormitory services and facilities for boarding students. Disproportionate numbers of students in BIA-funded schools also have learning problems and handicaps that require special attention.

The high cost of BIA schools also reflects the personnel structure of BIA schools. Excluding dormitory personnel, the ratio of pupils to total personnel in BIA-operated schools was 4.4 to 1 in 1987. By comparison, the ratio of pupils to total personnel in public schools was 9.6 to 1 in 1985. The chief explanation for the high number of personnel in BIA-funded schools is found in the nonprofessional categories of personnel such as education aides, clerical help, cooks, bus drivers, and others. Professional personnel represented 41 percent of all BIA instructional (nondormitory) personnel in 1987. In public schools, however, professional personnel represented more than 60 percent of total personnel in 1985. . . .

Spending for BIA education is only a limited part of total Federal spending for Indian education in the United States. In particular, the Department of Education (ED) provides special funding for Indian students in public schools through a variety of funding mechanisms. Total ED funding levels for the various programs providing assistance to Indian students have risen from $33 million in 1970 to $335 million in 1986. The largest source of such ED funds is Impact Aid, which in 1986 provided $226 million for the education of Indian students in public schools. The Impact Aid program involved greater total Federal funding than the total direct appropriations to BIA education for the operation of BIA-funded elementary and secondary schools.

Towards Effective BIA Schools

In light of the findings of this report with respect to BIA education, the Office of Indian Education Programs proposes to introduce into BIA-operated schools the educational lessons of the effective school movement. Recent educational research has demonstrated that effective schools have many characteristics in common, including:

• High expectations for student success.

- A clear sense of educational mission and purpose.
- Principals who provide strong leadership.
- A safe and orderly school environment.
- An emphasis on the learning of basic skills and the developing of a quality curriculum responsive to the academic and career development needs of the student.
- Students who are held academically accountable and whose progress is regularly monitored.
- Close involvement of parents and the local community in the educational process. Incorporation of the community milieu into content of curriculum.

The proposed overall goal of BIA education is to introduce and develop these characteristics of effective schools within all BIA-operated schools. In addition, a number of more specific goals are proposed in this Final Review Draft with respect to the operation of BIA schools. The Final Report will include a final set of goals, perhaps modified from the goals proposed here, depending on public review and comment. . . .

[*Report on BIA Education: Excellence in Indian Education through the Effective School Process* (Washington: Office of Education Programs, Bureau of Indian Affairs, March 1988), ix–xxi.]

195. Lyng v. Northwest Indian Cemetery
Protective Association
April 19, 1988

The American Indian Religious Freedom Act of 1978 set the policy of Congress but left the implementation of the act to the various agencies of the government. From time to time, Indians have complained that their religious rights still were not properly respected. The majority decision in this case, written by Justice O'Connor, seemed to many people to go against the principles set forth in the 1978 act, and it called forth a vigorous dissent.

This case requires us to consider whether the First Amendment's Free Exercise Clause forbids the Government from permitting timber harvesting in, or constructing a road through, a portion of a National Forest that has traditionally been used for religious purposes by members of three American Indian tribes in northwestern California. We conclude that it does not. . . .

Whatever may be the exact line between unconstitutional prohibitions on the free exercise of religion and the legitimate conduct by government of its own affairs, the location of the line cannot depend on measuring the effects of a governmental action on a religious objector's spiritual development. The Government does not dispute, and we have no reason to doubt, that the logging and road-building projects at issue in this case could have devastating effects on traditional Indian religious practices. Those practices are intimately and inextricably bound up with the unique features of the Chimney Rock area, which is known to the Indians as the "high

country." Individual practitioners use this area for personal spiritual development; some of their activities are believed to be critically important in advancing the welfare of the tribe, and indeed, of mankind itself. The Indians use this area, as they have used it for a very long time, to conduct a wide variety of specific rituals that aim to accomplish their religious goals. According to their beliefs, the rituals would not be efficacious if conducted at other sites than the ones traditionally used, and too much disturbance of the area's natural state would clearly render any meaningful continuation of traditional practices impossible. To be sure, the Indians themselves were far from unanimous in opposing the G-O [Gasquet to Orleans] road. . . , and it seems less than certain that construction of the road will be so disruptive that it will doom their religion. Nevertheless, we can assume that the threat to the efficacy of at least some religious practices is extremely grave.

Even if we assume that we should accept

312

the Ninth Circuit's prediction, according to which the G-O road will "virtually destroy the Indians' ability to practice their religion," ... the Constitution simply does not provide a principle that could justify upholding respondents' legal claims. However much we might wish that it were otherwise, government simply could not operate if it were required to satisfy every citizen's religious needs and desires. A broad range of government activities—from social welfare programs to foreign aid to conservation projects—will always be considered essential to the spiritual well-being of some citizens, often on the basis of sincerely held religious beliefs. Others will find the very same activities deeply offensive, and perhaps incompatible with their own search for spiritual fulfillment and with the tenets of their religion. The First Amendment must apply to all citizens alike, and it can give to none of them a veto over public programs that do not prohibit the free exercise of religion. The Constitution does not, and courts cannot, offer to reconcile the various competing demands on government, many of them rooted in sincere religious belief, that inevitably arise in so diverse a society as ours. That task, to the extent that it is feasible, is for the legislatures and other institutions. Cf. The Federalist No. 10 (suggesting that the effects of religious factionalism are best restrained through competition among a multiplicity of religious sects). . . .

The Constitution does not permit government to discriminate against religions that treat particular physical sites as sacred, and a law forbidding the Indian respondents from visiting the Chimney Rock area would raise a different set of constitutional questions. Whatever rights the Indians may have to the use of the area, however, those rights do not divest the Government of its right to use what is, after all, its land. . . .

Nothing in our opinion should be read to encourage governmental insensitivity to the religious needs of any citizen. The Government's rights to the use of its own land, for example, need not and should not discourage it from accommodating religious practices like those engaged in by the Indian respondents. . . . It is worth emphasizing, therefore, that the Government has taken numerous steps in this very case to minimize the impact

that construction of the G-O road will have on the Indians' religious activities. . . .

Justice BRENNAN, with whom Justice MARSHALL, and Justice BLACKMUN join, dissenting.

" '[T]he Free Exercise Clause,' " the Court explains today, " 'is written in terms of what the government cannot do to the individual, not in terms of what the individual can exact from the government.' " . . . Pledging fidelity to this unremarkable constitutional principle, the Court nevertheless concludes that even where the Government uses federal land in a manner that threatens the very existence of a Native American religion, the Government is simply not "*doing*" anything to the practitioners of that faith. Instead, the Court believes that Native Americans who request that the Government refrain from destroying their religion effectively seek to exact from the Government *de facto* beneficial ownership of federal property. These two astonishing conclusions follow naturally from the Court's determination that federal land-use decisions that render the practice of a given religion impossible do not burden that religion in a manner cognizable under the Free Exercise Clause, because such decisions neither coerce conduct inconsistent with religious belief nor penalize religious activity. The constitutional guarantee we interpret today, however, draws no such fine distinctions between types of restraints on religious exercise, but rather is directed against any form of governmental action that frustrates or inhibits religious practice. Because the Court today refuses even to acknowledge the constitutional injury respondents will suffer, and because this refusal essentially leaves Native Americans with absolutely no constitutional protection against perhaps the gravest threat to their religious practices, I dissent. . . .

Today, the Court holds that a federal land-use decision that promises to destroy an entire religion does not burden the practice of that faith in a manner recognized by the Free Exercise Clause. Having thus stripped respondents and all other Native Americans of any constitutional protection against perhaps the most serious threat to their age-old religious practices, and indeed to their entire way of life, the Court assures us that nothing in its decision "should be read to encourage governmental insensitivity to the religious needs of any citizen." . . . I find it difficult, however, to imagine conduct more insensitive to religious needs than the Government's determination to build a marginally useful road in the face of uncontradicted evidence that the road will render the practice of respondents' religion impossible. Nor do I believe that respondents will derive any solace from the knowledge that although the practice of their religion will become "more difficult" as a result of the Government's actions, they remain free to maintain their religious beliefs. Given today's ruling, that freedom amounts to nothing more than the right to believe that their religion will be destroyed. The safeguarding of such a hollow freedom not only makes a mockery of the "'policy of the United States to protect and preserve for American Indians their inherent right of freedom to believe, express, and exercise the[ir] traditional religions'" . . . , it fails utterly to accord with the dictates of the First Amendment.

I dissent.

[*Supreme Court Reporter*, Interim Edition, 108A:1321, 1326–28, 1330, 1339–40.]

196. Tribally Controlled Schools Act of 1988
April 28, 1988

The Indian Self-Determination and Education Assistance Act of 1975 enabled tribes to contract with the federal government to run the schools provided for Indian children. This principle was enlarged in 1988 by the provision of outright grants to tribes for their schools.

An Act to improve elementary and secondary education, and for other purposes (P.L. 100–297)
. . . .

TITLE V—INDIAN EDUCATION
PART B—TRIBALLY CONTROLLED SCHOOL GRANTS

SEC. 5201. SHORT TITLE

This part may be cited as the "Tribally Controlled Schools Act of 1988."

SEC. 5202. FINDINGS

The Congress, after careful review of the Federal Government's historical and special legal relationship with, and resulting responsibilities to, Indians, finds that—

(1) the Indian Self-Determination and Education Assistance Act, which was a product of the legitimate aspirations and a recognition of the inherent authority of Indian nations, was and is a crucial positive step towards tribal and community control;

(2) the Bureau of Indian Affairs' administration and domination of the contracting process under such Act has not provided the full opportunity to develop leadership skills crucial to the realization of self-government, and has denied to the Indian people an effective voice in the planning and implementation of programs for the benefit of Indians which are responsive to the true needs of Indian communities;

(3) Indians will never surrender their desire to control their relationship both among themselves and with the non-Indian governments, organizations, and persons;

(4) true self-determination in any society of people is dependent upon an educational process which will ensure the development of qualified people to fulfill meaningful leadership roles;

(5) the Federal administration of education for Indian children has not effected the desired level of educational achievement nor created the diverse opportunities and personal satisfaction which education can and should provide;

(6) true local control requires the least possible Federal interference; and

(7) the time has come to enhance the concepts made manifest in the Indian Self-Determination and Education Assistance Act.

SEC. 5203. DECLARATION OF POLICY.

(a) RECOGNITION.—The Congress recognizes the obligation of the United States to respond to the strong expression of the Indian people for self-determination by assuring maximum Indian participation in the direction of educational services so as to render

314

such services more responsive to the needs and desires of those communities.

(b) COMMITMENT.—The Congress declares its commitment to the maintenance of the Federal Government's unique and continuing trust relationship with and responsibility to the Indian people through the establishment of a meaningful Indian self-determination policy for education which will deter further perpetuation of Federal bureaucratic domination of programs.

(c) NATIONAL GOAL.—The Congress declares that a major national goal of the United States is to provide the resources, processes, and structures which will enable tribes and local communities to effect the quantity and quality of educational services and opportunities which will permit Indian children to compete and excel in the life areas of their choice, and to achieve the measure of self-determination essential to their social and economic well-being.

(d) EDUCATIONAL NEEDS.—The Congress affirms the reality of the special and unique educational needs of Indian peoples, including the need for programs to meet the linguistic and cultural aspirations of Indian tribes and communities. These may best be met through a grant program.

(e) FEDERAL RELATIONS.—The Congress declares its commitment to these policies and its support, to the full extent of its responsibility, for Federal relations with the Indian Nations.

(f) TERMINATION.—The Congress hereby repudiates and rejects House Concurrent Resolution 108 of the 83rd Congress and any policy of unilateral termination of Federal relations with any Indian Nation.

SEC. 5204. GRANTS AUTHORIZED

(a) In General.—

(1) The Secretary [of the Interior] shall provide grants to Indian tribes, and tribal organizations, that—

(A) operate tribally controlled schools which are eligible for assistance under this part, and

(B) submit to the Secretary applications for such grants.

(2) Grants provided under this part shall be deposited into the general operating fund of the tribally controlled schools with respect to which the grant

is provided.

(3)(A) Except as otherwise provided in this paragraph, grants provided under the part shall be used to defray, at the discretion of the school board of the tribally controlled school with respect to which the grant is provided, any expenditures for education-related activities for which any funds that compose the grant may be used under the laws described in section 5205(a), including but not limited to, expenditures for—

(i) school operations, academic, educational, residential, guidance and counseling, and administrative purposes, and

(ii) support services for the school, including transportation.

(B) Grants provided under this part may, at the discretion of the school board of the tribally controlled school with respect to which such grant is provided, be used to defray operation and maintenance expenditures for the school if any funds for the operation and maintenance of the school are allocated to the school under the provisions of any of the laws described in section 5205(a). . . .

(e) NO EFFECT ON FEDERAL RESPONSIBILITY.—Grants provided under this part shall not terminate, modify, suspend, or reduce the responsibility of the Federal Government to provide a program.

(f) RETROCESSION.—Whenever an Indian tribes requests retrocession of any program for which assistance is provided under this part, such retrocession shall become effective upon a date specified by the Secretary not more than 120 days after the date on which the tribe requests the retrocession, or such later date as may be mutually agreed upon by the Secretary and the tribe. If such a program is retroceded, the Secretary shall provide to any Indian tribe served by such program at least the same quantity and quality of services that would have been provided under such program at the level of funding provided under this part prior to the retrocession.

(g) NO TERMINATION FOR ADMINISTRATIVE CONVENIENCE.—Grants provided under this Act may not be terminated, modified, suspended, or reduced only for the convenience of the administering agency. . . .

[U.S. Statutes at Large, 102:385–87.]

197. Indian Gaming Regulatory Act
October 17, 1988

Many Indian tribes have found that sizable incomes can be obtained from bingo, for such gaming on Indian reservations is not subject to state regulations. But as the size of the operations increased and as fears developed that organized crime might be attracted, more detailed federal regulations were called for. Congress responded with this act.

An Act to regulate gaming on Indian lands.

FINDINGS

SEC. 2. The Congress finds that—
(1) numerous Indian tribes have become engaged in or have licensed gaming activities on Indian lands as a means of generating tribal governmental revenue;
(2) Federal courts have held that section 2103 of the Revised Statutes (25 U.S.C. 81) requires Secretarial review of management contracts dealing with Indian gaming, but does not provide standards for approval of such contracts;
(3) existing Federal law does not provide clear standards or regulations for the conduct of gaming on Indian lands;
(4) a principal goal of Federal Indian policy is to promote tribal economic development, tribal self-sufficiency, and strong tribal government; and
(5) Indian tribes have the exclusive right to regulate gaming activity on Indian lands if the gaming activity is not specifically prohibited by Federal law and is conducted within a State which does not, as a matter of criminal law and public policy, prohibit such gaming activity.

DECLARATION OF POLICY

SEC. 3. The purpose of this Act is—
(1) to provide a statutory basis for the operation of gaming by Indian tribes as a means of promoting tribal economic development, self-sufficiency, and strong tribal governments;
(2) to provide a statutory basis for the regulation of gaming by an Indian tribe adequate to shield it from organized crime and other corrupting influences, to ensure that the Indian tribe is the primary beneficiary of the gaming operation, and to assure that gaming is conducted fairly and honestly by both the operator and the players; and

(3) to declare that the establishment of independent Federal regulatory authority for gaming on Indian lands, the establishment of Federal standards for gaming on Indian lands, and the establishment of a National Indian Gaming Commission are necessary to meet congressional concerns regarding gaming and to protect such gaming as a means of generating tribal revenue.

DEFINITIONS

SEC. 4. For purposes of this Act—
. . . .
(4) The term "Indian lands" means—
(A) all lands within the limits of any Indian reservation; and
(B) any lands title to which is either held in trust by the United States for the benefit of any Indian tribe or individual or held by any Indian tribe or individual subject to restriction by the United States against alienation and over which an Indian tribes exercises governmental power.
(5) The term "Indian tribe" means any Indian tribe, band, nation, or other organized group or community of Indians which—
(A) is recognized as eligible by the Secretary [of the Interior] for the special programs and services provided by the United States to Indians because of their status as Indians, and
(B) is recognized as possessing powers of self-government.
(6) The term "class I gaming" means social games solely for prizes of minimal value or traditional forms of Indian gaming engaged in by individuals as a part of, or in connection with, tribal ceremonies or celebrations.
(7)(A) The term "class II gaming" means—
(i) the game of chance commonly known as bingo (whether or not elec-

316

tronic, computer, or other technologic aids are used in connection therewith) . . . , including (if played in the same location) pull-tabs, lotto, punch boards, tip jars, instant bingo, and other games similar to bingo. . . .

(8) The term "class III gaming" means all forms of gaming that are not class I gaming or class II gaming. . . .

NATIONAL INDIAN GAMING COMMISSION

SEC. 5.(a) There is established within the Department of the Interior a Commission to be known as the National Indian Gaming Commission. . . .

TRIBAL GAMING ORDINANCES

SEC. 11.(a)(1) Class I gaming on Indian lands is within the exclusive jurisdiction of the Indian tribes and shall not be subject to the provisions of this Act.

(2) Any class II gaming on Indian lands shall continue to be within the jurisdic-

tion of the Indian tribes, but shall be subject to the provisions of this Act. . . .

(3)(A) Any Indian tribe having jurisdiction over the Indian lands upon which a class III gaming activity is being conducted, or is to be conducted, shall request the State in which such lands are located to enter into negotiations for the purpose of entering into a Tribal-State compact governing the conduct of gaming activities. Upon receiving such a request, the State shall negotiate with the Indian tribe in good faith to enter into such a compact.

(B) Any State and any Indian tribe may enter into a Tribal-State compact governing gaming activities on the Indian lands of the Indian tribe, but such compact shall take effect only when notice of approval by the Secretary of such compact has been published by the Secretary in the Federal Register. . . .

[*U.S. Statutes at Large*, 102:2467–69, 2472, 2476.]

Appendix

Some laws omitted from the original edition have come to play an important role in Indian affairs. They are printed here as an appendix, rather than inserted in their proper chronological place, in order not to disturb the sequence, numbering, and pagination of the original collection.

A1. Winters v. United States
January 6, 1908

Water rights of Indians are a vital issue as Indians seek economic development of their reservations, and the basic document on Indian water rights is this 1908 Supreme Court decision, which decreed that where land was reserved for an Indian tribe, there was an implied reservation of the water necessary for the irrigation or other development of the reservation and that the tribe was not subject to the prior-appropriation rule of the state. This right to water was amplified in Arizona v. California (1963).

This suit was brought by the United States to restrain appellants and others from constructing or maintaining dams or reservoirs on the Milk River in the State of Montana, or in any manner preventing the water of the river or its tributaries from flowing to the Fort Belknap Indian Reservation. . . .

Under the just and reasonable construction of this agreement with the Indians [establishing the Fort Belknap Reservation], considered in the light of all the circumstances and of its express purpose, the Indians did not thereby cede or relinquish to the United States the right to appropriate the waters of Milk River necessary to their use for agricultural and other purposes upon the reservation, but retained this right, as an appurtenance to the land which they retained, to the full extent in which it had been vested in them under former treaties, and the right thus retained and vested in them under the agreement of 1888, at a time when Montana was still a Territory of the United States, could not be divested under subsequent legislation either of the Territory or of the State. . . .

The case, as we view it, turns on the agreement of May, 1888, resulting in the creation of Fort Belknap Reservation. In the construction of this agreement there are certain elements to be considered that are prominent and significant. The reservation was a part of a very much larger tract which the Indians had the right to occupy and use and which was adequate for the habits and wants of a nomadic and uncivilized people. It was the policy of the Government, it was the desire of the Indians, to change those habits and to become a pastoral and civilized people. If they should become such the original tract was too extensive, but a smaller tract would be inadequate without a change of conditions. The lands were arid and, without irrigation, were practically valueless. And yet, it is contended, the means of irrigation were deliberately given up by the Indians and deliberately accepted by the Government. The lands ceded, were, it is true, also arid; and some argument may be urged, and is urged, that with their cession there was the cession of the waters, without which they would be valueless, and "civilized communities could not be established thereon." And this, it is further contended, the Indians knew, and yet made no reservation of the waters. We realize that there is a conflict of implications, but that which makes for the retention of the waters is of greater force than

319

that which makes for their cession. The Indians had command of the lands and the waters—command of all their beneficial use, whether kept for hunting, "and grazing roving herds of stock," or turned to agriculture and the arts of civilization. Did they give up all this? Did they reduce the area of their occupation and give up the waters which made it valuable or adequate? And, even regarding the allegation of the answer as true, that there are springs and streams on the reservation flowing about 2,900 inches of water, the inquiries are pertinent. If it were possible to believe affirmative answers, we might also believe that the Indians were awed by the power of the Government or deceived by its negotiators. Neither view is possible. The Government is asserting the rights of the Indians. But extremes need not be taken into account. By a rule of interpretation of agreements and treaties with the Indians, ambiguities occurring will be resolved from the standpoint of the Indians. And the rule should certainly be applied to determine between two inferences, one of which would support the purpose of the agreement and the other impair or defeat it. On account of their relations to the Government, it cannot be supposed that the Indians were alert to exclude by formal words every inference which might militate against or defeat the declared purpose of themselves and the Government, even if it could be supposed that they had the intelligence to foresee the "double sense" which might some time be urged against them.

Another contention of appellants is that if it be conceded that there was a reservation of the waters of Milk River by the agreement of 1888, yet the reservation was repealed by the admission of Montana into the Union, February 22, 1889, c. 180, 25 Stat. 676, "upon an equal footing with the original States." The language of counsel is that "any reservation in the agreement with the Indians, expressed or implied, whereby the waters of Milk River were not to be subject of appropriation by the citizens and inhabitants of said State, was repealed by the act of admission." But to establish the repeal counsel rely substantially upon the same argument that they advance against the intention of the agreement to reserve the waters. The power of the Government to reserve the waters and exempt them from appropriation under the state laws is not denied, and could not be. . . . That the Government did reserve them we have decided, and for a use which would be necessarily continued through years. This was done May 1, 1888, and it would be extreme to believe that within a year Congress destroyed the reservation and took from the Indians the consideration of their grant, leaving them a barren waste—took from them the means of continuing their old habits, yet did not leave them the power to change to new ones. . . .
[207 *U.S. Reports* 565, 573, 575–77.]

A2. Authorization of Appropriations and Expenditures for Indian Affairs (Snyder Act)
November 2, 1921

In order to expedite legislation for Indian welfare, Congress in 1921 passed an act that gave general authorization for categories of Indian expenditures. While the law itself provided no funds, it continued to be used as the basis for appropriating money, and it stated the kinds of activities authorized for the Bureau of Indian Affairs.

An Act authorizing appropriations and expenditures for the administration of Indian affairs, and for other purposes.
Be it enacted. . . , That the Bureau of Indian Affairs, under the supervision of the Secretary of the Interior, shall direct, supervise, and expend such moneys as Congress may from time to time appropriate, for the benefit, care, and assistance of the Indians throughout the United States for the following purposes:

General support and civilization, including education.
For relief of distress and conservation of health.
For industrial assistance and advancement and general administration of Indian property.
For extension, improvement, operation, and maintenance of existing Indian irrigation systems and for development of water supplies.

For the enlargement, extension, improvement, and repair of the buildings and grounds of existing plants and projects.

For the employment of inspectors, supervisors, superintendents, clerks, field matrons, farmers, physicians, Indian police, Indian judges, and other employees.

For the suppression of traffic in intoxicating liquor and deleterious drugs.

For the purchase of horse-drawn and motor-propelled passenger-carrying vehicles for official use.

And for general and incidental expenses in connection with the administration of Indian affairs.

[*U.S. Statutes at Large*, 42:208–9.]

Selected Bibliography

The following bibliographies and reference works are essential for the study of United States Indian policy.

Felix S. Cohen's Handbook of Federal Indian Law, 1982 edition. Charlottesville, 1983. This detailed summary and analysis of legal questions and legal sources is a revised and updated edition of the original work of Felix S. Cohen, *Handbook of Federal Indian Law*, published in 1942.

Hill, Edward E. *Guide to the Records in the National Archives of the United States Relating to American Indians*. Washington, 1981.

Johnson, Steven L. *Guide to American Indian Documents in the Congressional Serial Set: 1817–1899*. New York, 1977.

Kappler, Charles J., ed. *Indian Affairs: Laws and Treaties*. 2 vols. Washington, 1904. Volume 2 is a standard edition of Indian treaties. The treaties also appear in *United States Statutes at Large*. *Indian Affairs: Laws and Treaties* has been expanded and now comprises seven volumes.

Kvasnicka, Robert M., and Herman J. Viola, eds. *The Commissioners of Indian Affairs, 1824–1977*. Lincoln, 1979.

Prucha, Francis Paul. *A Bibliographical Guide to the History of Indian-White Relations in the United States*. Chicago, 1977.

————. *Indian-White Relations in the United States: A Bibliography of Works Published 1975–1980*. Lincoln, 1982.

Royce, Charles C., comp. *Indian Land Cessions in the United States*. Eighteenth Annual Report of the Bureau of American Ethnology. Washington, 1899. A summary of treaty provisions with maps, by states, showing areas ceded.

There is an extensive literature on American Indian policy. The following titles will be helpful.

Beaver, R. Pierce. *Church, State, and the American Indians: Two and a Half Centuries of Partnership in Missions between Protestant Churches and Government*. St. Louis, 1966.

Berkhofer, Robert F., Jr. *Salvation and the Savage: An Analysis of Protestant Missions and American Indian Response, 1787–1862*. Lexington, Kentucky, 1965.

————. *The White Man's Indian: Images of the American Indian from Columbus to the Present*. New York, 1978.

Bolt, Christine. *American Indian Policy and American Reform: Case Studies of the Campaign to Assimilate the American Indians*. London, 1987.

Bowden, Henry Warner. *American Indians and Christian Missions: Studies in Cultural Conflict*. Chicago, 1981.

Burt, Larry W. *Tribalism in Crisis: Federal Indian Policy, 1953–1961*. Albuquerque, 1982.

Collier, John. *Indians of the Americas: The Long Hope*. New York, 1947.

Danziger, Edmund J., Jr. *Indians and Bureaucrats: Administering the Reservation Policy during the Civil War.* Urbana, Illinois, 1974.

Debo, Angie. *A History of the Indians of the United States.* Norman, Oklahoma, 1970.

Dippie, Brian W. *The Vanishing American: White Attitudes and U.S. Indian Policy.* Middletown, Connecticut, 1982.

Deloria, Vine, Jr., and Clifford M. Lytle. *American Indians, American Justice.* Austin, 1983.

———. *The Nations Within: The Past and Future of American Indian Sovereignty.* New York, 1984.

Downes, Randolph C. "A Crusade for Indian Reform, 1922–1934." *Mississippi Valley Historical Review* 32 (December 1945): 331–54.

Hagan, William T. *American Indians.* Rev. ed. Chicago, 1979.

———. *Indian Police and Judges: Experiments in Acculturation and Control.* New Haven, 1966.

———. *The Indian Rights Association: The Herbert Welsh Years, 1882–1904.* Tucson, 1985.

Hertzberg, Hazel W. *The Search for an American Indian Identity: Modern Pan-Indian Movements.* Syracuse, 1971.

Hoopes, Alban W. *Indian Affairs and Their Administration: With Special Reference to the Far West, 1849–1860.* Philadelphia, 1932.

Hoxie, Frederick E. *A Final Promise: The Campaign to Assimilate the Indians, 1880–1920.* Lincoln, 1984.

Hurt, R. Douglas. *Indian Agriculture in America: Prehistory to the Present.* Lawrence, Kansas, 1987.

Josephy, Alvin M., Jr., ed. *Red Power: The American Indians' Fight for Freedom.* New York, 1971.

Keller, Robert H., Jr. *American Protestantism and United States Indian Policy, 1869–82.* Lincoln, 1983.

Kelly, Lawrence C. *The Assault on Assimilation: John Collier and the Origins of Indian Policy Reform.* Albuquerque, 1983.

Lurie, Nancy Oestreich. "The Indian Claims Commission Act." *Annals of the American Academy of Political and Social Science* 311 (May 1957): 56–70.

McLoughlin, William G. *Cherokees and Missionaries, 1789–1839.* New Haven, 1984.

McNickle, D'Arcy. *Native American Tribalism: Indian Survivals and Renewals.* New York, 1973.

Murdock, Robert Winston. *The Reformers and the American Indian.* Columbia, Missouri, 1971.

Mohr, Walter H. *Federal Indian Relations, 1774–1788.* Philadelphia, 1933.

Otis, D. S. *The Dawes Act and the Allotment of Indian Lands.* Edited by Francis Paul Prucha. Norman, Oklahoma, 1973.

Peroff, Nicholas C. *Menominee DRUMS: Tribal Termination and Restoration, 1954–1974.* Norman, Oklahoma, 1982.

Philp, Kenneth R. *John Collier's Crusade for Indian Reform, 1920–1954.* Tucson, 1977.

Prucha, Francis Paul. *The Great Father: The United States Government and the American Indians.* 2 vols. Lincoln, 1984.

———. *Indian Policy in the United States.* Lincoln, 1981.

———. *Indians in American Society: From the Revolutionary War to the Present.* Berkeley, 1985.

———. *The Sword of the Republic: The United States Army on the Frontier, 1783–1846.* New York, 1969.

Prucha, Francis Paul, ed. *Americanizing the American Indians: Writings by the "Friends of the Indian," 1880–1900.* Cambridge, Massachusetts, 1973.

Satz, Ronald N. *American Indian Policy in the Jacksonian Era.* Lincoln, 1975.

Schmeckebier, Laurence F. *The Office of Indian Affairs: Its History, Activities and Organization.* Baltimore, 1927.

Sheehan, Bernard W. *Seeds of Extinction: Jeffersonian Philanthropy and the American Indian.* Chapel Hill, 1973.

Spicer, Edward H. *A Short History of the Indians of the United States.* New York, 1969.

Stuart, Paul. *The Indian Office: Growth and Development of an American Institution, 1865–1900.* Ann Arbor, Michigan, 1979

Szasz, Margaret. *Education and the American Indian: The Road to Self-Determination since 1928.* 2d edition. Albuquerque, 1977.

Taylor, Graham D. *The New Deal and American Indian Tribalism: The Administration of the Indian Reorganization Act, 1934–45.* Lincoln, 1980.

Trennert, Robert A., Jr. *Alternative to Extinction: Federal Indian Policy and the Beginnings of the Reservation System, 1846–51.* Philadelphia, 1975.

Tyler, S. Lyman. *A History of Indian Policy.* Washington, 1973.

Utley, Robert M. *The Indian Frontier of the American West, 1846–1890.* Albuquerque, 1984.

Van Every, Dale. *Disinherited: The Lost Birthright of the American Indian.* New York, 1966.

Viola, Herman J. *Thomas L. McKenney: Architect of America's Early Indian Policy.* Chicago, 1974.

Washburn, Wilcomb E. *The Indian in America.* New York, 1975.

White, Richard. *The Roots of Dependency: Subsistence, Environment, and Social Change among the Choctaws, Pawnees, and Navajos.* Lincoln, 1983.

Wilkins, Thurman. *Cherokee Tragedy: The Story of the Ridge Family and the Decimation of a People.* New York, 1970.

Wilkinson, Charles F. *American Indians, Time, and the Law: Native Societies in a Modern Constitutional Democracy.* New Haven, 1987.

Wooster, Robert. *The Military and United States Indian Policy, 1865–1903.* New Haven, 1988.

Index

Aberdeen, S.Dak., 238
Abiquiu Agency, 143
Abourezk, James, 272
Accounts, Bureau of Indian Affairs, 62
Acknowledgment of tribes. *See* Federal acknowl-
edgment
Administration for Native Americans, 306
Administration of Indian Service, 177–78. *See also*
Bureau of Indian Affairs
Adoptive homes. *See* Child welfare
Adult education, 263, 311
Advisory Board on Indian Affairs, 247
Agencies, 69, 76, 135, 141–43
Agency buildings, 101, 111, 166
Agency personnel, 195–97
Agents, Indian, 2, 12, 35, 38, 62, 64–65, 67, 70,
102, 104, 108, 134, 165–66, 172, 186; authori-
zation for, 19, 30, 35, 55, 69, 76, 81, 84, 111;
military officers as, 130, 135, 147, 186; pro-
hibited from trading, 2, 19, 70; school superin-
tendents as, 189. *See also* Subagents
Agents for trading houses. *See* Factors
Agricultural implements, 57, 72, 85, 93, 112,
126, 159
Agriculture for Indians, 21–22, 33, 78, 82, 88,
111, 125, 164
Agriculturists, rights to land of, 36
AIPRC. *See* American Indian Policy Review
Commission
Alaska Native Claims Settlement Act, 260–62;
amendments, 308–9
Alaska Native Fund, 261
Alaska Natives, 266, 267, 288, 298, 304, 308–9.
See also Aleuts; Eskimos
Albuquerque, N.Mex., school at, 164
Aleuts, 267, 288. *See also* Alaska Natives
Alienability restrictions, 309
Alienation of land, 15, 88, 116
Allotment formula for Indian schools, 292
Allotment of lands in severalty, 6, 74, 88, 93, 95,
111–12, 145, 149, 154–55, 155–57, 163, 165,
177, 183, 189–90, 197–98, 207, 225; ended,
222; equalization of, 184. *See also* Dawes Act
Allotment of trust funds, 210
All-Tribes American Indian Center, Chicago, 238

American Board of Commissioners for Foreign
Missions, 143
American Indian Chicago Conference, 244–46
American Indian Policy Review Commission,
272–74, 281–83
American Indian Religious Freedom Act, 312
American Indians, 304
American Indian School of Medicine, 280
Americanization of Indians, 177–78
Amnesty to Indians, 99
Anadardo, Okla., 238
Anadromous fish, 268
Annuities, 32, 34, 35, 37, 56, 66, 70, 72, 76, 85,
88, 89, 97, 101, 112–13, 127; criticism of, 82,
86, 92–93, 133, 156–57
Anti-poverty programs, 306. *See also* Poverty
Apache Indians, 117, 125, 137, 151, 224; agency
of, 143
Apprenticeship for Indians, 95
Appropriations, 33, 53, 106, 320–21
Arapaho Indians, 85, 103, 117, 125, 147, 224
Archaeological Resources Protection Act, 294–95
Archaeological sites, 295
Arikara Indians, 85, 237
Arizona v. *California*, 319
Army of the United States, 13, 159. *See also* Mili-
tary force
Articles of Confederation, 3
Arts and crafts, 228–29
Assiniboin Indians, 85
Assistant Secretary of the Interior, Indian Af-
fairs, 284, 292
Atkins, J. D. C., 169–71, 174–76
Atkinson, Henry, 40–41
Atlantic and Pacific Railroad, 106
Attorneys for Indians, 159
Authorization for Indian expenditures, 320–21
Avarice for lands, 11, 50, 90, 96, 106–7

Baptist Church, 142
Benevolence toward Indians, 32, 48, 93
BIA. *See* Bureau of Indian Affairs
BIA-funded schools, 310–11
BIA-operated schools, 310–11
BIA Profile, 304

327

Billings, Mont., 238
Bill of Rights, 250
Bingo, 307, 316–17
Blackfeet Agency, 143
Blackfeet Indians, 117
Black Hills, 295–96
Blacks, 7, 99–100. *See also* Freedmen
Black slaves, 7, 98, 99
Blacksmiths, 57, 70, 72, 89, 112, 114
Blood quantum, 303–4
Blue Lake lands, 258–60
Boarding schools, 179, 200, 211, 310. *See also* Education of Indians; Schools
Board of Indian Commissioners, 126–29, 131–34, 182
Boards of inspection, 105
Boatmen, foreign, 29, 64
Boldt, George, 267–68
Boldt decision, 267–68
Bonds, 70, 84
Boudinot, Elias C., 136
Boundary lines, 1, 4, 5, 6, 7, 11, 17, 42, 54, 85, 101
Bozeman Trail, 110, 114
Branch of Placement and Relocation, 238
Branch of Relocation, 238
British agents, 25
British traders, 25–26, 28–29
Brookings Institution, 219
Browning, Daniel M., 195–97
Bruce, Louis R., 264
Brunot, Felix R., 128
Buffalo, 103, 129. *See also* Game
Bureau of Indian Affairs, 37–38, 80, 83–84, 90, 118; authorized activities, 320–21; statement of policy (1984), 304–5. *See also* Independent Indian Department; Transfer of Bureau of Indian Affairs
Bureau Relocation Office, 237–38
Burke, Charles H., 208
Burke Act, 207, 208–9
Bursum, Holm O., 215–17
Bursum Bill, 215–17
Businesses, Indian, 269–70
Business sector on reservations, 307–8
Bylaws. *See* Constitutions and bylaws of tribes

Caddo Indians, 224
Calhoun, John C., 29, 31–33, 37–38
California, 86–87, 91, 94, 95, 233, 234
Camp Grant Agency, 143
Camp Verde Agency, 143
Carlisle Indian Industrial School, 164, 180, 210
Carpenters, 112, 114

Carson National Forest, 258
Cass, Lewis, 25–26, 29, 42, 64
Catholic Church, 143
Cattle. *See* Domestic cattle; Livestock
Cayuga Indians, 5
Census of Indians, 113
Central Superintendency, 142
Cession of lands, 3, 54, 87–88, 90, 98, 100, 114, 190, 277
CETA. *See* Comprehensive Employment and Training Act
Charters, British, 61
Cherokee Agency, 69, 142, 189
Cherokee cases, 58–62
Cherokee Indians, 6–8, 10, 11–12, 30, 44–48, 69, 74, 97, 124–25, 148, 174, 189, 194–95, 224
Cherokee Nation v. *Georgia*, 58–60, 285
Cherokee Tobacco Case, 136
Cheyenne Indians, 85, 103, 109, 117, 125, 147, 154, 224
Cheyenne River Agency, 143
Cheyenne River Reservation, 213
Chicago, 26, 30, 69, 238
Chicago Agency, 69
Chicago Field Relocation Office, 238
Chickasaw Indians, 12, 30, 69, 97, 124–35, 174, 189, 194, 224
Child custody, 293–94
Child welfare, 293–94
Chilocco School, 164
Chippewa Indians, 5–6, 42–43, 79, 82, 83, 143, 233
Chivington, John, 103
Choctaw Agency, 143
Choctaw Indians, 12, 30, 57–58, 74, 97, 124–25, 148, 174, 189, 194, 224
Christian Church, 143
Christianization of Indians, 63, 77, 92, 119, 124–25, 127, 133–34, 135, 157–58, 164, 166
Church buildings, 57, 72
Citizenship Act, 218
Citizenship for Indians, 55, 112, 133, 144–46, 163, 166, 167, 174, 175, 176–77, 178, 198–99, 207, 208, 215, 218, 219
Civilization Fund Act, 33, 38
Civilization of Indians, 16, 19, 22, 27–28, 32–33, 39–40, 47, 74, 77, 83, 85–86, 88, 91, 96, 104–8, 119, 123–29, 132–33, 135, 144, 146, 154–57, 169, 174–75, 177. *See also* Christianization of Indians; Education of Indians; Schools
Civil Rights Act of 1968, 249–52, 285, 287–88
Civil service, 182, 185–86, 195–97
Claims, 11, 38, 66, 140, 228. *See also* Indian Claims Commission

Clark, William, 25, 42, 64
Clarke, Sidney, 115–16
Clerks, 62, 87
Clothing for Indians, 56, 113, 117
Clum, John, 151
Coal, 306
Coeducation, 180
Cohabitation, 185
Coke Bill, 163
Colleges. *See* Community colleges; Higher education
Collier, John, 222, 225–28
Colliflower, Madeline, 247–48
Colliflower v. Garland, 247–48
Colonies for Indians, 77–80
Colorado River Agency, 143
Colorado troops, 103
Colville Agency, 143
Comanche Indians, 76, 97, 117, 125, 147, 224
Commissioner of Education, 263, 264
Commissioner of Indian Affairs, 62–63, 284. *See also names of commissioners*
Commissioners, 38, 40, 109–10, 182–83
Commission on the Rights, Liberties, and Responsibilities of the American Indian, 242
Commission to the Five Civilized Tribes. *See* Dawes Commission
Committee on Indian Affairs, 3–4
Communal land tenure, 74
Community colleges, 290–91
Community development, 249
Compact of 1802. *See under* Georgia
Competency of Indians, 213–14
Comprehensive Employment and Training Act, 266–67, 306
Compulsory education, 179
Concentration of Indians, 77–80, 83, 94, 125, 133, 148–49, 153–54
"Condition of the Indian Tribes." *See* Doolittle Committee
Confederate States, 97
Confederation of tribes, 74–75, 130
Congregational Church, 143
Congressional authority in Indian affairs, 3, 8, 10–11, 203. *See also* Plenary power
Consolidated government for Indians, 98
Consolidation of Indian lands, 300
Consolidation of reservations. *See* Concentration of Indians
Constitutions and bylaws of tribes, 224, 266
Continental Congress, 1, 3–4
Contracts, 275–76, 280, 304–5
Contract schools, 310–11
Contributions of Indians, 220

Cooley, Dennis N., 96–98, 99
Cooperative associations, 230–31
Corporations, 223, 230–31, 262
Corruption in Indian Territory, 193–94
Council houses, 57, 72
Court of Claims, 231, 295–96
Courts, 28, 35, 67, 134, 145, 150, 162–63, 174, 177, 198, 247, 285
Courts of Indian Offenses, 160–62, 186–89, 250–51
Cox, Jacob D., 129–31
Crawford, T. Hartley, 73–75
Crawford, William H., 26–28
Credit, 269, 308. *See also* Loans to Indians
Creek Agency, 142
Creek Indians, 10, 12, 30, 40, 97, 98–102, 124–25, 174, 189, 224
Crime, 6, 7, 15, 18, 20, 41, 54–55, 66, 68, 134, 145, 192, 278. *See also* Indian Crimes Act of 1976; Major Crimes Act
Criminal jurisdiction. *See* Jurisdiction
Crook, George, 151–53
Crow Agency, 143
Crow Dog (Sioux), 162–63, 167, 168. See also *Ex parte Crow Dog*
Crow Indians, 85, 109, 117
Culture of Indians, 63, 160–62, 204, 206, 220, 248
Curtis Act, 197–99

Dances, Indian, 160, 187
Dancing Rabbit Creek, Treaty of, 53–58
Dawes, Henry L., 165, 189
Dawes Act, 171–74, 181, 184–85, 199, 207, 208
Dawes Commission, 189–90, 190–95, 197, 198, 199
Day schools, 164, 178, 211, 310
Declaration of Indian Purpose, 244–46
Declaration of Policy in the Administration of Indian Affairs, 213–15
Decrease of Indian population, 102–3
Delaware Indians, 5–6, 79, 97, 224
Delegate of Indians in Congress, 8, 57–78, 130
Demoralization of Indians, 120
Department of Education, 311
Department of Indian Affairs, 68–71. *See also* Bureau of Indian Affairs
Dependence of Indians on the United States, 89, 168–69
Deputy Commissioner of Indian Education, 264
Destruction of property, 161, 187
Detroit, 6
Devils Lake Agency, 143
Devils Lake Sioux Tribe, 300

Discovery, right of, 35, 37
Disease among Indians, 102. *See also* Health of Indians
Distilleries, 67
Districts for Indian affairs, 8
Dole, William P., 95–96
Domestic arts, 22
Domestic cattle, 19, 71, 72, 85, 88, 93, 113, 126, 164. *See also* Livestock
Domestic dependent nations, 59, 117, 145
Doolittle, James, 102–5
Doolittle Committee, 102–5
Dormitories, criteria for, 291–92
Double jeopardy, 285–86
Drug traffic, 321
Duane, James, 1–2, 3
Due process for Indian students, 271
Dundy, Elmer S., 151–53
Dutch Reformed Church, 143

Eaton, John H., 44–47, 53
Economic development, 266–67, 269–70, 273, 302, 305–8, 310, 316
Economic Development Administration, 306
Educational facilities, 291. *See also* Schools
Education Amendments Act of 1972, 263
Education Amendments Act of 1978, 291–92, 309
Education functions of BIA, 292
Education of Indians, 33, 46, 57, 63, 73, 82, 88, 92, 112, 164, 177, 200, 201, 204–5, 219, 221–22, 241, 245, 263–64, 273, 274–76, 291–93, 307, 309–12, 314–15, 320; appropriations for, 311; grants for, 263; report on, 178–80, 253–56. *See also* Adult education; Boarding schools; Community colleges; Day schools; English language; Industrial schools; Manual labor schools; Schools; Student rights
Education programs, 309–12
Effective school movement, 311–12
Elk, John, 166–67
Elk v. *Wilkins*, 166–67
Emancipation of slaves, 98, 99
Emigrant Indians, 53, 91
Emigration of whites, 1, 79, 91, 102, 103
Emmons, Glenn L., 237–38, 240
Employment preference for Indians, 70, 223–24, 264, 266–67, 280. See also *Morton* v. *Mancari*
Encroachment of whites, 1, 3, 10, 11–12, 17, 90, 94
Engineers, 112, 114
English language, 73, 107, 112, 164, 174–76, 177, 179
Enrollment. *See* Rolls; School enrollment

Enterprise zones, 308
Episcopal Church, 143
Equal Employment Opportunity Act of 1972, 270
Eskimos, 267, 288. *See also* Alaska Natives
Executive orders, 143–44
Ex Parte Crow Dog, 162–63
Extinction of Indians, 27, 32, 33, 48
Extinguishment of Indian titles, 13, 36, 39. *See also* Treaties

Factors, 16–17, 23, 30
Factory system, 2, 16–17, 21–22, 23–24, 26–28, 31, 33–34
Families, Indian, 293–94
Family service programs, 294
Farmers, 70, 89, 112, 114, 321
Farming. *See* Agriculture for Indians
Federal acknowledgment, 289–90, 302–4
Federal Indian Law, 252
Federal land manager, 295
Fee simple title, 54, 55, 115, 207. *See also* Patents for land
Fever River, 42
Fiduciary relationship, 277
Field matrons. *See* Matrons
Fifteenth Amendment, 167
First Amendment, 241–42, 312–14
Fishing rights, 85, 267–68
Five Civilized Tribes, 169–71
Five Civilized Tribes, Commission to the. *See* Dawes Commission
Flandreau Sioux, 145
Flathead Agency, 143
Flathead Indians, 233
Florida Agency, 69
Florida Indians, 69, 233
Florida Territory, 68
Forbearance toward Indians, 139
Forest, Indian, 223
Forest Grove School, 164
Fort Belknap Reservation, 247–48, 319–20
Fort Berthold Agency, 143
Fort Hall Agency, 143
Fort Harmar, Treaty of, 5, 13
Fort Laramie, Treaty of: 1851, 84–85; 1868, 110–14, 295–96
Fort Lyon, 103
Fort McIntosh, Treaty of, 5–6
Fort Smith, 96
Fort Snelling, 82
Fort Stanwix, Treaty of, 5
Fort Sumner, 120
Fort Wayne, 30

330

Foster homes. *See* Child welfare
Fourteenth Amendment, 167, 248
Fractionalized land. *See* Heirship land problem
Freedmen, 194
Free Exercise Clause, 312–14
Fund for the Republic, 242
Furs, 24
Fur traders. *See* Traders

Gallup, N.Mex., 238
Game, destruction of, 13, 22, 37, 103, 129, 138, 141, 147
Gaming regulation, 316–17
Gasquet to Orleans road, 312–13
Gates, Merrill C., 182
General Allotment Act. *See* Dawes Act
General council of Indians, 101
Genoa, Nebr., school at, 164
Georgia, 10, 39, 46, 58–62; compact with United States in 1802, 39, 45, 47, 61
Gignaux, Edward T., 277
Good faith in dealing with Indians, 10, 11
Government for Indians, 39–40, 54, 145. *See also* Self-government; Wheeler-Howard Act
Government-to-government relationship, 290, 301, 305
Government trading houses. *See* Factory system
Governors of states and territories, 24, 68, 109
Grammar schools, 178
Grande Ronde Agency, 143
Grand Portage, 26
Grand River Agency, 143
Grant, Ulysses S., 127, 128–29, 135
Grants, 263, 269–70, 275–76, 279, 290–91, 294
Grazing leases, 185
Great Nemaha Agency, 142
Great Osages. *See* Osage Indians
Great Sioux Reservation, 296
Green Bay, 26, 30, 42
Green Bay Agency, 143
Gros Ventre Indians, 85, 117, 137
Guadalupe Hidalgo, Treaty of, 158, 216
Guarantee of lands, 53
Guardianship of Indians, 201, 214–15
Gunsmiths, 72

Habeas corpus, 247, 250
Half-Breed Tract, 42
Hampton Institute, 164, 180
Harrison, Benjamin, 182, 186
Harrison, William Henry, 22–23
Hawaiian Natives, 288
Hayt, Ezra A., 151
Health facilities, 276, 280. *See also* Hospitals

Health of Indians, 212–13, 214, 236–37, 273, 278–80, 298–300, 320. *See also* Medical services
Health Professions Preparatory Scholarship Program, 279–80
Heirs, 207
Heirship land problem, 207, 226–27, 247, 300
Henderson, John B., 105, 110
Herring, Elbert, 63
Hicksite Friends. *See* Quakers
Higher education, 179, 263, 311. *See also* Community colleges
High schools, 178
Hiring preference. *See* Employment preference for Indians
History of Indians, 76
Homesteads. *See* Allotment of lands in severalty
Hoopa Valley Agency, 143
Hoopa Valley Indian Reservation, 168
Hopewell, Treaty of. *See* Treaty of Hopewell
Hopi Indians, 220
Horses, 19
Hospitals, 236–37
Hostages, 5–6
Hostilities between tribes. *See* Intertribal hostilities
Houlton Band of Maliseet Indians, 296–98
House Concurrent Resolution 108, 233, 239, 240, 256, 302, 315
House of Representatives, 115–16
Houses, 57
Humanity toward Indians, 10, 28, 32, 43, 107–8, 146
Hunters, rights of, 36, 49
Hunting grounds, 13, 103
Hunting parties, 117
Hunting rights, 43, 85, 113, 114

IHS. *See* Indian Health Service
Illinois Territory, 30
Immorality, 187–88
Impact aid, 311
Implied reservation of water, 319–20
Improvements on land, 53
Inalienability of lands, 163. *See also* Dawes Act
Inconsistency in Indian policy, 137–38
Incorporation of Indians into white society, 23, 86. *See also* Civilization of Indians
Incorporation of tribes, 224
Indemnification, 20, 41–42, 66
Independent Indian Department, 109, 118, 121, 122–23
"Indian," definition of, 225
Indiana, Indians of, 69

Indiana Agency, 69
Indian Affairs: Laws and Treaties, 252
Indian agents. *See* Agents
Indian: America's Unfinished Business, The, 242
Indian Arts and Crafts Board, 228–29
Indian Business Development Program, 269–70
Indian character, 91
Indian Child Welfare Act, 293–94
Indian citizenship. *See* Citizenship for Indians
Indian Citizenship Act, 218
Indian Civil Rights Act of 1968. *See* Civil Rights Act of 1968
Indian claims. *See* Claims
Indian Claims Commission, 231–33, 239, 247, 259, 261
Indian Commissioners, Board of. *See* Board of Indian Commissioners
Indian country, 64. *See also* Boundary lines
Indian Crimes Act of 1976, 278
Indian Department. *See* Bureau of Indian Affairs; Independent Indian Department
Indian departments, 8
Indian Education Act of 1972, 263–64, 309
Indian Education Assistance Act, 276
Indian Financing Act, 269–70
Indian firms, preference for, 280
Indian Gaming Regulatory Act, 316–17
Indian Health Care Improvement Act, 278–80, 299
Indian Health Service, 298–300
Indian identity, 289–90
Indian Land Consolidation Act, 300
Indian land titles. *See* Lands of Indians
Indian Offenses, Courts of. *See* Courts of Indian Offenses
Indian Peace Commission, 105–6, 106–10, 116–17
Indian police, 151, 173, 321
Indian policy, 1–2, 3–4, 15–16, 92–93, 131–34, 137–41, 147–51, 177–78, 203–6, 213–15, 219–21, 248–49, 256–58, 273
Indian population (1980), 305–6
Indian removal, 23, 39–40, 44–46, 47–48, 49–52, 54, 56, 71–72, 82, 92, 165
Indian Removal Act, 52–53
Indian Reorganization Act. *See* Wheeler-Howard Act
Indian Revolving Loan Fund, 269
Indian Rights Association, 164
Indian scouts, 151
Indian Self-Determination Act, 275–76
Indian Self-Determination and Education Assistance Act, 274–76, 299, 301–2, 309, 314
Indian Territory, 148, 169–71, 190–95, 199

Indian trade. *See* Trade with Indians
Indian Trade, Superintendent of, 23–24
Indian Training School, 189
Indian values, 242–43
Indian wars. *See* Wars
Individuality of Indians, 177
Industrial schools, 164, 179
Industries, 146
Inherent tribal sovereignty, 283, 285–86. *See also* Sovereignty of Indians
Injustice toward Indians, 106, 139
Inspection of Indian affairs, 109
Inspectors, 321
Institute for Government Research, 219
Intemperance, 102. *See also* Liquor
Intercourse acts. *See* Trade and intercourse acts
Interior Department, 80, 122
Intermarriage, 28
International law, 281
Interpreters, 29, 63, 64, 70, 76
Intertribal hostilities, 42, 63, 79–80, 82, 85, 89, 98
Intoxication, 188. *See also* Liquor
Intruders on Indian lands, 47, 55, 65, 109. *See also* Encroachment of whites
Investigation of Indian affairs, 273
Iowa Indians, 42–43, 79, 224
Irrigation, 164, 174, 184, 320

Jackson, Andrew, 46, 47–48, 71–72
Jackson, Helen Hunt, 158–59
Jefferson, Thomas, 21–22, 22–23, 24, 51–52
Johnson, Emery A., 298–300
Johnson, Lyndon B., 248–49
Johnson and Graham's Lessee v. William McIntosh, 35–37, 284–85
Johnson-O'Malley Act, 221–22, 276
Joint Special Committee of Congress. *See* Doolittle Committee
Jones, William A., 199–202
Judges, 186–87, 321. *See also* Courts; Courts of Indian Offenses
Jurisdiction: over Indians, 59, 162–63, 198–99, 251–52, 273, 298; of tribal courts, 284–85
Justice toward Indians, 10, 12–13, 15–16, 43, 146

Kagama. *See United States v. Kagama*
Kansa Indians. *See* Kaw Indians
Kansas Territory, 89, 90
Kaw (Kansa) Agency, 142
Kaw (Kansa) Indians, 224
Kennedy, Edward, 253
Kennedy, Robert, 253
Kickapoo Agency, 142

Kickapoo Indians, 79, 224
Kinney, Abbot, 158–59
Kiowa Agency, 142
Kiowa-Comanche Reservation, 202
Kiowa Indians, 117, 125, 147, 224
Klamath Agency, 143
Klamath Indians, 233, 267
Klamath Reservation, 224
Knox, Henry, 11–12, 12–13, 14

Labor force, 307
Lacey, John F., 209
Lacey Act, 210
Laguna Pueblo, 220
Lake Mohonk Conference, 163–66
Lakes, agent to, 30
Land bounties, 4
Land grants, Pueblo, 215–17
Land monopoly, 115, 170
Lands, Indian, 6, 13, 21, 35–37, 55, 56–57, 59, 72, 92, 102, 115, 223, 226, 260–62, 276, 296–98, 300
Land speculators, 1–2
Land system, 104
Law for Indians, 32, 144–45, 150, 155, 157, 166, 273, 281–82
Lawrence, Kans., school at, 164
Lea, Luke, 81–83, 85–86
Leasing of lands, 185, 306
Legal counsel, 252
Legal status of Indians, 58–60, 270–71. See also Supreme Court cases
Leupp, Francis E., 203–6, 208, 210–12
Licenses for Indian trade, 8–9, 14, 18, 19, 28, 31, 34–35, 41, 64
Lincoln Institute, 164
Liquor, 21, 24, 31, 35, 44, 55, 62, 67, 76, 82, 89, 95, 188, 214, 321
Livestock, 65, 147. See also Domestic cattle
Loans to Indians, 223, 231, 269. See also Credit
Lone Wolf v. Hitchcock, 202–3, 288, 295–96
Looms, 57, 72
Los Angeles, 238
Los Pinos Agency, 143
Lummi Indians, 267
Lutheran Church, 143
Lyng v. Northwest Indian Cemetery Protective Association, 312–14

McKenney, Thomas L., 23, 33, 37–38, 43–44
Mackinac, agent at, 30
Maine, Indian claims in, 296–98
Maine Implementing Act, 297
Maine Indian Claims Land Acquisition Fund, 298

Maine Indian Claims Settlement Act, 296–98
Maine Indian Claims Settlement Fund, 297–98
Major Crimes Act, 167–68, 278
Maliseet Indians, 296–98
Mancari. See Morton v. Mancari
Mandan Indians, 85, 137
Manpower programs, 266–67
Manual labor schools, 73, 78, 93, 95, 164
Manypenny, George W., 87, 89–92
Marriage, 160–61, 176–77, 188
Marshall, John, 58, 60
Marshals, 145
Martinez. See Santa Clara Pueblo v. Martinez
Mason, John, 23
Matrons, 185–86, 321
Mechanics, 63, 70
Medical school, 280
Medical services, 221–22. See also Health of Indians; Hospitals
Medicine Lodge Creek, Treaty of, 117, 202
Medicine men, 161, 187
Medill, William, 77–80
Meeds, Lloyd, 281, 282–83
Menominee Indians, 42–43, 79, 83, 233, 239, 264–66, 267
Menominee Restoration Act, 264–66
Menominee Restoration Committee, 264–66
Meriam, Lewis, 219
Meriam Report, 219–21, 272, 281
Mescalero Apache Indians. See Apache Indians
Methodist Church, 73, 143
Miami Indians, 174
Michigan Agency, 143
Michigan Territory, 68
Michilimackinac, Mich., 6, 69
Military force, 12–13, 18, 20, 29, 35, 38, 65, 67, 95, 99, 108, 117, 118–19, 138–39. See also Army of the United States; Wars
Military posts, 6, 26, 85, 104, 114
Military roads, 55, 85, 114
Milk River, 319–20
Milk River Agency, 143
Millers, 112, 114
Mills, 72, 89, 111
Millwrights, 57, 72
Mineral resources, 306
Mineral rights, 197
Mining, 185
Minneapolis, 238
Minnesota, 84, 91, 234
Misdemeanors, 188
Missionaries, 78, 104, 126, 133, 142, 164, 175–76. See also Christianization of Indians; Religious societies

Missionary Society of the Methodist Church, 73
Mission Indians of California, 158–59, 182–84
Missouri, 30, 68
Missouri Indians. *See* Oto and Missouri Indians
Mix, Charles E., 92–95
Mohawk Indians, 5
Monopoly of trade, 31
Monroe, James, 39–40
Montana Territory, 114
Montana water rights, 319–20
Moqui Pueblo Agency, 143
Morgan, Thomas J., 177–78, 178–81, 186–89
Morton, Rogers C. B., 264
Morton v. Mancari, 264, 270–71
Muskogee, Okla., 238
Muskogee Nation. *See* Creek Indians

Narragansett Indians, 302–4
Nash, Philleo, 246–47
Natchitoches, La., 30
National Advisory Council on Indian Education, 264
National Council on Indian Opportunity, 248–49
National Federation of Federal Employees, 264
National holidays, 181
National Indian Gaming Commission, 316–17
National Plan (for Indian health), 300
Native American Church v. Navajo Tribal Council, 241–42
Native corporations (Alaska), 308–9
Natural resources development, 306–7
Navajo Agency, 143
Navajo Community College, 290
Navajo Indians, 104, 109, 285–86
Navajo Tribal Council, 241
Neah Bay Agency, 143
Nebraska, 89, 234
Negroes. *See* Blacks
New Mexico, 84, 91
New York (state), 233
Nez Perce Agency, 143
Niantic Indians, 303
Nixon, Richard M., 256–58
Nonfederally recognized Indians, 273, 277, 289–90
Nonintercourse acts. *See* Trade and intercourse acts
Nonreservation Indians, 267, 273
North Carolina, 10, 11
Northern colony for Indians, 79
Northern department, 3–4
Northern district, 8
Northern Pacific Railroad, 105, 140
Northern Superintendency, 142

Northwestern Indians, 12–13
Northwest Indian Cemetery Protective Association.
See *Lyng v. Northwest Indian Cemetery Protective Association*
Northwest Ordinance, 9–10
Northwest Territory, 9

Offenses, 187–88. *See also* Crimes
Office of Economic Opportunity, 249, 306
Office of Indian Affairs. *See* Bureau of Indian Affairs
Office of Indian Education, 263–64
Office of Indian Education Programs, 292, 309, 311
Officers of army, 130, 135, 147, 186
Off-reservation Indians, 305–6
Oil and gas, 306
Oklahoma Indian Welfare Act, 230–31
Oklahoma tribes, 224, 228, 267
Oliphant, Mark, 284–85
Oliphant v. Suquamish Indian Tribe, 284–85
Omaha Agency, 142
Omaha Indians, 79, 80
Oneida Indians, 5
Onondaga Indians, 5
Ordinance of 1786, 8–9, 31
Oregon, 80–81, 93, 234
Orthodox Friends. *See* Quakers
Osage Agency, 142
Osage Indians, 97, 115, 174, 224
Oto Agency, 142
Oto and Missouri Indians, 43, 79, 80, 87–89, 224
Ottawa Indians, 5–6, 42–43, 224
Outing system, 180
Outrages against Indians, 11–12

Paiute Agency, 142
Papago Indians, 137
Parental control of education, 274, 276, 312
Parker, Ely S., 99, 127–28, 134–35
Passamaquoddy Indians, 267, 277, 296–98
Passamaquoddy Tribe v. Morton, 277
Passports, 9, 17–18, 28, 65
Patents for land, 53, 89, 112, 154, 172–73, 183, 207, 208–9, 214
Paternalism, 304
Patriotism, 180–81
Pawnee Agency, 142
Pawnee Indians, 79–80, 148, 154, 224
Payments to Indians, 56, 57, 88, 100. *See also* Annuities
Pay of agents, 30, 84
Peace Commission. *See* Indian Peace Commission

Peace policy, 119, 126, 129–31, 135, 139
Peace with Indians, 2, 4, 5, 7, 8, 12, 22, 25, 42, 53, 98, 99, 110. *See also* Peace policy
Penalties, 15, 16, 19, 20–21. *See also* Punishments
Penobscot Indians, 267, 296–98
Peoria Indians, 174
Permits for archaeological work, 295
Person, Indian defined as, 152–53
Peyote, 241
Philanthropy, 16, 126
Phoenix, Ariz., 238
Physicians, 112, 114, 185, 213
Piegan Indians, 117
Pima and Maricopa Agency, 143
Pine Ridge Reservation, 213
Piqua, Ohio, agent at, 30
Plenary power, 272, 293, 309
Point Elliott, Treaty of, 284
Police. *See* Indian police
Political rights for Indians, 32
Political status of tribes, 60. *See also* Legal status of Indians; Self-government
Polygamy, 187
Ponca Agency, 143
Ponca Indians, 40–42, 79, 117, 137, 148, 151–53, 154, 224
Population, Indian, 305–6. *See also* Decrease of Indian population
Portage des Sioux, Treaty of, 25
Port Madison Reservation, 284–85
Post offices, 55
Posts. *See* Military posts
Potawatomi Agency, 142
Potawatomi Indians, 42–43, 79, 224, 233
Poverty, 305. *See also* Anti-poverty programs
Prairie du Chien, 26, 30, 42, 69
Prairie du Chien, Treaty of, 42–43
Preferential contracting, 307–8
Preferential employment. *See* Employment preference for Indians
Presbyterian Church, 143
Presents, 5, 6, 9
Presidential Commission on Indian Reservation Economies, 305
Price, Hiram, 155–57, 157–58, 158–59
Prisoners, 1, 5, 6, 7
Private businesses on reservations, 307
Private property, 27–28, 32, 63, 125. *See also* Allotment of lands in severalty
Private satisfaction, 20
Prizes, 114
Problem of Indian Administration, The, 219–21
Proclamations, 1–2, 11, 12
Program for Indian Citizens, 242–44

Property. *See* Destruction of property; Private property
Protection of Indians, 6, 7, 25, 41, 42, 53, 54, 71, 85, 92, 117
Protestant Episcopal Church, 143
Public domain, 115
Public Health Service, 236–37, 298
Public Law 280, 83rd Congress, 233–34
Public Law 93–638, 299, 274–76, 299, 301–2, 314
Public Law 94–437, 278–80, 299
Public Law 95–561, 291–93
Public Law 100–297, 314–15
Public schools, 214, 276, 310
Pueblo Agency, 143
Pueblo Indians, 170, 220
Pueblo land grants, 215–17, 218–19
Pueblo Lands Board, 218–19
Punishments, 7, 110. *See also* Crime; Penalties
Purchase: of goods for Indians, 19, 70, 127, 128; of lands, 2, 3, 4, 15, 19, 21, 65, 230

Quakers, 130, 135, 141, 142
Quapaw Agency, 142
Quapaw Indians, 97, 224
Quinaielt Agency, 143

Race, 107
Racial discrimination, 270–71
Railroads, 89, 91–92, 100, 103, 105–6, 113, 129, 140, 159, 174, 184
Ranges, 223
Rations, 30, 71, 113, 165, 200, 202, 221
Reagan, Ronald, 301–2, 304
Red Cloud Agency, 143
Red River of the North, 91
Regulation of gaming, 316–17
Regulatory relief, 307
Rehabilitation of Indian race, 225–26
Religious freedom, 241–42, 288–89, 312–14
Religious rights, 294–95
Religious sites, 288–89
Religious societies, 102, 107, 135, 141–43, 146, 157–58, 180. *See also* Missionaries
Relocation of Indians, 237–38
Removal. *See* Indian removal
Reservation Development Loan Fund, 246
Reservation economies. *See* Economic development
Reservation schools, 210–12
Reservations of land, 55, 81–83, 92–96, 105, 110, 114, 129–30, 139, 143–44, 153–54, 155, 159, 165, 177, 179, 182–83, 223
Retained sovereignty. *See* Inherent sovereignty

Retaliation, 7, 41
Retrocession, 315
Revolutionary War, 1
Revolving fund, 223, 226, 269
Rhode Island, Indians of, 302–4
Right of conquest, 4, 12, 36
Rights of Indians, 10, 11, 12–13, 49–52, 59, 92, 98, 153, 203, 219
Roads, 21, 89, 114, 174. *See also* Military roads
Rock Island Agency, 69
Rolls, 234–51, 261, 265
Roosevelt, Theodore, 258
Rosebud Reservation, 213
Ross, John, 44–47
Round Valley Agency, 143

Sac and Fox Agency, 142, 143
Sac and Fox Indians, 42–43, 79, 174, 224
Sacred objects, 288–89
Safe water facilities, 280
Saint Louis, Superintendent of Indian Affairs at, 35
Saint Peter's Agency, 69
Saint Peter's River, 42
Sale of Indian lands, 214
Sanborn, John B., 105, 110
San Carlos Reservation, 151
Sand Creek Massacre, 103, 109
Sanitary waste disposal facilities, 280
Sanitation, 213
Santa Clara Pueblo v. *Martinez*, 287–88
Santee Sioux Agency, 142
Sault Sainte Marie, 69
Savage state of Indians, 62, 177
Schofield, J. M., 117–18
Scholarships, 279–80
School enrollment, 310
Schools, 57, 72, 111, 133, 158, 159, 180–81, 247; standards for, 291–92. *See also* Boarding schools; Day schools; Education of Indians; Industrial schools; Manual labor schools; Public schools; Reservation schools
School superintendents, 185–86, 189
Schurz, Carl, 153–54
Scofield, Glenni W., 115–16
Scouts, Indian, 151
Seaton, Fred A., 240–41
Secretary of War, 8, 14, 62. *See also* War Department
Segregation of Indians, 77–80
Self-determination, 248–49, 250, 256–58, 301–2, 304–5, 310, 314–15. *See also* Indian Self-Determination and Education Assistance Act

Self-government, 270–71, 287–88. *See also* Self-determination
Self-help, 248–49
Self-support, 127, 161, 164, 199–202, 205–6, 209
Sells, Cato, 213–15
Seminole Agency, 143
Seminole Indians, 97, 101, 124–25, 174, 189, 224
Senate Special Subcommittee on Indian Education, 263
Seneca Indians, 5, 97, 174, 224
Settlement of whites, 3, 4, 6, 7, 18, 65. *See also* Encroachment of whites
Severalty. *See* Allotment of lands in severalty
Shawnee Agency, 142
Shawnee Indians, 97, 224
Sherman, William T., 110, 146–47, 159
Shoshone Agency, 143
Siletz Agency, 143
Sioux Indians, 25, 42–43, 79–80, 82, 84, 108, 110–14, 117, 125, 137, 147, 148, 202, 224
Sioux Nation of Indians. See United States v. Sioux Nation of Indians
Sioux Reservation, 165
Sisseton Agency, 143
Sites, religious, 288–89
Sites for trade. *See* Trading sites
Six Nations, 5
Skokomish Agency, 143
Slaves, 7, 98, 99
Smith, Edward P., 144–46
Smith, John Q., 147–51
Smith, Kenneth, 304
Snyder Act, 320–21
Social games, 316
Social welfare services, 221–22
Society of Friends. *See* Quakers
South Dakota, 110
Southern Department, 10–11
Southern district, 8
Southern Treaty Commission, 96–98
Sovereign immunity, 276, 287–88
Sovereignty of Indians, 135, 136, 145, 281–83. *See also* Inherent tribal sovereignty; Self-determination; Self-government
Sparks, W. A. J., 146
Special Subcommittee on Indian Education, Senate, 253–56
Speculators. *See* Land speculators
Spiritual rehabilitation of Indians, 227
Spotted Tail (Sioux), 162, 167
Spring Wells, Mich., 25
Standing army, 119, 122
Standing Bear v. *Crook*, 151–53

336

States and the Indians, 9, 10–11, 19, 24, 65, 96, 221–22, 233–34, 237, 251–52, 254. *See also* Governors of states and territories.
Statutory construction, 277
Stephens v. Cherokee Nation, 198–99
Stevens, Isaac I., 93, 268
Stuart, Robert, 43
Student rights, 271–72, 293
Subagents, 30, 38, 62, 69, 70
Superintendent of Indian Trade, 23–24, 30, 33–34
Superintendents, Indian, 8–9, 14, 31, 35, 64–65, 67, 69, 76, 81, 84, 86–87, 102, 104, 108, 134, 181, 245
Supplemental Report on Indian Education, 178–80
Supreme Court cases, 35–37, 58–60, 136, 162–63, 166–77, 168–69, 198–99, 202–3, 270–71, 284–85, 285–86, 287–88, 295–96, 312–14, 319–20
Suquamish Indians, 284–85
Suquamish Indian Tribe. See *Oliphant v. Suquamish Indian Tribe*
Surveys, 56, 101, 174
Syphilis, 120

Talton v. Mayes, 287
Taos Pueblo, 258–60
Tappan, S. F., 105
Task force on Indian affairs, 246–47
Task force on Indian economic development, 305–8
Task forces of AIPRC, 273, 281
Taxation, 136, 236
Tax incentives, 307
Taylor, Nathaniel G., 105, 110, 118–23, 123–26
Teachers, 70, 104, 112, 114, 126, 179, 263, 292–93
Technical assistance, 308
Telegraph lines, 174
Teller, Henry M., 160–62
Termination Act, Menominee, 234–36
Termination policy, 233, 234–36, 238–39, 240–41, 245, 248, 256–57, 264–66, 273, 276, 302, 315
Territorial government for Indians, 145, 169–71
Texas, 91, 95
Timber resources, 306
Titles to land, 37, 45, 61, 235. *See also* Lands of Indians
Tonkawa Indians, 224
Townsites, 197
Trachoma, 212–13

Trade and intercourse acts, 14–15, 17–21, 28–29, 38, 64–68, 81, 84, 87, 108, 128, 144, 277, 296–97
Trademarks, 229
Traders, 2, 4, 7, 32, 38, 132. *See also* Trade with Indians
Trade with Indians, 1, 2, 4, 7, 8–9, 14–15, 21, 23–24, 26–28, 28–29, 31–33, 34–35, 41, 55, 64, 109. *See also* Trade and intercourse acts; Traders
Trading houses. *See* Factory system
Trading sites, 38, 43–44, 64
Transfer of Bureau of Indian Affairs, 104, 108, 117–23, 146–47
Transfer of health services, 236–37
Treaties, 12, 34, 38, 51, 60, 81, 84, 89, 90, 93, 97, 115–16, 133, 134–35, 136, 165, 268, 273, 281. *See also individual treaties*
Treaty making, 136, 165
Treaty obligations, 101, 107, 117, 134, 136, 191, 203
Treaty of Dancing Rabbit Creek, 53–58
Treaty of Fort Atkinson, 84
Treaty of Fort Harmar, 5, 13
Treaty of Fort Laramie (1851), 84–85
Treaty of Fort Laramie (1868), 110–14, 295–96
Treaty of Fort McIntosh, 5–6
Treaty of Fort Stanwix, 5
Treaty of Guadalupe Hidalgo, 158, 216
Treaty of Hopewell, 6–8, 11–12, 45, 59
Treaty of Medicine Lodge Creek, 117, 202
Treaty of Paris (1783), 1, 13, 45
Treaty of Point Elliott, 284
Treaty of Portage des Sioux, 25
Treaty of Prairie du Chien, 42–43
Treaty with Creeks (1866), 98–102
Treaty with Poncas, 40–42
Treaty with Sacs and Foxes, 42
Tribal businesses, 307
Tribal governments, 273, 301–2, 316. *See also* Self-government
Tribally Controlled Community College Assistance Act, 290–91
Tribally Controlled Schools Act of 1988, 314–15
Tribal relations, 163, 170, 177, 180, 197–98, 222, 224, 227–28
Tribal-state compacts, 317
"Tribe," definition of, 225, 250
Trust funds, 209–10, 214, 235
Trust periods, 222
Trust responsibility, 267, 270, 272, 273, 274–75, 276, 277, 278, 279, 281–82, 293, 305, 315
Tuberculosis, 212–13

Tulalip Agency, 143
Tularosa Agency, 143
Tule River Agency, 143
Turtle Mountain Reservation, 233
Tuscarora Indians, 5

Udall, Stewart, 246
Uintah Reservation, 156
Uintah Valley Agency, 143
Umatilla Agency, 143
Unemployment, 305–6
Union Pacific Railroad, 105, 140
Unitarian Church, 143
United States Court of Claims. See Court of
    Claims
United States v. Kagama, 168–69
United States v. New England Coal and Coke Co., 277
United States v. Sioux Nation of Indians, 295–96
United States v. State of Washington, 267–68
United States v. Wheeler, 285–86
University of Chicago, 244
Upper Arkansas Agency, 142
Upper Missouri Agency, 69, 143
Urban Indians, 273, 280
Usual and accustomed grounds and stations, 267–
    68
Utah, 84, 91
Ute Indians, 156, 174

Valentine, Robert, 212–13
Veterans, 215
Vincennes, Ind., 30
Vocational training, 214, 246. See also Industrial
    schools; Manual training schools
Volunteer troops, 106, 109

Wabash Indians, 13
Wabash River, 12
Walker, Francis A., 137–41
Walker River Agency, 142

War Department, 14, 118–19, 122. See also Secre-
    tary of War
Wards, 59, 121, 133, 134, 171, 239
Warm Springs Agency, 143
War of 1812, 25
Wars, 2, 3–4, 11, 27, 102, 103, 109, 132, 138. See
    also Intertribal hostilities
Washington, George, 1–2, 14, 15–16
Washington Territory, 93
Washington v. Washington State Commercial Passenger
    Fishing Vessel Association, 267
Water rights, 174, 319–20
Watie, Stand, 136
Watkins, Arthur V., 238–39
Western Territory, 68, 69
Wheeler. See United States v. Wheeler
Wheeler-Howard Act, 222–25, 225–28, 230–31,
    239, 244, 264, 270, 281
Whetstone Agency, 143
White Earth Reservation, 148, 213
White Mountain Agency, 143
White River Agency, 143
Wichita Agency, 142
Wichita Indians, 97, 224
Winnebago Agency, 142
Winnebago Indians, 42–43, 79, 83
Winters v. United States, 319–20
Wisconsin, 234
Wisconsin River, 26
Witnesses, 188–89
Women's National Indian Association, 164
Worcester, Samuel A., 60–62
Worcester v. Georgia, 60–62
Work, Hubert, 219
Wyandot Indians, 5–6, 224

Yakima Agency, 143
Yakima Reservation, 148
Yankton Agency, 143
Yankton Sioux Indians, 42–43

Zuni Indians, 220